ETHNIC STUDIES
RESEARCH

ETHNIC STUDIES RESEARCH

Approaches and Perspectives

EDITED BY
TIMOTHY FONG

ALTAMIRA PRESS
A Division of Rowman & Littlefield Publishers, Inc.
Lanham • New York • Toronto • Plymouth, UK

ALTAMIRA PRESS
A division of Rowman & Littlefield Publishers, Inc.
A wholly owned subsidiary of The Rowman & Littlefield Publishing Group, Inc.
4501 Forbes Boulevard, Suite 200
Lanham, MD 20706
www.altamirapress.com

Estover Road
Plymouth PL6 7PY
United Kingdom

Copyright © 2008 by AltaMira Press

All rights reserved. No part of this publication may be reproduced, stored in a retrieval system, or transmitted in any form or by any means, electronic, mechanical, photocopying, recording, or otherwise, without the prior permission of the publisher.

British Library Cataloguing in Publication Information Available

Library of Congress Cataloging-in-Publication Data

Ethnic studies research : approaches and perspectives / edited by Timothy Fong.
   p. cm.
  Includes bibliographical references and index.
  ISBN-13: 978-0-7591-1141-7 (cloth : alk. paper)
  ISBN-10: 0-7591-1141-3 (cloth : alk. paper)
  ISBN-13: 978-0-7591-1142-4 (pbk. : alk. paper)
  ISBN-10: 0-7591-1142-1 (pbk. : alk. paper)
  1. Ethnology—Research. 2. Race relations—Research. 3. Minorities—Research. I. Fong, Timothy P.

GN316.E753 2008
305.80072—dc22
                                     2007041402

Printed in the United States of America

∞™ The paper used in this publication meets the minimum requirements of American National Standard for Information Sciences—Permanence of Paper for Printed Library Materials, ANSI/NISO Z39.48-1992.

CONTENTS

Preface   ix

CHAPTER 1
Introduction   TIMOTHY P. FONG   1

Part I: Perspectives
CHAPTER 2
Ethnic Studies: Preparing for the Future   OTIS L. SCOTT   17

CHAPTER 3
Crafting Ethnic Studies   GARY Y. OKIHIRO   33

CHAPTER 4
Ethnic or World Studies: A Historian's Path of Discovery
JACK D. FORBES   59

CHAPTER 5
Learning from the Outsider Within: The Sociological Significance of Black Feminist Thought   PATRICIA HILL COLLINS   93

Part II: Posing Questions, Approaching Research
CHAPTER 6
Research through Imperial Eyes   LINDA TUHIWAI SMITH   125

CHAPTER 7

Technique, Art, or Cultural Practice? Ethnic Epistemology in Latino Qualitative Studies   JULIE L. FIGUEROA AND PATRICIA SÁNCHEZ   143

CHAPTER 8

Riddles, Rhythms, and Rhymes: Toward an Understanding of Methodological Issues and Possibilities in Black/Africana Studies
JAMES B. STEWART   179

CHAPTER 9

Methodological Intersections of Race, Sexuality, and Ethnography
GINA MASEQUESMAY   219

Part III: Breaking Borders, Boundaries, and Color Lines

CHAPTER 10

Ethnic Studies and Interdisciplinarity   JOHNNELLA E. BUTLER   243

CHAPTER 11

Literary Matters: Research Methods in Reading Ethnic Literatures
KETU H. KATRAK   257

CHAPTER 12

Chicano/a Literary and Visual Arts: Intertextuality of Three Iconic Figures—La Llorona, La Malinche, and the Virgin of Guadalupe
MARÍA HERRERA-SOBEK   281

CHAPTER 13

Bricolage and the Quest for Multiple Perspectives: New Approaches to Research in Ethnic Studies   JOE L. KINCHELOE   313

Part IV: Teaching and Doing Ethnic Studies Research in the Classroom

CHAPTER 14

Lessons from an Activist Intellectual: Participatory Research, Teaching, and Learning for Social Change   JOSE Z. CALDERON   353

CHAPTER 15

Developing and Sustaining Community Research Methods and Meanings in Asian American Studies Coursework   PETER NIEN-CHU KIANG, KAREN L. SUYEMOTO, AND SHIRLEY SUET-LING TANG   367

CHAPTER 16

A Pedagogy for Ethnic Studies: Experiences and Methods for Teaching   PAMELA RALSTON   399

CHAPTER 17

Teaching about White Racism in the United States: Does It Make a Difference?   THEODORIC MANLEY, JR., JASON J. WASHBURN, AND FRANK HOLIWSKI   427

Part V: Epilogue: Community Praxis

CHAPTER 18

Ethnic Studies Community Collaboration and Activism: Bridging Theory and Practice   JAMES SOBREDO, LINDA REVILLA, AND GREGORY YEE MARK   453

CHAPTER 19

The Story of a Collaborative Project   LUKE ERIC LASSITER   469

Bibliography   491

Index   539

About the Editor and Contributors   555

Preface

THE PERSONAL GENESIS OF THIS BOOK evolved quite a long time ago. As an undergraduate student at California State University, Hayward (now California State University, East Bay), I majored in human development. Human development is an interdisciplinary field of academic study that grew out of traditional disciplines such as anthropology, biology, linguistics, theology, philosophy, psychology, and sociology. As a student majoring in human development, I explored people's lives from conception and birth through old age and death. I explored physical growth and change and the development of consciousness, knowledge, and relationships. In particular, I increased my understanding of myself and others in social, cultural, and historical terms. Very early in my academic career I learned to appreciate how change is the most important characteristic in our society, and individuals must develop skills not directly addressed in traditional programs. Among the department's learning objectives were for majors to show ability to access knowledge, design and carry out individual and group research projects, and present them clearly, logically, and persuasively. In addition, as a human development major, I was to show the ability to be self-reflective, be empathetic to others, and apply these skills to both academic and nonacademic contexts.

I earned my undergraduate degree in 1981 and, being the practical person that I am, went on for a master's degree in public administration at California State University, Hayward. In this program, the focus was on applied research intended to formulate public policy. After completing my master's degree in 1983, I spent a year in the Coro Foundation Fellowship in Public Affairs, where I participated in a series of intensive sequential internships in government, business, labor, media, and community-based organizations, as well as in a highly competitive political campaign. In addition, I engaged in special community problem-solving projects that required cross-sector organizing, negotiation, and coalition-building for successful resolution. The Coro fellowship was ideal in applying my interdisciplinary foundation and applied research interests in a nonacademic environment. Following my time at Coro, I decided I did not want to immediately work in government, so began working as a freelance video and radio documentary producer and as a writer with Pacific News Service in San Francisco. This was clearly a very impractical decision, especially since the only experience I had as a journalist was on my old high school newspaper. However, I was young and extravagant at the time, and I really wanted to try something different. It wound up changing my life.

I was researching a story when I met Gary Kawaguchi, a graduate student who had just entered the newly formed ethnic studies Ph.D. program at the University of California, Berkeley. I was not particularly interested in going back to school, but Gary talked with me at great length about the program and encouraged me to apply. My work as a journalist focused on race and ethnic relations and so the thought of advanced scholarly research in ethnic studies was attractive. The scholarly concern of ethnic studies at Berkeley was explicitly linked to the development of a social practice, and inquiries into the nature of racial, ethnic, and gender inequality are informed by a commitment to social change and social justice. Given my recent past, the interdisciplinary nature of ethnic studies, its challenge to traditional disciplinary boundaries and assumptions, the fact that it was the first ethnic studies Ph.D. program in the nation, and the thought that I would have a hand in helping to shape this new area of study were all extremely appealing to me.

I entered the ethnic studies Ph.D. program in 1987 and went through it without taking a single graduate course on ethnic studies research methodology. Instead, the advice was to have a "concentration" in a traditional discipline and take one or more methodology courses there. One of my former professors at UC Berkeley was very bitter about this fact, curtly complaining that in ethnic studies, "we study text to death." His words and tone stuck in my brain and the realities of ideal intentions versus real-life practice would continue to haunt me. Today most, but not all, ethnic studies departments and programs in the United States offer a methodology course as part of their curricula. Typically, these courses focus on the methodological background of whoever happens to be teaching the course at the time. This is admittedly the case in our home department of ethnic studies at California State University, Sacramento.

I have held this appreciation for the interdisciplinary approach to study, applied research, and social justice, along with my concern about the lack of a firm foundation for ethnic studies research and practice for over twenty years. That being said, I should clearly state I do not consider this book an endpoint to these conflicting impulses, but only a modest, introductory beginning. It is my hope that this book and the perspectives of the contributing authors reinvigorate discussion about ethnic studies as an interdisciplinary enterprise dedicated to social change among faculty and students. The ideas and opinions expressed in this book are not necessarily new, as I have talked to other ethnic studies colleagues about them before. At the same time, I believe attention to, and discussion of, this issue should never end.

I have briefly expressed my personal history in the development of this book. Now I want to express my appreciations. I first want to thank Julia Curry-Rodriguez, professor of Mexican American studies at San Jose State University. I first met Julia as a graduate student at UC Berkeley and I still do not know anyone who thinks about and cares about ethnic studies research methodology more than she does. She freely shared her ideas, syllabi, reading lists, and encouragement with me. She gives more to others than she gives to herself, and I admire her greatly.

I wish to thank the members of the informal advisory committee of ethnic studies scholars, each of whom helped shape this book at various stages of its evolution in their own special way. They also provided chapters, reviews of chapters, and sometimes both. They are: Edna Acosta-Belen, State University of New York, Albany (Latin American and Caribbean studies/Puerto Rican studies), Johnnella Butler, Spelman College (African American studies), Jose Z. Calderon, Pitzer College (Chicano/a studies), Evelyn Hu DeHart, Brown University (Asian American studies), Elaine Kim, University of California, Berkeley (Asian American studies), Charles Henry, University of California, Berkeley (African American studies), Keith Osajima, University of Redlands (Asian American studies), Luana Ross, University of Washington, Seattle (Native American studies), Matthew Snipp, Stanford University (Native American studies), Maria Hererra-Sobek, University of California, Santa Barbara (Chicano/a studies), John Stanfield, Indiana University, Bloomington (African American studies), and David Wilkins, University of Minnesota (Native American studies).

Local colleagues at California State University, Sacramento, also deserve thanks for their support and critical comments. Brian Baker, Manuel Barajas, David Covin, Julie Figueroa, Amy Liu Randall MacIntosh, Annette Reed, Otis Scott, and James Sobredo were around when I needed them. I can never say enough good things about Debbie James and Darcey Little, who provided excellent and efficient administrative assistance during the final stages of getting this book ready for the publisher. This book is now finished because of them. In addition, I am most grateful to the California State University, Sacramento, Research and Creative Activity Program, which provided funding for course reassignment to spend focused time to work on this project. It is important to emphasize that I am at a teaching institution and time to work on research is at an especially high premium.

Jennifer Collier, Rosalie Robertson, and Mitch Allen from AltaMira Press initially contacted me, and contracted me, to complete this book. Their support, confidence, and patience with me were extraordinary. Toward the completion of this book, I worked closely with Alan McClare, executive editor at Rowman & Littlefield Publishers, who gave me expert advice during the most trying times in this project. High praise goes to the Krista Sprecher and Amanda Gibson for their professional guidance throughout the production process.

Lastly, I save my most heartfelt thanks for my wife, Elena Almanzo, our sons Gabriel and Tomas, and our new baby girl, Mia. They do not really know what I do for a living, but they let me do it anyway. They keep life fun and in perspective.

Introduction 1

TIMOTHY P. FONG

*E*THNIC STUDIES RESEARCH: *Approaches and Perspectives* was created with several important purposes in mind. First, it is intended to reflect important trends in ethnic studies research and scholarship. Among the obvious trends in ethnic studies is its increasingly interdisciplinary nature. Besides the traditional fields of social sciences and humanities, the new fields of justice studies, multicultural education, and literary and cultural studies have also been incorporated in ethnic studies. This trend can be seen by the dramatic growth of interdisciplinary ethnic studies departments in public as well as private colleges and universities since the late 1960s and early 1970s. Second, this anthology is an invaluable resource to undergraduate students, graduate students, academics, and service practitioners in their understanding of the important issues and literature in ethnic studies. Third, this anthology synthesizes and benchmarks given modes or areas of inquiry by providing important summary articles on the key topics in the field.

Ethnic studies emerged as an academic discipline during an era of heightened civil rights activism, anti-Vietnam War protests, urban violence, and ethnic and feminist identity formation. This was the broader context that led to the 1968 boycott of classes at San Francisco State College (now University) led by students of color, along with supportive white students. Together, this multiracial coalition known as the Third World Liberation Front (TWLF) shut down the campus for five months and demanded dramatic changes in the college's education policies. One of the most important demands was for the creation of the first school of ethnic studies. The intensity of the San Francisco State strike captured the attention of the entire nation, and students at other colleges and universities began organizing and making similar demands.

Since that dramatic beginning hundreds of programs and departments have been created either under the broad umbrella of ethnic studies or individually as African American studies (a.k.a. black studies, Africana studies, pan-African studies), Asian American studies, Chicano studies (a.k.a. Chicano/a studies, Mexican American studies, Latino/a studies, Raza studies, as well as Puerto Rican studies), and Native American studies (a.k.a. American Indian studies, indigenous studies). These programs and departments offer general education service courses to their institutions as well as minors and undergraduate degrees. Now many offer master's degrees and a handful offer doctoral degrees as well. The University of California at Berkeley started the first ethnic studies Ph.D. program in 1983, while San Francisco State continues to place its emphasis on teaching and community service.

Ethnic studies grew out of student protest and sought specifically to challenge institutions of higher education, to oppose traditional disciplines, and to expand the curriculum to incorporate diverse perspectives and historical experiences. Ethnic studies also challenged the meaning and purpose of research, essentially asking the epistemological question: Research for whom and for what purposes? With this in mind, there are four interrelated founding concepts that distinguish ethnic studies research from other traditional disciplines.

Focus on Community

The pioneering founders of ethnic studies argued that research within traditional disciplines commonly privileged the scholar's viewpoints rather than the individuals or communities being studied. By comparison, the academic discipline of ethnic studies emphasizes giving a real voice to those who had been merely seen as "research subjects" for narrow academic publication purposes. Ethnic studies sought to break down the artificial barrier between researchers and the community and encouraged a "new breed" of researchers equally versed in rigorous applied data gathering and expansive information dissemination.[1] In an effort to further forward its methodological orientation, ethnic studies has sought to directly and actively involve the community in the research process. In other words, research work and community organizing go hand in hand and are not mutually exclusive endeavors.

Reinterpretive and Protective Agendas

Ethnic studies scholars also railed against research on communities and individuals of color that they considered high problematic and stereotypic, and sometimes quite harmful. For example, early research on African American and Mexican American families generally viewed them as culturally deviant and dysfunctional relative to white middle-class norms. Since the 1970s new research and interpretations led by a new generation of scholars of color have taken a more expanded view of African American and Mexican families to include external structural factors and their impacts on families.[2] Similarly, Asian American studies scholar Sucheng Chan noted that research on various minority groups and communities has generally fallen into four categories. The first category most common prior to the 1960s viewed racial minorities as deviant or deficient due to their inability or unwillingness to assimilate into the dominant society. The second category is celebratory, focusing on the accomplishments of various racialized groups in this country. The next category is the victim approach, which highlights the many ways specific groups have been exploited and their low position in the social structure in the United States. Lastly, and more recently, scholars have focused on racialized groups as agents of change who shape their individual and social lives in the face of the oppressive conditions they face.[3]

Research is not only a matter of perspective, but also one of life and death. Easily the most notorious case of harmful research is seen in the Tuskegee Syphilis Study (1932–1972) that involved some 400 African American men who were poor sharecroppers around Tuskegee, Alabama. These men were unaware they were being used to study the long-term progression of syphilis and were denied treatment widely and easily available to others at the time. The research was funded by the U.S. Public Health Service, which kept the study going to track how the disease spreads and kills. There was no consideration of the effects of this research on the men, their families, and their community until 1972, when news of the study was leaked to the press. In 1997 president Bill Clinton officially apologized on behalf of the nation to the remaining eight survivors of the study.[4] Revelations about the Tuskegee Syphilis Study led to many important recent reforms in both medical and social science research conducted on individuals. However, ethnic studies scholars have long been concerned with the social and ethical treatment of not only the people being studied, but the end-products of research as well.[5]

Questioning Objectivity and Neutrality

Ethnic studies research consciously offers a model that directly contrasts with positivist social science research commonly practiced in traditional academic disciplines. Positivist social researchers strive to develop precise rules that organize social interactions and relationships. Even more fundamental to the positivist approach is the general assumption that knowledge is, or can be, politically and socially neutral. Positivists believe that quantitative precision and an accumulation of detailed facts can reduce complex information and contextual factors into summary measures. Ethnic studies takes a more interpretive position toward research, openly acknowledging a strong political and what they see as a moral/ethical obligation to research. As a result, ethnic studies research is predominantly, though not exclusively, qualitative rather than quantitative, and welcomes interdisciplinary perspectives from both the social sciences as well as the humanities.[6] The interpretive approach does not accept that everything can be precisely measured and rather closely examines social context and individual experiences. The interpretative approach tries to give voice to individuals marginalized by society and works to develop a more empathetic understanding of people's lives. Particular attention is given to not only what types of questions are asked, but who is doing the asking, and how the questions are asked.[7]

Focus on Social Change

Ethnic studies formed to challenge the academic power structure and the prevailing approaches to knowledge at that time. Similarly, the most important hallmark of ethnic studies research is its intention for broader social change. The research findings in ethnic studies document injustice and survival, promote cultural tenacity and vibrancy, highlight unequal power relationships, influence policy, and work to provide a more accurate picture of the United States past and present. According to ethnic studies scholar Evelyn Hu-DeHart, the critical approach to teaching and research "is precisely what makes ethnic studies so exciting and powerful." She believes ethnic studies should "take seriously the edict that education's highest purpose is to liberate and empower (as opposed to socialize), then it becomes controversial and, frankly, threatening to the status quo."[8] The ethnic studies movement, both in terms of teaching and research, has sparked a new generation of young political activists. Many continue to make an impact after they have graduated from college, and many have returned to the community to start social service agencies and focus on grassroots organizing efforts. Others go on to obtain advanced degrees and move into mainstream positions of power and influence in government, business, law, and health care. Still others become involved in electoral politics in the belief that this is the best avenue to create social change.

Literature Review

It is surprising that there are relatively few books explicitly devoted to research focusing on race in the United States. The most notable early works were edited by John Stanfield. The first are *A History of Race Relations Research: First-Generation Recollections* and *Race and Ethnicity in Research Methods*, edited by Stanfield and Rutledge M. Dennis.[9] *A History of Race Relations Research* provides noteworthy biographical essays by important pioneers in this field. Perhaps as a product of the book's generation, all of the essays are written by men and there is no attention to issues of race and gender that are so prominent in the works of a new generation of race relations researchers. *Race and Ethnicity in Research Methods* was spawned during a 1984 meeting of the American Sociological Association when Stanfield organized a roundtable titled, "Methodological Innovations in Race Relations Research." According to Stanfield, "The purpose of the roundtable was to bring together several leading sociologists to reflect on the relevance of various methodological approaches for testing and modifying theories in race relations research and to recommend new approaches."[10] Not surprisingly, the book was clearly dominated by sociologists focusing on the social science research methodologies.

Two more recent anthologies in this area are France Winddance Twine and Jonathan W. Warren's *Racing Research, Researching Race: Methodological Dilemmas in Critical Race Studies* and Gerardo R. Lopez and Laurence Parker's *Interrogating Racism in Qualitative Research Methodology*. *Racing Research, Researching Race* provides insights primarily from a new generation of scholars from a variety of disciplines and includes two chapters on race relations in countries outside of the United States (Brazil, Cuba, and the Netherlands).[11] Since the chapters are written by younger scholars, they are heavily influenced by cultural studies theories and by white studies, which were both very much in vogue at the time. Indeed one review felt white studies was "over-represented" in this book.[12] This may well be the reason why the long-standing question/dilemma of "insider-outsider" perspectives between the research and communities being studied is a major theme that runs through this volume. What issues emerge when a white researcher studies communities and individuals of color? Conversely, what conflicts and ethical concerns arise when a researcher of color studies his or her own community or other communities of color?

The emergence of ethnic studies has slowly brought forth increased attention to the issues of race and racism within many traditional disciplines in a similar way that women's studies has raised consciousness over gender issues. *Interrogating Racism in Qualitative Research Methodology* is a brief volume from young education scholars who explore the links between the area of critical race theory and research methodology, critique the supposed neutrality of the researcher, and argue that race and racism are never absent from the research process.[13] It is striking to see articles in this book so consistent and aligned with the early ethnic studies stance on research. For example, Melanie Carter's "Telling Tales Out of School: 'What's the Fate of a Black Story in a White World of White Stories?'" which states: "We have a responsibility to resist the temptation to do 'hit and run' research that is unconcerned about the consequences of our work. Instead, as much as possible, we must encourage a researcher sensibility and ethic that expresses and demonstrates a collective good of our communities" (p. 3). Similarly, in "Race-Based Methodologies: Multicultural Methods or Epistemological Shifts?" Wanda Pillow writes: "Race-based methodologies are not a new tool or solution to simply add in, and thus take care of, oppressive privilege and racism in our research paradigms. Rather, they request something much more difficult than integration; they work to destabilize the very foundations for thinking about, doing, and writing up social science research" (p. 195).

Lastly, Chela Sandoval's *Methodology of the Oppressed* is the only single-authored book on this topic. Sandoval does not specifically focus on field research as much as she studies text. Her project concentrates on developing new theoretical frameworks challenging traditional disciplines as well as mainstream feminist and women's studies approaches to research. Sandoval centers her work on the subjective experiences of women of color in the United States and critiques various theoretical perspectives through what she calls the "five technologies" of methodology of the oppressed: semiotics, deconstruction, meta-ideologizing, differential movement, and democratics. It is the fifth technology that is most significant for Sandoval because democratics "permits, drives, and organizes the methodology of the oppressed: it is the moral and ethical commitment to enact any of its technologies with the aim of equalizing power between humans."[14] Sandoval's work is highly consistent with the concepts of ethnic studies mentioned above, and incorporates similar perspectives found in various oppositional feminist, postmodern, and poststructural theories.

More recently there have been a number of books focusing on European (primarily British) approaches to and experiences of the study of race and ethnicity. This has come as a result of increased immigration from Africa, Asia, and the Caribbean throughout Europe, which has led to an upswing of anti-immigrant sentiment and violence. *Comparative Perspectives on Racism*, edited by Jessika ter Wal and Maykel Verkuyten, is a compilation of papers from a 1998 conference, "New Directions in Comparative Research on Racism and Xenophobia."[15] While interesting, the volume does not offer an analysis of comparative research as much as it simply provides various essays about different geographic regions. Yasmin Gunaratnam's *Researching "Race" and Ethnicity: Methods, Knowledge and Power* and Caroline Knowles's *Race and Social Analysis* are short textbook primers (both published by Sage Publications) by British scholars focusing on the complex problems of clearly categorizing "race" and ethnicity globally.[16] Probably the most dynamic of the recent European-centered books on race and ethnicity is *Researching Race and Racism*, edited by leading British scholars Martin Bulmer and John Solomos.[17] This book provides provocative essays by both European and U.S. scholars of various disciplines discussing their experiences conducting research.

It should be noted that European interest in U.S. race and ethnic relations dates back to the work of Alexis de Tocqueville in his classic study, *Democracy in America*, first published in 1835. The second volume was published in 1840, and there have been various translations ever since. The examination of global race and ethnic relations is obviously significant, particularly in today's world of dramatically growing international migrations of people, capital, technology, and culture. It is obvious that racial and ethnic diversity is by no means a social feature unique to the United States. However, the development and evolution of ethnic studies (including its branches African American studies, Asian American studies, Chicano/Latino studies, and Native American studies) as a separate academic field of study *is* a phenomenon specific to the United States.

Arguably the most recognized book in the area of research on racialized groups and the one that has received a great deal of attention among ethnic studies scholars in the United States is Linda Tuhiwai Smith's *Decolonizing Methodologies: Research and Indigenous Peoples*.[18] One of the theoretical perspectives that dominated early ethnic studies thinking was "internal colonialism," which was an extension of the analysis of *external colonialism*—the imperialistic domination by European capitalist nations and the United States over "Third World" countries. Internal colonialism in the U.S. was defined as the oppression of racialized groups through forced entry (slavery and annexation), unfree labor (strict job segregation), and cultural destruction.[19] Ethnic studies started out challenging higher education and traditional academic research as a vehicle for domination and subordination of Third World people, or people of color, in the United States. In addition, Native American studies has long called for an "indigenous model" for research.[20] The ideas of decolonizing research methodology and for indigenous research are not new to ethnic studies, and Smith's clear and thoughtful articulation is very appealing.

Chapter Descriptions

The authors and chapters in this volume represent the diversity that is ethnic studies. There are works by pioneers in the field, seasoned scholars, as well as new assistant professors fresh out of graduate school. Also represented are scholars from research institutions, teaching institutions, and private colleges and universities. Some chose to write in a very personal and autobiographical fashion, while others chose to take a more formal academic and analytical style. The purpose of this collection is to provide perspectives, not necessarily to find agreement or complete uniformity. There are chapters that repeat consistent themes, but there are also chapters that offer challenging insights that question orthodoxy within the field itself. While early critics of ethnic studies have chided its interdisciplinary approaches to research as simply being chaotic and "undisciplined," the creative cross-pollination of disciplines is now quite fashionable.[21]

A unique feature of this book relative to others described above is that most, but not all, of the contributors teach in ethnic studies departments and programs. All had their advanced graduate training in traditional disciplines, but each came to this project with an understanding that ethnic studies has transitioned from being marginal, to establishing a space of its own, to now being mainstream. At the same time, ethnic studies needs to tread carefully into institutionalization, as not to dilute its critical thrust and attention beyond the halls of academe. Audre Lorde's famous quote, "the master's tools will never dismantle the master's house" is cited in several of the chapters in this book. But an expanded, less cited, quote from Lorde's 1979 speech is particularly relevant here because it is symbolic of the critical nature and perspective of ethnic studies. She states:

> *For the master's tools will never dismantle the master's house.* They may allow us temporarily to beat him at his own game but they will never enable us to bring about genuine change. And this fact is only threatening to those . . . who still define the master's house as their only source of support.[22]

Much has changed since the founding of ethnic studies, including the realization that the definition of what constitutes a "community" is far more problematic today than what was assumed in the past; nonetheless, maintaining the early inspired intentions of ethnic studies research, coupled with new insights from a new generation of ethnic studies scholars, is a continuous lofty process and a worthy goal.[23]

Part I (Perspectives) focuses on providing background and context for the emergence of ethnic studies. This begins with a chapter by Otis Scott, former chair of the Ethnic Studies Department and currently dean of the College of Social Sciences and Interdisciplinary Studies at California State University, Sacramento. Dean Scott is also the past president of the National Association for Ethnic Studies (NAES). His work provides an overview of the ethnic studies movement, the challenges it has faced in higher education, as well as in the broader society, and its future as an academic discipline. The following chapter by Gary Okihiro specifically examines the historical evolution of the "craft" of ethnic studies research. This chapter is valuable because it will help us to think about the general development of the field, but also to think critically, by extension, about the methodological directions that have come to ethnic studies out of various disciplines. Related to this is the chapter by Jack Forbes, a noted Native American historian, who provides a personal narrative on his approach to research. Forbes gives readers insight into the development of the field of ethnic studies in general, and Native American studies in particular, and his arguments demonstrate that the standard academic perspectives students hear from most of their instructors are not beyond question. Lastly, this section includes a classic article by Patricia Hill Collins that has been highly influential to both ethnic studies and women's studies. Like many ethnic studies scholars, Collins argues that black female intellectuals have made great creative use of their marginality. Her conclusion that researchers would benefit by placing greater trust in their own personal and cultural biographies can be seen as a fundamental element of ethnic studies research.

Part II (Posing Questions, Approaching Research) starts off with another important previously published work. This one, by Linda Tuhiwai Smith, is a chapter from her highly acclaimed book, *Decolonizing Methodologies: Research and Indigenous Peoples*, described above. The presentation here interrogates the cultural assumptions behind research by the dominant colonial culture, deconstructing the motivations and values that inform traditional Western research theories, methodologies, and writing. The next chapter by Julie L. Figueroa and Patricia Sánchez questions the metaphor of conducting research as an "art form" and how mainstream acadmic training as an undergraduate or graduate student is not always enough when conducting research within one's own ethnic community. Indeed, they see research as a process that can benefit from scholar's cultural practice. The authors share their own experiences and hope to validate others' efforts in seeking this alternative view of research. The following chapter by James B. Stewart focuses on the clear distinctions between black/Africana studies and traditional disciplines. According to Stewart, as Africana studies continues to evolve, it is imperative that researchers develop a familiarity with the intellectual history of the field, contemporary schools of thought, and methodological options available for studying various social phenomena. The work of Gina Masequesmay concludes this section and integrates her research involving race, gender, and sexuality. In addition, she provides some insights about the advantages and challenges of doing ethnography with a political agenda with a complex and multi-layered context. Her activist ethnography offers both methodological and theoretical justifications for an ethnic studies standpoint on epistemology and politics.

What is data? This is the theme to Part III (Crossing Borders, Boundaries, and Color Lines), where authors call for an interdisciplinary approach to ethnic studies research that incorporates the humanities as well as the social sciences. Johnnella Butler's chapter begins this section with an important discussion of what she calls "interdisciplinarity" for ethnic studies research that is an extension of her earlier work calling for a "matrix" approach to ethnic studies research. This work is followed up by two chapters by Ketu Katrak and Maria Herrera-Sobek, both former chairs of ethnic studies departments, who have firmly integrated their humanities backgrounds into their scholarship. Katrak's chapter focuses on critical reading practices and research methods used in the interpretation of ethnic literatures, with an emphasis on Asian American literature. She acknowledges there is no single theoretical or methodological approach that suffices for the interpretation of ethnic literatures. Rather the approaches used for literary texts overlap at times with overall interdisciplinary perspectives in ethnic studies as a whole. Herrera-Sobek examines how Chicano/a artistic expression can be analyzed and interpreted. She states that the Chicano/a population often perceives itself as a colonized people, both politically and culturally. As a result, Chicano/as have fiercely struggled since the 1960s, in particular, to decolonize themselves, and one of the most significant political actions taken was to reject Anglo-American/European aesthetics and embrace their indigenous Mexican cultural heritage. By focusing on three iconic images, Herrera-Sobek argues that art forms are another important way of conceptualizing social, cultural, and historical reality. The chapter by Joe Kincheloe concludes this section and is directly related to this interdisciplinarity of ethnic studies and its use of multiple methodological and theoretical tools. In this chapter Kincheloe introduces the notion of the bricolage, a French term describing a jack-of-all-trades worker who uses available tools to complete a task. Connecting the methodological and theoretical eclecticism of the bricolage bridges the mutually compatible goals of critical multiculturalism and ethnic studies. Both are concerned with the development of a literacy of power to help understand and take action in opposition to relations of inequality.

Part IV (Teaching and Doing Ethnic Studies Research in the Classroom) gives examples of ethnic studies research in college-level courses. Jose Calderon begins this section and highlights his work connecting abstract theoretical concepts in the classroom to lived experience and community engagement. Calderon states that his pedagogy is closely aligned with his approach to research methodology, which calls for students and faculty to join together with community participants in using research, teaching, and learning to bring about fundamental social change. Next, Peter Nien-chu Kiang, Karen L. Suyemoto, and Shirley Suet-ling Tang highlight activities of the Asian American Studies program at the University of Massachusetts, Boston, with particular emphasis on how students personally benefit from their positive classroom and research experiences. The authors inject comments from students and alumni who are quite often transformed by innovative new models of developing and sustaining community research methods and meanings in Asian American studies. Despite ethnic studies' proclamations of challenging traditional research methods, it is important to note that Kiang et al. recognize the importance of assessing their own program and activities to validate their impact. The chapter by Pamela Ralston looks at teaching research in a comparative ethnic literature course. Ralston seeks to integrate literature, culture, history, and theoretical research methods in a classroom that is focused on student involvement, in the form of discussion, presentation, research, and writing. Her course involves introducing students to the field of ethnic studies, introducing students to contemporary American ethnic voices in literary expression, and introducing students to literary theory and research methods useful for an interdisciplinary study of American ethnic literature. The chapter by Theodore Manley, Jr., Jason Washburn, and Frank Holiwski uses pre and post test measures to determine if there is a significant change in white student racial attitudes in a course designed to teach white racism and whiteness as an oppressive racial category, revealing significant attitude changes.

They seek to encourage professors who are teaching race and ethnicity courses at colleges and universities in the United States to use research methods creatively to integrate their teaching and research. They argue the need to systematically and effectively demonstrate that students and society benefit from race and ethnicity study courses.

Part V (Epilogue: Community Praxis) includes two chapters specifically focusing on concrete examples of research projects that involve strong community collaboration. The chapter by James Sobredo, Linda Revilla, and Gregory Yee Mark highlights a successful effort by the Ethnic Studies Department at California State University, Sacramento, that has become a model for the nation. Out of this community collaboration project came a $9 million federal grant to the Sacramento Unified School District and the creation of a Community Service Small Learning Community in one of Sacramento's most troubled high schools. The next chapter by Luke Eric Lassiter describes the research project from Ball State University in Muncie, Indiana, to correct the major omission in the 1929 sociological classic, *Middletown: A Study of a Modern American Culture*, which virtually ignored the vibrant African American community in town.[24] The original Middletown study can be seen as a metaphor for the invisibility of people of color in the social sciences for much of the twentieth century. To correct that error many years later, Lassiter, a professor of anthropology, students from various disciplines, and local African American collaborators of Muncie engaged in an unprecedented collaborative effort to shed light on a community so long ignored. The research work in Muncie is a prime example of what has been called Public Interest Anthropology (PIA), a field of inquiry and action within that discipline. Like ethnic studies, PIA is "motivated by the conviction that anthropology's effectiveness has been diluted by the unwillingness of its academic arm to insert itself into the public sphere of debate and action."[25] Clearly the ethnic studies approach to research is not unknown in other disciplines. However, community engagement and activism are central to the core of ethnic studies research, but marginalized and certainly under-utilized in other academic fields.

For ethnic studies, greater attention to specific methodologies and modes of inquiry is essential to several compelling projects. Among these projects are: (1) influencing research done in traditional fields; (2) strengthening and developing ethnic studies programs as independent entities with their own research traditions into the future; (3) sharing perspectives on research methods among ethnic studies scholars; and (4) creating a more reflexive, quality research—in collaboration with communities—that strengthen communities and proactively influence policy.

Notes

1. Chalsa Loo and Don Mar, "Research and Asian Americans: Social Change or Empty Prize?" *Amerasia Journal* 12:2 (1985–1986): 85–93.

2. Robert Staples and Alfredo Mirande, "Racial and Cultural Variations among American Families: A Decennial Review of the Literature on Minority Families," *Journal of Marriage and the Family* 42, no. 4 (1980): 887–903.

3. Sucheng Chan, *Asian Americans: An Interpretive History* (Boston: Twayne, 1991), xiii.

4. Alison Mitchell, "Survivors of Tuskegee Study Get Apology from Clinton," *New York Times,* May 17, 1997, 9.

5. Jesse M. Vasquez and Otis L. Scott, "Ethnic Studies More Timely Than Ever," *Black Issues in Higher Education* 13, no. 5 (1996): 72–73; and Lane Hirabayashi, *The Politics of Fieldwork: Fieldwork in an American Concentration Camp* (Tucson: University of Arizona Press, 1999).

6. Johnnella E. Butler, "Ethnic Studies as a Matrix for the Humanities, the Social Sciences, and the Common Good," in *Color-Line to Borderlands: The Matrix of American Ethnic Studies,* ed. Johnnella E. Butler (Seattle: University of Washington Press, 2001).

7. See Patricia Hill Collins, *Black Feminist Thought: Knowledge, Consciousness and the Politics of Empowerment* (New York: Routledge, 1991); and Cherrie L. Moraga and Gloria E. Anzaldúa, eds., *This Bridge Called My Back: Writings by Radical Women of Color,* 3rd ed. (Berkeley, Calif.: Third Woman Press, 2002).

8. Evelyn Hu-DeHart, "Ethnic Studies in U.S. Higher Education," in *Handbook of Research on Multicultural Education,* 2nd ed., ed. James A. Banks and Cherry A. McGee Banks (San Francisco: Jossey-Bass, 2004), 869–881.

9. John H. Stanfield and Rutledge M. Dennis, eds., *Race and Ethnicity in Research Methods* (Thousand Oaks, Calif.: Sage Publications, 1993); and John H. Stanfield, ed., *A History of Race Relations Research: First Generation Recollections* (Thousand Oaks, Calif.: Sage Publications, 1993)

10. John H. Stanfield, "Methodological Reflections," in Stanfield and Dennis, *Race and Ethnicity in Research Methods,* 3.

11. France Winddance Twine and Jonathan W. Warren, eds., *Racing Research, Researching Race: Methodological Dilemmas in Critical Race Studies* (New York: New York University Press, 2000).

12. Leslie A. Houts and Joe R. Feagin, "Review of *Racing Research, Researching Race,*" *Contemporary Sociology* 30, no. 5 (2001): 570–571.

13. Gerardo R. Lopez and Laurence Parker, eds. *Interrogating Racism in Qualitative Research Methodology* (New York: Lang, 2003).

14. Chela Sandoval, *Methodology of the Oppressed* (Minneapolis: University of Minnesota Press, 2000), 114.

15. Jessika ter Wal and Maykel Verkuyten, *Comparative Perspectives on Racism* (Aldershot, UK: Ashgate, 2000).

16. Yasmin Gunaratnam, *Researching "Race" and Ethnicity: Methods, Knowledge and Power* (Thousand Oaks, Calif.: Sage Publications, 2003); Caroline Knowles, *Race and Social Analysis* (Thousand Oaks, Calif.: Sage Publications, 2003).

17. Martin Bulmer and John Solomos, *Researching Race and Racism* (London: Routledge, 2004).

18. Linda Tuhiwai Smith, *Decolonizing Methodologies: Research and Indigenous Peoples* (New York: St. Martin's Press, 1999).

19. Robert Blauner, *Racial Oppression in America* (New York: Harper & Row, 1972).

20. M. Annette Jaimes, "American Indian Studies: Toward an Indigenous Model," *American Indian Culture and Research Journal* 11, no. 3 (1987): 1–16.

21. Sau-Ling Cynthia Wong, "Denationalization Reconsidered: Asian American Cultural Criticism at a Theoretical Crossroads," *Amerasia Journal* 21, nos. 1 and 2 (1995): 1–27.

22. Audre Lorde, "The Master's Tools Will Never Dismantle the Master's House," in *This Bridge Called My Back: Writings by Radical Women of Color*, 3rd ed., ed. Cherrie L. Moraga and Gloria E. Anzaldua (Berkeley, Calif.: Third Woman Press, 2002), pp. 106–109.

23. Lane Ryo Hirabayashi, "Back to the Future: Re-framing Community-Based Research," *Amerasia Journal* 21, nos. 1 and 2 (1995): 103–118.

24. Robert S. Lynd and Helen Merrell Lynd, *Middletown: A Study in Contemporary American Culture* (New York: Harcourt, Brace, 1929).

25. Yolanda T. Moses, forward to *The Other Side of Middletown: Exploring Muncie's African American Community*, ed. Luke Eric Lassiter, Hurley Goodall, Elizabeth Campbell, and Michelle Natasya Johnson (Walnut Creek, Calif.: AltaMira Press, 2004).

PERSPECTIVES I

Ethnic Studies: Preparing for the Future

2

OTIS L. SCOTT

ETHNIC STUDIES FORMATIONS on this nation's campuses have been in existence for over thirty years. The history of ethnic studies—to be sure not an even one—underscores the determination of faculty, students, and a few enlightened administrators to create and maintain a presence within the institutional framework of postsecondary institutions. And clearly those of us in this project have established a history—a record of our experiences which may be examined and evaluated as we carefully ponder the future of ethnic studies.

In broad strokes, this essay concerns the history and future of ethnic studies. My focus, however, is on moving the teaching, scholarly, and service agendas forward over the next, say, thirty years. I believe that a long look into the future is sharpened by a careful examination of the past and present. Given this, I am asserting the importance of a post-reflection on the first generation of ethnic studies programs. This is not meant to be a nostalgic revisit of an overly romanticized past. This exercise in critical reflection is meant to be a prompt for getting us to refocus, if needed, on the normative ideals shaping the formation of ethnic studies and to address the substantive conditions now facing ethnic studies. Both exercises are essential to preparing for the future.

I have divided this chapter into three major parts, exclusive of the introductory and concluding remarks. In part one, "Foundations in Transformation," I revisit key landmarks in the history of ethnic studies in an attempt to lay a conceptual foundation for understanding the origins and rationales for ethnic studies programs. I accept the risk of criticism by restating, what for some, is the obvious. I do so because I refuse to accept the premise that the history of the ethnic studies struggle for place and space in predominately white institutions is commonly known as we approach forty years from the beginnings of the struggle. In this section I discuss what I consider a defining feature of ethnic studies curricular and program efforts; its transformative objectives. Part two, "Facing the Wind," is a discussion of some major challenges—some old and continuing, others new—facing ethnic studies. In part three, "Toward a New Day," I discuss the responses ethnic studies programs must make in the face of continuing challenges. I argue that these responses should be part of a strategic plan intended to insure the discipline remains relevant to the needs of its historical constituencies and, importantly, keeps the discipline in alignment with its social change mission.

Part One: Foundations in Transformation

It can be asserted and ably defended that program formations constructed around the research, study, and teaching of the experiences of people of color represent—with no hubris intended—the most revolutionary changes to the curricula of higher education.[1] In the late 1960s, the development of ethnic-specific courses and programs, especially degree-granting programs, represented a clear oppositional presence to the hegemonic Eurocentrism which had shaped, and continues to shape and define the important enterprise of education in the United States. And nowhere has this grip been more visible and entrenched than in higher education.

In the late 1960s the curricular landscape of many colleges and universities was being altered. This was the direct result of the on-campus political activism which was situated within the moral postulates and social objectives of the larger national civil rights movement. The movement was a sustained and dramatic protest against the fundamental moral and ethical inconsistency between the pronounced democratic tenets of this society and its practices.[2] This protest dynamic was the context and the catalyst for the formation of ethnic studies programs. This spirit of change was infectious. It also raised the passions and commitment of those interested in developing new interdisciplinary programs, not only in ethnic studies, but also in women's studies, environmental studies, and peace and conflict studies. There are several informative studies and analyses of the struggles shaping the context of the beginning of what I'll refer to as the "ethnic studies movement."[3] I need not recapture the substance of these accounts here. However, it is interesting to note that there are several common themes arising from the various analyses of the history of ethnic studies. In summary fashion these are:

- *Ethnic studies has a transformative mission.* The most critical objective of the discipline is to bring about changes in what is taught about the social, historical, and cultural experiences of ethnic groups. The objective of research and teaching in ethnic studies is to provide a deeper and wider reservoir of knowledge and perspectives about the experiences of ethnic groups. Ethnic studies disciplinarians optimistically believe that with accurate knowledge about people of color, stereotypes, fears, prejudices, and discrimination will be reduced. Some scholars believe that new knowledge will bring about a change of consciousness which will compel the learner to become actively engaged in changing the negative aspects of one's institutional life.
- *Ethnic studies is a corrective and redemptive project.* This is another dimension of the transformative mission. Ethnic studies teaching and scholarship attempts to fill in the gaps in knowledge and correct misconceptions, half truths, and lies about ethnic groups. Ethnic studies scholarship also advances new paradigmatic approaches to both study and teaching which speak to the creative and innovative qualities of this discipline.
- *Ethnic studies has generative capacities.* As noted immediately above, ethnic studies researchers and teachers have developed and used social science and literary models, among others, to explain, describe, and represent ethnic group experiences. These models include those highlighting the resilience of ethnic families; *borderlands* constructs in literature and social science, which provide unique tools for knowing more about the insider experiences of Latinas; and diasporic and transnational models that allow us to draw connections and disconnections between the experiences of earlier generations of Asian and Pacific Island immigrants and their descendents. Such models also assist with developing more inclusive understandings of the world populations and their cultures and how groups have responded to the predations of other groups.

It should come as no surprise that these themes were embedded in the rhetoric of the social protest movements of the 1960s and early 1970s. Students, faculty, and community leaders all demanded a restructured American society, a reconstructed society more consistent in its practices with its democratic pronouncements. These themes also tended to be reflected in various iterations of the missions and goal statements of ethnic studies formations: programs, centers, institutes, departments, and, in one instance, a school.[4]

Needless to say, the development and implementation of ethnic studies programs were fraught with strife and conflict. Nathan Hare instructively comments on the substance of the struggle around instituting Black studies at San Francisco State.[5] The pitch and tenor of this struggle were replicated on countless campuses throughout the length and breadth of this nation. In a real sense the dynamic of change which brought about the Black Studies Program at San Francisco State served as the midwife for the birth of programs in Asian American and Asian Pacific American studies, Chicano/a and Latino/a studies, Native American studies, and women's studies.

An overarching and connecting theme throughout the majority of ethnic studies programs is that of *transformation*.[6] This becomes clear if one reviews the early program statements setting forth program objectives. The language of "change" is evident. This should come as no great surprise given that these programs were carved out of the dreams and aspirations of countless activists influenced by the spirit of social change emanating from the people movements of the 1960s. Transformationists of this early era were calling for substantial changes in America's treatment of people marginalized by those deeming skin color (and by extension: gender, lower social or economic status, and other cultural and or physical characteristics or lifestyles that were not valued) the mark of the *outsider*.

Before I go any further I want to offer an explanation of my meaning of the concept *transformation*. In its simplest root definition, transformation refers to a process of change; the altering of one form into another, or the change of one condition into another.

Transformation as used in this essay speaks to both the thesis and process resulting in change. That is, the process, which does not have to be linear, involves embracing the idea of change and developing the strategic approaches for breathing life into that idea. But transformation—and especially social transformation—represents first and foremost a change in one's consciousness to the extent that one is able to arrive at some basic interpretations and understandings of one's place in a larger institutional and cultural setting. In a very real sense, transformation in this context is a function of developing the capacity to understand the power of identifying and choosing preferences. Or, more simply put, recognizing the power of saying *yes* and *no*. In this regard the beginning of transformation must stem from a conscious willingness to pursue different ways of seeking knowledge and using it. In sum, transformation, the thesis and substance, means living a qualitatively different life.

At its social-cultural core, transformation speaks to an unwillingness to accept a status quo that is stultifying and limiting. On a personal and existential level transformation challenges us to re-envision ourselves as empowered beings having the agency to act positively on our environment, and in doing so, to cast off images and visages of powerlessness and victimhood.[7]

One has only to have a cursory understanding of the social histories of cultural groups *minoritized* in this society to understand how the social transformation process has functioned. People of color have consistently resisted the various representations of discrimination and the associated horrors of living lives of diminished opportunities. Indeed, each community of color in this nation, drawing from its cultural traditions, mother wit, and native genius, has continued to have to develop and implement modicums of positive changes—transformations—in the life circumstances of its members.[8]

Social transformation was a significant part of the ideology underlying many ethnic studies programs.[9] The institutional context within which people of color existed simply had to be changed from being discriminatory, alienating, and de-humanizing to one based on principles and practices recognizing the dignity and worth of human beings. An essential corollary of this was the fundamental belief that people in the American social order had a right to receive fair and equal treatment without regard to their cultural, physical, or other individual or group characteristics.

This basic understanding of the concept of transformation formed an essential part of the objectives and rationales of the advocates for ethnic studies programs. For example, early on ethnic studies scholars made demands for change. The demands were focused on loosening the canon-bound disciplines and the academic and administrative support structures upon which the disciplines rested. They were demands for space—physical and intellectual—where ethnic studies scholars could do their work. Many ethnic studies faculty still hold to the notion that our programs have a major role to play in forming a prescription for institutional transformation. As idealistic as it may still seem, the belief that the scholarly rebuttal of lies, stereotypes, and historical omissions will put into motion processes for disassembling the walls of oppression still holds sway. And yet, even in the face of this guarded optimism, most ethnic studies disciplinarians are also fully aware of the continuing challenges facing this project and its transformative objectives.

Part Two: Facing the Wind

To assert that the waters through which the diverse ethnic studies programs have navigated have hardly been placid is speaking to the obvious. Indeed, the histories of many, if not most, programs are written in styles similar to that written at San Francisco State, where the first degree-granting program in Black studies was founded in the mid-1960s. Critical examinations by and about people of color have not generally been welcomed to the table where Eurocentric ideas and perspectives about the human experience hold forth. Ethnic studies scholarship still elicits the rage of "cultural warriors."[10] This is to say that ethnic studies continues to face assorted difficulties on the way to becoming a full-fledged member in the academy. Suffice it to say that the specific challenges will vary from program to program. But in the main, ethnic studies' efforts to become fully institutionalized are made difficult by both structural and environmental factors. By structural factors I am referring to the formalized policy positions college and university officials (including faculty decision makers) take in response to ethnic studies' claims for first-class academic status. All too often both institutionalized attitudes and practices, ranging from patronizing to outright hostile, shape the context within which ethnic studies programs have had to function.

For purposes of clarification, some examples of structural challenges may be helpful. By no means are these meant to be all-inclusive. It is my experience that the examples noted are some of the more persistent and recurring ones. They demand much time and attention by heads of programs and their faculty. Budget allocations are public policy decisions, and ethnic studies program heads tend to be on the receiving end of policy statements and practices which threaten the program's life blood. Countless anecdotes from colleagues over the years attest to how their programs are marginalized through funding processes. I am aware that the extent to which this occurs varies across the nation. I am also aware that there are programs in public and private colleges and universities which are rather well-funded. I am also mindful of the fact that there are several examples of ethnic studies programs whose exemplary national status is—in large part—a function of strong institutional support. These are exceptions to the rule. In the main, ethnic studies must eke out an existence on budgetary support which, at best, allows for maintenance of a status quo existence. Such a status severely limits the possibility for program development and progress. Tragically, during austere budget times, ethnic studies programs are likely to lose even more of their subsistence-level support.

The placement of ethnic studies programs within academic units which may not have an affinity with the mission and goals of ethnic studies is another type of structural challenge to both programs and their faculty. Ethnic studies faculty in such circumstances too often experience difficulty receiving balanced retention, tenure, and promotion evaluations. A common feature of the malplacement of ethnic studies is assigning the program to another academic unit such as history, sociology, English, etc. In such arrangements ethnic studies programs become virtual wards of a guardian program. This lack of autonomy can have withering consequences for ethnic studies programs. Program heads too often find themselves having to work through the governance structures of the guardian department. These structures, due to priorities of the guardian department, often prove unworkable for ethnic studies because they invariably fail to adequately consider the program needs of ethnic studies and its faculty.

I believe that ethnic studies programs not having the autonomy necessary to function as do other academic programs remains a challenge and does not bode well for a healthy future for such programs. Program heads and their faculty must have the same degree and scope of "home rule" authority as provided to other, more "traditional" programs. Without this authority the ethnic studies agenda for curriculum development, vital personnel matters, student advising, service to the community, and other roles deemed important to the program will be crafted by others.

It must be mentioned here that there are ethnic studies programs which have weathered these and other challenges.[11] Several are as institutionalized as any other college or university program. That is, many ethnic studies programs have the essential element of autonomy. These programs have control over fiscal, personnel, and program matters. They are also able to place faculty on strategic governance structures in the academy, such as curriculum, budget, and faculty senate. Such successful programs award baccalaureate degrees; several have graduate programs; a very few, like UC Berkeley, have Ph.D. programs. The acknowledgement of successful programs and the contributions ethnic studies programs have made and continue to make to academia is a story in need of telling. I'll leave that project to someone else. The point here is that ethnic studies programs share a historical experience written by the pen of struggle. They also share a contemporary history shaped by a national civil rights antipathy which has shaped key public policy measures affecting communities of color in this society.

Contemporarily, ethnic studies is challenged by the politics of an environment where reactionary politics and public policy measures, led by anti-affirmative action and anti-immigration forces, have gained national prominence. In California, the Bakke case, Propositions 163, 187, 209, and most recently 54, have represented key policy measures contributing to sentiments ranging from indifference to hostility toward the social, cultural, and political interests of people of color.[12] Ideologues of this persuasion argue that this nation has paid much too much attention to the claims of "minorities," especially their leadership, and as a consequence, has contributed to creating conditions of "reverse discrimination." The charge is that the interests of people of color, particularly in hiring and college admissions, are privileged over those of white Americans.

Part and parcel of the present climate is the rhetoric of those advocating a "color-blind" society. While the concept has various meanings for different users, the consensual understanding among its anti-affirmative action users is that government enforcement of civil rights policy and programs undermines the norm of color blindness. In short, government and civil rights leaders are the targets of those aiming to dismantle programs and policy measures whose historical antecedents were the blatant racist policies and practices of the pre–civil rights era and their remnants in the post–civil rights era.

I suspect that many people have serious reservations about the need for remaking this nation into a society at odds with its racist past and present. They believe we live in a society where skin color is not an impediment to full enjoyment of rights, privileges, and amenities. However, given how deeply structured is the history of the subordination of people of color and other social groups scripted as "minorities" in the social order, creating a nondiscriminating society remains a dream deferred. Indeed, the color-blind concept has the currency of code speak. It argues against continuing to give credence to the claims of social groups which allege that they have been historically injured by America's institutional processes. And since there are no apparent new options or alternatives on the table to deal with continuing discrimination in this society, adherents of "color blindness" as social policy and practice are effectively calling for a maintenance of the status quo in race and ethnic relations.[13]

It is within this highly charged social and political environment that the activities of ethnic studies are carried out. Ours is an environment where expressions of dislike and even hate against people from different cultures speaking nonstandard English are commonplace. This is especially disturbing since the 2001 attacks against the World Trade Center in New York and the Pentagon in Washington, D.C. The representation of this nation's longstanding xenophobia has surged to a pitch unprecedented since World

War II. This is demonstrated by the racial profiling of Arabs and Arab Americans and others "appearing to look like Arabs" as "terrorists."

What does this have to do with ethnic studies? Much. We do our work within this environment. This is the social and political climate wherein we teach our students to be critical observers of society and urge them to become involved on some level, giving back to the communities from which they come or that they identify with. There is more. Given the scholarly and activist dimensions of the ethnic studies project, our work can and has been scapegoated as antithetical to creating a "color-blind" society. Proponents of this position argue that our continued emphasis on the experiences of ethnic and racialized groups contributes to the fragmenting and "balkanization" of the United States.[14] What is clear at this time is that ethnic studies is likely to be subjected to continued, if not heightened, attempts by critics to marginalize what we do and those who do it. I believe the challenges facing ethnic studies are considerable. How we might address and overcome them is my next concern.

Part Three: Toward a New Day

There are some areas of our endeavors which with some additional attention could have important payoffs for a meaningful ethnic studies future. I believe that given the political, economic, and social contexts of our lives over the last decade, ethnic studies is challenged to become more intimately involved in the day-to-day issues affecting the lives of the people who are the subjects of much of the work we do. I will return to this point after focusing on one of the important areas of ethnic studies work where continued scholarly activity will push this project forward.

Ethnic studies scholar-teachers must continue to do the deep conceptual work needed to sharpen the analytical tools necessary to more clearly and accurately represent the institutional and cultural lives, accomplishments, and challenges facing ethnic groups. Examples are noted in the work of scholars attempting to come to grips with mixed heritage and multi-raciality[15] and scholars delving into the concept of borders[16] and using it as a literary and social science tool for better knowing what it means to live in the "betweens" in this society. This work is joined by the ongoing efforts of scholars honing their analyses of the complexities of the lives of people of color by better understanding how class and gender affect the lives of both men and women in this nation.[17] And of course, these examples are within the new conceptual streams for explaining, describing, and prescribing responses to the challenges facing people of color forged by Molefi Asante and the school of Afrocentricity and those scholar-activists[18] arguing passionately on behalf of Native American sovereignty issues. This work must continue and be both sharpened and heightened.

There is still another consideration which must be made by ethnic studies. I will venture that most ethnic studies programs include in their program objectives some sort of statement of their commitment to social responsibility. Typically this statement is contained among a listing of program objectives which vow to build bridges of presence and service to communities of color. Ethnic studies programs invariably seek—at least normatively—to establish relationships with people of color outside the realms of academe. Generally the purpose of such bridge building—beyond simply establishing social and cultural ties—is to extend the resources of ethnic studies programs and faculty to people beyond the campus. These credos contain language recognizing the importance of reaching back and down to lift up others, as was strongly advocated by the late African American educator, Anna Julia Cooper.[19]

A practical way that ethnic studies programs implement this "lifting" occurs through a variety of service learning activities. Fieldwork, internships and special studies activities are also specific examples of how this service practicum can be experienced. I am aware that not all ethnic studies programs make this a requirement of completing the baccalaureate degree. From my experience, degree-granting programs are more likely to make community service a core requirement than is a program offering a minor or a certificate. I want to strongly urge that this feature of the preparation of undergraduate ethnic studies students continue. Not just for the practical purposes of serving others, which is noble in itself, but for the important purpose of modeling the value of service and the practice of serving others.

Requiring students to experience service learning should be a hallmark of the program. If no program exists, faculty should require service as part of the course(s) they teach. My experience with this form of "applied ethnic studies" is that both students and community members, or NGOs, or schools gain in the process. For example, college students serving in a mentoring program located at a local middle school gain important social and cultural skills, such as communication, time management, multicultural experiences, and so on, from such a learning opportunity. Further, they gain a real-world experience which gives them a chance to apply and evaluate some of the theories and concepts learned in lecture halls and laboratories. School children have a chance to interact with college students, perhaps of the same ethnic group, and learn something about what college is like. The school and the classroom teacher gain an additional interested adult in the life of the child. Ethnic studies' service role is another dimension of the transformative objective of the discipline. The work and dedication of eager and talented students and faculty can have, and has had, a positive effect on the lives of people. Change here is measured in small increments. These are increments of opportunity; increments evolving from seeking and finding new approaches to resolving persistent problems. Importantly, such collaborations can leave community residents and students with an important sense of agency. They understand that collective efforts can bring about positive changes in their life circumstances.

There is another important social role ethnic studies can and must play in the contemporary era. It is a role purposely intended to respond to the challenges facing communities of color and people in general who find themselves living unseen and unheard on the margins of life. The task of ethnic studies in large part today is to grapple with the issues and resulting sets of questions regarding how this discipline can be more socially relevant in this post–civil rights era. This is not a question which does not carry a heavy weight. It is not one on which all ethnic studies teacher-scholar-activists will agree as to its importance or, for that matter, relevance. But it is one which we must engage because it compels us to squarely face the history of this project. I do not mean its chronological history, that is, its beginnings. I am referring particularly to the moral bases underpinning the rationales for founding ethnic studies. Those foundations posited that a complete education must be culturally relevant to all learners.[20] And that a culturally relevant education was one which minimally presented opportunities to students for learning about their own and the social histories of people long not receiving serious consideration in academe. An important corollary of this thinking is that students, especially students of color, have a right to experience learning arenas where people of color—as authentic voices—preside over the learning process.

As I have earlier mentioned, ethnic studies courses and programs are largely creatures of struggle. Struggle for change in how and what postsecondary institutions offered up as social histories of people of color; struggle over the question of whether there was a place at the academic table for faculty and students of color. And in one fashion or another early programs have persisted and new programs have been initiated within this paradigm of struggle. This is another way of saying—perhaps reminding us—that activism is an inextricable part of ethnic studies. Further, this is also a way of reminding us of the theme of social responsibility. It is an ever-present thread woven into the multichromatic ethnic studies cloak. Of course, both activism and social responsibility can be and are carried out in different ways. Given the proactive history and the social change dynamic framing this history, it is crucial that we keep this legacy in mind as we approach the challenges of the current era. This necessarily means our being more proactive on behalf of our programs. We must be willing to use all strategies available to advance and protect our presence in the academy. In this vein, better networking efforts must be undertaken, both within and outside our institutions. Increased outreach efforts to our regional, state, and national colleagues are in order. This, for some of us, will mean leaving the comfort zones of our own ethnic home ground into realms of the unfamiliar. I believe such ventures are appropriate and necessary. Ethnic studies faculty cannot be timid about modeling new forms of coalitions and new forms of relationships, even if these take us across ethnic lines and borders. Such arrangements could very well result in faculty and curriculum sharing projects which could benefit the participating programs.

I strongly urge a more active role by ethnic studies faculty in public policy arenas. This includes local, state, and national venues. Especially needed is involvement in policy issues affecting communities of people whose opinions are neither heard nor solicited, or given serious attention, if solicited. I believe ethnic studies practitioners can fill important voids in this arena in any number of ways consistent with the roles expected of scholar-activists. A very basic role is that we will disseminate the results of their work. Merely sharing the results of, for example, a community-based study of homelessness could be of tremendous value to a community organization attempting to more effectively advocate for displaced individuals and families. And in this vein I also urge more networking between ethnic studies scholars and programs with policy makers at all levels.

For the sake of example I will use the urban area where I live, Sacramento, California. I think it a fair question to ask to what extent scholars of color—ethnic studies scholars in particular—are consulted on urban matters. To what extent are ethnic studies programs consulted on matters, such as transportation, crime, education, and employment, pertaining to people of color. I am contending here that ethnic studies scholars must be on any list of contacts regarding issues affecting people of color. It seems only logical that perspectives and views from those who research and teach about the life experiences and circumstances of people of color must inform the discourse—especially that having policy implications—affecting people of color. This, however, will not come to pass because it is a right, just, and proper relationship. It will come into being on the heels of ethnic studies faculty making purposeful steps toward building relationships with the folks in the communities which are the subjects of our scholarship and teaching.

This is likely not an observation which will be readily embraced by all. Some of us toil under the belief that neither our work nor our labors should be subjectified in this fashion. Some will vociferously argue that scholars should not wander into the forests of political issues, and certainly not community-based political activity.[21] Anything less than this risks, so the purists argue, compromising the level of objectivity which a scholar must always preserve.

I want to rebut this line of reasoning. It is not consistent with the social and intellectual history of ethnic studies programs. The social interventionist role of ethnic studies is one of its defining characteristics. The discipline was, to borrow a phrase commonly used during the struggles of the civil rights era, born of struggle. Ethnic studies scholar-activists have long records of activism through engagement with the issues, events, circumstances, and challenges facing people of color. This level of engagement should continue and, in selected instances, I would argue the level of social involvement must be raised.

I take this position because it is more than apparent that communities of color and other marginalized people are in need of voice, advocacy. Some of this can be provided by ethnic studies programs, faculty, and students. The unattended needs of people of color are not a new phenomenon. Discrimination, lack of economic opportunity, suspicion, alienation, xenophobia, and outright hate aimed at those scripted as "the other" have long shaped the experiences of tens of millions of Americans. Their lives have often been played out between the proverbial rock and hard place. But given this continuum of events and circumstances, this particular post–civil rights period is noteworthy. We live in the diminishing light of the dynamic era of social progress marked by the civil rights struggles of the 1960s. That span of time has long passed. The current post–civil rights era is disturbingly marked by clear and present antagonisms aimed at those living on the margins of institutional life in this nation. Assaults have been and are being made against such civil rights–inspired policies as affirmative action, immigration, and workers' rights.[22] California clearly upped the ante in the high-stakes anti–affirmative action game when voters in 1996 approved an amendment to the state constitution making any state-sponsored affirmative action programs unconstitutional.[23]

Added to this is the angst hanging over this nation in the wake of the September 2001 bombings of the World Trade Center and the Pentagon. The pall of nervous anticipation and the resulting hyper-patriotic nationalism generated in this society have chilled any real attention to the human needs of the disenfranchised. They remain locked out of any meaningful participation in American society. Never having much opportunity to voice their concerns even in the "best of times," in the current defense-orientated environment there is virtually no opportunity to have concerns about one's welfare paid any serious attention. There is a noticeable absence of voices in strategic positions both inside and outside government sectors working to translate concerns and needs of people into policies and practices that address those needs. Indeed, registering oppositional views to "official anti-terrorist" policy positions is likely to get the rapt attention of interconnected "homeland security" law enforcement agencies. And yet, in the face of this new oppression, arenas where these crucial issues can be aired and addressed must be found.

Concluding Observations

I believe that there is an important transformative role which can be played by ethnic studies faculty and students in this current milieu. Programs, faculty, and students in concert with various communities of people can become more active in planning and staging teach-ins, developing research projects, writing position papers, holding colloquia, and participating in other activities aimed at giving voice to the concerns of people unable or unwilling to speak for themselves. The fact that we academics function within a somewhat privileged venue where we can take unpopular positions affords us an arena for action and engagement not ordinarily provided to most others in this society.

It is in the creative space that this advantage provides that we must do the tough intellectual work necessary to bring about a change in attitudes and practices which diminish the humanity of too many people in this society. Alongside, and in some instances, in the absence of voices assuming the responsibility for humanizing the social culture of the United States, ethnic studies scholarship and activism as acts of social responsibility can be a welcome contribution to the age-old long march toward social justice.

Notes

1. Manning Marable, *Dispatches from the Ebony Tower* (New York: Columbia University Press, 2000).

2. An excellent study of the moral basis of the civil rights movement is Dr. Martin Luther King, Jr., *Why We Can't Wait* (New York: Mentor Books, 1964).

3. Evelyn Hu-DeHart, "The History, Development, and Future of Ethnic Studies," *Phi Delta Kappan* 75, no. 1 (1993): 50–54; Maulana Karenga, *Introduction to Black Studies* (Los Angeles: University of Sankore Press, 1993).

4. The School (now College) of Ethnic Studies was founded in 1969 at San Francisco State College (now University). See www.sfsu.edu/~ethnicst/.

5. Nathan Hare, "The Battle of Black Studies," *Black Scholar* (May 1972): 32–37.

6. I am indebted to the work Johnnella Butler has done on this subject. My thinking on the transformative role of ethnic studies is a work in progress and hopefully builds on her insightful work. See Johnnella Butler and John Walter, eds., *Transforming the Curriculum: Ethnic Studies and Women's Studies* (New York: SUNY Press, 1991); and Johnnella Butler, ed., *Color-Line to Borderlands: The Matrix of American Ethnic Studies* (Seattle: University of Washington Press, 2001.

7. Elizabeth Minnich, *Transforming Knowledge* (Philadelphia: Temple University Press, 1991).

8. Both Vincent Parrillo and Ronald Takaki make valuable contributions to our understanding of how and what people of color have done by way of helping themselves overcome the effects of race and ethnic discrimination. See their respective works, *Strangers to These Shores* (Boston: Allyn and Bacon, 2003); and *A Different Mirror* (Boston: Little, Brown, 1993).

9. The actual number of programs then and now deserves fresh research. Gretchen Bataille, Miguel Carranza, and Lauri Lisa report in *Ethnic Studies in the United States* (New York: Garland, 1996) some 800 very diverse ethnic studies programs.

10. Dinesh D'Souza, *Illiberal Education* (New York: Vintage, 1991); Arthur M. Schlesinger, *The Disuniting of America* (New York: Norton, 1992); and Alan D. Bloom, *Closing of the American Mind* (New York: Simon and Schuster, 1987).

11. Programs in ethnic studies have had to develop staying power to the *nth* degree. Most have had their ups and downs in both growth and support. It would not be far off the mark to suggest that most programs have significant histories of *crisis management* as they have attempted to survive and grow. Program heads have had to develop high-level negotiating and lobbying skills in order to stave off assorted predations. Ethnic studies' survival stories and strategies are begging research attention.

12. It deserves comment that California has a prominent place among those states where outright assaults against civil rights gains have been made. Most importantly, contemporary anti-affirmative action and anti-immigrant initiatives have originated in the Golden State. Among the instructive analyses of the phenomenon of resurgent racism in California is Adalberto Aguirre, Jr. and Jonathan H. Turner, *American Ethnicity: The Dynamics and Consequences of Discrimination* (Boston: McGraw Hill, 2001).

13. John Hope Franklin, *The Color Line* (Columbia: University of Missouri Press, 1993); and Ellis Cose, *Color Blind* (New York: HarperCollins, 1997).

14. Shelby Steele, *The Content of Our Character* (New York: Harper Perennial, 1991); Schlesinger, *The Disuniting of America*.

15. Maria P. P. Root, ed., *The Multiracial Experience: Racial Borders as the New Frontier* (Thousand Oaks, Calif.: Sage Publications, 1996); and Jon Michael Spencer, *The New Colored People: The Race Movement in America* (New York: New York University Press, 1997).

16. Gloria Anzaldúa, *Borderlands: The New Mestiza = La Frontera* (San Francisco: Aunt Lute Books, 1987).

17. Manning Marable, *The Crisis of Color and Democracy: Essays on Race, Class and Power* (Monroe, Maine: Common Courage Press, 1992); Leith Mullings, *On Our Own Terms: Race, Class and Gender in the Lives of African American Women* (New York: Routledge, 1997); and E. San Juan, Jr., *Racial and Cultural Studies* (Durham, N.C.: Duke University Press, 2002). Also see San Juan's *Racial Formations, Critical Transformations* (Atlanta Highlands, N.J.: Humanities Press, 1992).

18. Ward Churchill, *Struggle for the Land* (Monroe, Maine: Common Courage Press. 1998).

19. Anna Julia Cooper, *A Voice from the South, by a Black Woman of the South* (New York: Negro Universities Press, 1969).

20. Carter G. Woodson, *The Miseducation of the Negro* (Nashville, Tenn.: Winston-Derek Publishers, 1990); Paolo Freire, *Pedagogy of the Oppressed* (New York: Herder and Herder, 1970); and Ira Shor, *Critical Teaching and Everyday Life* (Boston: South End Press, 1980).

21. As is well documented in the history of the founding of ethnic studies programs, faculty activism has been a vital part of that history. This has subjected faculty to much criticism from non-ethnic studies faculty. They charge that activism makes ethnic studies more "political" than "academic." More than a few ethnic studies faculty have suffered grief through personnel processes because of their commitment to their roles as scholar-activists.

22. Stephen Steinberg, *Turning Back* (Boston: Beacon Press, 1995).

23. California voters by a 54 percent majority gave approval to the California Civil Rights Initiative—Proposition 209. This 1996 ballot initiative rendered all of California's affirmative action efforts unconstitutional.

Crafting Ethnic Studies　　　　　　　　　　　3

GARY Y. OKIHIRO

ETHNIC STUDIES SCHOLARS OF MY GENERATION, when reflecting upon our field, are wont to wax nostalgic about the originating spark of educational and social transformation. Back then, we might remember, we shared a common purpose and were energized by the injustices and inequities visited upon us and by the expansive promise of democracy. Born amidst the ruins of capitalist and imperialist "Amerika," ethnic studies emerged as an insistent and uncompromising demand of the masses, according to African American historian Vincent Harding. "Almost everywhere," he wrote, "women and men poured out into the streets and sent flames up into the sky. Almost everywhere a thousand black caucuses and conferences met. It was possible to hear the calls for our history. 'Give us back our history. Let us take our history. Let us use our history. Let us remake our history.'"[1]

This brief rendition of the "crafting" of ethnic studies conceives of that process of "making history" in several ways. Foremost, readers must appreciate that ethnic studies, like all fields of study, is constructed or made by individuals and groups in particular places and times. It matters who those creators are and the historical contexts and forces that constrain, enable, and inspire their works. Further, as a process, ethnic studies has antecedents as well as, hopefully, successors. The ethnic studies of today thus resembles as well as differs from its forebears, and a similar prospect awaits future versions. In tracing that genealogy, I highlight the historical nature of that crafting or the specificities of place and time along with the changes wrought by historical actors over time. Readers should know that the act of crafting might be purposeful and intentional, but it might also be situational and neglectful of introspection and self-criticism. Finally, I caution readers that this version of ethnic studies' pedigree is my crafting, and that my agenda includes the recognition of ethnic studies as a distinctive craft or art or field of study with its own practitioners, lineages, attributes, and integrity, and an appeal to the field to move toward a more self-reflective and generous apprehension of its subject matters and politics.

Crafting Pasts

Memories are short lived, and histories are created by actors and historians. Some remember ethnic studies as an aspect of the domestic U.S. struggle for civil rights. Access to the ballot and to equal opportunities comprised the broad social agenda for entry into higher education and its curriculum. Ethnic studies as remediation to correct past and present injustices and to end racism was cited by Yale University's provost, Charles H. Taylor, Jr., as a reason for instituting African American studies. Speaking at a conference organized by Yale's black students in 1968, Taylor explained: "The fact is that our society, our schools, our education, suffer from white racism. This racism is both conscious and unconscious—much of it unconscious, but nevertheless real. . . . What we are faced with then in our black students' protest is not simply, in some respects not even chiefly, their proper demand to know more about themselves, about *their* heritage and *their* tradition, but rather their consciousness of how important it is for American society, for us, the white majority, to know a lot more about them. We need this knowledge to attack not only conscious prejudice, which is easy to identify, but to overcome unconscious discrimination, that simple lack of awareness, the ignorance from which we all suffer in white America."[2]

Other accounts depict ethnic studies as a strand of identity politics arising during the 1960s among "blacks, Hispanics, women, and homosexuals." The breeding ground for this "victim's revolution," according to Dinesh D'Souza, himself an immigrant from India, was the browning of America through massive immigration from Asia, Latin America, and the Caribbean and their higher birth rates and the shrinking white population. "When America loses her predominantly white stamp," D'Souza asks, "what impact will that have on her Western cultural traditions?" Assuming the voice of an unbiased news reporter but with clear contempt for his subjects and their aspirations, D'Souza alleges that "powerful minority groups" were bent on insurrection "in the name of those who suffer from the effects of Western colonialism in the Third World, as well as race and gender discrimination in America. It is a revolution on behalf of minority victims. Its mission is to put an end to bigoted attitudes which permit perceived social injustice to continue, to rectify past and present inequities, and to advance the interests of the previously disenfranchised."[3]

Still others recall ethnic studies as the movement of "Third World peoples" for self-determination, to overthrow the yoke of colonialism both abroad and at home. Huge were the currency of the Algerian, Cuban, and Chinese revolutions and their luminaries—Fanon, Che, and Mao—and the determined struggles of Vietnamese women and men in their protracted wars for freedom inspired a generation of student activists. In a 1971 foundational text edited by a collective drawn from a course on Asian women at the University of California, Berkeley, a prominent section was devoted to "Third World women." The editors, in selecting chapters for that section, observed the connections among women in North America and Asia forged by the common threads of oppression and exploitation and resistance and liberation. Central was the Indochinese Women's Conference held in Vancouver, Canada in April 1971 that brought together Third World and women's liberation concerns and engaged over 150 Canadian and U.S. activists with a six-woman delegation from Viet Nam. "As Third World people," a conference report asserted, "we share similar struggles in fighting racist conditions and attitudes in our communities and our everyday lives. Our people—Blacks, Chicanos, Asians, Native Americans, and Native Hawaiians—have had our land ripped off by the whites, our women raped, our homes plundered, and our men drafted to further this country's imperialist ventures into Third World countries." Accordingly, "we see a need for learning about each other's history as Third World people and of informing each other about our movements for self-determination."[4]

Crafting Solidarities

Despite those women's internationalism, some men framed ethnic studies as a U.S. project. The wholesale exclusion of especially Asians and Latina/os, as "races," from American discourses of nation prompted a resistant, racialized nationalism that insisted on inclusion, not through absorption but as equal members of the nation state.[5] Nationalism, while racialized, was, in truth, simultaneously gendered in that manliness was recurrently crafted and reconstituted through nationalism and imperial expansion.[6] As I write in New York City about a month after the tragic events of September 11, 2001, I am confronted with a frenzied nationalism and the spectacle of manly reinventions, including New York City's policemen and firemen, the U.S. military, and even George W. Bush, who cast a furtive and slight shadow before the horrific and murderous acts of that day. And in making war on, in Bush's words, "evildoers," American men embark on a mission ("crusade") to rescue and uplift Afghan women, or "white men saving brown women from brown men."[7]

Seeking to counter anti-Asianists and the perpetual foreigner stereotype of Asians in the United States, liberal and Asian Americanist writers and scholars stressed that Asians lay claim to America by residency and birth, labor and community building, and extending the reach and ensuring the guarantees of the Constitution.[8] Perhaps the most emphatic about U.S. nationalism were the male writers who assembled the collections *Aiiieeeee! An Anthology of Asian-American Writers* (1975) and *The Big Aiiieeeee! An Anthology of Chinese American and Japanese American Literature* (1991). As plainly put by the editors about their selections for the Asian American literary canon, "Our anthology is exclusively Asian-American. That means Filipino-, Chinese-, and Japanese-Americans, American born and raised."[9] Paralleling the absence of Asians in American letters is the absence (or feminization) of Asian men. "The white stereotype of the acceptable and unacceptable Asian is utterly without manhood," the writers state. "Good or bad, the stereotypical Asian is nothing as a man. At worst, the Asian-American is contemptible because he is womanly, effeminate, devoid of all the traditionally masculine qualities of originality, daring, physical courage, and creativity."[10] And they underscore that theme, linking manliness with heterosexuality, in their second collection because, they write, "it is an article of white liberal American faith today that Chinese men, at their best, are effeminate closet queens like Charlie Chan and, at their worst, are homosexual menaces like Fu Manchu. No wonder David Henry Hwang's derivative *M. Butterfly* won the Tony for best new play of 1988. The good Chinese man, at his best, is the fulfillment of white male homosexual fantasy, literally kissing white ass."[11]

As feminist critics of colored men's patriarchal (and homophobic) responses to white racism have pointed out, resistance need not mimic the vocabulary and categories of oppression, but should work toward notions of gender and race (and sexuality) that are "nonhierarchical, nonbinary, and nonprescriptive; that can embrace tensions rather than perpetuate divisions."[12] Black power, writes bell hooks, was an effective antiracist idea, but it also forged a patriarchal bond between black and white men. "Militant black men were publicly attacking the white male patriarchs for their racism but they were also establishing a bond of solidarity with them based on their shared acceptance of and commitment to patriarchy," hooks observed. "The strongest bonding element between militant black men and white men was their shared sexism—they both believed in the inherent inferiority of woman and supported male dominance." Accordingly, black "manhood" was purchased with women's subordination.[13]

In addition to its rehabilitation of patriarchy, nationalism promoted homogeneity and repressed heterogeneities for the sake of union in the emergence of creole nation states in the Americas. Nationalism's suppression of difference, of course, sustained the status quo of race, gender, sexuality, class, and citizenship. And although anti-colonial struggles generally sought liberation from European colonizers, postcolonial states oftentimes copied the imagined original in putative revolutions that installed privileged classes—the bourgeoisie and military—over the masses.[14] Some ethnic studies scholars found attractive the idea of internal colonialism because it offered an alternative to the assimilation/integration model and aligned the struggles of peoples of color within the United States with those of Third World peoples against European and American hegemony.[15] Key elements of colonialism were forced entry, economic and political dependency, and racial and cultural oppression. The contest in this paradigm, whether within the nation-state (internal colonialism) or without (classical colonialism), was racialized dominance and resistance.[16] Largely absent were their gendered, sexualized, and classed natures, and hence their limitations as theoretical explanations and as liberation movements.

Transnational models of intellectual and political labors similarly reflected creole and European antecedents. During the late nineteenth century, in the noonday of U.S. and European imperialism, whiteness and white supremacy competed with narratives of nation and created homogenizing and universalizing racialized distinctions of white and nonwhite to sustain the new world order of empire.[17] Grand was the historical and prophetic vision of British historian Charles H. Pearson, who in 1893 published a book that divided the globe between the temperate or white zone and the tropics or nonwhite zone. Whites desired the products of the tropics, Pearson noted, and nonwhites sought the riches of the temperate areas. Empire, thus, created binary geographies—temperate and tropical zones—and racializations—white and nonwhite.[18] Equally essentializing was Germany's Kaiser Wilhelm II when in 1895 he conceived a European unity as whites and as defenders of civilization and Christianity against the invasive threat of the "yellow peril."[19] A decade earlier in the United States, Congregational minister Josiah Strong called for the Christian reconquest of America from the period's anxieties over industrialization and urbanization, immigration and class conflict. Diverse Europeans, melded in the United States as whites and keepers of the twin virtues of civil liberty and Christianity, would, in Strong's expansive rhetoric, "move down upon

Mexico, down upon Central and South America, out upon the islands of the sea, over upon Africa and beyond. And can any one doubt that the result of this competition of races will be the 'survival of the fittest'?"[20]

In opposition to that global whiteness arose negritude and pan-Africanism, the former, a reaction to an alleged European cultural superiority and the latter, a solidarity built upon the supposed unity of a race invented, enslaved, and dispersed by Europeans. Although politically potent, blackness mirrors an essentializing whiteness, and therewith bears the truths and falsehoods of its original. "Pan-Africanism seems to have originated with the awareness of Westernized Africans that all black people were suffering from the slave trade which tended to confer an inferior status upon all black people, whether slave or free, and regardless of the continent upon which they lived," explained a pioneering study of black nationalism. Enslavement, the work asserted, broke down ethnic loyalties and cultures, and endowed slaves with "a sense of common experience and identity." In addition, pan-Africanism, although manifest in struggles against European colonialism as in the maroon revolutions of Haiti, Jamaica, and Surinam, embraced Eurocentrism in its goal of employing Christianity and (European) civilization for the universal uplift of Africa and Africans.[21]

If pan-Africanism arose out of resistance to white supremacy, negritude provided an intellectual challenge to colonialism. First articulated by Afro-Caribbean and African intellectuals in Paris during the 1930s and named by the Martinican poet Aimé Césaire, negritude expressed a new consciousness among blacks of race and culture against the erasures of colonialism and white supremacy. Negritude advanced a defiant black pride in the face of white denigration, wholeness amidst fragmentation. Although primarily a movement of French-speaking blacks and at times at odds with English-speaking black nationalists, negritude offered a powerful antidote to assimilation by recapturing the "African personality," in the words of the West Indian educator Edward Blyden. But like the essentializing elements of pan-Africanism, negritude reflected the Eurocentrism that supported the ideology of white supremacy. African civilization, mainly black Egypt, the argument went, predated, exceeded, and lay the foundations for European civilization.[22]

Tunisian writer Albert Memmi agreed that in rejecting assimilation, as urged by negritude's proponents, "the colonized's liberation must be carried out through a recovery of self and of autonomous dignity." And yet, he observed, there was an intimate and "relentless reciprocity"[23] between colonizer and colonized. Liberation from the colonial condition, he testified, was fought "in the name of the very values of the colonizer," deploying the colonizer's "techniques of thought and his methods of combat. It must be added that this is the only action that the colonizer understands."[24] That conundrum of dismantling the master's house with his tools[25] has vexed black nationalism in its various versions throughout its history. A reflection of its time and contexts, according to a recent, provocative study, black nationalism's central political feature was its inability to create an alternative to the hegemonic politics of its day. "By accepting the notion that black people constitute an organic unit, and by focusing on the goal of nation building or separate political and economic development," the study concludes, "black nationalism *inadvertently* helps to reproduce some of the thinking and practices that created black disadvantage in the first place."[26]

The difficulty, it seems to me, rests not only in questions of methodology (the master's tools) but also in the social process. Those who hold power determine the field of contest. They define the nature and terms of the engagement. Accordingly, responses, comprehensible to the empowered as qualified by Memmi, are constrained by and limited to the original challenge. It is not surprising thus that white supremacy and nationalism is met by black or nonwhite supremacy and nationalism, or that patriarchy confronts another form of patriarchy. In addition, fields of conflict are never static, ever changing, and hence apprehensions of and resistances to oppression and exploitation must move constantly. Within living memory, for instance, the Irish and Jews, once nonwhite, have become white, changing relations in the U.S. racial formation,[27] and Asians and lighter-skinned Latina/os are dubious candidates for a similar transformation.[28] Not simply a moving target, racializations are multiply constituted and constituting. Race denotes not only phenotype and natures but also and simultaneously gender, sexuality, class, and nation. The ethnic studies' singular focus on race, thus, is impoverished and deficient. But its essentialist shortcomings notwithstanding, ethnic studies effectively challenged its equally essentialist creator, white supremacy, at particular historical junctures.

Crafting Ethnic Studies

A major paradigm shift instigated by ethnic studies, it seems to me, was the reversal of what I will call the "problems approach" to the study of race relations. That development was accompanied by the move from what I see as "race relations" to "ethnic studies." American sociology, according to a study, resulted from a mix of factors in the late nineteenth century. Urbanization and immigration from southern and eastern Europe and their attendant problems, including housing, sanitation, poverty, ethnic and labor strife, social disorganization, and crime and juvenile delinquency prompted the rise of the social gospel and various reform movements. The first courses in sociology in the United States offered during the 1880s and 1890s addressed the pathologies of contemporary American society as studies directed at problem solving.[29] Sociology was thus both a science of society and its management. As seen in the introductory textbook that established the direction and content of U.S. sociology after 1921, the discipline examined the individual and the group, social relations, social behavior and its control, and progress.[30]

Robert E. Park, a central figure in establishing an American brand of sociology at the University of Chicago, was interested in both the "Negro" and "Oriental" problems as samples to test his general propositions about modernity. As he observed, "The study of the Negro in America, representing, as he does, every type of man from the primitive barbarian to the latest and most finished product of civilization, offers an opportunity to study . . . the historic social process by which modern society has developed. The Negro in his American environment is a social laboratory."[31] Similarly, Park's first course at the University of Chicago, "The Negro in America," offered in 1914 sought "to estimate the character of the changes which race relations are likely to bring about in the American system."[32]

The consequences of Chicago sociology were both far-reaching and paradigmatic. Its students and faculty, notably Robert E. Park and William I. Thomas, who had recruited Park to Chicago, conceived of race relations and its subjects—problem minorities—as footpaths to understanding and offering cures for the ills of urbanization. The focus, thus, was on U.S. society and modernization broadly, and African and Asian Americans, like European ethnic groups, were mere transients and case studies in the advance of progress.[33] Additionally, Chicago sociologists sought to concoct a science of social research and a prescription to cure social ills and infirmities. As Park declared of his 1924–1926 Pacific Coast survey of race relations, the study, he recalled, was "primarily for the purpose of improving RACE RELATIONS."[34] And because Park believed that a recognition of a common humanity would reduce racial prejudice and conflict and hasten assimilation, he stressed the collection of life histories, as opposed to a study of social structure, and he initiated conversations between pro- and anti-Asianists.[35] Absent within that approach to the study of race relations were considerations of politics and power.

Race relations to sociologists at the University of Chicago were a subset of urban and spatial orderings of individuals and groupings. Within that flattened universe, race became synonymous with ethnicity, and European ethnic groups constituted the model for the progressive cycle of contact and interaction, competition and conflict, and accommodation and assimilation. African Americans from the rural South and Asian agrarian migrants in the West were like Polish peasants in urban centers in the North, according to the Chicago school. The urban environment and its civilizing modernity dissolved the affiliations of race and culture, enabling a single frame of reference and direction for disparate peoples.[36] That optimism was ultimately diminished by the durability of racial prejudice, evident in the histories of African and Asian Americans, by the racial solidarities advocated by nationalists, and by Chicago sociologists who modified their ideas of the ethnic cycle and assimilation in the light of contrary evidence.

Perhaps pivotal in that regard was the race riot in Chicago in July 1919 that lasted for over a week and resulted in the deaths of 15 whites and 23 blacks, injuries to 537, and left over 1,000 homeless. The Chicago riot was the worst of several instances of racial violence during the summer of 1919, in which 120 people died. In the wake of the riot, the state's governor appointed a commission to study the causes of the Chicago riot and to make remedial recommendations. An African American graduate student in the University of Chicago's sociology department, Charles S. Johnson, led the commission's research staff and was the principal author of the commission's report, *The Negro in Chicago*.[37] Although the Chicago school's cycle of migration, contact, competition, conflict, and assimilation formed the organizing framework of the report, *The Negro in Chicago* documented the persistence and deleterious effects of racial prejudice on African Americans as revealed in inferior housing, schools, and recreational facilities, and in poverty and unstable family life. It was clear to the report's authors that the African American experience failed to fit the European model as claimed by Chicago sociology.

The West Coast race relations survey headed by Robert E. Park similarly tested the applicability of the ethnic cycle to non-European groups. The assumption was that "the problems" of Europeans and Asians differed but were similar enough to sustain comparison. Instigated by the Institute of Social and Religious Research in New York City, the survey sought to ascertain the causes of anti-Japanese hatred on the Pacific Coast. Instead, Park conceived of the survey as a study in assimilation, especially of second-generation Japanese Americans. As was shown in later studies, however, notably by Emory Bogardus, a former Chicago student, social distance and discriminatory laws intervened in assimilation's advance, resulting in amalgamation but also in segregation. Even the so-called assimilated second generations among Chinese, Japanese, Filipinos, and Mexicans, Bogardus found, were partially alienated from both American culture and that of their immigrant parents, resulting in the marginal man.[38] As Park himself came to acknowledge, blacks and Asians were key to understanding U.S. society because they were racially distinctive from Europeans. "Japanese, Chinese, and Negroes cannot move among us with the same freedom as the members of other races because they bear marks which identify them as members of their race," explained Park. "This fact isolates them." Segregation and isolation lead to prejudice and prejudice, to isolation and segregation.[39]

The ideas bequeathed by Chicago sociology to succeeding generations of scholars and students are the ethnic cycle and the primacy and eventual triumph of assimilation, both derived from the attributed experience of European ethnic groups.[40] America's nation-of-immigrants ideology requires that all conform to the dominant pattern, America's indigenous peoples notwithstanding, for theoretical validation and political power. In the U.S. racial formation, it is no coincidence that whites constitute the subject and model, or that racialized minorities comprise object populations that conform to or deviate from the larger processes of social integration and modernization. They are sideshows and miners' canaries, curiosities to and litmus tests for the main attraction. Further, African and Asian Americans cannot assimilate with whites because of their badge of color and race prejudice, which, Park declared, was "a spontaneous, more or less instinctive defense-reaction." Segregation and even slavery, accordingly, were "natural" solutions to "the race problem," because both groups, masters and servants, knew their places. But racialized minorities became problems for the normative majority when they claimed democracy's promise and thereby asserted equality with whites and their entitlements to life, liberty, and the pursuit of happiness.[41]

Those core ideas of "natural" and instinctual reactions to perceived racial difference conformed to the Chicago school's analogy of social relations with ecological succession, biological competition, and evolution, procuring the vestment of science for sociology's still immature body. Thus, in the language of ecological succession, the "invading race," according to Park, whether black or brown, posed the problem and not white supremacy or the ideology and structures that sustained it.[42] And by resorting to universals and the inevitability of growth and progress, Chicago sociology slighted the historical (or the specificities of time and place), social, and political bases for human constructions of self and other, social relations, and institutions. Accordingly, despite sociology's initial attraction to activism and remediation derived from the social and religious reform movements of the period, its desire to institute an objective science exerted an opposite, if not contrary pull. Human nature rather than human institutions held the answer to the race problem.

Like sociology, ethnic studies drew its ideas from the politics of its times, when national liberation movements in the Third World pointed to European colonialism as the reason for their subjugation, underdevelopment, and twisted identities, and the domestic U.S. civil rights movement, to white supremacy and racism. The problem was European colonialism abroad and white racism at home, not the colonized or racialized minorities. The solution, accordingly, involved national liberation in the Third World and legislative and judicial redress in the United States, and not the altering of natural instincts or the assimilation of the subject peoples. Ethnic studies thus mirrored the civil rights movement's reversal of the source and definition of the problem as posited by the prevailing race relations paradigm from racism's victims to its perpetrators and from biology to sociology.

A landmark in that shift is the *Report of the National Advisory Commission on Civil Disorders* about the causes of and remediation for the "racial disorders" that hit American cities during the summer of 1967. Although initially criticized as composed of moderates, the commission, appointed by president Lyndon B. Johnson, issued a stinging rebuke not of the black rioters but of inequality in America caused by racism, segregation, poverty, and powerlessness. "This is our conclusion," the report stated succinctly, "our nation is moving toward two societies, one black, one white—separate and unequal." Moreover, "what white Americans have never fully understood—but what the Negro can never forget—is that white society is deeply implicated in the ghetto. White institutions created it, white institutions maintained it, and white society condones it."[43] Remediation, massive and sustained, thus was the responsibility of the government.

Another switch enjoined by ethnic studies was in situating the subject. Race relations, as advanced by Chicago sociology, focused on racialized minorities as mere case studies for its central project of documenting the relentless, triumphal march of modernity and democracy. African and Asian Americans exemplified and, because of their racial badges, deviated from those larger processes deemed central to the American pageant. Thus, for example, the mass removal and detention of Japanese Americans during World War II attracted wide scholarly interest, including from Chicago social scientists, not so much because of its impact upon the lives of Japanese Americans, but because it seemed an aberration in the prevailing narrative of American democracy.[44]

Ethnic studies, in contrast, positioned racialized minorities as the featured subjects and principal audiences of their research, writing, and teaching,[45] such that its practitioners claimed to produce results that were relevant to and for the benefit of their communities. This is a thoroughly commonplace contention, and I simply point out that although characteristic of the 1970s and 1980s, that idea about ethnic studies' subjects and its beneficiaries has a much deeper past. As early as 1938, for instance, Ernest K. Wakukawa published *A History of the Japanese People in Hawaii* because he hoped to nurture in the English-speaking second generation an "appreciation of the achievements and accomplishments of the pioneers and their forebears" and help them understand "their own status and problems in the light of history."[46]

In addition to reversing race relation's problematic subject matter, ethnic studies has insisted on the primacy of individual experience. In that, ethnic studies, like women's studies, sees experience as crucial to the recovery of voices and perspectives missing or distorted in the master narratives written mainly by white men.[47] As put by a study of African American women in the South, "black woman, silent, almost invisible in America, has been speaking for three hundred years in pantomime or at least in a borrowed voice." America "has never asked her to speak, to reveal her private history, her knowledge, her imaginings, never asked her participation in anything but maintenance of humanity by way of the back door."[48] Oral history, I argued some years ago, was both a method and theory in that it is a means by which to recover the history of women, racialized minorities, the working class, and people in non-literate societies, and it maintains that the masses as well as the elites are historical actors whose deeds are equally worthy of documentation and interpretation. Also, oral history links the academy with the community, and has the potential for raising social consciousness and enabling avenues for social change.[49]

Breaking the silence, wrote the historian Joan W. Scott in her important critique of experience, can be fraught with political possibility that might appear frightening and exhilarating. Visibility, another metaphor for empowerment, enables knowledge through an unmediated apprehension of what has hitherto been hidden from view. Experience, she continues, has been a principal means by which historians have given voice to or made visible those usually deemed inconsequential to orthodox history. Further, those experiences are deployed as evidence, uncontestable because of their authority and source—the person who has made and witnessed history. That variety of historical agency, Scott writes, removes experience from its discursive construction and decontextualizes it. Thereby "questions about the constructed nature of experience, about how subjects are constituted as different in the first place, about how one's vision is structured—about language (or discourse) and history—are left aside. The evidence of experience then becomes evidence for the fact of difference, rather than a way of exploring how difference is established, how it operates, how and in what ways it constitutes subjects who see and act in the world."[50] In that way, experience so-conceived reproduces rather than repudiates the very system that renders it invisible and silent in the first place.

Scott's corrective points to an essential difference, on the whole, between ethnic studies and race relations. As shown in Robert E. Park's race relations survey of the Pacific Coast, the focus was on individuals and mutual interactions and understandings. Group conflicts arose because of individual misapprehensions, rivalries, and fears. In contrast, ethnic studies seeks out the locations and articulations of power mainly in and among groups, institutions, and social relations. The contexts, the systems within which individual lives move, acquire meaning, and are constrained are the principal units of study and objects of transformation. While race relations might aspire toward the smooth assimilation of minorities into the majority, ethnic studies envisions a reconstitution of majority (or those who hold and exercise power) and minority (or those separated from power) and the very meanings and workings of America itself.[51]

Perhaps the main ethnic studies text today that poses a counter to the race relations approach is *Racial Formation in the United States* by sociologists Michael Omi and Howard Winant. The book, first published in 1986, describes a "racial formation" in the United States that stresses the social nature of race, its changes over time, and its contentious, political character. Moreover, *Racial Formation* arises from and poses a critique of contemporary conservative ideas of a color-blind society and the declining significance of race in American life.[52] Instead, they propose, the United States was and is an intensely color-conscious society, and race is central to American politics; it exhibits a unique historical flexibility and is immediate in everyday experience and social conflict. Even as racial formation does not displace class or gender systems and relations, Omi and Winant caution, it corrects the tendency of race relations to reduce race to a category of ethnicity and of Marxism, to class. Rather, race is autonomous, irreducible, and always at "the center of American political history."[53] It is ubiquitous and frequently determines access to employment, housing, goods, entitlements, and even identity itself.

Racial Formation rejects as ahistorical the race relations cycle of assimilation with its inevitability and universalism, and embraces a contrary theory of race that is contingent and malleable and hence emphatically historical and social. But it accepts Robert E. Park's notion of racial badges and the exceptional quality of race for peoples of color as opposed to Europeans. In fact, in arguing the centrality and salience of race, Omi and Winant neglect its intersections with gender, sexuality, class, and citizenship and its location within the broader contexts of power within the social formation. Racial meanings, they write, "pervade US society, extending from the shaping of individual racial identities to the structuring of collective political action on the terrain of the state." And although the concept of racial formation is but "a fundamental *organizing principle* of social relationships," they fail to describe the social formation as a whole or show how racial formation articulates with the other organizing principles.[54] Like many correctives, *Racial Formation* succeeds overmuch in making its case. It has become "natural" and a "common sense," Omi and Winant contend, like Park, that "one of the first things we notice about people when we meet them (along with their sex) is their race."[55]

Visibility, as Joan W. Scott has observed, possesses scant potential on its own for basic transformations of power. Ethnic studies, derisively called identity politics by those who invented identity politics, has been hijacked by visibility, voice, and presence in the recent upsurge of multiculturalism and diversity. A plethora of experiences, a palette of colors, a plenitude of cultures is the object of multiculturalism. A kind of capitalism—the united colors of Benetton—this amassing of variety brings strength and wealth, its proponents claim, and makes us feel good in this magnanimous process and gesture. Multiculturalism, in truth, is a latter-day descendent of race relations in that it approaches the "race question," disguised as a matter of culture, horizontally, or as the interactions among equals without consideration of the vertical, or as the hierarchies and relations among unequals. Further, the borders of race, gender, or sexuality are what separates and provokes conflicts, and thus their negotiation and even transgression are solutions to this problem of difference.[56] Under-examined are the powers that define and impose those strictures and designations in the first instance, and the "investments and privations" they install and perpetuate.[57]

Even as ethnic studies broke ranks with race relations, it kept several key aspects of the original faith. These include a continued focus upon urban communities, the idea of social change through research, and the exceptional quality of race for peoples of color. Each of those areas conjures a host of connections that have nurtured extensive and complex literatures. For example, the subject matter's spatial dimension involves not only the urban and rural distinctions and continuities but also regionalisms, nationalisms, and transnationalisms, the local and global, and diasporas, along with the cartographies of race, gender, sexuality, citizenship, and culture. And the notion of research's purpose has prompted debates on the politicization of the academy and culture wars over the canon and curriculum. Of course, ethnic studies, like sociology, has acquired the habits of the disciplines during its years in the university, although it has struggled over the troubling, if arbitrary and false, divides between activism and scholarship and community and academy.[58]

Crafting Social Formations

Ethnic studies has found institutionalization but in the course of the quest has lost its way. We, the founders, figured race as the central object of study and racial politics as the means toward our liberation. We diagnosed the problem correctly insofar as hegemony, in the form of white racial politics, mandated inclusions and exclusions in textbooks, the curriculum, and the racial formation, and we pursued its counter—colored racial politics that sought inclusion even as it excluded whites, those deemed inauthentic, and the wider social formation of gender, sexuality, class, and nation. We've since had diffident relationships with those constituent parts of the social formation, wedded as we are to the racial formation. The once radical expedient of colored politics, a strategic essentialism, plays into the hands of the dealer—white politics—by reifying race and its assumed salience, permanence, and solitude.

Instead, ethnic studies and its politics should embrace the social and not racial formation, and insist that race, gender, sexuality, class, and nation are related social constructions—the systematic exercise of power to maintain privilege and poverty. Those social constructions can be multiply or singly, simultaneously or serially expressed, and they constitute an interlocking whole such that race is gendered, classed, sexualized, and nationalized, while gender is raced, classed, sexualized, and nationalized, and so forth. In addition, those social categories and the hierarchies they produce have been defended by religion, genealogy and kinship, abilities and merit, and science, and they have been disguised as unstated assumptions and as universalisms common to all societies. They have also been muted as supposed singular entities, quarantined and unique, separate and distant one from another.

In calling for a movement beyond race, I am not vacating its premises. Albeit creations of the imagination, racializations persist because white racial politics mandates them. We also witness the power of racializations in how they have structured our lives and circumscribed our life's chances. They have material, palpable effects. We see these in the correspondences of race with income, education, health and wellness, and social mobility.

But our resistance against white racial politics needn't be solely or even principally colored racial politics. We must find alternative, radical ways to free ourselves from the bonds of white supremacy and our choices of the past. If we can construct solidarities made in America as "African Americans," "Asian Americans," and "Latina/os," "Native Americans," and "Pacific Islanders," we can reimagine more expansive unities for the new millennium.

Paul Gilroy, in his impassioned plea for freedom from the past and a rush to the future, argues for the abandonment of the entire, antiquated apparatus of race thinking, an admittedly utopian project. Escape, nonetheless, is a necessary precondition for a new humanism and democracy. Nationalism, he points out, was intimately tied to the notions of identity, belonging, and race. Union was a bond of blood. That was true of both white and black nationalisms. Instead of white nationalist appeals to sovereign states and national cultures and their assimilation by blacks in their aspirations for inclusion in modernity as citizens, Gilroy proposes transnational solidarities and cosmopolitan cultures as constituted by diasporic dispersal and estrangement. "Becoming oriented toward the idea of a cosmopolitan future, even as it recedes, involves a variety of political work around racial discourse and racial division that is very different from what has been practiced in recent periods," Gilroy writes. Raciology must be abandoned to the dustbin of the past for "a heterocultural, postanthropological, and cosmopolitan yet-to-come."[59] Although unclear about the actual strategy for achieving that future, Gilroy correctly exposes the intimacy of nationalism and racism (and sexism) and the complicity of whites and, in reaction, blacks in advancing those projects. Those connections and insights recall the beginnings of this essay and its critical accounting of ethnic studies' nationalist origins.

Perhaps exemplary in charting a new course for ethnic studies were the mappings of women of color toward Third World solidarities and cosmopolitan subject matters. I am thinking in particular of the 1971 *Asian Women* reader that sought common ground across race and nation and the 1977 statement of black feminists. The Combahee River Collective, named for the only military action in the United States planned and led by a woman, Harriet Tubman, in 1863, issued a statement after having met for three years in Boston. In it, they defined their politics as "actively committed to struggling against racial, sexual, heterosexual, and class oppression, and see as our particular task the development of integrated analysis and practice based upon the fact that the major systems of oppression are interlocking."[60] That conclusion, they testify, like the discovery of Asian American women in their 1971 text, derived from their political work and coalitions with other progressive groups. In retrospect, ethnic studies, led by men, erred when it chose race, patriarchy, and nation over the transnational "interlocking" systems of oppression as its theory and coalition politics as its practice.[61]

Ethnic studies must rethink its strategy for educational and social transformation in the light of growing diversity within racialized groups, the rise of multiracials, alienations among racialized groups, the intersections among race, gender, sexuality, class, and nation, and the global reorientations of capital, labor, culture, and our very identities as individuals and as peoples. Perhaps more compelling than the present circumstances are the exemplars of the past. In 1966, when SNCC (Student Nonviolent Coordinating Committee) turned from multiracialism to black power under the influence of Stokely Carmichael's (Kwame Toure) call "to reclaim our history and our identity" for racial self-determination and black liberation—entitlements demanded by ethnic studies—Bayard Rustin and Harold Cruse warned against what they saw as an introspective turn toward another kind of chauvinism. They argued that black racial politics would elide class oppressions and de-couple black poverty from white privilege. The black struggle, they proposed, should transform blacks, but also whites. We should also remember that Carmichael's black power was modeled after white power and the ethnic politics of the Irish and Jews.[62]

A stranger to itself, ethnic studies as an intellectual and political project flounders largely because of its unexamined career. There are few intellectual histories of the field, and even fewer attempts to assemble an ethnic studies epistemology. I suspect much of the blame for the field's seemingly erratic footprints stems from its almost constant siege mentality conditioned by the attacks from all sides, including from within. Ideological battles involved cultural nationalism and Marxism, race and ethnicity, American studies and area studies, the global and the local, the challenges from feminism and queer theory and postmodernism and poststructuralism, and so forth, along with the institutional and professional demands and the field's relations with and commitments to students and communities outside the academy. Self-reflection, under those strains, was a luxury that few could indulge in. Far from an extravagance, however, knowing oneself is rooted in necessity. Without clearly articulated methods and theories distinctive from those of other fields, ethnic studies remains not only undisciplined (perhaps a purposeful and healthy neglect) but without an intellectual genealogy and, hence, identity.

Ethnic studies as I know it, perhaps because of my grounding in Asian American studies, owes much to the Chicago school of sociology.[63] Despite the initial gestures to internationalism and Third World revolutionary movements, the field's instincts are introspective and centered firmly within the United States. It is an "American" project. Race, as manifested in the United States, is the field's central object of study and problematic, and, unlike Europeans who emerged from races to ethnic groups, peoples of color could never shed their racial badges. Urban communities and their plight are the focus, and remediation and redress, the desired ends of social research. Of course there are important differences between the race relations and ethnic studies approaches, as I've noted, and ethnic studies has made advances most notably in the idea of racial formation, but it has also been stuck in the rut of conventionalism. Binaries populate ethnic studies, notably the white/nonwhite formulation, and race is both assumed and normalized.[64] And like identities that collapse differences for the sake of union,[65] race thinking within ethnic studies suppresses and excludes critical considerations of gender, sexuality, class, and nation.

Although we now recognize that our thinking and politics need not be reduced to either/or, isolation or engagement, but could and should be either/or, both, and all, we must acknowledge that our decision to reclaim our history, our America for our liberation, has yielded us an unfinished revolution, like in much of the postcolonial world, that has transformed, but has also been complicitous with the designs of the ruling class. The journalist Robert L. Allen proposed thirty years ago that black power or racial solidarity was a vehicle by which the black middle class maintained class privilege, exploited African Americans, and conspired with capital.[66] Black racial politics, he argued, advanced the interests of capitalism.

And what George Lipstiz observed about the 1960s generally applies, I hold, to ethnic studies, another feature of the decade. The counterculture, he astutely noted, more closely resembled the system it claimed to be overturning than it opposed it, replicating rather than resisting the status quo.[67] Race-based ethnic studies is essentially conservative intellectually and politically. Adrienne Rich's criticism of U.S. feminism applies equally to ethnic studies. Rich scored feminism's retreat to "versions of female oppression which neglect both female agency and female diversity, in which 'safety' for women becomes valued over risk taking, and woman-only space—often a strategic necessity—becomes a place of emigration, an end in itself." Instead, she proposed, feminists should carry on "a conversation with the world."[68]

And that global conversation should be enjoined with the twin recognition of the falsity and reality of race. Although a fiction, we know that race structures self and self's choices. I am not calling for an end to race thinking. What I am advocating, already called for by many others before me, is the reorientation of our field away from "ethnic" studies to a study of social formations—a shift not only in name but also in substance. If the problem of the twentieth century was the problem of the color line, it was because white and, its opposition, colored racial politics made it so. By contrast, the problem of the twenty-first century for those of us in the newly constituted field of social formations will more accurately be the problem of our reconceptualized subject matter in all its confounded complexity and fetching fullness.

Notes

1. Vincent Harding, "Power from Our People: The Sources of the Modern Revival of Black History," *Black Scholar* 18, no. 1 (January–February 1987): 41.

2. Quoted in Armstead L. Robinson, Craig C. Foster, and Donald H. Ogilvie, eds., *Black Studies in the University: A Symposium* (New Haven, Conn.: Yale University Press, 1969), 1–2. See also Nathan Huggins, *Afro-American Studies: A Report to the Ford Foundation* (New York: Ford Foundation, 1985), 15–19, who sees the intersection of the university's turn toward utilitarianism and the civil rights movement.

3. Dinesh D'Souza, *Illiberal Education: The Politics of Race and Sex on Campus* (New York: Vintage, 1991), 13, 14.

4. *Asian Women* (Berkeley, 1971), 79, 80.

5. Carlos Muñoz, Jr., *Youth, Identity, Power: The Chicano Movement* (London: Verso, 1989); and Eugene E. Garcia, Francisco A. Lomelí, and Isidro D. Ortiz, eds., *Chicano Studies: A Multidisciplinary Approach* (New York: Teachers College Press, 1984). Cf. Wilson Jeremiah Moses, *The Golden Age of Black Nationalism, 1850–1925* (New York: Oxford University Press, 1978), who argues the Eurocentric and assimilationist cast of black nationalist ideology in the United States.

6. See, for example, Gail Bederman, *Manliness & Civilization: A Cultural History of Gender and Race in the United States, 1880–1917* (Chicago: University of Chicago Press, 1995); Anne McClintock, *Imperial Leather: Race, Gender and Sexuality in the Colonial Conquest* (New York: Routledge, 1995); and Dana D. Nelson, *National Manhood: Capitalist Citizenship and the Imagined Fraternity of White Men* (Durham, N.C.: Duke University Press, 1998).

7. Gayatri Chakravorty Spivak, "Can the Subaltern Speak?" in *Colonial Discourse and Post-colonial Theory: A Reader* (New York: Columbia University Press, 1994), 93.

8. For an expansion of these categories of anti-Asianist, liberal, and Asian Americanist, see Gary Y. Okihiro, *The Columbia Guide to Asian American History* (New York: Columbia University Press, 2001), 193–241.

9. Frank Chin, Jeffery Paul Chan, Lawson Fusao Inada, and Shawn Hsu Wong, eds., *Aiiieeeee! An Anthology of Asian-American Writers* (Garden City, N.Y.: Anchor, 1975), ix.

10. Chin et al., *Aiiieeeee!* 14.

11. Jeffery Paul Chan, Frank Chin, Lawson Fusao Inada, and Shawn Wong, eds., *The Big Aiiieeeee! An Anthology of Chinese American and Japanese American Literature* (New York: Meridian, 1991), xiii.

12. King-Kok Cheung, "The Woman Warrior versus the Chinaman Pacific: Must a Chinese American Critic Choose between Feminism and Heroism?" in *Maxine Hong Kingston's The Woman Warrior: A Casebook*, ed. Sau-Ling Cynthia Wong (New York: Oxford University Press, 1999), 127. See also David L. Eng, *Racial Castration: Managing Masculinity in Asian America* (Durham, N.C.: Duke University Press, 2001).

13. bell hooks, *Ain't I a Woman: Black Women and Feminism* (Boston: South End Press, 1981), 98–99. See also Cynthia Orozco, "Sexism in Chicano Studies and the Community," in *Chicana Voices: Intersections of Class, Race, and Gender*, ed. Teresa Córdova et al. (Austin: University of Texas, Center for Mexican American Studies, 1986), 11–18. For examples of black men's support of women's rights during the nineteenth century, see Rosalyn Terborg-Penn, "Black Male Perspectives on the Nineteenth-Century Woman," in *The Afro-American Woman: Struggles and Images*, ed. Sharon Harley and Rosalyn Terborg-Penn (Port Washington, N.Y.: Kennikat Press, 1978), 28–42.

14. Benedict Anderson, *Imagined Communities: Reflections on the Origin and Spread of Nationalism* (London: Verso, 1983). For a case study, see Percy C. Hintzen, *The Costs of Regime Survival: Racial Mobilization, Elite Domination, and Control of the State in Guyana and Trinidad* (New York: Cambridge University Press, 1989).

15. Influential was the concept of dependency drawn mainly from the post- (or neo-) colonial experiences in Latin America and Africa. This literature is extensive and complicated, and I must resist the temptation to mention even the most prominent works. Still, I cite Frank Bonilla and Robert Girling, eds., *Structures of Dependency* (East Palo Alto, Calif.: Nairobi Bookstore, 1973); and Richard White, *The Roots of Dependency: Subsistence, Environment, and Social Change among Choctaws, Pawnees, and Navajos* (Lincoln: University of Nebraska Press, 1983) because of their importance to the intellectual history of U.S. ethnic studies.

16. Robert Blauner, *Racial Oppression in America* (New York: Harper and Row, 1972); Rodolfo F. Acuña, *Occupied America: The Chicano's Struggle toward Liberation* (San Francisco: Canfield Press, 1972); Stokely Carmichael and Charles V. Hamilton, *Black Power: The Politics of Liberation in America* (New York: Vintage, 1967); John Liu, "Towards an Understanding of the Internal Colonial Model," in *Counterpoint: Perspectives on Asian America*, ed. Emma Gee (Los Angeles: UCLA Asian American Studies Center, 1976), 160–168; and Muñoz, Jr., *Youth, Identity, Power*, 146–149, 152–154.

17. For critiques of those racialized discourses, see Edward W. Said, *Culture and Imperialism* (New York: Vintage, 1993); Amy Kaplan and Donald E. Pease, eds., *Cultures of United States Imperialism* (Durham, N.C.: Duke University Press, 1993);

Richard C. Trexler, *Sex and Conquest: Gendered Violence, Political Order, and the European Conquest of the Americas* (Ithaca, N.Y.: Cornell University Press, 1995); and Ruth Roach Pierson and Nupur Chaudhuri, eds., *Nation, Empire, Colony: Historicizing Gender and Race* (Bloomington: Indiana University Press, 1998).

18. Charles H. Pearson, *National Life and Character* (London: Macmillan, 1893). For later versions of this theme, see Madison Grant, *The Passing of the Great Race; or, the Racial Basis of European History* (New York: Charles Scribner's Sons, 1916); and Lothrop Stoddard, *The Rising Tide of Color against White World-Supremacy* (New York: Charles Scribner's Sons, 1920).

19. Gary Y. Okihiro, *Margins and Mainstreams: Asians in American History and Culture* (Seattle: University of Washington Press, 1994), 118–119.

20. Josiah Strong, *Our Country: Its Possible Future and Its Present Crisis* (New York: Baker & Taylor, 1885), 159–161, 175.

21. Moses, *Golden Age of Black Nationalism*, 16, 18–22. For an example of Eurocentrism in early pan-Africanist writings, see George W. Williams, *History of the Negro Race in America from 1619 to 1880*, 2 vols. (New York: G. P. Putnam's Sons, 1883); and on African enslavement and resistance as the central features of the diaspora, see Vincent Bakpetu Thompson, *The Making of the African Diaspora in the Americas, 1441–1900* (New York: Longman, 1987).

22. Central are the writings of Cheikh Anta Diop, as in *The African Origin of Civilization: Myth or Reality*, edited and translated by Mercer Cook (Westport, Conn.: Lawrence Hill, 1974), and the more contemporary Molefi Kete Asante, *The Afrocentric Idea* (Philadelphia: Temple University Press, 1987).

23. From Jean-Paul Sartre's introduction to *The Colonizer and the Colonized*, by Albert Memmi (Boston: Beacon Press, 1967), xxviii.

24. Memmi, *Colonizer and Colonized*, 128, 129.

25. As noted famously by Audre Lorde, *Sister Outsider: Essays and Speeches* (Trumansburg, N.Y.: Crossing Press, 1984), 110–113.

26. Dean E. Robinson, *Black Nationalism in American Politics and Thought* (New York: Cambridge University Press, 2001), 1–2.

27. David R. Roediger, *The Wages of Whiteness: Race and the Making of the American Working Class* (London: Verso, 1991); Noel Ignatiev, *How the Irish Became White* (Cambridge, Mass.: Harvard University Press, 1995); and Karen Brodkin, *How Jews Became White Folks and What That Says about Race in America* (New Brunswick, N.J.: Rutgers University Press, 1998).

28. See, for example, Nancy Foner, *From Ellis Island to JFK: New York's Two Great Waves of Immigration* (New Haven, Conn.: Yale University Press, 2000). Cf. Clara E. Rodríguez, *Changing Race: Latinos, the Census, and the History of Ethnicity in the United States* (New York: New York University Press, 2000).

29. Fred H. Matthews, *Quest for an American Sociology: Robert E. Park and the Chicago School* (Montreal: McGill-Queen's University Press, 1977), 90–91.

30. Robert E. Park and Ernest W. Burgess, *Introduction to the Science of Sociology* (Chicago: University of Chicago Press, 1921).

31. Quoted in Winifred Raushenbush, *Robert E. Park: Biography of a Sociologist* (Durham, N.C.: Duke University Press, 1979), 50.

32. Raushenbush, *Robert E. Park*, 77. For a review of the Chicago school of sociology, see Andrew Abbott, *Department & Discipline: Chicago Sociology at One Hundred* (Chicago: University of Chicago Press, 1999).

33. See, for example, William I. Thomas and Florian Znaniecki, *The Polish Peasant in Europe and America: Monograph of an Immigrant Group*, 5 vols. (Chicago: University of Chicago Press, 1918–1920); and Henry Yu, *Thinking Orientals: Migration, Contact, and Exoticism in Modern America* (New York: Oxford University Press, 2001).

34. Quoted in Raushenbush, *Robert E. Park*, 117. See also Ernest W. Burgess, "Social Planning and Race Relations," in *Race Relations: Problems and Theory*, ed. Jitsuichi Masuoka and Preston Valien (Chapel Hill: University of North Carolina Press, 1961), 13–25.

35. Raushenbush, *Robert E. Park*, 114. See also Park's statement outlining the purpose and method of the Pacific Coast race relations survey in Robert E. Park, "Behind Our Masks," *Survey* 56, no. 3 (May 1, 1926): 138–139. This special issue of the *Survey* contains the results of the 1923–1924 phase of the study.

36. Stow Persons, *Ethnic Studies at Chicago, 1905–1945* (Urbana: University of Illinois Press, 1987), 34–35. Another midwestern idea was the frontier hypothesis that proposed the American frontier as the leveler of ethnic and class distinctions. See Frederick Jackson Turner, *The Frontier in American History* (New York: Henry Holt, 1920).

37. Chicago Commission on Race Relations, *The Negro in Chicago: A Study of Race Relations and a Race Riot* (Chicago: University of Chicago Press, 1922).

38. Emory S. Bogardus, "A Race-Relations Cycle," *American Journal of Sociology* 35, no. 4 (January 1930): 612–617; and Robert H. Ross and Emory S. Bogardus, "The Second-Generation Race Relations Cycle: A Study in *Issei-Nisei* Relationships," *Sociology and Social Research* 24, no. 4 (March–April 1940): 357–363. See also E. Franklin Frazier's version of Park's cycle in his "Theoretical Structure of Sociology and Sociological Research," *British Journal of Sociology* 4, no. 4 (December 1953): 293–311. Robert E. Park coined the term "marginal man" in his "Human Migration and the Marginal Man," *American Journal of Sociology* 23, no. 6 (May 1928): 881–893.

39. Robert E. Park, introduction to *The Japanese Invasion: A Study in the Psychology of Inter-Racial Contacts*, by Jesse Frederick Steiner (Chicago: A. C. McClurg, 1917), xvi.

40. See, for example, assimilation's resuscitation in Richard Alba and Victor Nee, "Rethinking Assimilation Theory for a New Era of Immigration," *International Migration Review* 31, no. 4 (1997): 826–874.

41. Park, introduction, xiii, xiv.

42. Park, introduction, xv.

43. *Report of the National Advisory Commission on Civil Disorders* (New York: Bantam, 1968), 1, 2.

44. For a discussion of this literature, see Okihiro, *Columbia Guide*, 100–127, 164–174.

45. See, for example, James H. Cone's *For My People: Black Theology and the Black Church* (Maryknoll, N.Y.: Orbis Books, 1984), which, he wrote, is for all people but "*primarily* addressed to the black church in particular and the black community in general" (2).

46. Ernest K. Wakukawa, *A History of the Japanese People in Hawaii* (Honolulu: Toyo Shoin, 1938), xvii, xix.

47. For examples of memoirs, biographies, and oral histories in Asian American studies, see Victor G. Nee and Brett de Bary Nee, *Longtime Californ': A Documentary Study of an American Chinatown* (New York: Pantheon, 1972); Akemi Kikumura, *Through Harsh Winters: The Life of a Japanese Immigrant Woman* (Novato, Calif.: Chandler and Sharp, 1981); James M. Freeman, *Hearts of Sorrow: Vietnamese-American Lives* (Stanford, Calif.: Stanford University Press, 1989); Mary Paik Lee, *Quiet Odyssey: A Pioneer Korean Woman in America* (Seattle: University of Washington Press, 1990); Usha Welarantna, *Beyond the Killing Fields: Voices of Nine Cambodian Survivors in America* (Stanford, Calif.: Stanford University Press, 1993); Sucheng Chan, ed., *Hmong Means Free: Life in Laos and America* (Philadelphia: Temple University Press, 1994); Steven DeBonis, *Children of the Enemy: Oral Histories of Vietnamese Amerasians and Their Mothers* (Jefferson, N.C.: McFarland, 1995); Yen Le Espiritu, *Filipino American Lives* (Philadelphia: Temple University Press, 1995); and Shamita Das Dasgupta, ed., *A Patchwork Shawl: Chronicles of South Asian Women in America* (New Brunswick, N.J.: Rutgers University Press, 1998). Two important books that skirt the borders of autobiography and fiction are Carlos Bulosan, *America Is in the Heart* (New York: Harcourt, Brace, 1943); and Maxine Hong Kingston, *Woman Warrior: Memoirs of a Girlhood among Ghosts* (New York: Random House, 1976).

48. Josephine Carson, *Silent Voices: The Southern Negro Woman Today* (New York: Delacorte Press, 1969), 1.

49. Gary Y. Okihiro, "Oral History and the Writing of Ethnic History: A Reconnaissance into Method and Theory," *Oral History Review* 9 (1981): 42, 43.

50. Joan W. Scott, "Experience," in *Feminists Theorize the Political*, ed. Judith Butler and Joan W. Scott (New York: Routledge, 1992), 25. See also Wendy S. Hesford and Wendy Kozol, eds., *Haunting Violations: Feminist Criticism and the Crisis of the "Real"* (Urbana: University of Illinois Press, 2001).

51. See, for example, Manning Marable, *How Capitalism Underdeveloped Black America: Problems in Race, Political Economy, and Society* (Boston: South End Press, 1983); Okihiro, *Margins and Mainstreams*; Coco Fusco, *English Is Broken Here: Notes on Cultural Fusion in the Americas* (New York: New Press, 1995); William V. Flores and Rina Benmayor, eds., *Latino Cultural Citizenship: Claiming Identity, Space, and Rights* (Boston: Beacon Press, 1997); Robin D. G. Kelley, *Yo' Mama's Disfunktional! Fighting the Culture Wars in Urban America* (Boston: Beacon Press, 1997); and George Lipsitz, *The Possessive Investment in Whiteness: How White People Profit from Identity Politics* (Philadelphia: Temple University Press, 1998).

52. A related contention in legal scholarship is advanced by critical race theory. For an introduction to this literature, see Richard Delgado, ed., *Critical Race Theory: The Cutting Edge* (Philadelphia: Temple University Press, 1995); Kimberlé W. Crenshaw, Neil Gotanda, Gary Peller, and Kendall Thomas, eds., *Critical Race Theory: The Key Writings That Formed the Movement* (New York: New York University Press, 1995); and Francisco Valdes, Jerome McCristal Culp, and Angela P. Harris, eds., *Crossroads, Directions, and a New Critical Race Theory* (Philadelphia: Temple University Press, 2002).

53. Michael Omi and Howard Winant, *Racial Formation in the United States: From the 1960s to the 1980s* (New York: Routledge & Kegan Paul, 1986), 4.

54. Omi and Winant, *Racial Formation*, 66.

55. Omi and Winant, *Racial Formation*, 62.

56. On multiculturalism's varieties, see Avery F. Gordon and Christopher Newfield, eds., *Mapping Multiculturalism* (Minneapolis: University of Minnesota Press, 1996); and David Bennett, ed., *Multicultural States: Rethinking Difference and Identity* (London: Routledge, 1998).

57. Hortense J. Spillers, "Mama's Baby, Papa's Maybe: An American Grammar Book," *diacritics* (Summer 1987): 65.

58. For an analysis of feminism's institutionalization, see Ellen Messer-Davidow, *Disciplining Feminism: From Social Activism to Academic Discourse* (Durham, N.C.: Duke University Press, 2002).

59. Paul Gilroy, *Against Race: Imagining Political Culture beyond the Color Line* (Cambridge, Mass.: Belknap Press of Harvard University Press, 2000), 334.

60. Combahee River Collective, "The Combahee River Collective Statement," in *Theorizing Feminism: Parallel Trends in the Humanities and Social Sciences*, ed. Anne C. Hermann and Abigail J. Stewart (Boulder, Colo.: Westview Press, 1994), 26.

61. Admirable recent studies include Evelyn Nakano Glenn, *Unequal Freedom: How Race and Gender Shaped American Citizenship and Labor* (Cambridge, Mass.: Harvard University Press, 2002); and Chandra Talpade Mohanty, *Feminism without Borders: Decolonizing Theory, Practicing Solidarity* (Durham, N.C.: Duke University Press, 2003).

62. Clayborne Carson, *In Struggle: SNCC and the Black Awakening of the 1960s* (Cambridge, Mass.: Harvard University Press, 1981), 220, 227–228.

63. For an account of Asian American intellectuals trained at Chicago and Chicago sociology's studies on Asian Americans, see Yu, *Thinking Orientals*.

64. Increasingly, ethnic studies scholars have begun to examine relations among peoples of color as mediated by white power. See, for example, Tomás Almaguer, *Racial Fault Lines: The Historical Origins of White Supremacy in California* (Berkeley: University of California Press, 1994); Neil Foley, *White Scourge: Mexicans, Blacks, and Poor Whites in Texas Cotton Culture* (Berkeley: University of California Press, 1997); Vijay Prashad, *Everybody Was Kung Fu Fighting: Afro-Asian Connections and the Myth of Cultural Purity* (Boston: Beacon Press, 2001); and Jacalyn D. Harden,

Double Cross: Japanese Americans in Black and White Chicago (Minneapolis: University of Minnesota Press, 2003).

65. For a critique of essentialized identities and the problems of difference, see Steven Seidman, *Difference Troubles: Queering Social Theory and Sexual Politics* (Cambridge: Cambridge University Press, 1997).

66. Robert L. Allen, *Black Awakening in Capitalist America: An Analytic History* (New York: Doubleday, 1969), 14–17. See also Kevin K. Gaines, *Uplifting the Race: Black Leadership, Politics, and Culture in the Twentieth Century* (Chapel Hill: University of North Carolina Press, 1996). Gaines notes that twentieth-century black leadership's invocation of racial politics advanced sexism and classism.

67. George Lipsitz, "Who'll Stop the Rain? Youth Culture, Rock 'n' Roll, and Social Crises," in *The Sixties: From Memory to History*, ed. David Farber (Chapel Hill: University of North Carolina Press, 1994), 224, 227.

68. Adrienne Rich, "Living the Revolution," *Women's Review of Books* 3, no. 12 (September 1986): 3.

Ethnic or World Studies
A Historian's Path of Discovery

4

JACK D. FORBES

The Origin of National/Ethnic Studies

ETHNIC OR NATIONAL STUDIES is certainly one of the oldest areas of scholarship, reaching back to the writings of Herodotus and beyond, to the chronicles of ancient Kem, Mesopotamia, and Mesoamerica. The rise of the modern "national" state and wars between fledging states have also encouraged the more recent trend of focusing most attention upon a single state or nationality. Thus we have chronicles and histories of Ireland, Scotland, England, France, et cetera, chronicles which became extremely important in the evolution of the national consciousness of their respective peoples. The purpose of such national histories was often to develop pride and to differentiate a given "people" from neighboring states or groups.

The tendency to be nation-centered is still very much with us. For example, the U.S. Public Broadcasting Service (PBS) has produced program after program on areas such as photography, poetry, and jazz, which almost inevitably stop at the U.S.-Canadian and U.S.-Mexican borders, as if pictures were never taken, nor jazz played, beyond those lines on a map. The people at PBS clearly are "nationalists" who seemingly cannot resist the impulse to focus upon their own territorial identity and history even if, as in the evolution of jazz, the phenomena has long been international.

In the United States white persons of European origin have long dominated higher education and scholarship. Thus United States history, literature, society, art, and so forth, were formerly always "white only" (and usually "male only"), with other groups included only as problems, enemies, or outsiders. Given this reality, efforts began to be made by non-Anglos to introduce Irish history (Catholic schools), "Negro" history (black colleges), Jewish history (yeshivas and Jewish schools), and so on. Many groups, such as Native Americans and some Asian Americans, were able to relate their own history, language, and values in traditional folk settings, religious schools, or community programs not sanctioned by the state (or even actively suppressed by the state, in the case of Indians).

The early twentieth century saw an increase of "assimilationist" Anglicization programs (called "Americanization" by advocates) and a corresponding decline in the ability of native people and others to offer their own versions of history and culture. World War I witnessed a rapid increase in Anglo-American paranoia and the teaching of German language and heritage especially suffered, along with a general phobia about those not speaking English. This situation continued on until the 1950s, when I began to grapple with it on a personal level as discussed below. (In the wake of the September 11, 2001 attack on the World Trade Center there were reports of people being attacked, physically and verbally, for speaking a non-English language or for being dressed in a non-Anglo style. But hostility to Indians speaking their own languages has long been known and we read reports of how even white schoolchildren attempted to attack physically and verbally native children who spoke an American language around school sites, as in Oklahoma. This undoubtedly has contributed to the decline in the use of American tongues in the United States.)

History has served as the "mother" field for much of what constitutes national or "ethnic" studies today. My personal approach to scholarship and program development arose out of my training as a historian (with one field in North American ethnography) and, in particular, as an "ethnohistorian." I am going to stress the evolution of my views on historical methodology because I believe that the latter is still at the core of any ethnic studies or national/cultural studies program.

Many persons associate the word "history" with the "past" but, in point of fact, everything that we might choose to seriously contemplate has already passed by or, at the very least, is in the process of passing the moment we fasten our attention upon it. Thus the old meaning of "learning by inquiry" from the Greek *histor:* "knowing, learned," needs to be kept in mind.

Many fields of study are branches of history, considered broadly. Our scientific fields were once referred to as "natural history" and that is still very apt, since the work of astronomers, geologists, botanists, zoologists, and many others has to do essentially with analyzing past events. Indeed, all information which we receive about the stars is very ancient history!

Of course, it is true that some fields, such as anthropology, sociology, political science, economics, and so on, try very often to see themselves as dealing with the present or even with the future, however, all of their data is, when analyzed, of necessity from the past, and all of their projections into the future are based upon past behavior. Perhaps such fields can be regarded as "applied history" or "projected history," or as dealing with selected historical issues.

My Path to History

My own interest in the past began very early, as I listened to the narrations of my parents, uncles and aunts, grandparents, and other elders. I liked older people and I loved to ask them about what had happened in a certain place or why things were like they were. My elders also loved to talk about their lives, their jobs, their personal history, their cars, and their horses. Of course, they also talked a lot about politics, union affairs, struggles with capitalism, Native American history, working-class history, and other aspects of their life experiences.

I suppose that I seriously started to become a historian in the 1940s when I began to cut out and save all of the maps of World War II combat fronts and began a scrapbook of "war criminals" with pictures of Nazi, Fascist, and imperial Japanese war leaders. This was soon followed by scrapbooks from 1945–1949 on railways, professional football, and sports generally with score charts. Soon also, as a Los Angeles Dons fan, I was recording the Don's football scores against other All-America Conference teams. By the years of 1948–1951 I had become an active historian of another type, observing our high school sporting events and writing articles about what had happened for the *Eagle's Scream*, our newspaper. This taught me a lot about how some things are forgotten, some things are overlooked, and other things are selected for recording and perhaps magnification. I started as a reporter but soon became sports editor and then associate editor, writing editorials and even a column which the principal censored!

But I became a more professional historian when, in November 1948, I began to do research in documentary sources on the past record of Eagle Rock High School teams playing against other schools. I examined old newspapers in the possession of "Auntie Bert" Morris, an elder who lived up on the hill behind my house. I interviewed coaches in our athletic department and, much to my surprise, found that they did not know very much! But I did find out that the City Schools' office in downtown Los Angeles was supposed to have the scores from all previous games. Soon I set out on an expedition via streetcar to the Fort Hill headquarters and there I was eventually able to copy down all of the past football scores for the Eagle Rock Eagles. This, in turn, led to a series of articles in the *Eagle's Scream* in which I gave all of the history of our contests with each particular school.

By the age of about fourteen I had thus discovered the value of primary sources and the method of going to the "archives" to find the original documents. In this period, incidentally, I read a great many books about ancient history the world over, about more recent history, and about Native Americans. I was especially interested in histories of Ataturk's Turkey, revolutionary Egypt, anti-colonialism, Trotsky, native peoples of Mexico and the Americas, and all aspects of ancient times. My father had purchased a used thirty-volume encyclopedia of British origin (c. 1875) with some U.S. material added (up to 1901), and I eagerly read article after article on Virginia history, American Indians, Scottish history, Irish history, and a multitude of other subjects. Although afflicted with the arrogant racism of the nineteenth-century white mind, the encyclopedia had tremendously detailed articles of a scholarly nature which were totally different from the common U.S. encyclopedias of the 1940s and 1950s. I feasted on it! And for about ten cents a volume, as I recall!

I also read Gibbon's *Decline and Fall of the Roman Empire*, which, like so many other works of earlier centuries, opened my mind to a kind of scholarship which was voraciously wide-ranging and which constantly pushed out from boundaries to explore what was beyond the edge. Such works were in sharp contrast to the extremely dull, narrow, and racist textbooks used in my high school history classes, as I will discuss later. Incidentally, I wish here to give my profound thanks to those librarians at the Eagle Rock Public Library who, in the 1930s and 1940s, built up an excellent collection of significant political, literary, and historical books, a collection which no longer exists in Eagle Rock (because of the purges of the McCarthy era and the "dumbing-down" of the branch library).

I was intrigued by electric railways from a very early age and by 1947 I had begun to photograph streetcars, car barns, right-of-ways, and the remains of abandoned rail lines all around the Los Angeles and San Diego areas. I collected old maps, timetables, and postcards, as well as printed histories of various railways. Downtown Los Angeles became a vast archive for me as I collected all kinds of materials and wandered around the Pacific Electric station at Sixth and Main, camera in hand. By means of historical research and hiking about I attempted to track down the old abandoned lines of the Mt. Lowe Railway, the Glendale and Montrose Railway, and other forgotten lines. For years, the sighting of rotting railroad ties or an old gravel roadbed or even the merest trace of a right-of-way would cause me to hike through forests or consult old maps to discover its route and history.

I also became a frequent visitor to the Southwest Museum, getting to know Ella Robinson, the wonderful librarian, and the curator, M. R. Harrington. In the desert I explored for Native American locations and carefully photographed the pictographs of Coyote Hole Canyon. Always an explorer of hidden places, I frequently crawled into caves and rocky labyrinths looking for signs and mysteries.

During my high school years (as noted above) and later, I became especially interested in works which dealt with decolonization efforts in Mexico, Africa, and Asia, as well as with revolutionary and liberation movements. I was also reading and learning about the lives of African Americans and Native Americans and was able to see the relevance of anti-colonialism to ethnic struggles within the U.S.A. Internal colonialism and such topics as the negative effects of colonialism on mental health and self-image were important concepts for me during the fifties and sixties and they related strongly with my understanding of what needed to be changed in academia.

By about 1950–1951 politics and liberation struggles had become very important to me, as my friend Richard Livingston and I attempted to found a journal (*National Report and Digest*) and participated actively in Democratic Party groups. But I continued to have many historical pursuits, including collecting old phonograph records and discovering the evolution of jazz from New Orleans to the California renaissance. Enrollment at Glendale College in the fall of 1951 gave me an opportunity to take a wonderful course in global history taught by professor Ellis Levine, a very fine teacher who used T. Walter Wallbank's *History of Civilization*. This text of two volumes was a real "turn-on" for one starved by racist, Eurocentric books. Wallbank and Alistair Taylor (his coauthor) actually included coverage of India, China, and ancient America in a fairly even-handed way! Unfortunately, the text in my U.S. history course (John Hick's *A Short History of American Democracy*) was anti-native and white-centered, which helped lead to an article I wrote a little later on "Lily-White History." My interests began to shift toward philosophy and the history of ideas as I transferred to the University of Southern California in 1953.

A Pan-American, Borderlands, Indigenous Perspective

By my senior year, 1954–1955, I had decided to return to history with a specialization in western North America, "borderlands," and Native American topics. At this time and as a first-year graduate student, I wrote several research papers, one of which was published in the *Masterkey* in December 1956 and January 1957 ("Anglo-Powhatan Relations in Virginia"). Other articles soon followed, including "A Historical Survey of the Indians of Sonora, 1821–1910," published in *Ethnohistory* (1957). I was greatly encouraged by my mentor, professor Donald C. Cutter (trained in the Boltonian tradition), and other fine scholars, including Russell Caldwell (who steered me into the American Indian Ethnohistoric Conference). I attended all of the early meetings of the Western History Association and some of the American Indian Ethnohistory meetings and helped to organize a Southwest branch. For a time I edited *El Tlatole*, the short-lived newsletter of the branch.

My research for the master's and doctor's degrees, as well as for shorter articles, was largely centered on the region from Coahuila, Durango and Sonora north into the Great Plains and westward through California. By focusing upon indigenous peoples and their relations with Europeans, I was led to the use of archaeological, ethnographic, oral-historical, and written sources without being limited by disciplinary or political boundaries. My projects soon caused me to climb on Greyhound buses to travel up the valley to Oakland for a few precious days of research in the Bancroft Library, using Spanish colonial documents. Don Cutter's help with early Castillian paleography proved extremely valuable, along with the Spanish I had learned as a child in El Monte del Sur. Working with old letters, reports, and diaries was a challenge and a thrill. Later, for the doctorate, I was able to spend almost a year in Madrid and Seville using bundles of old documents going back into the sixteenth century.

It is really interesting to stress that, unlike many later U.S.-trained Native American historians, I was exposed very early to a pan-American approach to native history in which the U.S. boundary (shifting as it was) was of no defining significance. Thus I never conceived that "American Indian history" was a subset within "United States history." I always saw it as a subject transcending modern political boundaries, and this perspective has influenced the way that I view most scholarship.

Since I believe that historical methodology forms a significant basis for other kinds of research in ethnic areas, I wish to devote some time to the manner in which I have learned to approach this topic. Because of my early interest in philosophy, I took a look at the epistemological aspects of historical research and writing. I began to incorporate this approach in my teaching of historical methodology in the 1960s. I was especially concerned that for many persons "the past" was a kind of "metaphysical object," an actual entity that one could study. Whereas I was persuaded that "the past" itself could *not* be studied since it was clearly gone, could never be retrieved, and, in fact, did not exist as a legitimate object of scholarly inquiry.

With my penchant as a youth for discovering original sources, remainders, and the refuse of past events, I was clearly destined to place an emphasis upon empirical research.

I want to pause and emphasize this theme because I am convinced that many academics (as well as laypeople) continue to believe that they can indeed examine "the past." It is especially important in connection with cultural studies and other "theory-driven" fields, because theories are apt to be particularly questionable when they are based upon intuitive or personalistic ("subjective") interpretations or are built upon layer after layer of equally interpretive theories, especially ones which use scattered "examples" to form their empirical connection. Some scholars have virtually abandoned comprehensive, open-ended empirical research in favor of the theory-driven collecting of only "selected" evidence. Perhaps much of this is related to a belief in the existence of a concrete "past" as opposed to a comprehensive collection of evidence which can be argued about.

I would argue, however, that our object of study consists solely in the residue of the past, and is not the past itself (which is unknowable by using the tools of the ordinary, rational mind at least). This is crucial, because if we believe that "the past" is our object, we can imagine that we are dealing with such a huge and unmanageable entity that we can, in fact, feel justified in saying whatever we want about it! But when we realize that it is *the residue* which is our object of study, then we must take a more empirical view of things because we do have, in fact, a fixed and limited set of evidence to look at (as huge as that pile of "remains" may be in some subject-areas).

Unfortunately, some disciplines have evolved with a methodology which encourages practitioners to be satisfied at finding selected bits of garbage which shed light upon or confirm a thesis which the scholar has already adopted (based on a hunch or the prevailing views of the field or, on the contrary, on a desire to perhaps disprove the prevailing view). This is also essentially the method of journalistic and polemical writers, who frequently use anecdotes and examples to try to prove a thesis, but it is also a model followed in academia as well. For example, the historian Arthur Schlesinger in his *The Age of Jackson* wrote a work which, in my opinion, is not an empirical history of the period but rather a pro-Democratic Party polemic which is at the same time pro-white, anti-native, and anti-black. He chose to ignore a great deal of data in order to set forth "a thesis with illustrations," as I see it.

I certainly am not opposed to "popular" writing or to personal writing (essays, autobiography, opinion editorials, and so on). I have authored quite a lot of them myself, but I like to believe that one should either base one's popularization upon sound research results or, if expressing opinion, one should make it rather clear that a strictly exploratory or personal viewpoint is being expressed. I would like to believe that my articles for newspapers on highlights of history, for example, have been based upon solid evidence from original sources or from reputable secondary works. Opinion articles and essays can also be very valuable resources, as long as the reader is encouraged to think independently and critically rather than to act blindly. Doctrinaire, one-sided advocacy is, of course, extremely common (especially in religious, sectarian, and political contexts). I should think that humility and reserve, with a deep awareness of and respect for the inherent fallibility of human beings, should be the hallmark of the scholar even when setting forth one's own judgments.

Clearly, when thinking about past events, it seems likely that our place of birth, our social class, our language heritages, our color, our national heritage(s), the quality of our schools, the books we have read, and so on, all determine how many "events" we can place in a given place in a given time-space. Thus, many eighteenth-century and nineteenth-century Europeans (such as David Hume, Immanuel Kant, Georg Hegel, and many others) assumed that because African or American history was largely a blank to them (that is, they knew of few if any events there in any time-period prior to Euro-invasion) that, in fact, it was really nothing but a blank. That was, of course, an extremely ignorant and naive way to think, but it was colored by self-interest and colonialist wishful thinking.

When I think of Central Asia at any time-period between, say 500 BC and 1917 CE, I have to be very careful because "the past" of that vast region is simply for me a collection of bits and pieces of information from diaries of travelers, historical writers, and television documentaries (let us say). Thus there are very many blanks. There are ethnic groups, states, nations, leaders, religious events, and so forth, which I have never heard of. Thus I am totally unequipped to construct theories about human history in the region because I have too many blanks. How would I correct this problem? Not by building a theory or pretending that "the past" is at my disposal. No, I would have to try to examine as much of the residue of activities in that region as I could or I might consult the works of others who had tried to do the task ahead of me. In any case, it is the "garbage" of Central Asia, its residue of evidence, which would flesh out its story of events, not "the past," blank or imagined as full, and certainly not some set of theories.

Our Evidence: All Kinds of "Garbage," Biased or Unbiased

By residue and "garbage," I mean, of course, the totality of information remaining about events, including the oral knowledge, traditions, and stories of the respective peoples themselves, as well as the character of their actions today as an expression of their historical evolution, and all of the hard objects left behind or still used, and so forth. In short, nothing can be without significance which provides us with empirical evidence of past events, even if it consists only of the scars left behind by oppression and denigration. Admittedly, not all kinds of evidence can be used in the same way, nor do all have equal value. Some residues suffer from manipulation, deletion, distortion, bias, disturbance (as in archaeological sites), selective memories, intentional propaganda, "true believer" advocacy, apologetics, and other impediments to use. But certainly one of the greatest handicaps has been the use of a priori theory to organize data in distorted ways in order to fulfill the needs of the overarching theory or belief system of the scholar/writer. It is this latter process which so often leads to the purposeful, but not always conscious, neglect of evidence which might have pointed in an opposite direction or which might have at least caused a cautious scholar to refrain from advocating a particular reconstruction or construction.

Here, for example, one can refer to the overarching biases of most early Spanish/Roman Catholic writers who possessed a theory of history which precluded giving voice to any non-Catholic, non-Spanish perspectives such as those of First Americans. Although certain Spanish Catholic writers gathered data from American persons (such as persons from Texcoco and other Nahua cities), they were unable to gather unbiased evidence for a number of reasons, not the least of which was the operation of the Holy Office (Inquisition) in Mexico and the possibility of torture and even death for any Americans who were suspected of relapse or secret adherence to indigenous religious beliefs. Most or all of the informants had been converted to Catholicism and were from cities which had fought against

Tenochtitlan in the conquest, and thus a critical analysis of their possible biases, and fears, must be part of any serious research project. In the end, however, few Spanish authorities could allow material to be preserved which would seriously challenge the basic apologetics of Spanish and Catholic imperialism and hegemony. (But, it has to be said, some material of an anti-Spanish nature did survive.)

Nonetheless, all of the texts produced by Spaniards and by Christianized Americans are of great value for researchers and must not be ignored, so long as one is aware of the a priori theories imbedded in the psyches of Iberian males and most Christian converts as regards religion, politics, gender, philosophy, and the purposes of the historical stream in relation to human destiny. The objectivity of colonial-era Roman Catholic priests and monks, all males theoretically dedicated to chastity, can certainly be doubted whenever such persons present evidence relating to non-Catholic men, and this in addition to their being imbedded in patriarchal Iberian or other European traditions very hostile to women, Muslims, Jews, nonconformists, and non-Christians.

In many situations involving non-Europeans or non-elites, we are faced with an absence or near-absence of written sources produced from the perspective of the latter groups (including workers, peasants, women in general, Americans, Africans, and so on). In such cases, the texts produced by the elites as rulers, invaders, exploiters, conquerors, masters, interpreters, scientists, philosophers, and so forth, tend to compose a thick layer of pavement, as it were, burying and crushing the viewpoints of the less-fortunate or oppressed or traditional indigenous peoples. The existence of this pavement has often so obscured the peoples below that many writers have not even imagined that anything existed beneath its opaque surface. Thus many European thinkers, such as Kant, Hume, and Hegel set forth opinions about Americans, Africans, and other non-Europeans which when seen today are an embarrassment and suggest incompetence. But the fact is that such writers chose to be totally dependent upon the pavement laid down by fellow Europeans, especially by travelers and imperialist soldiers or administrators, and did not apparently conceive of there being any evidence to the contrary. Perhaps racism and Eurocentrism led them to be predisposed to be less than scrupulous in their methodology, but for whatever reason they and thousands of other European writers failed to see beyond the overlays placed down by their own kind.

Of course, some white historians even went so far as to arbitrarily limit their work to the use of written texts alone, thus allowing themselves to ignore any evidence of a non-textual nature and therefore to totally exclude the perspectives of most women, non-elite males, and nonwhites from their "history." Moreover, in areas outside of Europe they were able to begin their works only with the arrival of literate white people, thus even erasing the centuries and epochs preceding. This is what most white historians did with the history of North America.

In fact, however, other kinds of evidence can be of vital and compelling importance. I mentioned earlier that one kind of evidence might even consist in the scars which exploitation or trauma has left upon a group of people. This can be a powerful line of evidence, as in the case of many modern Jews who clearly, in my opinion, carry with them the scars of Nazi persecution (in addition to the centuries of pogroms in various countries of Europe). There are pro-Nazis who would like to deny the reality of the incinerators and death camps of the Nazi regime, but, aside from extensive photographic, documentary, and other kinds of evidence, we have before us the almost universal conviction of Jews that they collectively passed through such an experience. Moreover, we also have the testimony of Jews and others who survived Nazi death camps and slave labor sites. That is one example of how the current beliefs and behavior of a people can be used as evidence. But specifically what I mean is that the physical and emotional scars carried by people are testimony about and confirmation of prior trauma. Other examples can be cited, such as the alcoholism and other symptoms exhibited by many First Americans and the often destructive self-deprecation experienced by some African-Americans, both responses to well-known experiences of systematic oppression and denial of self-worth.

Of course, the denial of Native American and African-American participation in the history of North America, except as impediments to European imperialism or as unpaid captive labor, rests on more than a mere equating of "history" with written evidence, since here there is a great deal of written evidence stemming from the pens of both whites and nonwhites. Thus, what is really at work in North American history is a conscious process of defining "American" history in such a manner as to make it a near-exclusive domain of only white Anglo-Americans. I have already written extensively on this subject and thus I will not review it here, but it is an example of how bias and theories created by biases can lead to the denial of conflicting evidence.[1]

The Use of Oral and Other Evidence

Thus while many historians and other white scholars assert that written evidence is the very definition of the discipline of history, the denial of non-European written evidence gives the lie to that definition. One of the world's early historians, Herodotus, made full use of oral traditions, oral testimony, and his personal observations of physical evidence (such as temples, statues, et cetera). Later European historians, when dealing with the history of their own countries, often make use of the evidence of archaeology, legend, oral tradition, art, philology, and linguistics in order to sketch out the full history of their land. They do not always begin with the most recent invasion by a currently dominant ethnic group, but deal with all peoples settled in the region, that is, they begin English history not with the Angles but with the most ancient inhabitants, the Celtic peoples, the Romans, the Germanic settlers, and the Norman-French conquerors of 1066. How different this is from the manner in which North American history has usually been written in my own day!

In any case, we have laid down the idea that in a fundamental work of scholarship one should use all kinds of evidence, written or otherwise. Of course, one may not always be an expert in dealing with each and every type of "garbage" in the historical pile, but quite often other scholars have already dealt with some of the highly specialized types of evidence (such as DNA or mtDNA or other kinds of genetic data) or someone can be found to consult with on such matters. Nonetheless, geneticists and physical anthropologists (for example) can make errors because they are often not highly prepared in relevant fields (such as in documentary evidence relating to human migrations in recent millennia) and, in any event, often suffer from biases of one kind or another. Often the requirements of natural science publishing (quick articles with new data hot off the press) sometimes lead to premature generalizations. So it is always necessary for the historian to adopt a critical posture even toward material which may be derived from a specialist, although one may have to make do with expert opinion in the end.

The Validation of Constructions

The products of historical effort are always "constructions" whenever a subject is being dealt with for the first time. One is always building something new from the evidence, something which has never existed before. Thus it is a construction. On the other hand, if one is redoing a subject which has already been constructed, perhaps in a preliminary, partial, or unsatisfactory way, then one can speak of a "reconstruction." In no case, however, are we "reconstructing the past." On the contrary, what we are building from the evidence has never existed before, to our knowledge, and no doubt it is quite different from the past itself since the evidence available to us will never equal the entire past, or reflect the total past moment, or, in some cases, the evidence might even exceed the past, since liars and theorists might have added information which never existed in the past itself. Thus we are always building something new, or revising something new, and our rules of procedure must relate to the careful adherence to the evidence. We will never be able to compare our constructions with the departed past, but we can compare our work with the residue left behind. It is the latter which forms our measure of validation.

In some of my most scholarly works (such as *Apache, Navaho and Spaniard*; *Warriors of the Colorado*; *Native Americans and Nixon*; and *Africans and Native Americans*) what I attempted to do, to the best of my ability, was to gather every bit of the pertinent evidence from all kinds of relevant sources. My technique was to allow the evidence to assemble itself, as it were, in such a way as to form a picture or a configuration. Ordinarily, I write each piece of evidence down on a single five-by-eight-inch card or paper, with the date in the upper left corner and the topic in the upper right. Each note, then, can be shuffled, reshuffled, laid out on a table, organized chronologically and/or topically, and given the freedom to influence directly what I ultimately will write.

In *Apache, Navaho and Spaniard* I acknowledge in the text or footnotes every fact, every bit of evidence, which I uncovered, even ones that might not be supportive of my general interpretation of events. Of course, my study of the southern Athapaskan nations was influenced by my being of Native American ancestry, especially in the sense that I did not accept all of the anti-Apache and anti-Navajo propaganda popular among many white writers, nor did I accept all of the assumptions of white archaeologists and ethnographers.

Did I have my own biases? Of course, we all do, and mine ran in the direction of not automatically accepting the claims of white imperialism (i.e., that the Spanish and Anglo invasions of the Southwest were part of civilization's forward march and, therefore, that Apaches and other Americans should have had the good grace to roll over and play dead!). I do not share the "imperialism is good" assumptions of most writers about the region (or about the world). In addition, as a person strongly attached to native tribes and as a believer in decentralized democracy, I was not particularly sympathetic to highly centralized, hierarchical structures or to land- and resource-grabbing aggressive kinds of people.

On the other hand, I did not set out to write a defense of Apaches and Navajos. Instead I set out to find out what really was to be revealed by a *full* examination of the evidence. I had no thesis to sell except for one: to see if the evidence, largely derived from Spanish documentary sources, would tell us if the Apaches and Navajos were truly the villains of southwestern history (as so often portrayed) or if they had behaved in the same general way as many small tribal societies, basically being non-imperialistic and non-aggressive until being forced by circumstances to change, perhaps into a more warlike and aggressive people.

In any case, since I chose not to ignore any evidence, and since I allowed the evidence to configure itself, I was largely able to avoid falling into traps which might have been set by any previous biases. The fact that *Apache, Navaho and Spaniard* has remained in print continuously since 1960 is, I think, testimony to my care and methodology.

In analyzing evidence, one must deal with the question of quality. Some evidence is likely to be less reliable than other evidence. For instance, in our own day, newspaper articles are apt to be extremely poor sources but memoirs written by participants in events are also apt to be biased and distorted by the writer's efforts to enhance his or her image for posterity.

Generally speaking, one tries to rely particularly on evidence which is closest to an event, such as a note in a diary written at the time, or the direct evidence of a Hohokam pottery sherd found at the Tujunga village site in the San Fernando Valley. On the other hand, all evidence must be weighed carefully and balanced against and with competing evidence. When one allows each datum to have a notecard and when one allows all such notes to have a role in creating a configuration, one sets up a situation in which the evidence itself is allowed to speak. But if one needs to insert one's own voice, as to note that a particular observer might have a strong bias, then that can be seen by the reader within the context of the total evidence.

The Hunter's Approach to Evidence

My approach to research often resembles that of a traditional hunter. As I have taught my students, a hunter ideally never goes directly into the center of a new territory, but rather circles about, becoming familiar with every canyon, watercourse, meadow, cliff-face, and ridge. A hunter watches closely the wind and its changes, watches the clouds, the sky, and the position of the sun. Only by testing the edges of the area can the hunter locate the "center," the best place to obtain food. (I might add that when I was young, exploring a new area in the desert or mountains, I used to often pause and listen carefully, as well as scan all directions. This process of pausing and scanning relates to what I will discuss below.)

When I wanted to research a topic, let us say the origins of Protestantism within Christianity, I was never content with the idea that Luther (or Zwingli, or Calvin, or even Huss) originated Protestantism. On the contrary, I "paused and scanned." I read about the Waldensians, the Albigenses, the Bulgars, the early Russian nonconformists, the Brethren of the Poor, and the Lollards. From them I explored Mani and Manicheanism, Arianism, the Nestorian Church, the Zoroastrian influence on early Christianity and Judaism, and so forth. I came to the opinion that the idea of a "Protestant Reformation" beginning in the 1500s was partly a myth, fostered perhaps by Lutheran and Calvinist central European historians who had a disinterest in what had transpired in Russia, for example. In any case, by exploring the edges beyond orthodox constructs, I believe that I was able to deliver much better and more valid lectures to my students.[2]

It is exploration to the edges of a subject which allows for the discovery of new insights and which guards against making mistakes relating to causation, sequence, roots, origins, and broad relationships. For example, one friend wrote an otherwise good article about Native American cowboys, but, because of his training perhaps, he totally ignored indigenous cowboys in Spanish-ruled and Mexican territories. He tended to regard cowboy "ways" as being a product of Anglo-American influence, whereas, in fact, the early Anglo-Texas cowboys learned everything from the indigenous cowboys of Texas, New Mexico, and Mexico.

One of the more dangerous mistakes in scholarship is to assume that one's topic or project has an iron-clad border which need not be examined critically as part of the research. Unfortunately, the walls which have been erected between our modern so-called disciplines not only encourage but often seem to demand the erection of boundaries. But borders also arise because of the narrowness encouraged by over-specialization, by "publish or perish" demands, and by ideological, political, and ethnocentric shallowness. Certainly, Christian writers often find it very difficult to surmount the boundaries at the edge of Christian thinking, even as Euro-Americans often find it very hard to conceive of events from an African, Asian, or Native American perspective.

Borders, after all, not only separate but, perhaps more importantly, can unite, just as a river usually unites the land on either shore with the opposite bank. In short, the method of the hunter requires that one sets borders aside in order to understand the connections which would otherwise be obscured. The borders of which I write are, of course, borders both in space and in time. But we must also question methodological borders, as between disciplines or subdisciplines, when a particular methodology requires or encourages the ignoring of relevant evidence. A methodology (as in traditional ethnographic writing) may also purposely destroy trails of evidence, as when the ethnographer fails to connect a particular description with a specific informant or other source. Ethnography is really no different from any other time-depth research, in that it is necessary that each significant assertion of fact or description be relatable to a particular source, or sources, in order that validation may occur.

An ethnography which simply lumps together all sources (or cites none of them) and which fails to identify divergent evidence can be a disservice to other scholars. One must then study the ethnographer's field notes, if available, in order to utilize the data in any significant way (unless one is willing to accept the authority of the researcher rather than the sources). Otherwise, one is forced to cite generalizations or constructions which have no known basis in any discernible empirical evidence. Ethnography without footnotes is, as it were, akin to good fiction in that one can cite fiction for the author's skill perhaps in hitting upon some significant theme or aspect of human existence; and one can also cite an ethnography for similar insights (as I have on occasion). But it is less satisfactory than a carefully documented work because of the inability to cross-check the evidence.

In other words, all kinds of literature presents us with impressive insights into behavior, insights which we may want to cite or which impress us with their value; but if we cannot check them out, that is, go to the evidence behind them, then should we not let our readers know that as impressive as the insights are, we cannot guarantee that they conform to any other body of evidence? They are like an equation which may not describe any aspect of the "real world" accurately, or perhaps like very compelling philosophical meditations which suggest deep truths without the possibility of proof.

Eurocentric Assumptions

In dealing with Native American topics one often finds that interpretations made by European or Euro-American scholars sometimes don't make much sense to an indigenous person, and yet these interpretations form the building blocks of all kinds of theoretical works and general studies. For example, certain anthropologists have developed the "chiefdom" concept to apply to small indigenous states such as are historically found in a variety of locales from Virginia south into Colombia and other parts of America. Archaeologists also speak of "chiefdoms" in discussing much of the Mississipian and other pre-1500 southeastern political groups.

But when one asserts that a given living-together group (a society) is a "chiefdom" one is not simply saying that a republic (a civil state) exists. On the contrary, one is asserting that a "chief" (from the French *chef*, head or top, from the Latin *caput*, the head) possesses ownership or dominion over a *dom*, short for domain or dominion, from *dominium*, ownership or property. In other words, one is duplicating the early English tendency to denominate virtually all principal native figures as "kings" or "queens" and chiefdom is simply a modernized or downgraded form of kingdom.

In the vast majority of cases, however, the precise power, ownership, and authority of any given American leader or spokesperson must be determined not from a priori assumptions but from a precise examination of the empirical evidence. Calling a state a "chiefdom" prejudges the nature of the political system in advance of gathering any evidence and is, therefore, inadmissible in scholarship.

I am personally interested in this matter because some of my late aunts believed that we are descended from "chief" or "king" Powhatan (Wahunsonacock), a leader of the Powhatan-Renápe people of Virginia. Certainly, Wahunsonacock has become one of the prototypes of the American "king" or "chief," except that in this case, he is alleged to have conquered or obtained hegemony over more than thirty separate small republics (tribes). In this instance, the scholar can examine the writings of John Smith along with much other evidence. What is interesting is that few if any scholars have critically examined the texts of Smith, John Strachey, and other principal sources, for evidence of the reliability of their statements about political structure. We must first assess if a given Englishman was able to understand the American language well enough to comprehend sophisticated political concepts. This seems very doubtful, since a perusal of Smith's use of Renápe and Strachey's dictionary of that language tends to indicate a very imperfect knowledge of words, a total absence of verbal comprehension, and an absence of complex concepts (such as conquest or inheritance).

When, therefore, we find English authors asserting that Wahunsonacock had "inherited" a certain number of kingdoms and conquered others, we have to adopt a very skeptical attitude, given the difficulty of making such inferences in the absence of suitable language. How does one imply "inheritance" with only gesture or signs, or with only the simplest of words (mostly names of objects or simple nouns) available?

We have also been informed that descent among the Powhatans was always through the female line. How did Wahunsonacock inherit many republics then? Did he have numerous sisters who each served as rulers of separate republics and all of whom conveniently died without any other heirs?

Also absent from most current work are any attempts to see how people behaved, as opposed to theoretical political structures. Did people obey Wahunsonacock? Did he have clear control over villages other than his own? Were subject groups anxious to rebel and go over to the English side? As an example, let me cite the alleged existence of a large Monacan population to the west of modern Richmond, a population allegedly hostile to the Renápe-Powhatan villages. If this was the case, then why did Wahunsonacock reportedly have his warehouse full of treasures located at the very edge of "his" territory, and very near to the region of the Monacans? This warehouse does not seem to have been especially guarded, which leads to many questions about just who the Monacans were, how numerous they were, and if, indeed, they were enemies at all. Certain it is that English sources make very little mention of the Monacans from Smith's time until 1676, with no references at all to warfare with Powhatan people.

Some scholars suppose that the Monacans and the similarly situated Manahoac to the north were Siouxan-speakers related to the later Saponi-Tutelo, however, the evidence on this is still not clear, especially for the latter group. In any case, the English do not make use of them as allies in their wars with the Powhatans, to 1676. Likewise, in 1656 the Richmond area was invaded by the Recahekrians (a Powhatan term, from *rikahak*, a fork, thus "People of the Forks") but only Totopotomoy (a Pamunkey leader) and Powhatans were recruited to fight them, even though they were close to, or in, Monacan territory.

I cite the above only to question the tendency of white writers to almost always accept John Smith and other early white sources without serious question. This same issue can be discussed in relation to the writings of Bernal Díaz del Castillo, Hernan Cortés, and other early Spaniards involved in the conquests of Mexico, Peru, and so forth. Not only do we witness problems of language, but also the biases, blind spots, and downright propaganda involved in most projects of imperialism (and especially where bloody warfare results in horrific numbers of victims).

It was certainly convenient, as well as culturally predictable, for Europeans to magnify the political authority of leaders whom they had defeated or whom they expected to force into cessions of land and resources. For the English, it was important to show that Wahunsonacock held sway over much of tidewater Virginia, since the English claim could be bolstered by tricking him into becoming a feudal subject of the English king or by forcing cessions of land after a military defeat.

Many Native Americans are very suspicious of Euro-American theories (such as the Bering Strait thesis), but all of us must become much more adept at textual analysis. In this, I find that the history of biblical scholarship is very helpful in setting an example of the close reading of texts and the development of methodologies for determining multiple authorship, additions, dates, and forgeries. But very often, Eurocentric texts have played major roles in the way that we look at the history and cultures of non-European peoples. Such "texts" also include novels, films, videos, radio broadcasts, plays (such as *The Tempest* and *Othello the Moor*) as well as diaries, memoirs, and books of all kinds. These texts or sources must often be deconstructed because one finds that anthropologists, archaeologists, historians, sociologists, and others (not to mention "popular" creators) continue to cite many of them as authoritative and reliable (e.g. Disney's *Pocahontas*).

Charging into Enemy Territory

I want to be very candid about some of the issues that I have faced over the years, hoping that they will be useful to others and will help to shed light on the larger struggles of emerging new fields. It may, at times, sound as if I am complaining about an unhappy fate (I hope not) but be assured that I feel very fulfilled as a scholar and innovator. One has to be able to "roll with the punches," so to speak, and to maintain a sense of humor and perspective if one is going to challenge powerfully entrenched groups and perspectives!

Being critical of Eurocentric writing may get one into trouble in one's field of study. For example, my early critiques of U.S. historiography, "western" history, frontier history, and "Gold Rush" historiography (written in the late 1950s) did not always gain me the "kudos" I might have expected as a frequent contributor to scholarly journals. Some of the major journals (such as *American Historical Review*, *Journal of American History*, the *Historian*, and the *American Scholar*) rejected my submissions and I was fortunate to be able to publish in less prestigious or newer quarterlies, such as the *Masterkey*, *Journal of the West*, *Arizona and the West*, *Ethnohistory*, and *Americas*.[3] Naturally, this circumstance influenced where I could be hired. I began my teaching at a community college rather than a major university. This was followed by some years at a state college and a small, but congenial state university. (Incidentally, I do not regret the above experiences, since I found my more working-class, "mature," and nonwhite students to often be the most rewarding to work with.)

By 1965–1966 I had two major scholarly books published (*Apache, Navaho and Spaniard* and *Warriors of the Colorado*), a textbook (*The Indian in America's Past*), and many articles, and had received a Guggenheim fellowship, but I still could not find a prestigious appointment. Partly this was due to the fact that native studies did not exist as a field and no history departments taught Indian history (outside of Oklahoma). Partly it was due to the fact that historians thought that I was an anthropologist because I wrote about native people, and because I incorporated an ethnohistorical perspective in my work. But also prejudice existed because of my working-class origin, my degrees from Glendale College (a community college) and the University of Southern California (which, at that time, lacked endowments, prestige, and a strong interface with the elite universities of the country), and my obvious failure to have been at the right places at the right time (Harvard, Yale, et al.).[4]

During the period when I was looking for a niche, say from 1959 through the late 1960s, the Berkeley history department, I understand, was essentially only hiring faculty from the elite New England schools, and, in any case, had chosen to eliminate California and U.S. western history out of animosity toward the earlier legacy of Herbert Eugene Bolton. The majority hadn't the least interest in North American Indian history (although I did develop a friendship with Woodrow Borah, who, of course, worked with Mexican-Indian history).

In this context, the development of Native American studies and similar fields not controlled by white scholars has been crucial, since it has allowed us to write articles that would never be accepted in the *American Anthropologist*, and so forth. We have been able to establish our own journals and write in ways that have much more validity and relevance (even if they have not altered many of the so-called "traditional" disciplines).

My high school courses were, on the whole, rather dismal and I cannot recall any material relating to Americans of color, whether in literature or history. In Spanish we did read an Argentine novel which made reference to Guaraní people as sort of fortune-teller types (as I recall), and I chose to read a very large number of books on my own relating to Native American, black, and worldwide subjects, for which I received no credit. As I have indicated, things changed somewhat at community college, where I did have the opportunity to use the world history texts of Wallbank and Taylor and where we had an outstanding, albeit all-white, faculty. The University of Southern California also had virtually an all-Caucasian faculty, except for one Chinese scholar in Asian studies, as I recall. Many of our courses made no pretense of looking at history from a black or other non-European perspective, and I believe it was very tough for nonwhite students to earn a doctorate if they exhibited any tendency toward a non-white ideology. I was fortunate, in that I had an exceptionally good group of faculty on my doctoral committee and an able mentor to guide me through the obstacles.

I was very much aware of the distortions in history to which I had been exposed and by 1955–1956, as noted, I was writing articles which attempted to offer a different perspective. Some were strictly focused on native people, while others offered a critique of racist historiography, a very dangerous thing for a young scholar to do, as noted above. My article on "Lily-White History," for example, was rejected by *American Scholar* and languished until being accepted, but never published, by the *Crisis*. But I did keep working away and my "Gold Rush" historiography critique appeared in the *Masterkey*, and my analyses of frontier and western history appeared in *Journal of the West* and *Arizona and the West*, both new journals outside of the establishment. My major critique of United States history, "An American Approach to American History," later revised as "The Historian and the Indian: Racial Bias in American History (which I had begun to sketch out as early as 1956) had to wait until 1963 to appear in the Academy of American Franciscan History's journal *Americas*. I was very pleased to have it finally published, but it did not have a chance to influence the field. In fact, I have found that my work of the early years has often been left out of digital databases and has been ignored by scholars offering critiques of history in general and western North American and Native American history in particular.[5]

I believe that I was a pioneer in attempting to introduce multiethnic history as well as multicultural approaches to curriculum, but I was certainly influenced by a group of outstanding African-American scholars teaching largely in black institutions such as Rayford W. Logan and E. Franklin Frazier. *Race and Culture Contacts in the Modern World* by Frazier provided a stimulating example for me, and others, I am sure.[6] We all owe a major debt to these black West Indian and African-American scholars, such as C. L. R. James, W. E. B. Du Bois, Carter G. Woodson, and others, who struggled for many decades under very adverse circumstances.

There were also some early Native American writers who pioneered the field of Native American studies, such as William Apess, Luther Standing Bear, Francis LaFlesche, D'arcy McNickle, and others, but few if any ever obtained an academic appointment, and most of their writings were out of print and hard to find when I was a youth. Fortunately, my local public library did have a few Indian sources, and I soon spent a lot of time at the Southwest Museum Library.

Proposals for Native Studies and Colleges
In any case, in 1961 I designed a proposal for a major in American Indian Studies at San Fernando Valley State College. It was patterned after a proposed program in Latin American Studies, but had little chance of being adopted. At the same time, off-campus, I proposed the creation of an independent American Indian university and formed a committee with Carl Gorman, the Navajo artist, and his wife Mary. Both of these ideas eventually bore fruit, but the former required about eight years and the latter eight to ten years, at Navajo Community College and D-Q University, respectively. During the period in between I campaigned consistently for native higher education, for changes in curriculum, and for the selection of multiethnic textbooks in the public schools.[7]

The Academy and the Community: Two Aspects of the Same Struggle
At the University of Southern California (USC) and Citrus College, 1957–1959, I introduced a great deal of Indian material into the courses which I taught, as well as black- and Chicano-oriented topics and readings where appropriate. My students at Citrus in "U.S. Government" had to read Milton Meyer's "The Issue Is Miscegenation," while at Valley State *Black Elk Speaks* was often required. I worked with students of diverse ethnic backgrounds at Citrus, building the United Nations Club into a strong and useful vehicle for helping Chicanas, African-Americans, Indians, and others to gain experiences normally unavailable to them.[8]

At Valley State, aside from teaching, I became very active in the development of a pan-Indian organization, the Native American Movement, which brought together U.S. Indians and Mexican-Americans in the San Fernando Valley and Ventura County areas. We were especially active in relation to the schools and education issues, but we also distributed political material to Mexican-American and tribal leaders throughout the Southwest and elsewhere. Fundamentally, our goal was to encourage Chicanos (a term not then popular) to become proud of their indigenous racial and cultural ancestry and to become proactive in their communities. We popularized the idea of "Aztlan" as a term for the Southwest and even proposed an "Aztec-American University." Thus, at the same time that I was becoming a Guggenheim fellow, I was not forgetting the people outside of academic settings. It seems that such has been true of my work since at least 1959, and I have no regrets on that score.[9]

During that same period I was writing popular articles for magazines such as *Frontier* (a California-based periodical of ideas and politics) and the *Humanist*, and for local newspapers, including *El Latino* (Oxnard). These articles attempted to argue for the use of Spanish in the schools and in elections, for multicultural approaches to the history of Los Angeles and California, and for respect for homosexuals, among other issues. While living in Nevada I wrote an article on Sarah Winnemucca as Nevada's outstanding female, and worked on Nevada land rights issues (a project which caused the University of Nevada president to order me to keep quiet, as I had offended some powerful white rancher-members of the Board of Regents). Still later, I published in the *Liberator* (a New York–based black magazine) and in local newspapers in the San Francisco Bay Area (after 1967).

All of the above activities relate to the emergence of nonwhite ethnic studies, since we were accumulating evidence and sensitizing all kinds of people to what should be possible. At the University of Nevada I was able to introduce a new course on "The Native in North American History," as well as sponsor the United Nations Club and help build up a group which was multiethnic. I also co-founded the new Nevada Civil Liberties Union and we worked often with African-American and indigenous leaders on relevant civil rights issues.

I have always been convinced that we academics should generate knowledge to be used by people, not just by other academics. I am uneasy with closed circles of jargon-using scholars forming self-styled elite groups, mystifying graduate students with long opaque sentences often devoid of factual meaning. Moreover, I feel that theory and abstract thought benefit greatly from hands-on experiences with real people in real-life circumstances. I have learned an immense amount from working with community people, as well as with undergraduate students and part-time students. At the University of Warwick (1981–1982) and at Oxford (1986–1987) I organized very rewarding Third World literature groups, modeled after ones which I had sponsored at UC Davis from about 1980. These groups have brought me friends of all races and from many continents, all very dear to me. All of this is a very essential part of how I relate to "world studies" and to history. (Since I am also a published poet, novelist, and short story writer, I give myself permission to cross many boundaries.)

Some Changes Come with the Mid-1960s

In any case, the late sixties brought an awakening among college-age youth, which allowed us to begin to bring about some institutional changes on a larger scale. In 1965 and 1966 I used to drive over the Sierras from Reno to do research in Berkeley, and there I saw the evidence of both the free speech movement and the organizing work of African-Americans. In January 1967 I moved to Berkeley to work for the Far West Laboratory, a federally-funded center for educational development. I became Research Program Director for the Multicultural Program and devoted my energies to developing curricular material for Native American, Mexican American, and African American units in the schools and colleges. These took many forms, but principally four publications: *The Education of the Culturally Different*; *Mexican Americans: A Handbook for Educators*; *Afro-Americans in the Far West;* and *Native Americans of California and Nevada*. Also, by helping to found the California Indian Education Association, we were able to facilitate the publication of *California Indian Education: The Report of the Statewide All-Indian Conference* (1967). This report specifically advocated the inclusion of Indian material and courses in higher education. We also conducted many workshops for teachers and community people and I lectured in college settings quite often. At the laboratory I also had a chance to critique school curricular units relating to African Americans and other related topics.[10]

One significant contribution was helping to bring Senator Robert Kennedy to San Francisco for hearings on Indian education and then accompanying him to visit Stewarts Point native community. We were able to insert a great deal of positive educational proposals into the final report of the Senate subcommittee, with the help of Adrian Parmenter, an aide to the subcommittee.

By 1968 the stage was set for student demands on higher education at San Francisco State, at UC Berkeley, and elsewhere. In Berkeley we organized United Native Americans, a new pan-Indian militant organization. We began working specifically on higher education. At the Far West Lab I secured a grant from the Donner Foundation to survey American Indian courses in colleges and to design community-developed courses as a prelude to creating an American Indian university or placing such courses in existing colleges. In any case, we began working closely with the handful of native students then enrolled at Berkeley, as well as meeting with Richard Oakes (Mohawk) and other students from San Francisco State. I located a vacant basement of a bungalow on the Berkeley campus in early 1969 and we proceeded to clean it up, occupying it as a native center. Subsequently, we secured official approval of our occupation and received money for a telephone. This office became central to much native planning for the Third World Strike which soon developed and provided a hub for Indian students.

Nineteen sixty-nine saw the beginning of nonwhite ethnic studies programs on several campuses, including both UC Davis and Berkeley. I was in a rather unique position because I had done a lot of the design work for Berkeley and had been offered the position as first chair of ethnic studies, but I ultimately chose to go to UC Davis in order to develop the Native American Studies program there. I was convinced that Berkeley was not willing to come up with enough money for a Third World college, and given that, I was persuaded that Davis would be a better site for California Indian students. (During the seventies and early eighties I was not sure that that I had chosen wisely, but in the long run we have been very successful at Davis, especially since 1988.)[11]

I have given this overview of my relationship with the early growth of ethnic studies in order to shed some light on what went into its origin but also to highlight the role of preparation, struggle, and intellectual commitment which had to occur for the successes of later years to become possible. I have left out many things, including the founding of our many journals and our frequent use of earlier periodicals, such as *Freedomways*, *Negro Digest*, *Phylon*, and many others. This latter has been very important for me personally and professionally, because almost all of my scholarly articles since the 1970's have been published in the *Journal of Ethnic Studies*, *Wicazo Sa Review*, *American Indian Quarterly*, *American Indian Culture and Research Journal*, *Phylon*, *Explorations in Ethnic Studies*, and other quarterlies not controlled by the traditional disciplines. My popular articles have usually also appeared in native newspapers, black periodicals, or publications controlled by politically progressive, grassroots groups. I find that since Carey McWilliams left as editor I haven't been able to be published in the *Nation* and, for some reason, my way of writing has never appealed to most white-controlled "old left" or "liberal" periodicals. I now have published about five hundred items, but as I go down the list, it is quite obvious that I have never made the literary or historical mainstreams. So I am in debt to all those intrepid souls who have developed alternative places for our voices.[12]

Obstacles Along the Trail

In terms of my writing, I find that whenever I have "strayed" from composing books on Native American historical subjects (or on native-black relations) I have discovered that commercial and university publishers were unwilling to print my works. In the mid-1960s I developed anthologies on very important and neglected topics: a history of race mixture in the United States, another on Native American current issues, and one on Mexican-American history and status. All were rejected by large numbers of publishers. It wasn't until 1973 that *Aztecas del Norte: The Chicanos of Aztlan* came out. The book sold 20,000 copies for Fawcett but after CBS took the house over, it and some other "radical" titles were shredded without warning. The race mixture book saw the light of day only as a reader for a course I taught from about 1970 to the mid-1990s ("Race and Sex: Race Mixture and Mixed-Blood Populations").

In about 1969 several of us were asked to put together a book on the struggles of people of color in the United States entitled "The Third World Within." Unfortunately, after many months of work and much correspondence the publisher canceled the project.

I wrote *A World Ruled by Cannibals* and edited *Tribes and Masses* in the mid-1970s. Both books were published in small editions by D-Q University Press after being turned down by commercial houses, as well as by Marxist and "new left" publishers. *Cannibals* was to have been published by the Mohawk Nation's *Akwesasne Notes* but they lacked the money in the end, and, while South End Press was interested, I lost my contact there. *Columbus and Other Cannibals*, a revised version, came out in 1992 from Semiotexte-Autonomedia and has had great success for a book printed with virtually no publicity and no review copies. (It is now being revised because of the continuing cannibalism in the world!)

Other writers seem to have had a lot more success at publishing in the "mainstream," and I find that this even applies to my poetry, which very seldom can be published in a white-edited poetry journal (except in special issues devoted to Native American writing). My poetry seems to resonate with Native Americans and other people of color, but not with Euro-American editors. I am persuaded that my "voice," the way I speak about issues, subjects, topics, and feelings, is somehow so divergent from what is acceptable in white-edited organs and houses, whether left, right, or center, that I am shunted aside. For example, I have been writing at least one op-ed each month but my only outlets are native newspapers and an occasional "progressive" or "grassroots" periodical. The *Los Angeles Times, San Francisco Examiner, Sacramento Bee, Washington Post,* and *New York Times*, among other dailies, have all uniformly rejected my articles (since the early 1970s in the case of the *Bee*) and only the *San Francisco Chronicle* (bless her heart) has published my work.[13]

What has all of this to do with ethnic studies? I believe that it may mirror our position in the academic world in that both the academy and the commercial press reflect much the same biases which are, at heart, ethnic and cultural. A wide range of opinion may be expressed in the press so long as Anglo-American nationalism and supremacy is the normative, the unstated, the assumed. In universities, this may range from economics departments which would never dream of departing from the kind of ideologies developed in western Europe and North America in the past five centuries, to philosophy departments loath to give any attention to Asian, African, Pacific, or Native American philosophies or to women's thought, and on to biology departments unwilling to consider non-European views on what constitutes "bios," life.

Anglo-American values are sanctified as "American" and other perspectives are often marginalized as non-American or "other."

Looking to the Future

Clearly, we have achieved a great deal in the past several decades. On many campuses we have strong academic departments, although it seems common to have experiences of decline or weakness as well. Our road to modest success is littered with failed dreams and we all have many aches and pains from the harsh battles we have often had to engage in. Having said that, though, I consider where we are today remarkable, given the context of the rigid and unbending resistance to multiculturalism evident in North American white academia and education generally since the 1620s. What I mean is that the "white supremacy" approach to curricula, which is also essentially an Anglo-American and Euro-Canadian approach, has not only been deeply entrenched, but is currently experiencing a resurgence supported not only by white "conservatives" but also by many "liberals" who, in this area, see multiculturalism as a threat to "Americanness" (by which they mean that "American" = Anglo-American).[14]

We often find few friends in academia outside of our own programs, I fear; although that varies from school to school, I am sure. At UC Davis, one thing that has happened is that non-European multiethnic approaches to subject matter are largely confined, I think, to our so-called ethnic units (with a few exceptions) and that this rather exactly corresponds with the process of racial desegregation. That is, the ethnic studies departments provide the great bulk of the only desegregation which has occurred. Many academic departments continue to be entirely Caucasian, while most others tend to have only one or two U.S.-born persons of color. Women (especially of color) are also underrepresented. In the climate of Davis, it seems difficult to persuade white faculty that they will benefit from the addition of an Asian American specialist, for example, when the kinds of problems to be studied through Asian American eyes may appear, let us say, much less significant than those that would be studied by another biological anthropologist, or another European art history scholar, or a Caucasian who has studied about Asian art or Asian history, and so forth. And, of course, the real pressure is to add more biological/engineering researchers/technicians to bring income into the university's coffers, even if one does not teach such major languages and cultures as Arabic, Hindi, Vietnamese, Indonesian/Malayan, Filipino, Iranian/Persian, Turkic, and so on.

By and large, we have failed to influence many of the white academic disciplines. Of course, they will deny their "whiteness" or Eurocentrism, but the truth is that most still study problems which are essentially of interest to Euro-North Americans, while overlooking or underrating issues of concern to many non-Europeans. For example, for Native Americans key questions in philosophy revolve around how we are to relate to the animals and to the earth, in short, how we are to live in this life. In economics Native Americans might wish to explore traditional economies based upon sharing and diversification, with ethical and spiritual questions being directly relevant to the practice of investment and "the market." Instead we now have dominant economic perspectives which seek to divorce how one makes money from any question of how one should behave, that is, as the head of the huge Teachers Insurance and Annuities Association has put it: there is no place for ethics in investment considerations. Thus if Texaco leaves an environmental mess behind when it pulls out of Ecuador, that is not an investment issue. The only issue is whether Texaco's investors secured a good return.

The point that I am trying to make is that the values of many disciplines reflect the values which have evolved within the moneyed classes of western Europe and North America since the 1500s. They by no means represent a world or global approach to the various fields of study, nor do they represent a multi-class or multiethnic approach from a North American perspective.

But in suggesting that we have failed to penetrate the white academy, I am not advocating the merger of our "ethnic" units with them. It would be unwise for us to advocate the disappearance of our studies programs and their absorption by traditional white departments. The reasons have already been stated above, but fundamentally we must survive with independence because that is the only way to hold out the opportunity of trans-ethnic thinking, global perspectives, and a degree of scholarly integrity and autodetermination. Of course, most of our programs remain underfunded and understaffed, and we are only now beginning to train our own doctoral candidates, people who will not have to "debrief" themselves from their often narrow anthropological, sociological, or historical training before being able to fully function in an interdisciplinary, cross-boundary manner.

We must also, in my opinion, make sure that our fields are grounded in a fundamental foundation of empirical research, with theory being based upon reasoning from widely-gathered data. We need to avoid apparently glamorous and/or faddish approaches to writing which can only discredit our work in the long run because of an absence of careful research or the use of obtuse language, which obscures meaning and avoids communication with our community bases.

Why Are We Ethnic Studies?

I have long viewed "ethnic" as a problematic and troublesome term, so long as it is restricted only to non-European or non-immigrant "minority" groups. When, in 1968, I prepared a proposal for a college of Third World studies at UC Berkeley, it was envisioned as being global in perspective, although beginning with foci on African Americans, Asian Americans, Native Americans, and Chicanos. Eventually, the term "ethnic" studies was adopted, in part because university administrators found it more acceptable, perhaps more manageable politically, than the Third World concept.[15]

The danger is, of course, that only nonwhites or recent immigrants are to be regarded as "ethnics," as having ethnicity, while Anglo-Americans and Europeans, in contrast, have "legitimate" and "normal" national cultures. Ethnic can become derogatory, similar to the sociological use of "subculture" to describe many of our cultural traditions, or the use of "subaltern" to refer to our populations. "Sub" is a root which leaves little ambiguity: it means under and below (as in substandard). Subaltern, in Latin, means subordinate.

Essentially, I would suggest that ethnic, subcultural, and subaltern, as well as minority, are terms popularized by persons from the politically dominant populations, and they are terms which we should regard with great suspicion. Our Native American Studies department at UC Davis is hemispheric and potentially global (since I personally have written about indigenous Americans in Europe and Africa, and indigenous peoples are found almost everywhere). African and African-American Studies are global at Davis and also on many other campuses. Asian American studies certainly has the potential of becoming hemispheric and even global if comparative studies are undertaken. Chicano/Raza studies has the potential of including Mexico, borderlands, and other parts of the hemisphere.

In any case, we must be perfectly clear: Native American studies is not a subset of United States studies. We are not a minority studies field. For this reason I have come to prefer the concepts of "global studies," "world studies," and/or hemispheric studies (at Davis we also have developed the Hemispheric Initiative of the Americas, HIA, which broadens Latin American studies to include all of the American hemisphere).

My preference is for the concept of world studies, which term could also include European, African, Asian, and Pacific study areas as well. Ethnic studies, of course, can also include the latter, properly speaking, but no one in power has wished to characterize French, British, or Italian studies as "ethnic," to my knowledge.

I might also suggest that we consider appropriating the term ethnology, although it is still used by a small group of anthropologists. It means "nation knowledge" or the "study of nations." An alternative might be "nations' studies," the Latin equivalent of Greek *ethniki*. While that would suit us in indigenous studies, some groups might not be thinking in terms of "nations," even though the term "ethno" is derived from exactly that meaning.

I have written elsewhere about how Anglo-Americans have attempted to literally appropriate the name of the continent or hemisphere (America) and apply it, not simply to the area of the United States as a physical country, but to whatever area they happened to politically control at any given time (i.e., the "thirteen colonies"). Moreover, they have attempted to extend the term "American" back in time to apply it to their colonial ancestors, often even before the latter reached our shores! In connection with this construction of a concept of "American" nationality extending back into the 1607–1620 period, a set of racial and cultural myths has been created, as noted earlier. Unfortunately, the Anglo-American ethnic myth has evolved as a highly xenophobic myth, in which "real Americans" are ones who resemble "the Brady Bunch" and who speak only Englatino (modern creolized English), dress in certain specified ways, and share a set of similar beliefs about other peoples and about the role of the United States as "the world's only super power."[16]

Since the 1960s we have been able to build upon a different heritage, the reality of a multicultural country, home to countless different linguistic and cultural traditions ranging from Pennsylvania German ("Dutch"), to Louisiana Cajun and Creole, to New Hampshire Quebecois, to New

Mexico "Hispanos," to Tejanos, and to numerous native nations, and to many other communities speaking Italian, Polish, Chinese, Japanese, Yiddish, and Arabic.

Our "world studies" programs have arisen directly out of the needs of these many communities, as well as out of the sincere efforts at multiethnic appreciation on the part of far-seeing Anglo-Americans. In the early 2000s we may see a new period of xenophobic nationalism and conformity, exemplified by many Middle Easterners and Muslims giving up their traditional dress in public in order to avoid persecution. Similarly, many may be pressured into not speaking a "different-sounding" language where it can be heard by airport security guards or by pseudo-patriotic bigots on the street corner. Nonetheless, I would argue that the momentum in favor of diversity will survive, and that the importance of globalism and international studies will grow in our universities, not diminish.

We need to position our departments and programs so as to participate in the obvious need for greater human understanding, on a global, international, and even interspecies scale. We must assume a central role on that stage. Internationalism and globalism should begin within the country, within the continent and hemisphere, going on to the globe and out into space.

Notes

1. See Jack D. Forbes, "The Hijacking of America," an unpublished article partly appearing as "The Name is Half the Game: The Theft of 'America' and Indigenous Claims of Sovereignty" in Mani Jo Moore, editor, *Eating Fire, Tasting Blood* (New York: Thunder's Mouth), 32–51. See also Jack D. Forbes, "The Historian and the Indian: Racial bias in American History," *Americas*, April 1963, and other works cited at nas.ucdavis.edu/Forbes/FORBES_PUBLICATIONS.html.

2. I did a lot of this initial research in 1959–1960 as a part of preparing lectures for my course in the history of civilization.

3. For titles of articles, see nas.ucdavis.edu/Forbes/FORBES_PUBLICATIONS.html

4. *Apache, Navaho and Spaniard* was published by the University of Oklahoma Press in 1960. It was my doctoral dissertation, with only one change requested by the editor, Savoie Lottinville. He asked me to drop the word "American" which I had used in the introduction to refer to American Indians. I complied reluctantly. Savoie told me later that he regretted not having submitted this book for a Pulitzer Prize. *Warriors of the Colorado* was also published by the University of Oklahoma Press in 1965. *The Indian in America's Past* was published by Prentice-Hall in 1964, and launched a totally new approach to Native American history writing. Although intended as a college supplementary text, it was also designed

to open up a whole new approach to indigenous studies, by including sections on Mexican-Americans, Puerto Ricans, Red slavery, race mixture, and by mentioning black/Indian mixture.

5. See citations for these articles at nas.ucdavis.edu/Forbes/FORBES_PUBLICATIONS.html

6. E. Franklin Frazier, *Race and Culture Contacts in the Modern World* (New York: Knopf, 1957).

7. See Jack D. Forbes, *Native American Higher Education: The Struggle for the Creation of D-Q University, 1960–1971* (Davis, Calif.: D-Q University Press, 1985). See also "Guide to the Jack D. Forbes Collection (Manuscripts) in the Special Collections Department, Shields Library, University of California, Davis" found on the website for Native American Studies, ucdavis.edu/nas/faculty.html. This guide references material relating to Native American higher education and native studies programs, among other educational issues.

8. Milton Mayer, "The Issue Is Miscegenation," *Progressive*, 23 (September 1959): 8–18; and John G. Neihardt, ed., *Black Elk Speaks* (Lincoln: University of Nebraska Press, 1961).

9. See the "Guide to the Jack D. Forbes Collection," cited above, for materials on the Native American Movement, Movimiento Nativo Americano, Chicano issues, Aztlan, and so forth.

10. *Education of the Culturally Different* (Berkeley, Calif.: Far West Laboratory, 1967); *Mexican-Americans* (Berkeley, Calif.: Far West Laboratory, 1967); *Afro-Americans in the Far West* (Berkeley, Calif.: Far West Laboratory, 1967); *Native Americans of California and Nevada* (Healdsburg, Calif.: Naturegraph, 1969). Revised edition 1982.

11. See Duane Champagne and Jay Stauss, eds., *Native American Studies in Higher Education: Models for Collaboration between Universities and Indigenous Nations* (Walnut Creek, Calif.: AltaMira Press, 2002), especially pp. 97–122.

12. See Jack D. Forbes, *Tribes and Masses: Essays in Red, Brown and Black* (Davis, Calif.: D-Q University Press, 1978); "The Barbarian Conquest of Ventura County," *Nation* 202, no. 5 (January 31, 1966): 128, 140; "Vietnam: What Role for the UN? Tactics for a Truce," *Nation* 202, no. 9 (February 28, 1966): 229–230; and "The Indian: Looking Glass into America," *Liberator* 6, no. 8 (August 1966): 6–9 and September 1966: 14–17 for examples of my many popular and political articles.

13. See Jack D. Forbes, "From Wounded Knee to Acteal," *San Francisco Chronicle*, December 30, 1998, p. A17; and "Do Homeless Human Beings Have a Right to Life?" *San Francisco Chronicle*, May 28, 2000, Sunday section 7, p. 9. Articles also appear regularly in *News From Indian Country*, *Bay Mills News*, *Micmac-Maliseet Nations News*, and other native or local newspapers.

14. See my article on "The Hijacking of America" as well as "Who Are the Americans?" *Akwesasne Notes* 8, no. 5 (Mid-winter 1976): 37–38; "How Europeans Have Stolen America," *Guardian* (Manchester and London), August 24,

1987, p. 19; "What Do We Mean by America and American?" *News from Indian Country* 8, no. 12 (Late June 1994): 16. Also see *Naming Our Land, Reclaiming Our Land* (Bandon, Ore.: Kahonkok Press, 1992) for poetic approaches to the subject.

15. See the "Guide to the Jack D. Forbes Collection (Manuscripts)," cited above, for numerous references to materials relating to ethnic studies at Davis and in general. These materials are largely available to researchers in the Shields Library, Special Collections.

16. I have introduced the term "Englatino" to refer to our contemporary creolized, mixed language of English, Latin, French, Native American, Spanish, Greek, and other tongues from all around the globe. See "English Only," *News from Indian Country* 10, no. 1 (mid-January 1996): 15A.

Learning from the Outsider Within   5
The Sociological Significance of Black Feminist Thought*

PATRICIA HILL COLLINS

> *Black women have long occupied marginal positions in academic settings. I argue that many black female intellectuals have made creative use of their marginality—their "outsider within" status—to produce black feminist thought that reflects a special standpoint on self, family, and society. I describe and explore the sociological significance of three characteristic themes in such thought: (1) black women's self-definition and self-valuation; (2) the interlocking nature of oppression; and (3) the importance of Afro-American women's culture. After considering how black women might draw upon these key themes as outsiders within to generate a distinctive standpoint on existing sociological paradigms, I conclude by suggesting that other sociologists would also benefit by placing greater trust in the creative potential of their own personal and cultural biographies.[1]*

AFRO-AMERICAN WOMEN HAVE LONG BEEN PRIVY to some of the most intimate secrets of white society. Countless black women have ridden buses to their white "families," where they not only cooked, cleaned, and executed other domestic duties, but where they also nurtured their "other" children, shrewdly offered guidance to their employers, and frequently, became honorary members of their white "families." These

---

*From: Patricia Hill Collins, "Learning from the Outsider Within: The Sociological Significance of Black Feminist Thought," *Social Problems* 33, no. 6 (December 1986): 514–532. Used by permission. This chapter was edited to conform with the format of this anthology.

women have seen white elites, both actual and aspiring, from perspectives largely obscured from their black spouses and from these groups themselves.[2]

On one level, this "insider" relationship has been satisfying to all involved. The memoirs of affluent whites often mention their love for their black "mothers," while accounts of black domestic workers stress the sense of self-affirmation they experienced at seeing white power demystified—of knowing that it was not the intellect, talent, or humanity of their employers that supported their superior status, but largely just the advantages of racism.[3] But on another level, these same black women knew they could never belong to their white "families." In spite of their involvement, they remained "outsiders."[4]

This "outsider within" status has provided a special standpoint on self, family, and society for Afro-American women.[5] A careful review of the emerging black feminist literature reveals that many black intellectuals, especially those in touch with their marginality in academic settings, tap this standpoint in producing distinctive analyses of race, class, and gender. For example, Zora Neal Hurston's 1937 novel, *Their Eyes Were Watching God*, most certainly reflects her skill at using the strengths and transcending the limitations both of her academic training and of her background in traditional Afro-American community life.[6] Black feminist historian E. Frances White (1984) suggests that black women's ideas have been honed at the juncture between movements for racial and sexual equality, and contends that Afro-American women have been pushed by "their marginalization in both arenas" to create black feminism.[7] Finally, black feminist critic bell hooks captures the unique standpoint that the outsider within status can generate. In describing her small-town, Kentucky childhood, she notes, "living as we did—on the edge—we developed a particular way of seeing reality. We looked both from the outside and in from the inside out . . . we understood both.[8]

In spite of the obstacles that can confront outsiders within, such individuals can benefit from this status. Simmel's essay on the sociological significance of what he called the "stranger" offers a helpful starting point for understanding the largely unexplored area of black female outsider within status and the usefulness of the standpoint it might produce. Some of the potential benefits of outsider within status include: (1) Simmel's definition of "objectivity" as "a peculiar composition of nearness and remoteness, concern and indifference"; (2) the tendency for people to confide in a "stranger" in ways they never would with each other; and (3) the ability of the "stranger" to see patterns that may be more difficult for those immersed in the situation to see.⁹ Mannheim labels the "strangers" in academia "marginal intellectuals" and argues that the critical posture such individuals bring to academic endeavors may be essential to the creative development of academic disciplines themselves.¹⁰ Finally, in assessing the potentially positive qualities of social difference, specifically marginality, Lee notes, "for a time this marginality can be a most stimulating, albeit often a painful, experience. For some, it is debilitating . . . for others, it is an excitement to creativity."¹¹

Sociologists might benefit greatly from serious consideration of the emerging, cross-disciplinary literature that I label black feminist thought, precisely because, for many Afro-American female intellectuals, "marginality" has been an incitement to creativity. As outsiders within, black feminist scholars may be one of many distinct groups of marginal intellectuals whose standpoints promise to enrich contemporary sociological discourse. Bringing this group—as well as others who share an outsider within status vis-à-vis sociology—into the center of analysis may reveal aspects of reality obscured by more orthodox approaches.

In the remainder of this essay, I examine the sociological significance of the black feminist thought stimulated by black women's outsider within status. First, I outline three key themes that characterize the emerging cross-disciplinary literature that I label black feminist thought.¹² For each theme, I summarize its content, supply examples from black feminist and other works that illustrate its nature, and discuss its importance. Second, I explain the significance these key themes in black feminist thought may have for sociologists by describing why black women's outsider within status might generate a distinctive standpoint vis-à-vis existing sociological paradigms. Finally, I discuss one general implication of this essay for social scientists: namely, the potential usefulness of identifying and using one's own standpoint in conducting research.

Three Key Themes in Black Feminist Thought

Black feminist thought consists of ideas produced by black women that clarify a standpoint of and for black women. Several assumptions underlie this working definition. First the definition suggests that it is impossible to separate the structure and thematic content of thought from the historical and material conditions shaping the lives of its producers.¹³ Therefore, while black feminist thought may be recorded by others, it is produced by black women. Second, the definition assumes that black women possess a unique standpoint on, or perspective of, their experiences and that there will be certain commonalities of perception shared by black women as a group. Third, while living life as black women may produce certain commonalities of outlook, the diversity of class, region, age, and sexual orientation shaping individual black women's lives has resulted in different expressions of these common themes. Thus, universal themes included in the black women's standpoint may be experienced and expressed differently by distinct groups of Afro-American women. Finally, the definition assumes that, while a black women's standpoint exists, its contours may not be clear to black women themselves. Therefore, one role for black female intellectuals is to produce facts and theories about the black female experience that will clarify a black woman's standpoint for black women. In other words, black feminist thought contains observations and interpretations about Afro-American womanhood that describe and explain different expressions of common themes.

No one black feminist platform exists from which one can measure the "correctness" of a particular thinker; nor should there be one. Rather, as I defined it above, there is a long and rich tradition of black feminist thought. Much of it has been oral and has been produced by ordinary black women in their roles as mothers, teachers, musicians, and preachers.[14] Since the civil rights and women's movements, black women's ideas have been increasingly documented and are reaching wider audiences. The following discussion of three key themes in black feminist thought is itself part of this emerging process of documentation and interpretation. The three themes I have chosen are not exhaustive but, in my assessment, they do represent the thrust of much of the existing dialogue.

The Meaning of Self-Definition and Self-Valuation

An affirmation of the importance of black women's self-definition and self-valuation is the first key theme that pervades historical and contemporary statements of black feminist thought. Self-definition involves challenging the political knowledge-validation process that has resulted in externally-defined, stereotypical images of Afro-American womanhood. In contrast, self-valuation stresses the content of black women's self-definitions—namely, replacing externally-derived images with authentic black female images.

Both Mae King's and Cheryl Gilkes's analyses of the importance of stereotypes offer useful insights for grasping the importance of black women's self-definition.[15] King suggests that stereotypes represent externally-defined, controlling images of Afro-American womanhood that have been central to the dehumanization of black women and the exploitation of black women's labor. Gilkes points out that black women's assertiveness in resisting the multifaceted oppression they experience has been a consistent threat to the status quo. As punishment, black women have been assaulted with a variety of externally-defined negative images designed to control assertive black female behavior.

The value of King's and Gilkes's analyses lies in their emphasis on the function of stereotypes in controlling dominated groups. Both point out that replacing negative stereotypes with ostensibly positive ones can be equally problematic if the function of stereotypes as controlling images remains unrecognized. John Gwaltney's interview with Nancy White, a seventy-three-year-old black woman, suggests that ordinary black women may also be aware of the power of these controlling images in their everyday experiences. In the following passage, Ms. White assesses the difference between the controlling images applied to Afro-American and white women as being one of degree, and not of kind:

> My mother used to say that the black woman is the white man's mule and the white woman is his dog. Now, she said that to say this: we do the heavy work and get beat whether we do it well or not. But the white woman is closer to the master and he pats them on the head and lets them sleep in the house, but he ain't gon' treat neither one like he was dealing with a person.[16]

This passage suggests that while both groups are stereotyped, albeit in different ways, the function of the images is to dehumanize and control both groups. Seen in this light, it makes little sense, in the long run, for black women to exchange one set of controlling images for another even if, in the short run, positive stereotypes bring better treatment.

The insistence on black female self-definition reframes the entire dialogue from one of determining the technical accuracy of an image, to one stressing the power dynamics underlying the very process of definition itself. Black feminists have questioned not only what has been said about black women, but the credibility and the intentions of those possessing the power to define. When black women define themselves, they clearly reject the taken-for-granted assumption that those in positions granting them the authority to describe and analyze reality are entitled to do so. Regardless of the actual content of black women's self-definitions, the act of insisting on black female self-definition validates black women's power as human subjects.

The related theme of black female self-valuation pushes this entire process one step further. While black female self-definition speaks to the power dynamics involved in the act of defining images of self and community, the theme of black female self-valuation addresses the actual content of these self-definitions. Many of the attributes extant in black female stereotypes are actually distorted renderings of those aspects of black female behavior seen as most threatening to white patriarchy.[17] For example, aggressive Afro-American women are threatening because they challenge white patriarchal definitions of femininity. To ridicule assertive women by labeling them Sapphires reflects an effort to put all women in their place. In their roles as central figures in socializing the next generation of black adults, strong mothers are similarly threatening, because they contradict patriarchal views of family power relations. To ridicule strong black mothers by labeling them matriarchs[18] reflects a similar effort to control another aspect of black female behavior that is especially threatening to the status quo.

When black females choose to value those aspects of Afro-American womanhood that are stereotyped, ridiculed, and maligned in academic scholarship and the popular media, they are actually questioning some of the basic ideas used to control dominated groups in general. It is one thing to counsel Afro-American women to resist the Sapphire stereotype by altering their behavior to become meek, docile, and stereotypically "feminine." It is quite another to advise black women to embrace their assertiveness, to value their sassiness, and to continue to use these qualities to survive in and transcend the harsh environments that circumscribe so many black women's lives. By defining and valuing assertiveness and other "unfeminine" qualities as necessary and functional attributes for Afro-American womanhood, black women's self-valuation challenges the content of externally-defined controlling images.

This black feminist concern—that black women create their own standards for evaluating Afro-American womanhood and value their creations—pervades a wide range of literary and social science works. For example, Alice Walker's 1982 novel, *The Color Purple*, and Ntozake Shange's 1978 choreopoem, *For Colored Girls Who Have Considered Suicide*, are both bold statements of the necessity for black female self-definition and self-valuation. Lena Wright Myers's work shows that black women judge their behavior by comparing themselves to black women facing similar situations and thus demonstrates the presence of black female definitions of Afro-American womanhood.[19] The recent spate of black female historiography suggests that self-defined, self-valuating black women have long populated the ranks of Afro-American female leaders.[20]

Black women's insistence on self-definition, self-valuation, and the necessity for a black female-centered analysis is significant for two reasons.

First, defining and valuing one's consciousness of one's own self-defined standpoint in the face of images that foster a self-definition as the objectified "other" is an important way of resisting the dehumanization essential to systems of domination. The status of being the "other" implies being "other than" or different from the assumed norm of white male behavior. In this model, powerful white males define themselves as subjects, the true actors, and classify people of color and women in terms of their position vis-à-vis this white male hub. Since black women have been denied the authority to challenge these definitions, this model consists of images that define black women as a negative other, the virtual antithesis of positive white male images. Moreover, as Brittan and Maynard point out, "domination always involves the objectification of the dominated; all forms of oppression imply the devaluation of the subjectivity of the oppressed."[21]

One of the best examples of this process is described by Judith Rollins. As part of her fieldwork on black domestics, Rollins worked as a domestic for six months. She describes several incidents where her employers treated her as if she were not really present. On one occasion while she sat in the kitchen having lunch, her employers had a conversation as if she were not there. Her sense of invisibility became so great that she took out a pad of paper and began writing field notes. Even though Rollins wrote for ten minutes, finished lunch, and returned to work, her employers showed no evidence of having seen her at all. Rollins notes,

> It was this aspect of servitude I found to be one of the strongest affronts to my dignity as a human being. . . . These gestures of ignoring my presence were not, I think, intended as insults; they were expressions of the employers' ability to annihilate the humanness and even, at times, the very existence of me, a servant and a black woman.[22]

Racist and sexist ideologies both share the common feature of treating dominated groups—the "others"—as objects lacking full human subjectivity. For example, seeing black women as obstinate mules and viewing white women as obedient dogs objectifies both groups, but in different ways. Neither is seen as fully human, and therefore both become eligible for race/gender-specific modes of domination. But if black women refuse to accept their assigned status as the quintessential "other," then the entire rationale for such domination is challenged. In brief, abusing a mule or a dog may be easier than abusing a person who is a reflection of one's own humanness.

A second reason that black female self-definition and self-valuation are significant concerns their value in allowing Afro-American women to reject internalized, psychological oppression.[23] The potential damage of internalized control to Afro-American women's self-esteem can be great, even to the prepared. Enduring the frequent assaults of controlling images requires considerable inner strength. Nancy White, cited earlier, also points out how debilitating being treated as less than human can be if black women are not self-defined. She notes, "Now, you know that no woman is a dog or a mule, but if folks keep making you feel that way, if you don't have a mind of your own, you can start letting them tell you what you are."[24] Seen in this light, self-definition and self-valuation are not luxuries—they are necessary for black female survival.

The Interlocking Nature of Oppression

Attention to the interlocking nature of race, gender, and class oppression is a second recurring theme in the works of black feminists.[25] While different socio-historical periods may have increased the saliency of one or another type of oppression, the thesis of the linked nature of oppression has long pervaded black feminist thought. For example, Ida Wells Barnett and Frances Ellen Watkins Harper, two prominent black feminists of the late 1800s, both spoke out against the growing violence directed against black men. They realized that civil rights held little meaning for black men and women if the right to life itself went unprotected.[26] Black women's absence from organized feminist movements has mistakenly been attributed to a lack of feminist consciousness. In actually, black feminists have possessed an ideological commitment to addressing interlocking oppression yet have been excluded from arenas that would have allowed them to do so.[27]

As Barbara Smith points out, "the concept of the simultaneity of oppression is still the crux of a Black feminist understanding of political reality and . . . is one of the most significant ideological contributions of Black feminist thought."[28] This should come as no surprise since black women should be among the first to realize that minimizing one form of oppression, while essential, may still leave them oppressed in other equally dehumanizing ways. Sojourner Truth knew this when she stated, "there is a great stir about colored men getting their rights, and not colored women theirs, you see the colored men will be masters getting their rights, and not colored women theirs, you see the colored men will be masters over the women, and it will be just as bad as before."[29] To use Nancy White's metaphors, the black woman as "mule" knows that she is perceived to be an animal. In contrast, the white woman as "dog" may be similarly dehumanized, and may think that she is an equal part of the family when, in actuality, she is a well-cared-for pet. The significant factor shaping Truth's and White's clearer view of their own subordination than that of black men or white women is their experience at the intersection of multiple structures of domination.[30] Both Truth and White are black, female, and poor. They therefore have a clearer view of oppression than other groups who occupy more contradictory positions vis-à-vis white male power—unlike white women, they have no illusions that their whiteness will negate female subordination, and unlike black men, they cannot use a questionable appeal to manhood to neutralize the stigma of being black.

The black feminist attention to the interlocking nature of oppression is significant for two reasons. First, this viewpoint shifts the entire focus of investigation from one aimed at explicating elements of race or gender or class oppression to one whose goal is to determine what the links are among these systems. The first approach typically prioritizes one form of oppression as being primary, then handles remaining types of oppression as variables within what is seen as the most important system. For example, the efforts to insert race and gender into Marxist theory exemplify this effort. In contrast, the more holistic approach implied in black feminist thought treats the interaction among multiple systems as the object of study. Rather than adding to existing theories by inserting previously excluded variables, black feminists aim to develop new theoretical interpretations of the interaction itself.

Black male scholars, white female scholars, and more recently, black feminists like bell hooks may have identified one critical link among interlocking systems of oppression. These groups have pointed out that certain basic ideas crosscut multiple systems of domination. One such idea is either/or dualistic thinking, claimed by hooks to be "the central ideological component of all systems of domination in Western society."[31]

While hooks's claim may be somewhat premature, there is growing scholarly support for her viewpoint.[32] Either/or dualistic thinking, or what I will refer to as the construct of dichotomous oppositional difference, may be a philosophical linchpin in systems of race, class, and gender oppression. One fundamental characteristic of this construct is the categorization of people, things, and ideas in terms of their difference from one another. For example, the terms in dichotomies such as black/white, male/female, reason/emotion, fact/opinion, and subject/object gain their meaning only in *relation* to their difference from their oppositional counterparts. Another fundamental characteristic of this construct is that difference is not complementary in that the halves of the dichotomy do not enhance each other. Rather, the dichotomous halves are different and inherently opposed to one another. A third and more important characteristic is that these oppositional relationships are intrinsically unstable. Since such dualities rarely represent different-but-equal relationships, the inherently unstable relationship is resolved by subordinating one half of each pair to the other. Thus, whites rule blacks, males dominate females, reason is touted as superior to emotion in ascertaining truth, facts supercede opinion in evaluating knowledge, and subjects rule objects. Dichotomous oppositional differences invariably imply relationships of superiority and inferiority, hierarchical relationships that mesh with political economies of domination and subordination.

The oppression experienced by most black women is shaped by their subordinate status in an array of either/or dualities. Afro-American women have been assigned the inferior half of several dualities, and this placement has been central to their continued domination. For example, the allegedly emotional, passionate nature of Afro-American women has long been used as a rationale for their sexual exploitation. Similarly, denying black women literacy—then claiming that they lack the facts for sound judgment—illustrates another case of assigning a group inferior status, then using that inferior status as proof of the group's inferiority. Finally, denying black women agency as subjects and treating them as objectified "others" represents yet another dimension of the power that dichotomous oppositional constructs have in maintaining systems of domination.

While Afro-American women may have a vested interest in recognizing the connections among these dualities that together comprise the construct of dichotomous oppositional difference, that more women have not done so is not surprising. Either/or dualistic thinking is so pervasive that it suppresses other alternatives. As Bonnie Thornton Dill points out, "the choice between identifying as black or female is a product of the patriarchal strategy of divide-and-conquer and the continued importance of class, patriarchal, and racial divisions, perpetuate such choices both within our consciousness and within the concrete realities of our daily lives."[33] In spite of this difficulty, black women experience oppression in a personal, holistic fashion and emerging black feminist perspectives appear to be embracing an equally holistic analysis of oppression.

Second, black feminist attention to the interlocking nature of oppression is significant in that implicit in this view is an alternative humanist vision of societal organization. This alternative worldview is cogently expressed in the following passage from an 1893 speech delivered by the black feminist educator, Anna Julia Cooper:

> We take our stand on the solidarity of humanity, the oneness of life, and the unnaturalness and injustice of all special favoritisms, whether of sex,

> race, country, or condition. . . . The colored woman feels that woman's cause is one and universal; and that . . . not till race, color, sex, and condition are seen as accidents, and not the substance of life; not till the universal tide of humanity to life, liberty, and the pursuit of happiness is conceded to be inalienable to all; not till then is woman's lesson taught and woman's cause won—not the white woman's nor the black woman's, nor the red woman's, but the cause of every man and of every woman who has writhed silently under a mighty wrong.[34]

I cite the above passage at length because it represents one of the clearest statements of the humanist vision extant in black feminist thought.[35] Black feminists who see the simultaneity of oppression affecting black women appear to be more sensitive to how these same oppressive systems affect Afro-American men, people of color, women, and the dominant group itself. Thus, while black feminist activists may work on behalf of black women, they rarely project separatist solutions to black female oppression. Rather, the vision is one that, like Cooper's, takes its "stand on the solidarity of humanity."

The Importance of Afro-American Women's Culture

A third key theme characterizing black feminist thought involves efforts to redefine and explain the importance of black women's culture. In doing so, black feminists have not only uncovered previously unexplored areas of the black female experience, but they have also identified concrete areas of social relations where Afro-American women create and pass on self-definitions and self-valuations essential to coping with the simultaneity of oppression they experience.

In contrast to views of culture stressing the unique, ahistorical values of a particular group, black feminist approaches have placed greater emphasis on the role of historically-specific political economies in explaining the endurance of certain cultural themes. The following definition of culture typifies the approach taken by many black feminists. According to Mullings, culture is composed of

> the symbols and values that create the ideological frame of reference through which people attempt to deal with the circumstances in which they find themselves. Culture . . . is not composed of static, discrete traits moved from one locale to another. It is constantly changing and transformed, as new forms are created out of old ones. Thus culture . . . does not arise out of nothing: it is created and modified by material conditions.[36]

Seen in this light, black women's culture may help provide the ideological frame of reference—namely, the symbols and values of self-definition and self-valuation—that assist black women in seeing the circumstances shaping race, class, and gender oppression. Moreover, Mullings's definition of culture suggests that the values which accompany self-definition and self-valuation will have concrete, material expression: they will be present in social institutions like church and family, in creative expression of art, music, and dance, and, if unsuppressed, in patterns of economic and political activity. Finally, this approach to culture stresses its historically concrete nature. While common themes may link black women's lives, these themes will be experienced differently by black women of different classes, ages, regions, and sexual preferences as well as by black women in different historical settings. Thus, there is no monolithic black women's culture—rather, there are socially-constructed black women's cultures that collectively form black women's culture.

The interest in redefining black women's culture has directed attention to several unexplored areas of the black female experience. One such area concerns the interpersonal relationships that black women share with each other. It appears that the notion of sisterhood—generally understood to mean a supportive feeling of loyalty and attachment to other women stemming from a shared feeling of oppression—has been an important part of black women's culture.[37] Two representative works in the emerging tradition of black feminist research illustrate how this concept of sisterhood, while expressed differently in response to different material conditions, has been a significant feature of black women's culture. For example, Deborah Gray White documents the ways black slave women assisted each other in childbirth, cared for each other's children, worked together in sex-segregated work units when pregnant or nursing children, and depended on one another when married to males living on distant farms. White paints a convincing portrait of black female slave communities where sisterhood was necessary and assumed.[38] Similarly, Gilkes's work on black women's traditions in the Sanctified Church suggests that the sisterhood black women found had tangible psychological and political benefits.[39]

The attention to black women's culture has stimulated interest in a second type of interpersonal relationship: that shared by black women with their biological children, the children in their extended families, and with the black community's children. In reassessing Afro-American motherhood, black feminist researchers have emphasized the connections between (1) choices available to black mothers resulting from their placement in historically-specific political economies, (2) black mothers' perceptions of their children's choices as compared to what mothers thought those choices should be, and (3) actual strategies employed by black mothers both in raising their children and in dealing with institutions that affected their children's lives. For example, Janice Hale suggests that effective black mothers are sophisticated mediators between the competing offerings of an oppressive dominant culture and a nurturing black value-structure.[40] Dill's study of the childrearing goals of black domestics stresses the goals the women in her sample had for their children and the strategies these women pursued to help their children go further than they themselves had gone.[41] Gilkes offers yet another perspective on the power of black motherhood by observing that many of the black female political activists in her study became involved in community work through their role as mothers. What typically began as work on behalf of their own children evolved into work on behalf of the community's children.[42]

Another dimension of black women's culture that has generated considerable interest among black feminists is the role of creative expression in shaping and sustaining black women's self-definitions and self-valuations. In addition to documenting black women's achievements as writers, dancers, musicians, artists, and actresses, the emerging literature also investigates why creative expression has been such an important element of black women's culture.[43] Alice Walker's classic essay, "In Search of Our Mothers' Gardens," explains the necessity of black women's creativity, even if in very limited spheres, in resisting objectification and asserting black women's subjectivity as fully human beings.[44] Illustrating Walker's thesis, Willie Mae Ford Smith, a prominent gospel singer featured in the 1984 documentary, "Say Amen Somebody," describes what singing means to her. She notes, "it's just a feeling within. You can't help yourself. . . . I feel like I can fly away. I forget I'm in the world sometimes. I just want to take off." For Mother Smith, her creativity is a sphere of freedom, one that helps her cope with and transcend daily life.

This third key theme in black feminist thought—the focus on black women's culture—is significant for three reasons. First, the data from black women's culture suggest that the relationship between oppressed people's consciousness of oppression and the actions they take in dealing with oppressive structures may be far more complex than is suggested by existing social theory. Conventional social science continues to assume a fit between consciousness and activity; hence, accurate measures of human behavior are thought to produce accurate portraits of human consciousness of self and social structure.[45] In contrast, black women's experiences suggest that black women may overtly conform to the societal roles laid out for them, yet covertly oppose these roles in numerous spheres, an opposition shaped by the consciousness of being on the bottom. Black women's activities in families, churches, community institutions, and creative expression may represent more than an effort to mitigate pressures stemming from oppression. Rather, the black female ideological frame of reference that black women acquire through sisterhood, motherhood, and creative expression may serve the added purpose of shaping a black female consciousness about the workings of oppression. Moreover, this consciousness is shaped not only through abstract, rational reflection, but also through concrete rational action. For example, while black mothers may develop consciousness through talking with and listening to their children, they may also shape consciousness by how they live their lives, the actions they take on behalf of their children. That these activities have been obscured from traditional social scientists should come as no surprise. Oppressed peoples may maintain hidden consciousness and may not reveal their true selves for reasons of self-protection.[46]

A second reason that the focus on black women's culture is significant is that it points to the problematic nature of existing conceptualizations of the term "activism." While black women's reality cannot be understood without attention to the interlocking structures of oppression that limit black women's lives, Afro-American women's experiences suggest that possibilities for activism exist even within such multiple structures of domination. Such activism can take several forms. For black women under extremely harsh conditions, the private decision to reject external definitions of Afro-American womanhood may itself be a form of activism. If black women find themselves in settings where total conformity is expected, and where traditional forms of activism such as voting, participating in collective movements, and officeholding are impossible, then the individual women who in their consciousness choose to be self-defined and self-evaluating are, in fact, activists. They are retaining a grip over their definition as subjects, as full humans, and rejecting definitions of themselves as the objectified "other." For example, while black slave women were forced to conform to the specific oppression facing them, they may have had very different assessments of themselves and slavery than did the slaveowners. In this sense, consciousness can be viewed as one potential sphere of freedom that may exist simultaneously with unfree, allegedly conforming behavior.[47] Moreover, if black women simultaneously use all resources available to them— their roles as mothers, their participation in churches, their support of one another in black female networks, their creative expression—to be self-defined and self-valuating and to encourage others to reject objectification, then black women's everyday behavior itself is a form of activism. People who view themselves as fully human, as subjects, become activists, no matter how limited the sphere of their activism may be. By returning subjectivity to black women, black feminists return activism as well.

A third reason that the focus on black women's culture is significant is that an analytical model exploring the relationship between oppression, consciousness, and activism is implicit in the way black feminists have studied black women's culture. With the exception of Dill, few scholars have deliberately set out to develop such a model.[48] However, the type of work done suggests that an implicit model paralleling that proposed by Mullings has influenced black feminist research.[49]

Several features pervade emerging black feminist approaches. First, researchers stress the interdependent relationship between the interlocking oppression that has shaped black women's choices and black women's actions in the context of those choices. Black feminist researchers rarely describe black women's behavior without attention to the opportunity structures shaping their subjects' lives.[50] Second, the question of whether oppressive structures and limited choices stimulate black women's behavior characterized by apathy and alienation, or behavior demonstrating subjectivity and activism is seen as ultimately dependent on black women's perceptions of their choices. In other words, black women's consciousness—their analytical, emotional, and ethical perspective of themselves and their place in society—becomes a critical part of the relationship between the working of oppression and black women's actions. Finally, this relationship between oppression, consciousness, and action can be seen as a dialectical one. In this model, oppressive structures create patterns of choices which are perceived in varying ways by black women. Depending on their consciousness of themselves and their relationship to these choices, black women may or may not develop black-female spheres of influence where they develop and validate what will be appropriate, black-female sanctioned responses to oppression. Black women's activism in constructing black-female spheres of influence may, in turn, affect their perceptions of the political and economic choices offered to them by oppressive structures, influence actions actually taken, and ultimately, alter the nature of oppression they experience.

The Sociological Significance of Black Feminist Thought

Taken together, the three key themes in black feminist thought—the meaning of self-definition and self-valuation, the interlocking nature of oppression, and the importance of redefining culture—have made significant contributions to the task of clarifying a black women's standpoint of and for black women. While this accomplishment is important in and of itself, black feminist thought has potential contributions to make to the diverse disciplines housing its practitioners.

The sociological significance of black feminist thought lies in two areas. First, the content of black women's ideas has been influenced by and contributes to ongoing dialogues in a variety of sociological specialties. While this area merits attention, it is not my primary concern in this section. Instead, I investigate a second area of sociological significance: the process by which these specific ideas were produced by this specific group of individuals. In other words, I examine the influence of black women's outsider within status in academia on the actual thought produced. Thus far, I have proceeded on the assumption that it is impossible to separate the structure and thematic content of thought. In this section, I spell out exactly what form the relationship between the three key themes in black feminist thought and black women's outsider within status might take for women scholars generally, with special attention to black female sociologists.

First, I briefly summarize the role sociological paradigms play in shaping the facts and theories used by sociologists. Second, I explain how black women's outsider within status might encourage black women to have a distinctive standpoint vis-à-vis sociology's paradigmatic facts and theories. I argue that the thematic content of black feminist thought described above represents elements of just such a standpoint and give examples of how the combination of sociology's paradigms and black women's outsider within status as sociologists directed their attention to specific areas of sociological inquiry.

Two Elements of Sociological Paradigms

Kuhn defines a paradigm as the "entire constellation of beliefs, values, techniques, and so on shared by the members of a given community."[51] As such, a paradigm consists of two fundamental elements: the thought itself and its producers and practitioners.[52] In this sense, the discipline of sociology is itself a paradigm—it consists of a system of knowledge shared by sociologists—and simultaneously consists of a plurality of paradigms (e.g., functionalism, Marxist sociology, feminist sociology, existential sociology), each produced by its own practitioners.

Two dimensions of thought itself are of special interest to this discussion. First, systems of knowledge are never complete. Rather, they represent guidelines for "thinking as usual." Kuhn refers to these guidelines as "maps," while Schutz describes them as "recipes."[53] As Schutz points out, while "thinking as usual" is actually only partially organized and partially clear, and may contain contradictions, to its practitioners it provides sufficient coherence, clarity, and consistency. Second, while thought itself contains diverse elements, I will focus mainly on the important fact/theory relationship. As Kuhn suggests, facts or observations become meaningful in the context of theories or interpretations of those observations. Conversely, theories "fit the facts" by transforming previously accessible observations into facts. According to Mulkay, "observation is not separate from interpretation; rather these are two facets of a single process."[54]

Several dimensions of the second element of sociological paradigms— the community formed by a paradigm's practitioners—are of special interest to this discussion. First, group insiders have similar worldviews, acquired through similar educational and professional training, that separate them from everyone else. Insider worldviews may be especially alike if group members have similar social class, gender, and racial backgrounds. Schutz describes the insider worldview as the "cultural pattern of group life"—namely, all the values and behaviors which characterize the social group at a given moment in its history. In brief, insiders have undergone similar experiences, possess a common history, and share taken-for-granted knowledge that characterizes "thinking as usual."

A second dimension of the community of practitioners involves the process of becoming an insider. How does one know when an individual is really an insider and not an outsider in disguise? Merton suggests that socialization into the life of a group is a lengthy process of being immersed in group life, because only then can one "understand the fine-grained meanings of behavior, feeling, and values . . . and decipher the unwritten grammar of conduct and nuances of cultural idiom."[55] The process is analogous to immersion in a foreign culture in order to learn its ways and its language.[56] One becomes an insider by translating a theory or worldview into one's own language until, one day, the individual converts to thinking and acting according to that worldview.

A final dimension of the community of practitioners concerns the process of remaining an insider. A sociologist typically does this by furthering the discipline in ways described as appropriate by sociology generally, and by areas of specialization particularly. Normal foci for scientific sociological investigation include: (1) determining significant facts; (2) matching facts with existing theoretical interpretations to "test" the paradigm's ability to predict facts; and (3) resolving ambiguities in the paradigm itself by articulating and clarifying theory.[57]

Black Women and the Outsider Within Status

Black women may encounter much less of a fit between their personal and cultural experiences and both elements of sociological paradigms than that facing other sociologists. On the one hand, black women who undergo sociology's lengthy socialization process, who immerse themselves in the cultural pattern of sociology's group life, certainly wish to acquire the insider skills of thinking in and acting according to a sociological worldview. But on the other hand, black women's experienced realities, both prior to contact and after initiation, may provide them with "special perspectives and insights . . . available to that category of outsiders who have been systematically frustrated by the social system."[58] In brief, their outsider allegiances may militate against their choosing full insider status, and they may be more apt to remain outsiders within.[59]

In essence, to become sociological insiders, black women must assimilate a standpoint that is quite different than their own. White males have long been the dominant group in sociology, and the sociological worldview understandably reflects the concerns of this group of practitioners. As Merton observes, "white male insiderism in American sociology during the past generations has largely been of the tacit or de facto . . . variety. It has simply taken the form of patterned expectations about the appropriate . . . problems for investigation."[60] In contrast, a good deal of the black female experience has been spent coping with, avoiding, subverting, and challenging the workings of this same white male insiderism. It should come as no surprise that black women's efforts in dealing with the effects of interlocking systems of oppression might produce a standpoint quite distinct from, and in many ways opposed to, that of white male insiders.

Seen from this perspective, black women's socialization into sociology represents a more intense case of the normal challenges facing sociology graduate students and junior professionals in the discipline. Black women become, to use Simmel's and Schutz's terminology, penultimate "strangers."[61]

The stranger . . . does not share the basic assumptions of the group. He becomes essentially the man

> who has to place in question nearly everything that seems to be unquestionable to the members of the approached group. . . . To him the cultural patterns of the approached group do not have the authority of a tested system of recipes . . . because he does not partake in the vivid historical tradition by which it has been formed.[62]

Like everyone else, black women may see sociological "thinking as usual" as partially organized, partially clear, and contradictory, and may question these existing recipes. However, for them, this questioning process may be more acute, for the material that they encounter—white male insider–influenced observations and interpretations about human society—places white male subjectivity at the center of analysis and assigns Afro-American womanhood a position on the margins.

In spite of a lengthy socialization process, it may also be more difficult for Afro-American women to experience conversion and begin totally to think in and act according to a sociological worldview. Indeed, since past generations of white male insiderism has shaped a sociological worldview reflecting this group's concerns, it may be self-destructive for black women to embrace that worldview. For example, black women would have to accept certain fundamental and self-devaluing assumptions: (1) white males are more worthy of study because they are more fully human than everyone else; and (2) dichotomous oppositional thinking is natural and normal. More importantly, black women would have to act in accordance with their place in a white male worldview. This involves accepting one's own subordination or regretting the accident of not being born white and male. In short, it may be extremely difficult for black women to accept a worldview predicated upon black female inferiority.

Remaining in sociology by doing normal scientific investigation may also be less complicated for traditional sociologists than for Afro-American women. Unlike black women, learners from backgrounds where the insider information and experiences of sociology are more familiar may be less likely to see the taken-for-granted assumptions of sociology and may be more prone to apply their creativity to "normal science." In other words, the transition from student status to that of a practitioner engaged in finding significant facts that sociological paradigms deem important, matching facts with existing theories, and furthering paradigmatic development itself may proceed more smoothly for white middle-class males than for working-class black females. The latter group is much more inclined to be struck by the mismatch of its own experiences and the paradigms of sociology itself. Moreover, those black women with a strong foundation in black women's culture (e.g., those that recognize the value of self-definition and self-valuation, and that have a concrete understanding of sisterhood and motherhood) may be more apt to take a critical posture toward the entire sociological enterprise. In brief, where traditional sociologists may see sociology as "normal" and define their role as furthering knowledge about a normal world with taken-for-granted assumptions, outsiders within are liable to see anomalies.

The types of anomalies typically seen by black female academicians grow directly from black women's outsider within status and appear central in shaping the direction black feminist thought has taken thus far. Two types of anomalies are characteristically noted by black female scholars. First, black female sociologists typically report the omission of facts or observations about Afro-American women in the sociological paradigms they encounter. As Scott points out, "from reading the literature, one might easily develop the impression that Black women have never played any role in this society."[63] Where white males may take it as perfectly normal to generalize findings from studies of white males to other groups, black women are more likely to see such a practice as problematic, as an anomaly. Similarly, when white feminists produce generalizations about "women," black feminists routinely ask "which women do you mean?" In the same way that Rollins felt invisible in her employer's kitchen, Afro-American female scholars are repeatedly struck by their own invisibility, both as full human subjects included in sociological facts and observations, and as practitioners in the discipline itself. It should come as no surprise that much of black feminist thought aims to counter this invisibility by presenting sociological analyses of black women as fully human subjects. For example, the growing research describing black women's historical and contemporary behavior as mothers, community workers, church leaders, teachers, and employed workers, and black women's ideas about themselves and their opportunities, reflect an effort to respond to the omission of facts about Afro-American women.

A second type of anomaly typically noted by black female scholars concerns distortions of facts and observations about black women. Afro-American women in academia are frequently struck by the difference between their own experiences and sociological descriptions of the same phenomena. For example, while black women have and are themselves mothers, they encounter distorted versions of themselves and their mothers under the mantle of the black matriarchy thesis. Similarly for those black women who confront racial and sexual discrimination and know that their mothers and grandmothers certainly did, explanations of black women's poverty that stress low achievement motivation and the lack of black female "human capital" are less likely to ring true. The response to these perceived distortions has been one of redefining distorted images—for example, debunking the Sapphire and Mammy myths.

Since facts or observations become meaningful in the context of a theory, this emphasis on producing accurate descriptions of black women's lives has also refocused attention on major omissions and distortions in sociological theories themselves. By drawing on the strengths of sociology's plurality of subdisciplines, yet taking a critical posture toward them, the work of black feminist scholars taps some fundamental questions facing all sociologists. One such question concerns the fundamental elements of society that should be studied. Black feminist researchers' response has been to move black women's voices to the center of the analysis, to study people, and by doing so, to reaffirm human subjectivity and intentionality. They point to the dangers of omission and distortion that can occur if sociological concepts are studied at the expense of human subjectivity. For example, there is a distinct difference between conducting a statistical analysis of black women's work, where Afro-American women are studied as a reconstituted amalgam of researcher-defined variables (e.g., race, sex, years of education, and father's occupation), and examining black women's self-definitions and self-valuations of themselves as workers in oppressive jobs. While both approaches can further sociological knowledge about the concept of work, the former runs the risk of objectifying black women, of reproducing constructs of dichotomous oppositional difference, and of producing distorted findings about the nature of work itself.

A second question facing sociologists concerns the adequacy of current interpretations of key sociological concepts. For example, few sociologists would question that work and family are two fundamental concepts for sociology. However, bringing black feminist thought into the center of conceptual analysis raises issues of how comprehensive current sociological interpretations of these two concepts really are. For example, labor theories that relegate Afro-American women's work experiences to the fringe of analysis miss the critical theme of the interlocking nature of black women as female workers (e.g., black women's unpaid domestic labor) and black women as racially-oppressed workers (e.g., black women's unpaid slave labor and exploited wage labor). Examining the extreme case offered by Afro-American women's unpaid and paid work experiences raises questions about the adequacy of generalizations about work itself. For example, black feminists' emphasis on the simultaneity of oppression redefines the economic system itself as problematic. From this perspective, all generalizations about the normal workings of labor markets, organizational structure, occupational mobility, and income differences that do not explicitly see oppression as problematic become suspect. In short, black feminists suggest that all generalizations about groups of employed and unemployed workers (e.g., managers, welfare mothers, union members, secretaries, black teenagers) that do not account for interlocking structures of group placement and oppression in an economy are simply less complete than those that do.

Similarly, sociological generalizations about families that do not account for black women's experience will fail to see how the public/private split shaping household composition varies across social and class groupings, how racial/ethnic family members are differentially integrated into wage labor, and how families alter their household structure in response to changing political economies (e.g., adding more people and becoming extended, fragmenting and becoming female-headed, and migrating to locate better opportunities). Black women's family experiences represent a clear case of the workings of race, gender, and class oppression in shaping family life. Bringing undistorted observations of Afro-American women's family experiences into the center of analysis again raises the question of how other families are affected by these same forces.

While black women who stand outside academia may be familiar with omissions and distortions of the black female experience, as outsiders to sociology, they lack legitimated professional authority to challenge the sociological anomalies. Similarly, traditional sociological insiders, whether white males or their nonwhite and/or female disciples, are certainly in no position to notice the specific anomalies apparent to Afro-American women, because these same sociological insiders produced them. In contrast, those black women who remain rooted in their own experiences as black women—and who master sociological paradigms yet retain a critical posture toward them—are in a better position to bring a special perspective not only to the study of black women, but to some of the fundamental issues facing sociology itself.

Toward Synthesis: Outsiders Within Sociology

Black women are not the only outsiders within sociology. As an extreme case of outsiders moving into a community that historically excluded them, black women's experiences highlight the tension experienced by any group of less powerful outsiders encountering the paradigmatic thought of a more powerful insider community. In this sense, a variety of individuals can learn from black women's experiences as outsiders within: black men, working-class individuals, white women, other people of color, religious and sexual minorities, and all individuals who, while from social strata that provided them with the benefits of white male insiderism, have never felt comfortable with its assumptions.

Outsider within status is bound to generate tension, for people who become outsiders within are forever changed by their new status. Learning the subject matter of sociology stimulates a reexamination of one's own personal and cultural experiences; and, yet, these same experiences paradoxically help to illuminate sociology's anomalies. Outsiders within occupy a special place—they become different people, and their difference sensitizes them to patterns that may be more difficult for established sociological insiders to see. Some outsiders within try to resolve the tension generated by their new status by leaving sociology and remaining sociological outsiders. Others choose to suppress their difference by striving to become bona fide, "thinking as usual" sociological insiders. Both choices rob sociology of diversity and ultimately weaken the discipline.

A third alternative is to conserve the creative tension of outsider within status by encouraging and institutionalizing outsider within ways of seeing. This alternative has merit not only for actual outsiders within, but also for other sociologists. The approach suggested by the experiences of outsiders within is one where intellectuals learn to trust their own personal and cultural biographies as significant sources of knowledge. In contrast to approaches that require submerging these dimensions of self in the process of becoming an allegedly unbiased, objective social scientist, outsiders within bring these ways of knowing back into the research process. At its best, outsider within status seems to offer its occupants a powerful balance between the strengths of their sociological training and the offerings of their personal and cultural experiences. Neither is subordinated to the other. Rather, experienced reality is used as a valid source of knowledge for critiquing sociological facts and theories, while, sociological thought offers new ways of seeing that experienced reality.

What many black feminists appear to be doing is embracing the creative potential of their outsider within status and using it wisely. In doing so, they move themselves and their disciplines closer to the humanist vision implicit in their work—namely, the freedom to be both different and part of the solidarity of humanity.

Notes

1. I wish to thank Lynn Weber Cannon, Bonnie Thornton Dill, Alison M. Jaggar, Joan Hartman, Ellen Messer-Davidow, and several anonymous reviewers for their helpful comments about earlier drafts of this paper. Correspondence to: Department of Afro-American Studies, University of Cincinnati, ML 370, Cincinnati, OH 45221.

2. In 1940, almost 60 percent of employed Afro-American women were domestics. The 1970 census was the first time this category of work did not contain the largest segment of the black female labor force. See Judith Rollins, *Between Women, Domestics and Their Employers* (Philadelphia: Temple University Press, 1985) for a discussion of black domestic work.

3. For example, in *Of Women Born: Motherhood as Experience and Institution*, Adrienne Rich has fond memories of her black "mother," a young, unstereotypically slim black woman she loved. Similarly, Dill's study of black domestic workers reveals black women's sense of affirmation at knowing that they were better mothers than their employers, and that they frequently had to teach their employers the basics about children and interaction in general. Even though the black domestic workers were officially subordinates, they gained a sense of self-worth at knowing they were good at things that they felt mattered. Bonnie Thornton Dill, "'The Means to Put My Children Through': Child-Rearing Goals and Strategies among Black Female Domestic Servants," in *The Black Woman*, ed. LaFrances Rodgers-Rose (Beverly Hills, Calif.: Sage Publications, 1980), 107–123.

4. For example, in spite of Rich's warm memories of her black "mother," she had all but forgotten her until beginning research for her book. Similarly, the black domestic workers in both Dill's and Rollins's studies discussed the limitations that their subordinate roles placed on them.

5. For a discussion of the notion of a special standpoint or point of view of oppressed groups, see Nancy M. Hartsock, "The Feminist Standpoint: Developing the Ground for a Specifically Feminist Historical Materialism," in *Discovering Reality*, ed. Sandra Harding and Merrill Hintikka (Boston: D. Reidel, 1983), 283–310. For an analysis of the potential contributions of insider and outsider perspectives to sociology, see Robert K. Merton, "Insiders and Outsiders: A Chapter in the Sociology of Knowledge," *American Journal of Sociology* 78 (1972): 9–47. For a related discussion of outsider within status, see his section "Insiders as 'Outsiders'" (29–30).

6. Hurston has been widely discussed in black feminist literary criticism. For example, see selected essays in Alice Walker's edited volume on Hurston, *I Love Myself When I Am Laughing . . . A Zora Neal Hurston Reader* (Westbury, N.Y.: Feminist Press, 1979).

7. E. Frances White, "Listening to the Voices of Black Feminism," *Radical America* 18 (1984): 7–25.

8. bell hooks, *From Margin to Center* (Boston: South End Press, 1984), vii.

9. Georg Simmel, "The Sociological Significance of the 'Stranger,'" in *Introduction to the Science of Sociology*, ed. Robert E. Park and Ernest W. Burgess (Chicago: University of Chicago Press, 1921), 322–327.

10. Karl Mannheim, *Ideology and Utopia: An Introduction to the Sociology of Knowledge* (New York: Harcourt, Brace, 1936).

11. Alfred McClung Lee, *Toward Humanist Sociology* (Englewood Cliffs, N.J.: Prentice-Hall, 1973), 64. By stressing the potentially positive features of outsider within status, I in no way want to deny the very real problem this social status has represented for large numbers of black women. American sociology has long identified marginal status as problematic. However, my sense of the "problems" diverge from those espoused by traditional sociologists. For example, in his *Race and Culture* (Glencoe, Ill.: Free Press, 1950), Robert Park states, "the marginal man . . . is

one whom fate has condemned to live in two societies and in two, not merely different but antagonistic cultures" (373). From Park's perspective, marginality and difference themselves were problems. This perspective quite rationally led to the social policy solution of assimilation, one aimed at eliminating difference, or if that didn't work, pretending it was not important. In contrast, I argue that it is the meaning attached to difference that is the problem. For a black feminist perspective on difference, see Audre Lorde, *Sister Outsider* (Trumansburg, N.Y.: Crossing Press, 1984), 114–123 and passim.

12. In addition to familiarizing readers with the contours of black feminist thought, I place black women's ideas in the center of my analysis for another reason. Black women's ideas have long been viewed as peripheral to serious intellectual endeavors. By treating black feminist thought as central, I hope to avoid the tendency of starting with the body of thought needing the critique—in this case sociology—and then fitting in the dissenting ideas, and thus, in the process, reifying the very systems of thought one hopes to transform.

13. Peter L. Berger and Thomas Luckmann, *The Social Construction of Reality* (New York: Doubleday, 1966); and Mannheim, *Ideology and Utopia*.

14. On this point, I diverge somewhat from Berger and Luckmann's definition of specialized thought. They suggest that only a limited group of individuals engages in theorizing and that "pure theory" emerges with the development of specialized legitimating theories and their administration by full-time legitimators. Using this approach, groups denied the material resources to support pure theorists cannot be capable of developing specialized theoretical knowledge. In contrast, I argue that "traditional wisdom" is a system of thought and that it reflects the material positions of its practitioners.

15. Mae King, "The Politics of Sexual Stereotypes," *Black Scholar* 4 (1973): 12–23; and Cheryl Townsend Gilkes, "From Slavery to Social Welfare: Racism and the Control of Black Women," in *Class, Race, and Sex: The Dynamics of Control*, ed. Amy Smerdlow and Helen Lessinger (Boston: G.K. Hall, 1981), 288–300.

16. John Langston Gwaltney, *Drylongso: A Self-portrait of Black America* (New York: Vintage, 1980), 148.

17. Gilkes, "From Slavery to Social Welfare"; Deborah Gray White, *Ar'n't I a Woman? Female Slaves in the Plantation South* (New York: W. W. Norton, 1985).

18. Elizabeth Higginbotham, "Two Representative Issues in Contemporary Sociological Work on Black Women," in *But Some of Us Are Brave*, ed. Gloria T. Hull, Patricia Bell Scott, and Barbara Smith (Old Westbury, N.Y.: Feminist Press, 1982), 93–98.

19. Lena Wright Myers, *Black Women: Do They Cope Better?* (Englewood Cliffs, N.J.: Prentice-Hall, 1980).

20. Paula Giddings, *When and Where I Enter: The Impact of Black Women on Race and Sex in America* (New York: William Morrow, 1984); and Bert Loewenberg, James Bogin, and Ruth Bogin, eds., *Black Women in Nineteenth-century Life* (University Park: Pennsylvania State University Press, 1976).

21. Arthur Brittan and Mary Maynard, *Sexism, Racism and Oppression* (New York: Basil Blackwell, 1994), 199.

22. Rollins, *Between Women*, 209

23. Joseph A. Baldwin, "The Psychology of Oppression," in *Contemporary Black Thought*, ed. Molefi Kete Asante and Abdulai S. Vandi (Beverly Hills, Calif.: Sage Publications, 1980), 95–110.

24. Gwaltney, *Drylongso*, 152.

25. See Frances Beale, "Double Jeopardy: To Be Black and Female," in *The Black Woman*, ed. Toni Cade (New York: Signet, 1976), 90–110; Angela Davis, *Women, Race and Class* (New York: Random House, 1981); Bonnie Thornton Dill, "Race, Class, and Gender: Prospects for an All-Inclusive Sisterhood," *Feminist Studies* 9 (1993): 131–150; bell hooks, *Ain't I a Woman: Black Women and Feminism* (Boston: South End Press, 1981); Diane Lewis, "A Response to Inequality: Black Women, Racism and Sexism," *Signs* 3 (1977): 339–61; Pauli Murray, "The Liberation of Black Women," in *Voices of the New Feminism*, ed. Mary Lou Thompson (Boston: Beacon Press, 1970), 87–102; Filomina Chioma Steady, "The Black Woman Cross-culturally: An Overview," in *The Black Woman Cross-culturally*, ed. Filomina Chioma Steady (Cambridge, Mass.: Schenkman, 1981), 7–42.

Emerging black feminist research is demonstrating a growing awareness of the importance of including the simultaneity of oppression in studies of black women. For example, Paula Giddings's history of Afro-American women emphasizes the role of class in shaping relations between Afro-American and white women, and among black women themselves. Giddings, *When and Where I Enter*. Elizabeth Higginbotham's "Race and Class Barriers to Black Women's College Attendance," *Journal of Ethnic Studies* 13 (1985): 89–107, examines race and class barriers to black women's college attendance. Especially noteworthy is the growing attention to black women's labor market experiences. Studies such as Dill's "'The Means to Put My Children Through'"; Rollins's *Between Women*; Higginbotham's "Laid Bare by the System: Work and Survival for Black and Hispanic Women," in *Class, Race, and Sex: The Dynamics of Control*, ed. Amy Smerdlow and Helen Lessinger (Boston: G.K. Hall, 1993), 200–215; and Leith Mullings's "Uneven Development: Class, Race and Gender in the United States before 1900," in *Women's Work, Development and the Division of Labor by Gender*, ed. Eleanor Leacock and Helen Safa (South Hadley, Mass.: Bergin & Garvey, 1986), 41–57, indicate a new sensitivity to the interactive nature of race, gender, and class. By studying black women, such studies capture the interaction of race and gender. Moreover, by examining black women's roles in capitalist development, such work taps the key variable of class.

26. Loewenberg, Bogin, and Bogin, *Black Women*, 26.

27. Davis, *Women, Race and Class*.

28. Barbara Smith, ed., *Home Girls: A Black Feminist Anthology* (New York: Kitchen Table, Women of Color Press, 1983), xxxii.

29. Loewenberg, Bogin, and Bogin, *Black Women*, 238.

30. The thesis that those affected by multiple systems of domination will develop a sharper view of the interlocking nature of oppression is illustrated by the prominence of black lesbian feminists among black feminist thinkers. For more on this, see Smith, ed., *Home Girls*; Lorde, *Sister Outsider*; and White, "Listening to the Voices of Black Feminism," 7–25, particularly 22–24.

31. hooks, *From Margin to Center*, 29.

32. For example, African and Afro-American scholars point to the role dualistic thinking has played in domestic racism (Molefi Kete Asante, "International/Intercultural Relations," in *Contemporary Black Thought*, ed. Molefi Kete Asante and Abdulai S. Vandi [Beverly Hills, Calif.: Sage Publications, 1980], 43–58; Baldwin, "Psychology of Oppression"; and Dona Richards, "European Mythology; the Ideology of 'Progress,'" in *Contemporary Black Thought*, 59–79). Feminist scholars note the linkage of duality with conceptualizations of gender in Western cultures (Nancy Chodorow, *The Reproduction of Mothering* [Berkeley: University of California Press, 1978]; Evelyn Fox Keller, "Gender and Science," in *Discovering Reality*, ed. Sandra Harding and Merrill Hintikka [Boston: D. Reidel, 1983], 187–206; Michelle Z. Rosaldo, "Moral/Analytic Dilemmas Posed by the Intersection of Feminism and Social Science," in *Social Science as Moral Inquiry*, ed. Norma Hann, Robert N. Bellah, Paul Rabinow, and William Sullivan [New York: Columbia University Press, 1983], 76–96). Recently, Arthur Brittan and Mary Maynard, two British scholars, have suggested that dualistic thinking plays a major role in linking systems of racial oppression with those of sexual oppression. In *Sexism, Racism and Oppression*, they note that

> there is an implicit belief in the duality of culture and nature. Men are the creators and mediators of culture—women are the manifestations of nature. The implication is that men develop culture in order to understand and control the natural world, while women being the embodiment of forces of nature, must be brought under the civilizing control of men.... This duality of culture and nature... is also used to distinguish between so-called higher nations or civilizations, and those deemed to be culturally backward.... Non-European peoples are conceived of as being nearer to nature than Europeans. Hence, the justification... for slavery and colonialism. (193–194).

33. Dill, "Race, Class, and Gender," 136.

34. Cited in Loewenberg, Bogin, and Bogin, *Black Women*, 330–331.

35. This humanist vision takes both religious and secular forms. For religious statements, see Andrews's collection of the autobiographies of three nineteenth-century black female evangelical preachers, William L. Andrews, ed., *Sisters of the Spirit* (Bloomington: Indiana University Press, 1986). For a discussion of the humanist tradition in Afro-American religion that has contributed to this dimension of black feminist thought, see Peter J. Paris, *The Social Teaching of the Black Churches* (Philadelphia: Fortress Press, 1985). Much of contemporary

black feminist writing draws on this religious tradition, but reframes the basic vision in secular terms.

36. Leith Mullings, "Anthropological Perspectives on the Afro-American Family," *American Journal of Social Psychiatry* 6 (1986): 13.

37. Dill, "Race, Class, and Gender," 132.

38. White, *Ar'n't I a Woman?*

39. Cheryl Townsend Gilkes, "'Together and in Harness': Women's Traditions in the Sanctified Church," *Signs* 10 (1985): 678–699. During a period when black women were widely devalued by the dominant culture, Sanctified Church members addressed each other as "Saints." During the early 1900s, when basic literacy was an illusive goal for many blacks, black women in the Church not only stressed education as a key component of a sanctified life, but supported each other's efforts at educational excellence. In addition to these psychological supports, the Church provided Afro-American women with genuine opportunities for influence, leadership, and political clout. The important thing to remember here is that the Church was not an abstract, bureaucratic structure that ministered to black women. Rather, the Church was a predominantly female community of individuals in which women had prominent spheres of influence.

40. Janice Hale, "The Black Woman and Child Rearing," in *The Black Woman*, ed. LaFrances Rodgers-Rose (Beverly Hills, Calif.: Sage Publications, 1980), 79–88.

41. Dill, "'The Means to Put My Children Through.'"

42. Cheryl Townsend Gilkes, "'Holding Back the Ocean with a Broom': Black Women and Community Work," in *The Black Woman*, ed. LaFrances Rodgers-Rose (Beverly Hills, Calif.: Sage Publications, 1980), 217–231.

43. Since much black feminist thought is contained in the works of black women writers, literary criticism by black feminist critics provides an especially fertile source of black women's ideas. See Claudia Tate, *Black Women Writers at Work* (New York: Continuum, 1983) and Barbara Christian, *Black Feminist Criticism: Perspectives on Black Women Writers* (New York: Pergamon, 1985).

44. Alice Walker, "In Search of Our Mothers' Gardens," in *In Search of Our Mothers' Gardens* (New York: Harcourt Brace Jovanovich, 1974), 231–243.

45. Marcia Westkott, "Feminist Criticism of the Social Sciences," *Harvard Educational Review* 49 (1979): 422–430.

46. Audre Lorde (*Sister Outsider*, p. 114) describes this conscious biding of one's self as follows: "in order to survive, those of us for whom oppression is as American as apple pie have always had to be watchers, to become familiar with the language and manners of the oppressor, even sometimes adopting them for some illusion of protection."

47. Westkott, "Feminist Criticism."

48. Dill, "Race, Class, Gender."

49. Mullings, "Anthropological Perspectives."

50. Higginbotham, "Race and Class Barriers"; Joyce Ladner, *Tomorrow's Tomorrow: The Black Woman* (Garden City, N.Y.: Anchor, 1971); Myers, *Black Women*.

51. Thomas S. Kuhn, *The Structure of Scientific Revolutions*, 2nd edition (Chicago: University of Chicago Press, 1970).

52. In this sense, sociology is a special case of the more generalized process discussed by Mannheim in *Ideology and Utopia*. Also see Morris Berman, *The Reenchantment of the World* (New York: Bantam, 1981) for a discussion of Western thought as a paradigm; Michael Mulkay, *Science and the Sociology of Knowledge* (Boston: Allen & Unwin, 1979) for a sociology of knowledge analysis of the natural sciences; and Berger and Luckmann's *Social Construction of Reality* for a generalized discussion of how everyday knowledge is socially constructed.

53. Kuhn, *Structure of Scientific Revolutions*; Alfred Schutz, "The Stranger: An Essay in Social Psychology," *American Journal of Sociology* 49 (1944): 499–507.

54. Mulkay, *Science and Society*, 49.

55. Merton, "Insiders and Outsiders," 15.

56. Merton, "Insiders and Outsiders"; Schutz, "Stranger."

57. Kuhn, *Structure of Scientific Revolutions*.

58. Merton, "Insiders and Outsiders," 29.

59. Jackson reports that 21 of the 145 black sociologists receiving doctoral degrees between 1945 and 1972 were women. Jacquelyn Jackson, "Black Female Sociologists" in *Black Sociologists*, ed. James B. Blackwell and Morris Janowitz (Chicago: University of Chicago Press, 1974), 267–298. Kulis et al. report that blacks comprised 5.7 percent of all sociology faculties in 1984. Stephen Kulis, Karen A. Miller, Morris Axelrod, and Leonard Gordon, "Minority Representation of U.S. Departments," *ASA Footnotes* 14 (1986): 3. These data suggest that historically, black females have not been sociological insiders, and currently, black women as a group comprise a small portion of sociologists in the United States.

60. Merton, "Insiders and Outsiders," 12.

61. Simmel, "Sociological Significance"; Schutz, "Stranger."

62. Schutz, "Stranger," 502.

63. Patricia Bell Scott, "Debunking Sapphire: Toward a Non-racist and Non-sexist Social Science," in *All the Women are White, All th Blacks are Men, But Some of Us Are Brave*, ed. Gloria T. Hull, Patricia Bell Scott, and Barbara Smith (Old Westbury, N.Y.: Feminist Press, 1982), 85–92.

POSING QUESTIONS, APPROACHING RESEARCH   II

Research through Imperial Eyes

LINDA TUHIWAI SMITH

MANY CRITIQUES OF RESEARCH have centered around the theory of knowledge known as empiricism and the scientific paradigm of positivism which is derived from empiricism. Positivism takes a position that applies views about how the natural world can be examined and understood to the social world of human beings and human societies. Understanding is viewed as being akin to measuring. As the ways we try to understand the world are reduced to issues of measurement, the focus of understanding becomes more concerned with procedural problems. The challenge then for understanding the social world becomes one of developing operational definitions of phenomena which are reliable and valid. The analysis in this chapter begins with a much broader brushstroke. Most indigenous criticisms of research are expressed within the single terms of "white research," "academic research" or "outsider research." The finer details of how Western scientists might name themselves are irrelevant to indigenous peoples who have experienced unrelenting research of a profoundly exploitative nature. From an indigenous perspective, Western research is more than just research that is located in a positivist tradition. It is research which brings to bear, on any study of indigenous peoples, a cultural orientation, a set of values, a different conceptualization of such things as time, space and subjectivity, different and competing theories of knowledge, highly specialized forms of language, and structures of power.

---

*From Linda Tuhiwai Smith, *Decolonizing Methodologies: Research and Indigenous Peoples* (London and New York: Zed Books, 1999), pp. 42–57. Reprinted by permission. This chapter was edited to conform with the format of this anthology.

In this chapter I argue that what counts as Western research draws from an "archive" of knowledge and systems, rules and values which stretch beyond the boundaries of Western science to the system now referred to as the West. Stuart Hall makes the point that the West is an idea or concept, a language for imagining a set of complex stories, ideas, historical events, and social relationships. Hall suggests that the concept of the West functions in ways which (1) allow "us" to characterize and class societies into categories, (2) condense complex images of other societies through a *system of representation*, (3) provide a standard *model of comparison*, and (4) provide *criteria of evaluation* against which other societies can be ranked.[1] These are the procedures by which indigenous peoples and their societies were coded into the Western system of knowledge.

Research contributed to, and drew from, these systems of classification, representation, and evaluation. The cultural archive did not embody a unitary system of knowledge but should be conceived of as containing multiple traditions of knowledge and ways of knowing. Some knowledges are more dominant than others; some are submerged and outdated. Some knowledges are actively in competition with each other and some can only be formed in association with others. Whilst there may not be a unitary system, there are "rules" which help make sense of what is contained within the archive and enable "knowledge" to be recognized. These rules can be conceived of as rules of classification, rules of framing, and rules of practice.[2] Although the term "rules" may sound like a set of fixed items which are articulated in explicit ways as regulations, it also means rules which are masked in some way and which tend to be articulated through implicit understandings of how the world works. Power is expressed at both the explicit and implicit levels. Dissent, or challenges to the rules, is manageable because it also conforms to these rules, particularly at the implicit level. Scientific and academic debate in the West takes place within these rules. Two major examples of how this works can be found in Marxism and Western feminism. Arguably, Western feminism has provided a more radical challenge to knowledge than Marxism because of its challenge to epistemology: not just the body of knowledge and worldview, but the science of how knowledge can be understood. Even Western feminism, however, has been challenged, particularly by women of color, for conforming to some very fundamental Western European world views, value systems, and attitudes toward the Other. Indigenous peoples would probably claim to know much of this implicitly but in this chapter some fundamental ideas related to understandings of being human, of how humans relate to the world, are examined. Differences between Western and indigenous conceptions of the world have always provided stark contrasts. Indigenous beliefs were considered shocking, abhorrent, and barbaric and were prime targets for the efforts of missionaries. Many of those beliefs still persist; they are embedded in indigenous languages and stories and etched in memories.

The Cultural Formations of Western Research

Forms of imperialism and colonialism, notions of the Other, and theories about human nature existed long before the Enlightenment in Western philosophy. Some scholars have argued that the key tenets of what is now seen as Western civilization are based on black experiences and a black tradition of scholarship, and have simply been appropriated by Western philosophy and redefined as Western epistemology.[3] Western knowledges, philosophies, and definitions of human nature form what Foucault has referred to as a cultural archive and what some people might refer to as a "storehouse" of histories, artifacts, ideas, texts, and/or images, which are classified, preserved, arranged, and represented back to the West. This storehouse contains the fragments, the regions and levels of knowledge traditions, and the "systems" which allow different and differentiated forms of knowledge to be retrieved, enunciated, and represented in new contexts.[4] Although many colonized peoples refer to the West, usually with a term of their own, as a cohesive system of people, practices, values, and languages, the cultural archive of the West represents multiple traditions of knowledge. Rather, there are many different traditions of knowledge and moments of history in which philosophical ideas are sometimes reformed or transformed, in which new knowledges lead to new sets of ideas.

Foucault also suggests that the archive reveals "rules of practice" which the West itself cannot necessarily describe because it operates within the rules and therefore takes them for granted. Various indigenous peoples would claim, indeed do claim, to be able to describe many of those rules of practice as they have been "revealed" and/or perpetrated on indigenous communities. Hall has suggested that the Western cultural archive functions in ways which allow shifts and transformations to happen, quite radically at times, without the archive itself, and the modes of classifications and systems of representation contained within it are destroyed. This sense of what the idea of the West represents is important here because, to a large extent, theories about research are underpinned by a cultural system of classification and representation, by views about human nature, human morality, and virtue, by conceptions of space and time, by conceptions of gender and race. Ideas about these things help determine what counts as real. Systems of classification and representation enable different traditions or fragments of traditions to be retrieved and reformulated in different contexts as discourses, and then to be played out in systems of power and domination, with real material consequences for colonized peoples. Nandy, for example, discusses the different phases of colonization, from "rapacious bandit-kings" intent on exploitation, to "well-meaning middle-class liberals" intent on salvation as a legitimation of different forms of colonization.[5] These phases of colonization, driven by different economic needs and differing ideologies of legitimation, still had real consequences for the nations, communities, and groups of indigenous people being colonized. These consequences have led Nandy to describe colonization as a "shared culture" for those who have been colonized and for those who have colonized. This means, for example, that colonized peoples share a language of colonization, share knowledge about their colonizers, and, in terms of a political project, share the same struggle for decolonization. It also means that colonizers, too, share a language and knowledge of colonization.

The Intersections of Race and Gender

David Theo Goldberg argues that one of the consequences of Western experiences under imperialism is that Western ways of viewing, talking about, and interacting with the world at large are intricately embedded in racialized discourses.[6] Notions of difference are discussed in Greek philosophy, for example, as ways of rationalizing the essential characteristics and obligations of slaves.[7] Medieval literature and art represent fabulous monsters and half-human, half-animal creatures from far-off places. According to Goldberg, concern about these images led to "observers [being] overcome by awe, repulsion and fear of the implied threat to spiritual life and the political state."[8] Goldberg argues that whilst these early beliefs and images "furnished models that modern racism would assume and transform according to its own lights," there was no explicit category or space in medieval thought for racial differentiation.[9] What did happen, according to Goldberg, was that the "savage" was internalized as a psychological and moral space within the individual that required "repression, denial and disciplinary restraint."[10] In Goldberg's analysis, modernity and the philosophy of liberalism (which underpins modernist discourses) transformed these fragments of culture into an explicit racialized discourse. Race, as a category, was linked to human reason and morality, to science, to colonialism, and to the rights of citizenship in ways that produced the racialized discourse and racist practices of modernity.[11]

Western concepts of race intersect in complex ways with concepts of gender. Gender refers not just to the roles of women and how those roles are constituted but to the roles of men and of the relations between men and women. Ideas about gender difference and what that means for a society can similarly be traced back to the fragmented artifacts and representations of Western culture, and to different and differentiated traditions of knowledge. The desired and undesired qualities of women for example, as mothers, daughters, and wives, were inscribed in the texts of the Greeks and Romans, sculptured, painted, and woven into medieval wall hangings, and performed through oral poetry. Different historical ideas about men and women were enacted through social institutions such as marriage, family life, the class system, and ecclesiastic orders.[12] These institutions were underpinned by economic systems and notions of property and wealth, and were increasingly legitimated in the West through Judeo-Christian beliefs. Economic changes from feudal to capitalist modes of production influenced the construction of the "family" and the relations of women and men in Western societies. Gender distinctions and hierarchies are also deeply encoded in Western languages. It is impossible to speak without using this language, and, more significantly for indigenous peoples, it is impossible to translate or interpret our societies into English, French, or Castilian, for example, without making gendered distinctions.

The process of engendering descriptions of the Other has had very real consequences for indigenous women in that the ways in which indigenous women were described, objectified, and represented by Europeans in the nineteenth century has left a legacy of marginalization within indigenous societies as much as within the colonizing society. In New Zealand many of these issues are the subject of a claim brought by a group of prominent Maori women to the Waitangi Tribunal. The Waitangi Tribunal was established to hear the claims by Maori relating to contraventions of the Treaty of Waitangi.[13] Before this tribunal, the Maori women making the claim have to establish and argue, using historical texts, research, and oral testimonies, that the Crown has ignored the *rangatiratanga*, or chiefly and sovereign status, of Maori women. To argue this, the claimants are compelled to prove that Maori women were as much *rangatira* (chiefs) as Maori men. At a very simple level the "problem" is a problem of translation. *Rangatiratanga* has generally been interpreted in English as meaning chieftainship and sovereignty, which in colonialism was a "male thing."

This claim illustrates the complexities which Stuart Hall raised. Several different and differentiated sets of ideas and representations are to be "retrieved" and "enunciated" in the historically specific context of this claim. In summary these may be classified as: (1) a legal framework inherited from Britain, which includes views about what constitutes admissible evidence and valid research; (2) a "textual" orientation, which will privilege the written text (seen as expert and research-based) over oral testimonies (a concession to indigenous "elders"); (3) views about science, which will allow for the efficient selection and arrangement of "facts"; (4) "rules of practice" such as "values" and "morals," which all parties to the process are assumed to know and to have given their "consent" to abide by, for example, notions of "goodwill" and "truth telling"; (5) ideas about subjectivity and objectivity which have already determined the constitution of the tribunal and its "neutral" legal framework, but which will continue to frame the way the case is heard; (6) ideas about time and space, views related to history, what constitutes the appropriate length of a hearing, the "shape" of a claim, and the size of the panel; (7) views about human nature, individual accountability, and culpability; (8) the selection of speakers and experts, who speaks for whom, whose knowledge is presumed to be the "best fit" in relation to a set of proven "facts"; and (9) the politics of the Treaty of Waitangi and the way those politics are managed by politicians and other agencies such as the media. Within each set of ideas are systems of classification and representation—epistemological, ontological, juridical, anthropological and ethical, which are coded in such ways as to "recognize" each other and either mesh together or create a cultural "force field" which can screen out competing and oppositional discourses. Taken as a whole system, these ideas determine the wider rules of practice which ensure that Western interests remain dominant.

Conceptualizations of the Individual and Society

Social science research is based upon ideas, beliefs, and theories about the social world. While it is acknowledged that people always live in some form of social organization (for example, a family unit, an efficient hunting and gathering unit, a pastoral unit, and increasingly larger and more effective and sophisticated variations of those basic units), Western forms of research also draw on cultural ideas about the human "self" and the relationship between the individual and the groups to which he or she may belong. Such ideas explore both the internal workings of an individual and the relationships between what an individual is and how an individual behaves. These ideas suggest that relationships between or among groups of people are basically causal and can be observed and predicted. Some earlier accounts of how and why individuals behave as they do were based on ideas which often began with a creation story to explain the presence of people in their specific environment and on understandings of human behavior as being connected to some form of external force, such as spiritually powerful beings, "gods," or sacred objects. Human activity was seen to be caused by factors outside the control of the individual. Early European societies would not have made much distinction between human beings and their natural environment. Classical Greek philosophy is regarded as the point at which ideas about these relationships changed from "naturalistic" explanations to humanistic explanations. Naturalistic explanations linked nature and life as one and humanistic explanations separate people out from the world around them and place humanity on a higher plane (than animals and plants) because of such characteristics as language and reason.[14] Socrates, Plato, and Aristotle are regarded as the founders of this humanistic tradition of knowledge.

Human nature, that is, the essential characteristics of an individual person, is an overarching concern of Western philosophy even though "human" and "nature" are also seen to be in opposition to each other. Education, research, and other scholarly traditions have emerged from or been framed by debates relating to human nature. The separation between mind and body, the investing of a human person with a soul, a psyche, and a consciousness, the distinction between sense and reason, and definitions of human virtue and morality are cultural constructs. These ideas have been transformed as philosophers have incorporated new insights and discoveries, but the underlying categories have remained in place. From Aristotle and Plato in Greek philosophy, the mind-body distinction was heavily Christianized by Aquinas. French philosopher Descartes developed this dualism further, making distinctions which would relate to the separate disciplines required to study the body (physiology) and the mind (psychology). His distinctions are now referred to as Cartesian dualism. Hegel reasoned that the split was dialectical, meaning that there was a contradictory interplay between the two ideas and the form of debate required to develop these ideas. It must be remembered, however, that concepts such as the mind or the intellect, the soul, reason, virtue, and morality are not in themselves "real" or biological parts of a human body. Whilst the workings of a mind may be associated in Western thinking primarily with the human brain, the mind itself is a concept or an idea. In Maori worldviews, for example, the closest equivalent to the idea of a "mind" or intellect is associated with the entrails and other parts of the body. The head was considered *tapu* for other reasons.

What makes ideas "real" is the system of knowledge, the formations of culture, and the relations of power in which these concepts are located. What an individual is—and the implications this has for the way researchers or teachers, therapists or social workers, economists or journalists might approach their work—is based on centuries of philosophical debate, principles of debate, and systems for organizing whole societies predicated on these ideas. These ideas constitute reality. Reality cannot be constituted without them. When confronted by the alternative conceptions of other societies, Western reality became reified as representing something "better," reflecting "higher orders" of thinking, and being less prone to the dogma, witchcraft, and immediacy of people and societies which were so "primitive." Ideological appeals to such things as literacy, democracy, and the development of complex social structures make this way of thinking appear to be a universal truth and a necessary criterion of civilized society. Although eighteenth- and nineteenth-century forms of colonization brought Christian beliefs about the soul and human morality to indigenous peoples, these concepts were discussed in Western traditions prior to Christianity. Christianity, when organized into a system of power, brought to bear on these basic concepts a focus of systematic study and debate which could then be used to regulate all aspects of social and spiritual life.

The individual, as the basic social unit from which other social organizations and social relations form, is another system of ideas which needs to be understood as part of the West's cultural archives. Western philosophies and religions place the individual as the basic building block of society. The transition from feudal to capitalist modes of production simply emphasized the role of the individual. Concepts of social development were seen as the natural progression and replication of human development. The relationship between the individual and the group, however, was a major theoretical problem for philosophy. This problem tended to be posed as a dialectic or tension between two irreconcilable notions. Hegel's dialectic on the self and society has become the most significant model for thinking about this relationship. His master-slave construct has served as a form of analysis which is both psychological and sociological, and in the colonial context, highly political.

Rousseau has a particular influence over the way indigenous peoples in the South Pacific came to be regarded, because of his highly romanticized and idealized view of human nature. It is to Rousseau that the idea of the "noble savage" is attributed. This view linked the natural world to an idea of innocence and purity, and the developed world to corruption and decay. It was thought that the people who lived in the idyllic conditions of the South Pacific, close to nature, would possess "noble" qualities from which the West could relearn and rediscover what had been lost. This romanticized view was particularly relevant to the way South Pacific women were represented, especially the women of Tahiti and Polynesia. The view soon lost favor, or was turned around into the "ignoble savage," when it was found that these idealized humans actually indulged in "barbaric" and "savage" customs and were capable of what were viewed as acts of grave injustice and "despicability."

Just as in the psychological traditions the individual has been central, so within sociological traditions the individual is assumed to be the basic unit of a society. A major sociological concern becomes a struggle over the extent to which individual consciousness and reality shapes, or is shaped by, social structure. During the nineteenth century this view of the individual and society became heavily influenced by social Darwinism. This meant, for example, that a society could be viewed as a "species" of people with biological traits.[15] "Primitive" societies could be ranked according to these traits, predictions could be made about their survival, and ideological justifications could be made about their treatment. Early sociology came to focus on the belief systems of these "primitive" people and the extent to which they were capable of thought and of developing "simple" ideas about religion. This focus was intended to enhance the understandings of Western society by showing how simple societies developed the building blocks of classification systems and modes of thought. These systems, it was believed, would demonstrate how such social phenomena as language developed. This in turn would enable distinctions to be made between categories which were fixed—that is, the structural underpinnings of society—and categories which people could create—the cultural aspects of the lifeworld. It also reinforced, through contrasting associations or oppositional categories, how superior the West was.

Conceptions of Space

Similar claims can be made about other concepts such as time and space. These concepts are particularly significant for some indigenous cultures because their language makes no clear or absolute distinction between the two: for example, the Maori word for time or space is the same. Other indigenous languages have no related word for either space or time, having instead a series of very precise terms for parts of these ideas, or for relationships between the idea and something else in the environment. There are positions within time and space in which people and events are located, but these cannot necessarily be described as distinct categories of thought. Western ideas about time and space are encoded in language, philosophy, and science. Philosophical conceptions of time and space have been concerned with (1) the relationships between the two ideas, that is, whether space and time are absolute categories or whether they exist relationally; and (2) the measurement of time and space.[16] Space came to be seen as consisting of lines which were either parallel or elliptical. From these ideas, ways of thinking which related to disciplines of study emerged (for example, mapping and geography, measurement and geometry, motion and physics). These distinctions are generally part of a taken-for-granted view of the world. Spatialized language is frequently used in both everyday and academic discourses.

Henri Lefebvre argues that the notion of space has been "appropriated by mathematics," which has claimed an ideological position of dominance over what space means.[17] Mathematics has constructed a language which attempts to define with absolute exactness the parameters, dimensions, qualities, and possibilities of space. This language of space influences the way the West thinks about the world beyond earth (cosmology), the ways in which society is viewed (public/private space, city/country space), the ways in which gender roles were defined (public/domestic, home/work) and the ways in which the social world of people could be determined (the marketplace, the theater).[18] Compartmentalized, space can be better defined and measured.

Conceptions of space were articulated through the ways in which people arranged their homes and towns, collected and displayed objects of significance, organized warfare, set out agricultural fields and arranged gardens, conducted business, displayed art, and performed drama, separating out one form of human activity from another. Spatial arrangements are an important part of social life. Western classifications of space include such notions as architectural space, physical space, psychological space, theoretical space, and so forth. Foucault's metaphor of the cultural archive is an architectural image. The archive not only contains artifacts of culture, but is itself an artifact and a construct of culture. For the indigenous world, Western conceptions of space, of arrangements and display, of the relationship between people and the landscape, and of culture as an object of study have meant that not only has the indigenous world been represented in particular ways back to the West, but the indigenous worldview, the land and the people, have been radically transformed in the spatial image of the West. In other words, indigenous space has been colonized. Land, for example, was viewed as something to be tamed and brought under control. The landscape, the arrangement of nature, could be altered by "man": swamps could be drained, waterways diverted, and inshore areas filled, not simply for physical survival, but for further exploitation of the environment or to make it "more pleasing" aesthetically. Renaming the land was probably as powerful ideologically as changing the land. Indigenous children in schools, for example, were taught the new names for places that they and their parents had lived in for generations. These were the names which appeared on maps and which were used in official communications. This newly named land became increasingly disconnected from the songs and chants used by indigenous peoples to trace their histories, to bring forth spiritual elements, or to carry out the simplest of ceremonies. More significantly, however, space was appropriated from indigenous cultures and then "gifted back" as reservations, reserved pockets of land for indigenous people who once possessed all of it.

Other artifacts and images of indigenous cultures were also classified, stored, and displayed in museum cases and boxes, framed by the display cases as well as by the categories of artifacts with which they were grouped. Some images became part of the postcard trade and the advertising market or were the subject of Western artistic interpretations of indigenous peoples. Still other "live" and performing examples were put "on stage" as concert parties to entertain Europeans. Indigenous cultures became framed within a language and a set of spatialized representations.[19]

A specific example of the colonization of an indigenous architectural space and of indigenous spatial concepts can be found in the story of the Mataatua, a carved Maori house built in 1875 as a wedding gift from one tribal group to another. The New Zealand government negotiated and gained agreement to send the Mataatua to the British Empire Exhibition at Sydney in 1879. The house was displayed according to the aesthetic and economic sense of the exhibition's curators:

> Finding that it would cost at least 700 pounds to erect it in the ordinary manner as a Maori house, the walls were reversed so that the carvings showed on the outside; and the total cost, including painting and roofing with Chinese matting was reduced to 165 pounds.[20]

A "Maori House," displayed inside-out and lined with Chinese matting, was seen as an important contribution by New Zealand to the Sydney exhibition. As argued by its original owners,

> The house itself had undergone a transformation as a result of being assimilated into a British Empire Exhibition. It changed from being a 'living'

meeting house which the people used and had become an ethnological curiosity for strange people to look at the wrong way and in the wrong place.[21]

Having gained agreement for this single purpose, the New Zealand government then appropriated the house and sent it to England, where it was displayed at the South Kensington Museum, stored for forty years at the Victoria and Albert Museum, displayed again at the Wembley British Empire Exhibition in 1924, shipped back to New Zealand for a South Seas exhibition in Dunedin in 1925, and then "given," by the government to the Otago Museum. Ngati Awa, the owners of this house, have been negotiating for its return since 1983. This has now been agreed upon by the New Zealand government after a case put to the Waitangi Tribunal, and the "door lintel" of the Mataatua has been returned as a symbolic gesture prior to the return of the entire house over the next two years.

Space is often viewed in Western thinking as being static or divorced from time. This view generates ways of making sense of the world as a "realm of stasis," well-defined, fixed, and without politics.[22] This is particularly relevant in relation to colonialism. The establishment of military, missionary, or trading stations, the building of roads, ports, and bridges, the clearing of bush and the mining of minerals all involved processes of marking, defining, and controlling space. There is a very specific spatial vocabulary of colonialism which can be assembled around three concepts: (1) the line, (2) the center, and (3) the outside. The "line" is important because it was used to map territory, to survey land, to establish boundaries, and to mark the limits of colonial power. The "center" is important because orientation to the center was an orientation to the system of power. The "outside" is important because it positioned territory and people in an oppositional relation to the colonial center; for indigenous Australians to be in an "empty space" was to "not exist." That vocabulary in New Zealand is depicted in table 2.1.

Conceptions of Time

Time is associated with social activity, and how other people organized their daily lives fascinated and horrified Western observers. The links between the industrial revolution, the Protestant ethic, imperialism, and science can be discussed in terms of time and the organization of social life. Changes in the mode of production brought about by the industrial revolution, an emerging middle class able to generate wealth and make distinc-

Table 2.1. The Spatial Vocabulary of Colonialism in Nineteenth-century *Aotearoa*

The Line	The Center	The Outside
maps	mother country	empty land
charts	London	*terra nullius*
roads	magistrate's residence	uninhabited
boundaries	redoubt, stockade, barracks	unoccupied
pegs	prison	uncharted
surveys	mission station	reserves
claims	Parliament	*Maori pa*
fences	store	*Kainga*
hedges	Church	*Marae*
stone walls	Europe	burial grounds
tracks	port	background
genealogies	foreground	hinterland
perimeters	flagpole	

tions in their lives between work, leisure, education, and religion, and a working-class evangelical movement which linked work to salvation contributed to a potent cultural mix. In Africa, the Americas, and the Pacific, Western observers were struck by the contrast in the way time was used (or rather, not used or organized) by indigenous peoples. Representations of "native life" as being devoid of work habits, and of people being lazy, indolent, and having low attention spans is part of a colonial discourse that continues to this day. There were various explanations advanced for such indolence; a hot climate, for example, was viewed as a factor. Often, it was a simple association between race and indolence, darker-skin peoples being considered more "naturally" indolent.

An example of how integral time is to social life can be found in the journals of Joseph Banks. Banks accompanied Cook on his first voyages to the South Pacific. The Royal Society supervised the Greenwich Observatory, which eventually set the worldwide standard of time measurement (Greenwich mean time) and was instrumental in organizing Cook's voyage to Tahiti in 1769 to observe the transit of Venus. Throughout this journey Banks kept a detailed diary which documents his observations and reflections upon what he saw. The diary was a precise organization of his life on board the ship, not only a day-by-day account, but an account which included weather reports, lists of plants and birds collected, and details on the people he encountered. Life on board the *Endeavour* was organized according to the rules and regulations of the British Admiralty, an adaptation of British time. Not only did the diary measure time, but there were scientific instruments on board which also measured time and place. As an observer, Banks saw the Pacific world through his own sense of time, his observations were prefaced by phrases such as "at daybreak," "in the evening," "by 8 o'clock," "about noon," "a little before sunset."[23] He confessed, however—after describing in detail such things as dress, ornaments, tattooing, house construction and layout, clothing, gardens, net-making, women, food, religion, and language, and after describing visits he and a companion made at particular times to observe the people eating, carrying out their daily activities and sleeping—that he was unable to get a "complete idea" of how the people divided time.

The connection between time and "work" became more important after the arrival of missionaries and the development of more systematic colonization. The belief that "natives" did not value work or have a sense of time provided ideological justification for exclusionary practices which reached across such areas as education, land development, and employment. The evangelical missionaries who arrived in the Pacific had a view of salvation in which were embedded either lower-middle-class English or puritanical New England work practices and values. It was hard work to get to heaven and "savages" were expected to work extra hard to qualify to get into the queue. This also meant wearing "decent" clothes designed more for hard labor in cold climates, eating "properly" at "proper" meal times (before and after work), and reorganizing family patterns to enable men to work at some things and women to support them.

Lineal views of both time and space are important when examining Western ideas about history. Here, the Enlightenment is a crucial point in time. Prior to this period of Western development was an era likened to a period of "darkness" (the "Age of Darkness") which "coincided" with the rise of power to the east. This era was followed by reformation within the Church of Rome. During these periods, which are social "constructions" of time, society was said to be feudal, belief systems were based on dogma, monarchs ruled by divine authority, and literacy was confined to the very few. People lived according to myths and stories which hid the "truth" or were simply not truths. These stories were kept alive by memory. The Enlightenment has also been referred to as the "Age of Reason." During this period, history came to be viewed as a more reasoned or scientific understanding of the past. History could be recorded systematically and then retrieved through recourse to written texts. It was based on a lineal view of time and was linked closely to notions of progress. Progress could be "measured" in terms of technological advancement and spiritual salvation.

Progress is evolutionary and teleological and is present in both liberal and Marxist ideas about history.

Different orientations toward time and space, different positioning within time and space, and different systems of language for making space and time "real" underpin notions of past and present, of place and of relationships to the land. Ideas about progress are grounded within ideas and orientations toward time and space. What has come to count as history in contemporary society is a contentious issue for many indigenous communities because it is not only the story of domination; it is also a story which assumes that there was a "point in time" which was "prehistoric." The point at which society moves from prehistoric to historic is also the point at which tradition breaks with modernism. Traditional indigenous knowledge ceased, in this view, when it came into contact with "modern" societies, that is, the West. What occurred at this point of culture contact was the beginning of the end for "primitive" societies. Deeply embedded in these constructs are systems of classification and representation which lend themselves easily to binary oppositions, dualisms, and hierarchical orderings of the world.

One of the concepts through which Western ideas about the individual and community, about time and space, knowledge and research, imperialism and colonialism can be drawn together is the concept of distance. The individual can be distanced, or separated, from the physical environment, the community. Through the controls over time and space, the individual can also operate at a distance from the universe. Both imperial and colonial rule were systems which stretched from the center outward to places which were far and distant. Distance again separated the individuals in power from the subjects they governed. It was all so impersonal, rational, and extremely effective. In research, the concept of distance is most important as it implies a neutrality and objectivity on behalf of the researcher. Distance is measurable. What it has come to stand for is objectivity, which is not measurable to quite the same extent.

Research "through imperial eyes" describes an approach which assumes that Western ideas about the most fundamental things are the only ideas possible to hold, certainly the only rational ideas, and the only ideas which can make sense of the world, of reality, of social life, and of human beings. It is an approach to indigenous peoples which still conveys a sense of innate superiority and an overabundance of desire to bring progress into the lives of indigenous peoples—spiritually, intellectually, socially, and economically. It is research which from indigenous perspectives "steals" knowledge from others and then uses it to benefit the people who "stole" it.

Some indigenous and minority group researchers would call this approach simply racist. It is research which is imbued with an "attitude" and a "spirit" which assumes a certain ownership of the entire world, and which has established systems and forms of governance which embed that attitude in institutional practices. These practices determine what counts as legitimate research and who count as legitimate researchers. Before assuming that such an attitude has long since disappeared, it is often worth reflecting on who would make such a claim, researchers or indigenous peoples? A recent attempt (fortunately unsuccessful) to patent an indigenous person in the New Guinea Highlands might suggest that there are many groups of indigenous peoples who are still without protection when it comes to the activities of research.[24] Although in this particular case the attempt was unsuccessful, it demonstrated yet again that there are people out there who, in the name of science and progress, still consider indigenous peoples as specimens, not as humans.

Notes

1. Stuart Hall, "The West and the Rest: Discourse and Power," in *Formations of Modernity*, ed. Stuart. Hall and Bram Gielben (Cambridge: Polity Press and Open University, 1992), 276–320.

2. B. Bernstein, "On the Classification and Framing of Knowledge," in *Knowledge and Control: New Directions for the Sociology of Education*, ed. Michael F. D. Young (London: Collier Macmillan, 1971), 47–69.

3. See, for example, Martin Bernal, *Black Athena: The Afroasiatic Roots of Civilisation* (London: Vintage, 1991).

4. Michel Foucault, *The Archaeology of Knowledge*, trans. A. Sheridan Smith (New York: Pantheon, 1972).

5. Ashis Nandy, *The Intimate Enemy: Loss and Recovery of Self under Colonialism* (Delhi: Oxford University Press, 1989), xi.

6. David Theo Goldberg, *Racist Culture: Philosophy and the Politics of Meaning* (Oxford: Blackwell, 1993).

7. Goldberg, *Racist Culture*, 23.

8. Goldberg, *Racist Culture*, 23.

9. Goldberg, *Racist Culture*, 23.

10. Goldberg, *Racist Culture*, 23.

11. Goldberg, *Racist Culture*, 41–60.

12. Mary Erler and Maryanne Kowaleski, *Women and Power in the Middle Ages* (Athens: University of Georgia Press, 1988).

13. The Treaty of Waitangi was signed between Maori chiefs and the British Crown in 1840. The Waitangi Tribunal was established by parliament under the Treaty of Waitangi Act of 1975. This act established the tribunal with the brief of

hearing claims by Maori that the Crown had contravened the principles of the Treaty of Waitangi. This applied to recent grievances. The tribunal was given powers to recommend actions to the Crown. The act was amended in 1985 in order to extend the scope of claims back to 1840.

14. James F. Brennan, "Racist Culture," in *The History and Systems of Psychology*, 3rd edition (Englewood Cliffs, N.J.: Prentice Hall, 1991).

15. Goldberg, *Racist Culture*, 62–69.

16. In the fifth century, Zeno, for example, posited a series of paradoxes which centered around two ideas, one which suggests that space and time are continuous, and one which suggests that they are made up of divisible parts. Others have argued since Zeno that there can be no such thing as 'empty' space because if it is empty, it does not exist.

17. Henri Lefebvre, *The Production of Space* (Cambridge, Mass.: Blackwell, 1991).

18. See, for example, Raymond Williams, *The Country and the City* (London: Paladin, 1973). See also Frantz Fanon, *The Wretched of the Earth* (New York: Grove Press, 1968), 30. Fanon talks about 'zones' where natives live and 'zones' where settlers live. For him, the border between the two is clear and there is no possibility of reconciliation.

19. See also Mick Gidley, ed., *Representing Others: White Views of Indigenous Peoples* (Exeter: University of Exeter Press, 1994).

20. Appendices to the Journals of the New Zealand House of Representatives, 1880, H5: 2.

21. Te Runanga o Ngati Awa (1990), *Nga Karoretanga o Mataatua Whare* [The Wanderings of the Carved House, Mataatua] (Whakatane, New Zealand: Ngati Awa Research Report 2, 1990).

22. Doreen Massey, "Politics and Space/Time," in *Place and the Politics of Identity*, ed. Michael Keith and Steve Pile, 141–161 (London: Routledge, 1993).

23. J. C. Beaglehole, *The Endeavour Journal of Joseph Banks* (Sydney: Angus and Robertson, 1962).

24. See the account of this attempt in *Third World Resurgence*, no. 63, 30.

Technique, Art, or Cultural Practice?
Ethnic Epistemology in Latino Qualitative Studies

JULIE L. FIGUEROA AND PATRICIA SÁNCHEZ

WHILE MANY SCHOLARS OF COLOR have often resisted the indoctrination of the academy—in particular positivist training in social science methods—we as Latina educational researchers have had a difficult time finding a researcher who speaks to the positive process of doing work with one's own community.[1] Though we are engaged with programs and departments that act as vital spaces of critical thought and have provided in many instances appealing alternatives to traditional research methods, we have been unable to find more works that affirm an ethnic epistemology when working in communities of color. In addition to not offering an affirmation of an ethnic epistemology, most qualitative method discussions do not consider the ways in which scholars of color approach their research and what exactly may inform this approach. By this, we do not mean to essentialize researchers of color or contribute to the "we vs. them" debate. Our interests are to more fully understand the role of qualitative researchers and what embodies the enactment of that role (e.g., training, prior knowledge, cultural or community resources).

While scholars define the nature and purpose of qualitative research differently, this difference often reflects the personal and political position scholars have on the research question as well as the community being researched. In other words, qualitative research serves a variety of purposes, depending on who conducts the research. To this end, we have found a plethora of books used in graduate seminars and training that depoliticize the act of conducting research by likening it to doing "high art" or traditional Western art that is often presented as apolitical. Often this type of conventional academic training that proposes specific techniques does not have the analytical power we need to study a community (namely our own) that lies beyond the cultural understandings of the institution. Therefore, when we are presented a set of decontextualized research techniques, how do we contextualize these in working within our communities? In this piece we articulate part of our experiences in doing research within a Latino context and what this means to academics who see themselves with a lifetime trajectory of working within the Latino community. What emerges is a discussion on qualitative research and the differences in approaching this work as an "art" (as expressed by several mainstream academics) and as women of color who rely heavily and unapologetically on cultural practice.

Our discussion begins by exploring the relationship between the term "art" and its use in qualitative research. We then turn to the contributions of Chicana/o researchers working within Chicano/Latino communities and build upon the Chicana/o epistemology voiced by our *compañeras/os*. By sharing our own theorizing on Chicana/o epistemology, we present the beginnings of a guiding metaphor for conducting research (*la vitrina*). We also attempt to define "cultural practice" in an effort to raise the important but often less-voiced issues of accountability and reciprocity in academic research. In the closing sections, we develop the notion of "cultural practice in action" by reflecting on experiences that occurred to us while in and out of the academy and in and out of "the field."

Research and the "Art of . . ."

One of the initial conversations we had regarding this piece was the prevalent use of the term "art" in research methods textbooks and how-to books. We found it striking to see so many social scientists liken conducting research to performing a special art form. A short list of such works includes: *Basic Research Methods in Social Science: The Art of Empirical Investigation*; *Social Science and the Self: Personal Essays on an Art Form*; *Learning from Strangers: The Art and Method of Qualitative Interview Studies*; *The Art of Fieldwork*; *Qualitative Interviewing: The Art of Hearing Data*; *The Art of Case Study Research*; *The Art and Science of Portraiture*; and "Interviewing: The Art of Science," in *Collecting and Interpreting Qualitative Materials*.[2] While space does not permit us to analyze each of these works' use of the art metaphor or fully address the analogies these authors create between social science methods and art, we do glean several similar themes from this convention and raise our own questions about the implications of using such a metaphor in research. Several questions we hope to raise are: Is the use of the art metaphor part of a white or racially-biased epistemology?[3] Do academics of color share a common "art" or set of unspoken techniques in approaching and conducting research? Or is this more akin to cultural practice? What then is the difference between "art" and cultural practice?

Perhaps the most salient theme that emerges in analyzing the art metaphor is the authority or voice of experience that comes across several of these works. It is impressed upon the reader or novice researcher that those who have developed an "art" for conducting a particular kind of research have mastered a set of techniques, practices, or skills with certain flair. There is an implicit message within some of these texts that is conveyed to the emerging researcher: Here are some words of wisdom, practical advice, and strategies that you will not hear anywhere else; these may help you in your pursuits, but remember that even after reading what I have written here, you still may not have what it takes to conduct research in an "art"-ful manner because that really cannot be taught, even though you should strive for it.

One author we reviewed is actually rather explicit in presenting his work and describes such methodological advice as "folk wisdom." Julian L. Simon explains in his social science methods book:

> This book is a textbook. Though some of the ideas in it are new, most are not. Like other textbooks it constitutes a sort of folk wisdom; the folk are the teachers, colleagues, and students who have discussed research with me. Some of this wisdom seems never to have been collected or transcribed from the oral tradition . . . To collect and discuss this wisdom is the aim of this book.[4]

Simon points out a gap in the social sciences between what is taught and what is not written down in terms of research methods.[5] That empty space or knowledge that goes unspoken is "folk wisdom" and its totality becomes the "art of empirical research."[6] In addition, Simon points out that the "folk" from whom he has learned a great deal are teachers, colleagues, and students; yet, he does not acknowledge learning from the "folk" many of us social science researchers turn to for data: the participants and community members of our studies.

As Chicana researchers who have worked in the academy on numerous studies pertaining to the Latino community—in fact, every research study we have been a part of was directly related to Latinos, whether it was on education, immigration, housing, or migrant farmwork—we both agree and disagree with Simon. In our estimation, there is in fact a rather large gap in our social science training—perhaps more akin to a silencing—but unlike Simon, we feel that which has gone unspoken is more than techniques or an "art"-ful way of conducting research. What is not taught in the majority of methods courses or textbooks are the epistemologies of scholars of color who come from many of the same communities in which social scientists conduct qualitative research. For us, working with and learning from "folk" in our Latino communities happen both in and out of research projects and overlap unconsciously during periods of scientific investigation and everyday practice. Voicing this reality is part of our aim in this piece, as well as trying to unpack the discourse researchers use to describe specialized techniques or methods that are based on "experience" (or the use of certain qualitative research techniques over and over again).

Part of the hidden discourse in the art metaphor is the distance it creates between those who are more experienced in a professional sense (or believe they are more experienced) and those of us who are emerging academics (and may have more experience in a real-world sense). While there are often seemingly sincere attempts to advise less-experienced colleagues, there is still a discourse embedded in this practical advice-giving. When research methods are presented as an established art form, these become difficult to replicate and can remain largely unobtainable. This discourse privileges the practice, flair, and "art" form that researchers develop *in* the academy and perfect with training, practice, and the use and re-use of techniques in the field. We as Latina researchers have found this discourse to be at odds with our own epistemology, which is grounded in the communities that we both "research" and live in and return to after every research project is completed.[7] In reality, as working-class Chicanas we never *leave* "the field." It may be the case that the Latino immigrant students we "studied" in an English-language learner study[8] are not much different from our present-day English-language learner neighbors, cousins, or siblings. While our cultural "training" and community experience may have been primarily forged prior to our entering the academy, some of us who maintain close relationships to the same or same type of Latino working-class neighborhoods, relatives, and friends, continue to develop this cultural "training" in the form of everyday practice and bring it with us to the officially designated "research site." *Somos los que estudiamos.*[9] This ongoing interaction with and understanding of our real-life communities is much different than the social science methods and epistemology traditionally espoused in the academy.

There are also several researchers who adhere to the art metaphor by describing their position as a painter or artist. In *The Art of Case Study Re-*

search, Robert E. Stake utilizes the art metaphor to represent numerous methods that the researcher has before him; it is he who chooses which of these will best fit a particular study:

> I will try to emphasize the arbitrariness of the methods from chapter to chapter, but I encourage you readers to be alert for tactics that do not fit your style of operation or circumstances. Before you is a palette of methods. There are many, many ways to do case studies.[10]

With this metaphor, Stake creates a picture of the researcher almost literally standing at a distance, deciding how to customize her or his methods to fit the "circumstances" of the impending research study (i.e., art project) while also selecting the most comfortable means of operating with the chosen methods. There is a sense of the researcher working from a distance, moving in and back out again, that portrays researchers with artist-like movements able to judge with artful precision what is appropriate for the study at hand. Again, the emphasis or priority here is the academy or researcher who is in charge and not the "subject" or "researched." This begs us to ask then, what is the most comfortable way for participants to be researched? What palette lies before them when a researcher suddenly approaches and asks them for their participation? The art metaphor helps the artist or researcher maintain power and wield considerable conscious control over those being studied while the entire process itself is veiled as a depoliticized act.[11] Stake also offers the following confirmation of this removed researcher-artist stance when he states:

> We tout case study as being noninterventive and empathetic. In other words, we try not to disturb the ordinary activity of the case, not to test, not even to interview, if we can get the information we want by discrete observation or examination of records. We try hard to understand how the actors, the people being studied, see things.[12]

Like a painter, the researcher here stands at a considerable distance from her or his "subject" and remains discrete and removed from the object being "studied." There is a certain omnipresence then that the researcher, like a master painter, may have in re-creating and transferring the observed world onto the academic canvas. In our estimation, this rings of positivism cloaked in humanistic aestheticism—the "truth" can be found with careful artistic and distant observation. In this way, the removed-ness of the researcher from the "researched" helps reinforce a severely imbalanced power relationship. There is no co-construction of knowledge or qualitative human exchange here.[13]

In her prologue to *Death without Weeping: The Violence of Everyday Life in Brazil*, Nancy Scheper-Hughes also describes the work of ethnographers as artists:

> The ethnographer, like the artist, is engaged in a special kind of vision quest through which a specific interpretation of the human condition, an entire sensibility, is forged. Our medium, our canvas, is "the field," a place both proximate and intimate (because we have lived some part of our lives there) as well as forever distant and unknowably "other" (because our own destinies lie elsewhere).[14]

In her metaphor, the field is actually the painter's or ethnographer's canvas. While this is an honest and reflective observation on the difficulty of representing the lives and experiences of others, it continues to portray the classic dilemma of (white) researchers and their traditional entries and exits in the field. What happened to the strokes painted by Scheper-Hughes and her participants while engaging in the field or canvas? When she returned to the ivory tower to write up this brilliant ethnographic account, where were her artistic partners from the field she alluded to and their contributions to this written representation?

The art metaphor in this example continues to provide authority to the lone artist-researcher as well as less accountability to research participants because as Scheper-Hughes states, sometimes researchers' "destinies lie elsewhere." However, as Chicana researchers whose destinies *do* in fact lie in the same communities we research, the practice of entry and exit is not experienced in the same manner, nor is accountability to the community being researched readily dismissable. What pulls us to do research in Latino communities are the same ties that bind us to the people and *el bienestar de nuestra comunidad*.[15] Research in this way is hardly depoliticized and hardly a lone act.

In addition to using an art metaphor to describe qualitative methods, several researchers have literally used art or aesthetic artifacts—such as pictures of famous paintings or essays on pottery-making—in order to convey their unique approach to social science research and art. Such authors include Sara Lawrence-Lightfoot, Jessica Hoffman Davis, and Susan Krieger. In *The Art and Science of Portraiture*, Lawrence-Lightfoot and Davis share their particular technique of ethnography—which they call "portraiture"—and explain how to replicate this methodology, often used to produce telling social portraits; they provide a framework through their own reflection and portraiture examples, as well as through artwork created by children and adults juxtaposed with paintings by famous artists such as Picasso.

For Lawrence-Lightfoot, portraiture makes a strong attempt to break from traditional positivist research by crafting art and science together: "With [portraiture], I seek to combine systematic, empirical description with aesthetic expression, blending art and science, humanistic sensibilities and scientific rigor."[16] In fact, Lawrence-Lightfoot roots the development of this methodology in her literal experiences as an artist's subject—how she was "attended to, recognized, appreciated, respected, scrutinized" by those painters who captured her in both pastels and oils during two distinct sittings in her lifetime. Based on these central encounters, Lawrence-Lightfoot believes that portraiture can merge "good ethnography" with "the evocative resonance of fine literature."[17] Indeed, while *The Art and Science of Portraiture* provides a broad range of techniques necessary in producing "portraiture," these techniques are not necessarily politically, socially, or historically grounded. In other words, Lawrence-Lightfoot and Davis may describe such things as creating a "central metaphor" or "shaping context," but they resist situating themselves in reference to the community which they study.

In her book, *Social Science and the Self: Personal Essays on an Art Form*, Susan Krieger uses the artistic lives and art of Georgia O'Keefe and Pueblo Indian potters to express an epistemology grounded in the self.[18] Like Lawrence-Lightfoot and Davis, Krieger places a premium on aesthetic (re)presentation. In addition, all three researchers discuss relying heavily on the self or "I" in their research. Lawrence-Lightfoot and Davis affirm the "explicit recognition of the use of the self as the primary research instrument."[19] For Krieger, a sociologist, infusing the "I" and self in her writing has produced considerable polemic in her discipline while at the same time has helped "free" some researchers to do more of this. Yet, the "I" that is included in describing this type of social science research remains enmeshed with the same "I" as artist, "I" as pioneer in painting, "I" as creator of this art project or research product. And unfortunately, this tends to reproduce the same "I" as in "Western *eye*," which stems from an academic social history that has been largely Eurocentric.

Scheurich and Young, in "Coloring Epistemology: Are Our Research Epistemologies Racially Biased?" discuss at length research epistemologies that have dominated the social sciences. These epistemologies (positivism to postmodernism/poststructuralism) are part of an academic and social history built upon a white, racially-biased, modernist civilization. Scheurich and Young refer to this as epistemological racism:

> Epistemological racism means that our current range of research epistemologies . . . arise out of the social history and culture of the dominant race. . . . Our "logics of inquiry"[20] are the social products and practices of

the social, historical experiences of whites, and, therefore, these products and practices carry forward the social history of that group and exclude epistemologies of other social groups.[21]

By examining the art metaphor, we have come to a similar conclusion as Scheurich and Young. The art metaphor in social science research is in fact part of a larger racially-biased epistemology that obscures other ways of knowing reality. In some ways, we can liken this to the "tools" of the "master's house"[22]: the art metaphor serves as a qualitative research discourse veiled as simple and harmless techniques when in fact this discourse provides license to many (white) social scientists to approach research without contextualizing their own social history or ways of knowing. As a result, an "un-colored" dominant epistemology continues to permeate research studies, methods courses, and textbooks.

It is not difficult to discern then that for scholars of color it has been a struggle to bring forth our own research epistemologies. Part of this difficulty lies within a two-pronged dilemma: First, as scholars of color, sometimes we are not aware that the different worldview we hold (in comparison to our white counterparts) will indeed affect the design and implementation of our investigations; often we are not aware of this before embarking upon research, and instead, we experience a serious disconnect from both our communities and academia while immersed in the research project or after completing the entire study. Second, even when we profoundly sense our misgivings about a particular research study that we are fully involved in, we lack the language or the ability to articulate this predicament because of our indoctrination or training in the academy (which has severely omitted the incorporation of epistemologies of color). Gloria Ladson-Billings captures this quandary or "limbo" well and describes it as a dilemma faced by veteran academics as well:

> This epistemological limbo—between the old discourse and the new—is the place where many scholars of color find themselves. The mechanisms for scholarly recognition, promotion, tenure, and publication are controlled primarily by the dominant ideology. Scholars of color find themselves simultaneously having been trained in this dominant tradition and needing to break free of it.[23]

We have found that this "breaking free" of traditional epistemologies would enhance the work of scholars of color who study the human condition within their own communities of color—communities which may be largely heterogeneous but are still sites of social injustice, economic instability, social immobility, and inequity. As two Chicana researchers speaking from lived experience, we hope to provide foresight to our *compañeras/os* who will also embark upon research with/in their own communities. In the following section, we examine how other Chicana/o researchers have approached (and reflected on) working within Chicano/Latino communities.

Chicana/o Epistemologies and Qualitative Research

While one of our aims in this piece is to contribute to the contours of a Chicana/o epistemology—in particular, one that is expressed by academics working in educational research—we believe that our dilemmas as researchers are shared across different disciplines and even by community members in different professions.[24] Thus, it is not our intention to omit the contributions of other scholars in this important endeavor, such as Patricia Hill Collins, Gloria Anzaldúa, Richard Delgado, Norma Alarcón, and Chela Sandoval.[25] In fact, we would like to point out that much theorizing on ethnic epistemologies has come from scholars working in many different fields and at different points in time. But, because our own research experience has been primarily in the area of educational studies, and because we come from a social history that is Chicana, bilingual, bicultural, working-class, second-generation immigrant, our focus in this piece remains largely on Chicana/o epistemology in Latino qualitative studies.

To this end, we chose to closely look at the work from the following educational researchers who primarily conduct research in Chicano/Latino communities: Concha Delgado-Gaitán, Sofia Villenas, Dolores Delgado Bernal, and Marcos Pizarro.[26] Their pieces highlight a Chicana/o epistemology and the process of "discovering" this epistemology while in the field and articulating it within a reflective space. In contrast to some of the lone artist-researchers mentioned in the previous section, these scholars found themselves pulled in different directions while working in the communities they were studying. Because these communities faced substantial marginalization and educational inequity, Delgado-Gaitán, Villenas, and Pizarro were either approached as a resource or offered assistance out of a cognizance that they themselves have a stake in the *bienestar* of that community. From their experiences, we understand that the role of participant-observer can intertwine considerably with that of community member. While it is clear that all four of these researchers were committed to studying different issues within the Chicano/Latino community, their awareness and readiness to move in and out of the role of researcher varied throughout different stages of their research projects. From their experiences, we were able to discern certain elements that constitute part of a larger Chicana/o epistemology as well as examples that support our notion of "cultural practice" (outlined in later sections).

Delgado-Gaitán, Villenas, and Delgado Bernal are *mujeres* in the field of qualitative research that challenge the proscribed roles of researcher and "the researched."[27] Each of their works questions the manner and method of inquiry undertaken, the analytical tools used for data interpretation, and the role of participants in the research process from inception to completion of the study. More importantly, their work recognizes the transformational experience that can occur for a researcher studying her own community. Although each of the three researchers responded to their communities in a variety of ways, they each came to understand that their research was much more enriched when they were willing to become involved with the community beyond their academic role.

Delgado-Gaitán's work with a parent group called COPLA (Comíte de Padres Latinos) in the city of Carpintería, California, helped her realize that a mutually beneficial partnership can emerge when the researcher moves beyond the non-interventive role of participant-observer. In her article, "Researching Change and Changing the Researcher," Delgado-Gaitán articulates this: the more involved she became with COPLA, the greater understanding she gained about how to go about interpreting what was unraveling. It was her role as a community member rather than that of a researcher that led her to decide to become involved. Yet, ironically, stepping out of that researcher role enabled her to become better informed and to create a methodology that would be more aligned with what was happening in that particular Latino community. Because knowledge was co-constructed between the researcher and the researched, there was an interconnectedness that generated a greater depth of understanding as opposed to the outcomes captured by traditional "objective" research methods. Delgado-Gaitán elaborates:

> Conducting the Carpintería study taught me that a researcher can only be an outsider; however, with insight, the researcher can encourage and foster the relational process between researcher and researched. In the Carpintería study, the reflective analysis between the parents and the researcher impacted the direction of the study; the researcher provided the community with specific data to develop their organization, while the parents changed the researcher's perception of the meaning of their activities.[28]

In other words, the researcher recognizes that as a lone researcher who works from a non-participant-observer role, she will have a limited understanding of the phenomenon she wishes to study. In this way, a researcher's epistemology informs her methodology. The way in which a researcher makes sense of the world—the reality she has lived and comes to understand—informs the ways in which she goes about asking questions.

Delgado-Gaitán also points out that "ethnography of empowerment" allows the researcher to bridge potential disconnects that influence the way we make sense of the lived realities of participants. She states:

> In the dilemma of being a member/non-member of the ethnic group, I recognized that I had to remain conscious of the insiders' perspective since, even though I belonged to the same ethnic group as the subjects of this study, I could not insure true understanding of the culturally bound practices of the parent group. My lack of understanding was due to both my acculturation into the dominant culture and my academic training.[29]

Rather than objectifying the lives of the researched, Delgado-Gaitán centrally works with her participants to create a certain level of reciprocity. And in this process, she becomes keenly aware that the cultural practice she brings has suffered dilution because of her acculturation to mainstream U.S. society and time spent in the academy.

Villenas's work also demonstrates how a researcher becomes the medium through which conflicting tensions get channeled, and unlike the "free," unaccountable artist-researcher, Villenas feels torn by a deep level of responsibility to the community she works with. Villenas's article "The Colonizer/Colonized Ethnographer: Identity, Marginalization, and Co-optation in the Field" provides an introspective look at her work with working-class, immigrant Latino families in rural North Carolina. This article reminds us that as scholars of color, we are forcibly placed by our academic institutions in the peculiar position of making research decisions around issues of loyalty and credibility rather than accuracy. Villenas believes that her role as a researcher is co-opted not just by the community but more directly by the academic institution. Because of this, Villenas stops to question the ways in which her academic training does not facilitate a scope of understanding but instead stymies her learning process by suggesting that she continue working with the popular and negative discourse that depicts Latinas/os:

> I was ready to learn from this Latino community, but in the process of seeking to reform my relationship with them, I failed to notice that I was

being repositioned and co-opted by the dominant English-speaking community to legitimate their discourse of "Latinas/os as problem." In the course of working with Hope City's non-Latino school and service professionals, I discovered that while I engaged in a rethinking of my own politics and the processes of empowerment with the Latino community, I was hiding my own marginality in relation to the majority culture.[30]

Villenas's positioning within the landscape of her embedded realities allowed her to recover a sense of self as a Chicana, researcher, and community member. In opposition to the well-known research technique of "making the familiar strange,"[31] Villenas recognized that to make the familiar strange disempowered her worldview, which is informed by the combination of lived experience and academic training: "The internalization of oppressive discourses in relation to oneself as a researcher, especially as a product of institutionalized education and university training, can lead to a disempowerment of the researcher and research process."[32]

Whereas Delgado-Gaitán and Villenas each come to realize their academic training does not speak to the process of conducting research in communities of color as scholars of color—after many moments of both internal and external struggle in the field—Delgado Bernal does not experience similar tensions when conducting research in the Chicano/Latino community. Delgado Bernal, in fact, had a highly positive experience working with eight Chicanas and their leadership roles in the 1960s and 1970s Chicano movement. In her piece, "Using a Chicana Feminist Epistemology in Educational Research," Delgado Bernal outlines a Chicana feminist epistemology based on this study. She asserts:

> A Chicana feminist epistemology arises out of a unique social and cultural history, and demonstrates that our experiences as Mexican women are legitimate, appropriate, and effective in designing and conducting, and analyzing educational research.[33]

According to Delgado Bernal, this Chicana feminist epistemology is supported and guided by what she terms "cultural intuition." The four tenants that form cultural intuition are personal experience, existing literature, professional experience, and the analytical research process itself. Delgado Bernal adopts this framework from Strauss and Corbin, who have the same four tenants under their rubric of "theoretical sensitivity."[34] According to Delgado Bernal, this newly revised framework "gives Chicana and Chicano education scholars some freedom to interpret their research findings outside of existing paradigms, and hopefully develop and propose policies and practices that better meet the needs of Chicanas and Chicanos."[35]

While the articulation of this epistemology is one more important step in encouraging Chicana/o researchers to recognize the ways in which their epistemologies directly inform the methodologies of their research studies, the essence of this framework is still rooted in a theoretical framework—grounded theory—developed *within* the academy. That is, the origin of this Chicana feminist epistemology does not come from a framework organic to the Chicana community (or any other community of color); instead it is based on academicians' theory-making—the same colonizing source many of our Chicana/o predecessors fought against. Why, we ask, must our insights rely so heavily on frameworks developed within the very institution we seek to change and redefine? Is it possible to break free and give credence to our own ways of knowing? In our estimation, in order for a framework, practice, or epistemology to truly become a platform for community social justice, it must be steeped in the experiences, practices, and social history of that community and its own knowledge-making practices.

Pizarro's article, "'Chicana/o Power!' Epistemology and Methodology for Social Justice and Empowerment in Chicana/o Communities," presents a closer approximation to a Chicana/o epistemology grounded in the Chicana/o community—much like Freire's work in *Pedagogy of the Oppressed*, which grounds itself in improving the lives of marginalized people.[36] Pizarro explicitly recognizes the political nature of research and utilizes this as a means to achieving social justice. Influenced by Delgado-Gaitán and Trueba's notion of "Ethnography of Empowerment,"[37] Pizarro echoes their own words by stating "that not only do we need research *on* empowerment but research *as* empowerment [his italics]."[38] Pizarro also describes how his academic training weakens his ability to think outside the traditional confines of qualitative research to enrich his own methodologies. Forced to search beyond his academic training, Pizzaro initiates a self-reflective critique and learns that as researchers, we must ground "our work and its underlying method and epistemology on the epistemology of those with whom we work."[39] That is, we begin with the perspectives, positioning, and social histories of the researched. For Pizzaro, then, Chicana/o epistemology stands

> in dramatic opposition to the dominant epistemology innovative researchers have been attempting to fight. I saw from my own experiences that love, family, and social justice are not only embodied in our goals but are the foundation to our epistemology itself. In addition, a central component of

this epistemology is the oral tradition through which Chicana/o epistemology is passed on in a context of respect and love.[40]

Pizzaro, therefore, begins to embrace and nurture the learning and experiences he acquired in his community and uses these to inform his methodological approach rooted in social justice. Because of the persistent problems challenging Chicanas/os, Pizzaro believes it is important "we consider how a Chicana/o epistemology can help us redefine our roles in the academy and reclaim our roles in Chicana/o empowerment."[41] It is within this process that Pizzaro reminds researchers of color, specifically Chicanas/os, that we can only initiate a social justice agenda by first figuring out our own positions relative to the predominant landscape.

Similar to the Chicana researchers previously discussed but more direct in his presentation, Pizarro believes we must self-interrogate and explore what informs our approaches and assumptions regarding the research we are doing:

> I suggest that we look at epistemology and the way that it actually shapes most of our efforts at innovation. Researchers who are challenging the oppressive tendencies of education and research must be willing to challenge their own approaches and assumptions if we are to move thought and action in a new direction.[42]

From this perspective, lived experience seems to serve as an important tool for scholars of color to modify and transgress qualitative pedagogies and methodologies. Like Pizarro, we believe that the union of lived experiences as Chicanas and our academic training is sorely disjointed. Through our working-class backgrounds, we experienced and witnessed the injustices that come from living that reality. Yet somehow, academic training is meant to catapult one into believing that to achieve legitimacy and credibility in academe, one must "check" that lived history at the door, as if that lived history has neither place in the ivory tower nor ability to generate critical thinking and a social critique.

Overall, all of these Chicana/o educational researchers and their experiences continue the articulation of a Chicana/o research epistemology. Delgado-Gaitán allows us to think deeply about the role of reciprocity and how stepping outside our roles as researchers supplements our understanding. Whereas Delgado-Gaitán focuses on her relationship with the researched, Villenas gives us an introspective view regarding the ways in which researchers of color can find themselves inadvertently caught between competing loyalties to the community and academy. Villenas evaluates her position and intentions with regards to the community she studied. In contrast to Delgado-Gaitán and Villenas, Delgado Bernal offers a framework—Chicana feminist epistemology—to better consider what it means to be a Chicana studying Chicana issues within the academy. Lastly, Pizzaro speaks forthrightly about qualitative research being informed by our own epistemologies as well as its politicized nature and how it can become a vehicle for attaining social justice.

Defining Cultural Practice

While we believe that the Chicana/o researchers discussed in the previous section respectfully serve as the beginning of the articulation of a coherent Chicana/o research epistemology, it would be naive to suggest that all Chicana/o or Latina/o researchers share these same experiences or epistemology. But, it is important to note that there is a growing number of Chicana/o academics in the field of education who are choosing to do work that does not leave their lived experience or commitment to their communities "checked" at the door.[43] Many of these researchers enrich their work and epistemologies with what we term "cultural practice."

Cultural practice originates from lived realities and therefore informs and orients our approach to conducting research. From our perspective, cultural practice 1) is constructed from the intersection of gender, class, immigration status, race, and sexual orientation; 2) creates a system of meaning and understanding of that intersected reality; and 3) positions oneself in the world in a way that frames both personal and professional interactions. Cultural practice emerges from a lived experience within a particular community. We each possess a cultural practice that is couched in our social histories. Therefore, it seems hardly plausible that we as researchers would somehow become disengaged from our cultural practice when we suddenly enter the academy and conduct research. At some level, we are either more or less aware of how cultural practice impacts the way we proceed as researchers. When we closely look at the academy's emphasis on learning and mastering a certain set of research techniques, the role of cultural practice is often omitted. While we understand this omission is not necessarily intentional, it perpetuates the notion that qualitative methods can be uniformly and universally applied without considering who the researcher is and who the community being researched is. For us, invoking cultural practice does not mean we discard our academic training, but rather, we recognize its limitations. Because the communities of color we choose to study are often located outside the cultural understandings of the institution, we must approach and conduct research in a way that utilizes both the strengths of our academic training and the strengths of our cultural practice—probably erring in favor of remaining loyal to our own communities of origin. However, for some researchers, at the end of the day, they easily step outside of their researcher roles and return to their homes; whereas for others, departure or exit from the research site is less self-evident or hardly possible because their own lives—families, friends, and/or neighborhoods—intimately resemble their research community.

The dividing line between community member and researcher is not always apparent. When researchers are actively engaged and invited to participate in community activities as community members, they have the opportunity to continue developing insight into both the community they belong to and the one in which they may stake their research interests. As Chicanas growing up in homes and neighborhoods that were different than the "official" knowledge transmitted to us (about us) in schools, we learned a great deal about who we were, where we came from, and what meaning this gave us in our lives from the human agents in our communities: our families, neighbors, parents, grandparents, *padrinos* (godparents), *tíos* (uncles and aunts), *primos* (cousins).[44] In our "home" spaces—which included the transnational experience of returning to our parents' natal communities in México—the repository of knowledge rested in the human resources of resistance and resiliency. In turn, this climate of survival greatly impacted the generous spirit of our communities, whether it was our *abuelita* (grandmother) sending us with an *ollita* of *atole* to a much older and widowed *viejita* who lived alone[45] or the collecting of bag after bag of clothing and goods at cheap Saturday yard sales—to be shipped with the first relative returning to México—or the $400 loan for a distant *primo* (cousin) to be able to cross and pay the *coyote*.[46] We learned about this knowledge or *conocimiento* primarily through everyday practice and in the form of *cuentos*, *dichos*, and *consejos* (stories, sayings, advice).

Today, this knowledge serves us well and has become the "cultural training" we bring to the academy. But it would be inaccurate to think that this cultural training only happened *before* we entered the academy.[47] As young scholars still intimately connected with our communities (in some cases with the same ones we grew up in and in other instances with ones very similar), we constantly develop cultural practice as we continue to live and practice in these communities. In our view, cultural practice is an ongoing process; it is practicing everyday life in our cultural community: what we live, experience, cherish, critique, and want to change. It also involves taking that cultural practice to our other communities of work, the university, and so forth. Our embedded knowledge, or *conocimiento*, of the Chicano/Latino community provides us with substantial insight into many of its needs. Our research, then, combines this *conocimiento* with action that will address the community's *bienestar*.

While we hope that we are not essentializing working within communities from which our cultural practice originates—nor do we mean to suggest that researchers cannot be effective or gain understanding about communities that are not their own—we do want to acknowledge that each of us is an agent in possession of a cultural practice that emerges from living within a particular cultural community and its social history. These cultural practices are embodied in the practices, intentions, and discourses we use in the social practice of research. As an example of this, we offer the following metaphor of *la vitrina* to further define how our cultural practice influences our epistemology and methodology.

Toward a Metaphor of Cultural Practice: La Vitrina

We began this piece by taking a close look at a common metaphor in qualitative research—the art metaphor that compares qualitative researchers to artists and their products (such as fieldwork or published studies) to artwork. If we extend this analysis, we also find that, traditionally, art in the Western world has primarily been a privilege for those who belong to the dominant group. In fact, in the modern world, many aspects of art have long been inaccessible to those without the financial resources to take part in its production, dissemination, consumption, or enjoyment.[48] As an elite social practice, Western art has been renowned for its exclusion of communities and artists that come from different traditions of artistic expression.

To disrupt part of this Eurocentric transmission in the arts and social sciences, we have developed a different metaphor for the way we conduct qualitative research in our own communities. Through a discussion we had early in the process of writing this piece, we found that we were both doing research in a very similar way that was not a part of our training (i.e., infusing cultural practice in the design and implementation of our research projects). During this conversation, we wondered if other scholars of color operated in the same way. As a starting point, we referred to Linda Tuhiwai Smith, who calls for a decolonization of research methods; as a Maori researcher working with her community, she carefully details a research agenda that reclaims control over indigenous ways of knowing and being.[49] This led to our creation of an organic research metaphor grounded in our experiences/ways of knowing and in the homes of many families in the Chicano/Latino community: *la vitrina*.

A *vitrina* (vee-tree-nah) is literally a cabinet with glass doors and windows that showcases or stores a family's fine china. In creating this metaphor, we recalled the *vitrinas* our *abuelitas*, *tías*,[50] and mothers keep intact for years, and where they collect different memories from major family events. A *vitrina* serves as a space where many Latino families keep their most important and special memories in addition to their fancy dishes. Each item in a *vitrina* tells a special story in a family's life—often celebratory and at times tragic. For example, the *vitrina* in one of our mother's homes has the family's fine china; *recuerdos* from baby showers, weddings, *bautizos*, and *quinceañeras*[51] (the small physical mementos Latino families hand-make and give to all attendees at special events); a plastic champagne glass from the first second-generation immigrant child who graduated from high school; two little vases one child made out of plaster and painted in third grade; a hollow Easter egg hand-painted by a German neighbor; the small flag used in a naturalization ceremony; decorative hand-crocheted doilies; and unframed photographs of new babies, special moments, and deceased loved ones.

Like the *vitrina*, we believe that people carry their life stories with them—sometimes "viewable" through transparent doors but often tucked away behind other objects. People and their life experiences and the ways they make meaning are part of larger stories kept in a human *vitrina*. When we speak with someone and ask them to "pour" their lives out to us, we are in essence asking them to share the items in their human *vitrina*. Some items are in easy view for them to bring out and others are carefully stowed deep and out of view. For us, then, it is important that the keeper of the *vitrina* be the one that decides which item to share.

In keeping with our beliefs about cultural practice and research, another set of questions emerges once an item is retrieved and shared from a person's *vitrina*. What do we then as "researchers" do with these special—often fragile—items our "informant" gives us? This special, individually sacred life story they have passed on to us is like one of those unique, delicate *recuerdos* or vases in our *tía's vitrina*. In which *vitrina* do we now place this precious gift our "informant" has given us? What kind of *vitrina* do we now create for its safekeeping and showcasing? Is this new *vitrina* as carefully constructed as the one our grandma has in her own home? Is it created with as much care as hers? Or is the academic *vitrina* we create and in which we place this item constructed with too much jargon, disconnecting this gift further from its organic origins? And when it is placed in this academic *vitrina*, how safe is it here? Who will see it through these new glass doors and will it be cherished as much as it was by its original keeper? How can we reconcile these different *vitrinas* and create one that addresses these multiple challenges?

Cultural Practice as Ethnic Epistemology and Methodology

As we saw in the metaphor of *la vitrina*, we strongly believe in and respect the knowledge and lived experiences of those that become involved in our research. Given the kinds of communities we have chosen to study throughout our academic careers, we have also chosen to make reciprocity and accountability an unquestioned condition in carrying out research. Several ways this has influenced the way we "practice" research can be found in our notion of "incentives," our commitment to a research process that brings immediate social change, and our belief that participants are knowledge creators outside of research projects.

Often a remunerated exchange between a traditional researcher and participant is carried out in the form of an incentive. This formal practice does not reflect the spirit of the exchange that happens in much of our work.[52] Participants in the studies we have led were not given incentives in direct relationship to the experiences they shared with us. Exchanges, instead, were facilitated by the reality of meeting community needs and improving its *bienestar*. Our connectedness to these communities and the accountability we felt in offering and sharing, at times, our social capital was motivated by a deep sense of reciprocity. We recognize this as *teniendo buena voluntad* (having good will), which means consistently offering good will from the beginning to those around you to acknowledge the formation of a relationship between two parties. This is not a discussion about incentives in exchange for information. *Buena voluntad* embodies the enactment of being mindfully courteous at all times to those around you to demonstrate your persona and intentions. This demonstration of good will allows the surrounding community to decide the value of your presence and the degree to which they would like to include and involve you in their everyday lives. Sometimes this involvement may entail a range of activities, such as helping someone's father create and type a résumé, looking for the best airfare via the Internet for a daughter to travel to México, accompanying a mother to sign up for cell phone service because she does not have the proper form of identification, or showing someone's cousin how to use an ATM because he or she just opened a bank account.

One of the tenants of our epistemology is that we are researchers because we believe research can be a vehicle for social change. More specifically, we believe that the actual process of conducting research can be a direct way to address immediate educational and social needs of our participants. For example, in a research project one of us has led, three Latina youth were at the center of designing and carrying out the entire research.[53] This collaborative process included over three years of weekly meetings, a field research trip with the three youth and adult researcher to México, as well as analysis, write-up, and presentation of data at several research conferences where the youth were integral.[54] The investigation of the particular phenomenon—transnationalism—was not the sole purpose but the vehicle for other areas of change, such as breaking the isolation of Latina youth in urban communities, co-authoring a bilingual and bicultural children's book, engaging "ordinary" people in the process of research which is usually left to "professionals," and creating an impact in the usually stagnant (or culturally exclusive) curricula of these girls' middle schools and high schools. While the art metaphor in research tends to promote and encourage a "free rein" of sorts in researching any topic within any community, cultural practice actually makes you seriously consider how the work you do will benefit participants and the community. Its utility is different from thinking how it will get you better data or advance your professional career. In other words, cultural practice embodies genuine commitment to your community.

As discussed in the previous two sections, we see members of our community as knowledge creators. It does not take their participation in a study for their lived experience and expression of it to become "knowledge"—though academia often does not consider community knowledge valid until it ends up as a transcribed quote in a published paper. It is profoundly disturbing that until a community member's knowledge is filtered through a professional researcher it isn't considered worthy or official. Even progressive researchers use language such as "sharing data with participants" or "involving them in data interpretation" to bestow participants as creators of knowledge. In our belief system, community members *are* knowledge creators long before we interview them.

Cultural Practice in Action: Moments in Academia and "in the Field"

In trying to theorize cultural practice, we have provided our analysis of other Chicanas'/os' reflective experiences in conducting research as well as a framework, metaphor, and approach to research based on our community experiences. However, we also recognize that one of the most effective ways to continue to define cultural practice is by providing extended examples of this dynamic. The first-person *testimonios*[55] written below are some of our personal experiences that best capture moments of cultural practice in action.

What Does It Mean to be Chicana?
Real Conversations with Real Women

This example comes from my first qualitative course in graduate school at a prominent public university in northern California. The course was taught by a well-known anthropologist who had years of "experience" conducting educational research in immigrant communities.

It was my very first qualitative course. While the first part of that semester required we understand the principles of observation and interviews, the second half of the semester required that we conduct a research project using what we learned. For my topic, I chose to explore the question: "What does it mean to be Chicana?" I arranged to interview eight self-identified Chicanas with college degrees. I also decided to choose women with whom I had good rapport. I arrived at each of our meeting spaces with the same set of questions.

The interviews themselves never began right away. The first twenty minutes were spent exchanging *saludos*. *Saludos* encompass more than a greeting and are more similar to a conversation in which people catch up with each other's lives and exchange current events happening within the respective family, neighborhood, city, and/or state; this process often takes place over something to eat or drink. *Dando saludos* was to be expected and to do otherwise would be considered rude. So, for me, this made interviews a very comfortable experience since the interviewee and I began with a familiar and common cultural practice.

I met with each of these eight women after work and mostly over dinner. At the time, I was trained to use a tape recorder and take field notes. And although I cannot explain why I decided against audio recording our conversations, to me, it seemed to compromise the integrity of the moment. In my mind, it seemed highly inappropriate to record our natural and genuine conversations over dinner. It was more than common courtesy; it was about paying respects to someone's living history (the precious and carefully arranged pieces inside of their *vitrina*).

Each woman was interviewed for approximately two hours. I jotted notes when something interesting was said that responded to or confirmed something in the existing literature on Chicanas. After each interview, I made a committed effort to immediately sit at my computer and type up all the interviews in a narrative fashion. I shared the interviews with participants to make sure that our conversation was accurate, which also helped me unpack their experiences if they felt that the discourse used to narrate their experience seemed to be inaccurate.

As part of the course's requirements, we were to submit weekly write-ups of our research interviews or as they took place. About four interviews into the cycle of submissions, I read a commentary in blue ink on the last page of my fourth interview: "Are these interviews real?" "Real?!?" I thought to myself. I finally went to the professor's office hours, and I asked what she meant by "real." She basically pointed to the fact that it was my first qualitative course and the quality of the interviews exceeded her expectations and my training. I responded by saying that these interviews were indeed real and that the renditions came from real individuals. Throughout the rest of the quarter, I continued submitting my interviews in the same format, but I was deeply skeptical about this professor's ability to train and work with someone like me because my approach to qualitative interviews was beyond and unlike her own academic training.

To this day, that particular conversation and experience lingers in my memory whenever I am conducting qualitative methods in my community. It lingers because I remain undecided as to whether this professor's comments were compliments or expressions of skepticism. Either way, one of the things that became clear to me then is that my cultural practice helped me conduct those first interviews. Yes, of course I also kept in mind certain qualitative conventions such as remembering to probe and making sure to pose questions that create building blocks to establish knowledge. But it was the manner in which the interviews were mediated through my understanding about what it means to be a Chicana community member that made a huge difference.

I grew up with a father who was an active storyteller, conveying all of his knowledge and wisdom in the form of real-life *cuentos*.[56] My father imparted to us our family history with its origins in Michoacán, México; Mexican history related to Jiquilpan, Michoacán; his personal migration history to the United States; how he met our mother; and what it was like for him to become a father. My upbringing was largely influenced by this tradition of oral history and *cuentos*. My father taught us through this storytelling to be active listeners, which immensely influenced me as a researcher to view the act of asking questions not as a device for acquiring lived experience but as a way to build understanding and appreciation about the lived experience. As children, we were not allowed to ask questions for the sake of asking questions. My father taught us to ask questions to gain greater depth of understanding and to be cognizant that not all questions have answers or should be answered. In this sense, knowledge and its power are maintained by the one telling the *cuento* or sharing his life story; knowledge remains sacred, intimate, and valued at all times.

In my familia, *cuentos*[57] were offered and shared to serve the purpose of remembering life experiences of the past to inform the decisions that needed to be made in the present. *Cuentos* imparted life lessons and outlined guiding principles that were to increase the well-being of my familia. *Cuentos* articulated experiences that highlighted life challenges and triumphs; they were meant to exemplify self-respect, dignity, and strength. For me, interviewing has always been foremost about gathering *cuentos* for the purpose of inserting greater clarity and gaining a closer approximation about a lived experience. I approach this work in much the same spirit as I was taught throughout my life: with a strong sense of reverence. This lived experience does not replace the fact that it is important to learn the conventions and practices that define qualitative research. Rather, cultural practice helped to compensate for the shortcomings in my academic training to help me understand lived experiences in their respective cultural contexts.[58]

I embraced and saw my cultural practice as being an asset to conducting academic work. It was the first time I realized that I had something to bring to my education that could not be taught in academia but only lived and learned from my community. With time, I realized I would never be complimented or acknowledged for bringing this contribution to my research. Nor would I be taught how to incorporate this insight into my academic training. Regardless of what my professor thought at the time, I never stopped to consider my family and community lessons outside of the academy to be less legitimate or credible: my academic training was enriched because of my outlook on *cuentos*. Upon taking my last course in qualitative research in graduate school, I maintained that who *I* was greatly influenced how I interviewed, analyzed, and represented data. In fact, years later when I found myself collecting data, I found myself understanding that what I knew about the world and my reality helped to inform my methodology. I had developed a greater sense of insight to ask the deeper questions.

Cruzando la Línea Otra Vez[59]: *Who Really Benefits from this Information Anyway?*

When my advisor invited me to attend a binational research colloquium on immigration between México and California, I was flattered and excited to meet the many scholars working in this area. In particular, I was looking forward to meeting those who worked at El Colegio de la Frontera Norte (College of the Northern Border). This conference took place in the spring of 2002 during our university's spring break. Immediately before the colloquium, I spent four days of my academic recess visiting my parents and family in El Paso, Texas.

What happened at the twenty-five-person colloquium is something I have a difficult time explaining. The two-day event was full of informative and interesting presentations; the researchers in attendance were predominantly on the "left" on issues of México-U.S. immigration; the size of the group was small enough for good follow-up discussion during and after each presentation. There was also a great deal of familiarity (and I would even say long-standing friendships) among participants, as well as a paid pair of highly trained translators that bridged the language barrier when necessary. The weather was sunny and pleasant those two days, the food was catered and actually very good. So why did I have such an adverse response to incorporating to this event and its dynamic?

I could say, academically, that there were a few key things that produced this result: 1) I was a graduate student and the majority of speakers were experienced scholars in their field, instilling at times an unspoken hierarchy; 2) I was technically an outsider to this group because I was invited to the colloquium to hear and discuss and not to present my own work on immigration and transnationalism; and 3) there was a large conference table in the middle of the room where all the presenters sat, with a ring of chairs outside this table for non-presenters like myself, creating a feeling, somewhat, of "not being at the table." But I think the greatest challenge for me was actually trying to decide where I fit in: as an academic or as a member of the population being studied.

I am the daughter of immigrants from México (the often-studied "second-generation"). I was raised along the México-U.S. border, where our home often served as a stop for family members ("undocumented laborers") along their U.S.-immigration journey. My entire life is steeped with this experience both personally and professionally, as my work involves issues of education and the Latino immigrant community. Immediately before this colloquium on immigration, I had been in El Paso where two key things were underway: My mother's relatives whom she had petitioned for U.S. residency fifteen years ago were about to be called for their interviews. I helped my father fill out the laborious paperwork for this process and repeatedly called the Immigration and Naturalization Service (INS) helpline for clarification. In addition, that same week, a cousin was preparing to cross into the U.S. via Texas but had undergone several thwarted attempts.

On a local front, my partner and I had just finished our interviews at INS for the processing of his green card, where we were grilled about the verity and legitimacy of our marriage. A close friend of ours was also in the process of bringing her three children across the border after not seeing them for over three years; this was going to cost her upwards of $3,000, let alone the emotional and psychological costs of entrusting their safety to strangers. Dealing with all of these personal stories involving U.S. immigration policy was not new to me or exactly difficult. But working through these issues while simultaneously hearing two consecutive days of abstract, distant presentations on phenomena that I was personally living was rather disconcerting. How could I engage in this intellectual exchange? Every presenter's findings were one more familiar and personal story to me.

I scribbled on my conference agenda, "Who's really crossing the border here?" There were studies on entry points and the beefed up border patrol and how this pushed migrants to cross at less safe points (such as the expansive and deadly hot desert); the protests by binational groups on this militarization; elections won and lost by transnational candidates; the unionizing efforts of certain immigrants and how organizing was more effective in their natal communities in México than in the U.S.; the results of a questionnaire given to migrant workers in the grape fields of Napa Valley; the participation of the second generation in hometown associations in the U.S.; the healthcare of immigrant families; and the role of youth in transnational events in small rural Mexican communities. I could not help but feel as if I were crossing in and out of multiple worlds as I heard data that was literally collected about members of my immigrant family. Many data points in a set could have easily been someone I knew or even me!

At one point during the colloquium, a policy analyst showed us a map of the most dangerous areas to cross along the México-U.S. border as well as the area least patrolled by the border patrol or *la migra*: Marfa, Texas. I thought to myself, "This is close to Ojinaga. I better call my mom." I called my mother during one of the breaks and asked her if our cousin had already crossed into the U.S. because if he hadn't, maybe he could try at Ojinaga. My mom said, "*No te preocupes. Ya cruzó la línea otra vez.*" (Don't worry. He already crossed the line again.) Our cousin had successfully gone through some agricultural fields at another entry point, carefully lodged himself inside the back of an unknown, large truck carrying used tires, and poked his head out at every freeway exit sign to see where the truck was taking him: Phoenix, Arizona. Though his intended destination was really elsewhere, he did not have a problem getting there because his U.S.-gringo boss personally drove two days to Phoenix to pick him up. For a moment, I just chuckled to myself. My cousin had beaten the stats.

"¿Por qué no vienes a comer?"[60]
Blurring Lines, Strengthening the Ties That Bind
In numerous decisions I made during the collection of my dissertation data, I chose to cross the boundaries of my researcher role despite feeling uncertain about the consequences. From a community standpoint, inclusion—not distance as in "making the familiar strange"[61]—felt more contextually appropriate when I was conducting a study on the educational experiences of three Chicano undergraduates attending a four-year institution.

I remember it was my plan to attend a conference on Latino teachers and teaching in San José, California, and then head on over to drop off a gift for my brother at my parents' since they would be going to Arizona to spend time with him. Days before the conference, I finished interviewing Antonio[62] and he asked if I was attending the conference in San José. I said yes. I asked if he was attending also. (At that point I remembered that Antonio did not have a car, and was probably going to be seeking transportation. He was the kind of person that reserved the number of personal requests he made of people until he really needed help.) Antonio said that he was going to attend if his friend was still going to offer to take him. I asked Antonio to call me if his friend did not follow through. About two days later, Antonio called me in the evening and asked if the offer for a ride was still on the table. Without hesitation, I said I would gladly take him to San José. I also let him know that I needed to stop by my parents' house to drop off a birthday gift for my brother. In that same breath, I said he was not obligated to come with me. I had planned to step out during the conference lunch break to drop off the gift at my folks' house. He said he would think about it. The next day I picked him up and we headed down to San José.

Our drive down became his opportunity to "interview" me and ask what it was like to be raised in San José. I shared my own history with him and what brought my parents to the city after so many years of working as migrant farm workers. We soon arrived at the conference site. When the lunch break arrived, I checked in with Antonio to see if he wanted to stay. I let him know that I would gladly come back to pick him up and then make the return trip back to our homes north of San José. He said that he preferred to come have lunch with me at my parents' house.

As we drove through the streets of San José, Antonio asked me what it was like to come home as a graduate student at one of the world's most prestigious universities. As we sat in my car waiting for the red light to change to green, I responded by saying, "Look around you. No one except you knows that I have such an education. We look like the people who are in the cars that surround us. There are no visible markers that would let people know I am college-educated." For the next couple of minutes, I realized that I really had no concerns about Antonio meeting my parents given that he spoke Spanish and that I considered him to be a really nice person based on our interviews. I parked the car and my parents came out to greet and welcome us. I exchanged hugs and kisses with my parents and introduced Antonio to them. My mom welcomed him and said, "*¿Por qué no vienes a comer?*"—she had just finished making "*unas sabrosísimas,*" chicken enchiladas. He smiled. We proceeded to sit down for lunch with my parents.

It was not long before my father asked him if his family was from México and whereabouts in México. Much of that lunch was spent witnessing the mutual exchange of family histories between my parents and Antonio. My parents gave Antonio a tour of the house and shared family photos in the home where I spent my childhood. Prior to leaving, my parents packed food for us so that we might have something to eat later on the drive home.

I remember driving away from my house thinking about the numerous ways I was led to believe (from my academic training) that I might have compromised my research because I chose to blur the lines of researcher and researched. However, I now realize that moments like these lend themselves to building reciprocity as well as a foundation of trust. Just as I came to know Antonio, Antonio also came to know me. This leveled the power imbalance of the researcher who usually "extracts" information from informants and shares nothing of her own life or background. The end result of this groundwork would inevitably better inform the means by which I could understand Antonio and his life history. Not only did he understand more about my history and intentions with the research I was conducting, but I also gained holistic insight into his outlook and participation in the world.

Continuing the Work in Our Communities (as "Researchers")

As Chicana researchers who live, work, and study (in) our communities, invoking an epistemology grounded in cultural practice means doing research where the stakes are high. Not only are we accountable to the academic machine, but also, and more importantly, we are accountable to the communities who have shaped us our entire lives, as well as to other academics of color who hold similar epistemologies. It is unfortunate that academia rarely creates a space where the researcher can openly discuss all the "home knowledge" that she brings to the field. Instead, in our experience, we have found that the spaces in academia too often try to diminish who we are and our lives. That is why we have come to believe that academic training alone does not always give a researcher the entitlement (or the best preparation) to examine the lives of communities like ours—though many academics feel otherwise. As Chicana scholars, we have taken "traditional" practices and discourses in qualitative research and transformed these to make them culturally responsive to and respectful of the communities we plan to spend the rest of our lives in. While we do not completely dismiss our academic training, our hope is to convey that as women of color—with particular social histories—we use a combination of academic training and cultural practice to transform and enrich our qualitative work, which most often happens (and will continue to happen) in our own ethnic communities.

For us, then, cultural practice embodies recognizing the knowledge and lived experiences of our community members and seeing the same human richness across different Chicano/Latino communities (which works to interrupt the transmission or reproduction of the cultural deficit theory).[63] Because of this, we feel that practicing research in the same traditional, objective way further fragments communities that are already torn and scarred by many existing injustices and social inequalities. Our cultural practice, therefore, does not allow us to be immobile, distanced, non-interventive participant-observers when we see and know that our communities are struggling. Instead, we attempt to create research projects that pay attention to multiple issues and meet some of the community's immediate needs because traditional methods rarely address (or condone) this in their process.

A question that arises for us, then, is "How do we work through these limitations in an authentic way that expands the existing conventions used in qualitative methods?" We believe that cultural practice holds part of the solution. Cultural practice becomes that missing tool that helps us fill the gaps of understanding that cannot be addressed solely by our academic training. Given the dynamic process with which knowledge is socially constructed in researched communities, the demands in the field should move researchers to not simply rely on techniques found within the latest how-to article. We believe that cultural practice stands to expand, enrich, and inform the traditions of qualitative methods.

In our experience, we were able to work through the traditions that bind us to academia and make our qualitative research a much more positive and organic process. We ask others who find themselves facing a similar situation to have the courage and seek the support to do the same.[64] Through our endeavors, we embraced the efforts of many scholars of color whose work encouraged us to think deeply about our responsibilities as researchers working within our own communities. We encourage all of our peers to think past methodological debates and instead think critically about two very important things: 1) the cultural practice that informs your research epistemology and 2) the kinds of communities you hope to work in during your "research" life's trajectory. In this way, qualitative research becomes more than the sum of techniques or art: qualitative research holds the rich possibility of being infused by cultural practice.

Closing Dicho[65]

Follow your epistemology even if it goes against your training (because your training may not be enough to work within your own community).

Notes

1. Often what is most circulated or cited are reflective pieces by scholars of color who have had a difficult time conducting research within their own community. For example, see Patricia Zavella, "Feminist Insider Dilemmas: Constructing Ethnic Identity with Chicana Informants," in *Feminist Dilemmas in Fieldwork*, ed. Diane L. Wolf, (Boulder, Colo.: Westview Press, 1996), 138–159; John L. Aguilar, "Insider Research: An Ethnography of a Debate," in *Anthropologists at Home in North America: Methods and Issues in the Study of One's Own Society*, ed. D. A. Messerschmidt (New York: Cambridge University Press, 1988), 15–26; Sofía Villenas, "The Colonizer/Colonized Chicana Ethnographer: Identity, Marginalization, and Co-optation in the Field," *Harvard Educational Review* 66, no. 4 (1996): 711–731; Brackette F. Williams, "Skinfolk, Not Kinfolk: Comparative Reflections on the Identity of Participant-Observation in Two Field Situations," in *Feminist Dilemmas in Fieldwork*, ed. Diane L. Wolf (Boulder, Colo.: Westview Press, 1996), 72–95.

2. Julian L. Simon, *Basic Research Methods in Social Sciences: The Art of Empirical Investigation*, 2nd ed. (New York: Random House, 1978); Susan Krieger, *Social Science and the Self: Personal Essays on an Art Form* (New Brunswick: Rutgers University Press, 1991); Robert S. Weiss, *Learning from Strangers: The Art and Method of Qualitative Interview Studies* (New York: Free Press, 1994); Harry F. Wolcott. *The Art of Fieldwork* (Walnut Creek, Calif.: AltaMira Press, 1995); Herbert J. Rubin and Irene S. Rubin, *Qualitative Interviewing: The Art of Hearing Data* (Thousand Oaks, Calif.: Sage Publications, 1995); Robert E. Stake, *The Art of Case Study Research* (Thousand Oaks, Calif.: Sage Publications, 1995); Sara Lawrence-Lightfoot and Jessica Hoffman Davis, *The Art and Science of Portraiture* (San Francisco: Jossey-Bass, 1997); Andrea Fontana and James H. Frey, "Interviewing: The Art of Science," in *Collecting and Interpreting Qualitative Materials*, ed. Norman K. Denzin and Yvonna S. Lincoln (London: Sage Publications, 1998), 47–78.

3. James J. Scheurich and Michelle D. Young, "Coloring Epistemology: Are Our Research Epistemologies Racially Biased?" in *Anti-Racist Scholarship: An Advocacy*, ed. James J. Scheurich (Albany, N.Y.: SUNY Press, 2002), 51–73.

4. Simon, *Basic Research Methods*, 10.

5. Though not a contemporary of Simon's, William I. B. Beveridge also points to a similar gap in his book, *The Art of Scientific Investigation* (New York: W. W. Norton, 1957). And while we offer our apologies for including in this discussion an adamant positivist from the mid-twentieth century, we think his comments make an interesting point about the way natural scientists have also connected scientific investigation to the art metaphor. Beveridge explains: "It is true that much time and effort is devoted to training and equipping the scientist's mind, but little attention is paid to the technicalities of making the best use of it. There is no satisfactory book which systematizes the knowledge available on the practice and mental skills—the art—of scientific investigation" (p. viii). Beveridge, professor of animal pathology, goes on to say that he apologizes for even writing this book: he feels terrible for proposing in essence an epistemology. However, he euphemizes such an epistemology by calling it "the psychological aspects" of research, as if these "aspects" can be measured precisely by another science—the science of the mind: psychology. Beveridge also apologizes for not being formally trained in psychology and for using his own experience as a source of information in his book (xi).

6. Simon, *Basic Research Methods*.

7. Miguel A. Guajardo, *Education for Leadership Development: Preparing a New Generation of Leaders*, unpublished doctoral dissertation, University of Texas, Austin, 2002, refers to this as "coming home" after a research project (53).

8. Emma Fuentes, Daniel Liou, Patricia Sánchez, and Andrea Dyrness, "Interim Report from the English Language Learner Committee," Diversity Project, University of California, Berkeley, Spring 2000.

9. We are who we study. Please note: we use Spanish words throughout this piece not with the intent of excluding any readers but rather to reflect the everyday discourse that frames the communities we belong to. The Spanish terms writ-

ten in this piece reflect the actual discourse used to think and discuss the topic being engaged. Just as it is the cultural practice to use academic language to discuss research issues, we see our use of Spanish as a part of our everyday practices that are at the root of our own cultural practice.

10. Stake, *The Art of Case Study Research*, xii.

11. For a keen example of this, see James J. Scheurich, "The Destructive Desire for a Depoliticized Ethnographic Methodology: Response to Harry Wolcott," in *Anti-Racist Scholarship: An Advocacy*, ed. James J. Scheurich (Albany, N.Y.: SUNY Press, 2002), 153–157.

12. Stake, *Case Study Research*, 12.

13. Fontana and Frey, "Interviewing," 47–78. Fontana and Frey offer a more humanizing approach toward interviewing, one where we as researchers "no longer remain objective, faceless interviewers, but become human beings and must disclose ourselves, learning about ourselves as we try to learn about the other [or the researched]" (73).

14. Nancy Scheper-Hughes, *Death without Weeping: The Violence of Everyday Life in Brazil* (Berkeley, Calif.: Unitersity of California Press, 1992), xii.

15. The well-being of our community.

16. Lawrence-Lightfoot and Davis, *Portraiture*, 3.

17. Lawrence-Lightfoot and Davis, *Portraiture*, 4.

18. Krieger, *Social Science and the Self*.

19. Lawrence-Lightfoot and Davis, *Portraiture*, 14.

20. John H. Stanfield, "Epistemological Considerations," in *Race and Ethnicity in Research Methods*, ed. John H. Stanfield and Rutledge M. Dennis (Newbury Park, Calif.: Sage Publications, 1993), 16–36.

21. Scheurich and Young, "Coloring Epistemology," 61.

22. Audre Lorde, "The Master's Tools Will Never Dismantle the Master's House," in *Sister Outsider: Essays and Speeches* (Freedom, Calif.: Crossing Press, 1984).

23. Gloria Ladson-Billings, "Racialized Discourses and Ethnic Epistemologies," in *Handbook of Qualitative Research*, 2nd ed., ed. Norman K. Denzin and Yvonna S. Lincoln (London: Sage Publications, 2000), 267.

24. On numerous occasions, we have heard about the same type of disconnect experienced by Latino peers working as lawyers, engineers, and social workers within their own communities. What made their work more effective was a combination of their professional training and their forms of cultural practice.

25. Patricia Hill Collins, *Black Feminist Thought: Knowledge, Consciousness, and the Politics of Empowerment*, 2nd ed. (New York: Routledge, 2000); Gloria Anzaldúa, *Borderlands/La Frontera: The New Mestiza* (San Francisco: Spinsters/Aunt Lute, 1987); Richard Delgado, *Critical Race Theory: The Cutting Edge* (Philadelphia: Temple University Press,1995); Norma Alarcón, "Chicana Feminism: In the Tracks of 'the' Native Woman," in *Living Chicana Theory*, ed. Carla Trujillo (Berkeley, Calif.: Third Woman Press, 1998); and Chela Sandoval, "Mestizaje as Method: Feminists

of Color Challenge the Canon," in *Living Chicana Theory*, ed. Carla Trujillo (Berkeley, Calif.: Third Woman Press, 1998), 352–370.

26. Concha Delgado-Gaitán, "Researching Change and Changing the Researcher," *Harvard Educational Review* 63, no. 4 (1993): 389–411; Villenas, "Colonizer/Colonized"; Dolores Delgado Bernal, "Using a Chicana Feminist Epistemology in Educational Research," *Harvard Educational Review* 68 no. 4 (1998): 555–582; and Marcos Pizarro, "'Chicana/o Power!' Epistemology and Methodology for Social Justice and Empowerment in Chicana/o Communities," *Qualitative Studies in Education* 11, no. 1 (1998): 57–80.

27. Delgado-Gaitán, "Researching Change"; Villenas, "Colonizer/Colonized"; and Delgado Bernal, "Chicana Feminist Epistemology."

28. Delgado-Gaitán, "Researching Change," 14.

29. Delgado-Gaitán, "Researching Change," 14.

30. Villenas, "Colonizer/Colonized," 4.

31. George Spindler and Louise Spindler, "Roger Harker and Schönhausen: From Familiar to Strange and Back Again," in *Doing the Ethnography of Schooling: Educational Anthropology in Action*, ed. George Spindler (Prospect Heights, Ill.: Waveland Press, 1988), 21–43. The Spindlers' concept about "making the familiar strange" does not always resonate in particular research settings. In our view, we are tied to communities by virtue of family, friends, spouses, partners, *tíos*, *tías*, *abuelos*, and *abuelas*. How can we make the familiar strange when we live in that space of strangeness that makes sense to us?

32. Villenas, "Colonizer/Colonized," 716.

33. Delgado Bernal, "Chicana Feminist Epistemology," 558.

34. Anselm Strauss and Juliet Cobin, *Basics of Qualitative Research: Grounded Theory Procedures and Techniques* (Newbury Park, Calif.: Sage Publications, 1990).

35. Delgado Bernal, "Chicana Feminist Epistemology," 575.

36. Paulo Freire, *Pedagogy of the Oppressed*, revised 20th-century edition (New York: Continuum, 1993).

37. Concha Delgado-Gaitán and Henry Trueba, *Crossing Cultural Borders: Education for Immigrant Families in America* (London: Talmer Press), 1991.

38. Pizarro, "'Chicana/o Power!'" 61.

39. Pizarro, "'Chicana/o Power!'" 64.

40. Pizarro, "'Chicana/o Power!'" 65.

41. Pizarro, "'Chicana/o Power!'" 65.

42. Pizarro, "'Chicana/o Power!'" 72.

43. Delgado-Gaitán, "Researching Change,"; Delgado-Gaitán and Trueba, *Crossing Cultural Borders*; Delgado Bernal, "Chicana Feminist Epistemology"; Dolores Delgado Bernal, "Learning and Living Pedagogies of the Home: The Mestiza Consciousness of Chicana Students," *Qualitative Studies in Education*, 14, no. 5 (2001): 623–639; C. Alejandra Elenes, Francisca E. González, Dolores Delgado Bernal, and Sofía Villenas, "Introduction: Chicana/Mexicana Feminist Pedagogies;

Consejos, Respeto y Educación in Everyday Life," *Qualitative Studies in Education* 14, no. 5 (2001): 595–602; Eugene E. Garcia, *Hispanic Education in the United States: Raíces y Alas* (New York: Rowman & Littlefield, 2001); Francisca González, "*Haciendo que hacer*—Cultivating a Mestiza Worldview and Academic Achievement: Braiding Cultural Knowledge into Educational Research, Policy, Practice," *Qualitative Studies in Education* 14, no. 5 (2001): 641–656; Norma González, *"I Am My Language": Discourses of Women and Children in the Borderlands* (Tucson: University of Arizona Press, 2001); Guajardo, "Education for Leadership Development"; Aída Hurtado, "Plenary Session on Chicana Positioning," National Association for Chicana and Chicano Studies Annual Conference, Los Angeles, Calif., April 5, 2003; Enríque Murillo, Jr., "How Does It Feel to Be a Problem?: 'Disciplining' the Transnational Subject in the American South," in *Education in the New Latino Diaspora: Policy and the Politics of Identity*, ed. Stanton Wortham, Enríque Murillo, Jr., and Edmund T. Hamman (Westport, Conn.: Ablex Publishing, 2002), 215–239; Pizarro, "'Chicana/o Power!'"; Luis Urrieta, Jr., "Las Identidades También Lloran, Identities Also Cry: Exploring the Human Side of Indigenous Latina/o Identities," *Educational Studies* 34, no. 2 (2003): 148–168; Angela Valenzuela, *Subtractive Schooling: U.S.-Mexican Youth and the Politics of Caring* (Albany, N.Y.: SUNY Press, 1999); Villenas, "Colonizer/Colonized"; Villenas, "Reinventing *Educación* in New Latino Communities: Pedagogies of Change and Continuity in North Carolina," in *Education in the New Latino Diaspora: Policy and the Politics of Identity*, ed. Stanton Wortham, Enríque Murillo, Jr., and Edmund T. Hamman (Westport, Conn.: Ablex Publishing, 2002), 17–35.

44. Delgado Bernal, in "Learning and Living Pedagogies," calls this "pedagogies of the home," where knowledge or *educación* for Latinos is passed on in places outside of a school context.

45. Our grandma sending us with a very small kettle filled with a popular Mexican drink made from warm milk, corn starch, and sugar to a widowed elderly woman living alone.

46. The person many undocumented immigrants pay to help bring them across the México-U.S. border.

47. Margaret E. Montoya, "Academic Mestizaje: Re/Producing Clinical Teaching and Re/Framing Wills as Latina Praxis," *Harvard Latino Law Review* 2 (1997): 349. As a Latina/o critical theorist, Montoya addresses many Latino academics who moved "out of the barrio" and how this distances them from the academic work that they are trying to do. Our argument here is that sometimes some academics do not move completely out of the barrio but remain strongly connected to it on a daily basis, which informs both their research and cultural practice.

48. However, we do recognize that art in some communities of color can be accessible and political because it is presented in a different venue and for a different purpose, such as the murals in the Mission District of San Francisco and Chicano Park in San Diego. This art is not usually found in mainstream galleries.

49. Linda Tuhiwai Smith, *Decolonizing Methodologies: Research and Indigenous Peoples* (New York: St. Martin's, 1999).

50. Grandmas, aunts.

51. Baptisms and the fifteenth birthday party for a teenage girl. For a broader definition of this second ritual, see Patricia Sánchez, "*Quinceañera*," in *Mexico and the United States*, ed. Lee Stacy Leney and Gordon Leney (Tarrytown, N.Y.: Marshall Cavendish, 2002).

52. See Julie L. Figueroa, "Out of the Neighborhood and Into the Ivory Tower: Understanding the Schooling Experiences of Latino Male Undergraduates as a Process of Negotiation and Navigation," unpublished dissertation, University of California, Berkeley, 2002; Patricia Sánchez, "Urban Immigrant Students: How Transnationalism Shapes Their World Learning," *Urban Review* 39, no. 5 (2007): 489–517; Patricia Sánchez, "Cultural Authenticity and Transnational Latina Youth: Constructing a Metanarrative across Borders," *Linguistics and Education* 18, no. 3–4 (2007): 258–282; Kysa Nygreen, Soo Ah Kwon, and Patricia Sánchez, "Urban Youth Building Community: Social Change and Participatory Research in Schools, Homes and Community-Based Organizations," *Journal of Community Practice* 14, no. 1–2 (2006): 105–121.

53. This type of research is referred to as participatory (action) research. For more detailed renderings of this type of work, see Orlando Fals-Borda and Muhammad Anisur Rahman, *Action and Knowledge: Breaking the Monopoly with Participatory Action Research* (New York: Apex Press, 1991); Budd L. Hall, "From Margins to Center? Development and Purpose of Participatory Research," *American Sociologist* 23, no. 4 (1992); Patricia Maguire, "Challenges, Contradictions, and Celebrations: Attempting Participatory Research as a Doctoral Student," in *Voices of Change: Participatory Research in the United States and Canada*, ed. P. Park, M. Brydon-Miller, B. Hall, and T. Jackson (Westport, Conn.: Bergin & Garvey, 1984), 157–178; and Rebecca S. Hagey, "The Use and Abuse of Participatory Action Research," *Chronic Disease of Canada* 18, no. 1 (1997).

54. See Tomasa Dueñas Tovar et al., "*Recordando Mis Raíces y Viviendo Mis Tradiciones* [Remembering My Roots and Living My Traditions]: The Making of a Transnational Bilingual Children's Book," panel at the Reading the World Conference, University of San Francisco, March 2003; Tomasa Dueñas Contreras et al., "Transnational Latina Youth and Low-Intensity Conflict: Tempering the Forces of Assimilation," paper presented as part of a panel, "Internal Wars in Education: *Llegaste a Jugar Entre Las Strawberry Fields y Nada*—You Walked into a Minefield," National Association for Chicana and Chicano Studies (NACCS) Annual Conference, Los Angeles, Calif., April 2003; Montserrat López et al., "*No me quiero ir pero no me quiero quedar*: Transnational Latina Youth and Participatory Research," panel at the Center for Popular Education and Participatory Research Annual Conference, Berkeley, Calif., February 2002; Patricia Sánchez et al., "Promoting the Life Experiences and Funds of Knowledge of Transnational Families: Writing Ourselves in(to) the Research and Children's Literature," panel at the

California Association for Bilingual Education (CABE) Annual Conference, Los Angeles, Calif., February 2003; Patricia Sánchez et al., "Achieving Equity in 'Other' Educational Sites: Re-distributing the Power of Knowledge through Youth Activism, Social Change, and Participatory Research," panel at the American Educational Studies Association (AESA) Annual Convention, Kansas City, Mo., November 2004.

55. For a broader example, discussion, and use of *testimonios*, see the Latina Feminist Group, *Telling to Live: Latina Feminist* Testimonios (Durham, N.C.: Duke University Press, 2001).

56. Elenes et al., "Introduction." The authors in this piece speak to the importance of education in the home and how *cuentos* (stories), advice, respect, and moral education form an integral component of Latino family life.

57. *Cuentos* in my home during these times seemed to resemble what are often referred to as *testimonios* in qualitative research. *Cuentos*, much like *dichos*, are elements that comprise *testimonios*.

58. Bringing cultural practice into the academy is not that dissimilar from the concept of bringing "funds of knowledge" to the classroom or to the concept of "pedagogies of the home" used by Delgado Bernal in "Living and Learning Pedagogies" to describe what Chicana undergrads bring with them to get through college. For a more detailed discussion on funds of knowledge, see C. Mercado and Luis C. Moll, "The Study of Funds of Knowledge," *Centro* 9, no. 9 (1997): 26–42; Luis C. Moll, C. Amanti, D. Neff, and Norma González, "Funds of Knowledge for Teaching: Using a Qualitative Approach to Connect Homes and Classrooms," *Theory into Practice* 31, no. 2 (1992): 132–141.

59. Crossing the line again.

60. Why don't you come over and eat?

61. See note 31 above.

62. This is a pseudonym.

63. Richard Valencia, ed. *The Evolution of Deficit Thinking: Educational Thought and Practice* (Washington, D.C.: Falmer Press, 1997).

64. A very special and humble *gracias* to the following *gente* who influenced, supported, and guided our growth in this area: Aída Hurtado, Gene García, Patricia Gándara, Miguel Guajardo, Juan Valadez, John Hurst, and the Center for Popular Education and Participatory Research (Berkeley, Calif.).

65. In Spanish-speaking communities, a *dicho* is a memorable saying embodying an important fact of experience.

Riddles, Rhythms, and Rhymes   8
Toward an Understanding of Methodological Issues and Possibilities in Black/Africana Studies

JAMES B. STEWART

THIS ANALYSIS COMPARES AND CONTRASTS various approaches to conducting theoretical and applied research under the aegis of black/Africana studies (the term Africana studies will also be used). The principal assumption undergirding this analysis is that it is possible to make clear distinctions between Africana studies research, per se, and traditional disciplinary research. Africana studies is treated as an enterprise embodying three interrelated dimensions: (1) an academic conception that treats the mission of Africana studies as researching the history of people of African descent and illuminating their contributions; (2) an ideological conception that identifies Africana studies as an instrument of cultural nationalism; and (3) an instrumental conception whereby the role of Africana studies is to serve as a vehicle for empowering communities.[1]

I use five characteristics to differentiate Africana studies analyses from traditional inquiries: (a) rejection of "victimology" orientations in favor of approaches focusing on efforts by African Americans to shape their own destiny (Africana agency); (b) interpretation of contemporary developments through a framework of analysis that explores the effects of historical forces in shaping current conditions (continuing historical influences); (c) use of multiple analytical methods and modes of presentation to understand and articulate the complexities of the experiences of peoples of African descent (wholism/multidimensionality); (d) exploration of policy implications (simultaneous pursuit of academic excellence and social responsibility); and (e) exploration of historical and continuing cultural and political linkages between Africans in Africa and Africans in the diaspora (pan-Africanism).[2] Obviously no individual investigation can be expected to incorporate all of these elements. However, the absence of characteristics (a) and (b) generally suggests that a particular research study is more appropriately identified with a field of inquiry other than Africana studies, per se. Conversely, studies incorporating more of these characteristics are more representative of the type of Africana studies scholarship envisioned by founders than studies possessing fewer of these elements.

The analysis focuses first on the original incarnation of Africana studies as "black studies," focusing largely on domestic blacks living in the United States. The methodological implications of several major epistemological issues embedded in that conception are explored. These issues can be framed in the form of a series of questions: How do preferences for historical explanations of current phenomena affect research designs and interpretation of research findings? How can the explicit political commitment of Africana studies be balanced with standard expectations regarding research protocols such that resulting research is accepted as "scientific" or "scholarly?" How does this issue affect the relative attractiveness of quantitative and qualitative research methods? How can the type of interdisciplinary research envisioned by black/Africana studies advocates be operationalized? Is it possible to articulate a relationship between social science–based and artistic/humanistic research that enables meaningful discussion of these two different modes of inquiry using some type of unitary methodological principles?

The second major thrust of this analysis is to examine methodological issues associated with several lines of research that are extending the original focus of Africana studies. The specific research thrusts discussed are Africana women's studies, African diaspora studies, and Afrocentricity. The final section discusses various challenges and opportunities associated with conducting research in Africana studies and some potential fruitful directions for the future.

The Original Vision of Black Studies: Problems and Potential

Maulana Karenga argues that the thrust of black studies is "to study the multidimensional aspects of Black thought and practice in their current and historical unfolding . . . in an inclusive and comprehensive manner."[3] This means, as Karenga insists, that black studies contains fields in the social sciences and in the humanities. History has always been accorded premier status by black/Africana studies proponents and Karenga insists "the core task of Black Studies . . . is the rescue and reconstruction of Black History and humanity."[4] In addition he maintains that black history is "indispensable to the introduction and development of all other subject areas. Black History places them in perspective, establishes their origins and development, and thus aids in critical discussion and understanding of them."[5]

The Primacy of History in Black/Africana Studies

The rescue and reconstruction of black history through black/Africana studies is necessary, in part, because of the limitations of both traditional and contemporary historiography for mobilizing the full potential of historical research to support efforts to enhance the well-being of people of African descent. Several ideological orientations have shaped the ways historians have approached the study of the experiences of peoples of African descent. Manning Marable identifies three ideologies: (1) the "negro has no history" school of thought, (2) the "individual contributions" approach, and (3) a modern school that treats the history of African Americans as "a history of struggle rooted in the concept that human beings collectively made their own history [throughout which they] fought to maintain their unique identity as a people and to secure by whatever means, the economic and political tools for self-determination [and] self-reliance."[6] Marable concludes correctly that only the third approach overlaps significantly with the vision of black/Africana studies. Examples of slavery-era historical research topics of special interest to black/Africana studies include studies of resistance among enslaved Africans, initiatives by free African Americans to overturn the slave regime, and attempts to establish and maintain African American families during slavery. Parallel themes during subsequent periods could include postbellum efforts to build self-sustaining communities, and the development and praxis of protest organizations in the battle to end Jim Crow.

Foreshadowing the later discussion of Africana women's studies, it is important to note the large body of historical literature written by Africana women scholars examining the lives of women of African descent.[7] In the same sense that historical studies support Africana studies as a whole, gender-specific historical studies are critical for engendering Africana studies.

The importance of the work of scholars of black history to Africana studies has increased over time as new areas of research and new techniques have emerged. Robert Harris observes:

> Afro-American historiography, with its own conceptual and methodological concerns, is now poised to illuminate the Afro-American past in a manner that will broaden and deepen our knowledge of black people in

this country. The writing of Afro-American History is no longer undertaken principally to revise the work of wrongheaded white historians, to discern divine providence, to show black participation in the nation's growth and development, to prove the inevitability of black equality, or to demonstrate the inexorable progress made by Afro-Americans. It is conducted as a distinct area of inquiry, within the discipline of history, with black people as its primary focus to reveal their thought and activities over time and place."[8]

The interest in the study of black history is, however, not limited to historians, per se, or to specialists in Africana studies. As an example, distinct approaches to historical inquiry focusing on the economics of slavery have been developed that use "cliometric" methods. Cliometrics is the application of the behavioral models and statistical methods of the social sciences to the study of history. The explosion of cliometric research has been made possible by the "vast expansion of information on the operation of slave systems and new techniques of analysis employed to assess this information."[9] Cliometric studies of slavery first received national attention with the publication of *Time on the Cross*.[10] Unlike the African American historians described by Harris, who have personal interests in historical research, most cliometricians took up this topic because it provided fruitful opportunities to test the application of cliometric methods. Some historical interpretations generated through cliometric research, such as the extent of economic exploitation and coercion experienced by enslaved African Americans, differ significantly from those produced by historians working in the tradition described by Harris.

Cliometricians often combine analytical and narrative historical methods, contributing to what Robert Fogel describes as an emerging synthesis that is "not only a fusion of various new analytical techniques, and various new bodies of evidence, and various new perspectives, [but] . . . also a fusion of past work and new work, of old perspectives and recent ones."[11] Paradoxically, the fusion of analytical and narrative techniques in cliometric research is similar to the type of fusion of techniques advocated by Africana studies. Obviously the motivations and commitments associated with the Africana and cliometric projects differ significantly. Thus the question arises as to how Africana studies can make use of these new historical techniques without distorting its emphasis on lived experiences. This is a case that fits Paul Robeson's call to examine closely the extent to which "mechanical technique [is external and thus] can be borrowed."[12] Rushton Coulburn and W. E. B. Du Bois faced a similar challenge in the early 1940s as quantification efforts in sociology threatened to displace traditional historiography. At that point in time they concluded that "how far . . . sociology comprehends society and history . . . depends upon belief rather than fact: a sociologist who has been trained in the natural sciences and regards sociology as one of them firmly believes—or at least dares not deny the conviction—that eventually all the facts of human action can be so measured and classified as to conform to natural law."[13]

Infusing new analytical techniques into black historiography, while necessary, is insufficient, in and of itself, to mobilize fully the potential contributions of historical research to the Africana studies project. The critical challenge is to identify ways in which historical research can contribute to contemporary liberation efforts. As noted previously, one of the tenets of black/Africana studies is that contemporary circumstances are influenced directly by historical developments. This means that evolutionary explanations of current events or those that focus on inter-temporal connections among social processes are privileged over ahistorical interpretations. One justification for this rule of evidence is provided by Du Bois's dictum "we can only understand the present by continually referring to and studying the past; when any one of the intricate phenomena of our daily life puzzles us; when there arises religious problems, political problems, race problems, we must always remember that while their solution lies in the present, their cause and their explanation lie in the past."[14]

The earlier discussion of the economics of slavery can be used to illustrate how the type of historical research outlined above can be approached. Black/Africana studies–inspired studies of the economics of slavery could be linked directly to the current debates about reparations. One objective could be the development of estimates of the amount of reparations that can be claimed for losses experienced during the era of slavery. Another objective could be the accumulation of detailed documentation of how losses by African Americans and gains by European Americans were transferred across generations. Computer simulation is one of the analytical techniques that could be marshaled to support this research.

There is also an ontological problem constraining the liberatory potential of contemporary historiography, namely an implicit commitment to a linear view of the forward flow of human history. This means every succeeding era is viewed as unique in its own right, even though the particular configuration of social forces and organizations at a particular point in time is influenced by preceding epochs. This ontological position is called into question by a body of research that explores the extent to which systematic cyclical variation in economic forces induces repeating patterns of social/political behavior and outcomes.[15] Similar to the thrust of cliometric research, this work uses models from the social and behavioral sciences to examine the social outcomes associated with repeating economic cycles occurring in capitalist economies. From the vantage point of black/Africana studies the potential power of this idea is the implication that historical analysis can be an important guide in the development of strategies to confront racial oppression in a world characterized simultaneously by change and stability.

This line of research can prove helpful in examining the effects of contemporary globalization on people of African descent. It can draw, for example, on the work of Du Bois that probed the effects of industrial transformation on African Americans in the early part of the twentieth century. Du Bois saw economic disfranchisement during this period as "a vital factor in . . . elimination [of blacks] from modern civilization" and he identified consolidations and mergers and the expansion of "holding companies and interlocking directorates" as major culprits.[16] The transformation of the global economy was such that "the great industries of the world are becoming integrated into vast private organizations, which means that the work of the world—the skilled work, the best paid work—in the vast majority of the cases, is subject to . . . racial exclusion, to this refusal to allow certain classes of men to earn a decent living."[17] For Du Bois this was

> the new slavery of black men in America—a new attempt to make degradation of social condition correspond with certain physical characteristics—not to be sure fully realized as yet, and probably unable for reasons of social development ever to become as systematized as the economic and physical slavery of the past—and yet realized to an extent almost unbelievable by those who have not taken the pains to study the facts—to an extent which makes the lives of thinking black men [and women] in this land a perpetual martyrdom.[18]

It does not require much extrapolation to recognize the parallels between the social developments described by Du Bois and contemporary social dynamics. This example illustrates the potential value of a forward-looking historiographic methodology as a powerful component of a multidimensional black/Africana studies methodology.

The legacy of modes of historical inquiry bequeathed by Du Bois has been preserved most effectively in the historiography of Marable and Lerone Bennett.[19] Both scholars have challenged conventional historical interpretations and linked historical factors to contemporary development. Their work also emphasizes Africana agency and treats the experiences of people of African descent as a major force shaping the broader social milieu. Marable has made his views accessible to the general public through a syndicated newspaper column and Bennett has reached millions through the pages of *Ebony*. Africana studies analysts use this same approach in establishing the historical foundations of the field and attempt to extend it by integrating it into social science–based research.

Social Science and the Politics of Africana Studies

Efforts to enhance the contribution of social science–based research to Africana studies are informed, in part, by the precedents set by W. E. B. Du Bois, who, at the dawn of the twentieth century, proposed a century-long research program in which ten topics would be studied in succession, one annually, for ten cycles. This proposed methodology can be described as a macro-level panel design that Du Bois believed would produce "a continuous record on the condition and development of a group of 10 to 20 millions of men—a body of sociological material unsurpassed in human annals."[20] This project would have, in essence, extended the approaches used in conducting the studies undertaken under the auspices of, and published by, Atlanta University (1897–1911). The design of these individual studies employed the holistic methodology exhibited in *The Philadelphia Negro*.[21] The methods developed by Du Bois in producing that classic study reflected his belief that "the student of the social problems affecting ethnic minorities must go beyond the group itself . . . [and] must specially notice the environment: the physical environment of city, sections and house, the far mightier social environment— the surrounding world of custom, wish, whim, and thought which envelops this group and powerfully influences its social development."[22] Central to Du Bois's approach was insistence that the research design focus on in-depth analysis of the black experience rather than on comparative research: "the careful exhaustive study of the isolated group, then, is the ideal of the sociologist of the 20th century—from that may come . . . at last careful, cautious generalization and formulation."[23]

This view of social science has important parallels to Karenga's vision of the social science dimension of black/Africana studies. Karenga asserts that "Black Studies, as both an investigative and applied social science, poses the paradigm of theory and practice merging into active self-knowledge which leads to positive social change."[24] Karenga further insists that black/Africana Studies "is a discipline dedicated not only to understanding self, society and the world but also to changing them in a positive developmental way in the interest of human history and advancement."[25] The self-knowledge to which Karenga refers is the in-depth investigation of the experiences of people of African descent, but in this case conducted by black/Africana studies specialists.

Other commentators have proposed radical changes to the manner in which social science research is conceptualized and conducted. In fact, the foundation for a radical view of how black/Africana studies "social science" is conducted was provided in the early 1970s by a group of black social scientists, trained in various disciplines, who called for the creation of a "black social science."[26] Terminology to be employed in research investigations under the purview of a black social science would reject sanitized descriptions and bring oppressive relationships into sharp relief. This transformative linguistic convention would reinforce political commitments to undertake social science–based research to counter racism and discrimination and improve the life circumstances of people of African descent. In the words of Abdul Alkalimat, "the conceptual approach of white social science is only useful on the analytical level of classification since for each term the social content must be specified."[27] In contrast, Alkalimat argues, "the concepts presented for a black social science clearly suggest a specific sociopolitical content to be understood as the race problem."[28] One of the challenges faced by such a thrust is the fact, as articulated by Stanfield, that "writing in the discourse style of the racially oppressed is viewed as unprofessional, as popular literature."[29]

Although the movement to create a black social science lost momentum, it provided a blueprint for the anticipated role of social science–based research within the field of black/Africana studies, per se. Preston Wilcox insists, for example, that generating this type of black studies knowledge base requires "the development of new definitions of old perspectives, an increasing reliance on black self-accreditation and the planful use of institutional understanding."[30] The types of theoretical research consistent with this black social science vision include development of new theoretical concepts, critique and deconstruction of theories used in traditional disciplines, and introduction of innovative observational language to guide applied research. Explicit criteria were to be employed to identify authentic "black/Africana studies" research. To illustrate, William McClendon declares "the relevance of each body of knowledge to black liberation can be determined only through obtaining an understanding of the substantive content."[31] It was clear to early black/Africana studies advocates that not all research would be applied in nature, but it was anticipated that theorists would provide guidance regarding potential applications. This would require, according to Maurice Jackson, "a close relationship between pure and applied roles of science, with a greater stress on application of knowledge."[32]

This vision is similar to that of E. Franklin Frazier, who advocated use of the method of cultural analysis that "takes into account all the factors, psychological, social and economic, which determine the character of any group."[33] Frazier used cultural analysis, coupled with the human ecology model developed at the University of Chicago, to produce path-breaking cross-sectional case studies of black communities in Chicago and New York. The interpretations of empirical data collected and analyzed in these studies were later integrated with quotations from personal documents generated during earlier periods to produce highly narrative-intensive treatises on black families and the "Negro" in the United States. Frazier's analyses subordinated the presentation of empirical data to a supporting role in clarifying the interpretative narrative.

In the vision of modern black social science advocates, producing research comparable to Frazier's requires engaged analysts who have organic ties to the community to be studied. Jerome Harris and William McCullough suggest "black communities must be studied by black people for our own self-interest [because] we cannot afford to be misled by the interpretations and conclusions of statistical studies done by whites who are interested in preserving the status quo. We must gather the data, analyze and interpret them for our own needs and purposes."[34] Contemporary perspectives echo these concerns. John Stanfield declares:

> Research in the social sciences is one of the last areas in U.S. society in which social inequality is taken as a given. It is assumed that researchers have expertise that is beyond the comprehension of those they study. . . . Unless we find adequate ways of liberating the research process in the social sciences, there will be mounting questioning of the relevance of scientific inquiry, especially from the empowering institutions and communities of people of color in the United States and abroad. No longer can social scientists hide behind the ivy-covered walls of academia and their research laboratories, assuming they can study whomever they want to, whenever they please.[35]

Harris's and McCullough's implicit prioritization of inductive, qualitative research approaches over statistical studies is consistent with the thrust of grounded theory, first introduced in the 1960s.[36] Grounded theory was developed as a non-discipline-specific approach to conducting qualitative research. As described by Brian Haig, "grounded theory research begins by focusing on an area of study and gathers data from a variety of sources, including interviews and field observations. Once gathered, the data are analyzed using coding and theoretical sampling procedures. When this is done, theories are generated, with the help of interpretive procedures, before being finally written up and presented."[37]

These techniques can be helpful in overcoming traditional gender biases in social science research, particularly if the research is conducted in sites in which Africana women are highly visible. Such qualitative research can support the work of a variety of analysts who are recovering and reinterpreting the role of Africana women in a variety of settings, including the economy, paid employment, and the professions[38] and politics.[39]

In addition to refining approaches to qualitative research, there are also opportunities to incorporate recent innovations in quantitative methods efforts to enhance the power of social science–based black/Africana studies research. One example is geographic information systems (GIS), which are specialized computer systems for the storage, retrieval, analysis, and display of large volumes of spatial or map type data. GIS allow researchers to integrate data and methods in ways that enable new types of analysis and modeling. With GIS it is possible to map, model, query, and analyze large quantities of data all merged within a single database. This technology allows refinement of both Frazier's ecological approach to black community research as well as a cross-sectional version of Du Bois's multi-panel design. The key is, in the spirit of Du Bois and Frazier, to avoid allowing the data and methods to drive the narrative components of the inquiry, as is the case in much contemporary empirical social science research.

Even with the refinements and extensions suggested above there is a lingering question as to whether the explicit political commitments of black/Africana studies make the use of the term "science" problematic even though research, per se, follows accepted protocols. Stewart proposes an alternative conceptualization of black/Africana studies as a "rational enterprise," using the terminology of Stephen Toulmin.[40] Toulmin argues that rationality is an attribute of procedures by which possible changes in concepts, judgments, and institutions are reviewed and accepted or rejected.[41]

Rationality as it operates in research related to social sciences in black/Africana studies includes the standard criteria applied to scientific research, including consistency, reproducibility, generalizability, coherence, and simplicity. In addition, however, supplemental criteria are employed, including degree of alignment with historical precedents and degree of applicability to community empowerment initiatives. To the extent that these additional criteria are clearly specified and systematically applied, any deviations from the standard scientific approach reflect the unique objectives of Africana studies, rather than underdevelopment of or aberrations from some idealized scientific model. Moreover, the conception of black/Africana studies as a "rational enterprise" provides the conceptual space that allows parallel consideration of the arts and humanities and the intersection of the scientific and artistic/humanistic modes of knowledge generation.

Art and Politics—The Black Aesthetic and Black/Africana Studies

Karenga asserts that "as a humanistic discipline, Black studies shares with other humanities disciplines a concern for and commitment to creative production . . . [and] [i]t shares with literature, art, music, and dance a definite concern with ongoing issues of aesthetics . . . but . . . Black Studies brings its own vision and voice to the discourse in the humanities, contesting the given, crossing boundaries and calling for a new way to understand and approach the human experience."[42] One of the "givens" contested by Africana studies proponents is the traditional view that political influences contaminate the purity of artistic expression. There are, in fact, strong similarities in how the political engagement issue is addressed vis à vis creative production and social science–based research. The Black Arts Movement of the 1960s and early 1970s provides a template for addressing the relationship between art and politics, paralleling the contribution of the black social science movement in clarifying the instrumental dimension of Africana studies.

The Black Arts Movement (BAM) roughly spanned the period 1964–1976 and was linked closely to the ethos of the Black Power movement. The BAM catalyzed the creation of a large body of poems, plays, and essays, much of which employed distinctive expressive modes. Hyperbolic language was marshaled in launching attacks on racism and the organic linguistic conventions associated with African American folk and urban lifestyles were celebrated. New forms of discourse were introduced, including techniques borrowed from various musical genres, especially jazz. Note how this praxis parallels the emphasis on linguistic transformation advocated by black social science proponents. However, the BAM had broader social impact than the efforts of social scientists, in part because cultural production is "polyvocal" and is disseminated by a variety of "cultural transmitters" such as scholars, writers, painters, editors, and popular culture media. African American poets, for example, performed readings for diverse audiences, including students on college campuses across the country, and produced recordings with musicians and choirs, paralleling the outreach initiatives of Africana studies.

The "methodology" employed by African American artists who were part of the BAM also illustrated important parallels to transformative social science initiatives. Black artists altered the traditional use of language, including the coining of new terms and the extensive use of words and phrases from various African languages. They also made special use of "black English." Many of the works that were produced embodied the Africana studies commitment to the primacy of history in examining social conditions, as, for example, in tribute poems celebrating heroic historical figures. The Africana studies emphasis on Africana agency was also reflected in works that celebrated how African Americans had struggled to overcome oppressive conditions.

If creative work, per se, is conceived as the equivalent of applied research undertaken under the auspices of a black social science paradigm component as I have implied in the preceding parallels, then the counterpart to theoretical social science research in artistic/humanistic inquiry is the collective effort to articulate and refine a school of artistic criticism characterized as the Black Aesthetic. Defining and refining a Black Aesthetic was a major focus of academic critics such as Addison Gayle and Stephen Henderson, cultural workers such as Larry Neal and Hoyt Fuller, and poets such as Amiri Baraka and Carolyn Rodgers. Karenga suggests that the Black Aesthetic had two distinct but interrelated meanings—a distinctive mode of aesthetic expression enabling identification of black art, and criteria for judging black art in terms of both creativity and beauty and also in terms of social relevance. The linkage to black/Africana studies per se can be seen from Karenga's observation that "if one combines these two interrelated definitions, the Black aesthetic can be defined as a distinctive mode of artistic expression and a distinctive standard by which Black art can be identified and judged in terms of its creativity and beauty as well as its social relevance."[43] Thus, what theorists sought was a type of rational enterprise, as described previously, with coherent standards and processes to enable judgments regarding content and aesthetic appeal. Consistent application of these standards would promote refinement and maturation of both the artistic and political aspects of cultural production.

Many of the artists who employed a "Black Aesthetic" used approaches that displayed important similarities to the efforts by Africana studies specialists to develop interdisciplinary modes of inquiry. Several of the BAM poets used jazz to frame their poetry, especially "free jazz." The BAM artists prioritized the militant dimensions of jazz, reinterpreted the music, and disseminated these interpretations through poetry.

This poetry-based musicology approach obviously differs dramatically from traditional musicological inquiries that examine jazz and other black musical genres.

However, the efforts of BAM poets do bear important similarities to approaches developed by some ethnomusicologists affiliated with Africana studies. These ethnomusicologists examine the functions of music within black cultures and how social forces shaped the content and form of the music. This ethnomusicological approach is reflected, for example, in the title of Jackson's edited volume, *More Than Dancing*.[44] Portia Maultsby and Mellonee Burnim at Indiana University are making important contributions to this mode of inquiry.

The BAM has been challenged by critics who oppose many of its dimensions and in particular some that are shared with Africana studies. In particular, the BAM has been criticized for its constructions of "blackness," manhood, and womanhood. One body of research focuses on excavating the distinctive literary and artistic traditions of Africana women.[45] There are also ongoing initiatives designed to establish the contours of a black feminist school of artistic and literary criticism reflecting the particular stance of Africana women.[46]

Some other contemporary critics champion a "new Black Aesthetic."[47] This new Black Aesthetic employs discourse analysis of texts in an attempt to explore dimensions of African American literature that go beyond "the race problem." While the right of creative artists and critics to approach their subject matter from any vantage point is not subject to challenge, this artistic and critical approach obviously lies outside the boundaries of the conception of Africana studies framed in the introduction. Africana studies is concerned especially with the products of cultural workers who self-consciously approach their craft as a vehicle to foster social change and whose cultural products embody themes, linguistic conventions, and images congruent with the vision of Africana studies.

Stewart suggests three general criteria for assessing the degree of alignment between specific creative/critical cultural products and black/Africana studies. The three proposed criteria are (1) the degree of complementarity between the values and images found in a work or approach and those undergirding black/Africana studies (discussed previously), (2) the degree to which the special significance of history and historical explanations of contemporary phenomena are reflected, and (3) the extent to which cultural workers self-consciously approach their craft as a vehicle to foster social change.⁴⁸ An historical precedent for this approach is provided by Du Bois, who spoke of "a certain group expression of Negro art which included essays examining Black life, aspirations and the problems of the color line, autobiographies of former slaves and notable Blacks, poetry, novels, paintings, sculpture, music, and plays which emerged organically from the collective experience."⁴⁹ Elaborating on this position, Du Bois emphasized the instrumental role of creative work:

> For the development of Negro genius, of Negro literature and art, of Negro spirit, only Negroes bound and welded together, Negroes inspired by one vast ideal, can work out in its fullness the great message we have for humanity. . . . For the accomplishment of these ends we need race organizations, a Negro school of literature and art, and an intellectual clearing house, for all these products of the Negro mind, which we may call a Negro Academy. Not only is all this necessary for positive advance, it is absolutely imperative for negative defense.⁵⁰

The preceding description of the parallels between approaches to artistic and humanistic research and cultural production and social science research in black/Africana studies establishes the foundations for the exploration of inter-modal (synthesis of social science–based and artistic/humanistic) research strategies. Preliminary efforts to outline such an approach have been undertaken by some Africana studies theorists, including Perry Hall.⁵¹ However, a functional synthesis of scientific and humanistic approaches to inquiry first requires an understanding of the possibilities and constraints associated with intra-modal interdisciplinary research, that is, research spanning several social science disciplinary boundaries and research spanning two or more artistic/humanistic disciplines.

The Rocky Road from Multidisciplinary to Interdisciplinary Research

W. E. B. Du Bois averred, "scientific work must be sub-divided, but conclusions that affect the whole subject must be based on study of the whole."⁵² The contours of Africana studies reflect ongoing efforts to implement Du Bois's dictum through the use of various strategies designed to overcome the constraints of traditional disciplinary boundaries.

Some early proponents conceived of the enterprise largely as a complement to traditional artistic/humanistic and social science disciplines.⁵³ Scholars operating from this mindset attempted to make the case for the existence of a distinct Africana studies enterprise using what has been characterized as a "value-added rationale" linked to a "weak conception of multi/inter-disciplinarity."[54] In this view black/Africana studies adds value by extending the explanatory power of traditional disciplines. Proponents of a weak multi/inter-disciplinary model of Africana studies take existing disciplinary demarcations as given and assume because the subject matter is examined by specialists trained in several disciplines, the collective product qualifies as multidisciplinary or interdisciplinary. As a consequence, virtually no attention is devoted to the comparative study of the underlying characteristics of research studies across disciplines.

Focusing on the social sciences, consider the following potential description of social science–based research in black/Africana studies: Black studies is the collection of social science–based studies generated by a distinct subset of analysts identified with various traditional disciplines using standard theories and observational languages to examine various aspects of the experiences of people of African descent. In this model the knowledge base of Africana studies is determined by forces internal to individual traditional disciplines, although a limited means exists based on authorship for identifying a set of studies that presumably could comprise the "core" of Africana studies. However, there is no procedure by which evidence is used to evaluate the distinct Africana studies explanatory power of research studies as opposed to the value to traditional disciplines. There is also no provision for reconciling differences in the theoretical and observational vocabularies across different disciplines. Resolving these issues involves developing decision rules regarding (1) what constitutes evidence for assessing theoretical coherence, and (2) what characteristics a theory must embody to make it a candidate for acceptance on the basis of the available evidence. In cases where conceptual change is involved, problems associated with the modification of the meanings of terms used to formulate theories also emerge. These issues cannot be resolved in this model, in part, because there is no vehicle for systematic collaboration among scholars from different disciplines. Even though analysts involved in conducting studies may interact at conferences and discuss strategies for moving toward a consensus in defining the scope and boundaries of Africana studies, there is no process whereby a unique body of knowledge or interdisciplinary methodology emerges.

To address the issues described above requires a conception of multi/inter-disciplinarity that rejects or ignores traditional disciplinary demarcations. One approach, suggested by Karenga, defines Africana studies as "an interdisciplinary discipline [with] seven basic subject areas." Karenga insists:

> These intradisciplinary foci which at first seem to be disciplines themselves are, in fact, separate disciplines when they are outside the discipline of

Black Studies, but inside, they become and are essentially subject areas which contribute to a holistic picture and approach to the Black experience. Moreover, the qualifier Black, attached to each area in an explicit or implicit way, suggests a more specialized and delimited focus which of necessity transforms a broad discipline into a particular subject area. The seven basic subject areas of Black Studies then are: Black History; Black Religion; Black Social Organization; Black Politics; Black Economics; Black Creative Production (Black Art, Music and Literature); and Black Psychology.[55]

The critical question raised by Karenga's assertions is, of course, "What exactly does the transformation from discipline to subject area involve and what are the implications for conducting research?" There is good reason to expect significant unevenness in the transformative process due to extensive variation across disciplines with respect to their interface with Africana studies. The specific character of disciplinary interfaces also affects both how, and the extent to which, Africana studies specialists are able to transform or translate discipline-generated constructs into forms appropriate to black/Africana studies. One consequence of these difficulties is that most subject matter investigations claiming multidisciplinary or interdisciplinary status are actually only loosely connected collections of studies performed by specialists in different disciplines. Such anthologies typically fail to present theoretical or empirical syntheses that unequivocally differentiate the product from discipline-based research.

The volume *Black Families: Interdisciplinary Perspectives* provides an interesting case study.[56] The examination of families fits under Karenga's "Social Organization" category. Consistent with the criteria suggested previously for identifying black/Africana studies research, the volume begins with an examination of historical approaches to the study of black families that identifies approaches consistent with the values of black/Africana studies. The organization of subsequent chapters is designed to incorporate Du Bois's view, noted previously, that studies of minority groups must be undertaken within the context of the larger environment with which they interact. Thus the second section of the book explores ecological perspectives, in the spirit of Du Bois and Frazier. The authors of the individual chapters represent various disciplines including child development and family relations, counselor education, education, economics, psychology, religious studies, social welfare/social work, and sociology. And the studies provide wide geographical coverage, including not only the United States, but also parts of Africa and the Caribbean. Consistent with the instrumental mission of Africana studies, the last section addresses policy and social service delivery implications. On all criteria that have been discussed, then, this work would seem to qualify as bona fide black/Africana studies research. Despite this fact, however, it fails the test of authentic interdisciplinarity. Only three of the studies are coauthored and only one of these by coauthors in different disciplines. In addition, the volume includes no attempt to produce the type of interdisciplinary theoretical or empirical synthesis described above.

The preceding self-criticism is designed to emphasize the difficulties associated with attempting to undertake interdisciplinary social science research. Achieving the ideal type of interdisciplinary synthesis outlined previously will require significant creativity and extremely innovative explorations. Experimental research involving multidisciplinary teams will be required to generate consensus around interdisciplinary observational categories. Qualitative research, especially that conducted by multidisciplinary teams employing grounded theory techniques, could play an important role in moving toward the desired types of syntheses. There are, in fact, techniques available to pursue these objectives.[57]

Experimental approaches are needed to develop interdisciplinary models and multidimensional outcome predictions that span several disciplinary boundaries. As an example, GIS methodologies, described previously, allow sequential or simultaneous layering of maps of a given geographical space, describing distributions of various measures on top of each other. Specialists, using analytical tools associated with several traditional disciplines, could map variables relevant to a particular topic, consistent with Karenga's subject matter approach to interdisciplinarity, for a defined geographical area. These maps could then be layered on top of each other and the overlaps in the distributions could be examined to identify interdisciplinary correlations. Since GIS also enables the development of new metrics, the overlapping map distributions could provide the content of new interdisciplinary metrics. These metrics could then be used to develop and test interdisciplinary theories exploring how the complex of factors influences the various outcome measures. Imagine the potential of a system in which dozens or hundreds of map layers are arrayed to display information about transportation networks, population characteristics, economic activity, political jurisdictions, and other characteristics of the natural and social environments.

Finally, experimentation is also needed to develop new approaches to multiple authoring of research studies. Specifically, online simultaneous multiple authorship strategies should be attempted in an effort to force researchers to write across disciplines rather than simply having authors from different disciplines write separate sections of joint research reports. The most useful starting point for initiating the type of interdisciplinary collaborations advocated here is increased use of multidisciplinary team teaching approaches in black/Africana studies classroom instruction.

Although the preceding discussion has focused on social science–related research, similar arguments can be made with respect to the arts and humanities. Houston Baker declares "the contextualization of a work of literary or verbal art, from the perspective of the anthropology of art, is an 'interdisciplinary' enterprise in the most contemporary sense of that word."[58] His approach is grounded in the "anthropology of art," which employs guiding assumptions that are "coextensive with basic tenets of the Black Aesthetic insofar as both prospects assert that works of Afro-American literature and verbal art can not be adequately understood unless they are contextualized with the interdependent systems of Afro-American culture." However, Baker also insists "the anthropology of art departs from . . . the Black Aesthetic . . . in its assumption that art cannot be studied without serious attention to the methods and models of many disciplines." He contends, "rather than ignoring (or denigrating) the research and insights of scholars in the nature [sic], social, and behavioral sciences, the anthropology of art views such efforts as positive, rational attempts to comprehend the full dimensions of human behavior. And such efforts serve the literary-theoretical investigator as guides and contributions to an understanding of the symbolic dimensions of human behavior that comprise Afro-American literature and verbal art."[59]

Baker's comments regarding the interface between social science and arts/humanities provide a useful transition to a more detailed exploration of the possibilities for inter-modal (scientific-artistic/humanistic) research in Africana studies.

Building a Bridge over Troubled Waters— Synthesizing Social Science–based and Artistic/Humanistic Research in Africana Studies

Several authors are attempting to develop new theoretical and operational approaches to conducting inter-modal research. As an example, Hall has proposed a set of principles to guide further development of Africana studies research that emphasize the interaction of external, objective (systematic) forces (or conditions) on social structure, with internal, subjective (thematic) forces (or conditions) on cultural sensibility, as the processes that are primarily responsible for shaping the lives of black individuals and black communities at any given historical moment.[60]

My own approach to establishing a foundation for inter-modal research involves challenging selected assumptions associated with social science research that create artificial barriers to dialogue and translation of information. One strategy involves reconceptualizing multi-person interdisciplinary scientific research using a "jazz" model of Africana studies.[61] The second strategy involves applying discourse theory to describe research by individuals or teams that combines social scientific and artistic/humanistic information sources using the work of Teun Van Dijk.[62]

The jazz model of Africana studies treats a musical composition performed by a jazz ensemble as the analog of an interdisciplinary investigation by a team of black/Africana studies specialists.[63] This model extends the approach to interpreting black music introduced by black poets involved in the BAM. Individual instruments are the counterparts to individual academic disciplines, with the unique sound produced by each corresponding to the specific emphasis of each academic discipline. The combined voice of the instruments tells a story in the same way as a narrative account produced by a research team. Although one instrument (discipline) may be showcased through solos, the basic model of the ensemble is democratic.

Polyrhythms in jazz compositions are the analogs of complex explanations of phenomena. And the role of history in Africana studies is reflected in jazz in the privileged role assigned to the drums and in the technique of "quoting," that is, playing portions of other pieces in a jazz composition. This practice obviously correlates to the standard practice of citing previous works in research studies. Improvisation in the jazz model can be interpreted as the exploration of new ideas, building on an established body of knowledge.

The different types of jazz, such as bebop, hard bop, and free jazz, are the equivalent of the different schools of thought or paradigms within Africana studies. From time to time paradigm shifts have occurred, as is the case in academic disciplines. And, as in scientific revolutions,[64] paradigm shifts in jazz have involved radical changes in style, content, and technique. When radical new styles emerge, traditional evaluative criteria become irrelevant, just as in the case of scientific revolutions.

The combination of the various characteristics discussed above enables jazz ensembles to create the equivalent of an interdisciplinary Africana studies analysis that is more than simply the sum of the individual performances. The composition is transformed into a collective statement that is irreducible to the contribution of individual instruments. Jazz performers face tripartite scrutiny from peers, audiences, and formal critics. The analogs for Africana studies specialists are academic peers, students, constituencies served through outreach, and academic administrators. Consistent with the instrumental focus of Africana studies, the audience is the most important source of evaluation. This does not mean that technical merit is irrelevant. Individual jazz performers and ensembles are formally and informally evaluated using various criteria, including technical precision, phrasing, and clarity of sound. In a similar vein, the peer review process used in scientific and artistic/humanistic research performs the same role of quality control. The political commitments of black/Africana studies are also found in jazz. Examples include Charlie Mingus's albums, *Fables for Faubus* and *Scenes of the City*, Max Roach's *We Insist: Freedom Now* and *Garvey's Ghost*, and Sonny Rollins's *Freedom Suite*. Consistent with the focus of BAM poets, revolutionary jazz forms such as free jazz are more representative of the type of Africana studies enterprise outlined in this analysis than more "mainstreamed" jazz genres.

This jazz model of Africana studies synthesizes the more useful features of scientific and humanistic approaches to inquiry while overcoming some of their most debilitating weaknesses. It relaxes the standard expectation in social science that research results be replicable if a work is to be accepted as valid. In its place the jazz model suggests an approach that assigns a crucial role to improvisation in a simultaneous process of generating new insights and implementing policies designed to enhance subjects' well-being. In other words, an individual researcher or research team is expected to conduct an interdisciplinary or multidisciplinary investigation using appropriate quantitative and qualitative methods, develop policy recommendations, work with subjects in designing an implementation plan, evaluate the outcomes, and perform a follow-up study to ascertain if the desired changes have occurred. In this model replication would produce a suboptimal inquiry. Improvisation is critical in designing interventions, evaluation criteria, and modifications to original interventions to increase program effectiveness. The second study and modified interventions constitute a different "performance" than the original undertaking.

While this model overcomes some of the methodological hurdles discussed previously, the jazz metaphor also reinforces the earlier cautions regarding gendered constructs. Both the expression of women's experiences and their roles have been circumscribed in jazz and in Africana studies. The role of women in jazz is disproportionately that of vocalist, rather than musician, paralleling the underrepresentation of Africana women as acknowledged theorists and analysts in Africana studies.

Discourse theory provides another means of dismantling disabling conceptions of differences between social scientific and artistic/humanistic investigations. Discourse analysis, according to Van Dijk, "has a double aim: a systematic theoretical and descriptive account of (a) the structures and strategies, at various levels, of written and spoken discourse, seen both as a textual 'object' and as a form of sociocultural practice and interaction, and (b) the relationships of these properties of text and talk with the relevant structures of their cognitive, social, cultural, and historical 'contexts.' In sum, discourse analysis studies texts in context."[65] Van Dijk argues that "discourse plays a central role not only in the 'text' studies of the humanities, but also in the social sciences" and that "the now fashionable 'postmodern' uses of the concept of 'discourse' have not always contributed to our understanding of the complex structures, strategies, mechanisms or processes of text talk in their socio-cultural or political contexts."[66]

From the standpoint of discourse analysis, we can treat a literary text or work of art as embodying information analogous to quantitative or qualitative data examined by social scientists. Conversely, a social science research report is a form of discourse with some characteristics similar to those of literary/artistic texts. The key is to develop a correspondence system that allows comparisons and cross-translation, that is, a type of multimodal triangulation approach to information verification. A key principle that can guide such translation efforts is that social science standards that define appropriate sample sizes in qualitative studies must be applied stringently to literary/artistic works. Thus, an individual character or aggregate character constitutes one observation or case and defensible generalizations can only be generated from comparative studies of sufficient artistic/literary works to satisfy social science guidelines. The growing digitization of artistic/literary works can enable the type of comparison of literary and artistic works necessary to satisfy traditional sample size guidelines.

As in earlier discussions, it is important to recognize the gendered character of discourse. As an example, Bettye Collier-Thomas has documented the distinctive approaches to sermons developed and delivered by black women preachers.[67] In a similar vein, Yvonna Johnson examines the distinctive use of narrative and authorial voice in the works of selected historical and contemporary black female authors.[68]

The potential power of synthesizing information generated through social scientific and literary/artistic inquiry is illustrated in the work of

W. E. B. Du Bois. As observed by Aptheker, Du Bois's works exhibited a "literary tendency . . . which took the form of rather exaggerated assertions or a kind of symbolism that in the interest of effect might sacrifice precision."[69] Du Bois characterizes the book *The World and Africa* as history even though he admitted that "the weight of history and science support me only in part and in some cases appears violently to contradict me."[70]

Du Bois's relaxation of the traditional guidelines governing historical and scientific research enabled him to explore potential complementarities between historical research and fiction in the analysis and portrayal of the experiences of people of African descent. In the postscript to the first volume of his fictional trilogy, *The Black Flame*, Du Bois laments that the work was not history in the strict disciplinary sense and cites limitations in terms of time and money as factors forcing him to abandon pure historical research in favor of the method of historical fiction "to complete the cycle of history which [had] for a half century engaged [his] thought, research and action."[71] At the same time, Du Bois insists that the foundation of the book was "documented and verifiable fact" although he freely admits that in some cases he had resorted "to pure imagination in order to make unknown and unknowable history relate an ordered tale to the reader" and in other cases small changes had been made in the exact sequence of historical events. Du Bois claims this methodology was superior to the tendency of historians to "pretend we know far more than we do," provided that the methodology was explicitly acknowledged beforehand. The characters in Du Bois's novels provided him with a means for developing a correspondence system between participant observation methodologies and representative depictions of the everyday life of black people. This linkage simply reflects his acceptance of a variant of phenomenological sociology as a critical element in his research design.[72]

Stewart offers an example of the synthesis of works by two different subjects working in different modalities in his comparison of the treatment of male sharing relationships (romantic triangles) in a qualitative social science study[73] and in the songs of rhythm and blues singer Millie Jackson.[74] He concludes that Millie Jackson's treatment of the sharing phenomenon embodies a nuanced and complex description comparable to that presented in the social science study. The content and structure of the interviews included in the social science study displayed significant parallels to the narrative discourse in Jackson's songs. Stewart argues that these parallels allow the treatment of the two sets of information as parallels.

Another study uses Du Bois's representations of the psychological conflicts of characters in his novels to compare the efficacy of three contemporary approaches to the analysis of African American identity dynamics developed by psychologists.[75] These fictional "cases" are used as analogs to qualitative data collected through traditional research methodologies, thereby dislodging the study of character development from traditional literary criticism. It also disconnects psychological discourse from its standard disciplinary moorings. The methodology also disregarded conventional conceptions of temporal boundaries on knowledge validity since the formal models of identity dynamics examined were developed to explore contemporary issues, while the data used to assess them are historical.

The increasing availability of both social science and literary texts in digital on-line formats enables more intense exploration of similarities across modes of inquiry through various types of string searches. Such searches can facilitate identification of common themes and enable new modes of structuring and disseminating research studies. Relaxing artificially imposed strictures on research designs and methods and making effective use of new information analysis techniques can promote the instrumental goals of black/Africana studies by speeding up the process of getting information into policy development and implementation channels.

Du Bois recognized the need for expedited research and dissemination processes, and he established forums for the direct sharing of academic research with practitioners involved in efforts to improve the status of black Americans as part of the design of the Atlanta conferences. However, he came to view these initiatives as insufficient: "I saw before me a problem that could not and would not await the last word of science, but demanded immediate action to prevent social death."[76] This conclusion led Du Bois, at least for a time, to abandon scientific research in favor of producing popularly-oriented propaganda treatises. It also catalyzed his experiments with conjoining scientific and literary/humanistic modes of knowledge generation and dissemination to reduce the time required for research to impact the lives of his constituents, which provide a model for those who believe that this is possible in Africana studies.

While the original vision and orientation of Africana studies continue to provide the foundation for the field, it is important to recognize that new areas of inquiry and competing ideological and ontological orientations have emerged. Some new approaches to inquiry challenge the validity of some core constructs underlying much of the Africana studies research conducted over the last thirty-odd years, such as postmodernist critiques of traditional racial classifications. Others challenge the emphasis on the experiences of African Americans in the United States compared to the experiences of people of African descent in other parts of the African diaspora. Researchers identifying themselves as Africana studies specialists should be aware of the thrust of these challenges as well as the implications for theory development, research design, information and data collection strategies, and interpretation of findings.

Contemporary Research Issues in Africana Studies

Africana women's studies, African diaspora studies, and Afrocentricity are three of the most widely discussed issues among scholars in Africana studies. While each constitutes a reaction to aspects of the original thrust of Africana studies, each also poses specific methodological challenges for researchers similar to those associated with the foundational perspective as discussed in previous sections.

Africana Women's Studies

There is no question that Africana studies faces a continuing challenge of combating the invisibility of Africana women in the public sphere and the marginalization of their historical and contemporary voices. This is, of course, not a challenge that is unique to Africana studies, rather it is one that derives from the patriarchal nature of most societies and is reflected in all fields and modes of inquiry. As Barbara Omolade argues:

> The historical oppression of black women and men should have created social equality between them, but even after the end of slavery when the white patriarch receded, maleness and femaleness continued to be defined by patriarchal structures, with black men declaring wardship over black women. In the black community, the norm of manhood was patriarchal power, the norm of womanhood was adherence to it, though both men and women selected which aspects of these norms they would emphasize.[77]

An Africana studies approach would be expected to reflect the emphases on agency and the importance of historical forces in shaping current conditions. Scholars associated with Africana studies must also be self-critical about the ways in which discussions of epistemological and methodological issues and research studies have marginalized Africana women. Given these requirements, the operative question is whether a distinct body of research exists that examines Africana women in a manner consistent with the view of Africana Studies outlined in the preceding sections. A corollary issue is, of course, how Africana studies–related gender-focused research differs from that associated with other disciplines or intellectual approaches.

There are two distinct contemporary approaches to the study of women of African descent that differ across all three dimensions of Africana studies discussed previously, that is, ideological, academic, and instrumental. Black feminism[78] is more closely aligned with feminism and women's studies than with Africana studies, per se. Ideologically, this feminist approach, while clearly recognizing the devastation associated with oppression based on race, prioritizes the issue of oppression based on gender and emphasizes the study of patterns of gender oppression among people of African descent. While Africana womanist scholars[79] also recognize the importance of gender-based oppression, they focus on its intersection and overlap with racial oppression as intertwined forces diminishing the well-being of Africana women. Their point of view is obviously much more closely aligned with the original vision of Africana studies.

The differences in views about the value of knowledge for social change, the instrumental dimension, flow directly from the differences in ideology. Black feminists focus their activism primarily in alliance with progressive elements of the women's movement. In contrast, Africana womanists work both collectively to address Africana women's issues and in cooperation with Africana men and Africana studies organizations to address racial oppression.

In the academic domain, both schools of thought draw upon the work by historians in excavating the history of Africana women in the United States, discussed previously. The Association of Black Women Historians has been an important catalyst, supporting efforts by black female historians to produce authentic historical research examining Africana women in the United States. Africana womanists and black feminists interpret the historical record through very different lenses and the same can be said of studies of traditional and contemporary African societies. As an example, Charlyn Harper-Bolton offers an Africana women's perspective of male-female relationships in traditional Africa that emphasizes collaboration and role flexibility.[80] In contrast, from a feminist perspective Filomina Chioma Steady has questioned the functionality of traditional gender roles in contemporary Africa.[81]

Much of the debate and discourse about the status and barriers to equality faced by Africana women reflect perspectives from the arts and humanities, including theological inquiries.[82] There is, surprisingly, relatively little social science–based research that can inform continuing efforts to refine the competing perspectives. The need for a more focused social science–inspired research effort is suggested by the comments of Patricia Hill Collins:

> On certain dimensions Black women may more closely resemble Black men; on others, white women; and on still others Black women may stand apart from both groups. Black women's both/and conceptual orientation, the act of being simultaneously a member of a group and yet standing apart from it, forms an integral part of Black women's consciousness.[83]

The absence of a significant body of social and behavioral science research examining identity dynamics among women of African descent clearly fuels some of the disagreement between Africana womanists and black feminists. Black psychologists have been largely silent on the issue of whether gender differences in socialization create variations in the process of developing self-efficacy and/or in cultivating racial identity. As an example, Adelbert Jenkins admits, "except at certain explicit points I do not distinguish between psychological issues affecting Black women as distinct from those affecting Black men."[84] In a similar vein, Cross acknowledges the possibility that there are gender-specific differences in the processes by which racial identity develops and changes, but fails to address this issue systematically.[85]

Efforts to address this research lacuna must make use of both quantitative and qualitative methods, as is the case for Africana studies generally. Such an approach is absolutely essential to overcome existing biases that constrain the understanding of the gender dimensions of identity development, especially as it relates to women of African descent outside metropolitan capitalist countries. As Kim Vaz opines, "alternative methods of carrying out research [are needed] that are not heavily dependent on technology, [so that] our information about women in developing countries [does not] become [simply] the study of women's behavior in the developed world."[86] Vaz's comments emphasize the need to extend the scope of inquiry beyond the experiences of people of African descent in the United States.

James Turner, director of Cornell's Africana Studies and Research Center, has spearheaded one of the most innovative contemporary efforts to increase the voice of women in Africana studies. Specifically, the Summer Institutes on Critical Theory, Black Women Scholarship, and Africana Studies, held in 2002 and 2003, have proved forums for the exploration of various research topics and the creation of new research collaborations that should facilitate the ongoing efforts to engender Africana studies.

African Diaspora Studies

Expanded study of populations of people of African descent living in parts of the African diaspora other than the United States is an important recent development in the continuing evolution of Africana studies. As is the case for the other issues discussed previously, there are multiple approaches to such inquiries. One of the most important contributions of this collective body of research has been to introduce a comparative perspective into discourses about race, identity, patterns of oppression and exploitation, liberation struggles, and other issues. Comparative perspectives are imperative for refining constructs and perspectives in Africana studies developed from studies focusing exclusively on descendants of Africans directly transported into what is now the United States through the Atlantic slave trade.

There are significant differences among the various approaches to African diaspora studies. The school of thought least aligned with the original vision of Africana studies has been advanced by "Black Atlantic" proponents, originating in the United Kingdom, whose work is informed by the European postmodernist "cultural studies" movement.[87] Misalignment with traditional Africana studies exists across several dimensions of this scholarly tradition. Postmodernists claim that texts have no fixed meanings and that readers supply their own meanings that diverge from authors' intentions. This attack on traditional linguistic conventions and modes of interpretation is advanced as an assault on the ways in which linguistic conventions are used to create and maintain hierarchial relations. This perspective challenges general assumptions associated with traditional historical and social science research. These viewpoints undergird Black Atlantic scholars' challenge to the usefulness of traditional racial classifications and their emphasis on hybridity as a construct for interpreting the experiences of people of African descent (outside of Africa). Interest in this approach within the United States has been fueled, in part, by the increasing contemporary immigration of people of African descent whose personal identities and reference group orientation differ from domestic African Americans and by the emerging domestic biracial movement.

In a historical and analytical sense, there is nothing particularly novel about the general concept of hybridity or attempts to use it as an alternative to traditional racial classifications. As an example in 1936, Edwin Embree proclaimed: "A new race is growing up in America. Its skin is brown. . . . The new race numbers 12 million in the United States, and other millions in the West Indies and Central America. The group is new in its biological make-up; in its culture it is almost entirely cut off from the ancient African home."[88] Similar views have been advanced in contemporary scholarship associated with traditional disciplines rather than cultural studies, as demonstrated, for example, by Joel Williamson's study of miscegenation in the United States.[89] In fact, African-centered authors writing outside the cultural studies tradition have recognized and incorporated notions of hybridity into their analytical frames of reference. As an example, comparing Paul Gilroy's framework of analysis with that of Ngugi wa Thiongo and Molefi Asante, Balogun observes, "Ngugi's and Asante's universalist particularism . . . recognizes a hybridity which does not preclude cultural rootedness . . . [and] promote[s] a literary criticism that frowns on racist essentialism at the same time as it encourages a discussion of both hybrid and culturally rooted literary elements . . . as fluid and coexistent cultural phenomena."[90]

The cultural studies–influenced approach to African diaspora studies can be usefully contrasted to one approach championed by Sheila Walker.[91] Walker's volume is the product of an international conference on the African Diaspora and the Modern World held in 1996. Contributors to the volume include historians; linguists; creative writers and literary scholars; social, cultural, and physical anthropologists; journalists; filmmakers; music and dance scholars; and political and cultural activists, reflecting the multidisciplinary emphasis of Africana studies. Walker describes the overall thrust of the volume as "the beginning of a comparative analysis of African diasporan societies and phenomena from an Afrogenic perspective that focuses on African and African diasporan agency, participation, and contributions."[92] For Walker, "Afrogenic simply means growing out of the histories, ways of knowing, and interpretations and interpretive styles of African and African Diasporan people."[93] The overall view of the African diaspora in the Americas, projected by Walker, is of "a vast, multidimensional puzzle in which some of the pieces were brought from Africa and have maintained recognizable identities, and other pieces were created in the Americas based on Afrogenic conceptual foundations."[94] Note that Walker's approach to the study of the African diaspora prioritizes the *original* involuntary formation of the diaspora rather than late twentieth-century voluntary migration that cultural studies adherents foreground. Collectively, Walker insists "the comparative study of African Diasporan societies and their roles in their nations, in addition to demonstrating similar patterns of misrepresentation, also highlights significant commonalities in both sociocultural forms and in the underlying principles that give them meaning."[95]

There is obvious alignment between Walker's conception of African diaspora studies and the vision of Africana studies described previously. Whereas Walker's approach emphasizes cultural similarities and historical continuities originating in Africa, the Black Atlantic model is an example of what Walker characterizes as the imposition of Eurogenic meanings rather than recognizing "the deep structural Afrogenic meanings of the same phenomena."[96]

In many respects, Walker's approach to Africana studies provides a blueprint for extending the original vision of Africana studies without the wholesale disruption reflected in the Black Atlantic approach. As discussed below, the concept of Afrogenic scholarship is also very similar to that associated with Afrocentricity. Interestingly, the Afrogenic approach to the study of the African diaspora has been very favorably received while Afrocentricity remains the most controversial construct within Africana studies.

Afrocentricity

Afrocentricity is one of the most discussed and least understood formulations that has been developed as part of the ongoing evolution of Africana studies. The confusion typically derives from concerns in some circles about some discourses that are assumed to be at the core of Afrocentric approaches to Africana studies. These discourses include those that focus on interpretations of classical and traditional African societies and those that offer prescriptions for transforming individual behavior that focus on reconstructing selected aspects of traditional African psychology, values, and behaviors in the present.

The essential claim of Afrocentrists is, however, simply that the liberation of people of African descent can be fostered if their interests are prioritized in personal and collective decision making. The critical issue then becomes (a) how to identify those interests, (b) how to cultivate a shared commitment to pursuing those interests, and (c) how to develop institutions and movements to operationalize those interests. To illustrate, Asante suggests that Afrocentricity entails "placing African ideals at the center of any analysis that involves African culture and behavior."[97] In a similar vein, Karenga suggests that Afrocentricity entails thought and practice "rooted in the cultural image and human interests of African people."[98] The work of Cheikh Anta Diop provides the foundations for contemporary Afrocentric theorizing and research.[99] Diop's work is multidisciplinary and incorporates biological, archaeological, anthropological, and linguisitic evidence to support a model of the cultural unity of black Africa.

In contrast to popular belief, Afrocentric theorists do not posit the existence of impermeable boundaries of race and culture as they relate to scholarly inquiry. To illustrate, Asante suggests that as a theory, Afrocentricity "is not, nor can it be based on biological determinism. Anyone willing to submit to the discipline of learning the concepts and methods may acquire the knowledge necessary for analysis."[100] Afrocentricity is linked integrally to what Asante describes as Africalogy. Africalogy is defined as "the Afrocentric study of African concepts, issues, and behaviors."[101] Asante asserts, in the spirit of Karenga,[102] that "Africalogy is a separate and distinct field of study from the composite sum of its initial founding disciplines,"[103] that is, seven subject fields comparable to those specified by Karenga.[104] In addition, the geographical locus of the field is defined as the African world, that is, "Wherever people declare themselves as African, despite the distance from the continent or the recentness of their outmigration," a concept that "includes Africa, the Americas, the Caribbean, various regions of Asia and the Pacific."[105] Africalogy is said to incorporate three paradigmatic approaches: functional, categorical, and etymological.[106] According to Asante, "The Afrocentrist seeks to uncover and use codes, paradigms, symbols, motifs, myths, and circles of discussion that reinforce the centrality of African ideals and values as a valid frame of reference for acquiring and examining data."[107] This approach is inspired by various critiques of the epistemologies and ontologies that undergird contemporary Western civilization. For example, Marimba Ani has provided an extensive critique of European cultural thought and behavior.[108]

Although there has been no overt cross-fertilization, the framing of methodological issues in Walker's Afrogenic approach to the study of the African diaspora, discussed previously, clearly overlaps with Asante's articulation of the principles of Afrocentric research. And Afrocentric and Afrogenic approaches also agree on the scope and foci of inquiry. Asante defines Africalogy as "systematic exploration of relationships, social codes, cultural and commercial customs, and oral traditions and proverbs, although interpretation of communicative behaviors, as expressed in discourse, spoken or written, and techniques found in jazz studies and urban street-vernacular signifying, is also included."[109]

A significant body of Afrocentric research literature examining a variety of topics is beginning to appear. Various authors, including Cecil Conteen Gray,[110] are exploring the intellectual foundations of Afrocentric thought. Topical and philosophical perspectives on historiography are offering new perspectives on the conduct of historical research on Africa and in the diaspora.[111] As an example, Barbara Faggins offers an interesting exploration of contacts between Africans and Native Americans in colonial Virginia. Several edited volumes attempt to demonstrate the wide potential reach of Afrocentric research, including James Conyers's *Afrocentricity and the Academy* and Ana Mazama's *The Afrocentric Paradigm*.[112] There is also specialized research focusing on the arts and aesthetics, including that by Kariamce Welsh-Asante.[113]

Despite these developments, the radical nature of the ontological, epistemological, and theoretical challenges to traditional modes of inquiry reflected by Afrocentricity needs to be articulated in a more coherent fashion that both facilitates the development of methodological guidelines and reduces the confusion that continues to cloud discussions of Afrocentricity. As an example, Stanfield insists "it is important to keep in mind that the major inroads Afrocentric reasoning has made in academic circles have been more in the humanities and history than in the social sciences" in part because "such inquiries do not need to be subjected to rigorous tests of empirical relevance to be acceptable in professional humanistic communities."[114] Afrocentric research can be guided by the suggestion offered by Duane Champagne, that it is necessary to study "group processes of institutional change within their transocietal and historical contexts" so that empirical knowledge can be accumulated "about specific processes of social change."[115] Based on this evidence, Champagne argues, "theory can be generated by inductive means, through comparisons of results from accumulated historical and comparative studies."[116] Champagne's comments suggest the potential power of synthesizing Walker's "Afrogenic" approach to comparative studies of communities in the African diaspora with Asante's more global Afrocentric orientation.

Emerging Methodological Challenges and Opportunities

As Africana studies continues to evolve, it is imperative that researchers develop a familiarity with the intellectual history of the field, contemporary schools of thought, and methodological options available for studying various social phenomena. Two publications by Delores Aldridge and Carlene Young and Nathaniel Norment provide important collections of historical and contemporary perspectives on Africana studies.[117] Further refinement of methodological approaches in black/Africana studies that build on the original vision will require changes in the focus of graduate training and targeted professional development efforts for existing faculty/researchers. Both students and current professionals must take up the challenge to contest conventional assumptions and experiment with unconventional methods of researching and interpreting the complex experiences of people of African descent throughout history and in all geographical spaces.

It is also important to recognize that unlike most traditional disciplines, non-authorial agents and institutions continue to shape directions and meanings related to Africana studies. As a consequence there is a disjunction between popular perceptions of the sociological and intellectual contours of the field and the actual significance of particular schools of thought to the overall evolution and direction of the enterprise. Research using meta-research techniques and citation analysis is beginning to facilitate an understanding of the implications of external and internal dynamics on patterns of published scholarship presumably identified with Africana studies.

Thomas Weissinger's citation analysis of periodical publications of eight "dream team" (Harvard) Africana American studies faculty and eight non-dream team Africana studies scholars at other institutions found that dream teamers published four times more often in discipline-specific periodicals than in Africana studies ones. In contrast, non-dream teamers published twice as much in Africana studies compared to discipline-specific periodicals. He also found that dream team members cited research in discipline-specific journals thirty-one times more often than work in Africana studies journals, while non-dream teamers cited discipline-specific periodicals only 1.15 times more often than black studies journals. These findings obviously have important implications for mapping the contours of the field and for young researchers seeking alternative approaches to those found in traditional disciplines. To illustrate, Weissinger found that dream teamers use very few constructs from interdisciplinary Africana studies sources. Weissinger concludes, "There is evidence that traditional academia suppresses the activist element of Black Studies research [and that] this element is forced 'off campus.'" He suggests that this activist dimension "resurfaces in Black Studies periodicals and mass culture popular periodicals . . . [and] conversely, traditional scholarship on Black Studies topics is shepherded through peer-review procedures endorsed by the disciplines."[118]

While some observers may welcome such a rupture between scholarship and activism, I have endeavored to demonstrate that the dichotomy between academic research and political advocacy can be bridged in Africana studies and further that scientific and humanistic inquiries can be integrated without making artificial choices that constrain the liberatory potential of the enterprise for enhancing the role of research in catalyzing social change. At the same time, it is important to recognize that there is a process of re-disciplinization occurring in which subspecialties exist or are emerging in certain fields such as ethnomusicology, literature, and psychology, as discussed previously. Some of these subspecialties are linked more closely to Africana studies, per se, than others, but all have the potential to both catalyze ongoing development of methodologies in Africana studies and challenge methodological approaches in traditional disciplines. The synergy between Africana studies and these subspecialties can also facilitate the development of more policy-oriented Africana studies research that specifically addresses problems of the day, including class schisms, globalization-induced marginalization, and intergenerational conflict.

Ironically, the contemporary subdisciplination of the quasi-African-centered research process brings us full circle back to the original black social science movement, discussed earlier, that informed the original vision of Africana studies. While some may see such a recycling as retrogression, I prefer to interpret it as the next step in the struggle to achieve Du Bois's objective of "the possession and conquest of all knowledge and reach[ing] modern science of matter and life from the surroundings and habits and attitudes of American Negroes . . . lead[ing] up to understanding of life and matter in the universe."[119]

Notes

1. Richard Allen, "Politics of the Attack on Black Studies," *Black Scholar* 6, no. 1 (1974): 2–7.

2. See James Stewart, "Reaching for Higher Ground: Toward an Understanding of Black/Africana Studies," *Afrocentric Scholar* 1, no. 1 (1992): 1–63.

3. Maulana Karenga, *Introduction to Black Studies*, 3rd ed. (Los Angeles: University of Sankore Press, (2002), 26–27.

4. Maulana Karenga, *Introduction to Black Studies*, 2nd ed. (Los Angeles: University of Sankore Press, 1993), 69.

5. Maulana Karenga, *Introduction to Black Studies*, 1st ed. (Los Angeles: University of Sankore Press, 1982), 43.

6. Manning Marable, "The Modern Miseducation of the Negro: Critiques of Black History Curricula," in *Black Studies Curriculum Development Course Evaluations*, Institute of the Black World, Conference I, C1–C28 (Atlanta, Ga.: Institute of the Black World, 1981).

7. For example, see Darlene Clark Hine, ed., *Black Women's History: Theory and Practice* (Brooklyn, N.Y.: Carlson Publishers, 1990); Darlene Clark Hine, Elsa Barkley Brown, and Rosalyn Terborg-Penn, eds., *Black Women in America: An Historical Encyclopedia* (Brooklyn, N.Y.: Carlson Publishers, 1993); Darlene Clark Hine and Kathleen Thompson, *A Shining Thread of Hope: The History of Black Women in America* (New York: Broadway Books, 1998); Sharon Harley and Rosalyn Terborg-Penn, eds., *The Afro-American Woman, Struggles and Images* (Port West, N.Y.: National University, 1978); and Deborah Gray White, *Ar'n't I a Woman? Female Slaves in the Plantation South* (New York: W.W. Norton, 1985).

8. Robert Harris, "Coming of Age: The Transformation of Afro-American Historiography," in *Paradigms in Black Studies. Intellectual History, Cultural Meaning, and Political Ideology*, ed. Abdul Alkalimat (Chicago: Twenty-First Century Books and Publications, 1990), 68.

9. Robert Fogel, *Without Consent or Contract: The Rise and Fall of American Slavery* (New York: W.W. Norton, 1989).

10. Robert Fogel and Stanley Engerman, *Time on the Cross: The Economics of American Negro Slavery*, 2 volumes (Boston: Little, Brown, 1974).

11. Fogel, *Without Consent*, 12.

12. Paul Robeson, "I Want Negro Culture," in *Paul Robeson Speaks: Writings, Speeches, Interviews, 1918–1974*, ed. Philip Foner (New York: Brunner/Mazel Publishers, 1978), 97. Originally published in the *London News Chronicle*, May 30, 1935.

13. Rushton Coulburn and W. E. B. Du Bois, "Mr. Sorokin's Systems," *Journal of Modern History* 14 (1942): 512.

14. W. E. B. Du Bois, "The Beginnings of Slavery," *Voice of the Negro* 2 (February 1905): 104.

15. See James Stewart, "Perspectives on Reformist, Radical, and Recovery Models of Black Identity Dynamics from the Novels of W. E. B. Du Bois," In *Flight in Search of Vision*, by James Stewart. Trenton, N.J.: Africa World Press, 2004, 107–127.

16. W. E. B. Du Bois, "Economic Disfranchisement," *Crisis* 37 (August 1930): 281.

17. Du Bois, "Economic Disfranchisement," 282.

18. W. E. B. Du Bois, "The Evolution of the Race Problem," *Proceedings of the National Negro Conference* (New York, 1909). Reprinted in *W. E. B. Du Bois Speaks: Speeches and Addresses 1890–1919*, ed. Philip Foner (New York: Pathfinder Press, 1970), 198.

19. Manning Marable, *From the Grassroots: Essays toward Afro-American Liberation* (Boston: South End Press, 1980); *How Capitalism Underdeveloped Black America: Problems in Race, Political Economy, and Society* (Boston: South End Press, 1983); and *Race, Reform and Rebellion: The Second Reconstruction in Black America, 1945–1982* (Jackson: University Press of Mississippi, 1984). Lerone Bennett, *Before the Mayflower: A History of the Negro in America, 1619–1962* (Chicago: Johnson Publishing, 1962); *Black Power, U.S.A., the Human Side of Reconstruction, 1867–1877* (Chicago: Johnson Publishing, 1967); and *Forced into Glory: Abraham Lincoln's White Dream* (Chicago: Johnson Publishing, 2000).

20. W. E. B. Du Bois, "The Atlanta Conferences," *Voice of the Negro* 1 (March 1904): 85.

21. W. E. B. Du Bois, *The Philadelphia Negro: A Social Study* (Philadelphia: University of Pennsylvania Press, 1899).

22. Du Bois, *Philadelphia Negro*, 5.

23. Du Bois, "Atlanta Conferences," 88.

24. Karenga, *Introduction*, 2nd ed., 19.

25. Karenga, *Introduction*, 2nd ed., 19.

26. See Abdul Alkalimat, "The Ideology of Black Social Science," in *The Death of White Sociology*, ed. Joyce Ladner (New York: Random House, 1973), 173–189;

Robert Staples, "What Is Black Sociology? Toward a Sociology of Black Liberation," in *The Death of White Sociology*, 161–172; Ronald Walters, "Toward a Definition of Black Social Science," in *The Death of White Sociology*, 190–212.

27. Alkalimat, "Ideology," 132.

28. Alkalimat, "Ideology," 132.

29. John H. Stanfield, "Methodological Reflections, an Introduction," in *Race and Ethnicity in Research Methods*, ed. John H. Stanfield and Rutledge M. Dennis (Newbury Park, Calif.: Sage Publications, 1993), 11.

30. Preston Wilcox, "Black Studies as an Academic Discipline," *Negro Digest*, March 1970, p. 78.

31. William McClendon, "Black Studies: Education for Liberation," *Black Scholar* 6, no. 1 (1974): 18.

32. Maurice Jackson, "Toward a Sociology of Black Studies," *Journal of Black Studies* 1, no. 2 (1970): 135.

33. E. Franklin Frazier, "Is the Negro Family a Unique Sociological Unit?" *Opportunity* 5 (1927): 165–168.

34. Jerome Harris and William McCullough, "Quantitative Methods and Black Community Studies," in *The Death of White Sociology*, 336.

35. Stanfield, "Methodological Reflections," 32–33.

36. Barney Glaser and Anselm Strauss, *The Discovery of Grounded Theory* (Chicago: Aldine, 1967); and Barney Glaser, *Theoretical Sensitivity* (Mill Valley, Calif.: Sociology Press, 1978).

37. Brian Haig, "Grounded Theory as Scientific Method," *Philosophy of Education* (1995), p. 1. www.ed.uiuc.edu/EPS/PES-Yearbook/95_docs/haig.html.

38. Delores Aldridge, ed., "Black Women in the American Economy," special issue, *Journal of Black Studies* 20 (1989): 2; Jacqueline Jones, *Labor of Love, Labor of Sorrow: Black Women, Work, and the Family from Slavery to the Present* (New York: Vintage, 1986); and Margaret Simms and Julianne Malveaux, eds., *Slipping through the Cracks: The Status of Black Women* (New Brunswick, N.J.: Transaction Books, 1986).

39. Bettye Collier-Thomas and Vincent Franklin, eds., *Sisters in the Struggle: African-American Women in the Civil Rights–Black Power Movement* (New York: New York University Press, 2001); and Lynne Olson, *Freedom's Daughters: The Unsung Heroines of the Civil Rights Movement from 1830 to 1970* (New York: Scribner, 2001).

40. James Stewart, "Alternative Models of Black Studies," *UMOJA* 5 (1981): 17–39; Stephen Toulmin, *Human Understanding*, vol. 1 (Princeton, N.J.: Princeton University Press, 1972).

41. Toulmin, *Human Understanding*.

42. Karenga, *Introduction*, 2nd ed., 24.

43. Karenga, *Introduction*, 2nd ed., 388.

44. Irene Jackson, *More Than Dancing: Essays on Afro-American Music and Musicians* (Westport, Conn.: Greenwood Press, 1985).

45. See, for example, Margaret Busby, *Daughters of Africa: An International Anthology of Words and Writings by Women of African Descent; From the Ancient Egyptian to the Present* (New York: Pantheon, 1992); and Frances Foster, *Written by Herself: Literary Production by African American Women, 1746–1892* (Bloomington: Indiana University Press, 1993).

46. See Barbara Christian, *Black Women Novelists: The Development of a Tradition, 1892–1976* (Westport, Conn.: Greenwood Press, 1980); and *Black Feminist Criticism: Perspectives on Black Women Writers* (New York: Teachers College Press, 1997). Also see Cheryl Wall, *Changing Our Own Words: Essays on Criticism, Theory, and Writing by Black Women* (New Brunswick: Rutgers University Press, 1989).

47. See, for example, Trey Ellis, "The New Black Aesthetic," *Callaloo* 38 (Winter 1989): 233–243.

48. Stewart, "Reaching for Higher Ground."

49. W. E. B. Du Bois, "The Social Origins of Negro Art," *Modern Quarterly* 3, no. 1 (1925): 54–55.

50. W. E. B. Du Bois, "The Conservation of Races," American Negro Academy Occasional Papers, no. 2, 1897. Reprinted in *W. E. B. Du Bois Speaks: Speeches and Addresses 1890–1919*, ed. Philip Foner (New York: Pathfinder Press, 1970), 79.

51. Perry Hall, *In the Vineyard, Working in African American Studies* (Knoxville: University of Tennessee Press, 1999).

52. W. E. B. Du Bois, "The Study of the Negro Problems," *Annals of the American Academy of Political and Social Science* 11 (January 1898): 12.

53. See Nick Ford, "Black Studies Programs," *Current History* 67, no. 399 (1974): 224–227; and Joseph Russell, "Afro-American Studies: From Chaos to Consolidation," *Negro Education Review* 26, no. 4 (1975): 181–89.

54. Stewart, "Reaching for Higher Ground."

55. Karenga, *Introduction*, 1st ed., 35–36.

56. Harold Cheatham and James Stewart, eds., *Black Families: Interdisciplinary Perspectives* (New Brunswick, N.J.: Transaction Books, 1990).

57. Stewart, "Alternative Models."

58. Houston Baker, "Generational Shifts and the Recent Criticism of Afro-American Literature," in *Paradigms in Black Studies: Intellectual History, Cultural Meaning, and Political Ideology*, ed. Abdul Alkalimat (Chicago: Twenty-First Century Books and Publications, 1990), 113.

59. Baker, "Generational Shifts," 113.

60. Hall, *In the Vineyard*.

61. James Stewart, "Foundations of a 'Jazz' Theory of Africana Studies," in Stewart, *Flight in Search of Vision*, 191–202.

62. Teun Van Dijk, "Analyzing Racism through Discourse Analysis," in *Race and Ethnicity in Research Methods*, ed. John H. Stanfield and Ruthledge M. Dennis, 92–134.

63. Stewart, "Foundations."

64. Thomas S. Kuhn, *The Structure of Scientific Revolutions*, 2nd ed. (Chicago: University of Chicago Press, 1970).

65. Van Dijk, "Analyzing Racism," 96.

66. Van Dijk, "Analyzing Racism," 94–95.

67. Bettye Collier-Thomas, *Daughters of Thunder: Black Women Preachers and Their Sermons, 1850–1979* (San Francisco: Jossey-Bass, 1998).

68. Yvonna S. Johnson, *The Voices of African American Women: The Use of Narrative and Authorial Voice in the Works of Harriet Jacobs, Zora Neale Hurston, and Alice Walker*, American University Studies 14: American Literature (Washington, D.C.: American University, 1999).

69. Herbert Aptheker, "Du Bois as Historian," in *Afro-American History: The Modern Era*, ed. Herbert Aptheker (Secaucus, N.J.: Citadel Press, 1971), 65.

70. W. E. B. Du Bois, *The World and Africa: An Inquiry into the Part Which Africa Has Played in World History*, originally published in 1946 (New York: International Publishers, 1968), viii.

71. W. E. B. Du Bois, postscript to *The Ordeal of Mansart*, originally published in 1957 (Millwood, N.Y.: Kraus Thomson, 1976), 316.

72. Du Bois, postscript, 315.

73. Joseph Scott, "Polygamy: A Futuristic Family Arrangement among African Americans," *Black Books Bulletin* 4 (1976): 13–19.

74. James Stewart, "Perspectives on Black Families from Contemporary Soul Music: The Case of Millie Jackson," *Phylon*, March 1980, 57–71.

75. Stewart, "Perspectives on Reformist, Radical, and Recovery Models."

76. W. E. B. Du Bois, "My Evolving Program for Negro Freedom," in *What the Negro Wants*, ed. Rayford Logan (Chapel Hill: University of North Carolina Press, 1944), 56–57.

77. Barbara Omolade, *The Rising Song of African American Women* (New York: Routledge, 1994), 15.

78. See, for example, Beverly Guy-Sheftall, introduction to *Words of Fire, an Anthology of African-American Feminist Thought*, ed. Beverly Guy-Sheftall (New York: New Press, 1995), 1–22; Patricia Hill Collins, *Black Feminist Thought: Knowledge, Consciousness, and the Politics of Empowerment* (New York: Routledge, 1991); and Gloria Hull, Patricia Bell Scott, and Barbara Smith, *All the Women Are White, All the Blacks Are Men, But Some of Us Are Brave: Black Women's Studies* (Old Westbury, N.Y.: Feminist Press, 1982).

79. See, for example, Aldridge, "Black Women"; *Focusing, Black Male-Female Relationships* (Chicago: Third World Press, 1991); "Womanist Issues in Black Studies: Towards Integrating Africana Women into Africana Studies," *Afrocentric Scholar* 1, no. 1 (1992): 167–182; Vivian Gordon, *Black Women, Feminism, Black Liberation: Which Way?* Rev. ed. (Chicago: Third World Press, 1987); Clenora Hudson-Weems, "Cultural and Agenda Conflicts in Academia: Critical Issues for Africana Women's Studies," *Western Journal of Black Studies* 13, no. 4 (1989): 181–189; *Africana Womanism: Reclaiming Ourselves* (Troy, Mich.: Bedford Publishers, 1993); "Africana Womanism

and the Critical Need for Africana Theory and Thought," *Western Journal of Black Studies*, Summer 1997, 70–84.

80. Charlyn Harper-Bolton, "A Reconceptualization of the Black Woman," *Black Male/Female Relationships*, Winter 1982: 32–42.

81. Filomina Chioma Steady, "African Feminism: A Worldwide Perspective," in *Women in Africa and the African Diaspora*, ed. R. Terborg-Penn et al. (Washington, D.C.: Howard University Press, 1987).

82. See, for example, K. Cannon, *Black Womanist Ethics* (Atlanta, Ga.: Scholars Press, 1988); and J. Grant, *White Women's Christ and Black Women's Jesus: Feminist Christology and Womanist Response* (Atlanta, Ga.: Scholars Press, 1989).

83. Hill Collins, *Black Feminist Thought*, 207.

84. Adelbert Jenkins, *Psychology and African Americans, a Humanistic Approach*, 2nd ed. (Needham Heights, Mass.: Allyn & Bacon, 1995), xi.

85. William Cross, *Shades of Black, Diversity in African American Identity* (Philadelphia: Temple University Press, 1991).

86. Kim Vaz, "Making Room for Emancipatory Research in Psychology: A Multicultural Feminist Perspective," in *Spirit, Space & Survival, African American Women in (White) Academe*, ed. Joy James and Ruth Farmer (New York: Routledge, 1993), 96.

87. See, for example, Paul Gilroy, *The Black Atlantic: Modernity and Double Consciousness* (Cambridge, Mass.: Harvard University Press, 1993).

88. Edwin Embree, *Brown America, the Story of a New Race* (New York: Friendship Press, 1936), 3.

89. Joel Williamson, *New People: Miscegenation and Mulattoes in the United States* (Baton Rouge: Louisiana State University Press, 1995).

90. F. Odun Balogun, "Hybridity, Neouniversalist Cultural Theory, and the Comparative Study of Black Literatures," in *African Visions, Literary Images, Political Change, and Social Struggle in Contemporary Africa*, ed. Cheryl Mwaria, Silvia Federici, and Joseph McLaren (Westport, Conn.: Praeger, 2000), 174–75.

91. Sheila S. Walker, ed., *African Roots/American Cultures: Africa in the Creation of the Americas* (Lanham, Md.: Rowman & Littlefield, 2001).

92. Walker, *African Roots*, 38.

93. Walker, *African Roots*, 8.

94. Walker, *African Roots*, 8.

95. Walker, *African Roots*, 41.

96. Walker, *African Roots*, 29.

97. Molefi Kete Asante, *The Afrocentric Idea* (Philadelphia: Temple University Press, 1987), 6.

98. Maulana Karenga, "Black Studies and the Problem of Paradigm: The Philosophical Dimension," *Journal of Black Studies* 18, no. 4 (1988): 403.

99. Cheikh Anta Diop, *The African Origin of Civilization, Myth or Reality*, ed. and trans. by Mercer Cook (Westport, Conn.: Lawrence Hill, 1974); *The Cultural Unity of Black Africa* (Chicago: Third World Press, 1990).

100. Molefi Kete Asante, *Kemet, Afrocentricity and Knowledge* (Trenton, N.J.: Africa World Press, 1990), 40.

101. Asante, *Afrocentric Idea*, 16.

102. Karenga, *Introduction*, 1st ed.

103. Asante, *Kemet*, 141.

104. Karenga, *Introduction*, 2nd ed., 26.

105. Asante, *Kemet*, 15.

106. Asante, *Kemet*, 12–13.

107. Asante, *Kemet*, 6.

108. Marimba Ani, *Yurugu: An African-Centered Critique of European Cultural Thought and Behavior* (Trenton, N.J.: Africa World Press, 1994).

109. Asante, *Afrocentric Idea*, p. 16.

110. Cecil Conteen Gray, *Afrocentric Thought and Praxis: An Intellectual History* (Trenton, N.J.: Africa World Press, 2001).

111. For example, Barbara Faggins, *Africans and Indians: An Afrocentric Analysis of Contacts between Africans and Indians in Colonial Virginia* (New York: Routledge, 2001); and C. Tsehloane Keto, *Vision and Time: Historical Perspective on an Africa-Centered Paradigm* (Lanham, Md.: University Press of America, 2001).

112. James Conyers, ed., *Afrocentricity and the Academy: Essays on Theory and Practice* (Jefferson, N.C.: McFarland, 2003); and Ama Mazama, *The Afrocentric Paradigm* (Trenton, N.J.: Africa World Press, 2003).

113. Kariamce Welsh-Asante, ed., *The African Aesthetic: Keeper of the Tradition* (New York: Greenwood Press, 1993); and *African Dance: An Artistic, Historical, and Philosophical Inquiry* (Trenton, N.J.: Africa World Press, 1996).

114. Stanfield, "Methodological Reflections," 28.

115. Duane Champagne, "Toward a Multidimensional Historical Comparative Methodology: Context, Process, and Causality," in *Race and Ethnicity in Research Methods*, ed. Stanfield and Dennis, 252–253.

116. Champagne, "Comparative Methodology," 253.

117. Delores Aldridge and Carlene Young, eds., *Out of the Revolution: The Development of Africana Studies* (Lanham, Md.: Lexington Books, 2000); and Nathaniel Norment, Jr., ed., *African-American Studies Reader* (Durham, N.C.: Carolina Academic Press, 2001).

118. Thomas Weissinger, "Black Studies Scholarly Communication: A Citation Analysis of Periodical Literature," *Collection Management* 27, nos. 3–4 (2002): 55.

119. W. E. B. Du Bois, "The Field and Function of the Negro College," alumni reunion address, Fisk University, 1933. Reprinted in *W. E. B. Du Bois: The Education of Black People, Ten Critiques 1900–1960*, ed. Herbert Aptheker (Amherst: University of Massachusetts Press, 1973), 5–6.

Methodological Intersections of Race, Sexuality, and Ethnography

9

GINA MASEQUESMAY

Using Sandra Harding's framework to distinguish some conflated concepts that have obscured discussion about methods, theories, and methodologies, I employ her definitions of *epistemology* as a "theory of knowledge" that examines how we know what we know, *methodology* as "a theory and analysis of how research does or should proceed," and *method* as a technique of data-gathering.[1] I concur with Nancy Naples's argument in *Feminism and Method* that our "epistemological stance profoundly shapes the methods we choose and employ."[2] In that sense, epistemology also shapes our methodological approach. Naples argues that how we interpret our roles as researchers, what we consider ethical research practices, what we count as data, and how these data are interpreted and reported are influenced by our epistemological assumptions. Given this premise, this methodological paper on race and sexuality[3] examines my implicit epistemological assumptions on conducting an ethnographic, participant-observation on Ô-Môi, a support group for Vietnamese lesbians, bisexual women, and female-to-male transgenders. As well, I discuss the theories on race and sexuality that inform my methodological approach. Highlighting some insights from my ethnographic data of Ô-Môi, I reexamine my original methodological and theoretical rationale to contend that there are both methodological and theoretical justifications for an ethnic studies standpoint epistemology and politics in conducting ethnographic studies with an activist agenda, which shall be termed *activist ethnography* in this paper.

An Underlying Epistemological Stance in Ethnic Studies

Although similar to women's studies in being an interdisciplinary field, ethnic studies does not have a philosophical treatise or manifesto on its epistemology and hence also does not have an agreed methodology or a clear set of methodologies.[4] Guided by the four principles of self-determination, educational relevance, solidarity with people of color, and interdisciplinary approach,[5] activist Asian American students and scholars and community people set out to fight against racial injustice, economic exploitation, government disenfranchisement, and other social injustices. In producing new knowledge that challenges the master's narrative or paradigm,[6] anti-racist scholars were constructing a new discourse on race that challenged the old racist assumptions. This epistemological position that the voice of the racially oppressed matters and that it adds conflicting, and hence more nuanced complexity to the old white supremacist paradigm, is parallel to what pioneering feminist theorists Sandra Harding, Dorothy Smith, Nancy Harstock, and Patricia Hill Collins call "standpoint theory."[7] While there are many interpretations of standpoint theory,[8] taken as a whole, this epistemology begins from the knowledge and experience of the oppressed. For feminists, women's experiences are the place from which knowledge is to be drawn; for ethnic studies, the experiences of people of color as racialized others are the starting point. For feminists of color, the point of analysis is the matrix of domination or the interlocking systems of race, class, gender, and sexual oppression.[9]

In conducting my dissertation research on race/ethnicity, gender, and sexuality, I started from the points of view of marginalized ethno-racial, gender, and sexual minorities. My politics was to bring in the perspective of the marginalized that would counter the dominant paradigm about race, ethnicity, gender, and sexuality. Trained in sociology to do ethnographic participant-observation, my original stance was to go into "a field" to learn from the people about their lives and to record that for analysis. It was important for me to document the lives of queer[10] Vietnamese females, because as a Vietnamese American lesbian, I saw the importance of making visible our marginalized community and countering a history of erasure. I also knew that as a researcher I had rare access to a somewhat hidden[11] network and that I could shed some light on the struggles of a community facing simultaneously racism, sexism, homophobia, and heterosexism of capitalist America. Having been politicized by my previous work in the Asian American social services field, I also incorporated some of the ethnic studies principles of self-determination and educational relevance[12] to guide me in doing research that would be "empowering" to my community of queer Vietnamese, a community that intersects race/ethnicity, class, gender, and sexuality. Originally, for me, empowering the community meant making visible our lives to normalize us. I will discuss later how this naive and simple notion of empowerment needs a clearer assessment to further develop a sound methodology and politics.

My Entrée and Alignment with Ethnic Studies Politics

Ô-Môi is a volunteer support group, founded in 1995,[13] for those who identify as Vietnamese lesbians, bisexual women, and female-to-male transgenders living in Los Angeles and Orange Counties. I became a coordinating member of this organization that was going through a lull in 1997–1998 of getting members to participate and organize activities. I was also a graduate sociology student thinking about a possible research project for my dissertation. My research interest had been in race, class, gender, and sexuality ever since I had come out as a lesbian in my second semester of graduate school. Thinking that I could save time by simultaneously working on Ô-Môi's behalf as its coordinator and needs assessment researcher, I chose Ô-Môi as my research site to examine the issues of race/ethnicity, class, gender, and sexuality. The needs assessment was to figure out how to involve and recruit members, because people who had made friends in Ô-Môi no longer felt the need to attend the larger meeting when they could just meet with their small group of friends. Ô-Môi's participation was down, and it needed resuscitation and new members. A needs assessment could document how Ô-Môi was meeting or not meeting the needs of members and potential members. As a coordinator, I needed to figure out a way to maintain the group's momentum, because without members' participation, there would be no group left.

Academically, I wanted a dissertation project that addressed the intersections of race/ethnicity, class, gender, and sexuality. Ô-Môi was an organization that was organized around marginalized racial/ethnic, sexual, and gender identities, and I wanted to know how successful it was in addressing the diverse needs of its lesbian, bisexual, and straight-identified female-to-male transgender members, some who are working class and many who are middle-class. Founded on identity politics that critiqued the homophobia of the mainstream Vietnamese community and the racism of the white-dominant queer community, Ô-Môi asserted itself as a support group for the multiply-marginalized. In contrast to its mission, I saw examples of Ô-Môi members marginalizing one another (not supporting one another's identity) at Ô-Môi events and in on-line Ô-Môi email list discussions, and that made me question the circumstances under which we would come together to support or not support each other and what the pattern of normalizing or marginalizing was in the group.

My other political and academic motivation followed the ethnic studies mission. Ethnic studies was born out of community activism and was part of a larger emancipatory project for the community of color. As a political project, its aim was to empower marginally racialized communities and disrupt the status quo by challenging mainstream knowledge production process with its own epistemology of truths.[14] Gathering voices that were long marginalized and/or excluded, scholars of color reinserted their agency into history and shifted the old Eurocentric, masculinist paradigm with voices and experiences of the oppressed, questioning old research questions that assumed white superiority.[15] They also challenged racist explanations of biological inferiority, subtler racist theories of cultural deficiency, and/or the color-blind assimilation model for ethnic minorities. Scholars of color replaced these racist explanations and race-blind predictions with social explanations and documentations of the effects of racial prejudice, discrimination, racist ideology, and institutional inequality.[16]

In the case of Ô-Môi, I wanted to document the multiply-marginalized queer Vietnamese lives so that our voices would be heard and our lives would no longer be invisible. As ethnic studies scholars before me documented the lives of people of color, I tried to document the lives of the multiply-marginalized so that our lives can become visible and demarginalized.

The next section discusses my theoretical and methodological framework for using ethnography to do activist research.

Conceptualizing Race and Sexuality

Social theories emerge within particular sociohistorical contexts. The sociology of knowledge asserts that these social theories are for the most part reflections of the time and place of their authors. Hence, the social positionings and privileged statuses of the theorists can create blind spots for many in constructing theories of human behaviors and group interactions. Shirley Hune in an essay on emergent paradigm discusses how the increasing presence of scholars of color has challenged the old (white) racial paradigm that sees only black and white and assumes white as normal and the standard for population comparison.[17] Specifically, in the post–World War II period, the increasing presence of scholars of color in the academy due to changes in politics and culture also led to their intervention on racist projects and their offer of new perspectives in viewing race, race relations, and racial inequality.[18]

A similar trend occurred in the studies on gender and sexuality, where gay, lesbian, bisexual, and transgender academics have depathologized alternative genders and sexualities that were once pathologized by sexologists and masculinist and sexist projects.[19] Gender and sexuality (and sex) are no longer static, taken-for-granted concepts reflecting nature. Rather, they are social constructions of ongoing negotiations in particular social, political, spatial, and temporal sites. As we shall see in the next two subsections, the successful constructionist challenges to the prevailing essentialist or primordial view of sexuality and race occurred around the social and political upheavals of the late 1960s and 1970s.[20] By the 1990s, AIDS activism with its new deconstructive politics ignited the emergence and proliferation of Queer theory as a critical, theoretical, and political inquiry into norms and institutions of heterosexuality. The emerging voices of queers of color insisted on another layer of "queering" not only about sexuality and gender but also race, class, ethnicity, and so forth. I now give a brief overview of the different developments and approaches to conceptualizing race and sexuality to help us reevaluate a theoretical framework in understanding their intersections.

Theoretical Development on Race

The conceptualization of race has changed in response to its sociopolitical contexts. Conceived as kinship, a quasi-biological notion, it was used to distinguish between people of different ethnicities, religions, and power relations (e.g., Irish versus English). During the colonial period, race became a biological fact, and racial theories (i.e., scientific racism) were created to justify colonialism.[21] Race was not just a marker of phenotypic distinctiveness but a reason for subjugation because racially categorized people were attributed particular social traits (e.g., Native Americans were savages and needed to be civilized). As an independent variable, it explained the behavior of a group of people. More importantly, the explanation implicated certain solutions such as enslavement (e.g., blacks are unintelligent and lazy and hence need subjugation to train them and maximize their worth).

Focusing on today's case of African Americans, racial inequality, defined as the racial gap in income, occupation, education, housing, and so forth, is still often explained as the result of African Americans' inherent inferiority in physical skillfulness, intelligence, and work habits.[22] These various explanations do not greatly depart from the original biological and moral justification of the conquest of the indigenous people of the Americas and the slave trade of Africans. Whereas, enslavement was explained as for "their own good," racial inequality in a non-slavery state occurred because "they're no good," be that biologically or culturally. In opposition to these views by the oppressors, W. E. B. Du Bois and others struggling for racial justice offered another compelling explanation, that of "the color line" or racism impeding African American progress. That is, racism (e.g., racial prejudice and racial discrimination) is the explanation for the racial gap. The concept "race" became a proxy for racism, not a group of people with inherent or learned inferiority.

An alternative model views racial groups as sites of resistance to racial discrimination, not the problem in itself. People facing discrimination and prejudice can organize as a collective to fight against their oppressors. Racism can be fought at the psychological, interpersonal, institutional, and discursive levels.[23] Here, race became an interdependent variable. No longer a given, race or racial groups were created in historical moments that could be reinvented in everyday interaction. In 1986, Michael Omi and Howard Winant offered racial formation as an approach to understand how the meanings of race changed over time.[24] In their formulation, what we need to examine are the macro and micro racial and racist projects that reinforce or challenge the racial status quo, respectively. Since their theoretical treatise on race as an organizing principle of society, sophisticated works have emerged to document the racialization processes or racial/racist projects in history as well as in contemporary time.[25] At a more mundane level, my own work on Ô-Môi and Asian Pacific AIDS organizations document the everyday "racial identity work," or everyday interaction that evokes notions of race, that can marginalize or normalize a social group or a social identity.[26]

Conceptualizing race as a social process opens our imagination to how other variables such as gender, class, and sexuality may interplay with race (as seen in works of Almaguer and Roediger). Works in feminism and by women of color have shown the experiential and epistemological importance of seeing the interconnections between race, class, gender, and sexuality. Using this framework, Joane Nagel, for example, demonstrates in *Race, Ethnicity, and Sexuality: Intimate Intersections, Forbidden Frontiers* how the construction of ethnicity and race is also a construction of sexuality.[27] That is, they are mutually constitutive, and it is imperative to examine race and ethnicity with an analysis of sexuality.

In short, the developments in race (and ethnic) studies have moved from a view of race/ethnicity as a biological fact and an independent variable in explaining behavior to a view of it as an interdependent variable that is mutually constitutive with other variables. Race as a social construct or process suggests that it is relational, tangential, and interdependent (a result of racialization and an organizing principle of society).

Theoretical Development on Sexuality

A similar conceptual development occurred in gender/sexuality studies. According to Stephen Seidman, past research in sexuality saw sex and sexuality as a given biological fact.[28] Most social theorists ignored sexuality per se as a social phenomenon to be investigated. Debates about birth controls and eugenics were viewed as the politics of biology, and the different norms of marriage and courtship were seen as varied kinship structures that control reproduction. That is, sexuality per se was seen as belonging to the biological realm and not that of sociological investigation. During the turn of the twentieth century, sexuality took center stage in theoretical development by psychologists and psychiatrists and empirical documentation by sexologists. Particularly interesting was Sigmund Freud's new view of gender and sexuality in stages of development.[29] Sexuality was not a given but a process that had to mature into "normal sexuality" (heterosexuality). Thwarted development in sexuality could lead to abnormal sexuality as seen in sexual inverts and homosexuals.

During the post–World War II era, Alfred Kinsey embarked on a historic survey of sexual behaviors among "normal" Americans[30] that went beyond clinical cases of "neurotic" patients. With empirical evidence, he and his associates dispelled many myths about sex and paved the way for a less Victorian approach to sexuality. He reframed homosexuality and heterosexuality as a variations on a spectrum of human sexual behaviors. By the 1950s, homosexuality became of interest to sociologists who were studying deviance. Partly due to the national public awareness of homosexuality and the rise in visibility of homophile organizations, homosexuals became another deviant group, like prostitutes and hustlers, for sociologists to study.[31] Applying labeling theory to study this marginalized group, sociologists added to the growing conceptualization of homosexuality in the 1960s and 1970s. Influenced by symbolic interactionism, the study of homosexuality became the study of the process of homosexual identity acquisition and management of a stigmatized identity. Like the critical studies on race, when the analysis focuses outward on the process that discriminates and deviantizes, the shift in examination helped to depathologize the group. In reverse, the problem became the external deviantizing and discriminatory processes.

This scrutiny of the process led to a reconceptualization of gender and sexuality as performativity and discourse.[32] By the mid-1990s, this new conceptualization has fermented into Queer theory, which insisted that the flip side of the deviantizing process was the normalizing process of heterosexuality. The study of sexuality became not just a focus on the deviantized but also on the normalized. Interrogating homosexuality also became interrogating heterosexuality, specifically examining heteronormativity, the norms and institutions that privilege heterosexuality and see it as natural and normal. Similarly in race studies, we see the current focus on interrogating whiteness or white privilege and not just the negative effect of racial discrimination.[33]

Converging Race and Sexuality

As we compare the developments in race and sexuality studies, we see similar shifts from taken-for-granted assumption of their ontology to problematizing them as variegated products of social interaction to viewing them as processes (racial/racist projects and racial identity work and gender-sexual performativity) that can overlap. Moving from endogenous factors to exogenous factors in explaining racial and sexual realities and differences, we also move from the focus on content (what the group is or has) to a focus on the process that racializes/sexualizes and demarcates people and aligns them with differential social and material resources. According to Joane Nagel, the studies on race and sexuality become an examination of the boundary constructions of insiders and outsiders and the conditions that would weaken or strengthen these boundaries. Applying Nagel's idea about the "ethnosexual frontiers," we have the racial-sexual frontiers, the borderlands where race is sexualized and sexuality is racialized. The "notion of racial and ethnic boundaries allows us to imagine ethnic-sexual police guarding ethnic-sexual borders, patrolling ethnic-sexual frontiers, directing ethnic-sexual checkpoints, demanding ethnic-sexual identification, and turning away or rounding up nonmembers."[34] The task of the analyst then is to research when and how these borders are patrolled as manifested "in patterns of dating, childbearing, marriage, and sexual relations, including sexual assault, rape, and sexual slavery, as well as in cosmologies—theories of ethnosexual attributes, practices, preferences and aversions" (p. 46). Another exemplary work that looks at this intersection is Eithne Luibhéid's 2002 study of U.S. immigration policies, *Entry Denied*. In sum, this convergence of conceptualizing race/ethnicity and gender/sexuality as mutually constitutive processes provides us with a new tool of analysis that considers these intersections in rereading historical and contemporary events[35] and in interpreting ethnographic data.

Before I begin discussing the development in ethnographic methodology, let me outline some implications in conceptualizing race and sexuality as processes.

Some Methodological Implications in Rethinking Race and Sexuality

By destabilizing race and sexuality into racial identity work and gender-sexual performativity, we force quantitative works on race and sexuality to also *not* take for granted these racial, sexual, and gender categories as natural. This demands studies that use racial categories to re-emphasize that the racial categories are proxies for racism and not for subcategories of human beings. This orientation also allows us to view the subjectivity of multiracial individuals in disrupting or reinforcing the racial taxonomy. In sexuality studies, the severance of identity label of behavior from ontology offers us insights to outreach to high-risk HIV-infected populations of men who have sex with men (MSM) but do not identify as gay. This also moves us away from viewing gays, lesbians, bisexuals, or transgenders as a sexual/gender minority group but as diverse sexual and gender beings in fluid spectrums of gender and sexual possibilities.

In qualitative research, the notion of racial identity work and sexual/gender performativity allows us to focus on the agency of people who face structural constraints and can reinforce or challenge the racial, gender, or sexual hegemony. Ethnography, in particular, allows us to see people, for the most part, as they are and as they experience and react to life. In other words, we can document their everyday racial-sexual projects or everyday racial-sexual identity work as they understand them and analyze whether the patterns of everyday projects are toward hegemony (dominant cultural norms and ideology) or counterhegemony. I next discuss the issues of reflexivity and the methodological breakthrough in ethnography to work toward an emancipatory project.

According to Stephen Pfohl, a critical approach analyzes a social phenomenon in its sociohistorical context and applies a power-reflexive method that acknowledges the power relationship between an understudied phenomenon and the researcher in producing knowledge and facts.[36] *Reflexivity* is the ability to step back and observe how one's social location and access to power affects one's engagement in challenging the existing structure of race, class, gender, sexuality, and age. In other words, we should critically examine how we, as individuals or in collectives, challenge or reinforce hegemony in our everyday experiences. Particularly as ethnographic researchers, we must be conscientious of how our presence influences the data we gather.

The revelation that we are all engaging in racial-sexual projects suggests that the researcher cannot hide behind the cloak of objectivity in examining everyday racial/sexual projects. The ethnographic works of people of color also challenge this false dichotomy of insider and outsider to the field or "homework."[37] Moreover, since both researcher and the researched are engaging in hegemonic or counterhegemonic projects in everyday interaction, ethnographic researchers need to be clear on their politics on these matters of race and sexuality vis-à-vis the people they research.

For ethnic studies scholars, their research has to be a political emancipatory project that empowers the researched and disrupts the status quo. Critical ethnography or participatory research, as interpreted by some sociologists, offers a way for an ethnic studies scholar to be both a researcher and an activist. For Alain Touraine and Gilbert Elbaz, a "critical ethnography" must also be an "emancipatory project" for the marginalized and disenfranchised and not just an edification process that has no implication for the people it involves.[38] An ethnic studies researcher thus must be aware of the politics he or she is bringing into an emancipatory project. Moreover, despite good intentions, he or she should ask how his/her everyday activities are hegemonic or counterhegemonic.

This involvement in one's community and politics can be critiqued as isolationist and bordering relativism, with critics questioning how such an ethnographic case study can contribute to the field of generalizable scientific knowledge. The answer lies with Michael Burawoy's extended case study.

In an edited volume of ethnographic case studies titled *Ethnography Unbound*, Burawoy advocates for the application of a set of methodological principles, which he calls the "extended case method."[39] Contrasting this methodology to grounded theory approach, symbolic interactionism ("interpretive case"), and ethnomethodology, Burawoy proposes a link between the best of macro- and micro-sociological worlds, between the rich data offered by micro-sociological methods in getting at the "lifeworlds" and the globally informed macro-sociological theories of current social structure and trends. Basically, Burawoy purports that one should extend one's ethnographic case study's findings to larger macro trends rather than rest in micro relativism of case studies and/or in the universalism of social processes that become ahistorical and apolitical in their rendering of social life. In this way, empirically sound data derived from ethnographic participant-observation are analyzed in contexts of macro-sociological theories on forms of domination.[40] Seeing the micro and macro as mutually determining, Burawoy nevertheless does not advocate for the other micro-sociological approaches (ethnomethodology, grounded theory, symbolic interactionism) but rather insists that macro-sociological theories be revisited and revised in the face of new empirical evidence or "anomalies"[41] from the micro world. Essentially, Burawoy is asking ethnographers to use C. Wright Mills's notion of the "sociological imagination" in examining their participant-observation's findings, linking between micro data and macro theories.

By combining ideas from critical ethnography and the extended case method, ethnic studies scholars can engage in an emancipatory project at the same time that they are conducting ethnographic research. The recent developments in race and sexuality studies will heighten their reflexivity of the everyday political projects of race and sexuality in which they engage. I call this reflexive ethnographic research with a political activist agenda *activist ethnography* for scholars who are activists. I discuss some implications of my findings in the next section.

Implications from My Ethnographic Findings on Ô-Môi

In the process of documenting voices, I also found that I had recorded particular voices more than others. This section discusses the findings and their methodological implications on standpoint epistemology.

As an organization that was predominantly lesbian, Ô-Môi's activities and plans were organized by lesbians with lesbian interests. Bisexual and transgender concerns were secondary to lesbian concerns. Most lesbian members assumed that other members were lesbians who were romantically interested in other lesbians despite the facts that bisexual women could be interested in men and that female-to-male (FTM) transgender members did not see themselves as women. In fact, the lesbian majority saw bisexual women as potential traitors (for their interest in men that garners them heterosexual privileges) and FTM transgender members as "really women who hate their bodies." Thus for bisexual and transgender members, they had to suppress their differences and play along the line of commonality with lesbian members to feel accepted and supported. When the transgender men asserted their "straight male" identification, they also disrupted the cohesion of the group as queer women interested in women.

In addition to the suppression of bisexual and transgender needs, I also noticed that middle-class and professional members were more involved in Ô-Môi's activities, planning organized activities that made it difficult for working-class members to participate because of limited time and money, such as events at dance clubs and restaurants that were in "gay" West Hollywood, Los Angeles, a half an hour to an hour one-way drive for members who were in "conservative" Orange County or in the San Gabriel Valley.

Furthermore, I observed that members who were bilingual benefited most from the group's activities. Although originally founded to support monolingual Vietnamese speakers who could not access mainstream queer organizations that were exclusively for English-speakers, Ô-Môi's activities were conducted almost entirely in English, because the majority of organizers as well as regular members spoke limited Vietnamese and could hardly write Vietnamese.

As an organization that claimed to represent the interests of a diverse group of members, Ô-Môi privileged the voices and interests of middle-class, professional, bilingual, and English-proficient Vietnamese American lesbians at the marginalization of working-class, Vietnamese monolingual lesbians and bisexual women and transgender men. The voice of Ô-Môi as represented in newsletters, email discussions, and activities meant a voice of members who were structurally more privileged and numerically dominant. These multiple and differentially privileged voices among the multiply-marginalized undermined a unified standpoint epistemology of the oppressed based on embodied or essentialized positionalities and pointed our attention toward the different processes that marginalize and normalize members. In my research, I discuss these processes as "identity work"[42] where members evoke notions of sexual, gender, racial, and/or ethnic identity as a means to coalesce or differentiate among each other. In "identity work," members also reinforce or challenge racial, sexual, gender, and class hegemony. Paying attention to these normalizing or marginalizing processes allowed me to begin mapping what Dorothy Smith calls "the relations of ruling."[43] Here, epistemology is "a site through which to begin inquiry"[44] and expose relations of ruling for resistance rather than a convoluted endless permutation of oppression.

What I observed at Ô-Môi is a pattern of identity work that normalizes English-Vietnamese bilingual (preferably English) lesbians while it marginalizes bisexual, transgender, working-class, and Vietnamese monolingual members. By viewing these queer females situationally as agents of change as well as reinforcers of hegemony, I am able to examine the complex interaction of agency and structure instead of making assumptions that members of a queer, Vietnamese, female support group would support all its members in a struggle against homophobia, racism, and heterosexism. At times, members reinforce/create new hierarchies among themselves.

Documenting the processes that marginalized some members while normalizing others also suggested to me that the notion of who is a member and who is not a member is always shifting, depending on the conscious and unconscious political decisions of people involved to be inclusive or exclusive. This also implies that I, a member of Ô-Môi and a voice in Ô-Môi, am not always an insider to represent the voice of the sexually and racially marginalized. This confirms other feminist and ethnic researchers who have discussed their shifting insider and outsider statuses.[45] It also underscores the importance of paying attention to the researcher's positionalities, which affect the types of data to which she has access or privy and the ones to which she does not. Thus, while research on Ô-Môi may represent the voices of the sexually and racially marginalized, if we closely examine the processes of identity construction and negotiation, we will see that these processes also intersect with class, language ability, and other social barriers that produce and privilege a particular type of voice at Ô-Môi. These processes are drawing and redrawing multiple boundaries in specific temporal spaces.

This section discusses my findings that influence and reshape my methodological analysis about power and representation. I now move to discuss the advantages and limitations of activist ethnography.

Specific Advantages and Limitations of Activist Ethnography on Race and Sexuality

Having outlined the need to combine critical ethnography, extended case method, and the deconstructive tendency of recent theoretical developments in race and gender-sexuality studies to arrive at a politically compatible methodology for the ethnic studies mission, I turn in this section to discuss the specific advantages and limitations of this methodological approach using my own ethnographic data and experience at Ô-Môi.

The idea of doing research on my own community had many benefits. Ô-Môi was an organization to which I had already belonged before deciding to conduct research on it. I was one of the main organizers, and we were running into difficulty keeping the membership active. I thought that by doing my dissertation research on Ô-Môi, I could also use my research as a needs assessment of the organization to redirect its energy in building and sustaining memberships. Having limited time as a graduate student, this solution maintained my involvement in Ô-Môi, which a regular volunteer participation would not have. I had a double mission. Working for the group was also working toward my dissertation. The two went hand in hand, but the blurry line between research and personal commitment also became overwhelming. There was no break between academic work and downtime. Every involvement in Ô-Môi that served as downtime (e.g., attending a party) had to be recorded; my life became occupied with journal writing about my Ô-Môi experience or my actual participation with Ô-Môi members. When friendships with some members went sour, I found myself reluctant to record what had happened and reflected on it for future analysis. I was probably also more diplomatic in my relationships with people than I normally would be, in fear that I might lose potential important interviewees and informants. The demands of research, in many ways, reinforced my commitment to Ô-Môi as I played the roles of organizer, counselor, facilitator, and secretary. I am no longer as active in Ô-Môi now that I am done with the research. In retrospect, I believe I have contributed much to the sustenance of the organization by providing my home as a space for members to meet and connect with one another. The objective of a needs assessment, on the other hand, did not contribute much to the organization because there were few active members left to implement any suggestions I made when I was busy writing up my dissertation. The moral here is that the actual participatory research is a benefit to the organization that is lacking in people and material resources. Suggestions of organizational changes, on the other hand, are lofty goals and not practical in an organization organized on volunteerism. In that sense, I should go back to implement the suggestions in order to be true to my activism now that my ethnographic research is done. That act of going back to help after my research is done would make that naive notion of "community empowerment" complete.

My entrée to the organization was my request to document our group interactions. There were no suspicions of my ethnicity (not being biracial), gender (not being transgender), or sexuality (not being bisexual). My identity as a Vietnamese lesbian was a definite advantage in my access to members. My loyalty was not questioned, unlike that of a bisexual woman in our group who discovered that despite being a co-founding member, her interests in men made her suspect to the group majority, which is lesbian.

My sanity was also not questioned because I identify as a woman. For the transgender men in our group, their sanity was questioned because most lesbians think that transgender people are "crazy" lesbians who hate their bodies. In other words, identifying as a lesbian, like the core majority, I was given the benefit of the doubt that I belonged.

Looking stereotypically "Asian," my ethnicity was also not questioned. Since I was able to speak and write basic Vietnamese, my ethnic capital fared well compared to other members who could not speak or write. There were two accounts, however, on which my ethnicity was questioned. For one, my strange non-Vietnamese last name usually became an initial conversation starter. The usual suspicions were that it was my name by marriage or that I was really biracial. Given that the majority of members were first generation Vietnamese, being "real Vietnamese" became a requirement for bonding with other members. The second questioning of my ethnic identity was because I'm partially Chinese. Being partially Chinese (my father and mother are each half Chinese), a few members thought that I should identify as Chinese Vietnamese instead of just Vietnamese.

The relative ease in entrée because of my racial/ethnic and sexual membership, however, could also create extra baggage. As an organization that operated to support marginalized racial, ethnic, gender, and sexual identities, the site came with high expectations of members receiving support from other members. When individual personalities clashed, this expectation became unfulfilled. I thus found myself received with open arms because "I'm one of them" and at the same time questioned for not wanting to be "best friends" with some members given our commonality. As one member puts it, "I wouldn't be friends with some of these people if it were not for Ô-Môi." The high expectation of support and friendship when unfulfilled indeed led to great disappointment and disillusionment by some members who have since departed from the group. Moreover, as one of the few places to offer a space for queer Vietnamese to meet to offset the homophobia and heterosexism in straight Vietnamese settings and the racism and cultural insensitivity in a queer (white) setting, Ô-Môi was a site of great promise for many individuals who were looking for romance. It could be sexually high-charged as old and new members scoped the field for potential partners, assuming that the commonality of being queer and Vietnamese would overcome other differences. This high expectation became taxing for me, a researcher who just wanted to document identity work.

In a group that supported stigmatized sexual-gender identities, the issues of privacy and secrecy were crucial. Many members did not want their sexual or gender identity revealed in a straight Vietnamese setting.

Many members were not out to their family, friends, and coworkers and were very cautious about being interviewed. They made sure I understood that none of the information would get back to them in the straight or queer Vietnamese community. In my write-up, I made sure I used non-identifying characteristics that would not out them to the straight Vietnamese community. More difficult was trying to do the same for the queer Vietnamese community. The community was small and most members in the network knew each other. When one member didn't have something nice to say about another and the information was important to cite in my analysis, it took double effort to obscure the identity of the speaker, especially when that identity was crucial in their critique of other members. For example, a transgender man criticized the group and a particular member about being transphobic. Given that there were only four transgender members, the obfuscation achieved little effectiveness because members of the community knew who among the transgenders were most vocal about their dissatisfaction.

As a social scientist, I see racial/ethnic, gender, and sexual identities as social constructs. Most Ô-Môi members, however, have an essentialist understanding of their ethnic/racial, sexual, and gender identities. These essentialist explanations by Ô-Môi members did not sit well with me. Given that one of the major tasks of the group was to explain and normalize their gender and sexuality, essentialist theses came to dominate conversations. The Queer[46] politics that informed my research project did not help me in my everyday cohesion building with members when I emphasized sexual preference instead of sexual orientation. This Queer inclination also did not mesh well with most members' politics or lack of progressive politics. While Queer activism had informed Queer theory about the praxis of destabilizing cultural space, this practice was only appreciated by a few queer activists in the group. For the majority, emphasizing difference and denaturalizing race, ethnicity, gender, and sexuality created conflict and negation of their identities. In short, while queer theory is good for analysis, its praxis in everyday settings may not help to create rapport for ethnographers who rely on such human connections for data gathering.

Conclusion

In summation, this paper reviews some of the developments in race and sexuality studies in sociology to argue their convergence in viewing race and sexuality as mutually constitutive processes (racial project, sexual performativity). From this conceptualization, we begin a different methodology in researching race and sexuality. Theoretically, seeing race and sexuality as processes means that we need a method that can capture these processes that racialize and sexualize. A rereading of past events or a documentation of everyday processes can achieve this. I thus turned to a discussion on ethnography that provided this type of documentation. I then discussed how critical ethnography and extended case method offer much potential to ethnic studies scholars who want to combine activism with academic work. I call this reflexive ethnographic approach with a progressive politics rooted in community activism, activist ethnography. I close with some detailed discussion about the advantages and obstacles of activist ethnography in the hope that they will give the reader some insights about its potentials and limitations.

While the developments in race and sexuality have theoretically illuminated our intellectual understanding of these processes, as seen in the rereading of history or in textual analysis, activist ethnography using the extended case study analysis on race and sexuality can connect the global and the local, the institutional and the representational, and the theoretical and the practical. It connects us to real people facing life struggles. Furthermore, it can also help us engage in current liberatory projects instead of just talking about them. In that sense, this methodology of activist ethnography has much to offer the mission of ethnic studies.

Ethnic studies, being an interdisciplinary or multidisciplinary[47] study, has never clearly articulated a methodology except for the fact that its methods are eclectic, given its multidisciplinary influences, and that its political projects are to challenge the cultural, economic, and political status quo. In my discussion of Ô-Môi, I shared some insights about the advantages and challenges of doing ethnography with a political agenda. Theoretically and methodologically, ethnography offers to document the intersection of race and sexuality through the observation of everyday racial-sexual projects or identity work. Politically, ethnographic participant-observations also allow ethnic studies scholars to intervene in everyday politics of identity. In this sense, activist ethnography offers both methodological and theoretical justifications for an ethnic studies standpoint epistemology and politics.

Notes

1. Sandra Harding, "Is There a Feminist Method?" in *Feminism and Methodology*, ed. Sandra Harding (Bloomington: Indiana University Press, 1987), 2–3.
2. Nancy A. Naples, *Feminism and Method: Ethnography, Discourse Analysis and Activist Research* (New York: Routledge, 2003), 3.

3. While I focus on race and sexuality, the study I am referring to deals with race, ethnicity, gender, sexuality, and class, because the people I am interviewing and working with are racialized ethnic minorities whose gender and sexuality are marginalized in a capitalist society that operates in gender-sex binaries.

4. Aside from the work of Omi and Winant on racial formation and the subsequent works of legal scholars of color in critical race studies, it appears that articulations about methodologies for race studies have come from women of color scholars like Gloria Anzaldua, bell hooks, and Patricia Hill Collins, who advocate for an analysis of the intersection of race, gender, class, and sexuality, where knowledge production centers on the perspectives of the oppressed.

5. Timothy P. Fong and Larry H. Shinagawa, eds., *Asian Americans: Experiences and Perspectives* (Upper Saddle River, N.J.: Prentice Hall, 2000).

6. Shirley Hune, "Rethinking Race: Paradigms and Policy Formation," in *Contemporary Asian America: A Multidisciplinary Reader*, ed. Min Zhou and James V. Gatewood (New York: New York University Press, 2000), 667–676; Audre Lorde, "The Master's Tools Will Never Dismantle the Master's House," in *Sister Outsider*. PBC Edition ed. Zami/Sister Outsider/Undersong. (New York: QPB, 1984), 110–113.

7. According to Sandra Harding, "feminist standpoint epistemology was evidently an idea whose time had come" since many of the theorists were working independently and were unaware of each other's work until Harding put together the 1983 anthology, *Discovering Reality: Feminist Perspectives on Epistemology, Metaphysics, Methodology, and the Philosophy of Science*. Quote from Sandra Harding, "Comment on Hekman's 'Truth and Method: Feminist Standpoint Theory Revisited': Whose Standpoint Needs the Regimes of Truth and Reality?" *Signs* 22, no. 2 (1997): 389. For more on the origin of standpoint theory/ies, please see the debate generated with Susan Hekman's article, "Truth and Method: Feminist Standpoint Theory Revisited" and responses back by Sandra Harding and Dorothy Smith. See Sandra Harding and Merrill Hintikka, eds., *Discovering Reality: Feminist Perspectives on Epistemology, Metaphysics, Methodology, and Philosophy of Science* (Dordrecht: Kluwer, 1983); Dorothy Smith, "Women's Perspective as a Radical Critique of Sociology," *Sociological Inquiry* 44 (1974): 7–14; Dorothy Smith, "Comment on Hekman's 'Truth and Method: Feminist Standpoint Theory Revisited,'" *Signs* 22, no. 2 (1997): 392–398; Nancy Hartsock, "The Feminist Standpoint: Developing the Ground for a Specifically Feminist Historical Materialism," in *Discovering Reality*, ed. Harding and Hintikka, 283–310; and Patricia Hill Collins, *Black Feminist Thought: Knowledge, Consciousness, and the Politics of Empowerment* (New York: Routledge, 1991).

8. Naples, *Feminism and Method*.

9. Hill Collins, *Black Feminist Thought*.

10. I use "queer" as a shorthand for lesbian/gay/bisexual/transgender (LGBT). It is also a shortcut term that encompasses sexual and gender minorities who do not conform to the binary sex-gender-sexuality regime. "Queer theory" or

"Queer praxis" with a capital "Q" refers to a specific set of deconstructive theories and practices that question cultural norms and interrogate what has been taken for granted as natural.

11. Many members in this group are not out for fear of rejections from family and community. As well, they fear being fired or harassed at work and home. Ironically, the support organization itself is publicly out as a means to recruit and support queer Vietnamese individuals who are often isolated and in the closet.

12. Fong and Shinagawa, *Asian Americans*.

13. A group of eight people met earlier in October 2004 to discuss the possible formation of a support group, but the group did not solidify and have a name until it met in 1995 with a core of twenty-eight members.

14. The Combahee River Collective, "A Black Feminist Statement," in *Capitalist Patriarchy and the Case of Socialist Feminism*, edited by Z. R. Eisenstein (New York: Monthly Review Press, 1979), 362–372; Hill Collins, *Black Feminist Thought*.

15. Hune, "Rethinking Race."

16. Eduardo Bonilla-Silva, *Racism without Racists: Color-Blind Racism and the Persistence of Racial Inequality in the United States* (Lanham, Md.: Rowman & Littlefield, 2003); Michael Omi and Howard Winant, *Racial Formation in the United States from the 1960s to the 1990s*, 2nd ed. (New York: Routledge, 1994).

17. Hune, "Rethinking Race."

18. Howard Winant, "Race and Race Theory," *Annual Review of Sociology* 26 (2000): 169–185.

19. Steven Seidman, "Introduction (Queer Theory/Sociology)," in *Queer Theory/Sociology*, ed. Steven Seidman, Twentieth-Century Social Theory (Cambridge: Blackwell, 1996), 1–29; Peter M. Nardi and Beth E. Schneider, eds., *Social Perspectives on Lesbian & Gay Studies* (London: Routledge, 1998); Harding and Hintikka, eds. *Discovering Reality*; and Hartsock, "Feminist Standpoint."

20. Joane Nagel, "Ethnicity and Sexuality," *Annual Review of Sociology* 26 (2000): 107–133; Seidman, "Introduction"; Winant, "Race and Race Theory."

21. Omi and Winant, *Racial Formation*.

22. Bonilla-Silva, *Racism without Racists*.

23. The four levels of oppression are borrowed from Gust A. Yep in his article "From Homophobia and Heterosexism to Heteronormativity: Toward the Development of a Model of Queer Interventions in the University Classroom," *Journal of Lesbian Studies* 6, no. 3–4 (2002): 163–176. While his focus is on gender and sexual oppression, we can also use his quadrant analysis (originally: internalized homophobia, externalized homophobia, institutional violence, and discursive violence) in looking at race (internalized racism, individual racial discrimination, institutional racism, and discursive racism or racist ideology).

24. Omi and Winant, *Racial Formation*.

25. For example, Tomas Almaguer, *Racial Fault Lines: The Historical Origins of White Supremacy in California* (Berkeley: University of California Press, 1994); Karen Brodkin, "How Jews Became White Folks," in *White Privilege: Essential*

Readings on the Other Side of Racism, ed. Paula S. Rothenberg (New York: Worth Publishers, 2002), 35–48; Neil Foley, "Becoming Hispanic: Mexican Americans and Whiteness," in *White Privilege: Essential Readings on the Other Side of Racism*, ed. Paula S. Rothenberg (New York: Worth Publishers, 2002), 49–60; Philip Kasinitz, *Caribbean New York: Black Immigrants and the Politics of Race* (Ithaca, N.Y.: Cornell University Press, 1992); David R. Roediger, *The Wages of Whiteness: Race and the Making of the American Working Class*, Haymarket Series, ed. Michael Davis and Michael Sprinker (New York: Verso, 1991).

26. Gina Masequesmay, "Everyday Identity Work at an Asian Pacific AIDS Organization," in *Cultural Compass: Ethnographic Explorations of Asian America*, ed. Martin F. Manalansan, IV, Asian American History and Culture (Philadelphia: Temple University Press, 2000), 113–138; Gina Masequesmay, "Negotiating Multiple Identities in a Queer Vietnamese Support Group." *Journal of Homosexuality* 45, nos. 2–4 (2003): 193–215.

27. Joane Nagel, *Race, Ethnicity, and Sexuality: Intimate Intersections, Forbidden Frontiers* (New York: Oxford University Press, 2003).

28. Seidman, "Introduction."

29. Rosemarie Tong, *Feminist Thought: A Comprehensive Introduction* (Boulder, Colo.: Westview Press, 1989).

30. Although Kinsey's population sample was revealed to be biased, it was the first national effort to find out what Americans were practicing sexually. His study shattered many sex-taboos and gave Puritanical and Victorian Americans an excuse to talk about sex.

31. Seidman, "Introduction."

32. Michel Foucault, *The History of Sexuality: An Introduction*, vol. 1. (New York: Vintage, 1978); Judith Butler, *Gender Trouble: Feminism and the Subversion of Identity* (New York: Routledge, 1990).

33. Paula S. Rothenberg, ed., *White Privilege: Essential Readings on the Other Side of Racism* (New York: Worth Publishers, 2002).

34. Nagel, *Race*.

35. A few examples of studies in Asian American studies are Jennifer Ting's historical study of the Bachelor Society (Jennifer Ting, "Bachelor Society: Deviant Heterosexuality and Asian American Historiography," in *Privileging Positions: The Sites of Asian American Studies*, ed. Gary Y. Okihiro, Marilyn Alquizola, Dorothy Fujita Rony, and K. Scott Wong [Pullman: Washington State University Press, 1995]); and David Eng's work in literature (David L. Eng, "Racial Castration: Managing Masculinity in Asian America," in *Perverse Modernities*, ed. Judith Halberstam and Lisa Lowe [Durham, N.C.: Duke University Press, 2001]). These works illustrate the usefulness of sexualizing or queering Asian American history and literature to give us a more in-depth understanding of how normal heterosexuality was implicated in the construction of Asians and Asian Americans.

36. Stephen Pfohl, *Images of Deviance and Social Control: A Sociological History*, 2nd ed. (New York: McGraw-Hill, 1994).

37. Linda Trinh Vo, "Performing Ethnography in Asian American Communities: Beyond the Insider-versus-Outsider Perspective," in *Cultural Compass: Ethnographic Explorations of Asian America*, ed. Martin F. Manalansan, IV, Asian American History and Culture series (Philadelphia: Temple University Press, 2000), 17–37; Martin F. Manalansan, IV, "Introduction," in *Cultural Compass*, 1–13.

38. Gilbert Elbaz, "The Sociology of Aids Activism: The Case of Act up/New York, 1987–1992," Ph.D. dissertation, City University of New York, 1992.

39. Michael Burawoy et al., *Ethnography Unbound: Power and Resistance in the Modern Metropolis* (Berkeley: University of California Press, 1991).

40. Burawoy uses "domination" to mean, as Jürgen Habermas had put it, "the colonization of the life world" by the system (1–2). That is, the invasion of everyday life by political and economic systems. It is a situation in which everyday life loses its autonomy and shared purpose with the continuous commodification of social life through money and ever-expansive administration of social life through power (2).

41. Whereas Harold Garfinkel's ethnomethodology creates "anomalies" in the field to find universal rules (and "theories") of interactions, Burawoy is proposing that the "anomaly" be located within existing theories and be explained by modifying relevant existing theories.

42. Masequesmay, "Everyday Identity Work"; Masequesmay, "Negotiating Multiple Identities."

43. Smith, "Comment."

44. Naples, *Feminism and Method*, 75.

45. Vo, "Performing Ethnography"; Naples, *Feminism and Method*.

46. I use "Queer" with a capital "Q" here to mean a politics of deconstruction that questions what is normal. In many queer personal narratives that attempt to normalize individual sexuality, the essentialist argument of being born gay/lesbian is given to naturalize the individual's non-straight sexual orientation. However, for Queer activists the argument for being treated equally because of one's natural gay/lesbian sexual orientation is problematic. As human beings, we should all be treated equally regardless of our sexual orientation or sexual preference.

47. It appears that the original effort of the field to be interdisciplinary is a trying project. My observation is that the trend of ever-increasing specialties has led to a congregation of disciplines under one roof of ethnic studies as seen in many departments of Asian American studies, Chicano studies, and so forth, whereby scholars of traditional disciplines follow their own discipline's methods and occasionally dabble with other disciplines' methods. Hence, it is more multidisciplinary than interdisciplinary, or integrating of methods and methodology. It also seems that there are more crossovers of theories than methods.

BREAKING BORDERS, BOUNDARIES, AND COLOR LINES   III

Ethnic Studies and Interdisciplinarity   10

JOHNNELLA E. BUTLER

ETHNIC STUDIES AND INTERDISCIPLINARITY is a complicated topic for two fundamental reasons. First, ethnic studies has no particular methodology which it identifies. I think it is fair to say, without doing an exhaustive study, that sociologists in ethnic studies tend to employ sociological methodology; literary scholars utilize the most current literary theories; historians the reigning theoretical approaches, and so on for the different disciplines, with all influenced greatly by feminists of color scholarship and theoretical stances as well as cultural studies and American studies. In addition many ethnic studies practitioners have embraced interdisciplinarity, as have many in the academy—incorporating it into disciplinary-based study to varying degrees—without significant reflection as to the whys and hows of interdisciplinarity.

Second, racial identity, a key theme, trope, and subject of investigation in ethnic studies, is heavily charged historically, politically, culturally, economically, and socially. It is so closely related to racism and ethnocentrism that ethnic studies has historically suffered a tension between the desire to engage the multiplicity of social identity and the impulse to give that multiplicity short shrift to address the immediacy and pervasiveness of racism. As Linda Martín Alcoff and Eduardo Mendieta state in the opening paragraph of their book *Identities: Race, Class, Gender, and Nationality*, the concept of identity is highly suspect:

> There is considerable interest in the question of identity today, perhaps equaled only by the considerable confusion around the question of why identities continue to exert such power, and whether they should be acknowledged and legally recognized or simply ignored in the hope that they

will disappear. Everyone seems to agree that social identities such as ethnicity, sexuality, and nationality have come to the center of political mobilization since the United States' cultural revolution of the 1960s, and many construe recent global conflicts as centered around differences in fundamental aspects of cultural identity. But there is little agreement about the true causes of this emerging importance of social identities or about its most likely enduring political effects. For some, the emphasis on identity is a threat to democracy and an incitement of ceaseless conflict; for others, it is a struggle long overdue.[1]

This chapter lays out the relationships among ethnic studies, identity, and interdisciplinarity, and argues that interdisciplinarity should become the hallmark of ethnic studies. Ethnic studies scholars and teachers are drawn to interdisciplinarity because identity is multiple and interconnected, as is life. The episteme of ethnic studies resides in the way people order and live their lives, and life is lived in interdisciplinarity. We make sense out of social, cultural, economic, and political realities, and therefore, interdisciplinarity is not only a humanities, social science, or scientific construct. It is the way we live our lives.[2]

When discussing interdisciplinarity, it is necessary to acknowledge that the discourses within and around ethnic studies inform its location in the academy. These discourses both necessitate and place obstacles to ethnic studies having an implicit theoretical base as a field of study, composed of disciplinary, multidisciplinary, cross-disciplinary, and interdisciplinary approaches, methodologies, research, and scholarship. Interdisciplinarity as a methodology for ethnic studies does not eradicate the necessity for other related discipline-based or multidisciplinary or cross-disciplinary methodologies. It does, however, seem to me to be the methodology that can give cohesiveness to the field and connect it most productively with other disciplines. It also follows logically that the theoretical foundation of ethnic studies, as implied above, rests in the lives of racialized ethnic Americans. What I offer here is a brief overview of the issues germane to ethnic studies in relation to interdisciplinarity. They are rooted in (1) the way the academy views identity, experience, and social location, the very real dimensions of human life that shape and inform ethnic studies; and (2) the skepticism about interdisciplinarity and the ability to be both a specialist and a generalist.

In her review of my edited volume, *Color-Line to Borderlands*, Marcia Marx,[3] citing her own tripart faculty appointment in two programs and one department, ethnic studies and women's studies and sociology, suggests that "the 'collisions' inherent in occupying such a position do not seem as daunting as they did before reading this book" (p. 113). Throughout her review, she invokes the language of "crossing borders," language which has become increasingly current outside discussions of borderland theory, as the sciences and social sciences, in particular, have recently begun to make concerted efforts to name and support interdisciplinarity in research and writing. While many humanists in cultural studies profess interdisciplinarity, there has been little attention to its institutionalization or methodology, perhaps given the overriding influence of theory that has become its own field of study. Similar to Professor Marx's assessment, I hope that this analysis suggests that the collisions brought about by the pursuit of both ethnic studies and interdisciplinarity are less daunting than they appear.

Ethnic Studies, Identity, and Objective Knowledge

The position of ethnic studies in higher education is vexed, as I see it, by confusions around the study of identity and conceptualizations of knowledge that disallow objectivity, particularly in American literary studies, whose methodologies tend to permeate the humanities and social sciences. Ethnic studies exists in stand-alone departments or centers devoted to both ethnic-specific and comparative study, and in departments and programs focusing on ethnic-specific groups. It examines racialized identity, experience, and social location in the multiple ways they are encountered, expressed, and represented domestically in the United States, transnationally, and diasporically. What has either not been made explicit or has been contested in ethnic studies is the epistemic status of identity as a source of valid knowledge. Instead, it has been debated, left to be "theorized in a wide range of idioms and through various methods and disciplines," as Henry Louis Gates, Jr. and Anthony Appiah offer in their influential 1995 volume, *Identities*.[4] Such an approach, I contend, is an inadequate effort to deal with the complexity of identity, its multiplicity, its intersections, its interconnections, and its relationships to other aspects of human reality. The theories implicit in the epistemic status of identity[5] aren't revealed and coded through unconnected and various idiomatic and disciplinary studies, but rather through a studied interdisciplinary methodology reflective of the complexity and multiplicity of identity and its effects in the world.

A consortium of scholars that formed "The Future of Minority Studies Project" is currently doing the most insightful and useful thinking about identity and its multiple manifestations, intersections, and layers.[6] Their work has significant theoretical implications for queer studies, women's studies, disability studies, ethnic studies, and any "minority studies." Paula Moya, one of the initiators of that project, in the first chapter of her book, *Learning from Experience: Minority Identities, Multicultural Struggles*, makes the case for postpositivist realism, "an epistemological position and political vision being articulated by a growing number of scholars in the United States and abroad who are developing an alternative to the reductionism and inadequacy of essentialist *and* postmodernist approaches to identity" (p. 27). After a brief discussion of Moya's argument in regard to postmodern conceptualizations of identity and a consideration of the implications of her argument to African American literature in order to make the case for interdisciplinarity in ethnic studies, I will discuss in the final section the institutionalization of interdisciplinarity in ethnic studies.

By no means do I mean to imply that ethnic studies is only concerned with identity. It is concerned with social location, experience, cultural identity, legacies of the past, legal and institutional structures and strictures, and all of their connections and interrelatedness. I am focusing on identity, however, for two reasons. First, identity is the one of multiple variables that has a defining role in all aspects of ethnic studies, from what is taught, to who is teaching. Second, the pervasive and misguided postmodern relegation of identity and identity politics has contributed more significantly to the arrested development of the field and its methodology than, I wager, administrators who ambivalently validate and support the field solely on the basis of campus demographics.

We are living through times in which dominant, mainstream scholarship—beginning with the backlash to the establishment of Black studies/African American studies/Africana studies—relegates serious study of identity by people of color in the United States to essentialist solipsism. It is enlightening to compare a quote from the editorial page of the first issue of the short-lived *First World, An International Journal of Black Thought* (Winter 1977) to contemporary observations by Paula Moya. The editor, the late Hoyte Fuller writes:

> In the January 19 issue of *Newsweek* magazine, one of the principal exponents of 'neo-conservatism,' Irving Kristol, defended his credo and offered definitions of its tenets. "Neo-conservatism tends to be respectful of traditional values and institutions: religion, the family, the 'high culture' of Western civilization," . . . Mr. Kristol said. "If there is any one thing that neo-conservatives are unanimous about it is their dislike of the 'counter-

culture' that has played so remarkable a role in American life over these past 15 years."... The erudite Mr. Kristol added that 'Values emerge out of the experience of generations and represent the accumulated wisdom of these generations; they simply cannot be got out of rap sessions about 'identity' or 'authenticity,'" and he is quite right, although not surprisingly, he deals in superficialities. If he could rise above his narrow-focused Europeanness, he might be able to understand that the Black Movement aimed, in fact, at an assertion of those values which had emerged 'out of the experience of generations.' As for rap sessions about 'identity' and 'authenticity,' that happens to be a manifestation of our culture and our particular needs (inside front cover).[7]

Moya continues in *Learning From Experience*:

> Within the field of U.S. literary and cultural studies, the institutionalization of a discourse of postmodernism has spawned an approach to difference that ironically erases the distinctiveness and relationality of difference itself. Typically, postmodernist theorists either internalize difference so that the individual is herself seen as "fragmented" and "contradictory" (thus displacing attention from the distinctions that exist between different kinds of people), or they attempt to "subvert" difference by showing that "difference" is merely a discursive illusion (thus leaving no way to contend with the fact that people experience themselves as different from each other). In either case, postmodernists inscribe, albeit unintentionally, a kind of universalizing sameness (we are all marginal now!) that their celebration of "difference" had tried so hard to avoid.... If, as Judith Butler and Joan Scott claim in their introduction to *Feminists Theorize the Political*, concepts like 'experience' and 'identity' enact a 'silent violence,'... then any invocation of these 'foundational' concepts will be seen as always already tainted with exclusionary and totalizing forms of power [p. xiv].... In the current theoretical climate within U.S. literary and cultural studies, the feminist scholar who persists in using categories such as race or gender can be presumptively charged with essentialism, while her appeals to 'experience' or 'identity' may cause her to be dismissed as either dangerously reactionary or hopelessly naïve. If, on the contrary, she accepts the strictures placed on her by postmodernism, the concerned feminist scholar may well find it difficult to explain why some people experience feelings of racial self-hatred while others feel a sense of racial superiority, some people live in poverty while others live in comfort, and some people have to worry about getting pregnant while others do not (pp. 24–25).

I am not suggesting neo-conservative ascriptions to postmodernism. Rather, I am suggesting that ethnocentrism can connect perspectives that see themselves as radically opposite, such as Kristol with Judith Butler and Joan Scott. Ethnic studies, itself, has not advanced to posit its theoretical positions (and they would vary somewhat to reflect the differing and similar realities of the racialized experiences studied), because at its core is the tension between the epistemic knowledge that identity and experience bring to the academy and the Eurocentric demand for objective knowledge that requires certainty. The kind of objective knowledge that ethnic studies requires is "a theory-dependent, socially realizable goal."[8]

For example, the genre and content of African American literature—very broadly stated as slave narrative, autobiography, oratory, poetry, historical fiction, signifying—and the call-response nature of the style and content—speak to reckoning with experience to understand the inherent multiplicity, complexity, and multi-layeredness as well as the imposed fixity of African American identity. This objective knowledge emerges from the critical interaction of parallel and counter-histories in texts, between the reader and the texts, and from the intersection of individual stories, group stories, local, regional, and national stories intersecting, overlapping, and complementing, interrogating, and conflicting with one another. The humanities often see African American literary study that reckons with identity, experience, and social location as socially and sociologically situated, or even as essentialist, rather than contextualized. The social sciences often view African American studies as a branch of its work, imposing sociological theory as the appropriate approach to the study of groups. In African diasporic work the arts frequently relegate ritual expression to non-contextualized play and performance.[9]

As a goal, objectivity facilitates expression, illumination, and an accuracy achieved by constantly identifying, examining, and working through error. Such an objectivity affirms a wholeness, the revision of the African American subject/self that understands his/her social location, the ways it changes as aspects of identity are foregrounded, and the ways to engage and reckon with the tensions of double-consciousness with agency because the dynamics that emanate from the past and the present are understood. This wholeness, or ability to identify and work with the knowledge that one's cultural identity, social location, and experience reveals as he or she interacts with reality ("a 'reality' that is, at least in part, causally independent of humans' mental constructions of it."[10]) is the springboard for agency, which includes the capacity to act on possibility. Ethnic studies, whether in courses on the Jazz Age and the Harlem Renaissance, on comparative studies of history, drama, film, or literature, or on Chicano/a autobiography, has as its goal an objective understanding of one's relationship with the world, through the engagement of error and fact, the possible and probable, and the impossible and improbable.

An objectivity that yields an accurate representation of racialized experience is achieved through the process of wholeness that Nella Larsen, Ralph Ellison, James Baldwin, Toni Cade Bambara, Toni Morrison, Gloria Naylor, and Paule Marshall, among others describe and analyze in their novels; it is the wholeness that Cherríe Moraga sees possible in coalition[11] and that the late Gloria Anzaldúa describes in her conceptualization of mestiza consciousness. Consistent with the Black feminist theory Patricia Hill Collins advances in her book, it is a palimpsestic, interactive, tension-engaging wholeness, one proposed and examined by feminist women of color.[12]

Moya discusses succinctly and accessibly the postpositivist realist theory of identity which has informed my discussion above and which I see as implicit in ethnic studies. She discusses six basic claims of a postpositivist realist theory of identity: First, that "the different social categories (such as gender, race, class, and sexuality) that together constitute an individual's social location are causally related to the experiences she will have"; second, "that an individual's experiences will influence, but not entirely determine the formation of her cultural identity"; third, "that there is an epistemic component to identity that allows for the possibility of error and of accuracy in interpreting the things that happen to us;" fourth, "that some identities, because they can more adequately account for the social categories constituting an individual's social location, have greater epistemic value than some others that the same individual might claim"; fifth, "that our ability to acknowledge and understand fundamental aspects of our world will depend on our ability to acknowledge and understand the social, political, economic, and epistemic consequences of our own social location; and sixth, oppositional struggle is fundamental to our ability to understand the world more accurately."[13]

The core questions of ethnic studies engage these claims. Their complexity and the complexity of identity, with its many dimensions, demands interdisciplinarity and comparative study in order to explore conflicts, error, similarities, and differences toward the end of a contextualized objectivity that yields knowledge.

Ethnic Studies and Interdisciplinarity

While I may be overlooking an important recent discussion on interdisciplinarity, I think it is safe to say it is just becoming a topic of serious consideration in many fields. An exception as well as an example may be American studies. Professing interdisciplinarity but recently, with impending and welcomed National Research Council rating, American studies is beginning to examine the methodological assumptions of the field and how those assumptions fit with institutional demands and structure.[14] American studies and women's studies, cognate fields to ethnic studies,[15] are far ahead of ethnic studies, so it seems at least to those of us who thirty-odd years ago envisioned that by now there would be, as a norm, B.A., M.A., and Ph.D. programs in ethnic studies in research institutions, and B.A. and M.A. programs in research-intensive, comprehensive, and liberal arts institutions. There exist to date only two Ph.D. programs in ethnic studies, and while there are a few M.A. programs, they are mostly through traditional, discipline-based departments. At the baccalaureate level, departments, programs, minors, and certificates appear to be stable and growing.[16] Given this landscape, future faculty in ethnic studies will be trained in American studies, women's studies, and in cultural studies in various discipline-based departments, with little, if any, attention to methodology or assumptions rooted in the episteme of ethnic studies, the lived lives of the peoples it studies.

The implications of this for the field are obvious and are most manifest in the fact that there is no term for ethnic studies methodology and theory as there is for women's studies methodology. Since the two fields, unlike American studies, address the study of specific groups, one might expect a methodology to be named. Women's studies named its methodology feminist: feminist theory (which is a field in itself), feminist perspectives, and so forth. The identification of a theory and methodology for ethnic studies is a complex problem, not easily solved. Women's studies "solved" the first and most important obstacle to establishing such a recognized theory and methodology—that of the multiplicity of women's locations and experiences—by defining "feminist" as white and largely middle-class, with marginal attention to domestic racialized minority women, and by locating programs and departments as unambiguously as possible in the humanities or social sciences. Its interdisciplinarity, then, locates itself within disciplines or cognate disciplines—literature, philosophy, and history; or sociology, anthropology, and political science, with cultural studies, of which feminist theory is a part, connecting the disciplines. Ethnic studies, on the other hand, while making significant inroads in literary studies and history, has been largely defined by sociology, where historically the study of "race relations" prevailed. That legacy places most ethnic studies units in the social sciences, relegating the humanities and the arts to tenuous ties with those units, as they locate themselves in discipline-based departments. This picture is further complicated by the cultural studies orientation of many ethnic studies units, which tends to displace the text-based, historically-located study of racialized ethnic representation and devalues or even dismisses the salience of the past and its legacies and identity. In addition, in programs and departments, faculty have formed courses of study, with little wrestling with the "collisions" inherent in bringing together either well-established disciplines with their attendant cultures or ladder and part-time faculty from various racialized ethnic, socioeconomic, and academic backgrounds with histories of tension and few models of collaboration. Well-meaning administrators, ruled by FTEs (full-time equivalents), discipline-based budgets, and either hesitant ignorance or latent racism, established programs with faculty lines in other departments and shared faculty lines—a structure that would either implode or remain in an arrested state because it was so poorly rooted in the institutional structure. Thus, for example, well-funded and well-intended efforts like the American Ethnic Studies Major Implementation Grant (funded by The Ford Foundation in the late 1980s at the University of Washington, my former institution), could not get beyond developing courses in disciplines, shying away from comparative, interdisciplinary teaching and scholarship, as it struggled with the tacit sociological methodology that pervaded the work, imposed in well-intentioned efforts by faculty in that or related disciplines. And, despite works of the early 1990s such as Ronald Takaki's masterpiece of interdisciplinary and comparative scholarship, *A Different Mirror: A History of Multicultural America*, and Maulana Karenga's well-stated attempt to lay out the unity of the field of Black studies by naming it a discipline with interdisciplinary methodology in his *Introduction to Black Studies*,[17] discipline-based or insufficiently defined multidisciplinary scholarship and methodology have prevailed in institutionally weak academic enclaves bursting with frustrated energy in the midst of arrested development.

The prevalence of discipline-based or multidisciplinary scholarship in ethnic studies is also symptomatic of the state of interdisciplinarity. In my article "Graduate Education and American Studies: The Implementation of Interdisciplinarity," I discuss strategies to enhance interdisciplinarity in American studies. They apply as well to ethnic studies. First, recognize the rigidity of the disciplines and the natural institutional resistance to change. Don't confuse the resistance with racism or ethnocentrism. Some of the most dedicated ethnic studies scholars defend disciplinarity to the death. Secondly, identify, think, and work through answers to questions interdisciplinarity raises. Those I listed in the American studies article hold here:

> How do we do interdisciplinarity research, scholarship, and teaching? What does it look like? How do we define it? What are its end products and how do we describe and name methodology that partakes of several disciplines, blurring boundaries? Does collaboration improve interdisciplinary research and writing? In fact, is collaboration a hallmark of interdisciplinarity? How do we assess collaborative work? Does interdisciplinary academic training prepare students for the work force? What norms are implicit in interdisciplinary work? Is interdisciplinarity counter to our binary-based logic that demands the resolution of opposites rather than both the resolution of opposites and the engagement of tensions of opposition over time? In other words, can we imagine an interdisciplinary methodology?[18]

Lisa R. Latucca's typology of interdisciplinarity helps us understand the dimensions of interdisciplinarity and demonstrates that often what we term multidisciplinary or cross-disciplinary can more precisely be described as a type of interdisciplinarity. She identifies the typology of interdisciplinarity as:

1. Informed Disciplinarity (disciplinary questions requiring outreach to other disciplines);
2. Synthetic Interdisciplinarity (questions that link disciplines);
3. Transdisciplinarity (questions that cross disciplines); and
4. Conceptual Interdisciplinarity (questions without a compelling disciplinary basis).[19]

The questions become, she says, more important than how they are answered.

Yet, to engage these typologies and even improve upon them through research and scholarship in ethnic studies, we would have to consciously identify the intersections of history, literature, politics, and economics, where one is foregrounded and better understood and illuminated by the others, in what ways, how, and why. Thus, we may find that in ethnic studies, as in American studies, we may move between synthetic interdisciplinarity and transdisciplinarity. At times, the questions, or parts of questions, may require an informed disciplinarity. To wrestle more productively with its foci of identity, experience, and social location, ethnic studies then must identify the questions most germane to each racialized group, to each manifestation of racialized experience in the various disciplines, and to each social location. Of course, these are not the only questions ethnic studies engages, but my point is that problem- or question-oriented research and teaching agendas relate more directly to the constantly emerging content of ethnic studies. And interdisciplinarity as a conscious methodology may well lead to ways of doing comparative study without imposing predetermined norms or reinforcing simplistic, surface comparisons.

Comparative study in ethnic studies has a complexity that demands disengaging imposed norms and utilizing interdisciplinarity and adds a layer to ethnic studies that interdisciplinarity can penetrate. As Latucca's typology indicates, different kinds of interdisciplinarity fit different purposes and questions. I propose that together with a realist theoretical understanding of identity that validates experience and views objectivity as possible, conscious interdisciplinarity will advance the field, whether it is located in departments or programs, whether it is ethnic-specific or comparative. It will also lend clarity and direction to questions of identity and methodology similar to those raised by Asian American studies regarding the complexity and multiplicity of those termed Asian American, and to questions of genre and literary device such as the ethnic bildungsroman and magical realism.

Ethnic studies arguably pioneered interdisciplinarity in the mainstream disciplines of the academy. As Andrew Carnegie reminded us, pioneering does not pay. However, now may be the time for ethnic studies to take seriously its implicit theory of identity and methodology. To do so means being open to different ways of teaching and doing scholarship rooted in interdisciplinarity. To do so also means that ethnic studies would be again at the nexus of insitutional changes—a difficult position but the only position, I think, that can advance the field. This would include problem-based research, teaching, and learning; research and writing teams that deliberately, consciously, and collaboratively cross boundaries of discipline, gender, ethnicity, race, class, and academic rank; addressing in courses and in research shared topics or problems from different perspectives and different methodologies; reorganizing curricula to emphasize communication and collaboration; and identifying and exploring boundaries within, among, and between groups as well as connections and analogous experiences. For the undergraduate curriculum, this would mean more deliberately informed and synthetic interdisciplinarity in introductory courses (questions that link disciplines and that allow students to see how ethnic studies is situated); transdisciplinarity would be more deliberately addressed in 200- and 300-level courses (questions that cross disciplines, examining the relationships among cognate disciplines, the questions they ask and the methodologies employed); conceptual interdisciplinarity would be introduced at the capstone level and further developed at the graduate level (how to proceed with all typologies available depending upon the question, developing new collaborative and comparative theoretical approaches to a question). Such a schema will allow for the generative tensions in identity, differences, experiences, and social locations to be seen as both constructed and real[20] and will open the theoretical space for ethnic studies to engage its contexts of Americanization and globalization more fully and profoundly.

While team-teaching and learning communities may come to mind as expensive ways to engage in interdisciplinarity, research and capstone seminars as well as introductory courses are established places to begin and indeed may be more appropriate. For faculty, encouraging collaborative research and writing means addressing the reward structure of an institution—a long and arduous process in which the sciences are leading the way.[21] The result of engaging interdisciplinarity deliberatively is the definition of the field in holistic, organic terms as well as a centering of the epistemic and theoretical status of identity, the crux of ethnic studies.

Notes

1. Linda Martín Alcoff and Eduardo Mendieta, *Identities: Race, Class, Gender, and Nationality* (Malden, Mass.: Blackwell, 2003), 1.

2. This is a conceptualization of interdisciplinarity that I have long held; however, I owe this paragraph to a generous anonymous reviewer of this chapter, who stated the connection between interdisciplinarity and human life so well that I could only paraphrase him/her. Thank you.

3. Marcia Marx, book review, *Journal of American Ethnic History*, Summer 2003, 113–114.

4. *Identities* (Chicago: University of Chicago Press, 1995) is a compilation of essays first published in *Critical Theory* in response to a call by Gates and Appiah. "The study of identity," the authors point out, "crosses a number of disciplines to address such issues as the multiple intersections of race, class, and gender in feminist, lesbian, and gay studies, the interrelations of postcolonialism, nationalism, and ethnicity in ethnic and area studies, and so on. These intersections provide a provocative site for the articulation and discussion of new theories and discourses of identity" (1). Yet, the final word is given to Judith Butler, who argues that "reading identities as they are situated and formed in relation to one another means moving beyond the heuristic requirement of identity itself" (446). The reader is left to ponder the essays without any substantive analysis by Gates and Appiah, suggesting that the subject of identity/identities is up for grabs. Given the institutional place of ethnic studies, in particular Chicano/a, Latino/a studies and African American studies, the sheer power of such postmodern analyses, adopted by cultural studies scholars in various disciplines, undermines the very project of ethnic studies. Hence, for example, I was told that an English department did not develop

its potential in American ethnic literature as a graduate concentration because to do so was essentialist and that the study of identities in relation to literary texts had been rightly displaced by cultural studies.

5. See Satya Mohanty, "The Epistemic Status of Cultural Identity: On *Beloved* and the Postcolonial Condition," in *Reclaiming Identity: Realist Theory and the Predicament of Postmodernism*, edited by Paula Moya and Michael Hames-García (Berkeley: University of California Press, 2000), 29–66.

6. The Future of Minority Studies Project is "a multi-year interdisciplinary national research initiative that seeks to explore the role of identity in the shaping of a progressive and intellectually rigorous vision of minority scholarship and education. The FMS project focuses on 'identity' and 'minority studies' in order to stimulate discussion about issues that are simultaneously theoretical and practical, ranging from ethics and epistemology to political theory, pedagogical practice, and political activism" (website: ccsre.stanford.edu/RI_rp_FutureMinor.htm). Satya Mohanty's *Literary Theory and the Claims of History* (Ithaca, N.Y.: Cornell University Press, 1997), Hames-García and Moya's *Reclaiming Identity*, Moya's *Learning from Experience: Minority Identities, Multicultural Struggles*, and Alcoff and Mendieta's *Identities* have charted directions for the project.

7. The editor, Hoyt W. Fuller, explained that the editorial that is on the inside front cover and page 64 first appeared in the next-to-last issue of *Black World*, and was one of the "unadmitted causes for the death of the magazine" (64).

8. Moya, *Learning from Experience*, 27.

9. Anecdotal evidence of these positions abound. While revising this article, three graduate students have come to me for advice regarding how to deal with potentially conflictual situations on committees. In one instance, a dissertation chair views ritual dance in the Caribbean as play and performative, despite observing it in the context of a sacred ritual; in two other instances, chairs purport that identity is solely performative and not particularly linked to historical, sociological, political, economic, and cultural contexts.

10. Moya, *Learning from Experience*, 27.

11. Moya's discussion of Moraga in *Learning from Experience* (45–57) is particularly useful here. See also Gloria Anzaldúa, *Borderlands/La Frontera: The New Mestiza* (San Francisco: Spinsters/Aunt Lute, 1987), in particular, chapter 7.

12. For extended discussion of objectivity and wholeness, see Johnnella E. Butler, "*Mumbo Jumbo*, Theory, and the Aesthetics of Wholeness," in *Aesthetics in a Multicultural Age*, edited by Emory Elliott, Louis Freitas Caton, and Jeffrey Rhyne, 175–193. (New York: Oxford University Press, 2002); and Johnnella E. Butler, "African American Literature and Realist Theory: Seeking the "True-True" in *Identity Politics Reconsidered*, edited by Linda Martín Alcoff, Michael Hames-García, Satya Mohanty, and Paula Moya. (Palgrave Press, forthcoming).

13. Moya, *Learning from Experience*, 39–44.

14. For example, see Barry Shank, "The Challenge to University Administration: Understanding Interdisciplinary Departments and Cross Departmental Programs in

the Humanities: Introduction"; Johnnella E. Butler, "Graduate Education and American Studies: The Implementation of Interdisciplinarity"; Simon J. Bronner, "American Studies and Humanities: The Challenge to University Administration"; and Michael Cowan, "Getting Respect," in the *American Studies Newsletter* 27, no. 1 (March 2004): 1, 4–12; also on the American Studies Association website, under archive for American Studies Association newsletter).

15. Here I am referring to both comparative ethnic studies which exists in departments and centers for the study of race and ethnicity, and to the ethnic-specific studies of African American studies, Asian American studies, Chicano/a, Latino/a studies, and American Indian studies, although American Indian studies does not identify as ethnic, but rather as the study of peoples of sovereign nations. Racialization and the oppression and containment it imposes link all these studies.

16. This assessment is solely from my own informed observations.

17. Ronald A. Takaki, *A Different Mirror: A History of Multicultural America* (Boston: Little, Brown, 1993) and Maulana Karenga, *Introduction to Black Studies* (Los Angeles: University of Sankore Press, 1993). For further consideration of this topic, see Floyd W. Hayes, III, *A Turbulent Voyage: Readings in African American Studies* (San Diego, Calif.: Collegiate Press, 2000); Lane Hirabayashi, ed., *Teaching Asian America* (Lanham, Md.: Rowman and Littlefield, 1998); Jean Yu-Wen Shen Wu and Min Song, eds., *Asian American Studies: A Reader* (New Brunswick, N.J.: Rutgers University Press, 2000); and Dennis J. Bixler-Marquez et al., eds., *Chicano Studies: Survey and Analysis*, 2nd ed. (Dubuque, Iowa: Kendall Hunt, 2001).

18. Butler, "Graduate Education and American Studies: The Implemantation of Interdisciplinarity" 6.

19. Lisa R. Latucca, *Creating Interdisciplinarity* (Nashville, Tenn.: Vanderbilt University Press, 2001), 81.

20. Moya, *Learning from Experience*.

21. The Integrative Graduate Education and Research Training (IGERT) program (www.igert.org/faqs.htm), funded by the National Science Foundation, funds programs in interdisciplinary, collaborative, and problem-centered research. Students from different disciplines tackle scientific research problems in organized interdisciplinary groups. Implications are considerable for emerging methodologies, structures for collaboration, pedagogy, and so forth. I discuss this at length in the American studies article cited above.

Literary Matters
Research Methods in Reading Ethnic Literatures

11

KETU H. KATRAK

> *Interdisciplinary studies disrupt the narrative of traditional disciplines that have historically subordinated the concerns of non-Western, racial and ethnic minority peoples, and women, insofar as they hold the potential to transform disciplinary divisions that guarantee the self-evidence of these narratives.*
>
> LISA LOWE, IMMIGRANT ACTS[1]

> *[Interdisciplinarity is] more than a compromised shuttling between two disciplines or a naïve reach for some organic wholeness of knowledge. [Rather] such simultaneous and conjoined investigations of history, culture, and political economy can also critically re-member the partiality of disciplinary divisions and their knowledge-making practices.*
>
> LAURA HYUN YI KANG, COMPOSITIONAL SUBJECTS[2]

THIS ESSAY EXPLORES CRITICAL READING PRACTICES and research methods used in the interpretation of ethnic literatures, with an emphasis on Asian American Literature. Critical approaches used for literary texts overlap at times with overall interdisciplinary perspectives in ethnic studies as a whole. There is no single theoretical or methodological approach that suffices for the interpretation of ethnic literatures. Rather, an eclectic multiplicity is both strengthening and challenging to literary scholars in ethnic literatures in contemporary times who may draw upon critical approaches derived from cultural studies,[3] critical race/legal theory,[4] and immigration studies,[5] which have emerged as some of the most influential in analyses of literary material. Literary research methods are also derived from theories of poststructuralism and postmodernism, cultural anthropology, and diaspora studies.[6] Significant intellectual contributions address the realities of globalization, shifting populations, and new diasporas in the late twentieth and into the twenty-first centuries. Several of these critical methodologies draw upon, and often revise, critical methods that were more prevalent from the early to mid-twentieth century, such as Marxist, New Critical, psychoanalytic, structuralist, and race theories.

In their more contemporary articulations, for instance, poststructuralism and postmodernism challenge and even rename concepts in structuralism; similarly, race studies are usefully modulated by critical advances in critical race and legal studies that formulate new methods of jurisprudence that question existing legal structures and confront racism that is structural in U.S. society and in its system of law. Research methods proposed by critical legal scholars such as Kimberly Crenshaw, Derrick Bell, and Patricia Williams, among others, purport to shift the power structures that determine how law is interpreted and practiced. However esoteric, legal decisions have huge impacts on racialized plaintiffs' futures—in prison, in regular society, or in state-sponsored limbo spaces such as parole or remediation locales. The interpretation of ethnic writers has gained significant new layers through insights in critical race and legal theory, where race is linked to the state as in David Theo Goldberg's text, *The Racial State*. He notes forthrightly that "the modern state is in short, nothing less than a racial state. . . . Race is integral to the emergence, development, and transformations (conceptually, philosophically, materially) of the modern nation-state." Critical race and legal theory has also enabled literary scholars to analyze issues of accountability and reparation, both material and psychological, for crimes committed by nation-states, particularly against its racialized citizens, such as historical scars left by the institution of slavery or the internment of American citizens of Japanese ancestry during World War II.[7]

Critical methods deployed by cultural studies that combine different methodologies often serve as an overarching umbrella to accommodate the many and varied shifts, debates, and controversies in literary theory that attempt to keep pace with new literary voices, and changing historical, economic, and political realities such as globalization and cosmopolitanism. As Donald Hall remarks in a useful text, *Literary and Cultural Theory: From Basic Principles to Advanced Applications*, "the millennia-long history of literary and cultural analysis is one of dramatic metamorphosis and expansion from aesthetics. . . . to an emphasis today on the study of culture and how aesthetic notions are produced in a given time and place."[8] Notions of "fixed standards" and "critical truths" are challenged increasingly in contemporary literary theory, and the inclusion of social and political forces and the interplay between text and context all lead to "the shift from strictly literary analysis to a more expansive notion of cultural studies" (3).

Even as a literary reading may begin with a hypothesis, with raising questions and posing problems, the actual process of arriving at a reading incorporates historical, archival, and ethnographic data, along with the common tools of literary analysis such as the interpretation of symbols, the meaning of images that may be repeated evocatively through the text, the representation of characters and how they change and grow, what they learn, and whether as readers we arrive at a satisfactory resolution by the end of the text. What I describe here is not very different from reading a canonic literary text that can certainly draw a reader into its written world through the power of its language and expression, but the process is also vastly enriched by the addition of historical material and where possible, ethnographic evidence. In fact, engaging with such data "external" to the literary text and using that to arrive at a complex reading of the text enables ethnic studies to make particular research method contributions to traditional disciplines such as literature departments.

The methods used to analyze ethnic writers do depend on qualitative (relying on humanistic approaches) rather than quantitative methods more commonly used in social science inquiries. However, it would be more productive not to hold these two methods in separate compartments, but rather to cross-fertilize and explore overlaps. For instance, quantitative date can be usefully subjected to qualitative analysis, and vice versa. Let me take a specific literary text, Joy Kogawa's novel, *Obasan*, and demonstrate how in the process of interpretation, which is central to analyzing creative writers, ethnic and others, certain data are extremely relevant. State documents, personal memories preserved in photographs and letters, interviews, and archival footage are key to interpreting Kogawa's literary representation of the Japanese-Canadian internment experience. "Official history" provides one point of view that has to be mediated and nuanced when confronted with the discovery of invisible, hidden histories that present different points of view: ethnographic materials, interviews, oral histories with survivors, and visual evidence in film footage. Such incorporation results in "thick" description, to use Clifford Geertz's phrase, and a layered and complex interpretation of a literary text.[9]

Reading ethnic literatures—novels, memoirs, poems—is enabled by various literary theories as well as by the old-fashioned tools of interpretation in analyzing the imaginative representation of society and conflicts faced by characters in their everyday recognizable worlds, or in fantastic and surrealistic realms. There is much scope for readers to use their own imaginations and come up with various responses since there is usually no one fixed answer to questions raised by complex texts, such as why Chin Gung in Genny Lim's play, *Paper Angels*, commits suicide,[10] or how Lilia in Jhumpa Lahiri's short story, "When Mr. Pirzada Came to Dine," understands the history unfolding halfway around the world as the nation of Bangladesh is born and how she connects with Mr. Pirzada, who is watching his nation's birth on American television even as his frantic gaze searches the screen for any news about the safety of his own family in the midst of the political turmoil.[11] Literary interpretation retains the excitement of suggesting fluid and open-ended responses along with incorporating relevant historical material, archival data, and ethnographic material.

Many of these emphases of multiple readings, revisionary histories, and open-ended resolutions are garnered from the insights of contemporary literary theories. For instance, there are several possible interpretations of texts such as the section entitled "No Name Woman" in Maxine Hong Kingston's *The Woman Warrior*.[12] The narrator creates several scenarios for her aunt who is ostracized since she became pregnant outside of marriage. The narrator images and imagines: Was she raped? Did she have a lover? Did he not have any responsibility about claiming fatherhood? Did she pay special attention to her personal appearance and stand out from the community? Did she flirt? These evocations give the reader a rich imaginative tapestry to dwell on, and it gives the narrator the defiant stance of telling this tale when her mother had told her categorically, "You must not tell anyone what I am about to tell you." The narrator also creates a history for this aunt, whose true history is deliberately suppressed. So, even without a name, she has an imagined history.

Interpretation is guided by different theoretical tools that may be available at different historical times, such as close reading, biographical criticism, New Historicism, structuralism, poststructuralism, postmodernism, and combinations of these theoretical methods. Since the late twentieth century, the cultural studies methods have been useful in interpreting ethnic writers, especially when combined with race theory by thinkers such as Stuart Hall, Paul Gilroy, and Hazel Carby, among others. Poststructuralism and postmodernism, for instance, have enabled productive theoretical moves such as questioning fixed and monolithic views of identity and decentering, or challenging authority. Now even as some of these concepts may emerge from European theorists such as Michel Foucault, ethnic studies has a lot to gain by drawing upon what is useful from these theoretical models and discarding what is not. By rejecting these methods as "Eurocentric" or "too theoretical," ethnic studies is the loser. It is more productive to think of theory as a tool and to use what is relevant for one's analysis than to dismiss it in an anti-theoretical stance. Admittedly, the use of insider jargon is often a problem. But this is not a universal reality. The study and scholarship in ethnic studies and ethnic literatures would be enhanced by engaging with a vast array of theorists—Lowe and Hall, as noted above; others in cultural studies, such as James Clifford and George Lipsitz; and feminist studies scholars Gayatri Gopinath, Rosemary George, and Purnima Mankekar, among others. I don't wish to present a free-market-economy type model, in terms of picking and choosing, since theories are produced and consumed differently even within academia—for instance, research resources vary widely between research institutions and state and community colleges. However, on a broad, philosophical plane, in terms of where ethnic studies belongs institutionally in this twenty-first century, it is incumbent upon scholars to be open to a variety of research methods, irrespective of their origins and locations, and without negating the centrality of race and ethnicity mediated through gender, class, and nation, among other crucial contemporary realities such as geography and diaspora.

It is important to recognize the distinctions between race and ethnicity and not use them interchangeably, as is often done. Race as a means of categorizing people in large groups based on biology and skin color is a concept that is heavily debated today, including studies that argue that race is no longer a viable category, such as Paul Gilroy's text, *Against Race*.[13] Ethnicity is understood generally as indicating differences of culture, national origin, ancestry, language, and other characteristics that distinguish peoples of color within broad racial groups such as blacks, Asians, or Latinos. Both concepts, race and ethnicity, when used with careful demarcations of their different meanings are important in ethnic studies. We do not live in a race-free or ethnicity-free society; in fact, the United States is one of the most racialized and race-conscious societies despite and perhaps because of its highly visible multiethnic population.

Race historians such as Howard Winant delineate changes in the concept of race in the United States prior to and after the civil rights movement of the 1960s.[14] "Enslavement, conquest, and exclusion," notes Winant, "were the chief means through which U.S. society was racialized beginning with its colonial origins" (43). The civil rights era was the first time that "the idea of equality—however fuzzy—has been coupled with notions of race in an accepted, commonsensical way" (38). Debates over what equality means continue to this day in anti–affirmative action attacks, charges of reverse discrimination, and racial quotas.[15]

Winant points out that, paradoxically, "white institutionalization of racial difference" and denial of basic civil rights to diverse peoples of color forced resistance and opposition and gradually "an ethnicity-based model of race" became more acceptable as "derived quite consciously from the 'immigrant analogy.'"[16] Ethnicity, based in cultural differences, becomes a less confrontational identity-space than the racial markings insisted upon by, say, the Black Power movement and other more in-your-face type struggles for equality. Even if ethnicity as a concept seems more acceptable than race to the power structures, it is important for peoples of color to re-appropriate the concept of "ethnicity" for their own purposes, especially in making distinctions among broad racial categories such as blacks, Asians, or Latinos. Each of these groups is vastly heterogeneous and differences via ethnicity, including national origin, language, ancestry, class, gender, and education are extremely important. However, I do not wish to advocate slipping into a comfortable ethnic corner in order to ignore race realities that are systemic in U.S. society. We need to struggle against this endemic disease of racism even as we keep our ethnic distinctions of native languages, expressive arts traditions, religions, clothing, food, and so on. Of course, we do not have much choice about being grouped racially in this hyper-color-conscious society where "racial lumping" is prevalent.[17]

Ethnic studies' engagement with race teaches mainstream disciplines to reframe their research questions in ways that shift the power structure and challenge hegemonic responses, whether to literary texts, the institutional status quo, or beyond into the nonacademic community. In the latter environment, scholars may share a common ethnic heritage and language with their community but remain separated in other crucial categories in terms of class, profession, education, and at times, the kinds of scholarly jargon used to describe everyday events.

The core difference between ethnic studies research methods and those used in traditional disciplines is interdisciplinarity, although it bears stating that even traditional disciplines in our contemporary era are becoming increasingly interdisciplinary, and intradisciplinary even within their own fields, such as new interdisciplinary B.A. degrees in "Global Cultures," or "Humanities and Arts." Borders are being crossed intellectually and ideologically from one discipline into another. In the best scenario, methodologies are also fluid, permeating rigid disciplinary boundaries.

Interdisciplinary Methods and Intersectional Approaches

Both interdisciplinary and intersectional research methods are significant in reading ethnic literatures. In a useful book, *Interdisciplinarity: History, Theory, and Practice*, Julie Thompson Klein undertakes a history of the concept "interdisciplinary" and its past and current definitions as understood within scholarly and non-scholarly communities.[18] Klein asks probing questions that are useful for this discussion of research methods in ethnic literature: "What is the relationship between disciplinarity and interdisciplinarity? What are the problems and implications of borrowing from other disciplines? . . . What happens when interdisciplinary fields begin to assume disciplinary characteristics?" (15). Later in her text, Klein asserts that "interdisciplinarity functions as a critique of disciplinary limitations. Although the critique is widespread, some of the richest examples are in ethnic, women's, and area studies" (95).

Interdisciplinary methods have been a part of ethnic studies from its inception as a field of scholarly study in the 1960s (a historical marker that I would distinguish importantly from the presence and history of ethnic peoples in the United States in the eighteenth and nineteenth centuries), out of the ferment of the civil rights struggle. According to Klein, interdisciplinarity evokes bringing together a plurality of disciplines with the aim of "fostering a new way of knowing, a new mode of intellectual discourse based on 'rediscovery'" (96). Laura Hyun Yi Kang, quoted in the epigraph, takes a more skeptical approach with her provocative phrase, "trenchant interdisciplinarity," and her critique of the usual association of the prefix "inter" with "spatial" movement among different fields, usually among disciplinary fields. Disciplines remain in their fixed space and valorize interdisciplinary studies moving around them, thereby denying interdisciplinarity "a temporal in-betweenness, as an interregnum."[19]

Interdisciplinarity also evokes a new linking of knowledge and action and introduces new evaluative standards of academic work. The linking of research to action and community has been an integral part of ethnic studies (as also of women's studies) from its inception during the civil rights movement. Balancing theory and practice, academia and community have varied at different historical times. As ethnic studies becomes more and more institutionalized there is increasing pressure to publish in prestigious venues and to professionalize knowledge, so much that communicating this work back to the community (and the time that takes) becomes increasingly challenging. And it is important to note here that research institutions in academia do not reward community work, and continue to place a high premium on publication.

A more contemporary research move in ethnic studies, since the 1980s and 1990s, is the theoretical category of intersectionality. This includes the analysis of a growing intersection of categories that are crucial in interpreting ethnic literary texts: the centrality of race and ethnicity as intersected and modulated by gender, sexuality, class, the state, and, increasingly, by nationality, immigration laws, and diasporic concerns. I assert further that intersectionality, in terms of the deployment of the categories of race, gender, and class, along with nation and diaspora, informs the use of interdisciplinarity. In contemporary reading practices for literary texts, scholars rely primarily on intersecting categories of race, gender, class, and nation, among others. The intersecting categories then guide scholars in their use of other disciplines such as history or politics. I posit that *intersectionality precedes interdisiciplinarity*, the former method leading and informing the latter. To concretize this theoretical premise further—when the intersectional research method for analyzing ethnic literature relies on the categories of gender, race, and class, then that analysis asks key questions of, and even challenges disciplinary frameworks. For instance, how are the intersecting formations of gender and sexuality in a particular literary text informed by the historical and legal disciplines? Or, how are intersecting categories of geography and nationality influenced by politics? What I am proposing is that the intersectional categories somewhat announce the critical approach and then this critical approach selects, questions, and, if necessary, revises the disciplinary frameworks from within which a text is analyzed. It is noteworthy that interdisciplinarity and intersectionality, even as they aim to challenge disciplinary knowledge and frameworks, often still deploy them because of the constraints of institutional positioning, the requirements for tenure and promotion, and the reality of material resources in terms of the growth of ethnic studies in academia.

Lisa Lowe, quoted at the outset, is one of the primary scholars in the literary field whose work of over a decade exemplifies the uses of both interdisciplinarity and intersectionality. Lowe's scholarship in Asian American and immigrant cultural politics brings together the intersectional, even interlocked categories of race, gender, immigration, and nation. Lowe's seminal and pathbreaking text, *Immigrant Acts*, is foundational in the field. Elsewhere, I have compared it in scholarly impact and influence to Edward Said's *Orientalism*. Lowe insightfully links Asian immigration to the United States to labor needs and a simultaneous exclusion from national citizenship. This paradoxical inclusion and exclusion marks the very history not only of Asian Americans, but also of the United States and its discriminatory policies of racialization and gendering of minority groups at different times.

Interdisciplinary and, more recently, intersectional approaches are used to address what Julie Thompson Klein describes as "a subtle restructuring of knowledge in the later twentieth century. New divisions of intellectual labor, collaborative research, team teaching, hybrid fields, comparative studies, increased borrowing across disciplines and a variety of 'unified,' 'holistic' perspectives have creased pressures upon traditional divisions of knowledge. There is talk of a growing 'permeability of boundaries . . . even a profound epistemological crisis.' To echo Clifford Geertz, there is indeed something happening 'to the way we think about the way we think.'" Klein demonstrates that the concept of interdisciplinarity has come into play in various fields, as in the hard sciences in areas such as biochemistry. Different disciplines have taken up interdisciplinarity and valorized it, and others have denigrated it as lacking scholarly rigor. Since there is no particular definition of the term, nor is there a single acknowledged method, the reception of the term varies widely. It is sometimes labeled as "suspicious" and useful to the "dilettante," or highly respected for collaborative research projects as in "environmental science" that bring together, as Klein points out "knowledge from disciplines of medicine, law, business, and social work." Klein does not include the voice of the creative artist. Let me cite only one example—Utah-based environmentalist writer Terry Tempest Williams, whose evocative poetry and poetic prose narratives have been embraced by environmentalists. Williams has even testified before Congress on matters of preserving habitats for endangered species. Like those of biologists, environmentalists, and botanists, Williams's imagination is also fired by the beauty of the monarch butterfly and its absolutely remarkable yearly winter migration from Canada into the southern United States.

Klein alerts us to the fact that there is no agreement on whether interdisciplinarity is "an old or new concept," and whether it is useful only in the academy, or only outside it in governmental and development areas. There is no commonly accepted body of material on interdisciplinarity since it serves disciplines as varied as medicine, sociology, and literary study. Klein calls for more dialogue across the fields that use interdisciplinarity in order to "provide a sound framework for future discussion and research" (14).

Klein presents a useful historical overview of where the term *interdisciplinary* comes from, even as far back as Plato and Aristotle, and its later evolution. Klein discusses how the concept was embraced in institutions of learning, and how disciplines such as theology became importantly articulated by the Middle Ages, although "the modern connotation of disciplinarity is a product of the nineteenth century and is linked with several forces: the evolution of the modern natural sciences, the general 'scientification' of knowledge, the industrial revolution, technological advancements, and agrarian agitation. As the modern university took shape, disciplinarity was reinforced in two major ways: industries demanded and received specialists, and disciplines recruited students to their ranks" (21). In the 1920s integrative thinking was encouraged by the reform-minded, interest in knowledge sharing, and even the evolution of certain "hybrid disciplines" such as "social psychology"; in general, "there was no challenge to the status quo of social science." Even today, there is much skepticism about interdisciplinary programs, even though the work of individual scholars may receive recognition. Klein indicates that even as the discussion of interdisciplinarity is becoming broader and deeper, institutional obstacles remain formidable. Often there is a retreat into the disciplines and "interdisciplinarity becomes a hostage to the disciplines" (39). The problem of how to delimit and categorize knowledge—through wholeness or through fragmentation—remains.

Klein points out a provocative paradox—namely that interdisciplinarity initially was used as a way to assert unity and synthesis—as in bringing together certain branches of science. In ethnic studies, on the other hand, one associates interdisciplinarity more with challenging traditional disciplines and using them in different, namely interdisciplinary, methods. Intellectual curricula are influenced ideologically and respond to political and historical factors. Ethnic studies grew out of demands to bring marginal texts into curricula and to teach them both in traditional departments as well as in ethnic studies units. American studies also comes out of a similar ferment of challenging traditional disciplines that may not encourage border crossings and speaking across disciplines.

Lisa Lowe's essay "The International within the National: American Studies and Asian American Critique" asserts that the research and teaching done in ethnic studies has the potential to challenge disciplinary boundaries. She further contextualizes this issue within the very function of a university in civil society: "The traditional function of disciplinary divisions in the university is to uphold the abstract divisions of modern civil society into separate spheres: the political, the economic, the cultural. The formation and reproduction of the modern citizen-subject is naturalized through those divisions of social space and those divisions of knowledge."[20] Lowe pinpoints in the same essay, that the exclusion of Asian immigrants and Asian Americans continues and is supported by "the relative invisibility of that history of racialization within the modern university" (36). Hence, universities reproduce the ideologies of the larger society, especially as they "form citizens through the education of students in national culture." The educational system "suppresses the history of racialization and racialized exclusion from citizenship" as that impacts Asians. Lowe places the very origins of Asian American studies, as other ethnic studies, not in the simplistic identity politics that its detractors criticize as limiting and insular, but in the very "voicing of racial consciousness that seeks to bring this history into the university, that seeks to refuse this disavowal" (37).

Even civil rights struggles and ethnic studies' efforts at demanding representation did not transform the teaching of culture, or the culture of the university that continues to center "Western culture" and accommodates multicultural curricula only when demanded by increasingly diverse students. In the late twentieth century and into the twenty-first, marginal spaces for ethnic studies are increasingly challenged, buttressed by the emergence of interdisciplinary fields such as Third World studies and cultural studies. "Interdisciplinary study," remarks Lowe, "may disrupt the empiricist paradigms of science and social science within which the disinterested scholar anatomizes, surveys, and classifies the non-Western, racialized, or female 'other' as objects of knowledge" (40). Lowe cites scholars Kimberly Crenshaw, Chandra Mohanty, and Rosa Linda Ferguso, whose works are attentive to race, class, and gender.

Asian American history in particular enables students to recognize, as Lowe remarks, that "the production of race is part of the contradiction between national economy and the political state, and in the contradiction between the U.S. nation-state and the global economy, and it rewrites the history of the United States as a complex racial history." There are important links to African American and other minorities, and a "comparative history of racialization" is useful. Lowe cites Grace Hong, who links the internment of Japanese Americans to the African American experience of discrimination, segregation, and exclusions.

Another important problem remains—institutionalizing ethnic studies by making it part of academia and providing it the material resources to mount courses and hire faculty goes somewhat inevitably with institutional demands as placed on traditional departments. While institutionalizing has all the dangers of co-optation and appropriation, it is possible for ethnic studies to remain oppositional and to train students in critical reading practices that make them question and rethink the larger social structures that in fact foster racism and sexism. Certainly, the pressures of institutionalization are real, especially when ethnic studies faculty positions are located in traditional departments. As Michael Omi and Dana Takagi, guest editors of the *Amerasia Journal*'s "Thinking Theory" volume, remark, ethnic studies in the 1980s and later, in becoming increasingly professionalized, did not "participate in new social movements of the previous decade. . . . [They] feel that the absence of a sustained and coherent radical theory of social transformation led to a retreat to more mainstream, discipline-based paradigmatic orientations."[21]

Even with increased professionalization, Asian American studies scholars attempt to maintain links outside the university, thereby fostering one of the key goals of ethnic studies. Academics participate in nonprofit organizations on health and legal services, serve on boards of arts groups, provide advice on public policy, share research strategies and data, and speak out against hate crimes and racial profiling.

Critical Reading Practices for Asian American Literature

Among scholars who use provocative critical reading practices for analyzing ethnic literatures, I include scholars such as Lisa Lowe, King-Kok Cheung, Cynthia Sau-Ling Wong, Elaine Kim, Laura Kang, and also those social scientists whose work creates most useful linkages with humanistic inquiries—scholars such as Yen Le Espiritu and Sandhya Shukla, among others. These thinkers creatively adapt, transform, and refashion contemporary theoretical concepts such as decentering, or de-totalizing, derived from European-origin theories such as poststructuralism and postmodernism, and make them relevant for literary analyses of ethnic literatures.

Ethnic studies, and ethnic literatures within it, has become more heterogeneous, with varied subgroups and numerous national origins in the last few years, so that in any area it is difficult to have a discrete ethnic-specific study. Increased numbers of the second-generation Asian Americans whose parents arrived here as part of post-1965 U.S. legislation that allowed entry to 170,000 immigrants from the Eastern Hemisphere make the Asia-born population, rather than the U.S.-born, the majority. This has put new pressures on the field as immigrants from South Vietnam, Cambodia, India, and Pakistan have "diversified" the Asian American population, dominated previously mainly by those of Chinese, Japanese, or Korean ancestry. This is not a new racialization of the field, as Lowe argues convincingly that it must be connected to the old racializing throughout the twentieth century. It is important to "'de-reify' the 'newness' of Asian immigration" (45).

Asian American literary scholarship in the twenty-first century is challenged in addressing a heterogeneous population that includes second-generation Asian American writers; first-generation immigrant writers, closely tied to homelands in Asia; 1.5 generation writers; and part-Asian writers with bi- and multiracial heritages. There are bound to be spills among and between ethnic groups. Such interethnic diversity certainly enriches the field while also making it theoretically difficult to hold ethnic differences in balance and establish common methodologies that address issues raised by a variety of U.S. ethnic literatures. The importance of border studies and the increasing need to place the United States as an empire-builder within a global context is important even in studies of literature and culture, especially with the United States' continuing ties—economic, military, and cultural—in parts of Asia. It is as significant to include the history of U.S. colonialism and wars in the Philippines, South Korea, Japan, and Vietnam. "The history of Asian American racialization," remarks Lowe, can be regarded usefully "as a critique of national history, so that it might be related to other histories of racialization, those of African Americans, Chicanos/Latinos, Native Americans, and 'white' Americans, in order to open possibilities of cross-race and cross-national projects" (44).

Lowe delineates the key links between literary studies and immigration policies, labor laws, and public policy, and further, how each of these arenas are both racialized and gendered. Lowe points out how "legal institutions reproduce the relations of production as racialized and gendered relations and therefore symptomatic and determining of the relations of production themselves" (32). Immigration law supports racial classifications in the interest of capitalism by disenfranchising certain populations, tactically and at different historical times, from citizenship. Lowe describes the study of Asian immigration based on this combination of inclusion and exclusion as both "a racial formation and an epistemological object." Lowe cites Omi and Winant's foundational analysis of "racial formation" and extends it in her inclusion of "cultural practices that continually redefine racial meanings in ways that seek to reorganize those racialized and gendered capitalist relations."

The great number of varied literary texts by individual writers, published in the 1990s in anthologies, scholarly books, and journal articles in the field of Asian American literature, has an "internal heterogeneity and disciplinary multiplicity."[22] Kang is skeptical about the "breaking silence" paradigm, since it is important to be aware of how minority voices, creative and scholarly, are misused at times in the service of a racist and sexist world. She questions how "this discursive proliferation," particularly about

Asian American women, is "more often bound up with, not liberated from, disciplinary regimes of codification and documentation.... There needs to be a sustained critique of the many possible redeployments of these knowledges that emerge in the name of women, racialized communities, or immigrant workers" (19).

As path-breaking as Kang's exposition of the scholarship on Asian American women, and complementing Lowe's distinctive analyses of cultural politics and the centrality of racial and gender formations of ethnic groups in the United States, has been literary scholar King-Kok Cheung's highly influential work for over a decade. Cheung's useful and extensively researched introduction, a must-read for students and scholars of Asian American literature, in her edited volume, the Cambridge *Interethnic Companion to Asian American Literature*, reviews the varying critical approaches in the field over the past forty years, the field's literary and theoretical antecedents, and the realities of the marketplace.[23] Cheung's is one of the best discussions of how the field's emphasis has changed from cultural nationalism in the 1960s, and the demanding of space for minority voices in the mainstream curricula and institutions, to the post-1980s perspectives influenced by the theoretical moves of poststructuralism and later of postmodernism wherein identity is no longer a single, monolithic category but fluid, multiple, and shifting, where a decentering of authority is more critically mediated than demanding a place at the table. Whereas earlier the emphasis was on sociopolitical issues, on establishing and proudly asserting racial identity, now a more useful stance lies in fragmenting the unitary subject, in decentering the subject, and in celebrating multiplicity. This is not to say that race is unimportant—it remains crucial. But race has to be analyzed as interlocked and intersecting with the categories of gender, ethnicity, class, nation, language, and geography. At times, racial realities and prejudices are even produced or are imbricated in interlocking categories of gender and class, or even nation and language (as is true for recent immigrants whose first language is not English and who may speak English with an "accent").

Cheung analyzes the shifts in critical practices as moving from "identity politics—with its stress on cultural nationalism and American nativity" to "heterogeneity and diaspora ... from centering on race and masculinity to revolving around the multiple axes of ethnicity, gender, class, and sexuality; from being concerned with social history and communal responsibility to being caught in the quandaries and possibilities of postmodernism and multiculturalism" (1). Although Cheung demarcates this "shift from the earlier one of "claim[ing] America" to the current one of "forging a connection between Asia and Asian America," she also points out in her carefully nuanced discussion that the "shift" does not necessarily replace the earlier with the later concerns. Rather, "the two phases of Asian American cultural criticism may more accurately be characterized as a dialectic that continues to spark debate" (1). For Cheung, continuing debate and dialogue are important. Hence, in the haste to adopt heterogeneity and diasporic perspectives as necessitated theoretically by Asian-born writers, scholarship should not simply privilege that perspective and marginalize American-born Asian Americans. The latter, after all, were in the forefront in establishing the field, and in claiming that Asian Americans were not "foreigners" but Americans, and an integral part of the U.S. multiethnic landscape. Cheung advocates "making room for reciprocal critique and multiple commitments" (10) both a national and a diasporic identity, where both possibilities of "claiming and disclaiming America" are possible.

Cheung's analysis sums up my emphasis on critical reading practices for ethnic literatures that rely both on interdisciplinarity (with historical, sociological, archival, and political material, and as Kang has suggested being attentive to the spaces "in-between" disciplinary fields), and on the increasing importance of intersectional perspectives (relying on theories of gender, race, class, sexuality, nation, language, and geography). Each of these areas certainly has its own scholarly developments and trajectories, for instance, the shifts in feminist theory from challenges by women of color in the United States and the Third World[24] who analyze gender along with nationalism, colonialism, and imperialism.[25]

Within the intersectional category of gender and class, the latter is often neglected. Theories of sexuality have become increasingly prominent and it is important to include perspectives of scholars such as David Eng and Russell Leong, and creative writers such as Jessica Hagedorn and David Henry Hwang in analyses of literary material. Increasingly, issues of class face a population that has somehow masked economic disparities in the "model minority" myth. And as Cheung indicates, class differences will become more apparent as the professional Asian American feels alienated from his/her working-class community, and because bilingualism can be both a privilege for a certain class and extremely disempowering for another class that often faces demotion in moving from Asia to America. Here transnational analyses of class and its intersection with gender, generation, and geography are key issues as explored by scholars such as Chandra Mohanty and Arjun Appadurai.

Inclusion of diaspora matters brings important perspectives of postcolonial theory into Asian American cultural criticism—a move that has been debated, for instance, in the "Thinking Theory" special issue of *Amerasia Journal*. Notions of diaspora and exilic identity versus national identity remain significant in Asian American criticism, especially for writers from Asian nations such as Vietnam, Korea, and the Philippines, where the United States has intervened militaristically, as well as for writers from the ex-British colonies of India, Pakistan, Bangladesh, and Sri Lanka. For immigrant writers from these regions who are tied to homeland the formation of diasporic ethnic communities and the practice of classical forms of music and dance need to include theoretical perspectives from geography, space, diaspora, and transnationalism into Asian American studies. Diasporic emphases serve as challenging reminders that the United States is part of a world community, specifically, in its own often dark history of military, economic, and cultural dominations in Asia. The history of U.S. imperialism, economic and cultural, needs to form a part of literary studies, especially where U.S. imperialism continues—in the form of International Monetary Fund–mandated policies of structural adjustment that perpetuate conditions of poverty, or in the form of cultural hegemony through popular TV shows such as *Baywatch* or *The Bold and the Beautiful*. To this day, high school students in U.S. public schools get a few paragraphs about the Vietnam War in their history texts. They do not hear about certain grim facts, for instance, of Operation Baby Lift, which brought children to the United States, many of whom were "orphaned" by U.S. military men who had fathered them. Such sad and sobering facts of history are often suppressed by racist states, and sometimes come to light via the imaginative work of novelists and poets.[26]

Theoretically, it is important that discussions of diaspora not supersede concerns of race and nationality. And in identity formations that are central to ethnic literatures (and ethnic studies), the recent assumptions of a diasporic identity, or what David Theo Goldberg terms evocatively "the romance with hybridity," should not elide the troubling aspects of nationalism. In fact, I would add a cautionary note to celebratory evocations of transnationalism, even cosmopolitanism, as though these new geographic realities enable a transcending of the old holds of fundamentalist nationalism and religious fundamentalism. Goldberg remarks that in the contemporary era of "expanding social mobilities" that have "produced increasingly heterogeneous societies globally, social order more locally was challenged to maintain homogeneity increasingly and assertively. The racial state is key to understanding this 'resolution' to this modern dilemma."[27] Hence, research methods that include diasporic concerns in reading ethnic literature, even as they recognize the openness and heterogeneity implied in studying multiple locations, need to remain cognizant of re-inscriptions into homogenous, racialized groups.

In analyzing ethnic literature, the complex and historically situated definitions and redefinitions of categories of feminism, or race, or sexuality are important. It is equally significant to include these categories intersectionally in our contemporary era, and in ethnic studies as a whole, since even fields such as cultural anthropology and qualitative models of sociological research have been impacted crucially by theoretical innovations in literary studies. Hence, just as feminist theory in the 1970s and 1980s infiltrated discipline-bound fields and insisted that scholars not add gender only tokenistically into their analyses, but that the inclusion of gender fundamentally transform the very hypotheses of their research projects, the scope of their fieldwork, and the results of their findings. Similarly, contemporary research methods from literary and cultural studies can usefully augment, and, at times, transform traditional, discipline-bound research methods in social sciences. The inclusion of ethnic material—literary or sociological—should ideally challenge mainstream disciplines and traditional research methods. For instance, including the literary text *Watermark*, an excellent anthology of Vietnamese American writers, not only in contemporary American literature classes but also in courses on Southeast Asian history, poses challenges in terms of the excellent stories and poems that elicit intersections of race, gender, sexuality, nation, and class.

In a discussion of critical reading practices, it is important to instill an awareness of literary tradition, namely, what traditions do Asian American and other ethnic literatures inhabit? Do they remain within their own ethnic subspecialties, and how do we make them part of mainstream American studies? How is this accomplished and what continuing battles remain in this kind of mainstreaming? How can minority voices be heard, appreciated, and analyzed with as much scholarly rigor and careful work as the numerous analyses of James Joyce's Dublin, or Shakespeare's Globe Theater, or T. S. Eliot's "Waste Land"? And is such belonging desirable? What are the gains and losses? Is the future to be worked toward more about challenging the ghettoization of ethnic subgroups and an attendant movement toward the mainstream? Are such moves inevitably institutionalized and then to a small or large extent co-opted? Are there ways to prevent such co-optation while still working within academic institutions? How should ethnic studies rethink its links to a nonacademic community? Are such links even more necessary today (with increasing institutionalization of ethnic studies), though differently articulated than the impetus of the civil rights period?

History speaks back to the present, and the lessons of the past bring new insights into the present. This is important even in the very constituting of literary traditions that reflect back and forth, that establish ways of intertextual referencing, and that encourage, in T. S. Eliot's terms, "individual talent" which is then integrated into a "tradition." The tradition of critical theory that influences the analysis of Asian American literature is a rich field reflecting different historical pressures from the 1960s into the twenty-first century. So, even as there was a place for cultural nationalism at a certain time, it has been timely for the past ten years and longer to challenge the limitations of cultural nationalism, to learn from new theoretical approaches. More relevant for our own time are the concepts of multiple nationalities (and emotional allegiances to more than one home and nation) and concepts of hybridity and diaspora, migration, postcolonialism, and new identity formations, quite different from the 1960s. Even the term "Asian American" remains contested though I would contend that it remains useful for a somewhat vigilant political solidarity that respects differences even as it struggles for common goals in matters of racial and gender equity and social justice. Among new theories, postcolonial and diasporic concerns remain a contested arena in Asian American studies, especially in dealing with Hawaii and the Pacific Islands. As Stephen Sumida usefully points out, there was no liberation in Hawaii from U.S. colonizers as in the case of South Asian nations gaining independence from the British.[28] Hawaii remains a colony of the U.S. and continues to have a sovereignty movement. Hence, even as certain advances made in postcolonial theory are useful in discussing Asian American diasporic writers, particularly those with histories of colonization and U.S. imperialism, I concede that postcolonialism is not applicable to every subgroup of Asian Americans. Postcolonial theory has brought important concepts to the forefront that are useful for diasporic writers, such as the significance of subaltern studies, or the studies of nationalism and cultural liberation, or the role of cultural tradition, not as fixed and unchanging, but as preserving ethnic heritages and providing emotional nurturing through the practice of music and dance and through the enjoyment of ethnic food, while creating a home in mainstream U.S. society.

Even as the term "Asian American" is debatable in terms of who is included and excluded, "pan-Asian ethnicity" is a useful and viable concept as proposed in ethnic studies scholar Yen Le Espiritu's path-breaking work. She notes that pan-Asian ethnicity "was the product of material, political, and social processes rather than cultural bonds" (164).[29] Even as Asian Americans come together to resist common forces of racism, endemic structurally in U.S. society, "a deeper sense of mutual understanding emerges," notes Cheung, "only after exposure to the different material histories, cultures, and literatures of the various groups" (27). Even learning about one's own ethnicity is instructive and there is nothing "natural" about somehow possessing such knowledge if one is an "insider" to the community.

In conclusion, critical reading practices for ethnic literatures can challenge disciplinary territories of literary study. The multiplicity of research methods discussed above, useful both for ethnic literature as well as for ethnic studies, suggests revisionary ways of reading that challenge the status quo and that shift power structures institutionally and intellectually. Several problems remain—for instance, the common practice of hiring the token black, or Hispanic, or Asian. More academic units in the United States have the *one* ethnic person covering entire fields, such as the one Asian Americanist or the one African Americanist in traditional departments. This places enormous pressures on individuals who are required to teach ethnic material, mentor students of color, and serve on committees, and all this very often at the pre-tenure level. Another paradoxical reality prevails in contemporary times, namely, that even as there is an increasing establishment of ethnic studies scholars and institutional stability for the field (including ethnic studies programs becoming departments, as is recently true for the Asian American studies programs at the University of California, Irvine, and at the University of California, Los Angeles), there is increasing ghettoization of ethnic enclaves in academia. Traditional disciplines do their work and ethnic studies does its "multi-culti" work, hence challenges to the institution are kept marginal. Ethnic studies still has much work to do in terms of integrating its materials and methods into mainstream disciplines, and transforming the knowledge bases and approaches used to read texts, both as active readers and as socially responsible citizens in this multiethnic society.

Notes

1. Lisa Lowe, *Immigrant Acts: On Asian American Cultural Politics* (Durham, N.C.: Duke University Press, 1996), 40.

2. Laura Hyun Yi Kang, *Compositional Subjects: Enfiguring Asian/American Women* (Durham, N.C.: Duke University Press, 2002), 19.

3. See selected texts in cultural studies: Simon During, ed., *The Cultural Studies Reader* (New York: Routledge, 1993); Michel Foucault, *Discipline and Punish: The Birth of the Prison* (New York: Vintage, 1977); Lawrence Grossberg, et al, *Cultural Studies* (New York: Routledge,1992); Cary Nelson and Dilip Gaonkar, eds., *Disciplinarity and Dissent in Cultural Studies* (New York: Routledge, 1996). Other prominent scholars whose work often enters cultural studies include Arjun Appadurai, Bruce Robbins, Inderpal Grewal, Purnima Mankekar, Andrew Ross, and Lauren Berlant, among others. Also seminal for studies of culture and issues of race, geography, and imperialism are Edward Said's *Orientalism* (New York: Random House, 1979); Said's *The World, the Text and the Critic* (Cambridge: Harvard University Press, 1983); and Said's *Culture and Imperialism* (New York: Vintage, 1993).

4. Michael Omi and Howard Winant, *Racial Formation in the United States: From the 1960s to the 1990s*, 2nd ed. (New York: Routledge, 1994); Richard Delgado and Jean Stefancic, *Critical Race Theory: An Introduction* (New York: New York University Press, 2001); Philomena Essed and David Goldberg, eds., *Race Critical Theories* (Malden, Mass.: Blackwell, 2002); David Theo Goldberg, *The Racial State* (Malden, Mass.: Blackwell, 2002); Anthony Appiah and Amy Gutmann, *Color Conscious: The Political Morality of Race* (Princeton, N.J.: Princeton University Press, 1996); Patricia Williams, *The Alchemy of Race and Rights* (Cambridge, Mass.: Harvard University Press, 1991).

5. Lisa Lowe, see note 1 above. Also Lowe and David Lloyd, eds., *The Politics of Culture in the Shadow of Capital* (Durham, N.C.: Duke University Press, 1997); Aihwa Ong, *Flexible Citizenship: The Cultural Logics of Transnationality* (Durham, N.C.: Duke University Press, 1999); Bill Ong Hing and Ronald Lee, eds., *Reframing the Immigration Debate* (Los Angeles: University of California, Los Angeles, Asian American Studies Center and LEAP, 1996).

6. See theorists such as Michel Foucault, and feminist critiques of Foucault such as Jana Sawicki's *Disciplining Foucault*. See also Arjun Appadurai, *Modernity at Large* (Minneapolis: University of Minnesota Press, 1996); Pheng Cheah and Bruce Robbins, eds., *Cosmopolitics: Thinking and Feeling beyond the Nation* (Minneapolis: University of Minnesota Press, 1998); Rob Wilson and Wimal Dissanayake, eds., *Global/Local: Cultural Production and the Transnational Imaginary* (Durham, N.C.: Duke University Press, 1996); May Joseph, *Nomadic Identities: The Performance of Citizenship* (Minneapolis: University of Minnesota Press, 1999).

7. There is a growing movement among black intellectuals for reparations and recompense for the outrages of slavery. There may be lessons to learn from another ethnic community, that of Japanese Americans who were wrongfully interned during World War II and have struggled for reparation and redress by the U.S. government. See an excellent documentation of the legal stages of this fight in a text edited by five Asian American lawyers, Eric Yamamoto et al., *Race, Rights and Reparation: Law and the Japanese American Internment* (New York: Aspen, 2001). See also a provocative new text by Anne Cheng, *The Melancholy of Race* (New York:

Oxford University Press, 2000), where she analyzes how a nation needs to come to terms with its past, especially its unjust dealings with its minority populations. See also Wole Soyinka's essays in *The Burden of Memory, the Muse of Forgiveness* (New York: Oxford University Press, 1999), where he discusses the pros and cons of the South African Truth and Reconciliation Commission. In terms of U.S. history of militarism, especially in Asia, see a volume of essays edited by Fujitani et al., *Perilous Memories: The Asia-Pacific War(s)* (Durham, N.C.: Duke University Press, 2001), especially essays by Marita Sturken, Arif Dirlik, Lisa Yoneyama, and George Lipsitz.

8. Donald E. Hall, *Literary and Cultural Theory: From Basic Principles to Advanced Applications* (New York: Houghton Mifflin, 2001), 1. See also Terry Eagleton, *Literary Theory* (Oxford: Blackwell, 1996); Michael Groden and Martin Kreiswirth, eds., *The Johns Hopkins Guide to Literary Theory and Criticism* (Baltimore: Johns Hopkins University Press, 1994); Frank Lentricchia and Thomas McLaughlin, eds., *Critical Theory for Literary Study* (Chicago: University of Chicago Press, 1995); Julie Rivkin and Michael Ryan, eds., *Literary Theory: An Anthology* (Oxford: Blackwell, 1998).

9. Clifford Geertz, *The Interpretation of Cultures: Selected Essays* (New York: Basic Books, 1973).

10. Genny Lim, *Paper Angels*, in *The Unbroken Thread: An Anthology of Plays by Asian American Women*, ed. Roberta Uno (Amherst: University of Massachusetts Press, 1993), 11–52. This anthology, along with Velina Hasu Houston's edited volume, *The Politics of Life: Four Plays by Asian American Women* (Philadelphia: Temple University Press, 1993), is a very useful text.

11. Jhumpa Lahiri, *The Interpreter of Maladies: Stories* (Boston: Houghton Mifflin, 1999). Winner of the Pulitzer Prize.

12. Maxine Hong Kingston, *The Woman Warrior: Memoirs of a Girlhood among Ghosts*, reprint (New York: Random House, 1976).

13. Paul Gilroy, *Against Race: Imagining Political Culture beyond the Color Line* (Cambridge, Mass.: Belknap Press of Harvard University Press, 2000).

14. Howard Winant, *Racial Conditions* (Minneapolis: University of Minnesota Press, 1994). Winant is also the coauthor, with Michael Omi, of their formative study, *Racial Formation in the United States* (New York: Routledge, 1986), with a second edition in 1994.

15. See Richard Delgado, *The Coming Race War? And Other Apocalyptic Tales of America After Affirmative Action and Welfare* (New York: New York University Press, 1996); Philip A. Klinkner and Roger M. Smith, *The Unsteady March: The Rise and Decline of Racial Equality in America* (Chicago: University of Chicago Press, 1999); Manning Marable, *Beyond Black and White: Transforming African-American Politics* (New York: Verso, 1995); Leslie G. Carr, *'Color-Blind' Racism* (Thousand Oaks, Calif.: Sage Publications, 1997); "How Race is Lived in America," *New York Times*, June 4, 5, 7, 11, 14, 16, 20, 22, 25, 29; July 2, 6, 9, 13, 2000. www.nytimews.com/race.

16. Omi and Winant, *Racial Formation*, 1st ed.

17. Winant, *Racial Conditions*, 52.

18. Julie Thomson Klein, *Interdisciplinarity: History, Theory, and Practice* (Detroit, Mich.: Wayne State University Press, 1990), 95. See also Klein's *Crossing Boundaries: Knowledge, Disciplinarities, and Interdisciplinarities* (Charlottesville: University Press of Virginia, 1996); and Ellen Messer-Davidow et al., eds., *Knowledges: Historical and Critical Studies in Disciplinarity* (Charlottesville: University Press of Virginia, 1993).

19. Kang, *Compositional Subjects*, 21.

20. Lisa Lowe, "The International within the National: American Studies and Asian American Critique," *Cultural Critique* 40 (Fall 1998): 29–47.

21. Michael Omi and Dana Takagi, eds., "Thinking Theory in Asian American Studies," special issue, *Amerasia Journal* 21, nos. 1–2 (1995), viii. I also recommend the many important essays in this volume as a whole, especially the essays by Cynthia Sau-Ling Wong, Kent Ono, and Dorinne Kondo.

22. Kang, *Compositional Subjects*, 16.

23. King-Kok Cheung, ed., *The Interethnic Companion to Asian American Literature* (Cambridge: Cambridge University Press, 1997).

24. Feminist theory within the United States has a long and complex history, including the work of scholars such as Annette Kolodny, Barbara Ehrenreich, Sandra Harding, bell hooks, Barbara Smith, Chandra Mohanty, Rosemary George, June Jordan, Gloria Anzaldua, and Cherrie Moraga, among others. Donald Hall's *Literary and Cultural Theory* usefully discusses various literary theories such as feminist theory, New Historicism, and so on, along with useful bibliographic material. This is a very approachable handbook for students and scholars of literary theory. Hall is also attentive, exemplarily so, to the applications of different theories to literary texts.

25. See Chandra Mohanty, *Feminism without Borders: Decolonizing Theory, Practicing Solidarity* (Durham, N.C.: Duke University Press, 2003); Mohanty et al., eds., *Third World Women and the Politics of Feminism* (Bloomington: Indiana University Press, 1991); M. Jacqui Alexander and Chandra Mohanty, eds., *Feminist Genealogies, Colonial Legacies, Democratic Futures* (New York: Routledge, 1997). See also Ketu H. Katrak, *Politics of the Female Body: Postcolonial Women Writers of the Third World* (New Brunswick: Rutgers University Press, 2006); Inderpal Grewal and Caren Kaplan, eds., *Scattered Hegemonies: Postmodernity and Transnational Feminist Practices* (Minneapolis: University of Minnesota Press, 1994); and numerous publications by postcolonial theorists such as Homi Bhabha and Gayatri Chakravorty Spivak. Also noteworthy are cultural anthropologists dealing with issues of postcolonialism and globalism such as Arjun Appadurai, Parama Roy, Sunaina Maira, Dipesh Chakravorty, Akhil Gupta, and Dilip Gaonkar.

26. Recently, I heard Aimee Phan read from her very moving first book called *We May Never Meet: Stories* (New York: St. Martin's Press, 2004). She talked about the need to research and write about historical facts such as Operation Baby Lift

and the difficulties of foster homes that many biracial children of the Vietnam War faced in the United States.

27. Goldberg, *Racial State*, 11.

28. Stephen H. Sumida, "Postcolonialism, Nationalism, and the Emergence of Asian/Pacific American Literatures," in *Interethnic Companion*, Cheung, 274–288.

29. Yen Le Espiritu, *Asian American Panethnicity: Bridging Institutions and Identities* (Philadephia: Temple University Press, 1992). Also see Espiritu's other texts: *Asian American Women and Men: Labor, Laws, and Love* (Thousand Oaks, Calif.: Sage Publications, 1997); *Home Bound: Filipino Lives across Cultures, Communities and Countries* (Berkeley: University of California Press, 2003).

Chicano/a Literary and Visual Arts 12
Intertextuality of Three Iconic Figures—La Llorona, La Malinche, and the Virgin of Guadalupe*

MARÍA HERRERA-SOBEK

EUROPEAN LITERARY AND ARTISTIC PRODUCTION, particularly during the Renaissance in the fifteenth and sixteenth centuries, the baroque in the seventeenth century, the neoclassic periods in the eighteenth century, and romanticism, realism, and modernism in the nineteenth, twentieth, and twenty-first centuries, derived much of its inspiration from the Greek and Roman classical periods. Greek art and architecture as well as Roman and Greek mythology are evident in the motifs, thematic subject matter, imagery, and representational forms in both the literary arts as well as the plastic arts. The figures of Jupiter, Venus, Aphrodite, Dionysus, Mars, Apollo, Minerva, Neptune, the sirens, water nymphs, and so forth are recurrent figures in European plastic arts. The prose, poetry, and literary productions emanating from Western Europe are equally imbued with the aesthetics of the classical Greek and Roman eras. These Roman and Greek influences evident in European artistic production were imported to Spanish America via heavy immigration, particularly from Spain during the colonial period. However, by the nineteenth century, after the wars of independence, the newly created Latin American republics sought to transform themselves both culturally and

---

*The author, editor, and publisher gratefully thank the following for their permission to reprint the poetry that appears in this chapter:
  Alurista. " Must Be the Season of the Witch." Floricanto en Aztlán. UCLA Chicano Studies Research Center, 1971, p. 26 [Formerly Chicano Cultural Center] Reprinted with permission of the Regents of University of California from UCLA Chicano Studies Research Center.
  Cordelia Candelaria. " Go 'Way from My Window, La Llorna." In *Infinite Divisions : An Anthology of Chicana Literature*, edited by Tey Diana Rebolledo and Eliana S. Rivero. Tuscon, Arizona: University of Arizona Press, 1993. pp. 215–16.
  "Legal Alien " is reprinted with permission from the publisher of *Chants* by Pat Mora (1984, Arte Público Press—University of Houston)

politically. By the second and third decade of the nineteenth century, Latin American artists such as those from Mexico, Chile, Cuba, Argentina, and Colombia began in earnest to look into their own historical and environmental contexts and found inspiration in American (used here in the broad sense of the word—the American continent) themes and subject matter. For Mexico, artists derived inspiration from their indigenous past. The glories of the Aztec and Maya empires were seen as appropriate subject matter that could be transformed into artistic cultural capital just as Greek and Roman cultures and civilizations had been appropriated during the Renaissance and thereafter by European artists.

For Mexico, the revolution of 1910–1917 exploding in the second decade of the twentieth century provided artists an impetus to further distance themselves from European themes and aesthetics and delve wholeheartedly into indigenous motifs. Diego Rivera, David Alfaro Siqueiros, and José Clemente Orozco, as well as Frida Kahlo and María Izquierdo later in the 1930s, 1940s, and 1950s turned their creative optic toward "lo mexicano" and indigenous cultures and civilizations, rejecting much of European motifs and subject matter for their artistic inspiration. The revolutionary fervor of the Mexican civil war of 1910 inspired artists and writers to reevaluate the artistic canon. In the realm of narrative fiction, Mariano Azuela broke with European literary aesthetics and introduced the novel of the revolution with *Los de abajo (The Underdogs)* (1915). Azuela's narrative initiated a new subgenre of novels having as their main subject matter the Mexican Revolution and generally known as *novelas de la revolución mexicana* (novels of the Mexican Revolution); this type of novel is still being produced in the twenty-first century. Numerous authors distinguished themselves with novels centering their narrative plot on some aspect of the Mexican Revolution; some of these authors included Agustín Yáñez, Carlos Fuentes, Juan Rulfo, Angeles Mastreta, Martín Luis Guzmán, Rafael Muñoz, Gregorio López y Fuentes, José Revueltas, and Elena Garro, among many.

In a manner analogous to that of the movements which appeared in Latin America and Mexico in the nineteenth and twentieth centuries, Chicanos/as during the civil rights movements in the 1960s also looked into their indigenous and Mexican past for both artistic and political inspiration and derived much of their aesthetic sensibility from these indigenous, autochthonous contexts. In this essay, I focus on Chicano and Chicana literary expressions and visual arts (paintings) in order to explore how in both of these very different genres motifs and themes are reiterated in word and canvas. I wish to explore the intertextuality and thematic connections between writing and painting via the use of three of the most popular iconic figures in Mexican/Chicano culture: La Malinche, La Llorona, and the Virgin of Guadalupe. My study underscores how these three mythic figures are incorporated within Chicano/a artistic production and are part of important political articulations such as those of gender equality and social justice relevant to this particular ethnic population. In particular, I point out how these figures articulate feminist concerns and issues and have been and continue to be iconic bulwarks of the Chicana feminist movement.

Given the search for independence from European artistic canons and aesthetic sensibilities, Chicano/a artistic production can be analyzed from the perspective of postcolonial theories such as those proposed by Edward Said in *Orientalism* (1979) and Frantz Fanon in *The Wretched of the Earth* (1994). Both Said and Fanon in their theoretical analysis of colonial cultures assert that the representation of the colonized (the Middle East for Said and Algeria for Fanon) is often rendered as Other—inferior, stupid, dirty, subhuman, and so forth. The colonizers distance themselves from the colonized by constructing them as Other—not like me. In this manner, the colonizer is able to dominate, exploit, and oppress what he/she deems to be the inferior races.

The Chicano/a population often perceives itself as a colonized people. This political viewpoint is most eloquently expressed in the work of Rodolfo Acuña, *Occupied America* (2000). A more generalized view of colonization is deemed to be via Western Civilization's pervasive cultural imperialism. Thus Chicanos/as not only perceive themselves to be politically colonized but also culturally colonized and have fiercely struggled since the 1960s, in particular, to decolonize themselves. When the Chicano movement exploded in the 1960s, one of the most significant political actions taken was to reject Anglo-American/European aesthetics and embrace their indigenous Mexican cultural heritage. It was a deliberate action taken in order to decolonize their imagination and is the principal reason that the Chicano muralist movement was inspired by the Aztec murals in Bonampak, Teotihuacan, and other Maya and Aztec archeological sites. These artists turned their eyes away from Europe and focused on Mexico and sought inspiration in the murals of Rivera, Orozco, and Siqueiros. Chicano/a artists such as Judy Baca, Santa Barraza, Irene Pérez, Emigdio Vásquez, and others derived a significant number of their themes, motifs, and aesthetics from indigenous and Mexican masters.

In an analogous manner to the visual artists, the Chicano/a literary movement rejected European mythological characters and writers and immersed themselves in indigenous philosophy and mythology. Indigenous deities such as Quetzalcoatl, Coatlicue, Tonantzin, Cihuacóatl, Coyolxauhqui, and Huitzilopochtli populated the pages and canvases of Chicano/a artists. Luis Valdez, the playwright, sought guidance in Maya and Aztec thought while Alurista embraced Aztec legends and mythological deities. Valdez's guiding principle was taken from the Maya "In lak ech," which can be translated into Spanish as "Tú eres mi otro yo" (You are my other self) while Alurista posited the mythological land of Aztlán as the Chicanos'/as' original homeland. The Maya concept of the world which views the Other as an integral part of oneself resonated within Chicano/a hearts and minds and was perceived as a superior philosophy than that of viewing the Other as subhuman, as not part of one's humanity. Similarly, the concept of the Chicano/a homeland being situated in Aztlán (the American Southwest) legitimized the Mexican American population as the original inhabitants of the Southwest and not as foreigners who had no right to live in the United States. The taunting, hateful words from racists of "Go back where you came from!" could be readily answered: "We came from here!" In this manner, the subtext of Chicano/a visual arts and literary writings has been, for the most part, highly politically engaged. This art has not been an "art for art's sake" as the modernists would have it but a committed art that has sought to transform a community, a nation, and indeed, the world. The European canon extolling the use of Greek and Roman mythology was challenged and ruptured. Chicanos/as insisted on a new canon (or no canon at all), and proceeded to show the world a fresh vision, a different way of conceptualizing reality. The Chicano movement provided this ethnic population with self-confidence and proceeded to construct and represent themselves as subjects rather than objects, that is, stereotypes. The primacy of the European and Anglo-American subject was deconstructed and de-centered and artists immersed themselves in creating alternate subjectivities.

In their explorations for artistic and literary expressions that spoke to them in a different key, Chicano/a artists discovered the three mythic/historical figures whose history, imagery, and politics resonated within their spiritual psyches and became splendid founts of artistic inspiration: La Llorona, La Malinche, and the Virgin of Guadalupe.

La Llorona

Historical Antecedents

Bacil F. Kirtley, in his excellent article "La Llorona and Related Themes," did a credible tracing of La Llorona's ancestry to both Germanic and Aztec cultural traditions.¹ Basically, he cites the existence of a Llorona-type legend in Germany "by at least 1486" as "Dia Weisse Frau" (Stith Thompson's Motif-Index classification number E435.1.1.) and recorded in writing by the poet Kaspar Brushchipus in his *Chronologia Monasteriorum Germaniae Praecipuorum*, written in 1552 and later published in Sulzach in 1682.² A second source of input contributing to the development of La Llorona, according to Kirtley, were the Aztec legends surrounding the goddess Cihuacóatl ("Snake Woman"). He further points out that Cihuacóatl was "among the earth goddesses the most famous . . . and whose voice, roaring through the night, betokened war."³

As might be expected, a controversy exists between those scholars espousing a Mexican origin and those that lean toward both Aztec and European influences. Those supporting an Aztec heritage generally base their theory, as Kirtley did, on such impeccable sources as Fray Bernardino de Sahagún, who in his *Historia de las cosas de la Nueva España* (*General History of the Things of New Spain*) (1950: book 1, chapter 4; first published in 1569) described the goddess Cihuacóatl as follows:

> Cihuacóatl appeared several times a year as a well-dressed woman. It was said she would cry out and howl at night. . . . Her clothing was white and her long hair was braided in such a manner as to appear like horns sticking out of her forehead.⁴

Furthermore, Sahagún lists in book 11 of his *General History* the different omens that foreshadowed the downfall of the great Aztec empire. Omen number six predicted that: "At night you will hear the anguished wailing of a woman who cries: 'Oh, my sons, your destruction is near.' On other occasions she will cry: 'Oh my sons! Where shall I take you so that you will not perish?'"⁵

Luis Leal, in his article "The Malinche-Llorona Dichotomy: The Evolution of a Myth," appearing in Rolando Romero and Amanda Nolacea Harris's edited collection of articles on La Malinche, *Feminism, Nation and Myth: La Malinche*, asserts that:

> The myth of La Llorona existed much earlier than the year of the Conquest or even the arrival of the Spanish in Mexico. . . . Malinche makes her appearance in 1519 and therefore could not have been the model for La Llorona. The model of La Llorona is to be found, rather, in pre-Conquest mythology, in the form of several old goddesses, among them the woman serpent, Chiuacóatl, who dates back to the time of the Toltecs; Xtabay among the Mayas; Quilaztli (a manifestation of Cihuacóatl); and Coatlicue among the Aztecs. These goddesses, in turn, are derived from

the Earth Mother, who appears in a cosmogonic myth transcribed in 1550 from oral tradition. (pp. 134–135)[6]

Leal refers to several sources from the colonial period which discuss the goddess Cihuacóatl, such as Sahagún's *General History of the Things of New Spain* and Juan de Torquemada's book *Monarquía Indiana*, as well as other books which posit mythological figures similar to Cihuacóatl such as the goddess Quilaztli described in Thomas A. Janvier's *Legends of the City of Mexico*. Of particular interest is the description offered by Fray Diego Durán in his work, *Historia de las Indias de Nueva España* (first published in 1579), and quoted in Leal's article cited earlier, "The Malinche-Llorona Dichotomy":

> The principal goddess was called Cihuacóatl, goddess of the Xochimilca and, although she was the particular deity of the Xochimilca, she was venerated in Mexico and in Texcoco. The goddess Cihuacóatl was made of stone. She . . . was dressed . . . all in white—skirt, blouse, and mantle. If [her priests] saw that eight days had passed and no one had been sacrificed, they took a baby's cradle and put in it a sacrificial flint knife, called "The Child of Cihuacóatl." . . . They wrapped it up in cloth. They would give the cradle to a woman so that she might take it on her back to the market place. They would instruct her to go to the most important merchant woman. She would carry the cradle to the market . . . asking her to look after it until she came back. . . . Surprised that, not having nursed all day, the baby had not cried, . . . [the merchant woman] would then open the cradle and find in it the sacrificial knife, the "child" of Cihuacóatl.
>
> The people, on seeing this, cried out that the goddess had come and had appeared in the market place. They would say that she had brought along her child to show her hunger and to reproach the lords for their neglect in feeding her.[7]

Although controversy exists with respect to La Llorona's origins, there is no hesitancy on the part of scholars to acknowledge similarities between this legend and other weeping woman–type legends. For example, many acknowledge a strong resemblance between La Llorona and the Hebrew Lilith. Lilith, according to tradition, was the first wife of Adam (Gen. ii., 27) and was created simultaneously with man. Because of this simultaneous creation, Lilith refused to acknowledge Adam as her superior and was subsequently expelled from Paradise. She reportedly cohabited with the Devil and gave birth to the jinn, or evil spirits. Her refusal to return to Adam brought upon her the wrath of God, who condemned her to lose one hundred of her progeny each day. In *Funk & Wagnalls Standard Dictio-*

nary of Folklore, we find a reference to Lilith, who is described as a "maid of desolation (ardat lili)" in the Babylonian tradition (this and all subsequent quotations in this paragraph are from page 622). She was thought of as a "wind spirit wild-haired and winged" in Assyrian belief. The Talmudic tradition, on the other hand, associated her with night (laylah) and in that tradition became a night demon, "a succubus who slept with sleeping men and whose offspring from these unions were the demons." In the Middle Ages Lilith became associated with a "Lamia-like creature who envied women their children (she had lost hers) and would take them unless prevented by specific charms."

In addition to Lilith and Lamia, several other weeping woman legends are found among other peoples. The Penobscot Indians, for example, have the Pskegdemus legend.

> Pskegdemus . . . is a swamp spirit who wails near camps to entice men and children. A man who shows any sympathy for her, even in thought, is lost, for he will never be satisfied to marry a human woman. Another such demon of the Penobscot, dresses in moss and cedar bark, likes children and pets them. But good willed though she be, children have a way of going to sleep forever where she fondles them.[8]

Other Mesoamerican Indian myths that share similarities with La Llorona apart from the Chiuacóatl myth include the Ciuateteo (or Ciuapipltin), which consisted of

> certain female spirits (literally "noble women") who had died in childbirth (or in their first childbirth) or who had been warriors. Their patroness was Cihuacóatl, the serpent woman, probably an aspect of Coatlicue. The Ciuateteo lived in the western sky, through which, from the time it reached the meridian, they carried the sun to deliver it to the lords of the underworld. From this connection with the underworld they probably derived their dangerous character. Sometimes they flew out of the west as eagles, bringing epilepsy to children and lust to men. At certain times they scared people on the roads. From the corpse of such a woman, the stupefying thieves' candle (hand of glory) might be made, hence great precautions in the form of armed guards and the like, had to be taken against the body being stolen or mutilated. Under Spanish influence, the Ciuateteo has developed into La Llorona, the weeping woman of folktale, who wanders through the streets seeking her lost children.[9]

Further studies such as Michael Kearney's "La Llorona as a Social Symbol" show that "a variant of La Llorona occurs in Ixtepeji (Zapotec-mestizo town in the Sierra Juárez of Oaxaca, Mexico) bearing the name Matlaziwa.

Matlaziwa is a spirit-being who is similar enough to La Llorona so that informants tend to equate them. Everyone knows of them and many people report having heard, seen, and having had direct encounters with them."[10]

A counterpart of Matlaziwa (also spelled Matlacihuatl), as pointed out by Elaine Miller in her book *Mexican Folk Narratives from the Los Angeles Area*, is Ixtabay, who is also a siren-type Llorona.[11]

Another interesting group of legends from the state of Veracruz bear a close resemblance to the siren-type Llorona. These legends are those related to the "Chanecas," who are:

> women living in the forest who try to get a traveler to lose his path so that they may live with him, have sexual relations with him and eventually kill him. When an Indian gets lost in the forest he fashions an instrument from the stem of a plant . . . and leaves it behind him. He believes that when the "chanecas" find it they will play with it and try to find out how it was carved and how it works. The instrument entertains them and they forget about the traveler who thus has an opportunity to escape and find his way back out of the forest.[12]

With respect to literary versions found in Mexico and the Southwest, Betty Leddy in her article "La Llorona in Southern Arizona" cites various adaptations such as a novel, drama, and a poem.[13] Two literary versions by Mexican authors consulted depict the life-history of La Llorona. The first, a long poem by Vicente Riva Palacio and Juan de Dios Peza, details the tragic love affair of Luisa with an aristocrat who abandons her so that he can marry someone from his own class. The anguished Luisa, beside herself from grief, stabs the children to death.[14] The second literary version appears in a collection titled *Leyendas y sucedidos del Mexico colonial*, edited by Artemio del Valle Arizpe in 1963. The texts in this collection are literary versions of popular legends from Mexico. The variant appearing in this collection of a La Llorona legend was written by del Valle Arizpe and is actually a summary of various versions extant in Mexico City. The principal variations recounted are:

1. La Llorona had been a woman deeply in love with her husband but lived far away from him. When she tried to join him, he was already married to someone else.
2. She was a woman who actually never married her fiancé because she died before their wedding and now returns to gaze at her beloved and cries upon seeing the wicked life he is living.

3. She was a widow with children living in poverty.
4. She was the mother of murdered children and came back to mourn them.
5. She was an unfaithful wife who returned crying for forgiveness.
6. She was a woman who was murdered by her jealous husband over unfounded suspicions.
7. She was doña Marina, the beautiful Malinche mistress of Cortez who came back to earth crying for forgiveness for having betrayed her race to the Spaniards.[15]

La Llorona and Chicano Writers

La Llorona or weeping woman, who wanders the earth in search of her orphaned children, is a recurring motif in Chicano/a literature and art. She appears in work by such important Mexican American poets and novelists as Alurista, Alejandro Morales, Rudolfo Anaya, Raul Salinas, Ana Castillo, Sandra Cisneros, Lucha Corpi, Cherríe Moraga, Helena María Viramontes, Naomi Quiñónez, and Cordelia Candelaria, among many others.

In Alurista's poetry, for example, La Llorona is depicted as a mother looking for her lost children in the mechanical labyrinths of United States industry. In a poem entitled "must be the season of the witch" the poet writes:

>must be the season of the witch
>> la bruja
>> la llorona
>
> she lost her children
>> and she cries
>
> en las barrancas of industry
>> her children
>
> devoured by computers
>> and the gears
>
> must be the season of the witch
>> I hear huesos crack
>
> in pain
>> y lloros
>
> la bruja pangs
>> sus hijos han olvidado
>
> la magia de Durango
> y la de Moctezuma
> —el Huiclamina

must be the season of the witch
la bruja llora
sus hijos sufren; sin ella[16]
[must be the season of the witch
the witch
la llorona
she lost her children
and she cries
in the canyons of industry
her children
devoured by computers
and the gears
must be the season of the witch
I hear bones crack
in pain
And cries
the witch pangs
her sons have forgotten
the magic of Durango
and that of Moctezuma
—the Huiclamina
must be the season of the witch
the witch cries
her sons suffer; without her] (my translation)

In Alejandro Morales's first novel, *Caras viejas y vino nuevo*, the motif of La Llorona serves to emphasize the barrio's (Mexican American neighborhood) loss of her children to drugs, police, and illness. The novel depicts barrio life in the 1950s and 1960s in its most grotesque, degraded, and violent moments. The constant fights and the poor health, both spiritual and physical, of the inhabitants of the area bring the mechanical cries of the sirens of an ambulance, a fire engine, or the police. It is the wail of La Llorona, who comes to take the "children," her sons, away. After a fatal car crash, the result of a drug-crazed driver, the following description appears:

> Lloronas everywhere; people here and there enjoying the scene, talking, rubber-necking, touching, not surprised at the agglutination of flesh and steel that was part of the intense colorings of the collage formed up, down and over the road. They could not open, they could not separate the mess. After about an hour the firemen took out what remained of Turco and Ramón.[17]

Similarly, La Llorona plays an important part in the structure of *Bless Me, Ultima*, a novel that has become a classic within the corpus of Chicano/a literature. In a penetrating analysis by Jane Rogers appearing in the *Latin American Literary Review* entitled "The Function of the La Llorona Motif in Rudolfo Anaya's *Bless Me, Ultima*," she asserts:

> A similar theme [as that in the Odyssey] is developed by Rudolfo Anaya's use of the *la llorona* motif in *Bless Me, Ultima*. In the novel, Antonio, symbolically both Christ and Odysseus, moves from the security and from the sweet-smelling warmth of his mother's bosom and kitchen out into light and experience. As he weighs his options—priesthood and the confinement represented by the farms of the Luna's or the Marezes' freedom and as he grows from innocence to knowledge and experience, the *la llorona* motif figures both on a literal mythological level and as an integral part of Antonio's life.
>
> As "literal" myth, *la llorona* is the wailing woman of the river. Hers is the "tormented cry of lonely goddess" that fills the valley in one of Antonio's dreams. *La llorona* is "The old witch who cries along the river banks and seeks the blood of boys and men to drink."[18]

La Llorona and Chicana Writers

Chicana writers have likewise incorporated the La Llorona motif within their literary works. In opposition to Chicano writers, however, they have redefined the La Llorona figure and provided a feminist perspective. Ana Castillo's Llorona, appearing in her novel *So Far From God*, is a friendly playmate to La Loca, one of the young women protagonists in the narrative. For Sandra Cisneros La Llorona serves as the title of her collection of short stories *Woman Hollering Creek and Other Stories*. The story by the same name has one of the characters in the narrative yell out a scream after crossing a creek. The scream is emblematic of freedom and liberation for women. The protagonist also screams and in the process finds her voice; she is no longer silent to the oppression she was suffering at the hands of her abusive husband.

Lucha Corpi in her detective novel *Black Widow's Wardrobe* has a La Llorona–like figure appear at the beginning of the novel. In this work, La Llorona is linked to La Malinche since the novel narrates the story of Licia Lecuona, who murders her husband and is "reincarnated" as La Malinche. Poets such as Naomi Quiñónez and Cordelia Candelaria have also incorporated La Llorona within their poetic discourse. Candelaria's poem seeks to abolish La Llorona from her nightmares and general consciousness in "Go 'Way from My Window, La Llorona." In no uncertain terms the poetic voice lashes at the ghostly figure:

> Get lost, lady! ¡Andale!
> Far away and forever, ¡Vete! But not
> Like sinks of dirty water swallowed by the drain
> To rise again in cesspools, not like
> A fat black roach swept away
> Returns with crowds at midnight. But vanish
> Weeping Bitch, out of my life.[19]

While Candelaria tries to vanish La Llorona, Quiñónez's poem, "La Llorona" is more conciliatory and evidences a compassionate understanding of the woman who is accused of having killed her children.

> When La Llorona comes to me
> Vulnerability turns compassion
> the haunting melody of her son
> wanders as wounded and random
> as her legend through the rivers
> and alleyway of my existence
> La Llorona—madre perdida
> who searches eternally.[20]

Cherríe Moraga in turn has written a play based on the La Llorona legend. Titled *The Hungry Woman: A Mexican Medea*, the play uses the Medea/Llorona myths to explore the Chicano/a politics of the future.

La Llorona and Chicano/a Visual Artists

Chicano and Chicana visual artists have likewise incorporated the figure of La Llorona within their canvases. Santa Barraza, an artist from Kingsville, Texas, has depicted several Llorona figures in her paintings. Some of these images appear in a book-length study on Santa Barraza's work titled *Santa Barraza: Artist of the Borderlands*, edited by this author. Barraza's Llorona at times appears within the context of other mythological figures such as the Virgin of Guadalupe and Coyolxauhqui, as for example in her painting *Cihuateteo con Coyolxauhqui y la Guadalupana*, painted in 1996 (see *Santa Barraza*, plate 12). At other times she appears as a beautiful mestiza woman with a maguey plant and water in the background, as for example in *La Llorona II/The Weeping Woman*, painted in 1995 (see *Santa Barraza*, plate 13). A third painting by Santa Barraza depicting La Llorona and titled *Ap-*

parition of La Llorona (1994) renders the woman with a double face and in a most vulnerable position. (See *Santa Barraza*, plate 34). That La Llorona is painted half sitting in water and with her arms and hands crossed around her stomach, protecting a fetus translucent in her uterus—her unborn child. Her face demonstrates the pain of seeing the future. An angel-infant hovers above the two heads of La Llorona as if protecting them with his/her wings. Two human hands framing the figure of La Llorona are seen extended and palms out toward the viewer as if gesturing those who would harm the child to stop. All of Barraza's La Llorona paintings connect her with bodies of water.

Rosa M., an artist from southern California, also connects her Llorona figure with an Aztec goddess, Cihuateteo, and depicts some of her Llorona figures exiting from a building with a sleeping (dead?) child under her arm.

"La Llorona, The Wailing Woman" (1979)
Artist: Alvaro Suman

She leaves behind the empty cradle with the obsidian knife in place of the child. This can be seen in her painting *Cihuacoatl, La Llorona* (See cover of the book *Chicana Literary and Artistic Expressions: Culture and Society in Dialogue*, María Herrera-Sobek, ed.).

Rosa M. includes Llorona figures hovering around lakes and forests with children depicted within the landscape. Chicano visual artists, on the other hand, have not focused on the La Llorona figure as a motif for their paintings as much as Chicana writers have done repeatedly. One Chicano artist that has depicted La Llorona is Alvaro Suman from Santa Barbara, California. His painting is titled "La Llorona, The Wailing Woman" (1979).

Suman's "La Llorona" features a ghostly white young woman in a field of mushrooms (or penis-like plants). It is dark and the moon shines brightly on the scene, which makes La Llorona look even more ghost-like with her bare white arms and white, mask-like face. Nevertheless, she is not a scary figure and unlike Chicana paintings of La Llorona the setting is not a body of water but an open farmland with trees and grass. The trees do seem to cast a dark shadow with their wavy forms, particularly the tree to the right of the viewer. She is more reminiscent of La Llorona and her encounters with inebriated men walking home in the dark at midnight after heavy drinking in the local bars or cantinas. They typically see a young beautiful girl walking in the farm fields and they run to see her, but when she turns around her face is that of an animal or a skeleton. The men then fall down sick with "susto," a folk illness similar to shock. (See Suman's image of La Llorona in Luis Leal's book, *Mitos y Leyendas de México/Myths and Legends of Mexico* [2002], p. 31.)

A Chicano scholar, José Limón, however, has written an excellent essay on the La Llorona legend titled "La Llorona, the Third Legend of Greater Mexico: Cultural Symbols, Women, and the Political Unconscious." In his study Limón explores the significance of this legendary figure and argues that La Llorona "may be understood at two levels: first, as a positive, contestative symbol for the women of Greater Mexico and second as a critical symbolic reproduction of a socially unfulfilled utopian longing within the Mexican folk masses who tell her story. She speaks to the social and psychological needs of both Greater Mexican sectors, needs yet unmet by the hegemonic, hierarchical, masculinized, and increasingly capitalistic social order imposed on the Mexican folk masses since their beginning."[21] More recently, Chicana and other scholars are focusing their research on La Llorona. Domino Renee Pérez from the University of Texas, Austin, presented a paper at the annual meeting of the Modern Language

Association in December 29, 2006 titled "Shared Spaces; or Toward a Process of Critical Interrogation: La Llorona in Two Short Films."

La Llorona is an important figure in the Chicano/a imagination. She is so popular that there are even two songs featuring her: "La Llorona" (in this song she appears as a beautiful lover) and "La Llorona Loca" (in this song she appears as a comic, "scary" figure).[22] La Llorona, as a shadowy figure of a mother crying for her lost children, resonates within the Chicano/a psyche since they view themselves as orphaned children, being that no "mother" country wants to claim them. In the United States they are perceived as Mexicans; in Mexico they are perceived as pochos—non-Mexicans. Pat Mora's poem "Legal Alien" encapsulates these feelings of alienation from both countries very well:

> Bi-lingual, Bi-Cultural,
> Able to slip from "How's life?"
> To "Me'stan volviendo loca,"
> Able to sit in a paneled office
> Drafting memos in smooth English,
> Able to order in fluent Spanish
> At a Mexican restaurant.
> American but hyphenated,
> Viewed by Anglos as perhaps exotic,
> Perhaps inferior, definitely different,
> Viewed by Mexicans as alien,
> (their eyes say, "You may speak
> Spanish but you're not like me")
> An American to Mexicans
> A Mexican to Americans[23]

The above section demonstrates how La Llorona is a multivalent figure that speaks at different levels and articulates multiple concerns: to some La Llorona makes anti-abortion statements—women should not commit infanticide. To others it offers a cautionary tale for wayward husbands since La Llorona appears to them in the dead of night when they are walking home drunk. Still others find in the La Llorona narrative a feminist statement of having a voice, of having agency (wailing) as in Sandra Cisneros's short story "Woman Hollering Creek," while others see it as a unique tool available to economically poor parents for socializing their children to stay away from dangerous canals and rivers to avoid drowning. La Llorona then has multiple faces and artists respond to this multifaceted iconic figure by repeatedly representing her in their works.

La Malinche

Historical Antecedents

A second important cultural icon appearing in Chicano/a works is La Malinche, sometimes perceived as another incarnation of La Llorona. La Malinche is a historical figure who rose to prominence during the Spanish conquest in 1519–1521. When Hernán Cortez, Mexico's conqueror, landed on the coast of the Gulf of Mexico in what is today the city of Veracruz, he received as a gift from the local cacique or Indian leader twenty young maidens. Among these girls whose ages were between fifteen and twenty years was Malintzín Tenepal, known by her Indian name as Malinche and her Spanish name as Doña Marina. Malinche's story reads like a fairy tale. According to the Spanish chronicler Bernal Díaz del Castillo, who wrote V*erdadera historia de la conquista de la Nueva España* (*The True History of the Conquest of New Spain*) (written in 1568 and first published in 1632 in Madrid), Malinche was an Aztec subject belonging to the upper classes. She was sold to Mayan merchants when she was about six or seven years old by her own mother, who, having remarried, wished to have her son by her second husband inherit the estate. Malinche grew up as a slave girl within the Maya culture in the town of Coatzacoalcos in the area around Veracruz and thus became fluent in the Maya language. When Cortez appeared on the scene, he needed translators in order to communicate with Moctezuma, the Aztec leader, who kept sending envoys to greet him. Among the soldiers accompanying Cortez was Gerónimo de Aguilar, who spoke fluent Maya, having been shipwrecked for several years on the Yucatan peninsula. Soon, it was learned that Malinche spoke Nahuatl, the language spoken by the Aztecs and her mother tongue. Since she also spoke Maya she was able to communicate with Aguilar and convey the messages coming from Moctezuma to Cortez. Del Castillo informs us that it was not long before Malinche, who was an extremely gifted person, learned to speak Spanish fluently and was able to translate directly to Cortez. Soon thereafter Cortez took her as his lover and she eventually bore him a son. Her translation skills led the indigenous population to refer to her as the Tongue, (La Lengua) and she became a cultural mediator between the Spanish and Aztec leaders. She was highly respected by both Spanish and Indians, for example she was referred to as Doña Marina by the Spaniards, granting her a title of respect. It was not until the Mexican Revolution (1910–1917) that Malinche began to be perceived in negative terms in the popular imagination. The term Malinche began to be used in a pejorative sense to mean a traitor, a sellout, one who betrays his/her country and his/her people. To be a Malinchista was to be one that favored foreigners over Mexico and anything that was Mexican. The negative perception of Malinche may be linked to the loss of Mexican territory to the United States in 1848 and with Santa Anna, the Mexican president at the time, being perceived as a traitor. A second major event that transpired in the second half of the nineteenth century was the French attempt to establish an empire in the 1860s and the importation of the Austrian-born Maximilian and Carlota to be the first rulers of Mexico. The members of the upper classes who supported the importation of foreign rulers were perceived as traitors to the Mexican nation. Nationalists after the defeat of the French and the execution of Maximilian on June 19, 1867 in the state of Queretaro, Mexico, seized upon the figure of La Malinche as a symbol of betrayal. John Taylor explains:

> Thus, the nationalists created a paradigm of Mexico with polarized perspectives of women: Malinche represented pure evil, the "Mexican Eve," on one side, and Mary the mother of Jesus represented supreme good, *La Virgen*, on the other. Virginity and fidelity were the highest womanly virtues: Malinche, therefore, was used as an example of a woman who deviated from expected female behavior. She was wrapped in negative symbolism and imagery, and associated with the negative aspects of national identity and sexuality. Her name became synonymous with "treason," "betrayal," and "sell-out." Malinche was suddenly portrayed as the beautiful temptress who conquered and destroyed her own people. She was objectified and "sexualized as the Indian woman who could not get enough of the white man." They effectively built this language and imagery around her in a deliberate campaign, with purely political objectives: to promote the Indian heritage of the Mexican people while making Malinche into an "anti-heroine, a national Judas," and the scapegoat for three centuries of colonial rule.[24]

Historians during the 1870–1880 decade such as Ignacio Paz wrote extensively on the history of Mexico and depicted Malinche in extremely pejorative and sexual terms, calling her the "barragana de Cortez," or Cortez's prostitute. Later in the 1950s, his son Octavio Paz would denominate Malinche as La Chingada or the "Fucked One" in his book *El laberinto de la soledad* (1950), translated as *The Labyrinth of Solitude*.

The third significant event that aided in the crystallization of the "Malinche-as-traitor" concept was the hated twenty-six-year Porfirio Díaz regime (the first term was served from 1876–1880; then the second to sixth consecutive terms were served from 1888–1910). Díaz's economic, social, and political policies sought to transform Mexico into a modern "European" country. Under the influence of his infamous *científicos* (scientists) and the positivist philosophy of August Comet, he subscribed to the Darwinian dictum of "survival of the fittest" and viewed the Indian population not as an asset but as a drag on Mexico's drive toward industrialization and modernization. He fomented and actively encouraged European and United States investment as well as immigration and in this manner sought to transform Mexico into a "white" country. His policies of favoring foreigners were so extreme that Mexico became popularly known as "the mother of foreigners." In fact, when the new revolutionary governments displaced Porfirio Díaz, the often-repeated theme was "México para los mexicanos" (Mexico for the Mexicans) and laws were instituted which forbade foreigners from owning more than 49 percent of Mexican investment holdings or land. It is in this manner that the pejorative term "Malinchista" was coined, most likely in the twentieth century, in response to Díaz's policies of favoring foreigners over Mexican citizens. Malinche, then, became the iconic figure through which resentment of foreign imperialism and the privileging of Europeans and Anglo-Americans and their cultures was vented. This resentment found expression in the symbol of La Malinche, through which it was explicitly articulated. Henceforth, Malinche began to be reconceptualized as a second Eve who aided the Spaniards in the conquest of Mexico. She became the fall guy within the lens of a patriarchal, misogynistic society.

La Malinche and Chicana Writers

The Chicana feminist movement began to revise Mexican history regarding La Malinche in the early 1970s. Adelaida del Castillo, in her article "Malintzin Tenepal: A Preliminary Look into a New Perspective" (1977), was the first Chicana scholar to explore in-depth Malinche's historical standing and reputation and to provide a Chicana feminist perspective on this unique female figure. For Del Castillo, Malinche was not a traitor, but a mediator who sought to make the best of a difficult situation. Other Chicana feminist scholars, such as Norma Alarcón, have likewise revised Malinche's role in the conquest. Alarcón's seminal article, "Traddutora, Traditora: A Paradigmatic Figure of Chicana Feminism" (1988), examines Malinche's role in history and her connection to modern Chicana feminists.

Feminist Chicana novelists and poets in particular have inscribed this iconic figure within their creative writings. Lucha Corpi's poem "Marina" poetically reconstructs Malinche's life. Malinche is first depicted as a victim of her own mother's machinations to deprive her of her inheritance and later as a victim of society who condemned her for giving life to the mestizo people.

Corpi continues to present Marina as a woman in love who worshiped the new Christian god as well as the woman who planted the seed for the future mestizo people. Other Chicana poets, such as Carmen Tafolla, Angela de Hoyos, Margarita Cota-Cárdenas, Pat Mora, and Alicia Gaspar de Alba, among others have written poems with Malinche as the main protagonist. Novelists such as Erlinda Gonzales-Berry also included a section on Malinche in her novel *Paletitas de guayaba* (1991). All of the writers present a positive view of Malinche. For Chicanas, Malinche is not a negative figure but a positive one; she is perceived as a strong, intelligent, linguistically gifted, diplomatically savvy individual who at the age of approximately twenty helped change the world. Chicano writers have not been as involved as Chicanas in revisioning Malinche. In this respect we see a gender difference in the response toward Malinche. Dan Banda, a Chicano film director, is one of the few Chicanos to evidence a strong interest in the Malinche figure. He produced and directed a documentary titled *Indigenous Always: The Legend of La Malinche* (2000), where he traces the journey Malinche took with Cortez from Veracruz to Mexico City. Banda interviews scholars as well as men and women on the street with respect to their views on Malinche. These interviews yielded various perspectives: most males viewed her as a traitor, as one who betrayed her people, while some of the women were more generous. One young lady opined: "Fue una persona muy hábil; supo conciliar intereses personales; sacar provecho." (She was a very clever woman who know how to reconcile her own interests in order to come out ahead.) An older woman stated: "Es el prototipo de la mujer mexicana. Yo la quiero." (She is the prototype of the Mexican woman. I like her.)[25]

Malinche has been depicted by many Mexican painters, including the early indigenous chroniclers. From the 1520s to the early 1900s, Malinche was not painted in a negative manner. However, after the Mexican Revolution, Diego Rivera depicted her in a very negative light—he portrayed her as a prostitute-looking woman beside a very ugly Cortez.

Orozco likewise drew Malinche in a negative pose. In the painting titled *Cortez and Malinche* (1926), she is presented as sitting at Cortez's side with an Indian facedown at their feet. (See image in Desmond Rochfort, *Mexican Muralists*, p. 46).

La Malinche and Chicana Painters

Chicana painters have not appropriated the Malinche icon as much as Chicana creative writers and scholars. One of the most beautiful renditions of Malinche was done by Santa Barraza. In her painting titled "La Malinche" (see *Santa Barraza*, plate 30), she has the Indian woman at the center of the canvass, half nude, and in front of her beautiful face and body is a maguey plant from whose center a newborn baby floats toward Malinche's face. In the background is Cortez; he is marginalized and appears as a secondary figure. The painting is an homage to Malinche as the mother of the future mestizo people.

Another Chicano painter who has rendered the image of La Malinche is Afredo Arreguín, in a painting titled "La Malinche" (1993). (See Lauro Flores's book *Alfredo Arreguín: Patterns of Dreams and Nature*, p. 109.) In a stunningly beautiful painting, Arreguín portrays Malinche as a three-faced woman, thus encompassing the mestizaje extant in Mexico as well as the many "faces" of La Malinche, since she is such a controversial figure.

La Malinche has made its strongest impact on scholarly writings and most specifically Chicana feminist theory. Adelaida del Castillo set the stage and Sandra Messinger Cypess (though not a Chicana) carried it forward with the publication of her book *La Malinche in Mexican Literature: From History to Myth* (1991). Norma Alarcón's theoretical work on La Malinche has further clarified the position of La Malinche within Chicana feminist thought. La Malinche has been conceptualized by patriarchal society as a traitor to the Mexican nation. However, Malinche was not a traitor since Mexico was not a nation during the colonial period—and certainly was not a nation in the modern sense of the word when Cortez landed in Veracruz in 1519. Malinche did not join Cortez voluntarily but was given as a slave to him. She had no say in the matter. On the other hand, we can admire Malinche for her linguistic skills, her skills as a diplomat, and her ability to function within two cultures. She was an exceptional woman who made history but since then has been erased from history. Her story is not completely known because a patriarchal society did not make it known. Chicana scholars and writers have tried to set straight the record on this woman through their creative works. Most recently there is a collection of creative and scholarly essays on La Malinche in Rolando Romero and Amanda Nolacea Harris's book titled *Feminism, Nation and Myth: La Malinche* (2005). The book includes an article by this author titled "In Search of La Malinche: Pictorial Representations of a Mytho-Historical Figure." In this essay I trace the various graphic representations of La Malinche from the 1500s to the present.

The Virgin of Guadalupe

Historical Antecedents

The third iconic female figure from the Spanish colonial period most popular in the writings and plastic arts of Chicanos/as that I explore in this essay is the Virgin of Guadalupe. According to tradition, the apparition of the Virgin of Guadalupe dates back to 1531, the date she is said to have appeared to the Indian Juan Diego, thirty-nine years after the conquistadores set foot in New Spain. From the very beginning the apparition of the Virgin of Guadalupe at the Hill of Tepeyac at the outskirts of Mexico City was perceived as an important sign, as an indication of the importance of the Mexican inhabitants and their role as a "chosen people." It was deemed that the apparition of the Virgin meant the Mexican people had a special role to play in the world since they had been favored by the Almighty. The portent was interpreted as a sign that Mexicans were a privileged people in which God was particularly pleased since he had sent his most beloved treasure—his own mother—to appear on Mexican soil. Even more surprising, if we adhere to the notion expounded upon by the French historian Jacques Lafaye in his book *Quetzalcoatl and Guadalupe: The Formation of Mexican National Consciousness 1531–1813* (1976), is the fact that this supernatural act became the catalyst which proved vital in the transformation of a peoples who were racially diverse and heterogeneous. Guadalupe's appearance aided proto-Mexicans to begin to form a national consciousness and crystallize as a political and social unit. Most significant was the fact that Guadalupe appeared to a humble Indian, Juan Diego. This simple act had profound ramifications in the construction of the ideological landscape, both racially and socially speaking, of the future Mexican nation.

All Mexicans, from an early age and even before learning their ABCs, are familiar with the story of the Virgin of Guadalupe. Basically oral tradition has it that in the early days in December a poor Indian by the name of Juan Diego was on his way to Mexico City to bring a doctor so that he could heal his ailing uncle. As Juan Diego approached the Hill of Tepeyac he saw the Virgin of Guadalupe, who began to speak to him. Guadalupe requested that Juan Diego deliver a message to the bishop of Mexico. The message was that she wished to have a church built in her honor at the Hill of Tepeyac. Poor Juan Diego was scared out of his wits but managed to respond that the bishop of Mexico would never believe him because he was a poor Indian. Nevertheless, the Virgin of Guadalupe insisted and Juan Diego went ahead and visited the bishop in Mexico City in order to deliver the message. As Juan Diego feared, the bishop did not believe him and sent him on his way. This event happened three times. On the third try, the Virgin told Juan Diego to pick a bunch of roses growing on the hillside. As this was the month of December, the fact that beautiful roses were growing on the hillside was another sign of the miraculous nature of the undertaking. Juan Diego picked the roses and placed them on his *tilma* or robe. He took the flowers to the bishop and when Juan Diego opened his robe to deliver the roses the image of the Virgin of Guadalupe was found imprinted on the white cotton *tilma*. The bishop acknowledged the miracle and a chapel was built on the Hill of Tepeyac. The *tilma* with the imprint of the Virgin of Guadalupe was framed and can be viewed today in the new cathedral at the Villa de Guadalupe in Mexico City.

Scholars have pointed out the connection between Guadalupe and the various native goddesses populating the Aztec pantheon before the conquest. At least six Aztec goddesses are associated with the name Tonantzin, "Nuestra Madre" (Our Mother): Cihuacoatl, Centeotl, Zilonen, Chicomecoatl, Toci, and Citlalicue. In fact the cult to some of these Aztec goddesses, particularly that of Tonantzin, took place in the Hill of Tepeyac. The transition from the cult of these goddesses to Guadalupe was relatively easy. The Native American pantheon of goddesses for many groups of Indians has been and is quite rich. The Aztecs and the Mayas, as well as other groups of Indians, house many female and male deities within their religious belief systems. When missionaries introduced the Virgin Mary, Indian tribes were generally receptive to accepting her. There was a flexibility within Native American religious worldview that facilitated the introduction of new gods and goddesses. Ethnographers and anthropologists point out that a significant factor in the syncretism and the easy acceptance of Tonantzin-Guadalupe was the racial makeup of Guadalupe, since the latter is often represented as an indigenous woman. Her skin color is brown and her racial features are indigenous.

The first basilica was constructed in 1555 under the jurisdiction of Archbishop Montufar at the Hill of Tepeyac. By 1622 this basilica was converted into a more substantial church with donations from the faithful. This indicates how rapidly the cult of Guadalupe was growing. The cult kept expanding and by 1694 church officials were forced to construct a new cathedral in order to keep up with the faithful. The 1694 cathedral still stands today and has recently been renovated and opened to the numerous people who come to visit the shrine of the Virgin of Guadalupe.

The cult of Guadalupe kept expanding and by the eighteenth century the shrine of Guadalupe was one of the most important sites in Mexico, where yearly celebrations took place on the twelfth of December to mark the anniversary of the apparition of the Virgin. Of particular note is the homage that has been paid to the Virgin of Guadalupe by the various indigenous groups in Mexico. But it was not only the indigenous populations who celebrated the apparition of the Virgin of Guadalupe. Creoles, mestizos (people of mixed blood), and others from all strata of society joined in the celebrations. The viceroys as well as humble servants all participated and vied with each other to honor the Virgin. These events demonstrate how the Virgin became associated with the political landscape of the country and why she is perceived by scholars as the incipient sprouting of a future Mexican nationalism.

When the wars of independence exploded in 1810, the Virgin of Guadalupe was ready to be used as a symbol of national unity. The Grito or the Cry that initiated the rebellion against the Spaniards given by Father Miguel Hidalgo y Costilla, the Father of the Mexican Independence Movement, on September 15, 1810, was "¡Viva México! ¡Viva la Virgen de Guadalupe!" (Long live Mexico! Long live the Virgin of Guadalupe!) This established a tradition within the Mexican people that at the inception of any revolutionary movement or social struggle the Virgin of Guadalupe would be brought forth to lead them. Guadalupe, then, becomes a multivalent symbol that can encompass within its sacred parameters a voice for social justice; a mantle of heavenly protection for those who feel marginalized, oppressed, exploited, and buffeted by hegemonic society. Thus the Virgin of Guadalupe was able to serve the cause of the peasant revolutionary movements that transformed Mexico during the violent decade of 1810–1821 and later during 1910–1920. She was equally at home, nevertheless, with the conservative, reactionary Catholic movement of the Cristero Rebellion (1926–1929), which sought to reestablish the power of the Catholic Church. The Cristeros felt they were fighting for a sacred cause and thus sought the protection of the Virgin of Guadalupe.

In the United States, during the civil rights movements of the 1960s and the drive to unionize the farm workers, banners with the figure of the Virgin of Guadalupe were at the forefront of various marches and demonstrations. The Virgin of Guadalupe, therefore, is not only a religious symbol but through the four centuries since her apparition she has acquired political and social dimensions. She has become to all Mexicans a plurivalent sign through which this ethnic group can identify and unite. The identification with this sacred symbol can take multiple forms: (1) as a cultural entity which can be represented or manifested through paintings, legends, literary works, history, rites, feasts, and the plastic arts; (2) as a political and/or ideological entity since she can encapsulate nationalist feelings of being Mexican and being privileged to be under the protection of the Mother of God; (3) as a psychological prop important to the self-esteem of Mexicans since they believe they are a "chosen people" by the Mother of God because she appeared to a Mexican Indian. This last point has the possibility of uniting Mexicans since being a country selected by the

Mother of God is a transcendental act that goes beyond race, color, or social status. Most importantly, the Virgin of Guadalupe encompasses the belief in social justice since she selected a humble Indian to be the bearer of her message and to whom she spoke directly. The act of the Virgin of Guadelupe choosing Juan Diego symbolizes her predilection for the poor and defenseless; for the downtrodden and those who yearn for social justice. She symbolizes the aspirations of a people who wish to break all social and racial barriers in order to attain a more just and equitable life for all humanity.

The Virgin of Guadalupe and Visual Arts

Given the above, it is not surprising to note that the Virgin of Guadalupe is the most popular iconic figure to be used in the plastic arts. Both Chicanos and Chicanas utilize the figure of the Virgin of Guadalupe in their paintings. From traditional representations to the most avant-garde depictions, the figure of this sacred image is both ever-present and ever-changing. The Virgin of Guadalupe has been a particularly malleable icon in the hands of Chicano/a visual artists. Yolanda M. López can be credited with initiating the explosion of Guadalupe paintings that have been gracing canvases and paper since 1978. López recalls the inspiring moment that led to the transformation of the iconic figure of the Virgin of Guadalupe that had remained practically static since 1531, when the image made its first appearance in the *tilma* of Juan Diego: "Looking at the image closely, I discovered that her dress was so long that it gathered at the feet, so I trimmed the cloth to let her feet and legs move. I felt that I had removed her from bondage, from having been trapped in her clothing."[26]

This simple act of clipping Guadalupe's long robes to mid-calf and having her wear slip-on, mid-heel sandals produced a great controversy in Mexico. The image was used for the cover of the June–July 1984 issue of *Fem* magazine and this elicited multiple bomb threats for the editors of *Fem*. López perceives the Virgin of Guadalupe as being a complex figure representative of the "Roman Catholic Church, Mexican nationality, Chicano spirituality, a role model for women, and a source of solace for men" (p. 80). She adds that she "started working with the image in 1978 because Guadalupe was the most popular female political image used by the United Farm Workers in demonstrations and in progressive immigrant support groups." (p. 80) López's Virgin of Guadelupe later that same year appeared as her grandmother, her mother working on a sewing machine as a seamstress, and as a portrait of the artist, featured as a powerful mini-skirted, tennis-shoes-wearing jogger.

The popularity of the image of Guadalupe is astounding. The image has metamorphosed into every conceivable possibility. The following are but a few; there are many, many more: Ester Hernández, "The Virgin of Guadalupe defendiendo los derechos de los chicanos," "La ofrenda/The Offering" (1988), and "La Virgen de las calles" (2001); Enrique Arciniega Campos, "Queen Bitch Goddess Success" (The Madonna) (1990); Cristina Cardenas, "La Virgen de los pescados" (1994); Margarita Mita Cuarón, "La Virgen de la sandía" (1997), "Virgen de Guadalupe baby" (1992); Richard Alvarez, "La Virgen de los muertos" (1996); Alfredo Arreguín, "Triología de la independencia de México" (1988); Meggan De Anza, "Las mujeres—mi familia" (1996); Alfred J. Quiroz, "Virgen de la muerte" (1997); Rosa M., "Mayahuel y Coyolxauhqui" (2000); Daniel Ponce Márquez, "Angelitos" (1995); Carlos Santistevan, "Nuestra señora de Guadalupe" (1996); Alma López, "Lupe y Sirena in Love" (1999) and "Our Lady," (1999); Eduardo Oropeza, "Untitled" (n.d.); María Almeida Natividad, "Virgen de las rosas" (1993); Ray Gaytán, "Sign of the Virgen Mary" (1996) and "V.G. Gets Variety" (1999); Wayne Alaniz Healy, "La Virgen de Venice" (1995) and "La Virgen de la cancha" (1995); Isabel Martínez, "The Virgin Crossing the River" (1998); Alfred J. Quiroz, "Goddess" (1991); Nephtali de León, "La Virgen de Guadaliberty" (1999).

Artists such as Yolanda M. López, Santa Barraza, Rosa M., and Alma López have created a whole series of Guadalupes in different poses and with various meanings encoded within the often startling images.

The image of Guadalupe has inspired a whole cycle of creativity surrounding the body of this sacred figure. Artists from the 1970s on have reconfigured, revisualized, reimagined, and reconceptualized the Virgin into a myriad of representations. The sacred image was secularized and converted into a more humane figure. She is represented by Chicano/a artists in numerous dynamic, everyday poses. She has descended from her pedestal to live, laugh, play, and work among Chicano/as. The Virgin of Guadalupe is no longer serene, untouchable, distant, and above the fray but is immersed in the everyday cares, sufferings, and worries of the Chicano population. Whether portrayed as a skater or playing basketball by Wayne Alaniz Healy, as a seamstress or jogger by Yolanda M. López, as a flower vender or karate figure by Ester Hernández, as the Mona Lisa by César González, as an immigrant by Isabel Martínez, or as a cool bikini clad chick by Alma López, the Virgin of Guadalupe will never be perceived the same again. She has been transformed and transported into the twenty-first century.

On the other hand, the social justice aspect that Guadalupe signifies continues to have meaning. Painters such as Rosa M. and Nephtali de

Victoria F. Franco: Our Lady of Guadalupe (1978)
Artist: Yolanda M. López

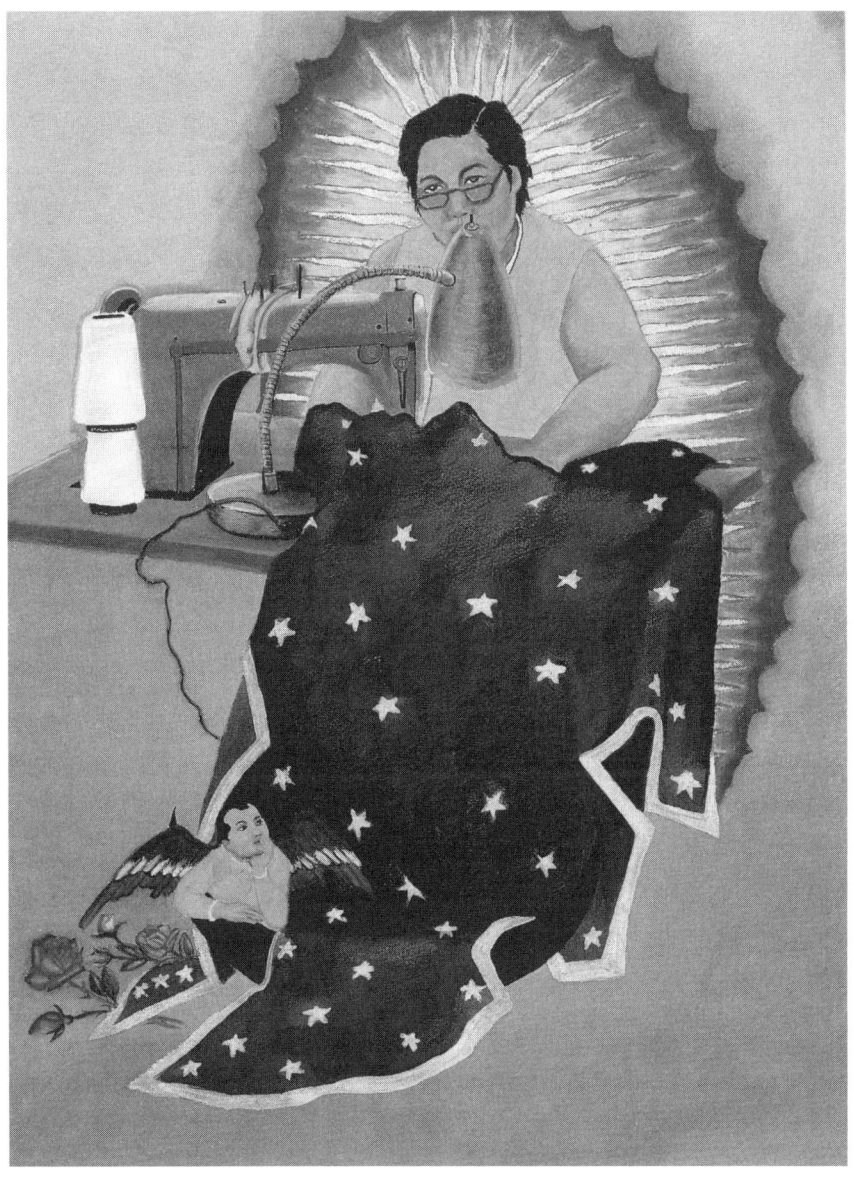

Margaret F. Stewart: Our Lady of Guadalupe (1978)
Artist: Yolanda M. López

Portrait of the Artist as the Virgin of Guadalupe (1978)
Artist: Yolanda M. López

León conflate the Virgin with the Statue of Liberty. Ester Hernández portrays her as a karate fighter defending the rights of Chicanos/as. The transformation of the Guadalupe image at the hands of Chicanos/as has not taken place without controversy. If in 1984 in Mexico City bomb threats were received by the editors of *Fem*, in 2001, twenty-three years later, Alma López received death threats from angry conservative Catholics after her work was put on exhibit in the Museum of International Folk Art in Santa Fe, New Mexico. Alma López's conceptualization of the Virgin as a lover of women as depicted in her "Lupe and Sirena in Love" and her portrayal of the Virgin dressed in a bikini made of roses elicited the ire of the Catholic Church clergy and some of the Catholic faithful, particularly men. (See Alma López's paintings in Gary Keller's *Contemporary Chicana and Chicano Art*, vols. 1 and 2.)

Nevertheless, Alma López is a highly respected artist whose "images are not merely enabled by technology, they stand as an active response to it. Through her calculating and poignant commingling of the classic, modern, and postmodern icons of an evolving Chicana history, López provides the viewer with an organizing and illuminating perspective on the political, social, and personal implications of a life lived in the ever expanding margins of the United States."[27]

Equally annoyed were some critics over Sandra Cisneros's written representation of the Virgin of Guadalupe as a sex goddess. Cisneros's article "Guadalupe the Sex Goddess," appearing in the anthology *Goddess of the Americas: La Diosa de las Américas; Writings on the Virgin of Guadalupe* (1990), edited by Ana Castillo, discussed the Virgin of Guadalupe in terms of indigenous, pre-Hispanic sex goddesses. The representation of Guadalupe associated with sexuality has not been well received. This position is exemplified by the article "Chicanos in Search of Their Souls," written by Héctor Carreón, a pugnacious and controversial journalist from the *La Voz de Aztlán*.[28] Nevertheless, Chicana writers and painters will not be silenced and will continue to represent the Virgin of Guadalupe in the manner they see fit, for Guadalupe speaks in many voices.

Conclusion

The three images discussed in this essay have been highly instrumental in developing the aesthetic and literary canon in Chicano/a art and literature. Upon analyzing the three icons within Chicano/a art and literary texts we find that La Llorona is playing a major role in literary expressions, La Malinche is finding a significant space in literature as well as Chicana feminist theory, while the image of the Virgin of Guadalupe is continually exploding on the visual artists' canvases. The Virgin of Guadalupe is being reconfigured as a feminist figure challenging patriarchal society and as a political icon signifying social justice for the poor and oppressed. Nevertheless, all three are connected to literary and artistic expressions. The three mythic icons continue to be major sources of creative energy and inspiration for Chicano/a artists. The icons are analogous to the classic Greek and Roman mythological figures which inspired artists in the Renaissance and later in the seventeenth and eighteenth centuries in the neoclassic period as well as the modernist movement in the twentieth century. In this essay, I posit that Chicano/a artists and writers rejected the Eurocentric images that were imposed on them during their training in colleges and universities in the United States and instead sought to find inspiration in autochthonous figures. Chicanos/as found it difficult to relate to a European heritage but flourished under the influence of a Mexican and Native American legacy. The themes, icons, images, and ways of cultural expression spoke to them in a loud voice. Chicano/a artists and writers listened to that loud voice and began to decolonize their imagination. The theoretical writings of Edward Said, Frantz Fanon, and Homi Bhabha resonated with respect to abandoning European indoctrinations and seeking inspiration and self-worth in their own autochthonous cultures. The link then between visual artists and writers, the thread that united them, was the new political awareness that Chicanos/as were not Europeans and that their cultures were worthy of study and representation not as objects, as for example the noble savage, but as subjects; as a people possessing a rich history and cultural heritage. The Chicano movement was the initial force that propelled visual artists and writers to look into their own historical specificity, to explore their own heroes, gods, and goddesses and to assert the newfound consciousness and newfound pride via the representation of Native American images. Visual artists and writers have found in the three iconic figures of La Llorona, La Malinche, and the Virgin of Guadalupe a rich vein of artistic inspiration encoding a multiplicity of messages, which will continue to be mined for generations to come.

Notes

1. Bacil F. Kirtley, "La Llorona and Related Themes," *Western Folklore* 19 (1960): 155–168.
2. Kirtley, "La Llorona," 157.

3. Kirtley, "La Llorona," 163–164.

4. As quoted in "La Llorona," *Leyendas y sucedidos del México colonial* (México: El Libro Español, 1963), 12.

5. *Leyendas y sucedidos*, 12.

6. Luis Leal, "The Malinche-Llorona Dichotomy: The Evolution of a Myth," in *La Malinche*, ed. Rolando Romero (Houston, Tex.: Arte Público Press, 2004).

7. Leal, "The Malinche-Llorona Dichotomy," 136–137.

8. *Funk & Wagnalls Standard Dictionary of Folklore, Mythology, and Legend* (New York: Funk and Wagnalls, 1950), 622.

9. *Funk & Wagnalls*, 236.

10. Michael Kearney, "La Llorona as a Social Symbol," *Western Folklore* 28 (1969): 200.

11. Elaine K. Miller, *Mexican Folk Narratives from the Los Angeles Area* (Austin, Tex.: American Folklore Society, 1973), 65.

12. Ralph Steele Boggs, *Bibliografía del folklore mexicano* (Mexico, D.F.: Instituto Panamericano de Geografía e Historia, 1939). In entry 1099 Boggs cites a study by Frans Blom, "Las Chanecas de Tecuanapa," appearing in the *Journal of American Folklore* 36 (1923): 200–202.

13. Betty Leddy, "La Llorona in Southern Arizona," *Western Folklore* 7 (1948): 272.

14. Vicente Riva Palacio and Juan de Dios Peza, "La Llorona," *Tradiciones y leyendas Mexicanas* (Mexico: Manuel Porrúa S.A., Librería, 1977), 79–95.

15. *Leyendas y sucedidos*, 7–12.

16. Alurista, "must be the season of the witch," in *Floricanto en Aztlán* (Los Angeles: Chicano Cultural Center, 1971), 26.

17. Alejandro Morales, *Caras viejas y vino nuevo* (Mexico, D.F.: Joaquín Mortiz, 1975), 14.

18. Jane Rogers, "The Function of the La Llorona Motif in Rudolfo Anaya's *Bless Me, Ultima*," *Latin American Literary Review* 5. no. 10 (Spring–Summer 1977): 64.

19. Cordelia Candelaria, "Go 'Way from My Window, La Llorona," in *Infinite Divisions: An Anthology of Chicana Literature*, ed. Tey Diana Rebolledo and Eliana Rivero (Tucson: University of Arizona Press, 1993), 215–216.

20. Naomi Quiñónez, "La Llorona," in *Infinite Divisions: An Anthology of Chicana Literature*, 218.

21. José Limón, "La Llorona, the Third Legend of Greater Mexico: Cultural Symbols, Women, and the Political Unconscious," *Renato Rosaldo Lecture Series Monograph* (Tucson: University of Arizona, Mexican American Studies and Research Center) 2, (Spring 1986): 59–93.

22. See *Cancionero mexicano*, tomo 1 (Mexico City: Editores Mexicanos Unidos, S.A., 1992), 587.

23. Pat Mora, *Chants* (Houston, Tex.: Arte Público Press, 1984), 52.

24. John Taylor, "Reinterpreting Malinche," userwww.sfsu.edu/~e-epf/2000/jt.html, 4.

25. Dan Banda, *Indigenous Always*. Milwaukee, Wis.: Bandana Productions, 2000.

26. Gary Keller, ed., *Contemporary Chicana and Chicano Art*, vol. 2 (Tempe, Ariz.: Bilingual Review/Editorial Bilingüe, 2002), 80.

27. Keller, *Contemporary Chicana and Chicano Art*, vol. 2, 76.

28. Héctor Carreón, "Chicanos in Search of their Souls," www.aztlan.net/souls.htm, 1.

Bricolage and the Quest for Multiple Perspectives

13

New Approaches to Research in Ethnic Studies

JOE L. KINCHELOE

AS A FIELD OF STUDY that has examined the social, historical, cultural, economic, educational, and political cosmos from the perspectives of particular, often marginalized racial/ethnic groups, the field of ethnic studies has often challenged the master narratives and the dominant discourses of more traditional academic disciplines. In this context the field has moved into a critical domain, as it challenges dominant racial ideologies that have inscribed both these disciplines and various social institutions. The study of such ideologies constitutes one dimension of ethnic studies' larger analysis of power and the complex ways it shapes the experiences of African Americans, Native Americans, Latinos/Hispanics, Asian Americans and other groups constructed around categories such as gender and sexuality. Thus, models of power have become profoundly important in the field of ethnic studies, especially as understanding them helps ethnic studies scholars better understand and act to subvert structures and inscriptions of social and cultural inequality. Central to the scholarship of ethnic studies has been an interdisciplinary orientation that is eclectic in its methodology and theory as it seeks new and better ways to accomplish the goals of the discipline.[1]

This chapter is directly related to this interdisciplinarity of ethnic studies and its use of multiple methodological and theoretical tools. In the effort to better understand structures and inscriptions of power and the ways they promote social and cultural inequality, I promote the notion of the bricolage. Connecting the methodological and theoretical eclecticism of the bricolage with critical multiculturalism's concern with the development of a literacy of power to help understand and take action in opposition to relations of inequality, this chapter contributes to the effort to more effectively accomplish the traditional goals of ethnic studies. Students of ethnic studies will find these concerns relevant to their scholarly, cultural, and political work. In this attempt to extend thought and action the chapter examines

- Ways social/cultural diversity expresses itself in the epistemological realm as it analyzes strategies that ethnic studies can employ to transcend Cartesian-Newtonian reductionism;
- More textured and rigorous (not in the positivistic sense) models of knowledge production;
- New modes of exposing and understanding the impact of tacit social forces, structures, and discourses overlooked by monological research methods;
- Multilogical articulations of epistemology, social theory, and methodology and their uses in ethnic studies;
- Subjugated and indigenous knowledges and the diverse forms of meaning making and knowledge production they bring to ethnic studies;
- New frames from which to conceptualize and extend the concept of interdisciplinarity;
- Multiple perspectives that help students of ethnic studies devise more compelling interpretations of the data they confront;
- Ways of deploying the multidimensional "power of difference" in ethnic studies;
- Modes of expanding what multiperspectval research in the interdisciplinary field of ethnic studies can become;
- The process a researcher might employ to enter the bricolage and engage its insight into conceptualizing and designing inquiry.

It is important to note in this context that the bricolage is not designed to create an elite corps of expert researchers in ethnic studies who deploy their authority over others by excluding them from the conversation about knowledge production. When critical scholars establish an exclusive "critical elite," they have fallen prey to the same power inequalities that motivated the founding of ethnic studies in the first place. When such domains of exclusion take shape around categories of status, class, race, gender, sexuality, and/or institutional affiliation, critical scholars have no moral or intellectual authority to produce knowledge in relation to the traditional concerns of ethnic study. Bricoleurs, as described here, are acutely aware of the dangers of such reproductions of inequality even among those studying and ostensibly challenging it. Thus, the bricoleur imagined in this chapter encourages scholars to claim the title who come from a wide diversity of social, cultural, and ethnic backgrounds, academic disciplines, educational and academic institutions, vocational roles, and activist groups.

Building the Critical Multiculturalist Theoretical Base in Ethnic Studies

In 1997 in *Changing Multiculturalism* Shirley Steinberg and I offered an evolving notion of critical multiculturalism that attempted to address and avoid the problems of more mainstream articulations of multiculturalism. Drawing upon critical theory and the tradition of an evolving criticality,[2] along with a variety of scholarship from ethnic studies, cultural studies, sociology, and education, critical multiculturalism is concerned with the ways that individuals are discursively, ideologically, and culturally constructed as human beings. Indeed, critical multiculturalism wants to promote an awareness of how domination takes place, how dominant cultures reproduce themselves, and how power operates to shape self and knowledge. This position—which theoretically supports this chapter on research in ethnic studies—makes no pretense of neutrality as it openly proclaims its affiliation with efforts to produce a more just, egalitarian, and democratic world that refuses to stand for the perpetuation of human suffering.[3] Critical multiculturalism is uncomfortable with the name multiculturalism, but works to redefine it in the contemporary era. Indeed, the first decade of the twenty-first century cannot be understood outside the framework of fast capitalism, transnational corporations, and corporatized electronic and ideologically-inscribed information, mutating more and more insidious forms of racism and ethnic bias, and a renewed form of U.S. colonialism and military intervention designed to extend the political, economic, and cultural influence of the twenty-first century American Empire.[4]

In particular, a critical multiculturalism is profoundly concerned with what gives rise to inequalities based on race, class, gender, sex, religion, culture, and ability. Critical multiculturalists focus their attention on the ways power has operated historically and contemporaneously to legitimate social categories and divisions. In this context we analyze and encourage further research on how in everyday, mundane, lived culture these dynamics of power play themselves out. It is at this ostensibly "innocent" level that the power of patriarchy and white supremacy, colonial assumptions of superiority, heterosexism, and class elitism operate. Critical multiculturalism appreciates both the hidden nature of these operations and the fact that most of the time they go unnoticed even by those participating in them and researching them. The invisibility of this process is disconcerting, as the cryptic nature of many forms of oppression makes it difficult to convince individuals from dominant power blocs of their reality. Such subtlety is matched by cognizance of the notion that there are as many differences within groups as there are between them.[5]

In the twenty-first century the increased influence of right-wing power blocs has elevated the need for a critical multiculturalist approach to knowledge production in ethnic studies. The geopolitical and military operations to extend the American Empire have been accompanied by disturbing trends in knowledge production that hold alarming implications for the future—the future of research in particular. Critical multiculturalists are aware that such knowledge work possesses a historical archaeology in Western culture and U.S. society. In this context David G. Smith contends that the U.S. Empire is constructed not only around territorial and natural resource claims, but in a hyperreal era it is grounded on epistemological claims as well.[6] Tracing the epistemological claims of the empire, Smith studies Western knowledge from the cogito of Descartes to Adam Smith's economics of self-interest. With the merging of Descartes rationalism with Adam Smith's economics, the West's pursuit of economic expansionism is justified by the concept of liberty. Ethnic studies cannot ignore these dynamics in the middle of the first decade of the twenty-first century.

Multicultural researchers who employ the bricolage described in this chapter have carefully examined this Enlightenment reason and its relation to oppression and social regulation. Proponents have maintained for centuries that it is this form of reason that frees us from the chaos of ignorance and human depravity. It is this reason, they proclaimed, that separates us from the uncivilized, the inferior. Smith argues that it is this notion that supports a philosophy of human development or developmentalism used in a variety of discourses to oppress and marginalize the cultural others who haven't employed such Western ways of seeing and being. Often in their "immaturity" these others, this rationalistic developmentalism informs us, must be disciplined, even ruled, in order to teach them to be rational and democratic.

The right-wing developmentalist story about the contemporary world situation conveniently omits the last five hundred years of European colonialism, the anti-colonial movements around the world beginning in the post–World War II era and their impact on the U.S. civil rights movement, the women's movement, the anti-war movement in Vietnam, Native American liberation struggles, the gay rights movement, and other emancipatory movements which inform our critical multiculturalism and have been traditional concerns of ethnic studies. In other work I have argued that the reaction to these anti-colonial movements has set the tone and content of much of American political, social, cultural, and educational experience over the last three decades.[7] In the middle of the first decade of the twenty-first century these forces of reaction seemed to have gained a permanent foothold in American social, political, cultural, and educational institutions. In this context ethnic studies finds itself in a precarious position.

The future of knowledge is at stake in this new cultural landscape. Few times in human history has there existed greater need for forms of knowledge work that expose the dominant ideologies and discourses that shape the information accessed by many individuals—especially in the United States. The charge of critical multiculturalists and scholars of ethnic studies at this historical juncture is to develop forms of knowledge work and approaches to research that take these sobering dynamics into account. This is the idea behind my articulation of the bricolage. Attempting to make use of a variety of philosophical, methodological, cultural, political, and epistemological discourses, the bricolage can be employed by critical multiculturalists and students of ethnic studies to produce compelling knowledges that seek to challenge the neocolonial representations of others at home and abroad.

Utilizing these multiple perspectives, the bricolage offers an alternate path in regressive times. Such an alternative path opens up new forms of knowledge production and researcher positionality that are grounded on more egalitarian relationships with individuals being researched. Bricoleurs, in their valuing of diverse forms of knowledge, especially those knowledges that have been subjugated, come to value the abilities and the insights of those whom they research. It is in such egalitarian forms of researcher-researched relationships that new forms of researcher self-awareness are developed—a self-awareness necessary in the bricoleur's attempt to understand the way positionality shapes the nature of the knowledge produced in the research process. The following section introduces the bricolage and begins a conversation about what are conceptualized as elastic and tentative dimensions of the concept.

Introducing the Bricolage

The French word *bricoleur* describes a handyman or handywoman who makes use of the tools available to complete a task. Some connotations of the term involve trickery and cunning and remind me of the chicanery of Hermes, in particular his ambiguity concerning the messages of the gods. If hermeneutics came to connote the ambiguity and slipperiness of textual meaning, then bricolage can also imply the fictive and imaginative elements of the presentation of all formal research. Indeed, as cultural studies of Western science have indicated, all scientific inquiry is jerry-rigged to a degree; science, as we all know by now, is not nearly as clean, simple, and procedural as scientists would have us believe. Maybe this is an admission many in social science would wish to keep in the closet.

In the first decade of the twenty-first century, bricolage is typically understood to involve the process of employing these methodological strategies as they are needed in the unfolding context of the research situation. While this interdisciplinary feature is central to any notion of the bricolage, I propose that critical multicultural and ethnic studies researchers go beyond this dynamic. Pushing to a new conceptual terrain, such an eclectic process raises numerous issues that researchers must deal with in order to maintain theoretical coherence and epistemological innovation. Such multidisciplinarity demands a new level of research self-consciousness and awareness of the numerous contexts in which any researcher is operating. As one labors to expose the various social, cultural, and political structures that covertly shape our own and other scholars' research narratives, the bricolage highlights the relationship between a researcher's ways of seeing and the social location of his or her personal history. Appreciating research as a power-driven act, the ethnic studies researcher-as-bricoleur abandons the quest for some naïve concept of realism, focusing instead on the clarification of his or her position in the web of reality and the social locations of other researchers and the ways they shape the production and interpretation of knowledge.

In this context bricoleurs move into the domain of complexity. The bricolage exists out of respect for the complexity of the lived world. Indeed, it is grounded on an epistemology of complexity. One dimension of this complexity can be illustrated by the relationship between research and the domain of social theory. All observations of the world are shaped either consciously or unconsciously by social theory—such theory provides the framework that highlights or erases what might be observed. Theory in a modernist empiricist mode is a way of understanding that operates without variation in every context. Since theory is a cultural and linguistic artifact, its interpretation of the object of its observation is inseparable from the historical dynamics that have shaped it. The task of the bricoleur is to attack this multicultural complexity, uncovering the invisible artifacts of power and documenting the nature of its influence on not only her own research, but on scholarship and knowledge production in general. In this process bricoleurs act upon the concept that theory is not an explanation of nature—it is more an explanation of our relation to nature. In the twenty-first-century neocolonial era this task becomes even more important.

Cultivating Agency: An Active View of Research Methodology

In its hard labors in the domain of complexity, the bricolage views research methods actively rather than passively, meaning that we actively construct our research methods from the tools at hand rather than passively receiving the "correct," transcultural, universally applicable methodologies. Avoiding modes of reasoning that come from certified processes of logical analysis, bricoleurs also steer clear of preexisting guidelines and checklists developed outside the specific demands of the inquiry at hand. In its embrace of complexity, the bricolage constructs a far more active role for humans both in shaping reality and in creating the research processes and narratives that represent it. Such an active agency rejects deterministic views of social reality that assume the effects of particular dominant social, political, economic, and educational processes. At the same time and in the same conceptual context, this belief in active human agency refuses standardized modes of knowledge production from particular power blocs.[8]

In many ways there is a form of instrumental reason, of rational irrationality in the use of passive, external, monological, monocultural research methods. In the active bricolage we bring our understanding of the research context together with our previous experience with research methods. Using these knowledges we *tinker* in the Levi-Straussian sense with our research methods in field-based and interpretive contexts. This tinkering is a high-level cognitive process involving construction and reconstruction, contextual diagnosis, negotiation, and readjustment. Researchers' interactions with the objects of their inquiries, bricoleurs understand, are always complicated, mercurial, unpredictable, and, of course, complex. Such conditions negate the practice of planning research strategies in advance. In lieu of such rationalization of the process, bricoleurs enter into the research act as methodological negotiators. Always respecting the demands of the task at hand, the bricolage, as conceptualized here, resists its placement in concrete as it promotes its elasticity. In light of Yvonna Lincoln's delineation of two types of bricoleurs, those who: 1) are committed to research eclecticism allowing circumstance to shape methods employed; and 2) want to engage in the genealogy/archaeology of the disciplines with some grander purpose in mind, I work to develop a critical vision of the bricolage.[9] My purpose entails both of Lincoln's articulations of the role of the bricoleur.

Research method in the bricolage is a concept that receives more respect than in more rationalistic articulations of the term. The rationalistic, colonialist articulation of method subverts the deconstruction of wide varieties of unanalyzed cultural assumptions embedded in passive methods. Bricoleurs in their appreciation of the complexity of the research process view research method as involving far more than procedure. In this mode of analysis bricoleurs come to understand research method as a technology of justification, meaning a way of defending what we assert we know and the process by which we know it. Thus, the education of ethnic studies researchers demands that everyone take a step back from the process of learning research methods. Such a step back allows us a conceptual distance that produces a critical consciousness. Such a consciousness refuses the passive acceptance of externally imposed research methods that tacitly certify modes justifying universal knowledges that are decontextualized and reductionistic.[10]

In this context it is important to note that the use of the term bricolage in relation to multimethod, multilogical interdisciplinary research is relatively new—emerging in the mid-1990s. Norm Denzin and Yvonna Lincoln, central figures in the development and sophistication of qualitative research in the social sciences, were the first to use the term in this specific context. In the domain of qualitative research and qualitative theory numerous scholars are beginning to use the term and employ the concept. In December 2001, *Qualitative Inquiry* published a special issue on the bricolage in which I took Denzin and Lincoln's delineation of the concept and detailed possibilities of what it might become.[11] Lincoln, William Pinar, and Peter McLaren responded to my essay, offering their own vision of the bricolage.[12] In addition to those directly involved with developing and enacting the bricolage, there are numerous researchers in the social sciences and interdisciplinary fields, such as cultural studies, education, and ethnic studies, who have already embraced multiperspectival inquiry.[13] Denzin and Lincoln describe it as a methodological diaspora where humanists migrated to the social sciences and social scientists to the humanities.[14] Ethnographic methodologists snuggled up with textual analysts; in this context the miscegenation of the empirical and the interpretive produced the bricoleur love child.

The Subversive Nature of Bricolage: Avoiding Reductionism

There's an impudent dimension to the bricolage that says "who said research has to be done this way?" Such impudence is based on a cynicism toward the notion that monological, ordered methods get us to the "right place" in academic research. To say it one more time with feeling: we should use the methods that are best suited to answering our questions about a particular phenomenon. For the bricoleur to use the means at hand, he or she must first be aware of them. Such awareness demands that the bricoleur devote time for rigorous study of what approaches to research are out there and how they might be applied in relation to other methods. Do not be deceived, this is no easy task that can be accomplished in a doctoral program or a post-doctoral fellowship.[15] Becoming a bricoleur who is knowledgeable of multiple research methodologies and their use is a lifetime endeavor.

Indeed, the bricoleur is aware of deep social structures and the complex ways they play out in everyday life, the importance of social, cultural, and historical analysis, the ways discursive practices influence both what goes on in the research process and the consciousness of the researcher, the complex dimensions of what we mean when we talk about "understanding." In this context the bricoleur becomes a sailor on troubled waters, navigating a course that traces the journey between the scientific and the moral, the relationship between the quantitative and the qualtitative, and the nature of social, cultural, psychological, and educational insight. All of these travels help bricoleurs overcome the limitations of monological reductionism and the empire's developmentalism while taking into account the new vistas opened by the multilogical and the pluralistic. Such victories provide entrée into the diverse community of inquirers—an inclusive group that comes from academia and beyond. Such individuals critique, support, and inform each other by drawing upon the diversity of their cultural backgrounds and concerns. In this process they expose and discuss one another's assumptions, the contexts that have shaped them, and their strengths and limitations in the exploration(s) at hand. The participants in this community come from a wide range of race, class, gender, sexual, ethnic, and religious groups and enter into their deliberations with humility and solidarity.

Norm Denzin and Yvonna Lincoln's work on the bricolage has profoundly influenced numerous researchers from a plethora of disciplines. Concerned with the limitations of monological approaches to knowledge production, we all subscribe to the "practical reason" of the bricolage that operates in concrete settings to connect theory, technique, and experiential knowledges. Here the theoretical domain is connected to the lived world and new forms of cognition and research are *enacted*. This improvisational enactment of the bricolage, buoyed by the insights of Francisco Varela and Humberto Maturana's Santiago theory of enactivism, moves research to a new level. This is the place where the multiple inputs and forces facing the researcher in the immediacy of her work are acknowledged and embraced. The bricoleur does not allow these complexities to be dismissed by the excluding, reducing impulses of monological methodology coming from particular power blocs.[16] Such a refusal is in itself an act of subversion.

The subversive bricolage accepts that human experience is marked by uncertainties and that order is not always easily established. "Order in the court" has little authority when the monological judge is resting in *his* quarters. Indeed, the rationalistic and reductionistic quest for order refuses in its arrogance to listen to the cacophony of lived experience, the coexistence of diverse meanings and interpretations in a socially, culturally, economically, and ideologically diverse world. The concept of understanding in the complex world viewed by bricoleurs is unpredictable. Much to the consternation of many there exists no final, transhistorical, transcultural, nonideological meaning that bricoleurs strive to achieve. As bricoleurs create rather than find meaning in enacted reality, they explore alternate meanings offered by others in similar circumstances. As if this wasn't enough, they work to account for historical, social, and cultural contingencies that always operate to undermine the universal pronouncement of the meaning of a particular phenomenon. When researchers fail to discern the unique ways that historical, social, and cultural context make for special circumstances, they often provide a reductionistic form of knowledge that impoverishes our understanding of everything connected to it—the process of research included.[17]

The monological, monocultural quest for order so desired by many social, political, psychological, and educational researchers is grounded on the Cartesian belief that all phenomena should be broken down into their constituent parts to facilitate inquiry. The analysis of the world in this context becomes fragmented and disconnected. Everything is studied separately for the purposes of rigor. The goal of integrating knowledges from diverse domains and understanding the interconnections shaping, for example, the biological and the cognitive, is irrelevant in the paradigm of order and fragmentation. The meaning that comes from interrelationship is lost and questions concerning the purpose of research and its insight into the human condition are put aside in an orgy of correlation and triangulated description. Information is sterilized and insight into what may be worth exploring is abandoned.[18] Ways of making use of particular knowledges are viewed as irrelevant and creative engagement with conceptual insights is characterized as frivolous. Empirical knowledge in the quest for order is an end in itself. Once it has been validated it needs no further investigation or interpretation. While empirical research is obviously necessary, its process of production constitutes only one step of a larger and more rigorous process of inquiry. The bricolage subverts the finality of the empirical act.

Bricoleurs make the point that empirical research, all research for that matter, is inscribed at every level by human beings. The assumptions and purposes of the researcher always find their way into a research act, and they always make a difference in what knowledge is produced. Even in the most prescribed forms of empirical quantitative inquiry the researcher's ideological and cultural preferences and assumptions shape the outcome of the research. Do I choose factor analysis or regression analysis to study the relationship of a student's SAT score to college success? The path I choose profoundly affects what I find. What about the skills and knowledges included on the SAT? Are they simply neutral phenomena free from inscriptions of culture and power? How I answer such a question shapes how my research proceeds.

Such inscriptions and the complexity they produce remind critical multicultural and ethnic studies bricoleurs of the multiple processes in play when knowledge is produced and validation is considered. They understand that the research process is subjective and instead of repressing this subjectivity they attempt to understand its role in shaping inquiry. All of these elements come together to help bricoleurs think about their principles of selection of one or another research perspective. Such decisions can be made more thoughtfully when a researcher understands the preferences and assumptions inscribed on all modes of inquiry and all individuals who engage in research. Thus, an important aspect of the work of the bricoleur involves coming to understand the social construction of self, the influence of selfhood on perception, and the influence of perception on the nature of inquiry.[19]

Moving to the Margins: Alternative Modes of Meaning Making in the Bricolage

In its critical concern for just social change the critical multicultural bricolage seeks insight from the margins of Western societies and the knowledge and ways of knowing of non-Western peoples. Such insight helps bricoleurs reshape and sophisticate social theory, research methods, and interpretive strategies, as they discern new topics to be researched. This confrontation with difference so basic to the concept of the bricolage—and central to this chapter—enables researchers to produce new forms of knowledge that inform policy decisions and political action in general. In gaining this insight from the margins bricoleurs display once again the blurred boundary between the hermeneutical search for understanding and the critical concern with social change for social justice.[20]

To contribute to social transformation bricoleurs in ethnic studies seek to better understand both the forces of domination that affect the lives of individuals from race, class, gender, sexual, ethnic, and religious backgrounds outside of dominant culture(s) and the worldviews of such diverse peoples. In this context bricoleurs attempt to remove knowledge production and its benefits from the control of elite groups. Such control consistently operates to reinforce elite privilege while pushing marginalized groups farther away from the center of dominant power. Rejecting this normalized state of affairs, critical multicultural bricoleurs commit their knowledge work to helping address the ideological and informational needs of marginalized groups and individuals. As detectives of subjugated insight, bricoleurs eagerly learn from labor struggles, women's marginalization, the "double consciousness" of the racially oppressed, and insurrections against colonialism.[21]

Thus, the bricolage is dedicated to a form of rigor that is conversant with numerous modes of meaning making and knowledge production—modes that originate in diverse social locations. These alternative modes of reasoning and researching always consider the relationships, the resonances, and the disjunctions between formal and rationalistic modes of Western epistemology and ontology and different cultural, philosophical, paradigmatic, and subjugated expressions. In these latter expressions bricoleurs often uncover ways of accessing a concept without resorting to a conventional validated set of prespecified procedures that provide the distance of objectivity. This notion of distance fails to take into account the rigor of the hermeneutical understanding of the way meaning is pre-inscribed in the act of being in the world, the research process, and objects of research. This absence of hermeneutical awareness undermines the researcher's quest for a thick description and contributes to the production of reduced understandings of the complexity of social life.[22]

The multiple perspectives delivered by the concept of difference provide bricoleurs with many benefits. Confrontation with difference helps us to see anew, to move toward the light of epiphany. A basic dimension of criticality involves a comfort with the existence of alternative ways of analyzing and producing knowledge. This is why it's so important for a historian, for example, to develop an understanding of phenomenology and hermeneutics. It is why it is so important for a social researcher from New York City to understand forms of indigenous African and Islamic knowledge production. The incongruities between such cultural modes of inquiry are quite valuable, for within the tensions of difference rest insights into multiple dimensions of the research act—insights that move us to new levels of understanding of the subjects, purposes, and nature of inquiry.[23]

Difference in the bricolage pushes us into the hermeneutic circle as we are induced to deal with diverse parts in relation to the whole. Difference may involve culture, class, language, discipline, epistemology, cosmology, ad infinitum. Bricoleurs use one dimension of these multiple diversities to explore others, to generate questions previously unimagined. As we examine these multiple perspectives we attend to which ones are validated and which ones have been dismissed. Studying such differences, we begin to understand how dominant power operates to exclude and certify particular forms of knowledge production and why. In the criticality of the bricolage this focus on power and difference always leads us to an awareness of the multiple dimensions of the social. Paulo Freire referred to this as the need for perceiving social structures and social systems that undermine equal access to resources and power.[24] As critical multicultural and ethnic studies bricoleurs answer such questions, we gain new appreciations of the way power tacitly shapes what we know and how we come to know it.

Absence Makes the Heart Grow Fonder: Research of the "Not Yet"

In their move to the margins and transcendence of reductionism, bricoleurs seek to identify what is absent in particular situations—a task ignored by monological, objectivist modes of research. In this context bricoleurs seek to cultivate a higher form of researcher creativity that leads them, like poets, to produce concepts and insights about the social world that previously did not exist. This rigor in the absence can be expressed in numerous ways, including the bricoleur's ability:

- to imagine things that never were;
- to see the world as it could be;
- to develop alternatives to oppressive existing conditions;
- to discern what is lacking in a way that promotes the will to act;
- to understand that there is far more to the world than what we can see.

As always bricoleurs are struggling to transcend the traditional observational constraint on social researchers, as they develop new ways and methods of exposing social, cultural, political, psychological, and educational forces not at first glance discernible. Pursuing rigor in the absence, bricoleurs document venues of meaning that transcend the words of interviewees or observations of particular behaviors.[25]

Of course, a central feature of this rigorous effort to identify what is absent involves excavating what has been lost in the naïveté of monological disciplinarity and Western rational developmentalism. As bricoleurs engaging in the boundary work of deep interdisciplinarity explore what has been dismissed, deleted, and covered up, they bring to the surface the ideological devices that have erased the lived worlds and perspectives of those living at the margins of power. In response to Yvonna Lincoln's question about the use or value of knowledge produced by the bricolage,[26] I maintain that as researchers employ the methodological, theoretical, interpretive, political, and narrative dimensions of the bricolage, they make a variety of previously repressed features of the social world visible. Because they are describing dimensions of the sociocultural, political, economic, psychological, and pedagogical cosmos that have never previously existed, bricoleurs are engaging in what might be termed the fictive element of research.

The use of the term fictive should not to be conflated with "unreal" in this context. Scientific inventors engaged in a similar process when they created design documents for the electric light, the rocket, the computer, or virtual reality. In these examples individuals used a fictive imagination to produce something that did not yet exist. The critical multicultural/ethnic studies bricoleur does the same thing in a different ontological and epistemological domain. Both the inventor and the bricoleur are future-oriented, as they explore the realm of possibility, a kinetic epistemology of the possible. In the process the sophistication of knowledge work moves to a new cognitive level; the notion of rigor transmigrates to a new dimension. As in a 1950s sci-fi movie, bricoleurs enter the 4-D—the fourth dimension of research.

In this way bricoleurs create a space for reassessing the nature of the knowledge that has been created about the social cosmos and the modes of research that have created it. In an era of information saturation and hegemony this space for reassessing knowledge production and research methods becomes a necessity for democratic survival, the foundation of a prodemocracy movement, and, as William Pinar correctly maintains, the "labor of educational scholarship in general."[27] Overwhelmed by corporate-produced data and befuddled by the complex of social issues that face us, individuals without access to the lenses of the bricolage often don't know how to deal with these debilitating conditions.[28] As the bricolage provides us new insights into the chaos of the contemporary, ethnic studies researchers become better equipped to imagine where we might go and what path we might take to get there through the jungle of information surrounding us. The bricolage is no panacea but it does allow us new vantage points to survey the epistemological wilderness and the possibilities hidden in its underbrush.

Power in the Ruins of Disciplinarity: Beyond the Epistemological Thunderdome

For those of us committed to theorizing and implementing the bricolage in ethnic studies, there are some profound questions that need to be answered as we plot our course. As we think in terms of using multiple methods and perspectives in ethnic studies research and attempt to synthesize contemporary developments in social theory, epistemology, and interpretation, we must consider the critiques of many diverse scholars. At the core of the deployment of the bricolage in the discourse of research rests the question of disciplinarity/interdisciplinarity. Bricolage, of course, signifies interdisciplinarity—a concept that serves as a magnet for controversy in the contemporary academy. Researching this chapter, I listened to several colleagues maintain that if one is focused on getting tenure he or she should eschew interdisciplinarity; if one is interested only in doing good research, she or he should embrace it.

Implicit in the critique of interdisciplinarity and thus of bricolage as its manifestation in research is the assumption that interdisciplinarity is by nature superficial. Superficiality results when scholars, researchers, and students fail to devote sufficient time to understanding the disciplinary fields and knowledge bases from which particular modes of research emanate. Many maintain that such an effort leads not only to superficiality but to madness. Attempting to know so much, the bricoleur not only knows nothing well but also goes crazy in the misguided process.[29] I respect these questions and concerns but argue that given the social, cultural, epistemological, paradigmatic, and neocolonial upheavals and alterations of the last few decades, rigorous researchers may no longer enjoy the luxury of choosing whether or not to embrace the bricolage.[30]

Once an understanding of the limits of objective science and its universal knowledge escaped from the genie's bottle, there was no going back. Despite the best efforts to recover "what was lost" in the implosion of social science, too many researchers understand its socially constructed nature, its cultural specificity, its value-laden products that operate under the flag of objectivity, its avoidance of contextual specificities that subvert the stability of its structures, and its fragmenting impulse that moves it to fold its methodologies and the knowledge they produce neatly into disciplinary drawers. My argument here is that we must operate in the ruins of the temple, in a postapocalyptic social, cultural, psychological, and educational science where certainty and stability have long departed for parts unknown. For some the absence of certainty makes the heart grow fonder, for the bricoleur it pushes him or her to gain new perspectives that challenge dominant ways of seeing.

In the best sense of Levi-Strauss's concept, bricoleurs pick up the pieces of what's left and paste them together as best they can. The critics are probably correct—such a daunting task cannot be accomplished in the timespan of a doctoral program; but the process can be named and the dimensions of a lifetime scholarly pursuit can be in part delineated. Our transcendence of the old regime's reductionism and our understanding of the complexity of the research task demand the lifetime effort. It is this lifetime commitment to study, clarify, sophisticate, and add to the bricolage that this chapter advocates.

As bricoleurs recognize the limitations of a single method, the discursive strictures of one disciplinary approach, what is missed by traditional practices of validation, the historicity of certified modes of knowledge production, the inseparability of knower and known, and the complexity and heterogeneity of all human experience, they understand the necessity of new forms of rigor in the research process. To account for such complexity bricoleurs seek a rigor that alerts them to new ontological insights. In this ontological context they can no longer accept the status of an object of inquiry as a thing-in-itself. Any social, cultural, psychological, or pedagogical object of inquiry is inseparable from its context, the language used to describe it, its historical situatedness in a larger on-going process, and the socially and culturally constructed interpretations of its meaning(s) as an entity in the world.[31]

Finding Rigor in Multiplicity: Postapocalyptic Knowledge Work

Thus, the bricolage in ethnic studies is concerned not only with multiple methods of inquiry but with diverse theoretical and philosophical notions of the various elements encountered in the research act. Bricoleurs understand that the ways these dynamics are addressed—whether overtly or tacitly—exerts profound influence on the nature of the knowledge produced by researchers. Thus, these aspects of research possess important lived-world political consequences, as they shape the ways we come to view the social cosmos and operate within it.[32] In this context Douglas Kellner's notion of a "multiperspectival cultural studies" is helpful, as it draws upon numerous textual and critical strategies to "interpret, criticize, and deconstruct" the cultural artifacts under observation.[33]

Employing Nietzsche's notion of perspectivism to ground his version of a multimethodological research strategy, Kellner maintains that any single research perspective is laden with assumptions, blindnesses, and limitations. To avoid one-sided reductionism, he maintains that researchers must learn a variety of ways of seeing and interpreting in the pursuit of knowledge. The more perspectival variety a researcher employs, Kellner concludes, the more dimensions and consequences of a text will be illuminated. Kellner's multiperspectivism resonates with Denzin and Lincoln's bricolage and its concept of "blurred genres." To better "interpret, criticize, and deconstruct," Denzin and Lincoln call for bricoleurs to employ "hermeneutics, structuralism, semiotics, phenomenology, cultural studies, and feminism."[34] Embedded in Kellner, Denzin, and Lincoln's call is the articulation of a new rigor—certainly in research but with implications for scholarship and pedagogy in general. As previously referenced, this multimethod research is already taking place.

Thus, in the early twenty-first century disciplinary demarcations no longer shape in the manner they once did the way many scholars look at the world. Indeed, disciplinary boundaries have less and less to do with the way scholars group themselves and build intellectual communities. Furthermore, what we refer to as the traditional disciplines in the first decade of the twenty-first century are anything but fixed, uniform, and monolithic structures. It is not uncommon for contemporary scholars in a particular discipline to report that they find more commonalities with individuals in different fields of study than they do with colleagues in their own disciplines. We occupy a scholarly world with faded disciplinary boundary lines. Thus, the point need not be made that bricolage should take place—it already has begun and is continuing. The research work needed in this context involves opening an elastic conversation about the ways such a bricolage can be rigorously conceptualized and enacted. Such cultivation should not take place in pursuit of some form of proceduralization but as an effort to better understand the beast and to realize its profound possibilities.[35]

Deploying Indigenous Knowledges in the Study of Disciplinarity: Questioning Monocultural, Monological Scholarship

Always looking for multiple perspectives, insight in diverse places, bricoleurs examine disciplinarity and interconnectedness via the lens of indigenous knowledges. Many systems of indigenous knowledge illustrate the *enaction* of interconnectedness and raise profound questions about the ways Western scholars have defined disciplinary knowledges. While there is great diversity in these so-called indigenous knowledges, most assume that humans are part of the world of nature. Extending this holism, many indigenous scholars maintain that the production and acquisition of knowledge involves a process of interactions among the human body, the mind, and the spirit.[36] R. Sambuli Mosha writes that among the East African Chagga peoples knowledge that is passed along to others must further the development of morality, goodness, harmony, and spirituality.[37] Indeed, he continues, in the Chagga worldview it is impossible to separate these domains. Such fragmentation simply does not make sense to the Chagga. Embedded in every Chagga child is a part of the divine dimension of reality, illustrating the interconnectedness of all aspects of reality. Thus, knowledge production cannot take place outside this intricate web of relationships.

In Cartesian-Newtonian modes of disciplinary thought the interrelationships cherished by the Chagga are not as *real* as their individual parts. For example, in Cartesian psychology, consciousness is often reduced to neural and chemical dynamics. Researchers in this context often study nothing outside the narrow confines of brain chemistry from graduate school to retirement. The notion that the understanding of human consciousness might be enhanced by anthropological, theological, or philosophical investigations rarely, if ever, occurs to such researchers over the decades of their research.

Making use of indigenous knowledges and the theological insights of Buddhism in this domain, cognitive theorist Francisco Varela employs the bricolage to develop a dramatically different concept of consciousness. Understanding the indigenous notion that the individual cannot be understood outside the community of which she or he is a part, Varela posits that human consciousness *emerges* from the social and biological interactions of its various parts. This understanding may over the next couple of decades revolutionize the fields of cognitive science, psychology, and even pedagogy. When scholars grasp the multilogical, interrelated nature of the bricolage, possibilities for dramatic changes in the ways disciplines operate emerge. Using the indigenous metaphor, knowledge *lives* in the cultures of indigenous peoples. As opposed to the disciplinary knowledges of Cartesian-Newtonianism, which are often stored in archives or laboratories, indigenous knowledges live in everyday cultural practices.[38]

Bricoleurs ask hard questions of indigenous knowledges. They know that folk knowledges—like Western scientific knowledges—often help construct exploitation and oppression for diverse groups and individuals. With this caution and resistance to essentialism in mind, bricoleurs study the ways many indigenous peoples in Africa construct the interrelationships of their inner selves to the outer world. This indigenous tendency to avoid dualisms that when unacknowledged undermine the balance of various relationships is important to bricoleurs. For example, the dualism between humans and nature can wreck havoc in an indigenous social system. In many indigenous African conceptions humanness is viewed as a part of nature, not separate from it. Unlike scholars in the Cartesian-Newtonian disciplines, the world was too sacred for humans to study and dominate or conquer. Once humanness and the environment were viewed as separate entities, forces were unleashed that could destroy the delicate ecological and social systems that sustained the indigenous culture. Thus, in the minds of many African peoples, to accept the dualism between humanness and nature was tantamount to committing mass suicide.

Another example of an indigenous culture whose knowledges bricoleurs deem valuable is the Andean peoples of South America. Everyone and everything in traditional Andean culture is sentient; for example, the rivers and mountains have ears and eyes. Acting in the world in this cultural context is a dimension of being in relationship to the world. In his or her actions within the physical environment, an Andean individual is in conversation with the mountains, rivers, trees, lakes, and so forth. In Andean culture, this language of conversation replaces a Western traditional disciplinary language of knowing. A profound epistemological shift has taken place in this replacement. In Andean culture the concept of knower and known is irrelevant. Instead humans and physical entities engage in reciprocal relationships, carrying on conversations in the interests of both.

These conversations have been described as mutually nurturing events, acts that enhance the evolution of all parties involved via their tenderness and empathy for the living needs of the other. Thus, the epistemology at work here involves more than simply knowing about something. It involves tuning oneself in to the other's mode of being—its ontological presence—and entering into a life-generating relationship with it.[39] Bricoleurs take from this an understanding of a new dimension of epistemology. Those working in the academic disciplines of Western societies must enter into relationships with that which they are studying. Such relationships should be enumerated and analyzed. How am I changed by this relationship? How is the object of my study changed or potentially changed by the relationship?

Great change occurs as a result of the Andean peoples' conversation with nature. Nature's voice is heard through the position and brilliance of planets and stars; the speed, frequency, color, and smell of the wind; and the size and number of particular wild flowers, to mention only a few. Such talk tells Andeans about the coming weather and various dimensions of cultivation, and they act in response to such messages. Because of the overwhelming diversity of ecosystems and climates in the Andes mountains and valleys, these conversations are complex. Interpretations of meanings—like any hermeneutic acts—are anything but self-evident. Such conversations and the actions they catalyze allow the Andean peoples to produce an enormous variety of cultivated plant species that amaze plant geneticists from around the world. As Frederique Apffel-Marglin describes this diversity:

> The peasants grow and know some 1,500 varieties of quinoa, 330 of kaniwa, 228 of tarwi, 250 of potatoes, 610 of oca (another tuber) and so forth.... The varieties differ according to regions, altitude, soils, and other factors. Such incredible diversity cannot only be due to ecological diversity. The manner in which peasants converse with plants and all the other inhabitants of the world, be they animate or inanimate, with not only an infinite attention to detail but with a receptive, open, and direct or embodied attitude is at the heart of such diversity.[40]

The Andeans actually have a word for those places where the conversation between humans and the natural world take place. *Chacras* include the land where the Andeans cultivate their crops, the places where utensils are crafted, and the places were herds and flocks live and graze. According to the Andeans, these are places where all entities come together to discuss the regeneration of life. The concept of interrelationship is so important in the Andean culture that the people use the word *ayllu* to signify a kinship group that includes not only other human beings but animals, mountains, streams, rocks, and the spirits of a particular geographical place. Bricoleurs adapt these indigenous Andean concepts to the rethinking of the disciplines as they identify the methodologies, epistemologies, ontologies, cultural systems, social theories, and so on that they employ in their multilogical understanding of the research act. Those who research the social, psychological, and educational worlds, bricoleurs conclude, hold a special responsibility to those concepts and the people they research to select critical and life-affirming logics of inquiry. Symbiotic hermeneutics demands that relationships at all levels be respected and engaged in ways that produce justice and new levels of understanding—in ways that regenerate life.

The Power of Difference in Knowledge Production: Mutualism and the Insight of Multiple Perspectives

The concept of difference is central to both critical multiculturalism and the bricolage. Gregory Bateson uses the example of binoculars to illustrate the power of difference. The image of the binoculars—a singular and undivided picture—is a complex synthesis between images in both the left and right side of the brain. In this context a synergy is created, where the sum of the images is greater than the separate parts. As a result of bringing the two different views together, resolution and contrast are enhanced. Even more important, new insight into depth is created. Thus, the relationship between the different parts constructs new dimensions of seeing.[41] Employing such examples of synergies, bricoleurs maintain that juxtapositions of difference create a bonus of insight. This concept becomes extremely important in any cognitive, social, pedagogical, or knowledge-production activity. Indeed, one of the rationales for constructing the bricolage in the first place involves accessing this bonus of insight.

This power of difference or "ontological mutualism" transcends Cartesianism's emphasis on the thing-in-itself. The tendency in Cartesian-Newtonian thinking is to erase this bonus of insight in the abstraction of the object of inquiry from the processes and contexts of which it is a part. In this activity it subverts difference. The power of these synergies exists not only in the cognitive, social, pedagogical, and epistemological domains but in the physical world as well. Natural phenomena, as Albert Einstein illustrated in physics and Humberto Maturana and Francisco Varela laid out in biology and cognition, operate in states of interdependence. These ways of seeing have produced perspectives on the workings of the planet that profoundly differ from the views produced by Western science. What has been fascinating to many is that these post-Einsteinian perspectives have in so many ways reflected the epistemologies and ontologies of ancient non-Western peoples in India, China, and Africa, and indigenous peoples around the world.

In the spirit of valuing difference, therefore, bricoleurs seek not only diverse research methodologies but search ways of seeing that provide a new vantage point on a particular phenomenon. As opposed to many mainstream Cartesian-Newtonian scholars, bricoleurs value the voices of the subjugated and marginalized. The idea of subjugated knowledge is central to the work of the bricoleur. With such an idea in mind, bricoleurs do not assume that experts in the disciplines possess the final word on a domain of study. Sometimes what such experts report needs to be reanalyzed in light of the insights of those operating outside the discipline. As a scholar of education I have often observed how some of the most compelling insights concerning pedagogy I have encountered come from those individuals living and operating outside the boundaries of educational scholarship. Sometimes such individuals are not formal scholars at all but individuals who have suffered at the hands of educational institutions. Such experiences provide them a vantage point and set of experiences profoundly different than those of more privileged scholars. This phenomenon is not unique to the study of education but can be viewed in a variety of disciplines, ethnic studies included.[42]

Thus, the concept of difference as employed by the bricolage provides new insights into the nature of rationality itself. As bricoleurs draw upon different knowledges, they begin to realize that there are many rationalities. When diverse rationalities are juxtaposed, insights into new ways of seeing emerge that may be greater than the separate parts. Thus, we return to the bonus of insight mentioned above. Transgression of traditional boundaries is an affirmation of the power of these different perspectives and the alternate rationalities they produce. Bricoleurs, in their omnipresent awareness of the hermeneutic circle, cross and recross the boundaries between the certified and the subjugated. This spiraling action of transgression disrupts calcified truths as it views them in the light of new horizons. In this context critical multicultural researchers in ethnic studies are empowered to make meanings that hold the power to transform society and self in ways that are more just and ethical.[43]

From the perspective of the bricoleur, rigor in research comes from an awareness of difference and the multiple perspectives it promotes. Indeed, what presently passes for rigor in many traditional disciplinary arrangements is a monological, uni-disciplinary pursuit of final truth. Under this regime of knowledge production the treasures of a multicultural society and the multiple ways of seeing of groups around the planet are dismissed. This concept, of course, is central to the concerns of this chapter. Emerging in place of such multiplicity is dominant power's effort to standardize truth, to provide monological answers to complex questions, and to mandate a universal set of steps necessary to the production of certified truth. This is the same logic that underwrites the effort to impose curricula on educational institutions under the name of content standards—a task nearly complete in U.S. elementary and secondary schools and in process in higher education. Why do educators need to be scholars who can interpret and produce knowledge when experts already know what constitutes the truth? Such absolutist epistemological orientations threaten the very notion of a democratic education, where students are exposed to diverse ideas and scholarly orientations taught in different ways by different teachers.[44]

Bricoleurs respect diversity and the kinetic power that accompanies it. They know that insights into solutions to the problems that face the planet and its peoples rest within diversity. Amazing things can happen when unconsidered perspectives and versions of the world around us are encountered. Indeed, when we see things differently and develop new connections between previously unconnected phenomena, our sense of who we are undergoes a process of metamorphosis. Because of our encounter with difference we emerge from our conceptual cocoons as different entities. Bricoleurs take the knowledge developed in the context of difference and synergy and run it through the filter of a literacy of power. Such an act helps them disclose the interests particular knowledges serve as well as expose the interests complicit with their production.

Such insights have numerous benefits, of course, especially in the realm of ideology and social transformation. They also aid individuals in better understanding the ways they have experienced the world. Indeed, bricoleurs define learning itself as a process of reshaping the world in light of understanding the ways other individuals in other times and places have shaped it. Thus, they come to see what they know and what "is known" in a new web of meaning. Operating in this multilogical manner, bricoleurs might study, for example, some women's capacity to understand the feelings of other individuals because in Western patriarchal cultures women often sense a greater need to develop this capacity. Such abilities often emerge in asymmetrical relations of power, as African American slaves understood their need to interpret their master's state of mind in order to escape punishment. Thus, researchers use diverse voices in differing historical situations to thicken the knowledges they produce.[45]

Using Subjugated Knowledges in the Bricolage

Cartesian rationalism has consistently excluded subjugated knowledges from validated databases in diverse disciplines. These local, unauthorized knowledges are central to the work of the bricolage. Too often in Western colonial and neocolonial history Europeans have viewed the knowledges and ways of seeing of the poor, the marginalized, and the conquered in a condescending and dismissive manner. Many of these perspectives, of course, were brimming with cosmological, epistemological, and ontological insight missing from Western perspectives. Western scholars were often simply too ethnocentric and arrogant to recognize the genius of such subjugated information. Bricoleurs unabashedly take a hard look at subjugated perspectives—not in some naïve romantic manner but in a rigorous and critical orientation. They are aware that Western scientific thinking often promotes contempt for individuals who have learned about a topic such as farming from the wisdom of their ancestors and a lifetime of cultivating the land. Many of the subjugated knowledges bricoleurs employ come from postcolonial backgrounds. Such ways of seeing force bricoleurs to account for the ways colonial power has shaped their approaches to research and has inscribed the knowledges they have produced.

Starting research with a valuing of subjugated knowledges, bricoleurs can spiral through a variety of subjugated discourses to weave a multilogical theoretical and empirical tapestry. For example, using a Hindu-influenced ontology that delineates the existence of a non-objective, purposely constructed reality; a critical theory that traces the role of power in producing this construction; a Santiago cognitive theory that maintains we bring forth this constructed world via our action within and upon it; and a poststructuralist feminist theory that alerts us to the ways patriarchal and other structures shape our knowledge about this reality, we gain a more profound understanding of what is happening when human beings encounter the world. The insights we gain and the knowledges we produce with these concepts in mind move us to new levels of epistemological and ontological awareness. Such an awareness may be similar to what the Vajrayana tradition of Buddhism calls "crazy wisdom." Bricoleurs seek the multilogical orientation of crazy wisdom in their efforts to push the envelope of knowledge production.[46]

With these insights in mind, bricoleurs can operate in a wide diversity of disciplines and use an infinite number of subjugated and indigenous forms of knowledge. Ethnomathematical knowledges can be used to extend understanding of and knowledge production about math and math pedagogy.[47] Organic African American knowledges of grandmothers, beauticians, and preachers can provide profound insight into the nature of higher order cognition.[48] Hip-hop musicians can help educators working to develop thicker and more insightful understandings of youth cultures and their implications for pedagogy.[49] Ancient African epistemologies and ontologies can help shape the theoretical lenses one uses to study contemporary racism and class bias.[50]

Feminist understandings are important to both male and female researchers, as they open doors to previously excluded knowledges. Such knowledges often point out the problems with the universal pronouncements of Cartesianism. The presence of gender diversity in this context reveals the patriarchal inscriptions on what was presented as universal, always true, validated knowledge about some aspect of the world. Indeed, this psychological pronouncement about the highest form of moral reasoning may apply more to men than it does to women—and even then it may apply more to upper-middle-class men than to men of a lower socioeconomic class or more to Anglo men than to Asian and African men. With these feminist insights in mind, bricoleurs find it easier to view the ways the knowledges they produce reflect the cultural, historical, and gendered contexts they occupy. In this context universality is problematized. Indeed, the more we are aware of those different from us on a variety of levels, the harder it is to produce naive universal knowledges. In our heightened awareness, in our crazy wisdom, we produce more sensitive, more aware modes of information.[51] Once the subjugated door is open the possibilities are infinite.

A Transformative Politics of Difference

Bricoleurs work with difference in a way that transcends liberal multicultural notions of simple toleration. Engaging difference in its lived expression so that social inquiry is connected to action in the world, they engage in knowledge work grounded upon a transformative politics of difference. In this context researchers study the ways difference is constructed by historical and social processes, in particular the ways power works to shape the meaning and lived expression of difference. In this context bricoleurs work to set up what Ray Horn calls postformal conversations where differences are acknowledged and used to address individual needs and systemic inequities.[52] All cultural groups differ in profound ways. Knowing this, bricoleurs who engage in the postformal conversation assume a radical humility that leads to a spirit of equality. Such a disposition allows bricoleurs the opportunity to begin the daunting task of developing genuine and egalitarian interactions among the various cultures of the planet.[53] Based on this foundation, the research in which they engage harbors a vision of what could be in the realms of race, class, gender, sexuality, and culture.

Thus, bricoleurs make organic connections with social, cultural, and historical traditions in a manner informed by understanding the power relations that shape them. In addition, bricoleurs are aware of where they stand in relation to these important power relations. With this insight they are better prepared to use the knowledges they produce to initiate critical action. Informed by local knowledges from multiple social and cultural locations, bricoleurs avoid the grand narratives of Western discourses that are monological in their dismissal of histories and the cultural concerns of non-Western peoples. In this context they are able to make use of multiple generative narratives emerging from diverse locales that are dedicated to the production of new ways of making meaning and being/becoming human. Difference in this context is negotiated in the womb of solidarity. These multiple generative narratives are central to the bricolage. Such narratives might include poststructuralist feminism, postcolonial discourses, various social theoretical analyses of macro-social structures vis-à-vis interactionist understandings of micro-dimensions of everyday life, critical hermeneutical ways of interpreting, Santiago enactivist cognitive theories, and so forth.

Bricoleurs who employ this transformative politics of difference, however, understand the difficulty of producing critical knowledges. In a globalized era marred by historical and contemporary power asymmetries, researchers interested in using their knowledges for social change face daunting obstacles. Difference in such contexts too often leads directly to tension and violence. In the post-9-11 landscape, dominated by U.S. military power, tension and violence escalate. From the international level to the national and local domains, difference in the twenty-first century is often not viewed as an opportunity for insight and social and personal transformation. Indeed, diversity without conversation, community, or a web of relationships can lead to hatred and misunderstanding. If a sense of the interdependence of all peoples has not been established, difference can lead to conflict and murder. In a situation where particular power groups have dominated specific peoples for centuries—as in European and U.S. colonialism and neocolonialism—the possibility for conflict increases manyfold. In this context difference for the colonized signifies the taking of political, social, epistemological, educational, and economic power and the imposition of culture.

European knowledges in these colonial and neocolonial contexts are often presented to the colonial other as the one correct point of view. The knowledges of the colonized are demonized and viewed as inherently inferior. Difference is viewed as a marker of deficiency. Indeed, in an epistemological context, more voices are not viewed as a benefit but as a cacophony of confusion undermining the scientific effort to get the correct answer. As such rationalism relegates the local knowledge of those low in status to the margins, it guarantees that official knowledge remains monological and unblemished by difference. In such a monological context Europeans could produce universal knowledge about the "true nature" of the world and its people. Using such knowledge to build theories delineating proper human behavior and development, Europeans gained the power to tell others what to do and how to organize their lives. Employing a transformative politics of difference, bricoleurs seek to throw a monkey wrench into such mechanistic operations.[54]

Bricoleurs make sure that Western rationalism is removed from its sacred sanctuary as the only legitimate mode of knowledge production. They take rationalism into the epistemological bazaar, where it assumes its place as simply another way of making meaning and producing knowledge about the world. Here it coexists with traditions coming from different places and times. It encounters modes of perceiving that utilize both rational and emotional dynamics and make use of context and interrelationship in unique ways. Bricoleurs like to hang out in the epistemological bazaar. In this locale they can engage in unimagined conversations that move them to new levels of insight derived from juxtaposing diverse forms of meaning making.

In addition to different cultural knowledges and modes of meaning making, bricoleurs study the history of European disciplines and the insights to be gained from traditions of dissent within such disciplines. Here they study the relationship of canonical and countercanonical ways of seeing. In this interactive setting bricoleurs are less interested in asking about the truth of other traditions and more concerned with inquiring about the origins of such perspectives and their implications for the larger act of knowledge production.[55]

Beginning the Process: The First Steps in "Doing" the Bricolage

In my work with Kathleen Berry on employing the bricolage, we suggest that beginning bricoleurs develop a point of entry text (POET) written, of course, from the perspective of one or more fields of study and from particular theoretical frames of reference.[56] While there are many possible ways of employing the bricolage, we suggest that researchers take their POET and *thread* it through a variety of conceptual maps, including, for example:

- Discourses of social theory—such as critical theory, poststructuralism, postcolonialism, complexity theory, ecological theory, and constructivism
- Research genres and methodologies—quantitative analysis, ethnography, phenomenology, psychoanalysis, historiography, semiotics, textual analysis, hermeneutics, and discourse analysis
- Cultural/social positionalities—racial (Afrocentric analysis, Chicano studies, Native American studies, indigenous studies, identity politics), class (materialist studies), gender (feminist theory, studies of alternate masculinities), sexuality (queer theory), ability, and religious (liberation theology, Islamic studies, Judaic studies)
- Disciplinary/interdisciplinary departmentalizations of knowledge: history, philosophy, sociology, anthropology, political science, economics, geography, psychology, literary criticism, aesthetics, cultural studies, and American studies
- Philosophical domains—epistemology, ontology, axiology, teleology, cosmology
- Power modes—hegemonic, ideologic, regulatory, discursive, disciplinary, coercive
- Knowledge sources—oral, print, photographic, Internet, and visual sources, as well as works of art, cartoons, popular culture, media, historical documents, daily life, books, and journals.

And there are many more categories such as these that can be enumerated.

In this context bricoleurs thread their POET through what they consider relevant conceptual maps. If my POET is an analysis of the ways contemporary racism in America is different than racism in the past, then each time I engage the conceptual map I encounter knowledges that complicate my original thesis. The POET has been subjected to multiple readings, conflicting discourses, and perspectives from diverse positionalities, epistemologies, modes of power, research methodologies, as well as a plethora of previously unconsidered knowledge sources. As the POET travels through these different domains, it circles back to its starting point. Each time it threads through the map the process looks more and more like a feedback loop. The bricolage process demands that this threading be repeated numerous times. The POET's interaction with the conceptual maps creates a state of turbulence, a disequilibrium that reflects a healthy feature of complexity and autopoiesis. Indeed, such turbulence sets up the possibility for discerning relationships and processes that open new conceptual vistas for the ethnic studies researcher. In this context conditions are created for analytical and interpretive spontaneity, random associations that yield profound insights and novelty.

The bricoleur's feedback looping process is disconcerting in its freedom from step-by-step linearity. Whereas more objectivist forms of empirical research attempt to reduce variables, the bricolage works to increase them. The feedback looping process can work to disrupt the researcher's train of thought and move it in an unanticipated direction. Monological knowledge is subverted, as the feedback looping process juxtaposes numerous perspectives and knowledge forms. Such juxtapositioning confronts the researcher with contradictions, unexpected relationships and unities, zones of interpretive possibility, disjunctions and fissures, and previously unseen processes at work. Every time the POET threads itself back through the concept maps its original composition changes. What emerges after a few loops may surprise the bricoleur in its uniqueness and unanticipated qualities. The POET's confrontation with these diverse knowledges and vantage points moves the researcher to a higher and more complex level of understanding. This level of understanding is characterized by unexpected turns, retraveled paths, reconceptualized assertions, bifurcation points, and encounters with equilibrium/near equilibrium in relation to agitation and disconcerting revelations. The bricoleur needs to develop a comfort with ambiguity.

Employing our POET on the uniqueness of contemporary racism, it may be helpful to thread it through the conceptual maps previously listed. As we examine the topic from diverse theoretical perspectives we come to ask new questions of our POET. In a critical theoretical perspective, for example, we ask questions about power theory. Does our text possess a sophisticated view of racial power, the power of white supremacy, and other dimensions of dominant culture that shape the nature of racism in the twenty-first century? In a postcolonial sense, does contemporary racism connect to issues of European/American colonialism and its long history of exploitation of nonwhite peoples? Is there insight to be gained by contextualizing the civil rights movement and the reaction to it within larger global issues of the colonial rebellion emerging in the middle decades of the twentieth century? Could use of constructivism in this context focus the bricoleur's attention on the social, cultural, and political economic forces that shape racial consciousness in the twenty-first century? Constructivism's focus on the production of consciousness/subjectivity could help raise unasked questions about white racism, the ways it is produced in the contemporary Zeitgeist, and the process of its mutation into new forms and articulations.

Looping her or her POET through diverse research genres and methodologies, the bricoleur asks what perspectives might be gained through the use of different primary research strategies. Is there need for an ethnographic study of African Americans' and/or Latinos' and other groups' perceptions of the differences between twenty-first-century racism and previous manifestations of racism? Is ethnography data essential in the effort to make such distinctions? Is the question so complex that ethnographic insights need to be supplemented by phenomenological and even psychoanalytical inquiries? Is there a logical ineffability to such insights that moves expression of them to the phenomenological realm of affect, emotion, and registers of feeling? Employing such phenomenological research, the ethnic studies bricoleur may open a new realm of insight into the nature of contemporary racism and its effects. Historiographical analysis in this research project in particular may be necessary for the researcher to gain the needed understanding of previous forms of racism. Might the use of semiotics with its study of cultural signs and signifiers contribute to an understanding of the ways contemporary racism is encoded in various cultural texts? Indeed, it may be semiotic analysis that exposes the subtlety of new forms of racism and the ways they are implanted unconsciously in popular social images. Using discursive analysis bricoleurs can make sure their POET is informed by discourses of contemporary "race talk." This process of looping the original text through other research genres can continue (or not) through even more methodologies.

Running the POET through the categories diverse social/cultural positionalities, bricoleurs review their work from the perspectives of racial, class, gender, sexual, religious, ability, and other groups for both the existential viewpoints they bring to observations and the theoretical orientations members of these groups have developed. In the case of our POET's focus on the difference between contemporary and historical manifestations of racism, class and gender perspectives provide new levels of insight and complexity to our study. Such perspectives undermine essentialist pronouncements that fail to understand the different relations of racism to individuals of color occupying differing rungs of the class ladder. When race intersects class (or gender, sexuality, religion, etc.) issues of racism may play out in quite different and often contradictory ways. With these understandings in mind, bricoleurs in ethnic studies are better equipped to turn out thicker and more complex research studies. In this context our study of the difference between contemporary racism and racism of previous eras is profoundly modified. Our feedback loop through social/cultural positionalities has informed us that contemporary racism manifests itself in multiple ways depending on its relationship to class, gender, and other positional factors.

A loop through diverse disciplinary frameworks opens our POET to more perspectives and possibilities. When previous insights are juxtaposed with, say, cultural studies and its emphasis on the discourses of popular cultural knowledges, important sources of previously unexplored information are brought to the bricoleur's attention. The study of contemporary movies, TV shows, video games, Internet websites, popular music, and so forth allows the bricoleur to explore what could be described as the "social dreams" of U.S. society in the twenty-first century. Within these unguarded social dreams of popular culture the researcher can begin to ask questions about new forms of racial representation, racial fears of the dominant culture, and the nature and meaning of the commodification and exoticization of "racial others." In this context the bricoleur finds unlimited resources to compare with data mined from other domains. What do these new knowledges tell us about the ways the new racism is constructed and disseminated? How do these media shape racial messages in ways that are different from more traditional sources of communication? Does racism in an electronic era (hyperreality) encounter unprecedented forces that fashion it in new and hard-to-discern ways?

Analyzing our POET in relation to the philosophical domains allows bricoleurs to embrace a form of philosophical research often missing from social research. Such insights remind bricoleurs of the complexity of the research act and the need to avoid monological forms of epistemology. Such monological forms of information are often based on the assumption that knowledge reflects objective reality. In this context the researcher understands that no objective, disinterested understanding of contemporary racism is possible. The distinctions we make between contemporary racism and prior forms of racism are interpretations, the researcher's constructions. In this context we understand the role that our diverse frames of reference have played in shaping these interpretations. Are we satisfied with this process? Do we sense that we have negated isolating and decontextualizing tendencies in epistemologically monological research and that in this process we have worked with multiple forms of knowledge about the uniqueness of contemporary racism? How has this exposure to epistemological difference changed the nature of our understanding of contemporary racism?

A central benefit of the bricolage's threading through the philosophical, specifically the epistemological domain for ethnic studies, involves the way the process works to bring previously excluded people and categories of people into the research process. "Exclude these uneducated upstarts," the blind monks of reductionism exclaim. Multilogical epistemological analysis reminds scholars of ethnic studies that their research is one aspect of a larger political process involved with apportioning power and resources. Bricoleurs know that racially, ethnically, and class-marginalized peoples have little to do with such a process. Once research is viewed as a humanly constructed process and not a transcultural and transhistorical universal enterprise, diverse and conflicting perspectives can be viewed as profound resources.

Threading our POET through the modes of power can provide compelling new insights into the uniqueness of contemporary racism. When researchers of contemporary racism pass their analysis through the filter of ideology, they begin to see the ways particular forms of Eurocentrism and white supremacy operate in contemporary society. Ideology is grounded on the notion that particular ways of seeing the world may work to sustain existing power relations. In a bow to complexity, these same ways of seeing may undermine dominant power relations in another context. A complex definition of ideology dismisses traditional viewpoints that define ideology as a coherent system of beliefs. Instead, bricoleurs move to a more complex, process-oriented, culturally sensitive perspective that views ideology in its dominant articulation as part of a larger process of protecting unequal power relations and maintaining domination. Specifically, a dominant cultural form of ideology involves sustaining these power asymmetries through the process of making meaning, producing a common sense that justifies prevailing systems of domination. Such a view of ideology corrects historical definitions of ideology as a monolithic, unidirectional entity that was imposed on individuals by a secret cohort of ruling-class tsars.

Understanding domination in the context of concurrent struggles among different classes, racial and gender groups, and sectors of capital, students of ideology analyze the ways such competition engages differing visions, interests, and agendas in a variety of social locales. Individuals use ideology to help them organize their lived experiences, to make sense of their predicaments. In this context bricoleurs studying contemporary racism in relation to ideology begin to discern an encoded ideology of white supremacy inscribed throughout the social and cultural landscape. Such a crypto-ideology often operates to naturalize the unequal relationships that structure racial and ethnic relationships in a way that erases the historical processes that have helped mould the present social order and extant racial dynamics within it. As bricoleurs in ethnic studies trace this ideology of white supremacy, they often discern that this discourse of whiteness induces many peoples around the planet to believe that the world could exist only in the way that it does today—what is had to be. Such ideological awareness moves our understanding of the uniqueness of contemporary racism to a new level of sophistication.

The last domain through which we will thread our POET in this example (there are many more) involves the category of knowledge sources. While there are many, we will focus here on works of art, the aesthetic realm. Exploring, for example, artistic and aesthetic styles that fall outside the confines of the Euro-canon, the bricoleur discerns a whole new domain where the uniqueness of contemporary racism can be analyzed. In numerous art shows illustrating, say, African or African American art,[57] guardians of the Euro-canon worked diligently to contain perceived threats to prevailing aesthetic standards and definitions of quality. The aesthetic orientations of such artists moved the priests of high art to equate difference with deficiency—a racist tendency that can be found in various social locales, including education, cognition, and religion. Indeed, the art of the racial other in this context is seen through the constructed lenses of the canon. That which is artistically transgressive is "tamed" and rendered harmless by including it as a primitive stage of canonical development.

Representatives of the dominant culture in this social domain claim the right to establish the universal characteristics of "good art." Bricoleurs in this example work to demystify these hidden cultural and ideological dimensions of high art. And what may be key to the study of the unique dynamics of contemporary racism, in this demystification process bricoleurs expose not only what is excluded but also the ideological precepts shaping the *inclusion* of the other. How can we talk about racism in the art world, many might complain in this context, if the contemporary canon includes the work of more Africans, African Americans, Latin Americans, and indigenous peoples than ever before? The aesthetic commitments required for inclusion, however, are profoundly revealing to the ethnic studies researcher studying the uniqueness of contemporary racism. The insight researchers develop into the terms of multiracial and multiethnic inclusion in the world of high art may help them discern similar patterns in other social, cultural, political, and economic domains.

Of course, these are merely a few of the domains bricoleurs in ethnic studies can use to inform their multilogical research. Bricoleurs have to make decisions about which domains to engage as they pursue new insights and exploit the conceptual power provided by the interaction of different perspectives. Understanding a phenomenon such as the uniqueness of contemporary racism is enhanced by exposure to these multiple categories of diversity. After the bricolage, ethnic studies researchers can never view the concept of diversity in the same light. Always devoted to the importance of diversity, ethnic studies scholars in this reconceptualized context move diversity into a new conceptual terrain.

Notes

1. Ling-chi Wang, "Curriculum Transformation at UC Berkeley: Our Past, Present, and Future," 1991, amercult/berkeley.edu/geninfo/wang.html; N. Banerjee, "Q and A with Ethnic Studies Pioneer Ronald Takaki," 2000, www.asianweek.com/2000_10_12/feature.html; H. Miramontes, "Requiring Ethnic Studies," 2003, gladstone.uoregon.edu/~hmiramon/writing%20121/esreqtograduate.rtf; Michael Elliott and Claudia Stokes, "What Is Method and Why Does It Matter?" 2003, www.nyupress.org/webchapter/0814722156intro.pdf.

2. Joe Kincheloe and Peter McLaren, "Rethinking Critical Theory and Qualitative Research," in *The Handbook of Qualitative Research*, ed. Norman K. Denzin and Yvonna S. Lincoln, 3rd ed. (Thousand Oaks, Calif.: Sage Publications, 2004).

3. Joe Kincheloe and Shirley Steinberg, *Changing Multiculturalism* (London: Open University Press, 1997).

4. Joe Kincheloe and Shirley Steinberg, *The Miseducation of the West: Constructing Islam* (New York: Greenwood, 2004).

5. W. E. B. DuBois, *The Education of Black People: Ten Critiques, 1906–1960* (New York: Monthly Review Press, 1973); Christine Sleeter, "How White Teachers Construct Race," in *Race, Identity, and Reproduction in Education*, ed. Cameron McCarthy and Warren Crichlow (New York: Routledge, 1993); Donaldo Macedo, *Literacies of Power: What Americans Are Not Allowed to Know* (Boulder, Colo.: Westview Press, 1994); George Yudice, "Neither Impugning nor Disavowing Whiteness Does a Viable Politics Make: The Limits of Identity Politics," in *After Political Correctness*, ed. Christopher Newfield and Ronald Strickland (Boulder, Colo.: Westview Press, 1995); and Ladislaus Semali, *Literacy in Multimedia America: Integrating Media across the Curriculum* (New York: Garland, 1997).

6. David Smith, "On Enfrauding the Public Sphere: The Futility of Empire and the Future of Knowledge after America," *Policy Futures in Education* 1, no. 3 (2004): 488–503.

7. Aaron Gresson, *The Recovery of Race in America* (Minneapolis: University of Minnesota Press, 1991); A. Gresson, *America's Atonement* (New York: Peter Lang, 2004); Joe Kincheloe, *Getting beyond the Facts: Teaching Social Studies/Social Sciences in the Twenty-first Century* (New York: Peter Lang, 2001); Kincheloe and Steinberg, *Changing Multiculturalism*; Joe Kincheloe, Shirley Steinberg, Nelson Rodriguez, and Ronald Chennault, *White Reign: Deploying Whiteness in America* (New York, St. Martin's Press, 1998); Nelson Rodriguez and Leila Villaverde, *Dismantling White Privilege* (New York: Peter Lang, 2000).

8. Bo Dahlbom, "Going to the Future," 1998, www.viktoria.infomatik.gu.se/~max/bo/papers.html; Cynthia Selfe and Richard Selfe, "The Politics of the Interface: Power and Its Exercise in Electronic Contact Zones," 1994, www.hu.mtu.edu/~cyselfe/texts/politics.html; John McLeod, "Qualitative Research as Bricolage" (paper presented at the Society for Psychotherapy Research annual conference, Chicago, 2000); and T. R. Young and James Yarbrough, "Reinventing Sociology: Mission and Methods for Postmodern Sociologists," Red Feather Institute, Transforming Sociology Series, 1993, 154.

9. Yvonna S. Lincoln, "An Emerging New *Bricoleur*: Promises and Possibilities—a Reaction to Joe Kincheloe's 'Describing the Bricoleur,'" *Qualitative Inquiry* 7, no. 6 (2001): 693–696.

10. Norman K. Denzin and Yvonna S. Lincoln, "Introduction: The Discipline and Practice of Qualitative Research," in *Handbook of Qualitative Research*, ed. Norman K. Denzin and Yvonna S. Lincoln. 2nd ed. (Thousand Oaks, Calif.: Sage Publications, 2000); McLeod, "Qualitative Research"; and Roxie Foster, "Addressing Epistemologic and Practical Issues in Multimethod Research: A Procedure for Conceptual Triangulation," *Advances in Nursing Education* 202, no. 2 (1997).

11. Joe Kincheloe, "Describing the Bricolage: Conceptualizing a New Rigor in Qualitative Research," *Qualitative Inquiry* 7, no. 6 (2001): 679–692.

12. Lincoln, "Emerging New *Bricoleur*"; William Pinar, "The Researcher as Bricoleur: The Teacher as Public Intellectual," *Qualitative Inquiry* 7, no. 6 (2001): 696–700; Peter McLaren, "Bricklayers and Bricoleurs: A Marxist Addendum," *Qualitative Inquiry* 7, no. 6 (2001): 700–705.

13. Douglas Kellner, *Media Culture: Cultural Studies, Identity and Politics between the Modern and Postmodern* (New York: Routledge, 1995).

14. Denzin and Lincoln, "Introduction."

15. Gary Thomas, "The Myth of Rational Research," *British Educational Research Journal* 24, no. 2 (1998): 129–146.

16. Frank Fischer, "Beyond Empiricism: Policy Inquiry in Postpositivist Perspective," *Policy Studies Journal* 26, no. 1 (1998): 129–146; Mark Weinstein, "Critical Thinking? Expanding the Paradigm," 1995, www.chss.montclair.edu/inquiry/fall95/weinste.html; Humberto Maturana and Francisco Varela, *The Tree of Knowledge* (Boston: Shambhala, 1987); Francisco Varela, *Ethical Know-How: Action, Wisdom, and Cognition* (Stanford, Calif.: Stanford University Press, 1999);

and D. Geeland and P. Taylor, "Writing Our Lived Experience: Beyond the (Pale) Hermeneutic," *Electronic Journal of Science Education* 5 (2000), unr.edu/homepage/crowther/ejse/geelanetal.html.

17. Nicholas Burbules and Rupert Berk, "Critical Thinking and Critical Pedagogy: Relations, Differences, and Limits," in *Critical Theories in Education*, ed. Thomas Popkewitz and Lynn Fendler (New York: Routledge, 1999); Pedro Marijuan, "Information Revisited" (paper presented to the First Conference on the Foundations of Information Science, Madrid, Spain, 1994); and Richard Cary, "Art and Aesthetics," in *Critical Thinking: An Encyclopedia*, ed. Danny Weil and Joe Kincheloe (New York: Greenwood, 2003).

18. Douglas Simpson and Michael Jackson, "John Dewey and Educational Evaluation," in *Standards and Schooling in the U.S.: An Encyclopedia*, ed. Joe Kincheloe and Danny Weil (Santa Barbara, Calif.: ABC-Clio, 2001).

19. Frank Richardson and Robert Woolfolk, "Social Theory and Values: A Hermeneutic Perspective," *Theory and Psychology* 4, no. 2 (1994): 199–226; John Pickering, "The Self Is a Semiotic Process," *Journal of Consciousness Studies* 6, no. 4 (1999): 31–47; and M. Allen, "Voice of Reason," 2000, www.curtin.edu.au/learn/unit/10846/arrow/vorall.htm.

20. Peter McLaren, Rhonda Hammer, Susan Reilly, and David Scholle, *Rethinking Media Literacy: A Critical Pedagogy of Representation* (New York: Peter Lang, 1995); Marjorie Devault, "Talking Back to Sociology: Distinctive Contributions of Feminist Methodologies," *Annual Review of Sociology* 22 (1996):29–50; Kristin Lutz, Kim Jones, and Judy Kendall, "Expanding the Praxis Debate: Contributions to Clinical Inquiry," *Advances in Nursing Science* 20, no. 2 (1997); Lourdes Soto, ed., *The Politics of Early Childhood Education* (New York: Peter Lang, 2000); Shirley Steinberg, ed., *Multi/intercultural Conversations* (New York: Peter Lang, 2001).

21. DuBois, *Education of Black People*; Young and Yarbrough, "Reinventing Sociology; Joe Kincheloe, Shirley Steinberg, and Patricia Hinchey, eds., *The Postformal Reader: Cognition and Education* (New York: Falmer, 1999).

22. Selfe and Selfe, "Politics of the Interface"; R. Paulson, "Mapping Knowledge Perspectives in Studies of Educational Change," in *Transforming Schools*, ed. Peter Cookson, Jr., and Barbara Schneider (New York: Garland, 1995).

23. Ladislaus Semali and Joe Kincheloe, *What Is Indigenous Knowledge? Voices from the Academy* (New York: Falmer, 1999); Burbules and Beck, "Critical Thinking."

24. Paulo Freire, *Pedagogy of the Oppressed* (New York: Herder and Herder, 1970).

25. Dahlbom, "Going to the Future"; Bella Dicks and Bruce Mason, "Hypermedia and Ethnography: Reflections on the Construction of a Research Approach," *Sociological Research Online* 3 (1998): 3.

26. Lincoln, "An Emerging New *Bricoleur*."

27. Pinar, "Researcher as Bricoleur," p. 698.

28. DeVault, "Talking Back to Sociology"; Denzin and Lincoln, "Introduction"; Dahlbom, "Going to the Future."

29. McLeod, "Qualitative Research"; Carole Palmer, "Information Work at the Boundaries of Science: Linking Library Services to Research Practices," *Library Trends* 44, no. 2 (1996): 165–192; Susan Friedman, "(Inter) Disciplinarity and the Question of the Women's Studies Ph.D.," *Feminist Studies* 24, no. 2 (1998).

30. McLeod, "Qualitative Research"; Friedman, "(Inter) Disciplinarity."

31. Jill Morawski, "The Science behind Feminist Research Methods," *Journal of Social Issues* 53, no. 4 (1997): 667–682.

32. Jan Blommaert, "Workshopping: Notes on Professional Vision in Discourse," 1997, africana_rug.ac.be/texts/research-publications/publications_on-line/workshopping.htm.

33. Kellner, *Media Studies*.

34. Denzin and Lincoln, "Introduction," 3.

35. Young and Yarbrough, "Reinventing Sociology"; Palmer, "Information Work"; and Friedman, "(Inter) Disciplinarity."

36. George Dei, "Indigenous Knowledge as an Empowerment Tool," in *Empowerment: Toward Sustainable Development*, ed. Naresh Singh and Vangile Titi (Toronto: Fernwood Press, 1995).

37. R. Sambuli Mosha, *The Heartbeat of Indigenous Africa: A Study of the Chagga Educational System* (New York: Garland, 2000).

38. Mark Woodhouse, *Paradigm Wars: Worldviews for a New Age* (Berkeley, Calif.: Frog, 1996); Dei, "Indigenous Knowledge"; and Mahia Maurial, "Indigenous Knowledge and Schooling: A Continuum between Conflict and Dialogue," in *What Is Indigenous Knowledge? Voices from the Academy*, ed. Ladislaus Semali and Joe Kincheloe (New York: Falmer, 1999).

39. Frédérique Apffel-Marglin, "Development or Decolonization in the Andes?" *Interculture: International Journal of Intercultural and Transdisciplinary Research* 28, no. 1 (1995): 3–17.

40. Apffel-Marglin, "Development or Decolonization," 11.

41. Gregory Bateson in Paul Newland, "Logical Types of Learning," 1997, www.envf.port.ac.uk/newmedia/lecturenotes/EMMA/at2n.htm.

42. Pickering, "Semiotic Process"; Edmund O'Sullivan, *Transformative Learning: Educational Vision for the 21st Century* (London: Zed, 1999); Erik Malewski, "Queer Sexuality—The Trouble with Knowing: Standards of Complexity and Sexual Orientations," in *Standards and Schooling in the United States: An Encyclopedia*, ed. Joe Kincheloe and Danny Weil, 3 vols. (Santa Barbara, Calif.: ABC-CLIO, 2001); and B. Thayer-Bacon, *Transforming Critical Thinking: Thinking Constructively* (New York: Teachers College Press, 2000).

43. Allen, "Voice of Reason"; Todd May, *Between Genealogy and Epistemology: Psychology, Politics, and Knowledge in the Thought of Michel Foucault* (University Park: Pennsylvania State University Press, 1993); and O'Sullivan, *Transformative Learning*.

44. Harold Berlak, "Standards and the Control of Knowledge," *Rethinking Schools* (1999), 13, 3, www.rethinkingscfhools.org/archieves/13_03/control.htm; C. Abel, C. Abel, V. Alexander, S. McCune, and P. Nason, "The ExCET Teacher Exams: History, Promises and Concerns," in *Standards and Schooling in the United*

States: An Encyclopedia, ed. Joe Kincheloe and Danny Weil, 3 vols. (Santa Barbara, Calif.: ABC-Clio, 2001).

45. Weinstein, "Critical Thinking?"; Lynne Noone and Patricia Cartwright, "Doing a Critical Literacy Pedagogy: Trans/forming Teachers in a Teacher Education Course," 1996, www.atea.schools.net.au/ATEA/96conf/noone.html; G. Scering, "Themes of a Critical/Feminist Pedagogy: Teacher Education for Democracy," *Journal of Teacher Education* 48, no. 1 (1997): 62–69; G. Hoban and G. Erickson, "Frameworks for Sustaining Professional Learning" (paper presented at the Australasian Science Education Research Association, Darwin, Australia, 1998); Kathy Hytten, "John Dewey and Critical Thinking," in *Critical Thinking: An Encyclopedia*, ed. Weil and Kincheloe; and Thayer-Bacon, *Transforming Critical Thinking*.

46. Thomas, "Myth of Rational Research"; Priya Parmar, "Critical Thinking and Rap Music: The Critical Pedagogy of KRS-One," in *Critical Thinking: An Encyclopedia*, ed. Weil and Kincheloe; Yusef Progler, "Social Studies—Social Studies Standards: Diversity, Conformity, Complexity," in *Standards and Schooling in the United States: An Encyclopedia*, ed. Kincheloe and Weil; Kathleen Berry, "Standards of Complexity in a Postmodern Democracy," in *Standards and Schooling in the United States: An Encyclopedia*, ed. Kincheloe and Weil; Fritjof Capra, *The Web of Life: A New Scientific Understanding of Living Systems* (New York: Anchor, 1996); and Francisco Varela, *Ethical Know-How*.

47. Peter Applebaum, "Mathematics Education," in *Critical Thinking: An Encyclopedia*, ed. Weil and Kincheloe.

48. Michael Dumas, "Critical Thinking as Black Experience," in *Critical Thinking: An Encyclopedia*, ed. Weil and Kincheloe.

49. Parmar, "Critical Thinking and Rap Music."

50. Rochelle Brock, "Using Critical Thinking to Understand a Black Woman's Identity," in *Critical Thinking: An Encyclopedia*, ed. Weil and Kincheloe.

51. Sally McRorie, "Pentimento: Philosophical Inquiry as Research in Art Education" (unpublished manuscript, 1999); Burbules and Beck, "Critical Thinking."

52. Raymond Horn, *Teacher Talk: A Postformal Inquiry into Educational Change* (New York: Peter Lang, 2000).

53. Richardson and Woolfolk, "Social Theory and Values"; Henry Giroux, *Pedagogy and the Politics of Hope: Theory, Culture, and Schooling* (Boulder, Colo.: Westview Press, 1997); and Allen, "Voice of Reason."

54. Allen, "Voice of Reason"; J. Degenaar, "Myth and the Collision of Cultures," *Myth and Symbol* 2 (1995): 39–61; Thayer-Bacon, *Transforming Critical Thinking*; and Thomas, "Myth of Rational Research."

55. Pickering, "Semiotic Process"; Thayer-Bacon, *Transforming Critical Thinking*; Degenaar, "Collision of Cultures"; and Allen, "Voice of Reason."

56. Joe Kincheloe and Kathleen Berry, *Rigour and Complexity in Qualitative Research: Conceptualizing the Bricolage* (London: Open University Press, 2004).

57. Karel Rose and Joe Kincheloe, *Art, Culture, and Education: Artful Teaching in a Fractured Landscape* (New York: Peter Lang, 2003).

TEACHING AND DOING ETHNIC STUDIES RESEARCH IN THE CLASSROOM   IV

Lessons from an Activist Intellectual   14
Participatory Research, Teaching, and Learning for Social Change*

JOSE Z. CALDERON

AS A PROFESSOR WITH A HISTORY in various social movements, I have often asked myself: How do I justify my teaching and research objectives without losing my values to advance progressive social change? How do I carry out research that does not belittle or hurt our communities? Is it possible to be a critical activist, a researcher, a committed teacher, and a dedicated learner?

Opposing the positivist view that academicians should remain neutral in the classroom and in their research, I suggest that connections can be made between research, teaching, and action.

My research and teaching correspond with aspects of the participatory action approach method, particularly the explicit connections made between classroom teaching and community-based social research and action.[1] Coming from an activist background, I have had to find a place for combining the roles of professor, researcher, and activist. In the area of research, I have had to resolve the issue that my data were collected in the dual roles of researcher and participant where one is involved in the process of social change while simultaneously describing the world of the participants through their eyes. In the area of teaching, I have implemented a style of critical pedagogy that involves the students both inside and outside the classroom.

The banking concept of pedagogy is still a widely used methodology in the college classroom. Teaching according to this method is based on the

---

*From: Jose Calderon, "Lessons from an Activist Intellectual: Participatory Research, Teaching and Learning for Social Change" in *Latin American Perspectives*, 134:31 (January 2004): 81–94. Copyright 2004 by Sage Publications. Reprinted by permission. This chapter was edited to conform with the format of this anthology.

premise that the teacher "educates" while the students "memorize" and feed back to the teacher whatever information is absorbed. With this type of pedagogy, there is little room for interaction among the students and between the students and the teacher. An alternative pedagogy involves participatory learning and research that fosters classroom collaboration and draws connections between lived experience and academic theories.[2]

Background to Connections between Action and Research

I have been part of various movements to create social change by combining participation, research, and action. Through the Coalition for Harmony in Monterey Park, I was involved in an effort to overturn an English-only resolution and in a larger movement to defeat the anti-immigrant and pro-growth trends in the city.[3] As president of the San Gabriel Valley Chapter of the League of United Latin American Citizens (LULAC), I helped promote more visibility of Latinos in all aspects of city and county government. As a co-chair of the Multi-Ethnic Task Force and chair of the Alhambra School District Human Relations Advisory Committee, I helped advance coalition-building efforts aimed at the establishment of multicultural and conflict resolution programs in the local high schools. In 1988 and 1990, I complemented this activity with work as a researcher with John Horton of the UCLA Department of Sociology in the community of Monterey Park. Over the next two years, our research was variously funded and supported by the Institute of American Cultures and by the Changing Relations Project of the Ford Foundation. In 1989, in conjunction with the Ford Foundation project, I became one of seven members of a local research team charged with studying political relations between newcomer immigrants and established community residents. Our research was part of a national study of the impact of immigration on everyday life in six communities: Miami, Houston, Philadelphia, Chicago, Monterey Park, and Garden City, Kansas. This national project emphasized the use of critical ethnography as a means of deciphering how day-to-day interaction was related to class and power. To avoid assuming static ethnic entities, we focused on the formation of political agendas through intergroup relations.[4] I incorporated these concerns into my own research by observing sites that were a part of my everyday life in the city, including: the neighborhood I lived in, the sports clubs in which my sons participated, and the community organizations and coalitions that I helped to organize. My observations were complemented by formal and informal interviews and consultation of work that grounds theory in data collected by participant-observation, interviewing, the writing and coding of field notes, and analysis.[5]

My work did not, however, entirely follow the grounded theory approach, because I was more than a participant-observer in the process. My prior involvement as a leader in various community neighborhood and civic groups made it impossible for me to be a neutral observer.

Gathering data in the dual roles of researcher and activist gave me special insight into activities and trends in the community, but it opened my work to criticism from some who disagreed with my public positions. For example, the former mayor of Monterey Park, Barry Hatch, openly stated in a *Los Angeles Times* article that the "Changing Communities" study would be biased because I was part of it.[6]

Linking Action and Research

The participants in the coalitions that I was involved in were less concerned about bias than about finding solutions to the many problems that they confronted in the community and schools. I was considered an "insider" by these coalitions, since I lived with my family in the community and had children in the district schools. They also knew that I was a researcher from my having told them or from having read about it in the local newspapers. What we had in common was the desire to find specific solutions to problems of ethnic/racial conflict in the community. When an all-White city council passed an English-only resolution calling for the use of English only in city literature, I was part of a group of multiethnic residents that formed the Coalition for Harmony in Monterey Park (CHAMP). Together, we were able to defeat the ordinance and eventually vote out of office its main proponents. Further, we were able to elect candidates that called for planned development without categorizing the issue of "growth" in anti-immigrant terms. By working actively in these coalitions, I was able to develop an ongoing dialogue with the participants that allowed me to serve as both active participant and researcher. In this dialogue we not only engaged in analysis and reflection but also challenged each other and began to develop theories and strategies for dealing with the rise of ethnic/racial divisions in the city.

As conflict moved from the city hall level to the schools, I was able to join in other coalition-building efforts. A series of fights between Latino and Chinese students at Mark Keppel High School led to the formation of two coalitions of parents. The Asian Coalition was led by the Chinese American Parents and Teachers Association of Southern California, including twenty-one Asian groups composed primarily of Chinese professionals, including teachers, teacher's aides, and bilingual social service workers. The other coalition, the Coalition for Equality, was predominantly Latino with a handful of White parents. At first these coalitions were unable to work together for what members of both coalitions pointed to as reasons of cultural and class difference. After numerous meetings between their leaders, they were able to overcome these differences to form one coalition, the Multi-Cultural Community Association.

Pressure by the association on school administrators led to the establishment of an official advisory group to the school board, the Alhambra School District Human Relations Advisory Committee. This thirty-member committee included representatives of groups, including the Multi-Cultural Community Association, the Parent-Teacher Association, the teacher's union, school staff and administrators, and student representatives from the district's three high schools.

I served as committee chair and worked alongside the community representatives to produce concrete evidence of ethnic/racial conflict in the school district.[7] Together, we carried out a survey of 1,500 students and 300 limited English-speaking students in English as a Second Language (ESL) programs. The results showed that 86 percent of the English-speaking students at Mark Keppel High School and a majority of the students at all three high schools perceived racial tensions as an important problem.

We also examined school district reports to establish that Latinos had a disproportionate percentage of student expulsions and that they were being tracked into the lower-level non-college-track courses. With this research in hand, the Multi-Cultural Community Association was able to rally the various ethnic groups around a ten-point plan that included the abolition of the tracking system.

Further, the committee wrote and the school board adopted a policy for dealing with hate-motivated behavior. This policy required principals to develop plans for creating an environment that would allow all persons "to realize their full individual potential through understanding and appreciation of society's diversity of race, ethnic background, national origin, religious belief, sex, age, disability, or sexual orientation." As part of this policy, the school district institutionalized conflict resolution classes and gave students the option of mediation as an alternative to expulsion.[8]

In these examples, the coalition leaders and researchers developed concrete theories through "cogenerative dialogue" to develop "empowering" plans of action.[9] In both the Monterey Park and Alhambra school district coalition efforts, participants went beyond cultural differences to find the structural foundations of the problems. Hence, the participants or "insiders" were not just sources of data but active participants in gathering the data and utilizing it to create institutional change.

At the same time, as both a participant and researcher in the process, I clearly influenced the process, the content of the research, and the outcomes.

Critical Pedagogy

When I began my academic career, I implemented a pedagogy that, similar to my research methodology, aimed at constructing a culture of connecting the classroom with participatory and lived experience. To advance a culture of action and participation, I practiced what Ira Shor, in his book *Empowering Education* (1992), calls "critical-democratic pedagogy." This technique seeks to place the readings and classroom activities in the context of the lived experience of the students. In creating dialogue on the subject matter, I have utilized generative themes that "grow out of student culture and express problematic conditions in daily life that are useful for generating critical discussion."[10] The topical and academic themes emerge from our readings or research in the field.

In my class on Race and Ethnic Relations, I have the students read sections from Paulo Freire's *Pedagogy of the Oppressed* (1993) to emphasize that we are all students and teachers who have the capacity to create culture. I then challenge the students to learn from each other, to share knowledge, and to consider where their experience fits in with that of the literature. I use a combination of readings that promote a comprehensive and critical study of the significant concepts and issues in the field: *Racial Formations in the U.S.* (Omi and Winant, 1994), *Racial and Ethnic Relation* (Feagin and Feagin, 2003), *A Different Mirror* (Takaki, 1993), *Racial Fault Lines* (Almaguer, 1994), *Race, Class, and Gender* (Andersen and Collins, 2003), and *Searching for the Uncommon Common Ground* (Blackwell, Kwoh, and Pastor, 2002). With the use of these readings as a foundation, I fashion this class as a society, purposely dividing the students into various types of "cultural" discussion groups. One type is randomly selected and usually multiethnic. Another is divided according to various novels that deal with the everyday lives of individuals that face the obstacles of racial, class, gender, or sexual inequality.

The discussion groups focusing on the novels are required to identify major themes, relate them to course concepts, and develop class presentations that creatively use multicultural media. In implementing this exercise, students have come up with all types of creative presentations that integrate critical dialogue and theory with life experiences. One group, focusing on Toni Morrison's *The Bluest Eye* (1972), combined original poetry, rap, and video to express their idea that "race is a pigment of our imagination." The video included interviews of shoppers at a nearby mall. After being shown pictures of various individuals representing different racial/ethnic groups, shoppers were asked to point out the one that they thought most represented their conception of "beauty." The results of this creative exercise sparked a dialogue on the role of society in the formation of ideas regarding race, class, gender, and sexual orientation. Another group, utilizing Sandra Cisneros's description of a barrio in *The House on Mango Street* (1991), presented a video comparing a nearby "Latino barrio" to the more affluent areas of Los Angeles. Students in another group utilized John Okada's *No No Boy* (1976) in a play about the troubles that Japanese Americans faced in the aftermath of Pearl Harbor. Yet another group, after reading Louise Erdrich's *Love Medicine* (1989), used poetry, film, and music to describe the relocation of Native Americans and the obstacles that they confront when they leave behind the familiarity of the reservation for the alienation of the city. A group of students from varied backgrounds read Maya Angelou's *I Know Why the Caged Bird Sings* (1996) and applied its content to various stratification theories. In the process of deepening their understanding of these theories, they found connections to their own lived experience and shared this collective interpretation through a mural. As they worked on the project, it became apparent that students of different ethnic and class backgrounds and genders could collaborate collectively to produce a masterpiece. Other works that students have used in their presentations include: Amy Tan's *Joy Luck Club* (1989), Alex Haley's *Malcolm X* (1965), Leslie Marmon Silko's *Ceremony* (1986), and Luis Rodriguez's *Always Running* (1993).

The grading for this exercise requires students to write a paper connecting the concepts outlined in the texts to the main themes of the novels. A group grade for the class presentations is based on the cohesiveness of the presentation, the connection of novel themes made to class concepts, and the effectiveness of the use of creative media.

The final research paper for this class requires students to utilize the ideas of Freire in examining whether a chosen site (institution, group, movement, or community) is advancing a process of "liberation" or merely a process of "domestication."

Partnership with the United Farm Workers' Union

Although the readings and exercises in my classes relate to the lived experiences of the authors and students, there is no comparison to the type of learning that involves the students outside the classroom. Having come from a farm worker background and having worked with the United Farm Workers' union in the early 1970s, I was moved to develop a class that could create dialogue on "new social movements" theory as applied to the farm workers' movement.[11] Utilizing union contacts from my early organizing efforts, I worked with them to develop a participatory action class that is now in its fourteenth year of implementation.

In that class, called Rural and Urban Social Movements, we spend the first half of the semester studying social movement theories and the historical foundations of farmworkers' unions in the United States.[12] Then, during the spring break, I take the students to the central headquarters of the United Farm Workers in La Paz to observe and experience firsthand how the union works. In return for the union's hospitality and shared knowledge, the students contribute their skills and abilities with the various segments of the farmworker community. Since the initial spring break in 1994, the students have worked in various offices of the union doing data entry, archive filing, law research, union by-laws collating, and advocacy planning. In addition, students have joined in organizing actions in nearby cities to support the contract efforts of the union. On the last day of the visit, the students present skits regarding their service learning experiences. One skit, for example, compared a spring break in Tijuana with the UFW alternative spring break. The Tijuana spring break depicted students lying on the beach, drinking beer, and partying. The UFW alternative spring break chronicled the student experience in cleaning up after a flood, carrying rocks from a creek, working in the UFW offices, and planting roses at Cesar Chavez's gravesite. In the past fourteen years, students have returned from La Paz and organized a campus commemoration of Cesar Chavez and all farmworkers. This day, conjoined to fall on the same day as Cesar Chavez's birthday, has included the student skits presented at La Paz, a pilgrimage march in the city of Pomona, speeches by representatives from the United Farm Workers, mariachi music, community *teatro*, and *ballet folklorico*.

In the spring of 1994, students organized a fast to boycott grapes in the college's cafeteria. Eighty-one-year-old Pete Velasco, one of the original Filipino strikers in the grape fields, joined the students in their negotiations with the Marriott Corporation.[13] With the president of the college supporting the fast, the corporation signed a letter that they would no longer serve grapes in the college cafeteria. When Brother Pete passed away in the fall of 1995, the union acknowledged the "deepness" of relations that had developed between the union and the students by inviting various Pitzer students to attend the funeral, to help carry his casket in a union procession, and to take turns in holding UFW flags at an all-night vigil.

The collaboration between Pitzer College students and the UFW is now a year-round activity. Every spring, the Pitzer College farmworker support networks have drawn hundreds of supporters to annual speeches by farmworker leaders such as UFW cofounder Dolores Huerta. In response to a UFW campaign in the strawberry fields, students negotiated the removal of all strawberries from the college's cafeteria. Some students committed themselves to the UFW's strawberry campaign through a "union summer" project and are now working full-time for the union. While some of the students have gone on to make presentations in local high schools about their experiences, others have written research papers for academic conferences. For example, various Pitzer College students have written thesis papers that have been motivated by their work with the union.[14]

Participatory Action Research in a Day Labor Center

A participatory style of activism and research has also been the foundation for the development of a day labor center in the city of Pomona, California.[15] In July 1997, Pomona passed an ordinance that prohibited "the solicitation of or for work on any street or highways, public area, or nonresidential parking areas in the city of Pomona."[16] The penalty for the violation of the ordinance was a $1,000 fine and up to six months in jail.

At the time I happened to have a group of students, part of a class called "Restructuring Communities," working with various community activists to study day laborers. To protest the city ordinance, we worked with these activists to organize the day laborers on various street corners and to pack city hall. When city officials defended their actions by claiming that all day laborers were undocumented, the students were able to present evidence from their research that permanent residents were also among those who solicited work on the street. The student researchers visited models of day labor centers organized by the Coalition for Humane Immigration Rights of Los Angeles. With the help of this research, a funding proposal was written and a nonprofit organization, the Pomona Economic Opportunity

Center, was formed. Subsequently, the city council allocated $50,000 to this nonprofit organization for the purpose of developing a day labor center. They also appointed a board of directors that included city commission members and representatives from the community.

Because of the involvement of our class, I was appointed to the board and so were various students. Fabian Nunez, a student at the time and now a state assemblyman and speaker, was elected president.

From the very beginning, two distinct philosophies emerged on the board. One view, backed by some city officials and consultants from a national hardware supply company, supported the ordinance and proposed using the police to get day laborers off the streets and into the center. Another view, which I supported along with Nunez, the students, the day laborers, and a community activist lawyer, opposed the ordinance while supporting the development of a day labor center. Rather than relying on the police to force the day laborers into the center, we proposed making the center a place that could help empower them through the establishment of employment training programs, language classes, health referral networks, immigration rights counseling, biweekly organizational meetings, and worker representation on the board

Presently, the students are not only continuing with their research, but they are implementing various projects to empower the day laborers.[17] In addition to holding language and computer classes every morning, the students have been instrumental in ensuring worker representation on the organization's board. Rather than allowing city officials or consultants to control the decision-making process, we have organized weekly meetings to build the "voice" of the workers in running the center. As a result, the center's board recently hired two coordinators from their own ranks.

When the city council decided to provide some funding for the day labor center, we employed surveys, questionnaires, and focus groups to determine how the resources of the day laborers could be maximized.[18] Our collaborative research has resulted in the acquisition of several grants from area foundations. One grant, in addition to helping pay the rent for the center, has allowed us to develop a health referral program for the day laborers and their families. Another has helped to support language, computer, and job training programs.

Moving beyond "Charity" Models
The examples presented here have the commonality of using critical pedagogy, participatory action research, and service learning as a means of

bringing students and faculty together with community-based organizations to work on common issues and to effect social change. These collaborative efforts are examples of policy-making models that go beyond charity and dependence on "experts" to get at the root causes of problems, and focus directly or indirectly on politically empowering the powerless."[19] These participatory action learning and research models require the faculty and students to immerse themselves alongside community participants collectively to develop theories and strategies and pursue common objectives. An essential component of this style of learning and research is its commitment to equality of interests between academicians and community participants. Participating students and faculty collaborate to "intentionally promote social learning processes that can develop the organizational, analytical, and communication skills of local leaders and their community-based organizations."[20]

It is essential for faculty members to make a long-term commitment to the sites and communities where they have placed their students. Although students can only make a commitment for a semester or until graduation, faculty participants are in a better position to sustain campus-community partnerships.

An example of this type of community-based partnering is the Center for California Cultural and Social Issues, created in 1999 at Pitzer College. This center, in addition to supporting research and education projects, has developed a number of core partnerships that at the minimum require a faculty member to make a four-year commitment to a community-based organization.[21] As these long-term campus-community partnerships are developed, students and faculty can become a political force in their communities. No longer limited to the role of visitors, they can see themselves as participants with a stake in the decisions being made.

Finally, in the participatory learning and research promoted here it is important to define "community." The community, as ordinarily understood, is made up of many competing interests. Those who are corporate growers, developers, and polluters call themselves part of the "community" even though their profit-making interests often place them in conflict with its "quality of life" initiatives. In contrast, "community" referred to in this article is a geographical, political, and spiritual body that is confronting inequality or trying to improve its quality of life. The research and learning described here focus on the sources of inequality and what can be done about it. The dominant understanding of inequality tends to blame "individuals" for their "inadequacies." Instead, the practices described here focus on the historical and systemic foundations of inequality and challenge students and faculty to find common ground with community institutions, unions, organizations, and neighborhood leaders to arouse social consciousness and effect long-term structural change.

Although considered outside the "objective" mainstream of social science, critical and participatory action research, teaching, and learning are gaining in acceptance.[22] This type of approach takes the academic beyond the traditional bounds of "community service" to a level at which students and faculty join community members in using research, teaching, and learning to bring about fundamental social change. Jim Thomas summarizes the distinction as follows: "Conventional ethnographers study culture for the purpose of describing it; critical ethnographers do so to change it. Conventional ethnographers recognize the impossibility, even undesirability, of research free of normative and other biases, but believe that these biases are to be repressed. Critical ethnographers instead celebrate their normative and political position as a means of invoking social consciousness and societal change."[23]

Conclusion

Participatory research, teaching, and learning constitute a viable alternative to the traditional "banking concept" of knowledge that connects abstract theoretical concepts to lived experience and community engagement; provides a meaningful and practical means for advancing positive social relations by building bridges between students, faculty, and community participants from diverse backgrounds; and moves beyond top-down charity and project development models to those based on collaborative action for social change.

Notes

1. Randy Stoecker, *Research Methods for Community Change: A Project-Based Approach* (Thousand Oaks, Calif: Sage Publications, 2005); Juana Mora and David R. Diaz, *Latino Social Policy: A Participatory Research Model* (Binghamton, N.Y.: Haworth Press, 2004); Kerry Strand et al., *Community-Based Research and Higher Education* (San Francisco: Jossey-Bass, 2003); David J. Maurrasse, *Beyond the Campus: How Colleges and Universities Form Partnerships with Their Communities* (New York: Routledge, 2001); Edward Zlotkowski, ed., *Successful Service-Learning Programs* (Bolton, Mass.: Anker Publishing Company, 1998); Philip Nyden, Anne Figert, Mark Shibley, and Darryl Burrows, *Building Community: Social Science in Action* (Thousand Oaks, Calif.: Pine Forge Press, 1997); James Ostrow, Gary Hesser, and Sandra Enos, *Cultivating the Sociological Imagination: Concepts and Models for Service-Learning in Sociology* (Washington, D.C.: American Association of Higher Education, 1999);

Orlando Fals-Borda and Mohammed Anisur Rahman, *Action and Knowledge: Breaking the Monopoly with Participatory Action Research* (New York: Apex Press, 1991); William Foote Whyte, *Participatory Action Research* (Newbury Park: Calif.: Sage Publications, 1989); and Davydd J. Greenwood and Morten Levin, *Introduction to Action Research: Social Research for Social Change* (Thousand Oaks, Calif.: Sage Publications, 1998).

2. Frances R. Aparicio and Christina Jose-Kampfner, "Language, Culture, and Violence in the Educational Crisis of U.S. Latino/as: Two Courses for Intervention." *Michigan Journal of Community Service Learning* 3 (Fall 1995): 128–138; Jeffrey A. Cantor, *Experiential Learning in Higher Education: Linking Classroom and Community*, report no. 7 (Washington, D.C.: George Washington University, 1995); Barbara Jacoby, *Service Learning in Higher Education* (San Francisco: Jossey-Bass, 1996); Michael Buroway, *Global Ethnography* (Berkeley: University of California Press, 2000); and Antonia Darder, *Reinventing Paulo Freire: A Pedagogy of Love* (Boulder, Colo.: Westview Press, 2002).

3. At the time I began living in the city with my family, the city had received the national designation of being an "All-America City," reflecting its volunteer and innovative programs in dealing with new Chinese immigrants. Concurrently, an organized backlash against the unbridled growth policies of the city council had also begun. A primary target of the "no-growth" movement came to focus on the city's growing Chinese population. Up until 1960, Monterey Park's population had consisted of 85 percent Anglo, 3 percent Asian, and 12 percent Latino. By the 1990 census, the Anglo population had dropped to 11.7 percent, while the Asian Pacific population had grown to 56 percent and Latinos to 31.3 percent. In the preliminary 2000 census, these rapid changes have continued, with Anglo numbers decreasing to 8.2 percent, the Asian Pacific population increasing to 63.7 percent, and Latinos to 26 percent (U.S. Census).

4. John Horton, *Politics of Diversity*, with the assistance of Jose Calderon et al. (Philadelphia: Temple University Press, 1995).

5. Robert M. Emerson, Rachel I. Fretz, and Linda L. Shaw, *Writing Ethnographic Fieldnotes* (Chicago: University of Chicago Press, 1995); John Lofland and Lyn Lofland, *Analyzing Social Settings: A Guide to Qualitative Observation and Analysis* (Belmont, Calif.: Wadsworth Publishing, 1995); and Anselm Strauss and Juliet Corbin, *Basics of Qualitative Research* (Newbury Park, Calif.: Sage Publications, 1990).

6. Berkley Hudson, "Monterey Park's Mix Lures Researchers," *Los Angeles Times* (October 23, 1988), IX, 1.

7. School officials and district level administrators had vehemently denied that the student conflicts were based on ethnic/racial tensions. One school principal blamed the fighting between ethnic groups on "machismo" while another explained to the press that it was the "hormones" of the teenagers that were responsible for the conflicts.

8. Jose Calderon, "Multi-Ethnic Coalition-Building in a Diverse School District," *Critical Sociology* 21 (Spring 1995): 101–111.

9. Max Eldin and Morton Levin, "Cogenerative Learning: Bringing Participation into Action Research," in *Participatory Action Research*, ed. William Foote Whyte (Newbury Park, Calif.: Sage Publications, 1991), 127–142.

10. Ira Shor, *Empowering Education: Critical Teaching for Social Change* (Chicago: University of Chicago Press, 1992), 55.

11. For new social movement theory, I used selected readings from Michael Buroway's *Ethnography Unbound* (Berkeley: University of California Press, 1991) and *Global Ethnography*; and Enrique Larana, Hank Johnston, and Joseph R. Gusfield's *New Social Movements: From Ideology to Identity*.

12. W. K. Barger and Ernesto M. Reza, *The Farm Labor Movement in the Midwest: Social Change and Adaptation among Migrant Farmworkers* (Austin: University of Texas Press, 1994); Devra Weber, *Dark Sweat, White Gold: California Farm Workers, Cotton, and the New Deal* (Berkeley: University of California Press, 1994); Miriam J. Wells, *Strawberry Fields: Politics, Class, and Work in California Agriculture* (Ithaca, N.Y.: Cornell University Press, 1996); Yolanda Broyles-Gonzales, *El Teatro Campesino: Theater in the Chicano Movement* (Austin: University of Texas Press, 1994); Richard Griswold Del Castillo and Richard A. Garcia, *Cesar Chavez: A Triumph of Spirit* (Norman: University of Oklahoma Press, 1995); Fran Leeper Buss, *Forged under the Sun/Forjado Bajo del Sol: The Life of Maria Elena Lucas* (Ann Arbor: University of Michigan Press, 1993); Marilyn Edid, *Farm Labor Organizing: Trends & Prospects* (Ithaca, N.Y.: ILR Press, 1994); Fred Ross, *Conquering Goliath: Cesar Chavez at the Beginning* (Keene, Calif.: Taller Grafico, 1989); Craig Scharlin and Lilia V. Villanueva, *Philip Vera Cruz: A Personal History of Filipino Immigrants and the Farmworkers Movement* (Los Angeles: UCLA Labor Center and Asian American Studies Center, 1994); Margaret Rose, "Traditional and Nontraditional Patterns of Female Activism in the United Farm Workers of America, 1962 to 1980," *Frontiers* 11, no. 1 (1990): 25–32.

13. Brother Pete developed a close relationship with Pitzer students during an alternative spring break in 1994 when they worked together in planting eighty rose cuttings at Chavez's gravesite. Upon learning that Brother Pete had terminal cancer, the students invited him to speak on the campus and to help in the negotiations with the Marriott Corporation.

14. Jill McGougan, "The Internal and External Factors Impacting a Day Labor Center as Part of a Social Movement" (senior thesis, Pitzer College, Claremont, Calif., 2000); Patricia Camacho, "An Interpersonal Process: Redefining Traditional and Nontraditional Roles of Women Supporters and Leaders in the UFW" (senior thesis, Pitzer College, Claremont, Calif., 1995); Alex Espinosa, "The Development of Critical Consciousness through a Praxis of Reflection and Involvement" (senior thesis, Pitzer College, Claremont, Calif., 1999).

15. The city of Pomona, located thirty miles east of Los Angeles and with a population of 149,473, is a very diverse community with 64.5 percent Latinos, 17 percent White, 9.3 percent African American, 7.2 percent Asian Pacific Islander, and .3 percent American Indian (U.S. Census, 2000).

16. Matthew Tresaugue, "Pomona OKs Labor Center," *Daily Bulletin*, July 31, 1997.

17. I had already begun to write this paper when I began to collaborate with two of these students (now alumni), Suzanne Foster and Silvia Rodriguez, on a much more comprehensive study of this topic for an anthology. The article, "Organizing Immigrant Workers: Action Research and Strategies in the Pomona Day Labor Center," appears in *Latino Los Angeles: Transformations, Communities, and Activism*, edited by Enrique and Gilda Ochoa (Tucson: University of Arizona Press, 2005).

18. Six students wrote their senior theses related to the day labor center while others made presentations at the National Association of Chicana and Chicano Studies (NACCS), the American Sociological Association, the American Association of Higher Education, and the Pitzer College Undergraduate Research Conference.

19. Keith Morton, "The Irony of Service: Charity, Project, and Social Change in Service Learning," *Michigan Journal of Community Service Learning* 2 (1995): 19–32.

20. Kenneth M. Reardon, "Participatory Action Research as Service Learning," *New Directions for Teaching and Learning* 73 (Spring 1998): 57–64.

21. In its three years of operation, the CCCSI has given over one hundred awards to students, faculty, and members of the community (these have included community-based summer projects and internships, academic-year course enhancement and senior year projects, and urban and community fellowships). In this relationship, the goal is to advance the empowerment of the campus participants as well as the community participants—together—and to build the utmost capacity of both.

22. Maurrasse, *Beyond the Campus*; Nyden et al., *Building Community*; Greenwood and Levin, *Introduction to Action Research*; and Laurel Richardson, "Narrative and Sociology," *Journal of Contemporary Ethnography* 19, no. 1 (April 1990): 116–135.

23. Jim Thomas, *Doing Critical Ethnography* (Newbury Park, Calif.: Sage Publications, 1993).

Developing and Sustaining Community Research Methods and Meanings in Asian American Studies Coursework

15

PETER NIEN-CHU KIANG, KAREN L. SUYEMOTO, AND
SHIRLEY SUET-LING TANG

THIS CHAPTER DOCUMENTS EFFORTS to engage students in meaningful and relevant community research with stance, methodology, and outcomes that reflect core commitments in Asian American studies courses to empower students and communities at one U.S. urban public university. Using case studies of an introductory course, a senior research seminar, and an applied research team-based course, we highlight a variety of specific pedagogical strategies, course assignments, student reflections, and research findings for others to consider as adaptable possibilities within their own institutional contexts. Though our focus is on teaching/learning and classroom-community connections, we recognize that the potential impact of such practices in individual ethnic studies courses also depends on the institutional structure/culture of one's campus and the commitments/coherence of the institution's overall ethnic studies curriculum. Our chapter begins with some brief reflections on these larger institutional challenges.

Structural Realities and Systemic Challenges

In their paper, "Curriculum Development in Asian American Studies," presented at the second national Asian American Studies conference in 1973, Lowell Chun-Hoon, Lucie Cheng Hirata, and Alan Moriyama anticipated:

> At some point, the lines between action and education, individual service to students and collective responsibility to communities may easily diverge. . . . It is a logical result of an attempt to create, within the structure of one of the dominant institutions of existing society, a form of education that

is aimed at specific advocacy rather than mythical objectivity; that tries to be accountable to groups traditionally unrepresented in the university structure and oppressed by society-at-large.[1]

These pioneers in the Asian American studies field correctly identified what has continued to be the central contradiction facing ethnic studies praxis in U.S. higher education after more than three decades of development: simply stated, schools and universities reflect and reproduce the structure and culture of inequality that define U.S. society, albeit with resources that still allow for the development of revolutionary visions and modest transformative practices.

By structure and culture of inequality, we are referring, for example, to the segmented structure of U.S. higher education in which resources, status, and influence are asymmetrically allocated (and assumed) such that elite private Ivy League and large Research I institutions are top-tier, while working-class state universities and community colleges are counterpositioned as bottom-tier. That same hierarchy of inequality then defines the day-to-day structuring of faculty work across and within institutions through differential teaching loads and the valuing of research/scholarship over teaching or service in faculty personnel reviews and hiring decisions.

Given these systemic challenges, we find it all the more necessary to connect and empower students and communities within our own underresourced, urban public university. We have, therefore, sought out innovative models, resources, and frameworks—including many outside of ethnic studies—that others have contributed in areas such as activist and feminist scholarship, educational ethnography, service learning, university-community collaboration and civic engagement, and community-based curriculum development in order to strengthen our own capacities.[2]

Broader conceptualizations of higher education reform, particularly as articulated by Ernest Boyer and our own late colleague Ernest Lynton of the New England Resource Center for Higher Education, have provided both the language and methods with which to transform how scholarship can be defined and assessed.[3] Inspired in part by Boyer's legacy, the sustained commitments of several national professional associations have improved the conditions for community-centered ethnic studies practitioners to develop our work. Examples include the Association of American Colleges & Universities' efforts to expand diversity and democracy in the curriculum (www.aacu.org/), the American Association for Higher Education's focus on transforming faculty roles and rewards and its evolution to the National Review Board for the Scholarship of Engagement (http://schoe.coe.uga

.edu/), the Carnegie Foundation's investments in pedagogical practice (www.carnegiefoundation.org/CASTL), and Campus Compact's leadership related to service learning and civic engagement (www.campuscompact.org/). Regrettably, too few ethnic studies researchers/teachers have been directly involved in any of these national networks or initiatives.[4] By aligning intentionally with these innovative higher education practices and policy developments, however, we have learned to ask larger programmatic and institutional questions that extend beyond our own classrooms. For example:

- How well do we engage in community-building practices internally?
- How do institutional reward systems for faculty concretely value our integration of community-centered service, teaching, and research?
- How has our collective work been informed by long-term, capacity-building perspectives and sustained community partnerships?
- How do we assess and share the impact of faculty and student work, particularly in relation to community constituencies?

Although our focus in this chapter is on micro-level curricular and pedagogical praxis within specific courses, the three cases presented below reflect larger programmatic commitments to student- and community-centered teaching and learning that we have evolved among ourselves and with other colleagues in Asian American studies, Latino studies, and Africana studies. Though trained in different fields and holding primary faculty appointments in different units (Kiang, education; Suyemoto, psychology; Tang, American studies), we have, nevertheless, each individually crafted research/teaching models in Asian American studies that reflect shared capacity-building agendas, community-building sensibilities, and commitments to generate grounded theory through practice.[5] Our efforts have also reflected and contributed to how Asian American studies has developed programmatically within our specific institutional setting.

Centering Community Commitments in a Program

We are based at an urban, public, commuter university that enrolls a diverse student body of approximately 13,000. The mean age of students is twenty-five and 60 percent are the first in their families to attend college. People of color comprise roughly half of the entering undergraduate class and most students work between half- and full-time while attending school. Survival and persistence are ongoing realities for our students, many of whom manage heavy responsibilities within their immigrant families and confront numerous barriers in school and society. Facing breathtaking inequities in resources and status, they, and we, take little for granted—whether in terms of students' and communities' continuing struggles for voice and power, or simply in having enough chalk for a classroom. The founding commitments of the Asian American studies field—to empower students and communities and to transform schools and society—still resonate here.

The immediate Boston neighborhood next to our campus (known as Fields Corner, Dorchester) is home to the largest concentration of Vietnamese residents, organizations, and businesses in the Northeast and the fifth largest in the United States. The second- and fifth-largest Cambodian communities in the United States are nearby in Lowell and Lynn, as are new Chinese/Vietnamese residential and commercial areas in Quincy and Malden and the 130-year-old Boston Chinatown. Asian American students, many of whom live and work in these concentrated communities, represent 15–20 percent of our entering undergraduate class each year.

But despite these impressive geocultural realities, most students and faculty do not have opportunities to engage with the historical presence, spectacular growth, or contemporary issues of Asian Americans locally or nationally. Our Asian American studies courses, therefore, are designed to intervene educationally by enabling students of all backgrounds to develop essential critical thinking skills as well as sensibilities for community building, community service, and social responsibility, particularly in relation to local Asian American populations. By grounding our curriculum, teaching, and applied research in the realities of these dynamic local communities and by respecting the knowledge and bilingual/bicultural skills that many of our students bring to the classroom, we create powerful learning environments for all students to gain critical understandings of the struggles, contributions, and voices of diverse Asian populations over time in the United States.

We offer a range of lower-level courses such as Cambodian American Culture and Community, Becoming South Asians, Asian Women in the U.S., Resources for Vietnamese American Studies, Asian American Psychology, Politics of the Japanese American Internment, and Introduction to Asian American Writing, along with more specialized, upper-level courses such as Asian Americans and the Law, Asian American Cultures and Health Practices, Asian American Literary Voices, Asian American Media Literacy, and Teaching & Learning in Asian American Studies. Students, in collaboration with faculty and community organizations, engage in internships and applied research project seminars each semester as well.

Our curriculum accounts for 75 percent of all Asian American studies courses offered throughout the entire system of public higher education in Massachusetts,[6] and should be understood, in part, as a systemic commitment to build the organizing, documentation, and research capacities of local Asian American communities. Enabling students—many of whom come from those communities—to engage in relevant Asian American community research is an important component of this explicit capacity-building commitment.

Indeed, rather than viewing our engagement with communities as "outreach"—a relationship that places the university at the center, we have framed the question differently by considering the communities as the defining center of the relationship. From that vantage point, we continually ask:

> What are the roles and resources represented by the university—and our Asian American Studies Program specifically—that can support the healthy, long-term development of Asian American communities and the ecological well-being of the larger urban environment?

At other institutions, many faculty are similarly engaged in passionate, purposeful community research, teaching, and especially service, but they typically do so as individuals, without the coordination, coherence, or collectivity that ethnic studies programs were originally intended to provide. Even when informed by Boyer's redefinition of scholarship as discovery, interpretation, integration, and application, it is difficult to sustain and share community-centered research and teaching amidst the fragmented, individualistic culture and structure of universities.[7] Meanwhile, alternative models of collective accountability intended to transform faculty role and reward structures in recent years have yet to take root or prove more effective.[8] Moreover, doctoral student training has continuously failed to prepare future faculty with the experiences or sensibilities needed to understand— much less undertake or lead—community-centered research and teaching.[9] Professional development and faculty-student-community collaborations are needed, therefore, to share innovative, practice-based approaches as well as conceptual models, institutional resources, and national networks.

In the following three cases that compose the body of this chapter, we offer examples of actual course assignments (primarily designed by Kiang) along with specific research findings and student reflections from three types of courses that have engaged students in Asian American community research. Our goal in being both meta-analytic and descriptively concrete in these cases is to assist practitioners who intend to develop their own context-specific curricular and pedagogical interventions. We seek neither to make big claims about transforming the structure/culture of inequality in U.S. higher education nor to suggest uncritical replication of specific course activities. We do wish to show, however, that interventions with long-term impact and larger institutional implications are possible, even through the modest efforts of particular faculty in individual courses.

Teaching/Learning Case #1: Student Research/Development in an Introductory Course

This first example describes a student research project from a fourteen-week introductory Asian American studies course that enrolls thirty-five to forty students each semester. Roughly 70 percent are immigrants and international students; most are Asian or Asian American. Motivated, in part, by hearing students' names being mispronounced at the university's graduation ceremonies, the Recognizing Names project asked students to produce a reference book for university personnel with guidelines for pronouncing common names of specific Asian linguistic/cultural groups, based on library research and interviews. Student work on the research project began during the second week of the semester with a reflective writing activity focusing on students' name stories:

Reflection Memo—The Meaning of Names

Parents give children specific names for many reasons. Sometimes the meaning of a name embodies qualities that parents hope their child will become. Sometimes a name is given in honor of another individual who has been important to the family or society. Sometimes a name is chosen simply because it sounds good. In any case, everyone has stories that accompany their names.

Furthermore, when immigrants and international students come to an English-dominant society like the U.S., they often face the dilemma of either having their names mispronounced (by teachers, neighbors, coworkers, friends, etc.) or having to change to new names in English. These experiences can be very powerful because one's name has such a close relationship to one's identity. With these ideas in mind, please address the following questions in a 2–4 page memo:

What is the meaning and origin of your full name? Why was it given to you?

DEVELOPING AND SUSTAINING COMMUNITY RESEARCH METHODS   373

> Were you ever embarrassed by your name? If so, describe some specific examples and how you dealt with them. Also, please include any examples that have occurred on campus.
>
> Did you ever change your name or adopt a new name? If so, describe when and why. What did you change it to and how did/do you feel about doing it?

Students respond to this assignment with breathtaking richness—sharing intimate, individual voices with compelling cultural insights and lessons about their social/historical contexts for teaching and learning. A Vietnamese female student, for example, wrote:

> The story behind my name ["Linh," which means a wishful thing that comes true] is very powerful and I am very proud to carry this name and its meaning as my mother told me. It was wartime and very intense before I was born. After she had my brother, my mother wanted a girl because she did not want her child to grow up and join the army and die like other kids in town. She said she did not really want to have my brother for that reason, but because having a boy first is good luck and blessing for a family, especially for my father who was also the first son, so it is very important for her to have a son. At that time my father was a "head-to-head" combat officer, twenty-five days out of a month he was five hundreds yards behind the enemy line and he could be death in any second. At home, my mother could do nothing but pray and wish for the best. Coming from a Catholic family and being a very religious person, my mother believed her prayer will come true and it did. She wished to have a son first; she got it. She wished safety for my father in the battlefield; he was doing fine. She wished to have a girl after my brother; she got me. Those are the reasons why I have my name. . . . I do not think I want to change my name, not just because of its meaning and the story behind it, but also because of identity; I want American people get used to say Vietnamese names instead of myself get used to American names.[10]

The meaning of names assignment served as an initial way for students to connect the course to important reference points in their own lives. From there, the research project (developed originally by Kiang in 1993) was introduced through the following guidelines:

> *Recognizing Names: A Guide to Asian Names for the*
> *University Community*
>
> Each small group of four people is responsible for developing one section of the Guide focusing on names for a specific language/culture different from your own. The groups include: 1. Chinese (Cantonese and Mandarin); 2.

Hindi (Indian); 3. Japanese; 4. Khmer (Cambodian); 5. Korean; 6. Lao; 7. Tagalog (Filipino); 8. Thai; 9. Urdu (Pakistani); 10. Vietnamese; and 11. Editing, Design, and Production.

Each specific language section should include:

- an overview about the particular language and culture along with some history and demographics about the ethnic group in the U.S.
- sample names, pronunciations, and helpful hints
- reflections about the significance and meaning of names based on interviews with at least two students from that language group
- listings of helpful references and resources

Each group must develop a timeline and plan for its own work that includes identifying campus resources (literature, students, faculty/staff), doing interviews with appropriate individuals, and deciding on names and pronunciation strategies. The groups will have to meet regularly outside of class in order to coordinate and complete the work. Each individual is responsible for the success of the group. Students who speak a particular Asian language are also expected to be a resource for the small group that is researching that language and culture. The Guide will also include a section that describes the significance and struggles of Asian names in school, based on selected Meaning of Names memos.

Given the reality of students' conflicting responsibilities between school, family, and work, regular class time for project work was allocated on Fridays during the Monday-Wednesday-Friday fifty-minute class schedule. To accompany the listings of names with romanized pronunciations, students in each group composed brief introductions based on their library and interview research about the social context and cultural meaning of names for the particular group they were assigned. Two volunteer teaching assistants and an exceptionally dedicated group of three students who served as project editors worked closely with each of the ten specific language/culture groups to complete and prepare the text for campus-based publication.

Lessons and Impact

Through the cross-cultural, collaborative learning process within each group and the jigsaw structure that connected groups together, students developed important skills in interviewing and editing, and successfully produced and disseminated a real publication that was clearly useful to others in the university. At the same time, students—especially those with immigrant/refugee or international backgrounds—were able to demonstrate that they had strengths and resources, including critically important linguistic and cultural knowledge that others, including most university faculty, urgently needed. Rather than being discouraged, humiliated, or penalized for their weaknesses and deficits as nonnative English readers, writers, and speakers in the classroom, they experienced a teaching/learning dynamic through the Recognizing Names project that concretely maximized their assets and capacities to contribute to the university community.

In order to have institutional impact beyond the teaching/learning goals of the course, we convinced the provost, who himself had struggled with pronouncing Asian names in classes and more public settings like graduation, to fund the printing of enough guides to distribute to every faculty member and every departmental or administrative unit on campus. The provost also hosted a campus reception to celebrate the guide's publication and to thank the students for their valuable research and development. For immigrant, working-class students whose educational experiences in urban public schools are mainly characterized by struggle and survival, this kind of positive institutional acknowledgement affirms a shared social and academic identification between them and the university—a critical factor in student persistence.[11]

Furthermore, their product continues to carry institutional value for staff in various offices ranging from Institutional Advancement to Public Safety more than ten years after its completion. In addition, the guide has been distributed regularly over the years to newly hired faculty who are grateful to receive a handy, user-friendly resource that helps them deal with an issue they will face throughout their teaching careers. Just as the guide explicitly warns, however, we ask them not simply to follow the suggested name pronunciations in a formulaic, uncritical way, but to pay special attention to students' essays about the significance of their names. Finally, we stress to new faculty that this is a concrete example of what they can also model as they develop their own classroom visions and practices of how to facilitate caring relationships, powerful teaching/learning opportunities, and long-term impact with students. Many faculty have not had opportunities to think about their teaching in these ways, so the act of distributing the guide opens possibilities for further faculty dialogue and development.

Research methods and semester-long student projects are typically not pursued in introductory courses because, by definition, the introduction to content is so important. Having a content priority is especially necessary in introductory ethnic studies courses both because the interdisciplinary, critical approaches that define these fields are so complex and because the prior miseducation of students about ethnic studies subject matter is usually so deep and problematic. Nevertheless, we have found in our own teaching that it is not only pedagogically possible, but consistent with the educational mission of ethnic studies to engage students actively in the production of relevant new knowledge and resources. Works such as *Roots* and *Counterpoint* that undergirded the first generation of introductory Asian American studies courses, after all, were mainly student-produced.

Furthermore, though the target of intervention in this example is campus-based, our reality as a commuter university without dormitory residences means that our students are themselves community members. Their development of collaborative research skills and cross-cultural competence from this project can then be applied in other settings such as their neighborhoods and workplaces. Sharing respect and understanding toward diverse groups' languages, cultures, and names, after all, is fundamentally necessary to initiate and sustain multicultural coalitions within and across communities, just as it is essential to effective teaching, learning, and community research.

Drawing from the details documented in the Recognizing Names research project, we note three broader qualities that reflect ethnic studies commitments in the teaching of research methods:

1. community-building through structures and processes of reflection, sharing, and collaborative learning;
2. empowering students by drawing on their strengths of culture, language, and lived experience as assets that directly contribute to the research process;
3. identifying authentic, socially relevant questions that, through research and development, lead to the generation of new knowledge and meaningful products or resources that connect clearly with course content and that have real external impact.

In this first case, the balance between these three commitments is relatively even, as one might expect in an introductory course. In the following second case—a senior-level seminar focusing on community research—these commitments are also interwoven, but with greater emphasis on the design of appropriate questions, methods, and outcomes.

Teaching/Learning Case #2: Advanced Undergraduate Community Research/Development

Like case number 1, this example presents some of the assignments and meta-analysis related to the teaching of research methods in a particular course, titled Boston's Asian American Communities. This course is intended as a culminating senior-level research seminar for majors and concentrators in the Asian American Studies Program. Inevitably, however, some take the course without having significant prior coursework in Asian American studies and need clear orienting to the purpose and practice of Asian American community-based research.

During the first week, following a sequence of short experiential exercises, students write an introductory essay that describes their own earliest memories or impressions of Asian American communities, along with their questions and initial ideas for research project topics. After their individual responses have been compiled, circulated, and reviewed by everyone, students then write and discuss their reflections about points of connection and difference they find meaningful. This contributes to the process of collectivizing knowledge and building relationships in the classroom. It also reveals students' involvement with and images of Asian American communities, and establishes an initial inventory of their prior knowledge and lived experience that may be important to affirm and/or challenge throughout the semester.

The next two weeks focus on assigned readings and discussion/analysis in order to provide a common knowledge base about the historical development and study of Asian American communities. Short-term small groups are formed with the responsibility to "teach/learn" one assigned reading with the whole class. The specific readings help students to look bifocally at both content and method: what important themes or insights about Asian American communities are described and what sources or approaches did the authors use to gather, interpret, and present their information?

For example, by reading and discussing a series of four readings about Chinese American communities, students gain content-focused insights about dynamics of class, cultural exchange, interracial conflict, and life cycles of development in various community settings during different time periods. They also see the advantages and limitations of various community research methods, ranging from ethnography and oral history to the use of census data, local/historical newspapers, artifacts of material culture (restaurant menus), and spatial/geographic information. From these and other assigned readings, students gain common perspectives and tools with which to begin seriously planning both the content and methods of their own research projects.[12]

During the fourth week, we view the film *The Fall of the I-Hotel*, by Curtis Choy, which records the historical presence, significance, and destruction of the International Hotel block in San Francisco's Manilatown, where many low-income Filipino immigrant elders once lived.[13] The purpose of showing this vivid documentary is twofold: to clarify that Asian American communities have struggled simply to survive—a reality that profoundly shapes the context for doing Asian American community research; and to highlight the farsighted contributions of the filmmakers who, like effective community researchers, realized the importance of documenting critical community issues as they happened. The vision and intervention of the filmmakers enabled later generations to have their own opportunities to witness and learn, just as the work of current students should produce resources for others to use in the future. Students then respond in writing to the following questions:

- What images/words from the film are most memorable and/or important to you?
- Were the eviction and destruction of the hotel inevitable? Did the violence surprise you?
- Could you see/imagine yourself in any of the scenes of the film?
- It has been over twenty years since the Fall of the I-Hotel. How do you think the space has been used from then until now?
- How does the I-Hotel story relate to Boston's Asian American communities (such as Dorchester, Revere, Malden, Quincy, Lowell, or Boston Chinatown)?
- What other questions or responses do you have regarding the film?

As students imagine themselves in *The Fall of the I-Hotel* and make connections to parallel social, cultural, political, and economic struggles over land in Boston's Asian American communities, they are developing both the affective and analytic foundations needed to ask and answer with passion and clarity: "Research for what?" Before deeply exploring this essential question, however, we ask students in class to shift their paradigm of "community struggle/defense/destruction" from the fall of the I-Hotel to healthy, alternative possibilities of "community development" through the following free-writing prompt:

"Development" is one of the most important words/concepts used in describing the life of people and communities. Yet, depending on the context, "development" can have many different meanings and implications. What does "development" mean to you?

- Brainstorm a conceptual web that starts with "development" at the center and branches out to related themes that you think have important connections.

- Write a 2–3 sentence definition of what you think "development" means in relation to people and/or communities.
- Based on your definition from #2, draw a picture to illustrate what "development" means.

After students explore, share, and critique various visions and possibilities for community development, the next major assignment over a two-week period asks them to use photography as a medium to document and/or express some aspect(s) of development in Boston's Asian American communities. Students choose the format for the photo-essay—a collage, a poster, a booklet, a map, a mobile, a website, and so forth—and compose five to twelve "good" photographs that present images from an Asian American community site that they find important for others to see. Initial questions that guide their planning include:

- What themes are you looking for?
- What are some examples of visual images that strike you?
- What is your relationship to your subjects and their environment?
- What format best presents your images/ideas?
- What are the relationships of the images to each other?
- What do you hope the audience sees, thinks, and feels from your work?

The photo-essay assignment challenges students not only to think visually but also to go beyond stereotypic images and tourist-like representations. Asian language signs and storefronts are easy to capture on film, for example, but what message do they convey? In contrast, pictures of immigrant elders working in a community garden, for example, document a significant aspect of daily life and also reveal a powerful relationship which that generation shares with nature, land, and peasant roots—a reality that is easily lost or devalued in urban settings. After showing their finished photo-essays in class, students recalibrate their expectations about the time, clarity, and focus needed to produce and present high-quality community research.

As students become more deeply immersed within Boston's Asian American communities through their projects and also through role-play activities, field trips, and guest presentations by practitioners in class, they then look comparatively at other ethnic and racialized communities. Specifically, they connect their own projects to the concepts of claiming "voice," "space," and "rights" outlined in an article by Chicano studies scholar Bill Flores, about Latino cultural citizenship.[14] Students might see, for example, the documentary video *Tales from Arab Detroit*[15] to explore specific images and themes in Arab American community life and analyze the similarities and differences with Boston's Asian American communities in relation to "development." Reflecting ethnic studies praxis, these instructional activities demonstrate the value of comparative analysis while also modeling solidarity between various immigrant communities and communities of color.

By this time, students must be intensely engaged in their own research projects. Without serious planning and disciplined attention, students realize they are unable to complete substantial work by the end of fourteen weeks. To motivate planning, students respond to the following questions in a memo during the fourth week of the semester:

- What is the main question you're trying to answer through doing your project?
- What do you already know that can help you complete your project?
- Who can help you complete your project?
- What methods of research/documentation are best suited to your topic and questions?
- What specific questions will you ask someone in an interview for your research?
- What is a realistic time line/workplan to complete and present your project?
- What obstacles are in the way of your project work right now?

By the fifth week, as they shape research plans based on their own ideas and collective discussion in class, students receive the following handout, which articulates the core philosophical commitments that we expect in our teaching and learning of community research methods and meanings:

Research Project Guidelines

Along with internships and independent studies, this course is the culmination of most students' coursework in Asian American Studies. The research project represents the primary way in which you can concretely show and synthesize what you have learned from all of the Asian American Studies and/or related courses you have taken. Your project grade will be based on whether your work is "outstanding," "adequate," or "not yet adequate" in relation to four criteria:

Depth—With limited time in one semester, it is far more productive to go deeply into a specific topic with very focused questions. If your topic is defined in a superficial, overly general way, you will probably not be able to learn much that is useful or original. Others will also find it more difficult to help you if you are not very clear and concrete in what you want/need/ask. It is important for researchers, especially those with social conscience, to ask how and why over and over again—to always dig deeper, as if you were peeling away the layers of an onion.

Relevance—Your research in this course is not meant to be abstract, distant, or "just a requirement to get a grade." The results of your project should be useful and relevant to others, including those who helped you to carry out the project (this is your reciprocity or "giving back" to them) and those whose lives are affected by the issue/question/need you are focusing on (this is your community responsibility or accountability). Your project might produce, for example, a print or on-line compilation of relevant resources or a series of recommendations for services or proposed policy changes or a continuing research agenda. You need to plan clearly how the process, format, and product of your project will be useful.

Multiple Perspectives—In order to understand something deeply, you need to apply multiple methods, consider multiple points of view, and hear multiple voices. Multiple methods might include a combination of interviews, survey data, narrative writings, photographs, analysis of newspaper articles and organizational archives, attending meetings and recording observations, etc. Multiple points of view might include examining the topic in terms of its history, economic implications, political realities, cultural meanings, etc. Multiple voices might take into account differences in gender, generation, race, culture, class, religion, etc. You will not be able to include all of these "multiples," but you must show how you have taken into consideration a range of perspectives that lead you to believe or conclude what you do. In research, this process is called triangulation—making sure that you have looked from at least three distinct vantage points in order to have confidence that what you see is really there.

Reflexivity and Integrity—While the findings of a research project are very important (assuming that the data are valid and reliable), your reflection on the research process is also essential. Reflexivity refers to the dialectical, back-and-forth ways in which the researcher affects the research and the research affects the researcher. Who are you as both an insider and outsider? What have been your biases and assumptions? How did you change and grow in the process of doing your research? Integrity refers to your being honest and explicit in describing what you have done, how you have done it, and why. This includes the ways in which you account for mistakes and weaknesses in your work (which everyone has, no matter how hard one tries). Especially in community research, why should someone believe that you are sincere and your work is trustworthy? Integrity is the heart of a researcher's relationship to her/his subjects of study and to the audiences with whom s/he shares her/his work.[16]

By the end of the semester, students present their projects in class and submit final reports and related products (websites, grant proposals, video documentaries, etc.). Students typically follow a generic format for presentations and reports while also seeking to infuse their work with the qualities of depth, relevance, multiple perspectives, and reflexivity and integrity described above. The suggested outline for presentations is as follows:

Introduction: Explain the focus, background, and purpose of your project.

Methods: Explain how you carried out your project:

- How did you get your information [interviews, surveys, observations, etc]?
- What were the limitations of your work and the methods you used?

Findings and Analysis: Explain and show what you learned and why it is important:

- What are the critical issues and themes which you discovered?
- Is this what you expected to find out? Why or why not?
- How can your findings be used by others? Be as specific as possible.

Evaluation and Reflection: Reflect critically on your learning:

- What was most successful in your project?
- What was most difficult about doing your project?
- If you had more time, how would you improve or continue your project?
- What did you learn about Asian American Studies and Asian American community development?
- What did you learn about the process of doing community research?
- What did you learn about your own interests, values, strengths and weaknesses, future plans, etc?

Lessons and Impact

Final projects in this course have focused on a wide range of subjects—some defined by students, others suggested and structured in collaboration with community-based organizations and/or former students who are active in local communities. Project topics have ranged from analyses of voting patterns and health insurance coverage in specific ethnic and geographic communities to profiles of community-based farming projects and Asian heritage language schools to mural design projects and bilingual oral histories with immigrant owners/workers in ethnic small businesses. Some projects, based on participant-observation, have captured and analyzed historic moments such as the 1999 city council campaign in Lowell, Massachusetts of Chanrithy Uong, who became the first Cambodian American elected official in the United States.

At times, projects also emerge organically without prior planning. For example, when the principal of a neighborhood K–8 school recently requested assistance related to the needs of his Vietnamese-speaking students, we responded to this authentically articulated community need by having seven students in Boston's Asian American Communities course design a collaborative community service and capacity-building project to connect Vietnamese bilingual/bicultural students from our university with classroom and school-based activities to support the social, cultural, and academic development of children identified by staff or parents at the school. As a class, we re-constructed our own teaching/learning praxis by designing a real program intervention with the following goals:

1. To assist those children facing language and culture barriers in the classroom so that they will be able to participate with the community, express themselves, and prepare to achieve their hopes and dreams in the future.
2. To engage students from the university in meaningful service-learning that connects them to issues and interventions related to the fields of education and Asian American studies.
3. To demonstrate ways that our Asian American Studies Program can serve as a resource and model for education and community development through working together with the school, the children and their families, and the local community.

After designing the intervention, five Vietnamese American students then implemented the project during the following semester while receiving internship or independent study credit. In addition to providing classroom support for Vietnamese-speaking children, these students produced three issues of a bilingual school newsletter to communicate with Vietnamese parents/families, and they helped teachers identify sources for culturally responsive books and curriculum materials. We also conducted a much-appreciated two-hour professional development workshop on

Vietnamese American cultural issues in the curriculum for all of the teachers in the school. Relationships with the school have continued since then as well.

Often, the most exciting and original projects are those in which students effectively connect meaningful questions and appropriate methods with their own community-based social networks, cultural understandings, and bilingual skills. For example, a deeply insightful study about Khmer youth gang involvement was produced in this course by a Cambodian American woman whose boyfriend was, at the time, a leading gang member. Her interviews, observations, and critical analysis presented a range and depth of data that other researchers simply could not produce. Similarly, an extensive and nuanced analysis of political dynamics in the local Vietnamese community was produced in this course by a student in his late fifties who had been an elite commando in the South Vietnamese army and a political prisoner in Vietnam for over twenty years. Because of his age, rank, and status, he was able to reach and interview every important leader of every political faction within Boston's Vietnamese community and offer his own comparative, critical, bilingual analysis of their various platforms. Outside researchers, including most Asian American studies students and faculty, simply cannot gain comparable access to these populations. At the same time, insiders with direct access also cannot produce such powerful work unless they are similarly trained in ethnic studies community research methods and stance.

Like the opening case of the introductory course, this second case illustrates how a culminating community research course can effectively draw on students' strengths of culture, language, and lived experience to enhance the quality and impact of their learning and research. The following case highlights a one-semester course dedicated to the design and implementation of specific ethnic studies applied research projects. While presenting aspects of the research and training process, this third case more fully documents students' research findings and reflections. This case also suggests one way to sustain the integration of teaching/learning and community research in the curriculum for both students and faculty.

Teaching/Learning Case #3: Applied Research Teams in Asian American Studies

To strengthen our ongoing, long-term commitments to the teaching and learning of community research, we established a new, upper-level pair of permanent courses titled Applied Research in Asian American Studies I/II

(AsAmSt 397/398) in 2003 to provide students with opportunities to work together on specific projects in faculty-led collaborative research teams. Coauthors Suyemoto and Tang have each offered the course twice between spring 2003 and fall 2004. Students working with Suyemoto's Asian American Student Needs Assessment Project team have become familiar with relevant literature, developed research skills in interviewing and data analysis, and recommended ways to analyze and improve the campus-based experiences of Asian American students. In her second offering of the course, students investigated the ways that Asian American Studies courses impact Asian American students and explored implications for supporting and engaging Asian American students in education more generally.

Tang's courses have enabled students to conduct documentary research about the development of the Cambodian community in Lynn, Massachusetts, and its relationship to other ethnic, racial, and immigrant communities in Lynn historically and comparatively through oral history interviews, visual representations, and archival analyses. Her students have contributed stories and analyses for a public exhibit produced by the local heritage museum in Lynn. Publications from both Suyemoto's and Tang's applied research course projects are forthcoming.[17]

Building on Suyemoto and Kiang's use of "diversity research teams," or DRTs, in their article about ethnic studies approaches to service learning and diversity research,[18] we similarly use the term "applied research team" (ART) in this chapter to refer to the collaborative teams of students and faculty who carry out semester-length segments of applied research projects that are led by individual faculty, typically over a one-to-two-year period.

The initial design for this ART model of teaching/learning community research was piloted in 1997 as a group independent study for a team of five undergraduates and two graduate students supported by a Ford Foundation grant-funded campus diversity research initiative.[19] The team's applied research project focused on how alumni viewed the long-term meaning and impact of their learning experiences in Asian American studies courses after they had graduated, but the project also contributed to community research because, given our institutional reality as an urban public commuter campus, most of our alumni were still members of local communities. By describing the process, outcomes, and reflections that emerged from this specific project, we suggest the broader potential of ARTs as a curricular intervention that supports both meaningful student learning and relevant community research.

Seven students were recruited for this initial applied research team based on their previous coursework in Asian American studies and their interest in the research question. One was a doctoral student who had served as a teaching assistant in several Asian American studies courses and was experienced with both quantitative and qualitative research. The other six students had not conducted extensive research before. All seven students in the group were bilingual in various languages (Cantonese, Vietnamese, Korean, Japanese, and Cape Verdean Creole). As an ART, we agreed on the following goals:

- to work and learn together as a team and share experiences and connections with each other;
- to develop an updated, accurate database and to renew connections with former Asian American studies students;
- to analyze how former students view the meaning and impact of their learning experiences in Asian American studies courses;
- to gain experience with qualitative research methods of data collection and analysis, including individual and focus-group interviewing, transcribing, and coding;
- to collaborate and share our learning with two other group independent study sections supported by the campus Diversity Research Initiative.

To achieve these goals, our team met for two and a half hours each Monday afternoon to discuss research methods and questions, share ideas and problems, provide feedback to each other, present data and findings, and reflect on the research and team process. To carry out the actual research, we formed two groups: one took responsibility for data entry and analysis of a nineteen-question survey (seventeen close-ended and two open-ended questions) designed by the entire team and mailed to a database of Asian American studies alumni; the other conducted, transcribed, and analyzed interviews based on protocols also designed by the full team. Team members conducted fifteen semi-structured individual interviews with alumni, and we participated as a full team in three focus-group interviews.

In weekly class sessions, we invested significant time in training and skill-building related to data collection and analysis (survey design, focus-group and individual interview design, interview practice, transcribing, coding, grounded theory, writing and presentation strategies, etc.). We emphasized, for example, the importance of learning how to do open-coding and thematic analysis of qualitative data, using both the interview transcripts and responses to open-ended survey questions. The team also used the survey data to learn how to do simple statistical calculations of percentages and means with sorting by variables such as race, gender, number of courses taken, and year of graduation.

Significant class time was also devoted to group critique, problem-solving, and reflection related to the actual research activities of that week. Participants each kept reflective journals, maintained communication during the week through email or office visits or by phone, and developed a variety of individual and collective documents to support our research process (memos, maps, field notes, meeting transcripts, graphic charts to illustrate etic and emic analytic frameworks, etc.). The purpose of keeping a journal, for example, was to record impressions, questions, insights, and concerns as they arose in the project and to help make sense of what we were doing/learning in this research. We stressed the value of researchers' ongoing reflections as an important source of data to complement the interview transcripts and surveys. Weekly journal questions included:

- How do you feel about the way we are working together as a group? How can we improve?
- What seems important to learn from the data (interviews, surveys, etc.)? What impresses or surprises you?
- What are some questions or problems that you want/need to address?
- What connections are you finding between the research and your own experience?
- How are your ideas and perspectives about the research changing? How do you think you are changing?
- What are your next steps for the coming week?

By the end of the semester, each student had fulfilled aspects of our original ART goals, particularly in gaining experience with research methods and generating significant findings related to the continuing impact of Asian American studies. An immigrant student from Hong Kong, for example, commented critically on his own growth as a researcher:

> Personally, I am still learning how to do the analysis. I am confused about how to interpret and analyze the quotes from the interviews. I feel like my analysis is not in-depth enough. . . . When reading the transcript, I need to read carefully and think about what the person was trying to tell me.

A Korean student emphasized the importance of the team's shared learning from each other:

> The findings of a research project are very important and also the gaining of knowledge and research method skill. However, to me, reflections and

insights from each group member are much more valuable and meaningful because it is alive information and can't get from anywhere, even textbooks.

In their evaluations, each student noted that time was too limited to carry out the ambitious research and development agenda we had envisioned. They noted how difficult it was in only one semester to develop a caring research team while learning about research methods and also producing meaningful research with real products. A Cape Verdean student, for example, described some of the pain involved in trying to achieve such high expectations across our five ART goals:

> Something that I will never forget about this research process is the feeling of letting the group down. I never thought that I would feel that way until I realized I was falling behind. I did not know what was going on at times and sometimes felt frustrated with the entire project. I found myself panicking and feeling like everything was falling apart.

In fact, attending to the team's dynamics emerged as the single most important lesson from our work, as the doctoral student explained in her reflection paper about the training process:

> For researchers, it is normal to confront unpredictable elements in the process of doing research. Research strategies need to be flexible to allow for changes in the process, especially when initiating a new research project. Appropriate methods need to be developed from practice rather than following standard or traditional methods uncritically, even if they have been successful or tested by others. But for our students, the unclarity and flexibility inherent in real research directly conflicts with their assumptions about work to fulfill requirements of a course. They wanted to know specifically and well in advance what to complete in terms of assignments during the semester. Because their expectations about doing research differed with ours, they became frustrated when we could not provide simple, clear guidelines to follow, especially in analyzing the data. This added to their stress levels and further lowered their motivation. As our work became more difficult (when we began coding data, for example), students began to negotiate the extensions for their research in order to complete assignments for other classes which seemed "clearer."

Despite their difficulties, students recognized the importance of sustaining the research beyond one semester for the sake of our own continued learning and program development as well as to support comparable efforts at other institutions. After much struggle with the process, for example, a Chinese Vietnamese refugee student reflected:

> At different times during this research project, I have wondered about "Why are we taking so many little steps in this gathering of data? It's such a waste of time!" I thought we could just do the interview and pick out lines or quotes that are important to answering the questions we were asking. But now that we are at the end of the semester, I realize that all those steps were important because we are not the only people working with the data, and that people from other semesters might be looking at these also [as the research continues]. I feel now that I was somewhat selfish before; I didn't think about who else might benefit from the hard work we have done to find out all this information.

Reflecting on the findings, the Cape Verdean student in the team proudly asserted: "Maybe other universities will follow in our footsteps and pay close attention to our research. . . . These findings are a way for professors, deans, department heads, students and President to know what needs to be done and how to do it."

Lessons and Impact

To continue the project's research/development and reach broader audiences, we gained grant funding from the Ford Foundation and National Association of Student Personnel Administrators (NASPA) to extend the work for an additional three semesters. Although we could not replicate the intense ART environment shared by the original team, we were able to continue using the ART-generated research instruments (interview protocols and survey questions) by assigning alumni research projects to interested students in the introductory Asian American studies courses. With this came a shift in emphasis from teaching/learning to prioritizing data collection and analysis.

At the end of the second year of research, a total of eighty-eight alumni had completed the survey. Respondents' years of graduation ranged from 1988 to 1999 with a mean of 1995. Roughly half (47 percent) had taken only one Asian American studies course and the other half (53 percent) had taken more than one course. We also conducted seventy structured individual interviews with alumni, including fifty-eight in person and twelve via email. Nearly all interviews were conducted and transcribed by students, including several that were conducted in native languages (Chinese, Vietnamese, Japanese, Korean) and translated to English as part of the transcription process.

Women comprised 57 percent of the interviewees; 43 percent were men. The racial backgrounds of the interviewees were 69 percent Asian, 4 percent black, 6 percent Latino, and 21 percent white. Two-thirds of the Asian informants were refugees/immigrants, 19 percent were U.S.-born, and 14 percent had matriculated as international students with visas from Japan, Korea, and Hong Kong. This profile is similar to the student composition in Asian American studies courses. The ethnic profiles of the Asian interviewees included 15 percent Cambodian, 35 percent Chinese, 6 percent Chinese Vietnamese, 2 percent Filipino, 10 percent Japanese, 4 percent Korean, 2 percent Lao, and 25 percent Vietnamese, which also matches well with the demographics of our student body.

From both quantitative and qualitative data, we found that Asian American studies courses had direct relevance and meaning to alumni in their jobs or careers, continued education, family life, interpersonal relationships, community involvement, and personal identities. Ninety-one percent of respondents said they had gained a better understanding of the immigrant experience; 86 percent stated that they had a better awareness of racial stereotypes; 65 percent said that their writing and thinking skills had improved; 70 percent noted that an Asian American studies course had enabled them to make friends outside of their race or ethnic group; and 83 percent indicated that an Asian American studies course had helped them to interact more comfortably with Asian Americans.

In analyzing the data by race, Asian alumni noted that the impact of becoming more aware of who they are in U.S. society was nearly as powerful as gaining social awareness about the immigrant experience and racial stereotyping. Interestingly, Asian men—far more than Asian women—indicated that their learning had a strong impact on their family life. In contrast, Asian women, far more than Asian men, indicated that their learning from Asian American studies courses had affected their jobs and careers. These results suggested that Asian American studies courses not only had long-term effects on the social awareness and identities of Asian alumni, but also contributed to their redefining of gender roles and relationships.

Black and Latino alumni also noted that taking an Asian American studies course had influenced their level of social awareness, and, to a higher degree than whites, had also influenced their identity. White alumni noted long-term effects of the course on their academic interests, relationships with friends, and level of community involvement. Asians and Latinos, to a higher degree than blacks or whites, indicated that Asian American studies coursework enabled them to become more aware of their own status in U.S. society and to feel more comfortable speaking up.

Complementing the survey results, qualitative data from the seventy interviews were remarkably consistent for both Asian and non-Asian alumni. For example, a Latina who graduated in 1996 and works as a job developer for low-income communities recalled:

> I learned that I have a lot more in common with the Asian community. . . . I found a lot of pieces of my identity with my friends of countries like China, Korea, Japan, etc. . . . I felt connected and it was very exciting to feel and know that I had friends who are Asian American who really care for me. . . . I can communicate and relate to people when I have knowledge of their history and struggles as well as achievements. This is what I learned and pass on to others.

An African American alumna who graduated in 1990 was one of many informants who described the significance of cross-racial learning:

> As a Black person, I hate to be stereotyped, and I'm sure that Asians feel the same way. . . . When people of different races have an opportunity to interact and get to know each other, they often like each other. Like I met many people I probably would have never had the opportunity to meet and get to know [from the courses]. I learned that I liked them and respected them as people.

Similarly, a white alumna from 1989 who became a public school teacher reflected:

> Generally, I am much more comfortable around Asians than I used to be. I don't view them as the "others" anymore. . . . I finally decided to become a teacher of English as a second language, and I am sure that the Asian American course had some effect on that decision, partly by giving me a stronger sense of empathy for the immigrants' experience and at the same time giving me a greater sense of respect.

Alumni were also able to apply their learning from Asian American studies courses in their roles as parents. For example, a Cambodian interviewee who took one Asian American studies course in 1989 and is raising two children explained:

> [My studies] have an effect on my way of raising my children. I will raise my children to be aware of their parents' root and to respect others, regardless of race, class, and gender. . . . I gained a lot of knowledge from Asian American studies courses and it will always stay with me.

These cross-racial and cross-generational effects involving alumni as teachers and parents represent some of the exciting qualitative findings that emerged from the study. Their voices illustrate powerful ways in which Asian American studies teaching and learning contribute to longer-term civic life and community capacity-building, and suggest the need for further interventions within and across multiple domains ranging from teacher preparation and parent organizing to voter registration and community cultural development.[20]

Though difficult to complete within one semester, the alumni research process modeled those same three qualities described in the first and second cases that characterize the nature of ethnic studies commitments in the teaching of research methods. In each case, students and faculty constructed collaborative learning communities based on individual and collective reflection and action. While gaining familiarity with various methods of research and analysis, students enhanced the research process by developing strategic ways of engaging their cultural and linguistic competence, social networks, and lived experience. Most importantly, students in each case were able to pursue socially relevant questions, produce important resources, and present significant findings that various university and community constituencies continue to find meaningful.

The alumni research process also clarified other aspects that have proven to be essential in designing effective ARTs since then, such as the critical involvement of graduate students as team members and mentors working with the faculty and undergraduates. In a recent Suyemoto-led ART, for example, a Korean immigrant doctoral student in clinical psychology reflects:

> As a first year graduate student in a new school, the team provided me with a community and support system I did not expect. I learned a tremendous amount about mentoring and being mentored . . . about balance, keeping people accountable, and sharing knowledge and resources. It was cool to be in a position where I can impact someone's personal and educational growth.

Although Asian American Studies does not itself offer a graduate degree at our university, we are each affiliated with graduate programs (education, clinical psychology, and American studies) and have successfully created intersecting circles of support and shared learning between the faculty with both graduate and undergraduate students through the ARTs. These kinds of powerful learning communities are typically difficult to establish at urban commuter institutions, and contribute not only to student learning but also increased student persistence for everyone involved. Thus, ARTs can be important contexts for preparing graduate students to be more effective as faculty in the future and for recruiting underrepresented undergraduates into graduate programs where they can play similar mentoring roles while participating in meaningful research and development. We will continue to extend and adapt this model in our future work.

Conclusions

At the turn of the new century, the blue-ribbon Kellogg Commission on the Future of State and Land-Grant Universities called on public higher education institutions to become "engaged" by responding to the diverse demographic profiles of students, by connecting students' learning with real-world research and practice, and by allocating resources to address the critical issues of communities.[21] Their call, though urgent and appreciated, merely restated some of the core commitments that ethnic studies programs have struggled to sustain, albeit from marginal positions, within universities throughout the past three decades. Nevertheless, it is one of many recent examples in mainstream higher education institutional reform—along with community service learning, global education, diversity research, collaborative learning communities, and civic engagement, to name a few—that should recognize (and reward) ethnic studies praxis for its continued modeling of innovative best practices.

In that spirit, the three cases of teaching and learning highlighted in this chapter are meant to illustrate some of the specific ways faculty and students have engaged with the methods and meanings of doing community research through Asian American studies courses at our urban public university. These curricular and pedagogical practices reflect a foundation of earlier work,[22] but articulate well with current visions such as those recommended in *Greater Expectations*, a national report by the Association for American Colleges & Universities, to revitalize liberal education by enabling college students to become informed, empowered, and responsible learners.[23]

Through continued curricular and program development in Asian American studies, we have developed a range of individual tactics and shared strategies within our particular institutional context in order to:

- facilitate socioculturally responsive and academically relevant learning communities that support student persistence, mentoring, and connection at our urban, working class, commuter university;
- document significant issues, needs, and interventions in local Asian American communities and on campus, recognizing that our own students and alumni are themselves members and participants

within local neighborhoods, workplaces, and community-based institutions;
- develop scholarly resources in our fields and research capacities in local Asian American communities through connecting ethnic studies methods, stance, and analytic frameworks with students' indigenous social networks and cultural/linguistic knowledge;
- sustain faculty engagement with community research through the curriculum, particularly by supporting the work of applied research teams as core commitments of regular faculty teaching loads over multiple semesters.

Although some of the teaching/learning examples in the three cases reflect more than a decade of curricular and pedagogical development, primarily by one person, the more recent design and implementation of the applied research course model reflects shared visions and collective contributions within our program. ARTs, in particular, have emerged as productive and sustainable forms through which to connect scholarship, service, and teaching. Given that service activities are not as highly valued as scholarship or teaching in the evaluation of faculty for tenure and promotion, there are structural barriers and systemic challenges that discourage faculty engagement with community-based activities. Even if institutional rhetoric supports civic engagement, the service and outreach mission of institutions is typically left to the ad-hoc initiative of individual faculty.[24] Moreover, faculty at lower-tier, underresourced institutions with heavy instructional loads may find it difficult to balance or integrate teaching with scholarship and community involvement. Our current work suggests, however, that ARTs can bring together community-centered realities with the regular teaching of research methods and field-specific content as well as the possibilities of scholarly outcomes that reflect linguistically and culturally responsive research methodologies and community-based processes of knowledge production.[25]

Finally, we are arguing that under-resourced, urban, public institutions like our own—or others such as community colleges that have even less prestige and flexibility—are actually critical sites for ethnic studies research and development as well as teaching and learning of ethnic studies research methods because our student populations are so deeply grounded within their communities' pasts, presents, and futures. When guided by a curriculum and pedagogy that connect students' (and faculties') strengths, passions, and questions with meaningful projects and powerful practices defined by depth, relevance, multiple perspectives, and reflexivity and integrity, then the impact of our shared teaching/learning and research is often tangible, if not transformative.

At the same time, we recognize that the working-class and immigrant/refugee students who are critical to the success of our courses and applied research teams will most likely not gain access to major research grants or Ph.D. programs or publishing opportunities—despite their remarkable strengths and skills—because their backgrounds do not match well with the norms and priorities of resource-rich foundations, research universities, and academic presses. This is a great loss, not only for those individuals who deserve such opportunities, but more importantly for the fields of study that continue to go uninformed by their compelling and original contributions to Asian American community research and development.

Despite (or because of) this, however, we appreciate with even greater clarity our opportunities to teach and learn with students like the thirty-five-year-old mother of three who noted after an intense semester in Suyemoto's most recent ART:

> I really felt this source of pride in my work and the attachment began to grow even more. . . . I had never had this kind of experience, in such depth. . . . It is like having a child. Suddenly, one day there is a new life in the room, a life which previously did not exist, and this life depends on me. This is how I felt about my contribution to the research.

Having graduated after taking Asian American studies courses with each of us and now pursuing her M.Ed with plans to become an urban high school history teacher, this student's comparison of her ART experience to that of having a child is neither abstract nor fanciful. Indeed, her groundedness in the experience of giving life enables her to echo and add to the voices of our Cambodian refugee students from more than a decade ago who—after having profoundly witnessed death—described their experiences in Asian American studies courses specifically in terms of being "educated for life" and "coming alive, full of life!" In the same way, the emergence of Suyemoto's and Tang's ART courses reflects not only innovative new models of developing and sustaining community research methods and meanings in Asian American studies, but also the legacy and continuing construction of our program's much-needed "pedagogies of life and death."[26]

Acknowledgments

The authors thank our reviewers for their helpful suggestions and the editors for their enormous patience. We also express deep appreciation to our students, colleagues, community partners, and alumni associated with the Asian American Studies Program at UMass Boston.

Notes

1. Lowell Chun-Hoon, Lucie Hirata, and Alan Moriyama, "Curriculum Development in Asian American Studies," in *Proceedings of National Asian American Studies Conference II*, ed. George Kagiwada, Joyce Sakai, and Gus Lee (Davis, Calif.: University of California, Davis, 1973), 83–90.

2. Charles R. Hale, ed., *Engaging Contradictions: Theory, Politics and Methods of Activist Scholarship* (Berkeley: University of California Press, forthcoming, 2008); José Z. Calderón, "Partnership in Teaching and Learning: Combining the Practice of Critical Pedagogy with Civic Engagement and Diversity," *Peer Review* 5 no. 3 (Spring 2003): 6–9; Yali Zou and Henry T. Trueba, eds., *Ethnography and Schools: Qualitative Approaches to the Study of Education* (Lanham, Md.: Rowman & Littlefield, 2002); Linda Trinh Vo and Rick Bonus, *Contemporary Asian American Communities: Intersections and Divergences* (Philadelphia: Temple University Press, 2002); Felix M. Padilla, *The Struggle of Latino/Latina University Students: In Search of a Liberating Education* (New York: Routledge, 1999); Janet Eyler and Dwight E. Giles, *Where's the Learning in Service Learning?* (San Francisco: Jossey-Bass, 1999); Lane Ryo Hirabayashi, ed., *Teaching Asian America: Diversity & the Problem of Community* (Lanham, Md.: Rowman & Littlefield, 1998); Timothy P. Fong, "Reflections on Teaching about Asian American Communities," in *Teaching Asian America: Diversity & the Problem of Community*, ed. Lane Hirabayashi (Lanham, Md.: Rowman & Littlefield, 1998), 143–150; Zelda F. Gamson, "Higher Education & Rebuilding Civic Life," *Change*, January–February 1997, 10–13; Elsa Auerbach, *From the Community to the Community*, Community Training for Adult and Family Literacy Project Final Report (Boston: Boston Adult Literacy Fund, 1994).

3. Ernest L. Boyer, *Scholarship Reconsidered*, Carnegie Foundation for the Advancement of Teaching (San Francisco: Jossey-Bass, 1990); C. E. Glassick, M. Taylor Huber, and G. I. Maeroff, *Scholarship Assessed*, Ernest L. Boyer Project of the Carnegie Foundation for the Advancement of Teaching (San Francisco: Jossey-Bass, 1997); Ernest A. Lynton, *Making the Case for Professional Service* (Washington, D.C.: American Association for Higher Education, 1995).

4. Some notable exceptions who have bridged these worlds of higher education innovation and ethnic studies praxis include: José Calderón, Nadinne Cruz, Evelyn Hu-DeHart, Gregory Yee Mark, and Danny Teraguchi.

5. James D. Bui, Shirley Suet-Ling Tang, and Peter N. Kiang, "The Local/Global Politics of Boston's Viet-Vote," *AAPI Nexus: Policy, Practice & Community* 2, no. 2 (2004): 10–18; Karen L. Suyemoto and Peter N. Kiang, "Diversity Research as Service Learning," *Academic Exchange Quarterly* 7, no. 2 (Summer 2003): 71–75; Peter N. Kiang, "Long-Term Effects of Diversity in the Curriculum: Analyzing the Impact of Asian American Studies in the Lives of Alumni from

an Urban Commuter University," in *Diversity on Campus: Reports from the Field* (NASPA: Student Affairs Administrators in Higher Education, 2000), 23–25.

6. Amanda Yu, "Asian American Studies Course Offerings in Massachusetts Colleges and Universities" (unpublished document, University of Massachusetts, Boston, 2002); Peter N. Kiang and Kenneth Wong, "The Status of Asian Americans in Public Higher Education in Massachusetts: Asian American Studies in the Curriculum," unpublished report, (Institute for Asian American Studies, University of Massachusetts, Boston, 1996).

7. Judith A. Ramaley, "Supporting Public Scholarship," *Peer Review* 2, no. 1 (Fall 1999): 13–14.

8. D. Hiley, S. Kennedy, and S. Robbins, "Faculty Roles and Collective Responsibilities," *Metropolitan University* 8, 1997, 242–252.

9. Carol Geary Schneider, "Changing Practices in Liberal Education; What Future Faculty Need to Know," *Peer Review* 6, no. 3 (Spring 2004): 4–7.

10. Peter N. Kiang, "Voicing Names and Naming Voices: Pedagogy and Persistence in an Asian American Studies Classroom," in *Crossing the Curriculum: Multilingual Learners in College Classrooms*, ed. Vivian Zamel and Ruth Speck (Mahwah, N.J.: Lawrence Erlbaum, 2003), 207–220.

11. Suyemoto and Kiang, "Diversity Research"; Peter N. Kiang, "Stories and Structures of Persistence: Ethnographic Learning through Research and Practice in Asian American Studies," in *Ethnography and Schools: Qualitative Approaches to the Study of Education*, ed. Yali Zou and Henry T. Trueba (Lanham, Md.: Rowman & Littlefield, 2002), 223–255; Peter N. Kiang, "Persistence Stories and Survival Strategies of Cambodian Americans in College," *Journal of Narrative and Life History* 6, no. 1 (1996): 39–64.

12. See Victor Nee and Brett de Bary Nee, "Grant Avenue," in *Longtime Californ': A Documentary Study of an American Chinatown* (Palo Alto, Calif.: Stanford University Press, 1986), 117–122; Imogene L. Lim and John Eng-Wong, "Chow Mein Sandwiches: Chinese American Entrepreneurship in Rhode Island," in *Origins and Destinations* (Los Angeles: Chinese Historical Society of Southern California, 1994), 417–436; K. Scott Wong, "'The Eagle Seeks a Helpless Quarry': Chinatown, the Police, and the Press—The 1903 Boston Chinatown Raid Revisited," *Amerasia Journal* 22, no. 3 (1996): 81–103; and David C. Lai, "Introduction" and "Retrospect and Prospect," in *Chinatowns: Towns within Cities in Canada* (Vancouver: University of British Columbia Press, 1988), 1–11 and 273–285.

13. Available from the Center for Asian American Media, asianamericanmedia.org/.

14. William V. Flores, "Citizens vs. Citizenry: Undocumented Immigrants and Latino Cultural Citizenship," in *Latino Cultural Citizenship: Claiming Identity, Space, and Rights*, ed. William V. Flores and Rina Benmayor (Boston: Beacon Press, 1997), 252–277 and 289–290.

15. Available from New Day Films, www.newday.com.

16. Students in this course have typically not been asked to gain Institutional Review Board approvals for research with human subjects, though this depends on the specific project. The policy decision by the U.S. Office for Human Research Protection (OHRP) of the Department of Health and Human Services (HHS) that oral history interviewing projects in general do not involve the type of research defined by HHS regulations and are therefore excluded from Institutional Review Board oversight is noteworthy here. See: omega.dickinson.edu/organizations/oha/org_irb.html.

17. Shirley Tang, "Challenges of Policy and Practice in Under-Resourced Asian American Communities: Analyzing Public Education, Health, Development Issues with Cambodian American Women," *Asian American Law Journal* 13 (Spring 2008).

18. Suyemoto and Kiang, "Diversity Research."

19. Center for Improvement of Teaching, *Diversity Research at an Urban Commuter University*, monograph (Boston: University of Massachusetts, Boston, 1999); Peter N. Kiang, "After the Initiative: Envisioning Diversity Research Sustainability," in *Diversity Research at an Urban Commuter University*, Center for the Improvement of Teaching (Boston: University of Massachusetts, Boston, 1999), 85–104.

20. Peter N. Kiang, "Linking Strategies and Interventions in Asian American Studies to K–12 Classrooms and Teacher Preparation," *International Journal of Qualitative Studies in Education* 17, no. 2 (2004): 199–225; Bui, Tang, and Kiang, "Boston's Viet-Vote."

21. Kellogg Commission on the Future of State and Land-Grant Universities, *Returning to our Roots: The Engaged Institution*, 3rd report (February 1999).

22. Kiang, "Effects of Diversity"; "Writing from the Past, Writing for the Future: Healing Effects of Asian American Studies in the Curriculum," *Transformations: A Resource for Curriculum Transformation and Scholarship* 9, no. 2 (Fall 1998): 132–149; "Pedagogies of Life and Death: Transforming Immigrant/Refugee Students and Asian American Studies," Duke University Press, *Positions* 5, no. 2 (1997): 529–555.

23. Association of American Colleges & Universities, *Greater Expectations: A New Vision for Learning as a Nation Goes to College*, National Panel Report (Washington, D.C., 2002). Also see: www.greaterexpectations.org.

24. Sharon E. Singleton, Cathy A. Burack, and Deborah J. Hirsch, *Faculty Service Enclaves: A Summary Report*, New England Resource Center for Higher Education, February 1997.

25. Suyemoto and Kiang, "Diversity Research"; Tang, "Challenges of Policy and Practice"; and *An Assessment of Khmer American Community Needs in Lynn, Massachusetts*, research report (Lynn, Mass.: Khmer Association of the North Shore, 2005).

26. Kiang, "Pedagogies of Life and Death."

A Pedagogy for Ethnic Studies
Experiences and Methods for Teaching

16

PAMELA RALSTON

IN THINKING ABOUT THE USE and integration of research methods in an ethnic studies classroom, I have struggled over some of the disciplinary-specific issues inherent in our interdisciplinary field of study. As a literary critic who teaches Comparative American Ethnic Literature, I rarely articulate our work in the classroom as "research methods." Rather, I work consciously to foreground my own theoretical and ideological perspective and to help students to formulate their own theories and perspectives. I also teach disciplinary-specific methods and theories alongside a history of the development of ethnic studies as an interdisciplinary field of study formed around the notions of social justice, social change, and the cultural imperative of revealing ethnic difference and experience. Grounded in this history, this essay clarifies a pedagogy based on the experience of teaching large, introductory courses on Comparative American Ethnic Literature. Drawn from that experience, a practical, albeit partial, pedagogy is outlined, which explores how to integrate literature, culture, history, and theoretical research methods in a classroom that is focused on student involvement in the form of discussion, presentation, research, and writing. Paula Moya and Satya Mohanty's postpositivist realism provides this essay with a framework for theorizing the classroom as a space within ethnic studies that responds to the crucial inclusion of experience and identity in a theoretically mediated interpretation of American ethnic groups. This pedagogy strives to make transformative scholarship a reality in the classroom. Over the last three decades, scholars in ethnic studies have worked to transform our curricula, and by doing so have changed the institutions where we teach. In addition to changing the curriculum, I have sought to change my approach to teaching: from theorizing about texts to allowing texts to offer up theory, and from theorizing about the classroom to encouraging the members in the classroom to theorize.

Course Context: Teaching after Curriculum Transformation

The pedagogy I argue for here is one developed while teaching an introductory-level course in comparative American ethnic literature at a large research university in the Northwest. This course is a requirement for our majors, and is linked with two other required introductory courses, one comparatively treating the history of American ethnic groups and one addressing contemporary social and cultural conditions of American ethnic groups through a social science and cultural studies perspective. Set alongside these courses, the goals of the comparative American ethnic literature course are: introducing students to the field of ethnic studies; introducing students to contemporary American ethnic voices in literary expression; and introducing students to literary theory and research methods useful for an interdisciplinary study of American ethnic literature. I do this by organizing the course around a series of connected themes: identity, community, individualism, and family, as well as assimilation, double consciousness, and epistemology. I approach these themes through the connecting rubric of storytelling. Throughout the 1990s, feminist and/or ethnic studies scholars called for the transformation of the curricula of our classes, arguing for a reconfiguring of the canon of classical, white, Western, and/or European texts by either integrating texts by writers who had been marginalized or by shifting the curriculum entirely to consider culture and art through those previously marginalized texts. The ethnic literature classroom is a place to enact that alternative to the traditional canon, but simply changing what we teach is not enough; we need to change how we teach.

As I construct the reading list for this course, and others, I choose texts that represent the literary heritages of people of color in the United States. The role of the first-person narrative in the form of slave narratives and spiritual conversion narratives in these literary legacies is a crucial element in the literature of this course. The role of testimonial literature, particularly that which bears witness for a collective experience, is central in the literary and political history of the struggle by people of color to evidence subjectivity and voice. Beyond evidencing humanity in the face of dehumanizing racism, this literature interpellates its audience, rhetorically constructing nations of readers and discursively locating people of color as subjects in writing and in the literary landscape. While the reading for this introductory course is primarily contemporary novels and first-person narratives, we approach these readings with a literary history of the emergence and variety of earlier works by ethnic writers. I explain both in the syllabus and in class meetings how the chronologies and cross currents of our literary past inform and are represented in the works we read. As part of their research, students investigate historical and biographical information for the writers we read and for the authors who have influenced them. Students share their findings with the larger class in the form of group presentations, introductions to various discussions, and study guides, as well as referring back to this history as cultural context for the analyses both in discussion and in the expository writing. In a technologically viable setting, a class such as mine could create a series of related websites that serve to represent the backgrounds and areas of interest for the course. Multiple resources are now available, such as the Schomburg Center for Research in Black Culture's photo archives and digital collections, as well as a variety of resources detailing the history of Native Americans and immigrants.[1] We use these resources to provide the background stories and the histories behind the literature we read.

A pedagogy appropriate for teachers in ethnic studies with its multidisciplinary perspective has specific goals, objectives, and learning outcomes: provide students with critical experience with the cultures, histories, and literature of people of color in the United States; provide the history and theoretical perspectives of the discipline; provide students opportunities to read, research, write critically about what they learn; and provide a forum in the classroom for enacting change inside and outside the classroom. As Johnnella E. Butler describes teaching in our field, we work to teach the substance, "the content and the perspective to help them understand the complexity of the United States, its values, its conflicts, and it potential, so that students can move to the *significance* of their education."[2] The pedagogy advanced here is one that integrates research methodology in the forms of literary theory and criticism into the classroom discussion and into the requirements and learning outcomes of study in ethnic studies. Such a rigorous method of teaching foregrounds the hope that "students will inevitably encounter the nation's diversity and the need to maintain equity and social justice as active goals."[3] Ethnic studies engages students in conscious interactions with diversity, equity, and social justice. The study of ethnic literature should help to ground those goals in writing that can fill teachers and students with joy, wonder, and critical insight in a plurality of voices, cultural expressions, and ideas.

In *Teaching to Transgress*, bell hooks argues for a "liberatory pedagogy," one that counteracts a binaristic relationship between student and teacher and mind and body.[4] A liberatory pedagogy exposes the classroom as a site of work, of labor, asking students and teachers to engage in that work together. In addition to the work of transforming curricula that scholars in ethnic studies have worked toward for over three decades, hooks calls for a transformation of classroom practices. She underscores the importance of sharing perspectives, experiences, and speaking. Hooks bases her pedagogical process in the recognition and valorization of the crucial intersections between race, class, and sexuality. She asks teachers to not only include those issues in reading lists and syllabi, but also to develop courses designed to empower students within a learning community to actively engage in discussion, analysis, and scholarship about those concerns and our relationships to them. As an example of the importance of changing not only classrooms but also the institution itself, she encourages placing:

> the emphasis on creating in classrooms learning communities where everyone's voice can be heard, their presence recognized and valued. . . . When those of us in the academy who are working class or from working-class backgrounds share our perspectives, we subvert the tendency to focus only on the thoughts, attitudes and experiences of those who are materially privileged. (184)

Using class positions as the focus here, hooks argues for dramatic reconfiguring of two crucial issues concerning identity and the academy: firstly, once those of us who are not materially or racially privileged enter the classroom, we enact some level of transformation, but secondly, we must share those experiences in fully elaborated ways in order to engage in subverting dominant tendencies. For those of us whose subject positions may well contribute to the tendency to focus on the privileged, we must find ways to counteract that tendency by creating classrooms that promote sharing multiple perspectives.

I work under the premise that students who sign up for my course and who have not yet met me probably hope that their new class will be taught by a person of color, perhaps by someone who looks like them. The first few minutes before the bell rings on the first day, several students will ask me if they have the right room, even though I've written the course title and number on the board, along with my name. I begin immediately to foreground a theoretically informed perspective as I introduce myself in a classroom. As a white scholar trained in comparative literature, I enter into ethnic studies as an already comparative space, and I make explicit my positionality in relation to the people in the classroom and in relation to the writers, texts, and cultures we read and discuss. I am both a white body and a white perspective occupying space that has been made difficult for people of color to access (my particular position is complicated by being the only white faculty member in a department of people of color on a campus largely populated by whites). I speak directly about whiteness with students, about how the privilege of being a member of the dominant culture informs my experience of our collective society, academia, the literature we are reading, and the conversations we are having. As part of the pedagogical process, I refer to myself as an embodied person. I can refer to whites as "my people" (on occasion with derision or pain) or to connect a reference in a text to me as a body (such as Jean Toomer's starkly imagistic image of a white man, interestingly named Art, whom he describes as "a purple facsimile . . . a purple fluid, carbon-charged that effervesces" revealing that for "some reason white skins are not supposed to live at night").[5] In a pedagogical process, making this identification overt requires conscious grace. Students of color immediately recognize the erasure of difference that strives to make the classroom a "safe" place, but namely safe for the instructor. Conflict and dissension, however, are part of the constitutive elements of a course treating identity, ethnicity, class, and gender; what we read and discuss replicates and challenges the very history and social constructions we work to dismantle. To ignore or strive to eradicate (superficially) these points of difference undermines the project and stops transformation and removes part of the very language necessary for the discussion. My potential discomfort with my racialized body plays a role; whiteness has power most when it succeeds in erasing itself.

I walk a fine line in this classroom conversation with this clarification, however, as I do here in this essay; my whiteness needs to be addressed, but, as whiteness often does, it threatens to take over any discussion of ethnicity and positionality. In a discussion of ethnicity in the United States, however, we must contend with the topic of "whiteness" in order to examine adequately the historical "cultural imperative" to whiteness that has conditioned the construction and continued enforcement of racist ideologies and white supremacy. We discuss on that first day how to begin to change the body of academia, considering what it means to have teachers of color and/or teachers from working-class backgrounds on campus, in primary and secondary school. As a white ally, a part of my pedagogical practice is to mentor students of color to promote education as a means of changing academia and other institutions. I am unabashed in my recruitment of students into education. Ethnic studies is not simply a field of study; it is a studied account of bringing about social change, starting with classrooms, curricula, and campuses. As an example of transforming the classroom space, hooks calls for movement in the classroom, where the teacher moves physically to underscore embodiment and engagement. A seemingly simple solution, moving away from podia and lecterns is a symbolic move that decentralizes authority in the classroom and authorizes other voices as valid and teacherly. Despite two decades of feminists calling for reconfigured classroom spaces, however, I still encounter rooms (even in an expensive new building donated by computer magnates) where seats are bolted to the floor and where the front of the room is filled with a podium (now electronically and digitally reconfigured). Moving around in these rooms, sitting with students and underscoring, as hooks suggests, that teachers are bodies who labor does begin to desediment the traditional focus of the classroom on the droning lecturer and students' passive learning. Symbolic moves of this sort, however, never succeed in completely de-authorizing the role and voice of the teacher in our courses, nor should they. Expertise is an important component that can situate student experience and observation in a larger theoretical and historical framework, as well as serve to facilitate conversations toward larger goals. It is my job to add to the theoretical frameworks with which students enter the classroom, working to reveal the various epistemologies and ideological frames that may ground our conversations and the literary texts we read.

I also model and work to enact ways to bring the multiplicity of voices and experiences of the students in our learning community to the center of our course. As Paula M. Moya makes clear in *Learning from Experience: Minority Identities, Multicultural Struggles*, experience and perspective are theoretically mediated and provide epistemologically viable tools through which we can begin to read literature that makes voicing experience and testimonial arts discursive. As a theorist, hooks explains that theorizing is crucial to the pedagogical process as well as to her own survival, explaining that theory can "be a location for healing," although "theory is not inherently healing, liberatory, or revolutionary. It fulfills this function only when we ask that it do so and direct our theorizing toward that end" (60). The ethnic studies classroom can be a location for theorizing, voicing, and revolutionizing, and the teaching and learning that can happen there is the work of a learning community dedicated to social, political, and personal change.

Postpositivist Realist Theory and the Literature Classroom

The theoretical underpinning of this pedagogy is one that seeks to bridge notions about the issues and articulations of identity. Literature provides an excellent arena for the interrogation, analysis, and interpretation of identity, experience, and society for the field of ethnic studies. Informed by Paula M. Moya's work, *Learning from Experience: Minority Identities, Multicultural Struggles*, and the work of other realists,[6] I argue that postpositivist realism provides a framework for theorizing the classroom as a space within ethnic studies that responds to the crucial inclusion of experience and identity. Postpositivist realist theory provides for experience as a theoretically mediated interpretation of American ethnic groups, our students and ourselves as scholars and/or as people of color in the United States, without limiting our interpretations by essentializing our experiences or succumbing to a poststructuralist relativism that incapacitates. In this way, postpositivist realism can be defined as the philosophical perspective that, contra positivism, which claims that rational assertions are only those that can be scientifically verified or are capable of logical or mathematical proof, assertions can be seen as real with other forms of evidence, and that objective truth can be proven with experiential evidence. Realism accounts for the necessity of additional information beyond mere "facts" in order to account for the possibility that reality transcends human analysis and that propositions must be evaluated in terms of truth to reality, rather than in terms of simple verifiability. Moya clarifies that

> first and foremost, realism about identity involves a commitment to the idea that identities refer outward—albeit in partial and occasionally inaccurate ways—to the social world within which they emerge. Contra postmodernist theorists, who argue that the relationship between identities and the "real" or "material realm" is arbitrary, I argue that the "real" is causally relevant to our epistemic endeavors (including the formation of our identities) because it shapes and limits our knowledge-generating experiences. (13)

In the classroom, studying American ethnic literature reveals this commitment, foregrounding for our students the social constructivist theoretical position of poststructuralism with an understanding of the importance and very real implications of identity. This commitment furthermore reveals that "identities [are] socially significant and context-specific ideological constructs that nevertheless refer in non-arbitrary (if partial) ways to verifiable aspects of the social world" (13).

Challenging poststructuralism, Moya claims that "The failure to attend to the question of identity formation is a characteristic weakness of postmodernist theories of subjectivity: they are unable to explain the persistent correlation between certain kinds of bodies and certain kinds of identities" (18). This is clear to anyone introducing students to the concept of social construction of identities, for example. Students are often quite willing to accept the postulate that race as a category is socially constructed once we interrogate racial stereotypes and their history and construction. However, students (of color, in particular) immediately seek to challenge the premise of the argument, because they experience the "reality" of the socially constructed categories on a daily basis. The empirical data that students have collected challenges, for them, the theory of social construction. Overt discussions of stereotypes help this conversation: students are much more willing to accept the construction of racial stereotypes than they are the category "race;" and they are much more willing to imagine gender as a construction over the category of "sex." In this way, the use of postpositivist realism helps students to move through the thinking between the more readily apparent empirical understanding of social construction and an embedded social understanding of "physical" versus ideological constructions of categories of identity.

Satya P. Mohanty further explains the postpositivist realist reconsideration of "experience," working to establish

> a realist theory of social or cultural identity, in which experiences would not serve as foundations because of their self-evident authenticity but would provide some of the raw material with which we construct identities[, . . . for in order] to say that experiences and identities are constructed is not to prejudge the question of their epistemic status. Radical skepticism [as poststructuralists would have us believe] is not the only alternative to an ahistorical essentialism.[7]

Reading literature that enacts and interrogates these categories of identity serves to make apparent for students how both the construction of and the experience of living out these categories is "real." It is in this way that, as Moya states above, "the 'real' is causally relevant to our epistemic endeavors (including the formation of our identities) because it shapes and limits our knowledge-generating experiences." Students encouraged to engage academically in epistemological analyses already have access to "theory" and are able to think critically about their experiences and knowledge of the world, which they can bring to bear on their interpretations of literature and their interactions with academic discourse.

Despite her radical stance, Moya is not a "naive empiricist" and is not simply opposing poststructuralism by upending it, but rather is working against both "an uncritical belief in the possibility of theoretically unmediated knowledge" and "a denial of the possibility of objectivity" (13). Instead, she argues for a defining of the term *experience* that

> refers to the fact of personally observing, encountering, or undergoing a particular event or situation. By this definition, experience is admittedly subjective. Experiences are not wholly external events [and they] happen to us, and it is our theoretically mediated interpretation of an event that makes it an "experience." The meanings we give our experiences are inescapably conditioned by the ideologies and "theories" through which we view the world. [Thus] experience *in its mediated form* contains an epistemic component through which we can gain access to knowledge of the world (38–39, italics in the original).

Thus, a classroom with a pedagogy based in postpositivist realist theory and ethnic studies is well suited to addressing the intersections of identity, experience, ideology, and theories of socially constitutive categories and consequences. As Moya explains: "when realists say that something is 'real,' they do no mean that it is *not* socially constructed; rather, their point is that it is not *only* constructed." She explains that "while realists . . . acknowledge that ideologies have constitutive effects on the social world such that 'the world' is what it is at least partially because of the way humans interact with and understand it, they will insist that reality is not exhausted by how any given individual or group perceives it ideologically" (27).

As a consequence of using postpositivist realist theory in my classroom, I am able to introduce students to competing theories and ideologies, allowing for comparative readings and analyses. In turn, students are able to use their "real life" experiences in ways that go beyond simple expressivist articulations or reductions of their experiences to a "self-evident authenticity" of racial identity. Such a pedagogical approach creates a large basis for teaching "core knowledge" in the field of ethnic studies, introduces students to the intersections of interdisciplinary foci in the field, and prepares students to be able to face accusations of engaging in "identity politics" and "essentialism" by being able to argue against poststructuralist theories of relativism and neoconservative dismissals of the reality of identity and experience. Furthermore, using realism in this way in the classroom allows students to grasp that

> there are processes of the natural world which operate independently of the human mind, and which both *shape* and *place a limit on* humans' ability

to "construct" or "produce" the world. Second, because the sheer variety of conflicting ideologies extant in a global society such as ours precludes any one ideology from "producing" the entirety of the social world (27).

Such an understanding exposes students to a sophisticated and practical theoretical lens for viewing their own experiences, their scholarship, and their abilities to work toward social change. Satya P. Mohanty argues that such a perspective of the theoretical constructedness of identities encourages us to enter an epistemological position that allows us to read ourselves in the world in specific ways. He claims that such readings "in and through" identities and their epistemic status are valuable because "we learn to define and reshape our values and our commitments, we give texture and form to our collective futures. Both the essentialism of identity politics and the skepticism of the postmodernist position seriously underread the real epistemic and political complexities of our social and cultural identities" (43). Moya's and Mohanty's articulations of postpositivist realist theory are compelling arguments for reading experience through theory and vice versa. Furthermore, postpositivist realist theory articulates a method for thinking concretely about the transformative potential for theorizing identity and experience in an effort to enact social change, which is a primary goal for an ethnic studies classroom and which validates the inclusion of students' knowledge and analytical frames while promoting rigorous scholarship.

Given the relatively new development of postpositivist realist theory, I have located very few critical treatments that challenge what I find to be an effective way of reading and thinking about "the world." Ramón Saldívar offers some critical questions in reading postpositivist realist theory in "Multicultural Politics, Aesthetics, and the Realist Theory of Identity: A Response to Satya Mohanty." Saldívar challenges the goal of "objectivity" that Mohanty advances, asking:

> Is this Real that the realist theory equates with social location, lived experience, and knowledge of the world available postpositively as well as empirically? . . . In other words, Mohanty's postpositivist position rightly allows room for empirically verifiable assessments of truth claims. And so, if indeed some ethical and aesthetic judgments are better than others (which might also imply that some identities are better than others), then what counts, objectively, as better or worse?[8]

As he finds inadequate response to the issues he raises, Saldívar opts to wait rather than embrace postpositivist realist theory. He declares, "In the absence of answers to these questions, one can only remain unconvinced that it is time to abandon the hard-won position that value and judgment—ethical, aesthetic, and political—must be made from within the context of local conditions of knowledge" (854). Choosing the importance of a localized epistemology over Mohanty and Moya's efforts at a broad-reaching epistemology based in objectivity locates Saldívar within poststructuralism's relativism, as does recognizing the value of identity and experience advanced by scholars and activists of color. His refusal to reject postpositivist realist theory wholesale, despite his concerns voiced above, is seconded by Linda Martín Alcoff, who paraphrases Mohanty's pursuit of objectivity as she describes his nominalism: "Our social and political conditions set out what we look for, . . . and what we consider important today, and thus we are not simply discovering values so much as our inquiry arises from our own concernful engagement with the world, and each other."[9] While we continue to work toward theories that adequately account for our "engagement with the world," we as scholars in ethnic studies must find ways in which we can challenge our students to consider what they know as they come to know it. Storytelling in the form of literature and in classroom discussion provides students with opportunities to read the production and representations of ways of knowing.

Bringing Theory into the Classroom

This liminal space evinced by Alcoff and Saldívar, while not advocated by postpositivist realist theory, is one which still serves at this juncture as we, as scholars in ethnic studies, work to interrogate knowledge, identity, and power formations, particularly in our classrooms. In making the series of statements I have described above about my identity, experience, and relationship to dominant culture, I have already inserted a theoretically mediated perspective into the classroom. As an example of underscoring a theoretical perspective within the field of ethnic studies, I explain in class how and why I have begun with a discussion of my position and connections between whiteness and ethnicity. I provide a historical context describing how women of color have worked to disrupt white feminist scholarship and scholarship by men of color to make clear that their voices and concerns be clearly and powerfully heard. (I refer to bell hooks's early works, the now classic text *This Bridge Called My Back*, and more contemporary projects by David Roediger and Robyn Weigman, for example.) I explain that by marking where I stand in relationship to these challenges, I have learned from these scholars and activists that who I am plays a critical role in how I am perceived and how I am able to function in the world. I open the conversation up for a discussion (which continues throughout the quarter) about how subject positions play active roles in our interpretations, social interactions, conditions, and media representations, particularly for our purposes, in literature. As a class, we are engaged in the discussion and analysis of both identity and experience. Throughout the quarter, we read literary and cultural theory written by people of color and we interpret it in relation to the literary texts we read and to our experiences, inside and outside the university. This introduces students to the disciplinary subfield of literary critical studies within ethnic studies and reveals how literary critical theory has informed ethnic studies as a whole. For me, this approach also serves to make transparent the theoretical underpinnings of my work as a scholar and teacher, which we as scholars often embed in our teaching.

These theoretical underpinnings are often evoked in the construction of syllabi and reading lists, as well as in the direction teachers take in conversations in classrooms. Ethnic studies courses, by virtue of their very origins in student revolts and activism, should, by all rights, be sites of active learning and discussion, not lecture halls of passive assimilation of information. I construct my syllabi and reading lists with this notion of active learning at the core. The texts we read work to represent a literary history of people of color in the United States; this literature is a cacophony of people entering discourse, elevating their individual voices into representation of lived experience as art. For this introductory and comparative course, I choose texts that make that entry overt; most of the novels we read are written as first-person narration or use extensive dialogic strategies that foreground speaking and subjectivity and that articulate other accounts of history and reality that challenge dominant culture's version. The reading list for the course on which this essay is based includes: Ernest Gaines's *A Lesson before Dying*; John Okada's *No-No Boy*; Ana Castillo's *So Far from God*; Linda Hogan's *Mean Spirit*; Carlos Bulosan's *America Is in the Heart*; Toni Morrison's *Beloved*; and readings from several collections of short stories, Sherman Alexie's *The Toughest Indian in the World*, Jhumpa Lahiri's *Interpreter of Maladies*, and Jessica Hagedorn's edited collection, *Charlie Chan is Dead: An Anthology of Contemporary Asian American Fiction*. I have chosen more or less contemporary texts for this course, but all of the works focus on historical issues and can be read in light of the overall objectives of an introductory course in ethnic studies. All of the texts we read not only enact the power of storytelling for us as their audience, but also provide theories of how the telling of stories creates a means for disrupting hegemonic discourse by telling the stories of those dominant culture has sought to marginalize. Read comparatively, these texts can introduce students to a vibrant and lengthy literary and cultural history that will also engage them in reading literature that is enjoyable, challenging, and disruptive of dominant paradigms.

Early in the quarter, I begin to introduce key terms and theoretical ideas that serve to ground our discussions across the texts that we read, which enables our comparative readings of American ethnic literary texts and works to solidify our literary approach within a multidisciplinary field. I pair texts with smaller sections from larger theoretical or secondary literary critical pieces that require us to conceptualize and expand our conversations across texts, and across cultures. In addition to familiarizing students with the discourse of ethnic studies and other academic writing, this terminology serves other purposes as well: I teach this course (and all of my courses) as a writing course, working to evaluate students' critical thinking through the writing of expository, literary critical essays. Not only am I teaching works that convey the power of writing as social change, I am working to engage students in writing as their own entry into discourse and logic in order to access academic discourse. We as teachers often expect students to enter into these discursive strategies and codes as we did: through immersion and by osmosis. Instead of this sink-or-swim method of learning, we should be modeling how to appropriate this discourse, how to unpack and evaluate its efficacy and utility, and by doing so, help students to use language and logic to improve their experiences in the university and beyond. David Bartholomae, in his now classic composition studies essay, "Inventing the University," claims that a student

> has to learn to speak our language, to speak as we do, to try on the peculiar ways of knowing, selecting, evaluating, reporting, concluding, and arguing that define the discourse of our community. . . . The student has to appropriate (or be appropriated by) a specialized discourse, and he [sic] has to do this as though he were a member of the academy . . . ; he has to invent the university by assembling and mimicking its language while finding some compromise between idiosyncrasy, a personal history, on the one hand, and the requirements of convention, the history of a discipline, on the other."[10]

The university requires students to be scholars already, to exist within a discursive framework without having entered fully. Ethnic studies is an ideal site for working with students to learn, interrogate, and appropriate this discourse, for, as a discipline, we have challenged much of academia's discourse and disciplinarity during our push into academia.

I often direct our discussions to rhetorical analyses of the literature as well as to examining the logic in secondary critical and theoretical pieces we read. I encourage students to approach our readings from a variety of analytical starting points: informal logical argumentation (what is the author arguing to us?); rhetorical persuasion (how and why are we moved and/or convinced by this piece?); experiential constructions of identity (in what ways do we feel connected to this author's claims and what does it mean if we don't?) and via postpositivist realist theory, how accurately or suggestively does the work construct the "real" (does the author, through the use of both logic and evidence, and image and art, portray a reality beyond empirical "fact"?). We discuss these analyses in relation not only to the texts we read, but also in relation to our own arguments, in the classroom and in our various writings for the course. I ask students to engage with writing in a series of assignments: informal and personal writing outside the classroom in response to reading, upon entering the classroom before discussion in order to have an opportunity to formulate ideas (this is particularly effective on days when I anticipate conflict between interpretations or positions), as a means of solidifying a group work experience (presenting a report of sorts after working together closely on an issue), and as more traditional expository essays, three of which are assigned during the quarter and two of which can be revised as many times as a student might choose.

One of the ways that I work to introduce students to the field of ethnic studies is to ask them to work with key terms as entry into theoretical analysis of the literature they read. A useful strategy for this is to begin with a term students believe they are familiar with, asking them to generate a definition as a class. We have begun with the term "racism," using *The Oxford English Dictionary* definition: racism is "the theory that distinctive human characteristics and abilities are determined by race."[11] I ask students to think about what this definition accomplishes and what it lacks. In order to understand so literal a definition, we put it into context, discussing our experiences and understandings of the term and reality of racism. Our discussion foregrounds how objectivity and experience intertwine in order to attain understanding and in order to construct an argument. Following this discussion about the inadequacy of a literal definition of racism, I introduce an abstract definition of racism provided by philosopher Lewis Gordon.[12] Gordon argues:

> Racism is a form of dehumanization. That dehumanization is a form of bad faith—for to deny the humanity of a human being requires lying to

ourselves about something of which we are aware. . . . Racism is a context marked by a paradox of being a human relation of inhumanity. It is a human act of denying the humanity of other groups of human beings.[13]

This definition becomes part of our "working definition" for racism for the remainder of the quarter. We discuss how Gordon's abstract term is in fact an argument that is "ideational," and as such is more general and supported by ideas rather than "fact." From here, we proceed to interrogate Gordon's description of racism, walking through it to open up his language and philosophical constructs of paradox and bad faith. In order that our understanding of racism is marked by the abstract and ideal as well as by experience and a relation to identity, we explore Gordon's idea of dehumanizing racism in more concrete discussions. Ernest Gaines's *A Lesson before Dying* makes radically apparent the ways in which Lewis Gordon has clarified the full ramifications of how racism is "a human act of denying the humanity of other groups of human beings." Over several class meetings we analyze this novel, connecting the theoretical structures in which we are reading it to other issues and concerns that the novel might serve to exemplify. From working together as a large class, to interacting in small groups, to writing responses to significant issues in the novel, we critically examine and expound upon Gaines's concerns, many of which recur throughout the quarter in other texts we examine. We examine how meaning is constructed in this novel by using our own experiences as the theoretical frame for analysis, adding history and contemporary social issues. A pedagogy that promotes the ideals and expectations of ethnic studies is one that affirms Paula Moya's argument about postpositivist realist theory outlined above:

> Experiences happen to us, and it is our theoretically mediated interpretation of an event that makes it an "experience." The meanings we give our experiences are inescapably conditioned by the ideologies and "theories" through which we view the world. [Thus] experience *in its mediated form* contains an epistemic component through which we can gain access to knowledge of the world.[14]

Published in 1993, but set in 1948, *A Lesson before Dying* is set in Ernest Gaines's fictive Louisiana parish, St. Rafael.[15] It is the story of two African American men learning what constitutes manhood and constitutes learning while living with a Du Boisean "double consciousness." At the level of the plot, Gaines's novel provides an analysis of dehumanizing racism, as well as an examination of epistemology, identity, and experience. *A Lesson before Dying* plots the course of social change and its relationship to teaching and learning. When Grant Wiggins returns to St. Rafael after his education in the North, he is embittered by the restrictions on his person under Jim Crow and the legalized segregation of his school. He is failing in his job as teacher in the local school for sharecroppers when his great aunt demands that he teach an accused murderer to "become a man" before his execution. Wiggins changes his thinking about learning and teaching after studying humanity as dialogic with his former student, Jefferson, after they each learn from by listening to music together and spending time with the school children outside the classroom. As a result, Wiggins comes closer to members of his own family, the community, and the children he teaches as he learns how to be a man from them. While the "lesson" before death at first seems to be Jefferson's, it becomes clear that Wiggins, too, has engaged in lessons about learning by the close of the novel.

Told in first person, the novel begins in a courtroom where Wiggins explains, "I was not there, yet I was there. No, I did not go to the trial, I did not hear the verdict, because I knew all the time what it would be. Still, I was there."[16] These opening sentences immediately challenge a reader's expectation of knowledge and objectivity, and create a series of compelling questions for students in ethnic studies: Can one trust an account told by someone who "was not there"? How could Wiggins be present at the trial when he never attends? Why does he already know the outcome? The following narration of the event that he knows about but does not witness provides answers to the preceding questions. This narrative strategy convinces readers that local and cultural knowledges are accurate, even when disputed by official versions sanctioned by dominant culture and its institutions. As Moya claims, "the 'real' is causally relevant to our epistemic endeavors (including the formation of our identities) because it shapes and limits our knowledge-generating experiences" (13). A close reading of the first chapter of Gaines's text reveals dehumanizing racism and opens powerful conversations inside and outside a classroom.

During the trial, the prosecutor alleges that Jefferson conspired with Brother and Bear to rob the store and kill Mr. Gropé so he could not identify the robbers. The most disturbing version of the story, however, lies in the defense's argument, supposedly designed to exonerate Jefferson. It is here that Gaines makes apparent the paradox of racism described by Gordon and how it pervades our judicial system. The white defense attorney defends Jefferson first by claiming that he is a boy, despite his being over 21. He next refers to him as a fool, claiming, "'I would call it a boy and a fool. A fool is not aware of right and wrong. . . . A fool stood by and watched this happen, not having the sense to run'" (7). The defense uses the historical and contemporarily pervasive racist rhetorical strategy of equating grown African American men and women to children who need to be protected from themselves by the white patriarch. Furthermore, in the midst of this "defense," he moves on from infantilizing Jefferson to dehumanizing him fully. He appropriates nineteenth-century phrenological racism, arguing that Jefferson could not have planned the robbery and using the shape of Jefferson's head as evidence. He explains to the jury that seated before them is "'a cornered animal [that could] strike quickly out of fear, a trait inherited from his ancestors in the deepest jungle of blackest Africa—yes, yes, that he can do but to plan? . . . No gentlemen, this skull here holds no plans'" (28). The final blow for Jefferson's humanity as defined by whites is struck as the defense fires off its final argument: "'What justice would there be to take this life? Why, I would just as soon put a hog in the electric chair as this'" (28). Compared now to a hog, Jefferson is found guilty by the all-white, all-male jury and sentenced to death by electrocution.

At the close of the novel, Wiggins gives Jefferson a pad and pencil, and Jefferson, who is barely literate, begins to write a diary of his final days. Here Jefferson comes to voice, articulating his subjectivity and representing himself in discourse as a human, not as the hog image that he had internalized previously. His reactions to those around him change and he begins to think of himself in relation to others. The diary also represents the possibility of offering an official account of Jefferson's time in the jailhouse and the treatment he receives from the sheriff and his deputies. Sheriff Guidry worries that his actions be recorded "accurately" and that Jefferson's portrayal of him show him to be humane, which Jefferson recounts as "he say good put that in yo tablet I tret you good all the time you been yer" (233). Jefferson recognizes that his writing will outlive him and he does not hesitate to record his experiences as the truth, as an objective recounting of his time between sentencing and execution. The entries are discursive representations of Jefferson's "theoretically mediated" experiences, his lessons before dying, and in this way support the relevance of a postpositivist realist perspective in both analyzing ethnic literature and enacting ethnic studies scholarship. Gaines's novel provides students, at the very level of plot, an example of how learning and speaking aloud can begin a process of social and personal change. Gaines does not portray the actual execution, providing only individuals' responses to the execution, from passersby hearing the generator for the electric chair to the deputies and others in the jailhouse. It is here that as a class we discuss more fully the death penalty, researching resources about the history of the death penalty and the recent controversies over racial inequalities and wrongful execution.[17] Reading *A Lesson before Dying* through a multidisciplinary set of lenses makes apparent to students how experience is connected to epistemology and how knowledge and experience can inform concrete claims in discursive argumentation and social activism that work to bring about dramatic social justice. Knowledge and theory are revealed throughout the text, and asking students not only to analyze these issues inside the text but to bring their own experiences and those of our communities to bear on their analysis of the novel provides opportunities to bring the theory in the novel to bear on our "real" world.

I work to pair texts for comparison, using theoretical claims as starting points for our comparison. I have used W. E. B. Du Bois's articulation of "double consciousness" to link *A Lesson before Dying* to *No-No Boy* by John Okada to explore the protagonist's struggle with family, identity, and citizenship. Du Bois defines double consciousness as:

> this sense of always looking at one's self through the eyes of others, of measuring one's soul by the tape of a world that looks on in amused contempt and pity. One ever feels his two-ness—an American, a Negro; two souls, two thoughts, two unreconciled strivings; two warring ideals in one dark body, whose dogged strength alone keeps it from being torn asunder.[18]

Ernest Gaines's *A Lesson before Dying* is an examination of working with and possibly through "double consciousness." As Wiggins and Jefferson struggle with dehumanizing racism, they come to understand that to continue to view themselves through the eyes of whites is to struggle with "two warring ideals" and that the lesson to be learned is how to resist being torn asunder. Learning and teaching are clearly linked here as tools of resistance. Du Bois's idea of double consciousness is a clear argument for how epistemology is informed by positionality and experience. Working comparatively, we transition from Gaines's novel to John Okada's *No-No Boy*, the story of Ichiro Yamada, a nisei in Seattle who refuses both to leave the United States for Japan and to join the U.S. military during World War II. In the course of analyzing this novel, we explore Gordon's claims about acts of "bad faith" as we read an original archival copy of the U.S. government's loyalty questionnaire, titled "Application for Leave Clearance," focusing on the wording of questions 27 and 28. This document is the basis for Okada's novel, which constructs Ichiro's conundrum of answers, refusing to be deported and repatriated to a country he has never seen and refusing to give up allegiance to an empire that he had never claimed in the first place. We examine both the history of the internment and its theoretical implications, connecting Ichiro's subjectivity to Jefferson's and Wiggins's.[19] Theoretically, we move from Du Bois's claim into Lisa Lowe's argument that the Asian American experience is one of a palimpsest, a very clear example of a "double consciousness," as we begin to read Okada's novel. In *Immigrant Acts*, Lowe argues that:

> narratives of immigrant inclusion—stories of the Asian immigrant's journey from foreign strangeness to assimilation and citizenship—may in turn attempt to produce cultural integration and its symbolization of the national political terrain. Yet these same narratives are driven by the repetition and return of episodes in which the Asian American, even as a citizen, continues to be located outside the cultural and racial boundaries of the nation.... Rather than expressing a "failed" integration of Asians into the American cultural sphere, this distance preserves Asian American culture as an alternative site where the palimpsest of lost memories is reinvented, histories are fractured and retraced, and the unlike varieties of silence emerge into articulacy.[20]

This alternative space that Lowe envisions is a space of storytelling, where history is reconstituted through the act of the story being told and where integration and periphery are located. A course treating comparative readings of ethnic studies theory and literature must take into consideration the experience of duality, of multiple configurations of identity, reinforcing that a social construction of that multifaceted identity does not render identity relativistic, but rather reinforces how interconnected individuals are to the world in which they live. Lowe's construction of an alternative site where memories are written over and over again, bringing silenced voices into articulation, can be a metaphor for the ethnic studies literature classroom as well as the literature we study.

Bringing the Classroom into Theory

In an effort to clarify some of the theories and issues in this pedagogy I've been outlining, I am including a story from early in my teaching that helped me put theory into practice, theorize from my own experience, and listen to others' experiences in order to make changes, both in my teaching and learning processes. The first time I taught a version of Comparative American Ethnic Literature, I chose to focus our inquiry around the question: "What constitutes ethnic literature?" I designed a reading list that I believed would challenge our assumptions and require us to formulate a definition (or a series of definitions) that would account for complexity of experience and plurality in cultural identity and ask us to think beyond literature to consider market forces, publication, and reader reception across ethnicity.[21] In light of that decision, I included a controversial writer, selecting one of her less controversial texts, locating the reading mid-quarter, after we had read a series of other novels and before we turned to short fiction. While I anticipated a strong reaction to the inclusion of Amy Tan in the course, I was unprepared for the dramatic and powerful responses from many of the students in the course. Rather than teach the often discussed and frequently maligned *The Joy Luck Club*, I had chosen Tan's *The Hundred Secret Senses*. The rationale behind my choice of Tan, which I explained to students on the first day as I introduced myself, the course, and our other readings, was to study in an academic context an ethnic author who had broad appeal to dominant culture, whose work was widely anthologized, and about whom much critical discourse had been written. I planned for us to consider the themes we would have developed prior to our reading of Tan: Gordon's notion of bad faith and dehumanizing racism, Du Bois's "double consciousness," Lisa Lowe's conception of narratives as a palimpsest and alternative sites for storytelling and historical analysis. I chose the text I did because Tan sets the story of a Chinese American woman in relation to historical events in China, and it appears to be a more researched and historically accurate depiction than her other texts. My hope for our reading of Tan's work in a comparative setting was to examine the responses of Asian American critics and more general readers in relation to the conversations and analyses we were creating around the other texts, most of which were considered more radical, more literary, and less "popular" with mainstream (read white) readers. In short, I wanted us to consider what promotes wide-scale popularity of ethnic literature and what happens when ethnic literature becomes so popular that one can pick it up in the fiction rack at the local grocery store, where it might sit next to Harlequin romances and post–Cold War spy novels.

Midway through the quarter, we had established a level of trust in the classroom. Students addressed each other by name, had worked together in small groups in the classroom and outside it, and had contended with several challenging texts, many of which had hit close to home for many of us. We had accomplished what I had hoped we might by this point in the quarter: we were analyzing ethnic literature in an interdisciplinary context, considering storytelling as an alternative site for truth telling—a place to reconsider "truths" and challenge them, and reading fiction that students connected to and, perhaps most importantly, enjoyed. *The Hundred Secret Senses* challenged the calm that had settled into class. A student emailed me the day before we began our discussion to ask me again to explain why Tan was included in the course, going on to explain that he and other students had been engaged in a letter-writing campaign to two professors on campus who had included *The Joy Luck Club* in an American history course and an American literature course, both treating twentieth-century America. I wrote him back with some version of the explanation above and began preparing for the discussion with this letter campaign in mind. I came to class with excerpts of articles criticizing Tan's stereotyping of Chinese Americans in particular and Asian Americans in general, both from academic journals and from non-academic sources, as well as with an interview between Tan and several Asian American students who were raising some of the concerns voiced by the student's email. I was confident that I had the matter in hand.

I learned more at this juncture about how much my sense of self as a teacher derives from the automatic respect afforded me as the person paid to be in the room (as opposed to those paying, i.e., students). Much of the earlier calm was simply a result of the ways, subtle and covert, that I had been exercising my authority in the classroom, and the student response to Tan and her work revealed to me and to everyone in the classroom that my authority was completely open to question. During the first day of our discussion of *The Hundred Secret Senses*, I presented the controversy and issues surrounding Amy Tan's place in ethnic literature. Some students began to argue that Amy Tan's stereotypical portrayal of Asians was so egregious that she should never be included in a college syllabus and my inclusion of her work revealed that I was: 1) not an Asian Americanist and therefore not qualified to assess Asian American literature; 2) guilty of reinforcing the stereotypes that Tan constructs by including her in the syllabus; and 3) racially divisive in a mixed race class, as I had included worthwhile texts written by people of color who were not Asian American. While I had included multiple texts by a variety of writers of a diverse Asian American background, including Southeast Asian and South Asian and Filipino American as well as Japanese and Chinese American, my inclusion of Tan's work seemed to negate those inclusions. As a white teacher, I embodied the nameless, faceless, white audience who bought Tan wholesale (along with people of color, given the extent of her sales); worse yet, I was legitimizing her work in an academic context.

Our schedule had five class meetings allotted to the conversation of Tan's *The Hundred Secret Senses*. We spent the first day discussing the controversy behind Amy Tan. The second day, we broke into small groups to try to do a close reading of the first few chapters to either support or challenge some of the charges against her work. The third day, when I attempted to move the conversation beyond the discussion of stereotyping, the students most disturbed by the work effectively stalled the discussion. Working together, they turned any conversation back to issues of negative representation. I tried a series of traditional academic dodges, I'm embarrassed to admit, when my decisions were so soundly challenged. First, I listened and tried to clarify, and when that didn't work, I tried to take us "back to the text," I sought other "authorities" to validate my position, and I stood up in front of the classroom, standing as straight and tall and commanding as I could. Responding to the students resisting discussion of Tan's work, some students charged others with essentialism for asserting the existence of one "authentic" Chinese identity (the one that Tan failed to represent). Others tried to reason about why one writer had to speak for all Chinese Americans, when as a class no one had analyzed the literature by African Americans and Chicano/as in this way. The lowest point was when a student charged that the only reason some students were angry was that they themselves fit one of the stereotypes by dating "outside the race." By the fourth day, the room had rearranged itself into racial zones, where groups of students seemed to ally based around shared concerns over what could be called the Ralston/Tan controversy (white students hid in the back, as far away from me as possible). Two students cried. I wanted to be home in bed. A rumor of a boycott of my course circulated. That afternoon, students from class got together with students in a group called Ethnic Studies Student Association, a student-sponsored group of our department's majors who work to represent student concerns in the department and on campus. Together they called for a student-only meeting to discuss the issues raised in my class. On the fifth day, I dragged myself into class and apologized. We had never gotten past chapter three of the novel. We talked together about how to move on as a class and how we might salvage the rest of the quarter. We talked about what we had learned, and I shared what I had realized (which I will unpack later in this essay). I asked for suggestions for how to deal with the "loss" of Tan as part of our assigned work. Students voted and as a result, I changed the assignment series to make writing about Tan optional, created an extra credit assignment where students could discuss the Ralston/Tan controversy as an example of concerns in the ethnic literature classroom, and called the bookstore to see if students who wanted to could return the unread text for full price.

I tell this unflattering and problematic story to elucidate three sets of points: first, to underscore what I didn't do well and what works better; second, to show how students are ready for a liberatory pedagogy and are already theorizing and practicing ethnic studies before and during our courses; and third, to establish how postpositivist realist theory and a liberatory pedagogy would have helped me as a teacher to listen to students, facilitate their theorizing in discussion, and be able to respond to identity claims that included self-evident "authenticity" and an uncritical negation of an individual perspective (in this case, Amy Tan's). Using Moya's establishment of the claims of postpositivist realist theory in *Learning from Experience* (a fitting title for reviewing this set of issues above) helps to provide responses and directions for the problems I created and faced above. Moya establishes that

1. The different social categories (such as gender, race, class, and sexuality) that together constitute an individual's social location are causally related to the experiences she will have.
2. An individual's experiences will influence, but not entirely determine, the formation of her cultural identity.
3. There is an epistemic component to identity that allows for the possibility of error and of accuracy in interpreting the things that happen to us.
4. Some identities, because they can more adequately account for the social categories constituting an individual's social location, have greater epistemic value than some others that the same individual might claim.
5. Our ability to understand fundamental aspects of our world will depend on our ability to acknowledge and understand the social, political, economic, and epistemic consequences of our own social location.
6. Oppositional struggle is fundamental to our ability to understand the world more accurately (39–43).[22]

Moya's first premise, "The different social categories (such as gender, race, class, and sexuality) that together constitute an individual's social location are causally related to the experiences she will have" (39), is evident in the conflict. Our different positions created part of the tension in considering the issue, in interpreting it, and in failing to communicate well across our differences. Furthermore, my social location, white, female, teacher, informed my decision to include Tan in the course and my whiteness was irrevocable for some students in relation to this conversation. My body belied my words and intentions, which is an unusual space for a white person in a world of white privilege, or as George Lipsitz terms it, "a possessive investment in whiteness." Here was a place to open the conversation back up to differences in subject positions, embodiment, and experience. Such a conversation could take up Moya's second claim, "An individual's experiences will influence, but not entirely determine, the formation of her cultural identity" (40), in relation to students' relationships to the novel and the discussion as well as my own, and most importantly for our inquiry of "what constitutes ethnic literature?" in relation to Tan as a writer. Such questions in discussion encourage students (and teachers) to examine their expectations of what qualifies as ethnic literature suitable for academic study and what seems to appeal to publishers and a more generalized audience that seeks universalism over particularity. Students' initial reaction to Tan's work, that she misrepresents or stereotypes Asian Americans, is validated by Moya's third claim, "There is an epistemic component to identity that allows for the possibility of error and of accuracy in interpreting the things that happen to us" (40). While an objective truth may be nearly impossible to imagine or attain, the possibility of it encourages us to think critically about claims of truth in representations of identity. Students who investigate discomfort with Tan can go beyond claims of stereotyping to include an analysis of why her works are widely read and received and extensively promoted and published. In light of the concerns of the course, we could have investigated the potential danger and hegemonic power of universalism in light of *The Hundred Secret Senses*.

Moya's fourth premise is perhaps the most challenging for poststructuralists in claiming that "some identities, because they can more adequately account for the social categories constituting an individual's social location, have greater epistemic value than some others that the same individual might claim" (41). In the midst of tension, students angry with me for choosing Tan evaluated my social location and established that my category of whiteness superseded my categories marked as female, teacher, and ethnic studies scholar and conferred greater epistemic value on the knowledge gleaned from their experience in their social locations marked by ethnicity. The epistemology used in this conflict became focused around knowledge constructed through ethnicity. Our conversation could have benefited by finding ways to move all of the way through the conversation with that in mind, rather than using that epistemology only as a direct counter to stereotypes in Tan's novel. Jumping ahead to the sixth claim, "Oppositional struggle is fundamental to our ability to understand the world more accurately" (42), in part reveals why we were able to salvage the quarter. The students worked together to learn from the opposition in class, bringing in other student-driven resources and creating a student-only space to discuss the issues away from the classroom and me as the teacher. For my part, rather than simply attempt to apologize and move on, I worked to continue our discussion throughout the remainder of the quarter, resisting the desire to pretend that our conflict had not happened.

Asking students to help reconfigure the remainder of the quarter and the assignments worked to mitigate some of the powerlessness students might have felt and put their perspectives even more fully into the new design of the course. We also used the conflict and the ensuing tension as a way to go back to the issues about representation we had raised and to investigate them in light of other texts (Sherman Alexie's *The Toughest Indian in the World* was particularly useful for this). Finally, Moya's fifth premise encapsulates why I choose to study and teach ethnic literature: "Our ability to understand fundamental aspects of our world will depend on our ability to acknowledge and understand the social, political, economic, and epistemic consequences of our own social location" (43). To this claim, I would add, as a comparatist and a teacher of ethnic studies, that following our learning about "the social, political, economic, and epistemic consequences of our own social location," we need to learn about other locations and consequences. This experience has taught me about the reality of a liberatory pedagogy and provided me with more tools for engaging with it. The students learned a great deal about the power available to redirect the learning environment to reflect more of their interests and experiences.

Pedagogies for ethnic studies theory and literature should consider the experience of duality, of multiple configurations of identity, reinforcing that a social construction of that multifaceted identity does not render identity relativistic, but rather reinforces how interconnected individuals are to the world in which they live. Teaching and studying American ethnic literature comparatively is a struggle to reveal shared and disparate histories and social connections. In "Postcolonial Authority and Postmodern Guilt," Homi K. Bhabha provides a useful model for the examination of the space created when cultural differences collide in texts. He postulates that:

> At the point at which the hierarchy and the subordinations of the sentence are replaced by the definitive discontinuity of the text, at that point, the subject of discourse spatializes and moves beyond the sententious. It turns "outside" the sentence to inscribe the boundaries of meaning (but not its depth) in the "affective" language of cultural difference.[23]

In other words, writers and readers can decenter discourse that uses hierarchical structures at specific moments through the incorporation of disruptive non-hegemonic or non-formulaic methods. Reading for understanding both subjecthood and experience can lead to an emotional or "affective" space that conveys difference outside the written realm of the text and the proscribed realm of hegemony and hierarchy. American ethnic literature challenges the sentence and creates a new space for the subject outside the sentence. Comparative readings in a postpositivist realist classroom reveal the potential of the voice exploding the "sentence" or judgment conferred by the power of hegemonic discourse and the society that utilizes and reinscribes such power. Bhabha explains, "There is continual tension between the spatial incommensurability of the articulation of cultural differences and the temporal non-synchronicity of signification as they attempt to speak, quite literally, in terms of each other" (58). The tension that exists between the incommensurable and the social is realized in literature, classroom discussions, and student writing that make audible enunciations of identity. In the classroom, our work as scholars embodied and socially constituted is to convey the means for working with the tension as students enter into discourse—academically, politically, and socially.

Notes

1. The Schomburg Center is located in the Harlem branch of the New York Public Library and holds the largest collection of texts of all kinds relating to the black experience in the Americas. The Center is online at www.nypl.org/research/sc/exhibitions.html. Other sites, such as those chronicling the histories of Angel Island and Tule Lake, mark histories that might have been lost (Angel Island was declared a historical monument after much effort by the Angel Island Association members) but are now available to people across the United States and beyond. See www.sandiego-online.com/forums/chinese/htmls/angel.htm and www.gaylonn.com/tulelake/history.html as examples of how progressive representations of histories are being reconstituted on the Internet.

2. Johnnella E. Butler, "Ethnic Studies as a Matrix for the Humanities, the Social Sciences, and the Common Good," in *Color-Line to Borderlands: The Matrix of American Ethnic Studies* (Seattle: University of Washington Press, 2001), 20. Italics in the original.

3. Butler, "Ethnic Studies as Matrix," 21.

4. bell hooks, *Teaching to Transgress: Education as the Practice of Freedom* (New York: Routledge, 1994).

5. Jean Toomer, *Cane* (1923, New York: Liveright, 1993), 73.

6. Paula M. Moya, *Learning from Experience: Minority Identities, Multicultural Struggles* (Berkeley: University of California Press, 2001). The postpositivist realist theory of identity is an "adaptation" and an "extension of the epistemological framework known as philosophical realism." It is derived from a philosophy of science and analytic philosophy. Moya makes clear that "while disagreement exists among those who would call themselves realists, the most sophisticated versions of realism today entail a postpositivist conception of objectivity, together with the anti-idealist thesis that the world exceeds humans' mental conceptions of it" (12).

7. Satya Mohanty, "The Epistemic Status of Cultural Identity," in *Reclaiming Identity: Realist Theory and the Predicament of Postmodernism*, ed. Paula Moya and Michael R. Hames-García (Berkeley: University of California Press, 2000), 32.

8. Ramón Saldívar, "Multicultural Politics, Aesthetics, and the Realist Theory of Identity: A Response to Satya Mohanty," *New Literary History* 32 (2001): 853.

9. Linda Martín Alcoff, "Objectivity and Its Politics," *New Literary History* 32 (2001): 846.

10. David Bartholomae, "Inventing the University," in *When a Writer Can't Write: Studies in Writer's Block and Other Composing-Process Problems*, ed. Mike Rose (New York: Guilford Press, 1985), 134–135.

11. "Racism," in *The Oxford English Dictionary*, dictionary.oed.com/cgi/entry/00195909, [cited 9/1/2002].

12. In this introductory course, I often approach the inclusion of theoretical writings by bringing in a short passage of a longer, denser piece. I often introduce theorists' ideas by working with students on understanding the role of abstract terms in discourse. In my upper-division courses, we read these literary critical and theoretical pieces in their entirety; often I have students present the works in small groups.

13. This is from "Black Consciousness, Bad Faith and the Human Genome," an unpublished talk by Gordon, delivered at "Black Identity in Theory and Practice," University of Washington, 1999, 10. See *Bad Faith and Anti-Black Racism* (Atlantic Highlands, N.J.: Humanities Press, 1995), where Gordon defines racism as "the self-deceiving choice to believe either that one's race is the only race qualified to be considered human or that one's race is superior to other races" (2).

14. Moya, *Learning from Experience*, 38–39 (italics in the original).

15. Thematically, this incredibly rich and didactic novel can be read many ways: as a historical analysis of the last years of official Jim Crow; a geographical analysis of deep southern African American and white communities; a gender analysis of African American men and women's relationships; an analysis of generational differences before the civil rights era; an indictment of racism in the justice system; a condemnation of execution; and a graceful treatment of the role of the African American church in community and religious life in the 1940s.

16. Ernest Gaines, *A Lesson before Dying* (New York: Vintage, 1993), 3.

17. Some excellent resources on this subject can be found on the World Wide Web: Southern Poverty Law Center at www.splcenter.org; the Illinois Report of the Governor's Commission on Capital Punishment, April 2002, at www.idoc.state.il.us/ccp/ccp/reports/commission_report/index.html; death penalty issues at www.truthinjustice.org; and David J. W. Vanderhoof, assistant professor of the University of North Carolina at Pembroke, maintains an excellent website at: www.uncp.edu/home/vanderhoof/death.html.

18. W. E. B. Du Bois, *The Souls of Black Folk* (New York: Library of America, 1986), 364–365.

19. There are now many excellent resources for this history; one notable among other electronic resources is the Smithsonian National Museum of American History's website, "A More Perfect Union: Japanese Americans and the U.S. Constitution," which contains oral histories, an archive of documents, and access to electronic collections. The site can be found at: americanhistory.si.edu/perfectunion/experience/index.html.

20. Lisa Lowe, *Immigrant Acts* (Durham, N.C.: Duke University Press, 1996), 6.

21. In considering text selection, teachers should avail themselves of the now many resource guides in ethnic literature. One in particular would have helped me considerably had it been published before I taught this version of this course: editors Sau-Ling Cynthia Wong and Stephen H. Sumida's excellent text, *A Resource Guide to Asian American Literature* (New York: MLA, 2001), provides teachers with excellent historical contexts, biographical material, and strong pedagogical suggestions targeting the teaching of specific Asian American authors.

22. I am responsible for isolating these claims and numbering them in this fashion. Moya is much more subtle in her treatment of these premises.

23. Homi K. Bhabha, "Postcolonial Authority and Postmodern Guilt," in *Cultural Studies*, ed. Lawrence Grossberg et al. (New York: Routledge, 1992), 56.

Teaching about White Racism in the United States
Does It Make a Difference?

17

THEODORIC MANLEY, JR., JASON J. WASHBURN, AND
FRANK HOLIWSKI

THE CIVIL RIGHTS MOVEMENT OF THE 1950s and 1960s in the United States ushered in a new sense of hope for African Americans and liberal white Americans who struggled side by side for equality, fairness, and justice for all. Various leaders of the civil rights movement exposed the blatant and overt symbols of racial discrimination and white supremacy in the South and the North. It became no longer acceptable for public and private businesses to blatantly promote blacks as less than equal by posting signs that read "whites only."[1] The civil rights movement denounced forms of blatant white hostility toward black Americans and led the way for the passage of the Civil Rights Act of 1964 and the Voting Rights Act of 1965.

One of the few successes of the civil rights movement was characterized by a reform in white social and racial attitudes toward African Americans. Whereas in the early 1900s whites held an extreme stereotypic and negative image of African Americans as lazy, shiftless, and unmotivated,[2] today a growing percentage of whites responding to national opinion polls on racial attitudes are more accepting of African Americans as equals.[3] Moreover, whites are now more likely to open their once all-white neighborhoods to prospective African American neighbors and other racially identified groups of home-seekers.[4] Because of these dramatic changes in white racial and social attitudes toward black Americans, some scholars began in the late 1970s to develop the thesis that race was no longer an important issue for America.[5] Indeed, the topic of race that seemed paramount to anyone interested in understanding anything about America had now been defined as the declining significance of race and the rise of the "new" black middle class.[6] Could it be true that white Americans genuinely have changed their negative attitudes and opinions about African Americans? Do white Americans feel that African Americans are genuinely equal to them regardless of the color of their skin? Are white Americans truly antiracists and therefore able to judge African Americans and persons of color by the content of their character?

Politically Correct Movement

In the 1980s a new term was born that challenged white liberals, conservatives, and radicals at predominantly white colleges and universities to confront their pedagogical biases and stereotypes. The concept of political correctness, or the acronym "PC," stood for a movement that had an ideological commitment to represent difference—the individual right to choose an identity to one's own likeness. On predominantly white college campuses in the United States, political correctness challenged the language of white professors, instructors, and students. When white students on university and college campuses in the United States began to claim shared identities with racial, gender, class, or any other social groups, college professors and students that benignly mentioned and classified people into generic categories of black, white, female, Asian, Latino, Native American, gay, lesbian, biracial, working-class, disabled, and so forth, were accused of stereotyping and bias. Those who were politically correct decided to no longer passively observe and tolerate college professors, instructors, and students who made generic and sweeping statements about an individual because of his or her "alleged" membership in some group based on race, gender, class, or other physical or cultural markers.

The politically correct movement began an assault on stereotyping biases. If political correctness meant tolerating and respecting difference, then unintended and intended forms of stereotyping and prejudging were no longer acceptable during informal and formal college discourses. Racial generalizations were denounced and challenged. White college professors who contradicted themselves by treating white students as individuals and blacks, Latinos, Native Americans, and Asian Americans as groups were told that they were denying individual rights to persons of color. As college professors, instructors, and, more importantly, college students began to think more carefully about what they said to each other in the university milieu, the politically correct challenge hid from full view the genuine and authentic expressions of their thoughts, feelings, and behaviors toward people of color.[7] Indeed, a form of social desirability was developed as college professors, instructors, and students began to avoid the appearance of expressing stereotypes and their own biases for fear that they might be called racist. The politically correct movement ushered in a new form of racism.

The New Racism

The new racism became more symbolic,[8] subtle, and semantic but nevertheless painfully damaging to the self-esteem and the character development of those it was and still is directed toward.[9] The new racism, sometimes referred to as aversive, modern, symbolic, subtle, or unconscious,[10] embraces "individualistic, egalitarian, achievement oriented values institutionalized in the United States."[11] Race talk is avoided at the expense of having any real national dialog about race.[12] And yet, since the founding of the United States "race will *always* be at the center of the American experience."[13] Institutions from the federal to the state, county, and local governments were *racialized* by a core commitment to protecting white interest and advancement over all other groups typically defined as nonwhite.[14] The recent comments made by Senator Trent Lott (R-Mississippi) are critical reminders of the role that *race* and *being raced* play in the drama of state and federal institutions in the United States.[15] Senator Lott's bigoted comments made while honoring the one-hundredth birthday of Senator Strom Thurmond—a noted bigoted white southern segregationist who ran for president in 1948—are not isolated. In 1980 Senator Lott advocated the views of white southern segregationists by stating on numerous occasions how the United States would be "better off" if we had supported Strom Thurmond's election for president in 1948.[16] Moreover, in 1997 Senator Lott was shown posing with officials of the pro-white Council of Conservative Citizens.[17] Lott had insisted a month before that he had "no firsthand knowledge" of the group. The Southern Law Poverty Center, which tracks hate groups, described the council as the "incarnation of the infamous White Citizen's Councils" that enforced segregation in Mississippi and other Southern states in the 1950s and 1960s.[18] The recent comments made by Senator Lott reinforce a profound legacy of bigotry and white supremacy in the United States. Thus, some whites continue to see blacks and the policy of integration as *the* problem facing the United States.[19]

The *new racism* contains an appeal to reason and justification, and some putative grounding in rational calculation and thought.[20] The new racism treats all people as equal and yet, when certain individuals like blacks and other minorities don't "make it" the reasoning is not tied to the fault of the society they live in but to their alleged individual inadequacies that can be attributed to their group membership.[21] But what is said about whites that don't "make it"? Statistically speaking, there are more whites in the United States who don't make it than there are people of black, Latino, Native American, or Asian descent who don't.[22] The fact that there are whites that don't "make it" has never led white Americans to utter generalized statements like "whites don't try hard enough." Imagine how just a few statements like "whites can make it if they try hard enough" or "whites can be just like blacks if they try hard enough" sound when we use the logic of the new racism. They approach the absurd. Few who identify as white accept these statements as valid because seldom are they treated as a group—they are individuals.

Much of the new racism is associated with a conscious effort to eliminate societal racism as a cause of group or individual position in society.[23] The egalitarian, individualistic, achievement-motive premise of the new racism creates a color-blind mentality—all people have the same opportunities in society.[24] This kind of rational calculation hides from full view the authentic and genuine attitudes whites hold toward African Americans.

In an effort to reduce the existence of contemporary societal racism, whites appear to be conscious of the past by arguing that society is no longer like it was "back then." The blatant, overt, and egregious forms of racism appear eliminated, but have the cultural meaning of those stereotypes dissipated? Whites who claim to be more conscious of societal racism appear to be less likely to attribute any action they commit toward African Americans as racist. Have whites unlearned the cultural meaning and behavior associated with past stereotypes perpetrated on African Americans and all other persons of color?

Unconscious Racism

What is the relationship between white internalized cultural meanings of stereotypes and unconscious racism? Does the new racism allow whites to assume the position that they are not racist? Does not being racist mean whites or people who self-identify as white do not attribute their conscious actions and behaviors toward African Americans as prejudiced by past or current stereotypes and stigmas? Have whites overcome past internalized stereotypes of African Americans such that they judge their current behavior and attitudes toward African Americans as non-racist? Could whites still harbor racist stereotypes of African Americans and not know it?

Race is paramount in the United States. So much of what we do in our daily lives is unconsciously centered on race. Racism, the ideological justification of superiority and inferiority, is a crime and disease.[25] It is a crime because it violates the implementation of equal rights and opportunities under the Constitution of the United States. It is a disease because it cannot be separated from its psychic costs.[26] Whites would have no strong sense of their whiteness if they had no sense of a denigrated and hated blackness. This denigration takes a heavy toll not only on black bodies but also on the character development of people who self-identify as white. A moral dilemma faces all whites that are aware at some level of the incalculable damage they and their ancestors have repeatedly done to fifteen generations of African Americans and other people of color. Racism has become a thing and its costs have grown exponentially.[27]

Much of our inability to know racial discrimination when we see it results from failure to recognize that racism is both a crime and a disease. This failure is compounded by a reluctance to admit that the illness of racism infects everyone. Acknowledging and understanding the malignancy are prerequisites to the discovery of an appropriate cure. The diagnosis is, however, difficult because our own contamination with the very illness for which a cure is sought impairs our comprehension of the disorder. Americans share a common historical and cultural heritage in which white racism has played a paramount role. This shared experience attaches significance to a white individual's race and induces negative feelings and opinions about all other racialized and raced groups (e.g., poor white, black, Indian, Asian, Hispanic, biracial, etc.). The influence of the culturally embedded racist belief system in the United States reproduces racist institutions and their victims. At the same time, most of us are unaware of everyday societal racism. We do not recognize the ways in which our internalized cultural experiences and beliefs affect our everyday actions. In simple terms, a lot of the behavior that produces racial discrimination is today influenced by unconscious racial motivation.

There are two explanations for the unconscious nature of our racially discriminatory beliefs and ideas. First, Freudian theory states that the human mind defends itself against the discomfort of guilt by denying or refusing to recognize those ideas, wishes, and beliefs that conflict with what the individual has learned is good or right. While our historical experience has made racism an integral part of our culture, our society has more recently embraced the idea that racism is immoral. When an individual experiences conflict between racist ideas and the societal ethic that condemns those ideas, the mind excludes racism from consciousness. Second, a theory of cognitive psychology states that culture—including, for example, the media and an individual's parents, peers, and authority figures—transmits certain beliefs and preferences. This theory embraces the ecology of the individual social formation, asserting that what we come to be most aware of are those things external to us that reinforce our internal notions of self.[28]

> Sarah: At age sixteen, Sarah brought her best friend home with her from high school. After the friend left, Sarah's mother told her not to invite her friend home again. "Why?" Sarah asked, astonished and confused. "Because she is colored," her mother responded. That was not an answer, Sarah thought to herself. It was obvious that her friend was colored, but what kind of reason was that for not inviting her? So Sarah persisted, insisting that her mother tell her the real reason. None was forthcoming. The indignant look on her mother's face, however, made Sarah realize that if she persisted, she would jeopardize her mother's affection toward her. Horrified by what she had just glimpsed, Sarah severed her friendship with the girl. Sarah told me she had not thought of this incident in twenty years. She also said that until now, she had never consciously said to herself that her deepest tragedy in this incident was her loss of trust in her mother's love. Sarah . . . began to cry.[29]

As in the above situation, parental, peer group, and media preferences and influences are so much a part of our lives and culture that we don't experience them as explicit lessons until much later in life.[30] In our daily lives we are unaware of the ubiquitous presence of cultural stereotypes and how they influence our perception that people of color should not be invited to white peoples' homes.[31] Because racism is so deeply ingrained in our culture it is unlikely to be transmitted by tacit understanding. Even if a child is not told that blacks are inferior, he or she learns that lesson by observing the behavior of others.[32] These tacit understandings, because they have never been articulated, are less likely to be experienced at a conscious level.

Strategies to Reduce Racism

Numerous strategies have been implemented over the last several decades to reduce racism in the United States. At the political and societal level, strategies have included reactive policies, such as anti-discrimination laws, and proactive policies, such as affirmative action.[33] Corporations have responded to these changes with diversity and anti-discrimination training for their employees.[34] Efforts to reduce racism have also entered primary, secondary, and higher education classrooms through school desegregation and exposure to multicultural curricula.[35] While many opinions and commentaries have been published about the effectiveness of corporate anti-discrimination training programs, multiculturalism within schools, and college courses on race and ethnicity, little systematic research has been conducted.[36] For instance, a recent survey of 281 U.S. colleges and universities found that while an overwhelming majority of educational institutions have conducted diversity programs, none of the institutions reported conducting systematic efficacy evaluations.[37] Of the research that has been conducted on multicultural education, the findings tend to show non-significant or even paradoxical effects.[38]

Methods

Current Study

The current study presents preliminary analyses from a sample of university students and community people who elected to participate in courses on white studies and white racism. Colleges and universities in the United States that have offered race and ethnic courses seldom evaluate how these courses have affected student racial attitudes and behavior. In contrast to courses that teach about multiculturalism or how to *manage diversity*,[39] the course taught in this study focused specifically on teaching white participants about the new modern white racism and the affect of the materials used in course instruction on white participant racial attitudes and behaviors. Thus, the main purpose and focus of the course and study was to evaluate the impact of those materials used in the course on white participants' racial identity using a quasi-experimental model. We seek to encourage, by example, other professors who are teaching race and ethnicity courses at colleges and universities in the United States to use research methods creatively to integrate their teaching and research. That way, we can systematically and effectively demonstrate that students and society benefit from race and ethnicity study courses. This is important for the future of ethnic studies and the accepting of diversity in the United States.

Course Description

The primary instructor of the course was a male, African American associate professor with a doctorate in sociology. The research and teaching assistant for the course was a European American male working on his doctorate in clinical psychology. Additional instructors were utilized during the weeklong summer institute. These included an African American male working on his doctorate in history, an Asian American female with a background in secondary education, a white female with a background in union organizing, a Latino male with a background in community development, and an African American male with a doctorate in clinical community psychology.

The course was offered in three formats: A one-week intensive course during the summer that met six hours a day for five days; a three-week course that met three times a week for three hours; and a ten-week course that met twice a week for one and a half hours. The required reading for the course included Joe Feagin et al.'s *White Racism: The Basics* (second edition), Richard Delgado and Jean Stefancic's *Critical White Studies: Looking behind the Mirror*, and Ian F. Lopez's *White by Law: The Legal Construction of Race*. The first presents a compelling case for the existence of white racism while the last two provide a set of articles and case studies that relate to key areas dealing with how whites see themselves and others, and the roles of culture, law, white privilege, white mobility, supremacy, and what shall we do? Although lecture and discussion were the primary tools for delivering course content, several other teaching formats were used.

All students completed pretest scales before course instruction. After completing the outcome measures, participants reviewed the video *White Identity Theory: Origins and Prospect*,[40] which discusses Rita Hardiman's theory of white racial identity development. The stages discussed included pre-socialization, active and passive acceptance, resistance, redefinition, and integration. After the video, each student is asked to self-identify with one or more of the stages. One student wrote in her journal the following:

> After our first class session, I was forced to think about issues that I had never thought about before. The one issue that struck me most is the fact that I am *White*, and I have never thought about being *White* before. It never occurred to me that I am White and just being White I belong to a race? Just that fact alone makes me feel sort of racist. I have never thought of myself as a racist before, I've always seen people of other races as equal, but I think what I really need is to stop seeing color.

All students wrote weekly or daily journals to log their daily feelings, reactions, and thoughts about the reading and other course materials. Quotes from the journals were arbitrarily selected and read at the beginning of class to provide ways for students to hear different thoughts from their fellow peers in the classroom. Quotes from the first journal were often based on the experience of avoiding discussions on race or on being unaware of the origins of race in the United States:

> To be honest I really wanted to avoid this class and the topic of race altogether. For me the issue of race seemed just too politically "charged." For some reason, going into the class I didn't want to think about the issue of race because I didn't want to "strain my brain." It sounds so stupid to say that, but I know myself well and I tend to avoid conflict, confrontation, and any other highly controversial, charged, and debatable issue.
>
> I'm more confused now than ever before. I've spent most of my life believing that racism was the result of the hatred and evilness and insecurities of a few sick people. I had no idea that it is the result of people dating back to the beginning of civilization.

Before the start of class a poster-size piece of paper with "grass catcher" written on top in bold letters was taped to classroom walls for student access (e.g., on the door, on the back and side walls). At the beginning of each class students received a small post-it sheet of adhesive paper. These were distributed to solicit from students the questions or comments *not* made during class discussion. All students were encouraged to stick all comments and questions on the grass catcher. The grass catcher was read either the next class time or after a break in ten-week or three-week courses.

Participants also viewed the video *Death Runs Riot*, which focuses on the violent conflict between the pro-slavery and the ideological abolitionist Free-Soilers movements.[41] The video portrays the conflict of white liberalism by depicting the challenge ideologically committed abolitionists made to the extension of slavery in the Kansas and Nebraska territories while simultaneously barring black settlement. Additional videos were also used to show the impact of white racism on people of color.[42]

Several additional instruments were used throughout the course. For instance, participants engaged in an outside activity that exposed racial and socioeconomic differences in privilege between participants in the class.[43] Participants shared the following comments about their reactions to this exercise.

> My reaction to having such a head start was a feeling of embarrassment. I don't even know why though. Maybe it was because I didn't realize how good I have it, and really took things for granted. It seemed very unfair to me that I was so far ahead of other people just due to my financial upbringing and class, and my race.

> I don't think we even start out in the same place, that from the beginning minorities are placed in the back and the Whites closer to the "finish" [American Dream]. We're not born into the same affluent communities, given the same quality of education, and minorities are not able to access

resources like Whites. These situations and more have us in a staggered formation from the start.

The importance of this activity for me is that it allowed me to feel anger. As I got further and further [back], I began to feel scornful towards the factors that kept me from moving up with the mostly White members of the class. For a moment I blamed my parents for not taking me to a museum or the bookstore to provide the experience the White students had to move up a step. I also felt anger towards the designers of this "American system" that halted my advancement.

Participants also completed checklists to measure white privileges and the cost of white racism.[44] The results of the checklists were made available to students during the following class session. For example, one item frequently endorsed by participants on the "Cost of Racism for White People Checklist"[45] is "I have been in situations where I heard derogatory jokes and remarks about people of color and did nothing." In some sense this item confirms the "passive observer" role of students in the class.[46]

My wife never liked it when I would participate in racist jokes, either by laughing or telling them. I always told her that it was only a joke. Nobody had ever been hurt by laughing or telling a racist joke, I would tell her. Man, was I wrong. The last seven weeks I have learned that I was definitely wrong, by participating in these jokes, I was just as guilty as any racist living in America. The worst part was that I believed that telling these jokes did not make me a racist, at all. Learning this about myself scares me, and makes me mad because just like me there are many people in America that are living their lives in ignorance. I consider myself lucky because I have this class to guide me in my quest to become a better human being. Unfortunately, there are many people in America that are not as lucky as I am, and that makes me very sad."

Finally, music and slide presentations were used to show the symbolic forms of whiteness in ancient Greek and Roman art compared to contemporary images of power, strength, control, and dominance; and segregation in Chicago followed by a song by Tracy Chapman called "Across the Lines." In addition, the last scene in the film *Do the Right Thing* is used to highlight the confrontation between private property and collective rights.[47] After reviewing this scene, which ends in a riot, students listen to the song by Tracy Chapman called "New Beginning." Provocative and emotional discussions have usually occurred using this teaching format for the course.

Participants

A total of 233 European Americans volunteered to participate in the current study, with 151 participants enrolled in the white racism course, referred to as the treatment group, and 82 participants in the introductory course, referred to as the comparison group. Participants in the treatment group were recruited from a course titled White Studies and Eradicating White Racism offered by the sociology department at a large, urban college in the Midwest. Participants included 104 female and 47 male university students and community members who were enrolled in the course during one of nine different sessions, starting with the spring session of 1999 and ending with the summer session of 2002. The course was offered as a traditional ten-week course in the spring quarter, a three-week intensive course between the fall and winter quarters, and a weeklong institute during the summer quarter. Participants in the comparison group were recruited from undergraduate students enrolled in two Introduction to Sociology classes. Participants included 51 female and 31 male students enrolled in the course during the spring quarters of 1999, 2000, and 2001.

Missing Data

Three participants at pretest and 54 participants at posttest did not complete the measures due to absences on the day of the evaluations. Missing data analyses did not reveal any patterns among those who were present for the evaluation versus those who weren't. One participant in the treatment group agreed to the study and completed demographic information, but did not complete pretest or posttest measures. Two participants were eliminated from the treatment group due to an excessive number of missing items. Twenty-one participants (9 percent of the sample) had no more than two missing items and were included in the analyses. Missing data for these participants were replaced with the entire sample's median score for each item. Missing data analyses did not reveal any patterns or significant differences between those who fully completed the scale and those who required median substitution. The final total sample size for pretest and posttest analyses was 173, with 121 participants in the treatment group and 52 participants in the comparison group.

Measures

WHITE RACIAL IDENTITY ATTITUDE INVENTORY (WRIAI).[48] This measure was used to assess the level of racial awareness of the white participants. The fifty self-report items of the WRIAI were originally designed to measure the stages of racial identity development for whites based on the model proposed by Helms and by Helms and Carter.[49] The WRIAI measures racial identity attitudes for whites on five subscales, specifically: (a) contact—naïveté and lack of awareness of the sociopolitical significance of racial-group membership (e.g., "In my family, we never talked about racial issues"); (b) disintegration—confusion and self-disorientation with respect to one's own whiteness as well as other racial groups (e.g., "I do not feel that I have the social skills to interact with black people effectively"); (c) reintegration—active and passive endorsement of white superiority and black inferiority (e.g., "I believe that blacks are inferior to whites"); (d) pseudo-independence—white liberalism characterized by an intellectualized acceptance of one's whiteness and quasi-recognition of the sociopolitical implications of racial differences (e.g., "It is possible for blacks and whites to have meaningful social relationships with each other"); and (e) autonomy—racial humanism expressed from a positive white (non-racist) orientation (e.g., "I seek out new experiences even if I know a large number of blacks will be involved in them"). The WRIAI also includes ten experimental questions that are not included in the subscales. These questions assess participants' dedication to challenging racism and understanding more about "being white."

The five subscales are each composed of ten, five-point Likert-style items ranging from *strongly disagree* (1) to *strongly agree* (5), with higher scores representing greater endorsement of each attitude. Alpha coefficients have been reported by Helms and Carter as the following: contact, .55; disintegration, .77; reintegration, .80; pseudo-independence, .71; and autonomy, .67. For this sample, alpha coefficients for the subscales were as follows: contact, .32; disintegration, .70; reintegration, .79; pseudo-independence, .65; and autonomy, .44. Investigations of construct validity provide initial support for content, construct, and criterion validity,[50] particularly in prediction of self-reported racism[51] and multicultural counseling competencies.[52]

WHITE RACIAL ATTITUDES SCALE (WRAS).[53] This experimental measure was used to assess the racial attitudes of white participants. The measure was derived from a synthesis of existing theoretical perspectives pertaining to racial attitude development among European Americans toward African Americans. A principal components factors analysis resulted in six factors, specifically: (a) separatist and superior—preference for racial separatism predicated on the notion of white racial superiority; (b) pluralistic—belief that unique strengths could be observed in both African American

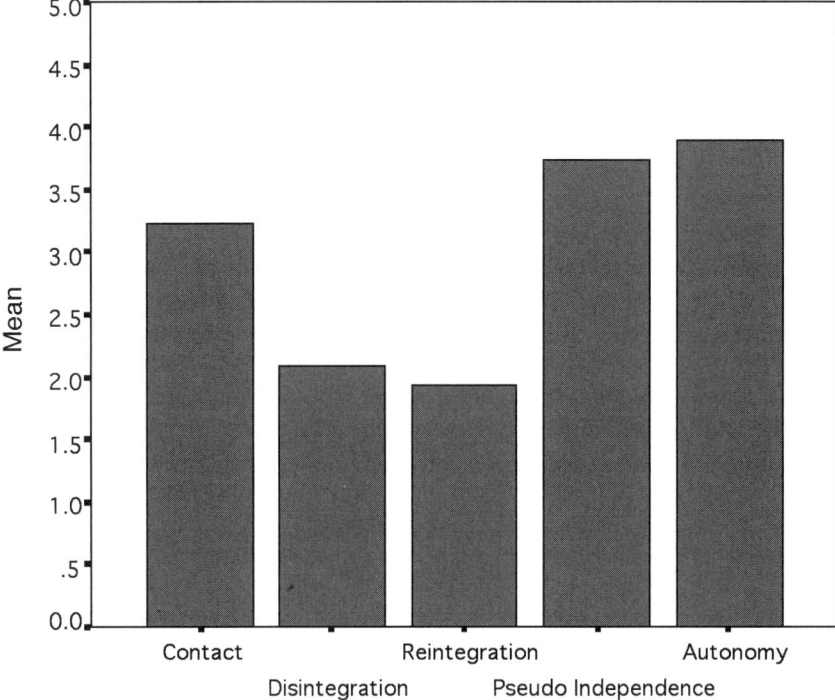

Figure 17.1. Profile for the Means of All Subtests on the WRIAI

and white cultural practices; (c) obliviousness—desire to focus on similarities between races and a limited understanding of the need for differentiation on the basis of race; (d) self-doubt—uncertainty and concern regarding social interactions with African Americans; (e) paternalism—belief that African American people can benefit from the cultural guidance and education in the ways of a superior white culture; and (f) other-identification—preference for the company of African American friends and the selection of social activities designed to expose the individual to African American people and culture.

The six subscales are each composed of ten, five-point Likert-style items ranging from *strongly disagree* (1) to *strongly agree* (5), with higher scores representing greater endorsement of each attitude. Internal consistency reliability coefficients have been reported by Galloway et al. between .65 and .80. For this sample, alpha coefficients for the factors were as follows: separatist and superior, .83; pluralistic, .74; obliviousness, .74; self-doubt, .81; paternalism, .69, and other-identification, .63. An initial investigation of the WRAS provides initial empirical support for the validity of the WRAS.[54]

Demographic Subscale: An eight-item personal data form was also completed for this study in order to obtain participants' demographic information, such as sex, age, race, class in school, environment grown up in (e.g., size of town, zip code, state), and parents' occupation.

Procedure

Students were informed of the research project and invited to voluntarily participate in the project by the class instructor (black/African American) and research assistant/instructor (white/European American) on the first day of the class.[55] Specifically, students were informed that the primary investigators were interested in better understanding the dynamics of white racism and attempts to intervene in white racism. The investigators emphasized that participation was voluntary, and that a decision to participate had no effect on course grade. Students were informed data would be collected on the first day of the class and on the second-to-last day of the class. Printed consent forms were provided and read to the students by the research assistant. After consents were completed, participating students were asked to self-identify based on race or ethnicity. All participants who identified as white European American were provided the WRIAI. Due to the more recent availability of the WRAS, those who identified as white European American after the winter 1999 course were provided the WRAS in addition to the WRIAI. Therefore, 173 participants completed the WRIAI, whereas 127 participants completed the WRAS.

Results

Preliminary Analyses

Multivariate analyses of variance were first performed to test for any pretest differences in WRIAI and WRAS scores between treatment and comparison groups. No significant differences were found for the WRIAI, Wilkes = .94, $F (5, 167) = 2.06$, $p = .072$, or the WRAS, Wilkes = .93, $F (6, 120) = 1.59$, $p = .16$. Demographic variables had no significant effect on pretest scores on the WRIAI or the WRAS.

Course Outcomes

A 2 × 2 repeated measures MANOVA was utilized to examine the impact of the course on the dependent measures. Group (treatment, comparison) was the between-subjects variable, and time of administration (pretest, posttest) was the within-subjects variable. The dependent variables were

Table 17.1. Pretest and Posttest Means and Standard Deviations for WRIAI Subscales

Subscale	Group	Pretest M (SD)	Posttest M (SD)
Contact	Treatment	3.18 (.37)	3.28 (.40)
	Comparison	3.13 (.39)	3.13 (.36)
Disintegration***	Treatment	2.18 (.47)	2.00 (.49)
	Comparison	2.18 (.50)	2.29 (.48)
Reintegration***	Treatment	2.00 (.53)	1.82 (.48)
	Comparison	2.09 (.61)	2.18 (.55)
Pseudo-Independence	Treatment	3.68 (.44)	3.78 (.43)
	Comparison	3.65 (.47)	3.64 (.44)
Autonomy**	Treatment	3.84 (.36)	3.92 (.37)
	Comparison	3.94 (.41)	3.84 (.40)

Notes:
** $p < .01$
*** $p < .001$

the WRIAI subscale scores and the WRAS factor scores. The mean response to a subscale, rather than the total subscale, was used in the means and analyses and therefore scores range from 1 to 5.

For the WRIAI, a multivariate within-subjects main effect was not found for administration time, Wilks' $\Lambda = .96$, $F(5, 167) = 1.35$, $p = .245$, $\eta^2 = .04$, however a significant multivariate within-subjects effect was found for the interaction of administration time and group, Wilks' $\Lambda = .89$, $F(5, 167) = 4.03$, $p = .002$, $\eta^2 = .11$, allowing for an examination of univariate findings. Univariate within-subjects analyses indicated a significant effect of administration time by treatment group only for the disintegration subscale, $F(1, 172) = 12.79$, $p < .000$, $\eta^2 = .07$, the reintegration subscale, $F(1, 172) = 15.62$, $p < .000$, $\eta^2 = .08$, and the autonomy subscale, $F(1, 172) = 7.69$, $p = .006$, $\eta^2 = .04$. Refer to table 17.1 for the pretest and posttest WRIAI means in the treatment and comparison groups.

The 10 experimental questions on the WRIAI were also examined separately for treatment and comparison groups using paired samples t-tests. Results for the treatment group indicate significant increases for 8 out of the 10 items, as presented in table 17.2. No significant changes for the comparison group were found for any of the 10 experimental items.

For the WRAS, a multivariate within-subjects main effect was not found for administration time, Wilks' $\Lambda = .92$, $F(6, 120) = 1.80$, $p = .105$, $\eta^2 = .08$, however a multivariate within-subjects effect was found for the interaction of administration time and group, Wilks' $\Lambda = .85$, $F(6, 120) = 3.62$, $p = .002$, $\eta^2 = .15$, allowing for examination of univariate findings.

Table 17.2. Pretest and Posttest Means, Standard Deviations, and t-tests for WRIAI Experimental Questions

Item	Pretest M (SD)	Posttest M (SD)	t'' test (df = 120)
I am making a special effort to understand the significance of being white.	3.52 (1.08)	4.07 (.97)	−5.73, p > .000
Rather than focus on other races, I am searching for answers about my own race.	3.07 (1.01)	3.52 (1.10)	−2.43, p = .017
I am making an effort to decide the type of person I want to be in terms of my race.	3.37 (1.10)	4.11 (.98)	−7.57, p > .000
I am becoming aware of the strengths and limitations of my white culture.	3.65 (.96)	4.20 (.83)	−5.82, p > .000
I am taking definite steps to define an identity for myself that includes working against racism.	3.80 (.93)	4.41 (.74)	−7.62, p > .000
I am examining how racism relates to who I am.	3.89 (.96)	4.35 (.80)	−5.85, p > .000
I am involved in discovering how other white people have positively defined who they are in terms of their race.	3.13 (.99)	3.65 (1.05)	−5.34, p > .000
I am considering changing some of my behaviors and practices because I think they are racist.	3.21 (1.11)	3.96 (1.07)	−6.56, p > .000

Table 17.3. Pretest and Posttest Means and Standard Deviations for WRAS Factors

Subscale	Group	Pretest M (SD)	Posttest M (SD)
Separatist and Superior*	Treatment	1.62 (.47)	1.52 (.60)
	Comparison	1.66 (.62)	1.79 (.57)
Pluralism***	Treatment	4.21 (.53)	4.43 (.45)
	Comparison	4.10 (.56)	3.90 (.69)
Obliviousness*	Treatment	2.98 (.97)	2.65 (.91)
	Comparison	3.18 (.72)	3.19 (.69)
Self-Doubt	Treatment	3.26 (1.01)	3.55 (1.01)
	Comparison	2.96 (1.02)	2.87 (1.04)
Paternalism	Treatment	2.55 (.69)	2.70 (.74)
	Comparison	2.32 (.62)	2.45 (.66)
Other-Identification	Treatment	2.61 (.62)	2.69 (.59)
	Comparison	2.66 (.60)	2.58 (.65)

Notes:
* $p < .05$
** $p < .01$
*** $p < .001$

Significant univariate effects for administration time by treatment group were found for the separatist and superior factor, $F(1, 126) = 6.30$, $p = .048$, $\eta^2 = .05$, the pluralistic factor, $F(1, 126) = 15.87$, $p < .000$, $\eta^2 = .11$, and the obliviousness factor, $F(1, 120) = 5.63$, $p = 019$, $\eta^2 = .04$. Refer to table 17.3 for the pretest and posttest WRAS means in the treatment and comparison groups.

Discussion

The results suggest that teaching white racism and white studies on a predominantly white college campus has several significant effects on white racial identity and attitudes. Specifically, the results indicate that, in comparison to students enrolled in an Introduction to Sociology course, the white racism course significantly increases participants' endorsement of attitudes that are consistent with racial humanism and pluralism, while decreasing participants' endorsement of traditional and modern racist attitudes, and obliviousness and confusion regarding racial issues.

The results of this study are provocative and encouraging. The results are encouraging in the sense that they demonstrate attitudinal change in a direction designed to address the issues of white racism. These results suggest that courses that directly address white racism, even at varying lengths of time and intensity (i.e., one week, three weeks, and ten weeks), can impact the attitudes of self-identified white European Americans (no data is available for understanding the *attitudes* of other ethnic groups). Furthermore, the results are encouraging because they suggest some, albeit modest, attitudinal change at posttest toward greater social action, as evidenced by the experimental questions on the WRIAS. In conclusion, the results are encouraging because they provide tangible hope for changing and ultimately eradicating the perpetuation of white racism in the United States of America.

We believe our findings may assist in the development of a theory of social action to reduce white racism in the United States. The results of the measures and questionnaires from this course clearly demonstrate that white European American students endorse an ideology of equality and reject active, conscious racism. This is evident in the strong endorsement of the autonomy, pseudo-independence, and pluralism subscales in the current study. However, the results also suggest that the behavior and feelings of these students were not always congruent with this ideology. Thus, some of the students' behavior might be incongruent with the ideology of equality and, in certain instances, can be interpreted as aversive/modern racism. As presented in figure 17.1, how can participants strongly endorse items that indicate support for racial humanism (i.e., autonomy), an understanding of the sociopolitical significance of race (i.e., pseudo-independence), and an appreciation of cultural diversity (i.e., pluralism), while also endorsing items that suggest a naïveté and lack of awareness of racial issues? It is possible that racist attitudes and beliefs, which are obtained through everyday socialization in a racist world, are out of the awareness of conscious thought. By acknowledging and understanding these unconscious attitudes and beliefs in classroom situations, it is then possible to *choose* action and react to feelings based on one's ideology.

Two concerns limit the generalizability and implications of these results. First, it is important to note that the sample was self-selected. It is possible that students who enroll in a course entitled "White Racism" are different from students who choose not to enroll in such a course. Specifically, it is likely that students in the treatment group are more interested in racial issues, and thus are more amenable to efforts to intervene in racism at both the social and personal levels.

The measures utilized in this study also pose an additional concern. The questions in the WRIAI and the WRAS are vulnerable to the influences of social desirability and political correctness. In addition, they measure conscious attitudes and beliefs, and are therefore not specific measures of unconscious racism. While the measures do suggest that students endorse an ideology of equality while also endorsing behaviors or feelings that are inconsistent with that ideology, they do not provide a direct assessment of unconscious racism. Recent technologies, such as the Implicit Association Test (IAT),[56] may prove promising in assessing change in unconscious racism. Indeed, recent research supports the validity of the IAT in measuring automatic prejudicial evaluations of others,[57] and has been used in at least one published evaluation of a multicultural seminar.[58]

Conclusion

Does teaching white racism make a difference? Over time we believe it does. The long-term effect is difficult to assess and we hope to incorporate into our research design a random panel study to follow up with students on the long-term impact and effect of being taught white racism and whites studies on predominantly white college campuses. The challenge is in determining whether participants in the course actually change their behavior and actions toward racism in society on a daily basis. We are unable in our analysis to test whether in fact participants taking the course actually changed in an affective way.

Throughout the course we stress the importance of social action and require students to write a social action paper stating what activities in the literature they have read they would endorse and how they would participate. These papers have generally been good exercises in fleshing out the social actions of the new abolitionist society and understanding the existence of white privilege.[59] However, most students are unable, beyond the cognitive, to offer a set of steps and goals they would accomplish on a daily basis to participate in the eradication of white racism. Some of their inability to find steps that fit their actions in daily life is challenged by the absence of support groups and role models where the behavior and actions of such can be linked to the potential actions of the class participants. Furthermore, there are too few places and spaces where whites can discuss these issues among other whites. We encourage participants to continue to read antiracist literature and attend antiracist workshops to foster support for their "new" assessment of race in America. But this is the ideal. Moving from ideology and cognitive capacity to behavior and action requires considerable investment toward creating and sustaining a social network where one can constantly discuss the daily trials of race in the United States. Until these spaces become available for a vast majority of whites, our goal is to continue to teach white racism. Perhaps, in the end, it will make a difference.

Notes

1. Lawrence Bobo, James R. Kluegel, and Ryan A. Smith, "Laissez-Faire Racism: The Crystallization of a Kinder, Gentler, Anti-Black Ideology," in *Racial Attitudes in the 1990s: Continuity and Change*, ed. Steven A. Tuch and Jack K. Martin (Westport, Conn.: Praeger, 1997), 15–42.

2. D. Katz and K. W. Braly, "Racial Prejudice and Racial Stereotypes," *Journal of Abnormal and Social Psychology* 30 (1935): 175–193; and Howard Schuman, Charlotte Steeh, Lawrence Bobo, and Maria Krysan, *Racial Attitudes in America: Trends and Interpretations*, revised ed. (Cambridge, Mass: Harvard University Press, 1997).

3. Patricia G. Devine and Andrew J. Elliot, "Are Racial Stereotypes Really Fading? The Princeton Trilogy Revisited," *Personality and Social Psychology Bulletin* 21 (1995): 1139–1150; and Schuman et al., *Racial Attitudes*.

4. Douglas S. Massey and Nancy N. Denton, *American Apartheid: Segregation and the Making of the Underclass* (Cambridge, Mass.: Harvard University Press, 1993); and Schuman et al., *Racial Attitudes*.

5. Thomas Sowell, *Ethnic America* (New York: Basic Books, 1981); and William J. Wilson, *The Declining Significance of Race: Blacks and Changing American Institutions* (Chicago: University of Chicago Press, 1978).

6. Wilson, *Declining Significance of Race*; Bart Laundry, *The New Black Middle Class* (Berkeley: University of California Press, 1987).

7. Leaf Van Boven, "Pluralistic Ignorance and Political Correctness: The Case of Affirmative Action," *Political Psychology* 21 (2000): 267–276.

8. Joe R. Feagin, Hernan Vera, and Pinar Batur, *White Racism: The Basics*, 2nd ed. (New York: Routledge, 2001).

9. Margo J. Monteith, Julia R. Zuwerink, and Patricia G. Devine, "Prejudice and Prejudice Reduction: Classic Challenges, Contemporary Approaches," in *Social Cognition: Impact on Social Psychology*, ed. P. G. Devine, D. L. Hamilton, and T. M. Ostrom (New York: Academic Press, 1994), 323–346; Michael Omi and Howard Winant, *Racial Formation in the United States*, 2nd ed. (New York: Routledge, 1994).

10. Feagin, Vera, and Batur, *White Racism*, 2nd ed.; Samuel L. Gaertner and John F. Dovidio, "The Aversive Form of Racism," in *Prejudice, Discrimination, and Racism*, ed. John F. Dovidio and Samuel L. Gaertner (San Diego, Calif.: Academic Press, 1986), 61–89; John B. McConahay, "Modern Racism, Ambivalence, and the Modern Racism Scale," in *Prejudice, Discrimination and Racism*, 91–125; David O. Sears, "Symbolic Racism," in *Eliminating Racism: Profiles in Controversy*, ed. Phyllis A. Katz and Dalmas A. Taylor (New York: Plenum, 1988), 53–84; Thandeka, *Learning to Be White* (New York: Continuum, 1999).

11. Mark Gould, "Race and Theory: Culture, Poverty, and Adaptation to Discrimination in Wilson and Ogbu," *Sociological Theory* 17, no. 2 (1999): 191.

12. Toni Morrison, *Playing in the Dark: Whiteness and the Literary Imagination* (Cambridge, Mass.: Harvard University Press, 1992); and bell hooks, *Killing Rage: Ending Racism* (New York: Henry Holt, 1995).

13. Omi and Winant, *Racial Formation*, 5; Lani Guiner and Gerald Torres, *The Miner's Canary: Enlisting Race, Resisting Power, Transforming Democracy* (Cambridge, Mass.: Harvard University Press, 2002).

14. Omi and Winant, *Racial Formation*; David R. Roediger, *Colored White: Transcending the Racial Past* (Berkeley: University of California Press, 2002); Guinier and Torres, *Miner's Canary*.

15. Guinier and Torres, *Miner's Canary*; Roediger, *Colored White*.

16. Carol Hulse, "Lott's Praise for Thurmond Echoed His Words of 1980," *New York Times*, December 10, 2002. Retrieved December 16, 2002, from www.nytimes.com.

17. John Kifner, "Lott, and the Shadow of a Pro-White Group," *New York Times*, Nation, July 14, 1999.

18. Kifner, "Lott."

19. Guinier and Torres, *Miner's Canary*; Roediger, *Colored White*.

20. Bobo et al., "Laissez-Faire Racism."

21. Thomas F. Pettigrew, "Race and Class in the 1980s: An Interactive View," *Daedalus* 110, no. 2 (1981): 233–255.

22. Martin Gilens, *Why Americans Hate Welfare: Race, Media, and the Politics of Antipoverty Policy* (Chicago: University of Chicago Press, 1999).

23. Feagin, Vera, and Batur, *White Racism*, 2nd ed.

24. Guinier and Torres, *Miner's Canary*.

25. Joel Kovel, *White Racism: A Psychohistory* (New York: Columbia University Press, 1984); Joe R. Feagin, Hernan Vera, and Pinar Batur, *White Racism: The Basics*, 1st ed. (New York: Routledge, 1995); Feagin, Vera, and Batur, *White Racism*, 2nd ed.; Charles Lawrence, "The Id, the Ego, and Equal Protection: Reckoning with Unconscious Racism," *Stanford Law Review* 39 (1987): 317–322; Pettigrew, "Race and Class."

26. Feagin, Vera, and Batur, *White Racism*, 1st ed.; Feagin, Vera, and Batur, *White Racism*, 2nd ed.

27. Feagin, Vera, and Batur, *White Racism*, 1st ed., 171.

28. Lawrence, "Id."

29. Thandeka, *Learning*, 34.

30. Robert M. Entman and Andrew Rojecki, *The Black Image in the White Mind: Media and Race in America* (Chicago: University of Chicago Press, 2000); Thandeka, *Learning*.

31. Debra Van Ausdale and Joe R. Feagin, *The First R: How Children Learn Race and Racism* (New York: Rowman & Littlefield, 2001).

32. Van Ausdale and Feagin, *How Children Learn*.

33. R. A. Lee, "The Evolution of Affirmative Action," *Public Personnel Management* 28 (1999): 393–408; and Lani Guinier and Susan Sturm, *Who's Qualified?* (Boston: Beacon Press, 2001).

34. J. M. Ivancevich and J. A. Gilbert, "Diversity Management: Time for a New Approach," *Public Personnel Management* 29 (2000): 75–92.

35. R. S. Bigler, "The Use of Multicultural Curricula and Materials to Counter Racism in Children," *Journal of Social Issues* 55 (1999): 687–705; and M. A. Wittig and L. Molina, "Moderators and Mediators of Prejudice Reduction in Multicultural Education," in *Reducing Prejudice and Discrimination*, ed. S. Oskamp (Mahwah, N.J.: Lawrence Erlbaum, 1999), 295–318.

36. M. Bendick, M. L. Egan, and S. Lofhjelm, *The Documentation and Evaluation of Anti-discrimination Training in the United States*. Retrieved July 26, 2002, from the International Labour Organization website: www.ilo.org/public/english/protection/migrant/research/imp/29/index.htm; Bigler, "Multicultural Curricula"; Ivancevich and Gilbert, "Diversity Management."

37. Clark McCauley, M. Wright, and M. Harris, "Diversity Workshops on Campus: A Survey of Current Practice at U.S. Colleges and Universities," *College Student Journal* 34 (2000): 100–114.

38. J. A. Banks, "Multicultural Education: Its Effects on Students' Racial and Gender Role Attitudes," in *Handbook of Research on Multicultural Education*, ed. J. A. Banks and C. M. Banks (New York: Macmillan, 1995), 617–627; Bigler, "Multicultural Curricula"; and H. A. Neville and M. Furlong, "The Impact of Participation in a Cultural Awareness Program on the Racial Attitudes and Social Behaviors of First-Year College Students," *Journal of College Student Development* 35 (1994): 371–377.

39. Ivancevich and Gilbert, "Diversity Management"; and John Naisbitt and Patricia Aburdene, *Megatrends 2000, Ten New Directions for the 1990's* (New York: William Morrow, 1990).

40. Rita Hardiman and William Cross, *White Identity Theory: Origins and Prospect*, videorecording (North Amherst, Mass.: Microtraining, 1991).

41. Insignia and WETA, producers, *Death Runs Riot*, television series episode. In *The West*, ed. West Film Project and WETA (Washington, D.C.: Insignia and WETA, 1996).

42. These include *Who's the Savage*, about the massacre of Cheyenne indigenous people at Sand Creek, for which the perpetrator, Samuel Chittingon, was never put on trial; *Days of Waiting* (a film by Steven Okzaki, Farallon Films), the story of Estelle Ishigo and her Japanese internment camp experience; and *Ethnic Notions: Black People in White Minds* by Marlon Riggs (California Newsreel, 1987)

43. Anti-Defamation League, A World of Difference Institute. Teacher/Student Resource Guide: Greater Chicago Region, 1995.

44. Paul Kivel, *Uprooting Racism: How White People Can Work for Racial Justice* (Philadelphia: New Society Publishers, 1996).

45. Kivel, *Uprooting Racism*.

46. Feagin, Vera, and Batur, *White Racism*, 1st ed.

47. Theodoric Manley, Jr., "Teaching Race and Ethnic Relations: Do the Right Thing," *Ethnic and Racial Studies* 17, no. 1 (1994): 135–163.

48. Janet E. Helms and Robert T. Carter, "White Racial Identity Attitude Inventory," in *Black and White Racial Identity: Theory, Research and Practice*, ed. Janet E. Helms (Westport, Conn.: Greenwood Press, 1990), 62–80.

49. Janet E. Helms, "Toward a Theoretical Explanation of the Effect of Race on Counseling: A Black and White Model," *Counseling Psychology* 12 (1984): 153–165; Helms, *Black and White Racial Identity*; and Helms and Carter, "Attitude Inventory."

50. Helms and Carter, "Attitude Inventory."

51. Robert T. Carter, "The Relationship between Racism and Racial Identity among White Americans: An Exploratory Investigation," *Journal of Counseling and Development* 69 (1990): 46–50; and D. B. Pope-Davis and T. M. Ottavi, "The Relationship between Racism and Racial Identity among White Americans," *Journal of Counseling and Development* 72 (1994): 293–297.

52. H. A. Neville et al., "The Impact of Multicultural Training on White Racial Identity Attitudes and Therapy Competencies," *Professional Psychology: Research and Practice* 27 (1996): 83–89; and T. M. Ottavi, D. B. Pope-Davis, and J. G. Dings, "Relationship between White Racial Identity Attitudes and Self-Reported Multicultural Counseling Competencies," *Journal of Counseling Psychology* 41 (1994): 149–154.

53. A. M. Galloway et al., "White Racial Attitudes: A Synthesis of Extant Literature and Scale Development" (poster presented at the American Psychological Convention, Boston, Mass., August 1999).

54. Galloway et al., "White Racial Attitudes."

55. A former research assistant for the course co-taught the course as a part-time instructor in July 2002.

56. For example, S. C. Draine and A. G. Greenwald, "Replicable Unconscious Semantic Priming," *Journal of Experimental Psychology* 127 (1998): 286–303; A. G. Greenwald, D. E. McGhee, and J. L. K. Schwartz, "Measuring Individual Differences in Implicit Cognition: The Implicit Association Test," *Journal of Personality and Social Psychology* 74 (1998): 1464–1480.

57. N. Dasgupta et al., "Automatic Preference for White Americans: Eliminating the Familiarity Explanation," *Journal of Experimental Social Psychology* 36 (2000): 316–328; and L. A. Rudman et al., "Measuring the Automatic Components of Prejudice: Flexibility and Generality of the Implicit Association Test," *Social Cognition* 17 (1999): 437–465.

58. Rudman, Ashmore, and Gary, 2001

59. Noel Ignatiev, "Abolitionism and the White Studies Racket," *Race Traitor: Treason to Whiteness Is Loyalty to Humanity* 10 (1999): 3–7.

V

EPILOGUE
Community Praxis

Ethnic Studies Community Collaboration and Activism
Bridging Theory and Practice*

JAMES SOBREDO, LINDA REVILLA, AND GREGORY YEE MARK

CALIFORNIA HAS ONE OF THE MOST DIVERSE ethnic and linguistic communities in the United States. Examining demographic data gathered in the 2000 census, researchers at UCLA's Lewis Clark Center for Regional Policy Studies concluded that "California is the most diverse of the 50 states."[1] In California, the "minority population" is now "squarely in the majority."[2] According to the *San Francisco Chronicle*, "California's Anglo population has officially dipped under 50 percent and is no longer a majority."[3] Hispanics now make up 34.4 percent of California's population. At 10.8 percent of the state's population, Asians are now the second largest ethnic group in California. The significance of this diversity, however, is rarely integrated successfully in a K–12 school curriculum. Furthermore, "diversity" curricula are generally inadequate because of their brevity and lack of in-depth analysis.

In December 2001, the Department of Ethnic Studies at California State University at Sacramento (CSUS), Hiram Johnson High School (HJ), and Healthy Start (HS), a Sacramento school district program teamed up to develop and incorporate an "ethnic studies service-learning project" (ES/SL project) which involved creating a comprehensive program of teaching an ethnic studies curriculum and providing tutoring and mentorship for Sacramento high school students. In spring 2003, Will C. Wood Middle School (WCW), a feeder school to Hiram Johnson, joined our ES/SL collaborative project.[4]

---

*From: James Sobredo, Linda Revilla, and Gregory Yee Mark, "Ethnic Studies Community Collaboration & Activism: Bridging Theory and Practice," in *Introduction to Ethnic Studies*, ed. Brian Baker, Boatamo Masupyoe, and Julie Figueroa (Dubuque, Iowa: Kendall Hunt Publishing, 2004), pp. 289–302. Reprinted by permission. This chapter was edited to conform to the format of this anthology.

Background

Built in 1958, Hiram Johnson High School was a high school with a solid academic curriculum serving a predominantly middle-class neighborhood. Named after the former governor of California (1910–1916) who later became a U.S. senator, Hiram Johnson High School currently serves an ethnically diverse, multilingual, working-class community in Sacramento. The neighborhood was heavily affected by a booming aerospace industry and the nearby military air base, which contributed to its middle-class population. In the late 1960s and throughout the 1970s, however, the demographic composition of the neighborhood and the high school changed.

One major factor that caused the change was the burgeoning redevelopment programs occurring in the downtown Sacramento area. Sprawling concrete buildings were being constructed to accommodate the growth of state government, which led to further economic expansion, and until the late 1990s, the state of California remained the largest employer in the Sacramento metropolitan area. Aside from government building projects, housing redevelopment was also displacing many African Americans from the downtown area. As they moved away from the downtown area, blacks were moving into the outlying affordable neighborhoods such as Oak Park, Tahoe Park, and Del Paso Heights. These changes in the neighborhood eventually caused a white flight out to newer, more middle-class suburban developments.

The changing demography around the Hiram Johnson community was also affected by the civil rights movement, affirmative action policies, and major changes in immigration laws. People of color were able to afford to move into this middle-class neighborhood and wanted to send their kids to a decent high school. The demographic changes in the community were accelerated in the 1980s as more ethnically diverse populations moved into the surrounding neighborhoods around Hiram Johnson. Today, areas along main arteries such as Stockton Boulevard and Franklin Boulevard hold a large concentration of newly arrived Asian Americans of Vietnamese, Cambodian, Hmong, and Mien origins. The Elder Creek and Oak Park neighborhoods continue to receive African Americans and Southeast Asian residents. The community's demographic changes were also represented in the ethnic composition of Hiram Johnson. Established teachers were not prepared to deal with an ethnically diverse student population. To make the process more complicated, in the last thirty years, there were no new high schools built in the city of Sacramento. The state's budget crisis and shifting educational priorities have further exacerbated the school system. Hiram Johnson was used as a dumping ground for incoming new students.

Overcrowding became a familiar experience. The overcrowding led to a high student-to-teacher ratio. Furthermore, cultural and linguistic gaps between students and teachers worsened the learning process. As a consequence, talented and experienced teachers left the high school and went to more racially monolithic institutions. The new incoming teachers were inexperienced and oftentimes ill-prepared. Those teachers who were well-prepared and talented would not stay at Hiram Johnson and transferred out to more stable, middle-class schools, leading to a "revolving door" system of teachers. These combined factors led to an educationally underperforming school and increased tensions among students, which in turn led to frequent cases of student violence.

Today, students at Hiram Johnson have low scores on standardized tests, have low graduation rates, rarely go to college, and are severely overcrowded—in the fall of 2002, for instance, a school designed for 1,700 students had an opening day registration of over 3,300 students. Not surprisingly, there are high rates of student truancy and youth violence (fights and youth gang activities). One recent television report referred to Hiram Johnson as a "gladiator school" where things are "just plain scary." In the fall of 2002 it was within this context that Dr. Gregory Yee Mark, chair of the Department of Ethnic Studies, approached Dr. Andre Douyon, then principal of Hiram Johnson, with the plan of creating a community partnership and service-learning program between CSUS and HJ.

Mark had initially surveyed principals in Sacramento with the purpose of developing a community collaboration and service-learning project. After meeting Dr. Douyon, however, Dr. Mark chose Hiram Johnson High School as our principal partner for a community collaboration and service-learning project.

Mark is one of the key participants of the "Third World" student movement at the University of California, Berkeley, which culminated in the famous 1969 Third World Strike for the purpose of establishing an "ethnic studies" curriculum and program at the university. One of the key goals of the strike was to bridge the divide between university and community by establishing a "community service" component to the academic curriculum, a goal which grew out of the recognition that ethnic communities were in dire need of social services. Mark would spend a lifetime serving ethnic communities—in his case, focusing on the Asian American community—beginning with establishing the East Bay Chinese Youth Council in Oakland, citizenship programs in Honolulu, and eventually becoming principal investigator/director of the Asian Pacific Islander Youth Violence Prevention Center at the John Burns School of Medicine, University of Hawaii.

Demographically, Hiram Johnson goes against the common perception of inner-city schools comprising mostly African Americans and Hispanics. At Hiram Johnson, it is Asian/Pacific Islander and white students who are the majority: 27.9% Asian Americans, 2.5% Pacific Islanders, and 1.7% Filipinos, for a total of 32.1%. European Americans, particularly those of Russian descent, make up the next largest student group at 27.2%. In contrast, Hispanics make up 22.4% of the school's population and African Americans, 16.3%.

In terms of academic performance, in 2001 only 18% of ninth graders were achieving at the "Proficient" or "Advanced" level in English language arts, 24% of tenth graders, and 21% of eleventh graders. In reading, only 25% of ninth graders scored above the fiftieth percentile, 26% of tenth graders, and 29% of eleventh graders. In mathematics, 46% of ninth graders scored above the fiftieth percentile, 42% of tenth graders, and only 42% of eleventh graders. In one of our classroom visits to Hiram Johnson, a ninth-grade teacher stated that some of the students in class were only at a fifth-grade reading level. In 2001, the school suspended 597 students and expelled 6 students. Not surprisingly, the school has a very low graduation rate of 45%.

Will C. Wood Middle School, a feeder school to Hiram Johnson, also had similar statistics in 2001. It has an ethnically diverse student population with Hispanics and Asians comprising the majority: 32.1% Hispanics, 29.1% Asian Americans (predominantly Southeast Asians), 18.1% African Americans, 15.8% Caucasians, 2.6% Native Americans, and .9% for both Pacific Islanders and Filipinos. In 2001, it had a population of 1,210 and 958 incidents of suspension were reported. Only 13% of seventh and eighth graders were achieving at the "Proficient" or "Advanced" level in English language arts; 28% of seventh graders and 27% of eighth graders were scoring above the fifty-ninth percentile in reading, and 32% of seventh graders and 28% of eighth graders scored above the fiftieth percentile in mathematics.

The major goals of this ES/SL collaborative program were (1) to provide a service-learning component to the ethnic studies curriculum at California State University at Sacramento, (2) to provide an integrative and community-based approach to teaching ethnic studies, (3) to prevent youth violence and promote tolerance of different ethnic groups, and (4) to bring a community-based research model into practice in an ethnically diverse community.

Service-Learning Research Project

Our research project goal was to assess the needs and assets of an ethnically diverse, working-class community and then conduct both a short-term and a long-term longitudinal study of the effectiveness of our service-learning program. Our research tools were surveys (multilingual format), focus groups comprised of community members and students (also multilingual format), oral history interviews, and participant observation.

Our ES/SL collaborative project started in early 2002, when a needs assessment research project (NAR) was conducted from March to April. The research project was in partnership with Healthy Start, a Sacramento school district program designed to help schools that are officially classified as having high poverty and crime rates. Healthy Start is based on the recognition that educational achievement, physical and emotional health, and family strength all depend upon each other. Its mission is to promote and facilitate the integration of community and school resources to better serve students and their families and to promote academic success. Healthy Start encompasses an array of prevention and intervention services for youth and their family members. During the 2001–2002 school year, the Healthy Start program at Hiram Johnson served 370 students, over 75% of whom were low-income. Mary Struths is the Healthy Start coordinator at Hiram Johnson.

The NAR project was intended not only to assess the needs of the community but also the *assets* of the neighborhoods around Hiram Johnson High School and Will C. Wood Middle School. On Saturday, March 16, 2003, a four-hour "walk-the-block" community survey was conducted by CSUS students (many of whom are multilingual), Healthy Start staff, and participants from VISTA, AmeriCorps, and the National Civilian Community Corps, all working in teams of two and three. Dr. Mark and Mary Struths were on-site, supervising the fifty-seven volunteers. The community survey teams took advantage of several community events occurring that day—a community health fair at Lincoln Village, a neighborhood association pancake breakfast at the Colonial Heights Library, and a Southeast Asian community resident forum at the George Sim Community Center. At the end of the day, 359 surveys were completed.

Students in Dr. Gregory Mark's Research Methodology course (Ethnic Studies 194) were trained to assist Healthy Start to design, conduct, and analyze a field survey. After the survey, Struths noted the invaluable research and translation assistance provided by CSUS students. The survey was distributed in English, Vietnamese, Chinese, and Spanish. Because they were able to speak Vietnamese, Hmong, Mien, Laotian, Cambodian, Chinese, and Spanish, CSUS students were better able to approach non-English speakers, provide translation for Hmong, Cambodian, and Mien speakers, and explain the importance of the survey. Here are the results of the needs assessment research project.

Table 18.1. Ethnic Composition of the Respondents

Ethnic Composition of Respondents	Percentage
Asian	15
Native Hawaiian or Pacific Islander	2
African American or Black	11
Hispanic or Latino	26
American Indian or Alaska Native	2
Caucasian/White	39
Other	6.8

Table 18.2. Languages Spoken at Home

Language Spoken Most Often at Home	Percentage
English	73
Spanish	18
Russian	.3
Vietnamese	4
Mien	3
Cantonese	3
Laotian	.3
Other	3

[Note: Figures do not add up to 100 because respondents were allowed to choose more than one language.]

Table 18.3. Age and Gender of the Respondents

Age	Percentage
Under 20 years of age	11
21–30 years old	16
31–40 years old	19
41–50 years old	15
51–60 years old	10
61–70 years old	3
71 years and older	5.6

[Note: Figures do not add up to 100 because some respondents declined to state his or her age.]

Gender	Percentage
Female	55
Male	40
Unknown (left blank)	5

Table 18.4. "Top 10" Serious Issues Facing Youth in Their Neighborhoods

Top 10 Most Serious Issues Facing Teens in Your Neighborhood	Percentage
Drinking/drugs	69
Fighting/violence	47
Lack of safe places to play and hang out	44
Lack of supervision/parental involvement	43
Gang involvement	42
Family problems	40
Early sexual activity	40
School failure/dropping out	37
Lack of employment	30
Suicide	25

[Note: Respondents were allowed to choose more than one issue.]

Of the respondents surveyed, 13% mentioned that they or their children attended Hiram Johnson High School, and 11% attended Will C. Wood Middle School. The survey respondents were most concerned about drinking and drugs (69%), followed by fighting/violence (47%). These results were similar to the results of the student focus group conducted at Hiram Johnson.

Aside from a field survey, CSUS students also conducted several focus groups from March to May 2002: Four groups at WCW for twenty-four students and four groups at HJ for thirty-six students. CSUS students facilitated the focus group discussions, half of which were for students only and the other half for parents only. The research goals of the focus group were to gain student perceptions of the needs, strengths, and challenges facing students and their families.

For both WCW and HJ students, the top concerns were gang violence and fighting at school and in the neighborhood. Next were street-safety concerns for WCW students, and mental health and health access issues for the HJ students. When asked the question, "What is your estimate of the percentage of students at your school that are involved in gangs?" the average response for both schools was 50%. Students in both schools also referred to the very low level of parent participation in school activities and indicated how discouraging this is to them. Many of the students expressed concerns that they were not respected by most school staff and that their individual needs were of little consequence to the majority of their teachers.

Partly as a result of the NAR project, Healthy Start received a $9 million Department of Education federal grant for the Sacramento Unified School District. Mary Struths specifically mentioned and acknowledged the important role that CSUS students played.

I could not have pulled off something this broad-based and labor- and time-intensive without the direct involvement of the Ethnic Studies Research class. My program, although a program of Sacramento City Unified School District, is in many respects, very similar to a grassroots nonprofit organization. At the moment, we have very few actual dollars to implement programs and services. My staff is small. . . . The partnership with Professor Mark and his class has allowed me to reach far more people with the needs assessment than I had initially envisioned and has provided me with the technical support and expertise that I needed. I've been so impressed with his students that I'd like to recruit a few of them for AmeriCorps positions at my Healthy Start for next year. Of course, it is only through Professor Mark's leadership and support of community engagement that my contact with the research class was made possible. The nice thing for me is that I foresee an on-going relationship with the Ethnic Studies Department and Healthy Start long after the needs assessment project is completed.

An Ethnic Studies Model of Community Collaboration

The Healthy Start survey identified that an immediate need at Hiram Johnson was a tutorial program for students in math and English. Other programs would develop in response to the needs identified by professors, teachers, administrators, and CSUS student-teaching interns. Here are our programs, along with a brief description:

Student Tutoring

A key component to our community collaboration and service-learning project involves a tutorial program in which CSUS students tutor in math, science, and English at HJ and WCW. In spring 2003, we started out with thirty-five CSUS student interns providing tutorial services at HJ, and the following semester WCW was added to our tutorial program.[5]

The major goals of the program were:

1. To tutor the students of Hiram Johnson High School in predominantly English and math.
2. To promote interethnic agency, community, and university collaboration.
3. To raise the consciousness of college students concerning the issues facing the youth in inner-city schools.
4. To promote and facilitate the empowerment of the youth and communities at large.

Training Workshops

It is difficult for any program to succeed without the proper orientation and training. In this light, we created three "training workshops" to provide an introduction to our ES/SL project, to explain how CSUS got involved with HJ, to provide training in teaching in high school versus at the college/university, and to meet the CSUS and HJ faculty. Mark and James Fabionar presented and facilitated the major portion of the training workshops, and they were assisted by CSUS and HJ faculty and "veteran" CSUS student-teaching interns. Students were also introduced to the CSUS students who were coordinating our ES/SL program in HJ and WCW. In order to participate in the student-teaching internship, tutorial, and peer mentorship programs, all CSUS students were required to attend the three workshops.

CSUS student tutors were recruited from ethnic studies classes to serve between twenty and thirty hours per week as tutors. The first of the training sessions was designed to familiarize the potential tutors with the schools' histories and cultures. This training session discussed the racial and economic shifts that have occurred at Hiram Johnson and in the surrounding communities. The second training session focused on the history of service learning in ethnic studies. Students were given a detailed account of the creation of ethnic studies and the Third World Liberation Front, and ethnic studies' strong ties to serving the community. The third training session provided students with the tools they would need when they entered the classroom. At this point students were introduced to the principal and teachers and given preliminary tutoring assignments. Students were also given instructions concerning common lesson-planning structures and participated in workshop sessions with teachers to discuss common issues facing instructors in the classroom. At the end of the semester, all tutors were required to attend a "reflection session" to discuss and share any observations and problems that may have arisen in the course of the semester.

Because both HJ and WCW students performed below the "Proficient" level of the California Standards Test, principal Lynne Tafoya of HJ and principal James Wong of WCW requested that CSUS interns also provide service as tutors in math, science, and English. Our tutorial program at HJ and WCW provided direct tutoring services to approximately 900 students. We are currently in the midst of evaluating the effectiveness of our tutorial program, and hope to have more substantial survey results as well as be able to demonstrate a rise in test scores.

Small Learning Communities

This academic year, Hiram Johnson switched to a "small learning communities" (SLC) model. The idea is that students will receive more personalized instruction when they belong to a small learning community that, aside from fulfilling the necessary educational requirement for graduation, will also provide instruction in their areas of interest. For instance, HJ has the following small learning communities: Arts, Multimedia, and Entertainment; Business and Information Technology; Health and Medical Services; Human and Legal Services; Humanities, Education, and Leadership; Engineering and Industrial Technologies; Government and Public Administration; and International Cultural Community. Our collaboration with HJ has led to the creation of a Community Studies (CS) small learning community, which is based on an ethnic studies/community studies model of conducting research: "The Community Studies SLC focuses on the cultural, historical, and social experience of ethnic groups both nationally and within the Hiram Johnson surrounding community. This SLC will be a collaboration with CSUS and includes Ethnic Studies classes."

Community Studies SLC

Aside from teaching the basics of math, science, social science, English, and language, the Community Studies SLC also teaches ethnic studies and a documentary arts curriculum. James Fabionar, our community partner from the inception of the ES/SL project, is the lead instructor of the Community Studies SLC. In fall 2002, he taught the first ethnic studies class, which had an enrollment of one hundred students. Fabionar was assisted by fifteen student-teaching interns from the CSUS Ethnic Studies Department. Ethnic studies undergraduates, most of whom were taking Dr. Mark's research methodologies class, helped in designing and implementing an ethnic studies curriculum by planning and creating lesson plans, selecting readings, creating handouts and overheads, and assisting in classroom instruction. CSUS students worked as teaching assistants in the classroom and occasionally lectured on the day's lesson plan. The ethnic studies course at Hiram Johnson High School is offered as an elective to ninth-grade students. The class is a yearlong course, with part one in the fall, and part two completed in the spring.

Community Celebration

At the end of the 2002–2003 academic year, CSUS students planned a community celebration which was intended to mark the implementation of the first ethnic studies class at HJ as well as provide an opportunity to thank students, faculty, and staff for their help and participation in the ES/SL project. CSUS students sent letters home to parents and did follow-up telephone calls to personally invite parents and students to the community celebration. James Fabionar had to prepare CSUS students to make sure to say the correct greetings in their phone calls. Most HJ parents are so accustomed to hearing only bad news when the high school calls, so CSUS students were coached on how to inform parents that the phone call was for the purpose of delivering "good news" about their son or daughter. At the community celebration, CSUS students served dinner to the evening's participants, which included the ES faculty, CSUS administrators and staff, and principals from HJ and WCW. Aside from faculty, staff, and CSUS students, more than 200 HJ parents and students attended the event. This is significant in light of the fact that HJ has very low parent participation in school activities, to the extent that there is currently no parent teacher association at HJ. Thus, this was the first time that something close to a PTA meeting had been held in recent years.

Documentary Arts

In fall 2003, a documentary arts component was added to the CS curriculum. The goal was to make the class enjoyable for students and allow them to utilize their assets in conducting the documentation of communities. The course was taught by Ms. Teresa Barnett, a computer teacher and graduate of CSUS who worked in close collaboration with Dr. James Sobredo, assistant professor in ethnic studies, in designing and implementing the curriculum. The documentary arts curriculum included these four main components: (a) oral history; (b) photo editing; (c) community photo documentary; and (d) video documentary and production. Under the guidance of Dr. Sobredo, CSUS teaching interns lectured on the background and importance of oral histories, gave workshops and demonstrations on conducting oral histories, explained the importance and proper procedure of obtaining signed consent forms, demonstrated how to type transcripts and narrative summaries, and gave workshops on how to scan/digitize photographs, edit and crop photographs, and prepare and mount documents and photographs for public exhibition. At the end of the winter semester, students gave a public exhibit of their oral history projects, which included edited oral history narratives accompanied by family photographs.

Peer Helpers

This semester we started our student "peer helper" program. Under the guidance of Ms. Julia Hedstrom, English teacher at HJ, and with the help of Mr. Andres Victorio, a CSUS ethnic studies major and associate pastor at a community church, we had thirty-five students who were participating in a Peer Helping course. Students studied and examined basic principles of counseling and peer mentorship, role-play scenarios that cause conflict (especially among students, teachers, and parents), and learned effective, nonviolent ways of dealing with the situations. A major goal of this program was to reduce the level of conflict and violence in HJ, which was especially needed given the amount of violence occurring at HJ, as well as student indications that violence and fights are among their top concerns at school.

Significance and Relevance

The majority of research in ethnic studies remains a top-down model: Scholars research their subjects in the comfort of a university, institute, or library. Furthermore, when the research project is completed, it generally has very little application or benefit to the community. In contrast, this ethnic studies community-based research project has measurable and beneficial applications: research data that CSUS ethnic studies students collected and analyzed was instrumental in the district receiving the $9 million federal grant. Our community-based research project utilized community surveys and focus group discussions. We are currently in the midst of implementing an oral history project and a longitudinal study of the effectiveness of the ESHS program. Smaller versions of our project have been implemented by other professors in other CSU departments. Several universities have individual professors working on internship programs with community organizations (schools, nonprofits, businesses, and government agencies). What is unique and significant about our ES/SL project, however, is that it has involved the participation and commitment of the *entire department*. We are recognized system-wide by the California State University Chancellor's Office as an "engaged" department; that is, the entire faculty, not just a few individuals, is involved in a collaborative service-learning project. Our ESHS program is a collaboration between professors, university students, high school teachers, high school counselors, social service providers, and high school students. For ethnic studies student-teaching interns, their participation in the ESHS project has changed their traditional views of "ethnic community" and ethnic studies "activism." As one CSUS teaching intern stated, "Teaching can be a radical and revolutionary act."

Here are some of the comments from teachers regarding CSUS tutors:

> This is a very beneficial program. The students really gain from individual attention.
> Kara Synhorst, language arts and reading teacher, Will C. Wood Middle School

> My students looked up to the college students. They are good role models to high school kids. Thanks.
> Lorene Matsumoto, algebra teacher, Hiram Johnson High School

Here are the comments that CSUS students shared regarding their experience as tutors:

> These students taught me things about myself. This class has changed my life, and I hope [the students I worked with] can say the same of me.
> Kara Meador

> I found that when I allowed myself to open up to these students most did the same in return. I think this affected the way they acted in class after this. Knowing that they could relate to me in a number of ways in which they probably never imagined, made them a little more comfortable with me and settled in class.
> Silva Martinez

> For many of the Spanish-speaking students, I have become something more [than a tutor], perhaps a friend or maybe someone they know will listen.
> Eduardo Sevill

> To be able to reach out to these students and know that I've gained a new level of respect from them really meant a lot to me.
> Jason Kondi

Through end-of-semester course evaluations handed out to high school students, we evaluated the effectiveness of our ethnic studies student teachers and the Hiram Johnson High School seniors who served as teaching assistants. Using Hiram Johnson records, we evaluated the effectiveness of the program in terms of the incidences of youth violence and gang activity.

Theory and Conceptual Framework: Community-Based Research

Historically, ethnic studies programs on the West coast have developed as a result of student and community involvement and participation. This was particularly the case during the 1968 Third World Strike in San Francisco State College and the 1969 student strike at UC Berkeley, which gave rise to the formal institution of ethnic studies programs.[6] Today, as ethnic studies programs have been institutionalized in major research and comprehensive universities, the central role of students and ethnic communities have been diminished. Scholars such as Lane Hirabayashi and Marilyn Alquizola have pointed out the historical divergence between scholars, students, and community.[7] Moreover, as Hirabayashi points out, some scholars have taken an even stronger view and argued that "in terms of the will to pursue community-oriented, community-based research in the academic setting, Asian American Studies faculty have 'dropped the ball.'"[8]

This ethnic studies community service-learning program has tilted the balance back toward student participation, serving the needs of ethnic communities, and conducting community-based research. Hiram Johnson serves a diverse ethnic population of Hispanics, Asians, African Americans, Native Americans, and Eastern Europeans. Our program involves ethnic studies majors taking classes that prepare them for teaching ethnic studies in high school. Under the close supervision of a high school teacher and ethnic studies professors, CSUS students began teaching at Hiram Johnson in the fall of 2002. The first ethnic studies class comprised five ninth-grade sections, serving more than 125 students. We are now teaching an ethnic studies curriculum to all levels, grades nine through twelve, and our collaborative program currently serves more than 250 students. CSUS ethnic studies students—some of whom are themselves graduates of Hiram Johnson—are teaching Hiram Johnson students history, culture, social science theory, community-based research and photo-documentation, and ways to create and exhibit oral history projects.

An immediate goal of the service-learning project was to assist the Healthy Start program to conduct a needs and assets assessment of the community, parents, and students. CSUS ethnic studies students and Hiram Johnson students participated under the auspices of Healthy Start. Student volunteers conducted more than 368 surveys in the surrounding community; Hiram Johnson parents submitted 390 surveys; and so far ethnic studies students have facilitated eight focus group discussions (four comprised of students only and four of parents only). The service-learning participation of ethnic studies students and professors filled an immediate research need of Hiram Johnson High School.

Summary

Our ES/SL project is unique because our entire department is engaged in the project. In further recognition of our program's success, in 2003 the

Corporation for National Service awarded the CSUS Ethnic Studies Department a Serve and Learn Grant of $375,000 to support our community collaboration and service-learning project at Hiram Johnson High School and Will C. Wood Middle School.

The ethnic studies community program's ultimate goal is to attract Hiram Johnson students to CSUS, and to encourage them to major or minor in ethnic studies, earn a teaching degree, and return to their communities as teachers and mentors who promote a community-based model of teaching and learning. This goal will not only produce more college-bound students, promote tolerance, reduce youth violence, and address California's pressing need for more teachers, but it will also fulfill the original vision of ethnic studies as service to the community.

Notes

1. We are thankful for the generous grant support from the Corporation for National and Community Service in providing funding for our program.

2. Carol Ness, "S. F.'s Diversity Comeuppance," *San Francisco Chronicle*, April 1, 2000.

3. Tanya Schevitz, "California Minorities Become Majority: Census Reflects Surge among Latinos, Asians," *San Francisco Chronicle*, August 30, 2000.

4. Carol Ness, "33,871,648 Hispanics Now Make Up Third of Californians," *San Francisco Chronicle*, March 30, 2000.

5. "Hiram Johnson High School & Will C. Wood Tutorial Program," a report by Kyle Meador, project coordinator, Ethnic Studies Department, California State University, Sacramento, Fall 2003. The following information regarding the tutorial programs at Hiram Johnson and Will C. Wood is taken from Meador's report.

6. William Wei, *The Asian American Movement* (Philadelphia: Temple University Press, 1993).

7. Lane Hirabayashi and Marilyn Alquizola, "Asian American Studies: Reevaluating for the 1990s" *The State of Asian America: Activism and Resistance in the 1990s*, ed. Karin Aguilar-San Juan (Boston: South End Press, 1994).

8. Lane Hirabayashi, "Back to the Future: Re-framing Community-Based Research," *Amerasia Journal* 21, nos. 1–2 (1995).

The Story of a Collaborative Project*   **19**

LUKE ERIC LASSITER

ON A COLD AFTERNOON IN EARLY JANUARY 2003, a group of Ball State University faculty and students gathered at the Virginia B. Ball Center for Creative Inquiry to talk about beginning the collaborative ethnography that lies before you—the brainchild of retired seventy-seven-year-old Indiana state legislator Hurley Goodall. After making some introductions, I asked Hurley to talk about the work that lay ahead: "I wondered if Hurley could talk a little about his vision for this project and how it is we're here now."

"Okay, I'm Hurley Goodall," he began. "I'm a native of Muncie, and that's one of the reasons I'm extremely interested in what you're doing. On behalf of the community, I'd like to thank you." Hurley pulled out a piece of paper from a folder that sat on the table in front of him. It was a selection from his own writing. "I would just like to read you part of the original Lynd plan—to tell you why this project is being done."

Hurley began reading: "In 1929, Robert S. Lynd and Helen Merrell Lynd [published] . . . what they called an 'objective study' of American society. The method they used was to come and live in that American community, observe the people, the institutions, and the forces that made the community work. The effort was also designed to show how communities change over time, but also how certain things did not change. The choice of the Muncie community was determined, in part, by population . . ."

---

*From: Luke Eric Lassiter, "Introduction," in *The Other Side of Middletown: Muncie's African American Community*, ed. Luke Eric Lassiter, Hurley Goodall, Elizabeth Campbell, and Michelle Natasya Johnson, pp. 1–24 (Walnut Creek, Calif.: AltaMira Press, 2004). Reprinted by permission. This chapter was edited to conform to the format of this anthology.

Hurley looked up from his reading. "And this is the part I'm interested in," he said, ". . . a homogeneous native-born population, a small foreign-born and Negro population that could basically be ignored." After a short pause, Hurley added, "That was the standard the Lynds set. So, in essence, the African American community here . . . was completely ignored by that study. And, hopefully, some of the things you'll be doing will fill that void."[1]

When Robert S. and Helen Merrell Lynd first published *Middletown: A Study in Modern American Culture* in 1929, it was immediately heralded for its unprecedented survey of a "typical" American city. With few exceptions, social scientists had never attempted an American-based study so broad in its scope.[2] Influenced by anthropologists such as Clark Wissler (who wrote the book's foreword), the Lynds used anthropological research methods to organize their fieldwork (long-term participation and observation in one locality).[3] The Lynds also applied the theoretical approaches to culture in use among the day's social anthropologists to organize their writing: they split their study into six broad cultural categories (with each receiving treatment in individual chapters)—Getting a Living, Making a Home, Training the Young, Using Leisure, Engaging in Religious Practices, and Engaging in Community Activities—categories that social anthropologists used as guiding categories to explain human behavior cross-culturally.[4] Wrote the Lynds:

> Whether in an Arunta village in Central Australia, or in our own seemingly intricate institutional life of corporations, dividends, coming-out parties, prayer meetings, freshmen, and Congress, human behavior appears to consist in variations upon a few major lines of activity: getting the material necessities of food, clothing, shelter; mating; initiating the young into the group habits of thought and behavior; and so on. This study, accordingly, proceeds on the assumption that all the things people do in this American city may be viewed as falling under one or another of [these] . . . six main-truck activities.[5]

At a time when anthropology had its sights set on non-Western tribal peoples, *Middletown* became a sociology classic, and remains so today. It has never gone out of print.

The Lynds chose Muncie because they perceived it to be a relatively homogeneous community. In many ways it was. In the 1920s, Muncie was a medium-sized city "large enough to have put on long trousers and to take itself seriously, and yet small enough to be studied from many aspects as a unit," was relatively self-contained and not "a satellite city" of a larger metropolis, and had "a small Negro and foreign-born population."[6] Although Muncie's black population was indeed a small percentage of the overall Muncie population, importantly, the Lynds missed that Muncie's black community was growing at a faster rate, and was indeed larger "as a proportion of overall population" in Muncie than in such major cities as Chicago, New York, or Detroit.[7]

One can almost excuse the Lynds for missing this, especially because, in recognizing their omissions of "racial change" in lieu of their focus on the larger "base-line group," they acknowledged that they were ignoring significant heterogeneities such as race, and thus encouraged that "racial backgrounds may be studied by future workers."[8] Several researchers took up the Lynds' call, focusing on different minority groups in Muncie, including its African American population.[9] But even so, when one reads the corpus of Middletown literature—for this literature is much larger for Muncie than for any other town of its size—one still may be struck by how the contributions of African Americans to the larger Muncie community are so often categorically ignored, even dismissed. The most recent study of Middletown, *Back to Middletown: Three Generations of Sociological Reflections*, does just this, for example. The author, Rita Caccamo, writes that "only a small group of intellectuals associated with the college is active in the fight for civil rights."[10] As we argue in the following chapters, black Muncie has been at the heart of a vibrant civil rights movement in the city for the past several decades, continuing to this day (albeit in different forms). To place that civil rights activity solely in the hands of college professors is to seriously—and inexcusably—miss the role of Muncie's African American community here. For civil rights activists like Hurley Goodall, who, with many others, has spent nearly his entire adult life organizing the African American community around civil rights issues, such omissions of the African American community and its contributions forcefully echo "the standard the Lynds set."

From Idea to Project: Some Background

This book is thus an attempt to fill the void about which Hurley Goodall spoke on that January afternoon. It is, however, only a small part of a much larger effort to document the history and contributions of the African American community in Muncie—a small part because Hurley, for one, has collected community photographs, church histories, newspaper clippings, and individual narratives for well over three decades. In addition to this, he has written extensively about Muncie and the African American experience here; much of these writings remain archived in Ball State's Archives and Special Collections.

In 2001, Hurley and I began to discuss combining his own research and writing with an ethnographic perspective. But the roots of this conversation had begun much earlier—specifically during a museum exhibit on early African American pioneers and farmers in Indiana, an exhibit organized for Muncie's Minnetrista Cultural Center (a local museum) by folklorist and ethnographer Elizabeth (Beth) Campbell. Both Hurley and I served as consultants for the project, and through Beth, Hurley and I first met. Soon after this time, all three of us were also involved in a project sponsored by Ball State's Virginia B. Ball Center for Creative Inquiry—a unique and innovative educational program privately funded by Virginia B. Ball that allows Ball State faculty and students to design a collaborative and community-based project on which both the students and faculty focus solely for one semester (with no other course commitments for either faculty or students). The project, entitled "Transformations" and headed by Ball State English professor Lee Papa, brought together students, faculty, and community members to explore their memories of Muncie's 1967 race riots, on which they built an ethnographically and collaboratively based play.[11] Beth and I were hired as consultants for the ethnographic part of the project; Hurley as a consultant on Muncie's black community. It was during this time that I learned of Hurley's extensive collections and writings on Muncie's African American community, a collection that served as the basis for a third project in which Beth and Hurley, in particular, put together a photo exhibit entitled "The Other Middletown."

With all of this in mind, Hurley, Beth, and I began to envision an extension of the "The Other Middletown" project: a Ball State University seminar that would bring a student-based and ethnographic perspective to Hurley's work. In collaboration with Hurley and Beth, I proposed the project to the Virginia B. Ball Center, and with their generous support (in cooperation with the Muncie Commission on the Social Status of Black Males, the Center for Middletown Studies, and the Community Foundation of Muncie and Delaware County, Inc.), we designed a collaboratively based project to involve local experts, ethnographers, and Ball State students to add to and complete this part of Goodall's work for publication.

The work would be the quintessential collaborative project—between faculty, students, and community consultants; the students would conduct the research for and write part II of the book. In particular, the role of the students would be twofold. First, they would conduct ethnographic research in the community for a semester: that is, they would participate in Muncie's African American community by attending, for example, community meetings, church services, or family events; taking photographs; observing social landscapes; and, most importantly, conducting interviews. Second, the students—in teams, supported by community advisors—would combine their own ethnographic research with Goodall's and other historic materials archived in Ball State's Bracken Library (which includes an unpublished 1986 University of Virginia and Virginia Commonwealth University study of Muncie's African American community) to write their ethnographic contributions for the larger book project. Throughout this phase the students would work closely with the community and with faculty and independent researchers to learn and participate in the process of publishing an actual ethnographic manuscript.

Recognizing this unique opportunity for a "quintessential" collaboration between faculty, students, and community members, I also wanted someone to closely study the collaborative process itself, to understand more deeply just how collaboration works and how we (and others) could learn from it. With the Department of Anthropology and the Virginia B. Ball Center's combined financial support, I put out a national call for a graduate student to do just this. Several students from all over the country applied but one stood out: Michelle Natasya Johnson, whose intense interest in African American studies and collaborative models made her an ideal addition to the project. She joined us in August 2002, took up the project's collaborative process as the topic of her master's thesis, closely studied our collaborative approach throughout its development, and provided some preliminary reflections.

Our Collaborative Methodology from Beginning to End

The collaborative methodology for this project began in the months before the Virginia B. Ball Center seminar began (January 2003). Hurley, Beth, and I—now along with Michelle—called two community meetings to outline our plans for the project. Our main purpose at these meetings was to find community advisors who could serve as both mentors and facilitators—that is, key consultants who could lead students to further contacts within their subject area. We asked community members to volunteer for those subject areas in which they felt they could make the best contributions. For example, business owners volunteered to assist the Making a Living student research team; ministers volunteered to assist the Engaging in Religious

Practices team; current and former political leaders volunteered to assist the Engaging in Community Activities team; and so forth.

Thanks mostly to Hurley and his wife Fredine, who spread the word throughout Muncie, the enthusiasm shown by the African American community was extraordinary. Numerous people agreed to help the students in any way they could; after our second community meeting, in addition to Hurley and Fredine, twelve community advisors eagerly agreed to work with the students full time throughout the seminar: Renzie Abram, Jr., Julius Anderson, Phyllis Bartleson, Geraldine Burns, Edgar Faulkner, Eric Johnson, Edward McNeary, Delores Pryor, Carl Rhinehart, Dolores Rhinehart, Phyllis Joanne White, and John Young-El.

Meanwhile, I set about finding students who would be interested in the work, and who could, for an entire semester, focus solely on the project.[12] The team had to be interdisciplinary as a requirement of the Virginia B. Ball Center, so, in addition to a core of anthropology students, I sought out students from disciplines that were closely related to anthropology—especially disciplines that counted "culture" and/or "ethnography" as among their key concepts. The obvious choices were sociology and history. But I also drew students from philosophy, journalism, English, education, urban planning, and telecommunications, believing such an interdisciplinary group would only help enhance the project. (Indeed it did.)

After interviewing each student, and after much thinking about the class's composition (including its racial diversity), by early January we had our student team: Michelle Anderson (anthropology), Jessica Booth (journalism), Brandy Bounds (urban planning and sociology), Sarah Bricker (anthropology and Spanish), Carla Burke (English and education), Abigail Delpha (sociology and Spanish), Jarrod Dortch (history), Eric Efaw (anthropology and history), Mia Fields (English), Danny Gawlowski (anthropology and photojournalism), Carrie Kissel (anthropology), Anne Kraemer (anthropology and history), Ashley Moore (telecommunications), and Cari Peterson (organization communication and philosophy).

With the students' individual interests in mind (for example, in education or family life or religion), we organized the students into six teams, teams that would focus their research and writing on the subject areas set out in the original Lynd study: again, Getting a Living, Making a Home, Training the Young, Using Leisure, Engaging in Religious Practices, and Engaging in Community Activities. (One student, Danny Gawlowski, an award-winning photographer, was assigned as an auxiliary member of each group and worked with teams to illustrate their chapters with his photographs.) These teams paralleled the teams of community advisors that had been already organized along similar lines. The next step was to bring these two groups together.[13]

The Student–Community Advisor Teams
On that January afternoon—the first day of spring semester 2003 classes—when Hurley reminded us why we had come together in the first place, the faculty and students met to learn about what lay ahead of us. That evening we met at Shaffer Chapel, a place that is steeped in history and meaning. There the students and community advisors met each other for the first time and ate dinner together. After introductions, they split up into their respective groups and by the end of the evening our collaborative project had officially begun.

We (Hurley, Beth, Michelle, and I) recognized early on that having the students research and write fully exhaustive chapters of Muncie's African American experience (including all of its social, economic, and political dimensions) was not only theoretically suspect but pragmatically impossible for one semester's work. Recognizing that the groups' composition was established along lines of common interest, we instead wanted the teams to define their own subjects for study: they were to focus, within their respective topic areas, on those parts of Muncie's black experience that interested them the most.

This was a particularly difficult challenge for the students at first. Several, for example, wanted clear guidelines for what they were supposed to look for and write about. A collaborative ethnographic methodology, we explained, centered on defining the questions of study with our community advisors, not imposing research questions on them from the outside.[14] It was to be an inductive process, not a reductive one. Although we had indeed chosen to stick with the Lynds' original six categories to remain consistent with the classic study, these six categories would serve only as a loose guide—a springboard to the larger issues that mattered to the people with whom we were working. To illustrate this, and to initiate talk between the students and community advisors about the topics and issues that would direct their writing, the students read *Middletown*, with each student research team focusing on their respective chapters and making notes of the subject areas within those chapters that the Lynds had originally explored. After discussing these at length as a group, the students took their reading of *Middletown* back to their community advisors, asking them to what extent the Lynds' discussion represented their own experiences in Muncie. In some cases, the Lynds' focus was similar to that of our community advisors; in others, however, they were quite different. For example, the Getting a

Living student team learned that while the Lynds had made much of the divisions between the business and working class in their original study, the divisions were never as pronounced in Muncie's black community, especially because the city's wealthy business class was (and remains) almost entirely made up of white Munsonians. The community advisors, as we'll see, thought the students should focus instead, among several other things, on the businesses that had a particular significance to the black community, past and present.

Interviews/Conversations

Through this exercise and subsequent conversations, the student/advisor teams began to define the issues that they thought were most important to explore. This was no easy task, however. The community advisors led the students to other consultants, who, like the community advisors, had topics and issues of their own that they thought were important to the study. For example, the community advisors for the Making a Home team encouraged the students to focus on single mothers, who, in turn, led the students to other single parents, including single fathers. Many of these consultants encouraged the students to focus, as well, on dual-parent homes lest the students stereotype the community in their writings and forego the actual diversity of families.

We encouraged students to begin identifying themes (as well as important exceptions to those themes) so that they might develop more directed research questions about the topics and issues that were emerging in their field conversations. These they took back to their community advisors, who helped them further develop their questions. These questions were regularly revamped and revised as the research progressed, however. The Engaging in Religious Practices student team, for example, began with a long list of questions the students had first hammered out on their own, and then with their community advisors during their first meeting. Many of these questions were very general in their scope and served as a guide in their earliest field conversations, but as the students learned more about the role of the church in Muncie's African American community (such as in the civil rights movement) their questions became much more refined, centering around specific topics and issues (such as the ministers who were also civil rights activists).

The students' interviewing methods, then, were simple but time-consuming: the students asked community advisors about the topics they thought were most important for them to explore; they developed research questions along these lines; and they structured interviews around these research questions. These interviews led to new topics and issues to explore, which in turn led to new questions upon which to structure interviews. These interviews, actually, were more like conversations in that they were much more free-flowing than structured interviews often are. On many occasions, the community advisors and students met to talk—sometimes for hours—about the project, about their respective interests, or just to visit. And each time, the students learned a little more about what it was like to live in African American Muncie.

The students recorded most of their conversations either as field notes or, most often, on analog tape, using a Marantz PMD-201 professional field recorder with an external microphone (important for canceling out internal motor noise from the recording). The Virginia B. Ball Center provided each student research team with its own field recorder "kit" (which included a laptop computer) so competition for equipment between groups would be kept to a minimum. After each interview/conversation was complete, the students labeled their tapes (with a numbering system that we developed for archiving), and meticulously logged their recorded conversation. We did not ask the students to transcribe their conversations for several reasons. Most importantly, we wanted the students to regularly return to the original recordings—especially as they began to write (more on this below). Moreover, because we wanted the students to focus on listening, we wanted them to forego a dependency on written transcripts—that is, a prolonged focus on written transcriptions begins to yield a more narrowed focus on the content of speech (especially when the interview/conversation is long over) at the expense of its intent—such as its veiled, often more subtle meanings. Regularly returning to the original recording forces one to listen for both content and intent. Thus student logs generally looked like this excerpt from a taped log entry by the Training the Young team:

Tape #:	M03TY14-I-02/27 (tape 1 of 2)
What:	Conversation with Phyllis Bartleson
Who:	Phyllis Bartleson
Where:	Human Rights Commission, City Hall, Muncie, Indiana
Time:	10:30 A.M.
Recorded by:	Carla Burke, Carrie Kissel
Specs:	Marantz, external mic
Notes:	Done in Phyllis's office; logged by Carrie

Side A
(000) Discussion of training the young. Carla asks for definition. Phyllis says it takes a strong fortitude due to really adverse outside influences in society today. Sons twenty-eight, twenty-two; daughter thirty-five.

(027) Phyllis gets out picture of her first grade class at Garfield Elementary (over fifty years ago). Remembers the teacher—seemed tall, must have been about 5 foot, 10 inches, but seemed like a giant to first graders. Carla asks if we can get a copy of it later, when we start getting pictures together.

(072) A lot more difficult in raising youngsters than it was when my children were small. Single parent, worked with young people a good portion of her life. When she was going full time to Ball State, worked at Youth Detention Center (now the Youth Opportunity Center). Children went to Burris then, probably about first grade, sixth grade. Worked nights, best for education, but sometimes got to work with the kids—got her interested in working with young people.

(102) Was director of a summer youth work program for ages fourteen through twenty-one: Partnership for Progress, mid-late 1980s. Taught adult responsibilities, good work ethic, also other problems, job training.

(122) Been Human Rights Commission Director for about fifteen years, has worked with other groups who serve youth. . . .[15]

In the end, the students conducted more than 150 hours of interviews/conversations with well over sixty people, including their community advisors and other consultants (about two-thirds of these interviews/conversations were tape-recorded, logged, and archived). That the students completed this many interviews in one semester's time is an amazing feat in and of itself. But conversing was not all they were doing.

Participant-Observation / Observant Participation

The students' intensive interview agenda was heavily supplemented with participant-observation, that staple of all ethnography: intensive participation and observation in a particular locality. At the beginning of the semester, we required the students to attend at least one community event (broadly defined) each week, but after the first few weeks, their community advisors were inviting and taking them to numerous family gatherings, school meetings, sporting events, church services, political rallies—you name it. Indeed, after the first month, many of the students had become a regular part of the "Muncie scene."

The purpose of this intensive participation was for the students to observe the larger social context in which their consultants lived their lives. But, as our students came to understand, a significant by-product of this intensive participation is recognizing how the "observer" is similar to and different from the people with whom she or he works: as we learn about others, we learn about ourselves; and as we learn about ourselves, we learn about others. This is extremely important for the serious field-worker. One must recognize where Self leaves off and Other picks up. But, more importantly, one must also recognize how one's experience shapes one's interpretation of others. We thus encouraged the students to be, more precisely, "observant participants," to observe their own participation just as closely as they were observing others; to fully embrace fieldwork's "intersubjectivities" (put simply, the "co-experiences" and "co-understandings" that developed between and among the students and their Muncie collaborators); and to recognize the points when deeper understandings of Muncie's African American community began to emerge within this experiential context.[16]

With this in mind, we required the students to keep detailed field notes (a journal of sorts) of all of their activities and experiences; we also expected them to reflect openly in this writing about what they were learning about themselves and how this was shaping what they were discovering about Muncie's black community. This would be extremely important, we explained, for writing an honest and responsible ethnography. They often used this material (excerpted straight from their field notes) to situate their discussions of their individual topic areas. Field notes thus took an open-ended form, much like these excerpts from the notes of Sarah Bricker (of the Using Leisure team):

Researcher's name:	Sarah Bricker
Date of visit:	2/9/03
Date recorded field notes:	2/9/03
Event:	Sunday Morning Worship
Place:	Shaffer Chapel A. M. E. Church
Documentation materials:	Notepad and pen; service bulletin and calendar of events

On the way to the service I felt some anxiety. I've been to more Christian services lately than usual, and in some ways feel like an outsider.... I wondered if there was a parking lot somewhere behind the church? I always park at the annex for class—but how can everyone fit on the streets on Sunday? As I neared the church there was plenty of space. I was surprised that there weren't more cars. I arrived close to 11 A.M. and as I walked toward the church, Eric Efaw pulled in. I waited for him and we walked together, passing the African Methodist Episcopal Church sign and walking up the few steps. Two people greeted us at the door, with bulletins, and "good morning." The woman asked for my coat which took me by surprise I guess—felt like being a guest at someone's home. We took a seat in one of the pews on the right side, closer to the back than the front. I noticed the windows right away—letting the sunlight into the church. Then I saw Carl and Dolores Rhinehart further back on the left side. It was great to see them, as I thought Eric Johnson would be the only person I'd know—I didn't see him yet. And Hurley and Fredine were sitting in front of us, and soon Geraldine was behind us! I loved it, so many people were here that I recognized, it made me a lot more comfortable. Everyone waved or said hello.

One of the choir members comes to the pulpit and brings praise. Talks about the Spirit. The choir begins in song, the drums, the piano, the song's upbeat. . . . Then a praise song, "Jesus in Heaven" and tambourines start in, the drums, the voices, the piano. Some claps from the congregation—about twenty-five people in the pews, mostly women, a couple of kids, a few men. Some voices say "Jesus." A woman comes in and sits behind Phyllis and the kids. She leans over the pew and hugs the young girl, and kisses her on the cheek, her lipstick stays and the girl tries to rub it off with the help of Phyllis. Later she moves back to sit by the woman. In the fourth pew from the front, a woman sits alone, she often sways from side to side in her seat, and claps moving her shoulders. . . . Eric Johnson comes to the podium, his Bible looks well-read, the papers scraggly coming out of it. He talks about the Middletown project, about Hurley's work in the community, about needing to document history, about working with the leisure group. He encourages people to stay after, and says my name, that I'll be staying after to do interviews, and if anyone can stay, especially women, please stay. . . . I felt connected to him there, how much he wants these stories written down, even though he works in Indianapolis, commuting every day to take care of his mom and brother, he's taking time to do this project. That's what it means.[17]

Students turned in field notes like these at the start of each week, adding exponentially to their growing corpus of fieldwork materials. In order to help the students recognize their emergent understandings, these field notes were, during the project's earliest stages, discussed among the group as a whole or in smaller consultations between the individual research teams and either Beth, Michelle, or myself.

Reading and Researching Texts

In addition to the texts produced by the students as a result of their interviews and observant participation, they also read and researched extensive background materials on Muncie's African American community. Much of their historical research, in particular, had already been done for them by Hurley. Before the seminar began, Hurley compiled a summation of his research to date for each category (Getting a Living, Making a Home, etc.), which he placed in individually labeled folders for use by each team (these folders also included original photographs). These materials provided direction to the much larger collection on Muncie's African American community held in Ball State University's Archives and Special Collections, which housed a plethora of materials. Of particular note were two manuscript collections, both in which Hurley was closely involved: the Black Muncie History Project Records, which included newspaper clippings, pamphlets, and interviews collected by Hurley in the 1970s; and the Black Middletown Project Records, interview transcripts from a 1981–1982 University of Virginia and Virginia Commonwealth University study of the black community (which was never published).[18]

Some student research teams depended more on this archived material than others, mainly because the student teams focusing on areas that had formal institutional histories (such as churches, schools, and businesses as studied by the Engaging in Religious Practices, Training the Young, and Getting a Living research teams, respectively) found more materials at their disposal; the student teams focusing on areas with less formal institutional histories (such as family, recreation, and public events as studied by the Making a Home, Using Leisure, and Engaging in Community Activities research teams, respectively) depended more on oral histories through their conversations with their community advisors and consultants to establish their historical understandings in this regard. Perhaps the largest formal institutional history was church history. Early on in their research, members of the Engaging in Religious Practices student research team found the archived materials particularly helpful to their growing understandings of how the present-day churches had emerged from their previous role in the civil rights movements of earlier eras.

Added to this archival reading was the students' reading of newspaper articles, pamphlets, and other community materials that they collected. They also read a number of texts to help them contextualize their work within larger currents. In addition to reading *Middletown*, the students read various excerpts from the larger Middletown literature (e.g., the Lynds' *Middletown in Transition*); general anthropological texts such as my own *Invitation to Anthropology* (to help them more fully understand the role of ethnography in larger discussions of culture and society); books on doing fieldwork such as Bonnie Stone Sunstein and Elizabeth Chiseri-Strater's *Fieldworking: Reading and Writing Research* (to provide models for specific research strategies);

ethnographies that we sought to emulate (such as Glenn Hinson's *Fire in My Bones: Transcendence and the Holy Spirit in African American Gospel*); and, most especially, our guide for writing nonfiction to general audiences, William Zinsser's *On Writing Well*.[19]

Writing Ethnography

Simply put, ethnography is the description of culture; but it also implies both a field method and a method for writing. In this case, the students were practicing ethnography as a method as they sought to understand the culture of Muncie's African American community through their conversations with their community advisors and other consultants, through their observant participation, and through their intensive reading of historical and contemporary texts. Perhaps the biggest challenge was translating this work into an actual written ethnography.

Throughout the project, each student team compiled all of their research (particularly tape logs, field notes, and archival and other materials) into portfolios upon which they based their writing.[20] Early on, however, we encouraged the students to de-emphasize the separations between "collecting data" and "writing up the results"—indeed, such divisions have very little use and meaning to contemporary ethnography (especially in doing collaborative ethnography, which I will discuss below). Throughout the semester, then, we also conducted writing exercises (in addition to their instruction on writing field notes) so that students would be better prepared to translate their emergent understandings into an ethnographic text when the most intensive writing came. For example, during the third week of the seminar, we all attended a Martin Luther King, Jr., celebration at Christ Temple Apostolic Church. I recorded the entire service, excerpted a few minutes from the sermon, and asked each research team to translate the excerpt as poetic transcription—a writing method developed by sociolinguists to more closely represent both the intent and content of speech in the final written ethnography.[21] Student teams chose to use poetic transcription (which is also called "ethnopoetics") where it was most appropriate for translating and writing particular types of speech that did not translate easily to the written page.

Soon after the first month of the seminar, we asked students to construct rough outlines for their chapters based on the themes they had discovered so far. These they shared with one another as a group. Much of their material overlapped, as expected, so they spent some time discussing which team would write about what, as well as how to best create transitions between chapters. While in the process of continuing their ethnographic research, they shared these outlines with their community advisors, which created further discussion about the direction the students' writing would take. These collaborative discussions thus distinguished gaps in the students' understandings and defined new trajectories for further research.

Near midsemester, the students began writing their first drafts, all the while continuing with their interviews and other research. Discussing their writing with their community advisors, each student team began to forge their chapters. They spent long days and nights at the Virginia B. Ball Center (some groups worked as much as eighteen hours per day), and within a week they had their first drafts completed. These we discussed as a group, and with the group's suggestions, the student teams began their writing and rewriting anew. By the time they left for their well-deserved spring break, the students had submitted their final "first drafts." While they vacationed (or should I say, slept), Beth, Michelle, and I (along with Ball State English professor Robert Nowatzki), heavily edited these drafts and made suggestions for rewriting. When we finished, we sent these drafts to Rosalie Robertson, editor-in-chief at AltaMira Press, who then flew out to Muncie to meet with the students after they returned from spring break—she added still more suggestions.

This initial editing process was perhaps the hardest part of the seminar for the students. We wanted big changes, really big changes; indeed, we were a long way from completing our ethnography. Some of the students, as expected, were angry and hurt; they had never had their writing critiqued like this before. But they had also never been part of an actual publishing process. This project was becoming a much larger group effort, we explained, which now included the book's publisher. Our sights had to be set accordingly.

After a few days, the students' anger subsided (in fact, I encouraged them to be mad at us—particularly me—this was part of the publishing process); and the group was back to intensive writing and rewriting. Our next step would be to present our chapter drafts to our community advisors and other consultants.

Writing Collaborative Ethnography

In that ethnographers work with local communities to construct their texts, the approach to ethnography, as a method, is essentially collaborative. But what makes ethnographic writing collaborative is closely involving consultants in the actual writing of the text. For this project, that meant taking the developing chapters back to community advisors and other consultants for corrections, clarifications, and commentary.

Within a few weeks after Rosalie Robertson had visited the seminar, the students had written new drafts and distributed them among all of their community collaborators (that is, both the community advisors and other consultants), all the while continuing to conduct interviews and other research. At the end of March, we met for a light dinner and an open forum to discuss the chapter drafts. The gathering was largely celebratory, with our collaborators praising the students for all of their hard work. But it also initiated the serious work of integrating consultant commentary into the chapter drafts. During the meeting, for example, community advisors voiced, in addition to corrections, that they wanted material that had been deleted through the editing process reintegrated back into chapters, and that they wanted the students to elaborate certain points even more than they already had.

This forum was only the beginning, however, of writing our collaborative ethnography. The more directed and intense discussions came after our public forum as the students met with their community advisors and other consultants individually, and in private, to talk about their developing chapters. Importantly, talk about the students' texts spawned deeper co-interpretations of each chapter's content—a discussion that lasted until the students finished their final chapter drafts and continues with me even now.

Ultimately, writing a collaborative ethnography depends upon a trust relationship between ethnographer(s) and consultant(s), a moral and ethical "co-commitment" to one another as "co-intellectuals." To keep this co-commitment in the forefront of our collaborative ethnography, early in the semester the students reviewed several different professional ethical codes (such as that of the American Anthropological Association) and from these, they designed their own "statement of ethics" that reflected the particular contours of this specific project.[22] That statement is as follows:

1. Our primary responsibility is to the community consultants with whom we work.
2. We shall maintain academic integrity by creating faithful representations.
3. We shall establish good rapport with the community so that future collaborative studies can be undertaken. This project is not just about our book.

4. All project participants should be aware of the study's products. Materials are only archived with the participants' consent. Participants have rights to have copies of their own interviews.
5. We shall willingly and openly communicate intentions, plans, goals, and collaborative processes of the project.
6. We shall remain open to our consultants' experiences and perspectives, even when their views are different from ours.
7. We have a responsibility to the community, our respective disciplines, and our future audience to fulfill our commitment to finish what we have started: the book *The Other Side of Middletown*.

This statement of ethics was specific to our particular collaborative ethnography in several different ways, but a couple of these points need clarification. Point 7, for instance, emerged from our discussions with our community advisors—especially Hurley—who had worked with teams of researchers before and had been extremely disappointed that they had never produced their results for either Muncie's black community or the general public. I, for one, had promised Hurley when the project began that I would do everything in my power to get our work published. And the students agreed.

Perhaps the most important part of this statement—"our primary responsibility"—is point 1. Being committed to our community collaborators first and foremost meant several things, but most prominent among these were (1) fully recognizing the contributions of our consultants, unless they preferred otherwise (that is, fully attributing knowledge to them as community experts, not as anonymous contributors); (2) representing our consultants the way they wanted to be represented (that is, as authors—we work very hard to present ourselves in the best possible light; our consultants should have that right also); and (3) allowing our consultants, as collaborative coauthors, to review, comment on, or change their contributions (quotations, for example) as they saw fit—all of which are indeed central to writing a collaborative ethnography.

On the Book's Goals and Purposes

From the very beginning, our goal for this project was, simply, to build our research upon a set of mutual relationships (framed by moral and ethical responsibilities to one another), and, in turn, to build our co-understandings around these relationships. We never asserted—and we still do not assert—that we were researching and writing an "exhaustive" or "objective" study (ours is indeed a humanistic effort, not a scientific one). Our purpose was to fully embrace the experiences of our consultants, their memories, and their stories, and to use our coexperience (as engendered by our relationships with one another, particularly between the students and their community collaborators) as the foundation for creating our collaborative ethnographic text.

Being Honest about Our Ethnography's Potentials and Limitations

Building our collaborative ethnography around these relationships provided definite and clear potentials for in-depth co-understandings of our collaborators' experiences, memories, and stories. Our particular relationships, to be sure, engendered a very particular dialogue about the Muncie community. Had those relationships taken any other form, a very different dialogue would have emerged, and our collaborative ethnography would have thus looked very different. But, in the end, it would still point us to a deeper understanding of Muncie's African American community (as we believe this ethnography does in its current form).

As such, the final product is not so much an ethnography of Muncie's African American community as it is a dialogue about Muncie's African American community. Of course, all dialogues, and thus all ethnographies, have their boundaries, and ours is no exception. In that we base this ethnography on information collected in a very short amount of time (about four months) and that we primarily, although not exclusively, worked with older (often retired) middle-class collaborators (who had the time to work intensively with us within this short time frame), our ethnography also has very clear limitations. Hence, we view this research not as a conclusive statement, but rather as a beginning to new study and new conversation.

This research project is unique in two key ways. First, it is among the very few widely published, full-length ethnographies written mostly by undergraduate college students.[23] Several anthropologists, in particular, have written books with their students (most posed as instruction manuals for doing ethnography).[24] These, however, feature student essays on disparate "subcultures" rather than on a single, local community. Second, and more obvious, we believe that this work is a significant contribution to the overall Middletown literature. In addition to the few works that take up the experiences, memories, and stories of Muncie's African American community, this research seeks to add to the growing Middletown literature that gives a "face" to the people who live here and that situates this place in real people's experience.[25] The Lynds' *Middletown*, for example, was a product of its time. It offered a "distanced" and "normalized" description of Muncie (the people and their quotations, for example, were nameless). We wanted to write a very different kind of ethnography. And that we did.

Notes

1. Class conversation, Virginia B. Ball Center for Creative Inquiry seminar titled The Other Side of Middletown, Ball State University, Muncie, Indiana, January 6, 2003.

2. An important exception is W. E. B. Du Bois's *The Philadelphia Negro: A Social Study* (Philadelphia: University of Pennsylvania Press, 1899).

3. In fact, when the study's sponsors questioned the validity of the study (the Lynds had been charged to study religion in Muncie, not the entire community) and threatened to terminate its publication, Wissler convinced them otherwise and agreed to write the book's foreword (Theodore Caplow, personal communication, May 3, 2003).

4. On this point, the Lynds were primarily influenced by W. H. R. Rivers's *Social Organization* (New York: Knopf, 1924) and Clark Wissler's *Man and Culture* (New York: Crowell, 1923). See Robert S. Lynd and Helen Merrell Lynd, *Middletown* (New York: Harcourt, Brace, 1929), 4.

5. Lynd and Lynd, *Middletown*, 4.

6. Lynd and Lynd, *Middletown*, 8.

7. Jack S. Blocker, "Black Migration to Muncie, 1860–1930," *Indiana Magazine of History* 92 (1996): 297–320.

8. Lynd and Lynd, *Middletown*, 8.

9. See, for example, Dan Rottenberg, ed., *Middletown Jews: The Tenuous Survival of an American Jewish Community* (Bloomington: Indiana University Press, 1997) and Xiaozhao Huang, *A Study of African-American Vernacular English in America's "Middletown": Evidence of Linguistic Convergence* (Lewiston, N.Y.: E. Mellen Press, 2000).

10. Rita Caccamo, *Back to Middletown: Three Generations of Sociological Reflections* (Stanford, Calif.: Stanford University Press, 2000), 121.

11. This project is documented in Lee Papa and Luke Eric Lassiter, "The Muncie Race Riots of 1967, Representing Community Memory through Public Performance, and Collaborative Ethnography between Faculty, Students, and the Local Community," *Journal of Contemporary Ethnography* 32 (2003): 147–166.

12. As I've already mentioned, Virginia B. Ball Center seminars provide the resources for Ball State University faculty to teach the seminar, and only the seminar, for an entire semester. Students, too, take the seminar as their only course. But in order for students to take the course without losing credit for their majors and/or core curriculum, the center arranges for seminar credit to replace needed classes that are closely related. For example, students enrolled in The Other Side

of Middletown seminar substituted courses such as ethnographic methods, race and ethnicity, cultural anthropology, sociology, Middletown studies, or African American studies.

13. The composition of these teams generally remained the same through the semester, with one exception. Due to medical problems, Brandy Bounds had to pull out of the class about a month into the seminar.

14. See Luke Eric Lassiter, "From 'Reading over the Shoulders of Natives' to 'Reading alongside Natives,' Literally: Toward a Collaborative and Reciprocal Ethnography," *Journal of Anthropological Research* 57 (2001): 137–49.

15. The numbers to the left represent the recorder's tape counter. No standard exists for tape counters, but Marantz field recorders are very common, still in use among fieldworkers and archivists (hence the importance of the "specs" line at the beginning of the log). Generally, students made note of the tape counter with a change in conversation topic.

16. See Barbara Tedlock, "From Participant Observation to the Observation of Participation: The Emergence of Narrative Ethnography," *Journal of Anthropological Research* 47 (1991): 69–94.

17. Generally, we asked the students to make short notes during their visits to community events, if possible, and then to expand on these brief notes in longer form as soon as possible after attending the event.

18. As Hurley was closely involved in this study (called the "Black Middletown Project"), he is, to this day, extremely disappointed that the research team never published their results as promised. They "came to Muncie in the middle 1980s with a sizeable federal grant and spent one year here in our city," he writes. "I, among others, spent many hours helping to open doors in homes, places of business, churches, clubs, and other venues. One of the persons interviewed at the time was my mother, who was in her late eighties. No product of any kind was produced by this team. Frustrated, I wrote to the president of the University of Virginia and expressed my feelings, especially after I found through research that they had expended $250,000 while here. I felt sure that no other study of the African American community in Muncie would be possible." (Hurley Goodall, comments at "Writing Muncie's African American Community: How We Wrote the Other Side of Middletown," Union Baptist Church, Muncie, Indiana, April 17, 2003.)

19. See Robert S. Lynd and Helen Merrell Lynd, *Middletown in Transition: A Study in Cultural Conflicts* (New York: Harcourt, Brace, 1937); Luke Eric Lassiter, *Invitation to Anthropology* (Walnut Creek, Calif.: AltaMira Press, 2002); Bonnie Stone Sunstein and Elizabeth Chiseri-Strater, *Fieldworking: Reading and Writing Research*, 2nd ed. (Boston: Bedford/St. Martin's, 2002); Glenn Hinson, *Fire in My Bones: Transcendence and the Holy Spirit in African American Gospel* (Philadelphia: University of Pennsylvania Press, 2000); and William Zinsser, *On Writing Well: The Classic Guide to Writing Nonfiction*, 25th ed. (New York: Quill, 2001).

20. See Sunstein and Chiseri-Strater, *Fieldworking*, in which building a research portfolio is a major component of their approach.

21. See, for example, Dennis Tedlock, *The Spoken Word and the Work of Interpretation* (Philadelphia: University of Pennsylvania Press, 1983). This exercise is also featured in Sunstein and Chiseri-Strater, *Fieldworking*, 300–301.

22. This exercise we pulled from Sunstein and Chiseri-Strater, *Fieldworking*, 116–118.

23. See, for example, Mary LaLone, ed., *Appalachian Coal Mining Memories: Life in the Coal Fields of Virginia's New River Valley* (Blacksburg, Va.: Pocahontas Press, 1997).

24. See, for example, James P. Spradley and David McCurdy, *The Cultural Experience: Ethnography in Complex Society* (Prospect Heights, Ill.: Waveland Press, 1972).

25. See, for example, Dan Rottenberg, *Middletown Jews*.

Bibliography

Abbott, Andrew. *Department & Discipline: Chicago Sociology at One Hundred.* Chicago: University of Chicago Press, 1999.

Abel, C., C. Abel, V. Alexander, S. McCune, and P. Nason. "The ExCET Teacher Exams: History, Promises and Concerns." In *Standards and Schooling in the United States: An Encyclopedia,* edited by Joe Kincheloe and Danny Weil. 3 vols. Santa Barbara, Calif.: ABC-Clio, 2001.

Acuña, Rodolfo F. *Occupied America: The Chicano's Struggle toward Liberation.* San Francisco: Canfield Press, 1972.

——. *Occupied America: A History of Chicanos.* 3rd ed. New York: Harper and Row, 1988.

——. *Occupied America: A History of Chicanos.* 4th ed. New York: Longman, 2000.

——. *Sometimes There Is No Other Side.* Notre Dame, Ind.: University of Notre Dame Press, 1998.

Aguilar, John L. "Insider Research: An Ethnography of a Debate." In *Anthropologists at Home in North America: Methods and Issues in the Study of One's Own Society,* edited by D. A. Messerschmidt, pp. 15–26. New York: Cambridge University Press, 1988.

Aguirre, Adalberto Jr. and Jonathan H. Turner. *American Ethnicity: The Dynamics and Consequences of Discrimination.* Boston: McGraw Hill, 2001.

Alarcón, Norma. "Chicana Feminism: In the Tracks of the 'Native Woman.'" In *Living Chicana Theory,* edited by Carla Trujillo Berkeley Calif: Third Woman Press, 1998.

——. "Tradutora, Traditora: A Paradigmatic Figure of Chicana Feminism." *Cultural Critique,* Fall 1989, 57–87.

Alba, Richard, and Victor Nee. "Rethinking Assimilation Theory for a New Era of Immigration." *International Migration Review* 31, no. 4 (1997): 826–874.

Alcoff, Linda Martín. "Objectivity and Its Politics." *New Literary History* 32 (2001): 846.

Alcoff, Linda Martín, and Eduardo Mendieta. *Identities: Race, Class, Gender, and Nationality*. Malden, Mass.: Blackwell, 2003.

Aldridge, Delores, ed. "Black Women in the American Economy." Special issue, *Journal of Black Studies* 20 (1989): 2.

———. *Focusing, Black Male-Female Relationships*. Chicago: Third World Press, 1991.

———. "Womanist Issues in Black Studies: Towards Integrating Africana Women into Africana Studies." *Afrocentric Scholar* 1, no. 1 (1992): 167–182.

Aldridge, Delores, and Carlene Young, eds. *Out of the Revolution: The Development of Africana Studies*. Lanham, Md.: Lexington Books, 2000.

Alexander, M. Jacqui, and Chandra Mohanty, eds. *Feminist Genealogies, Colonial Legacies, Democratic Futures*. New York: Routledge, 1997.

Alkalimat, Abdul. "The Ideology of Black Social Science." In *The Death of White Sociology*, edited by Joyce Ladner, pp. 173–189. New York: Random House, 1973.

Allen, M. "Voice of Reason." 2000. www.curtin.edu.au/learn/unit/10846/arrow/vorall.htm.

Allen, Richard. "Politics of the Attack on Black Studies." *Black Scholar* 6, no. 1 (1974): 2–7.

Allen, Robert L. *Black Awakening in Capitalist America: An Analytic History*. New York: Doubleday, 1969.

Almaguer, Tomás. *Racial Fault Lines: The Historical Origins of White Supremacy in California*. Berkeley: University of California Press, 1994.

Altbach, P. G., and Kofi Lomotey, eds. *The Racial Crisis in American Higher Education*. New York: SUNY, 1991.

Alurista. "must be the season of the witch." In *Floricanto en Aztlán*, p. 26. Los Angeles: Chicano Cultural Center, 1971.

Anaya, Rudolfo. *Bless Me, Ultima*. Berkeley, Calif.: Quinto Sol, 1972.

Andersen, Margaret L., and Patricia Hill Collins. *Race, Class, and Gender*. Belmont, Calif.: Wadsworth Publishing, 1995.

Anderson, Benedict. *Imagined Communities: Reflections on the Origin and Spread of Nationalism*. London: Verso, 1983.

Andrews, William L., ed. *Sisters of the Spirit*. Bloomington: Indiana University Press, 1986.

Angelou, Maya. *I Know Why the Caged Bird Sings*. New York: Chelsea House, 1996.

Ani, Marimba. *Yurugu: An African-Centered Critique of European Cultural Thought and Behavior*. Trenton, N.J.: Africa World Press, 1994.

Anti-Defamation League. A World of Difference Institute. Teacher/Student Resource Guide: Greater Chicago Region, 1995.

Anzaldúa, Gloria. *Borderlands: La Frontera = The New Mestiza*. San Francisco: Spinsters/Aunt Lute, 1987.

Aparicio, Frances R., and Christina Jose-Kampfner. "Language, Culture, and Violence in the Educational Crisis of U.S. Latino/as: Two Courses for Intervention." *Michigan Journal of Community Service Learning* 3 (Fall 1995): 128–138.

Apffel-Marglin, Frédérique. "Development or Decolonization in the Andes?" *Interculture: International Journal of Intercultural and Transdisciplinary Research* 28, no. 1 (1995): 3–17.
Appadurai, Arjun. *Modernity at Large*. Minneapolis: University of Minnesota Press, 1996.
Appelbaum, Peter. "Mathematics Education." In *Critical Thinking: An Encyclopedia*, edited by Danny Weil and Joe Kincheloe. New York: Greenwood, 2003.
Appiah, Anthony, and Amy Gutmann. *Color Conscious: The Political Morality of Race*. Princeton, N.J.: Princeton University Press, 1996.
Aptheker, Herbert. "Du Bois as Historian." In *Afro-American History: The Modern Era*, edited by Herbert Aptheker. Secaucus, N.J.: Citadel Press, 1971.
Asante, Molefi Kete. *The Afrocentric Idea*. Philadelphia: Temple University Press, 1987.
———. *Afrocentricity, the Theory of Social Change*. Revised ed. Trenton, N.J.: Africa World Press, 1988.
———. "International/Intercultural Relations." In *Contemporary Black Thought*, edited by Molefi Kete Asante and Abdulai S. Vandi, pp. 43–58. Beverly Hills, Calif.: Sage Publications, 1980.
———. *Kemet, Afrocentricity and Knowledge*. Trenton, N.J.: Africa World Press, 1990.
Association of American Colleges & Universities. *Greater Expectations: A New Vision for Learning as a Nation Goes to College.* National Panel Report. Washington, D.C., 2002.
Auerbach, Elsa. *From the Community to the Community*. Community Training for Adult and Family Literacy Project Final Report. Boston: Boston Adult Literacy Fund, 1994.
Azuela, Mariano. *Los de abajo*. (1915). Mexico City: Fondo de Cultura Económica, 1995.
Baker, Houston. "Generational Shifts and the Recent Criticism of Afro-American Literature." In *Paradigms in Black Studies: Intellectual History, Cultural Meaning, and Political Ideology*, edited by Abdul Alkalimat, pp. 71–117. Chicago: Twenty-First Century Books, 1990.
Baldwin, James. "A Talk to Teachers." In *Graywolf Annual Five: Multi-Cultural Literacy*, edited by Rick Simmons and Scott Walker. St. Paul, Minn.: Graywolf Press, 1988.
Baldwin, Joseph A. "The Psychology of Oppression." In *Contemporary Black Thought*, edited by Molefi Kete Asante and Abdulai S. Vandi, pp. 95–110. Beverly Hills, Calif.: Sage Publications, 1980.
Balogun, F. Odun. "Hybridity, Neouniversalist Cultural Theory, and the Comparative Study of Black Literatures." In *African Visions, Literary Images, Political Change, and Social Struggle in Contemporary Africa*, edited by Cheryl Mwaria, Silvia Federici, and Joseph McLaren. Westport, Conn.: Praeger, 2000.
Banda, Dan. *Indigenous Always*. Milwaukee, Wis.: Bandana Productions, 2000.
Banerjee, N. "Q and A with Ethnic Studies Pioneer Ronald Takaki." 2000, www.asianweek.com/2000_10_12/feature.html.

Banks, James A. "Multicultural Education: Its Effects on Students' Racial and Gender Role Attitudes." In *Handbook of Research on Multicultural Education*, edited by James A. Banks and Cherry McGee Banks, pp. 617–627. New York: Macmillan, 1995.

Barger, W. K., and Ernesto M. Reza. *The Farm Labor Movement in the Midwest: Social Change and Adaptation among Migrant Farmworkers.* Austin: University of Texas Press, 1994.

Bartholomae, David. "Inventing the University." In *When a Writer Can't Write: Studies in Writer's Block and Other Composing-Process Problems*, edited by Mike Rose, pp. 134–135. New York: Guilford Press, 1985.

Bataille, Gretchen, Miguel Carranza, and Lauri Lisa. *Ethnic Studies in the United States.* New York: Garland, 1996.

Bateson, Gregory. In "Logical Types of Learning," edited by Paul Newland. www.envf.port.ac.uk/newmedia/lecturenotes/EMMA?at2n.htm

Beaglehole, J. C. *The Endeavour Journal of Joseph Banks.* Sydney: Angus and Robertson, 1962.

Beale, Frances. "Double Jeopardy: To Be Black and Female." In *The Black Woman*, edited by Toni Cade, pp. 90–110. New York: Signet, 1976.

Bederman, Gail. *Manliness & Civilization: A Cultural History of Gender and Race in the United States, 1880–1917.* Chicago: University of Chicago Press, 1995.

Bendick, M., M. L. Egan, and S. Lofhjelm. *The Documentation and Evaluation of Anti-discrimination Training in the United States.* Retrieved July 26, 2002, from the International Labour Organization website: www.ilo.org/public/english/protection/migrant/research/imp/29/index.htm.

Bennett, David, ed. *Multicultural States: Rethinking Difference and Identity.* London: Routledge, 1998.

Bennett, Lerone. *Before the Mayflower: A History of the Negro in America, 1619–1962.* Chicago: Johnson Publishing, 1962.

———. *Black Power, U.S.A., the Human Side of Reconstruction, 1867–1877.* Chicago: Johnson Publishing, 1967.

———. *Forced into Glory: Abraham Lincoln's White Dream.* Chicago: Johnson Publishing, 2000.

Bennett, W. "Seizing This Teachable Moment." In *September 11: What Our Children Need to Know.* Thomas B. Fordham Foundation. 2002, www.edexcellence.net/sept11/september11.pdf.

Berger, Peter L., and Thomas Luckmann. *The Social Construction of Reality.* New York: Doubleday, 1966.

Berlak, Harold. "Standards and the Control of Knowledge." *Rethinking Schools.* 1999. www.rethinkingscfhools.org/archieves/13_03/control.htm.

Berman, Morris. *The Reenchantment of the World.* New York: Bantam, 1981.

Bernal, Martin. "Black Athena." In *The Afroasiatic Roots of Civilisation.* London: Vintage, 1991.

Bernstein, Basil. "On the Classification and Framing of Knowledge." In *Knowledge and Control: New Directions for the Sociology of Education*, edited by Michael F. D. Young, pp. 47–69. London: Collier Macmillan, 1971.

Berry, Kathleen. "Standards of Complexity in a Postmodern Democracy." In *Standards and Schooling in the United States: An Encyclopedia*, edited by Joe Kincheloe and Danny Weil. Santa Barbara, Calif.: ABC-Clio, 2001.

Beveridge, William I. B. *The Art of Scientific Investigation*. New York: W. W. Norton, 1957.

Bhabha, Homi K. "Postcolonial Authority and Postmodern Guilt." In *Cultural Studies*, edited by Lawrence Grossberg et al., pp. 437–465. New York: Routledge, 1992.

Bickman, Martin. Review of *The Art and Science of Portraiture*, by Sara Lawrence-Lightfoot. *TC Record*, 2003. Retrieved from www.tcrecord.org/Content.asp?ContentID=11067 on March 13, 2003.

Bigler, R. S. "The Use of Multicultural Curricula and Materials to Counter Racism in Children." *Journal of Social Issues* 55 (1999): 687–705.

Bixler-Marquez, Dennis J., et al., eds. *Chicano Studies: Survey and Analysis*. 2nd ed. Dubuque, Iowa: Kendall Hunt, 2001.

Blackwell, Andrea Glover, Stewart Kwoh, and Manuel Pastor. *Searching for the Uncommon Ground: New Dimensions on Race in America*. New York: W.W. Norton, 2002.

Blauner, Robert. *Racial Oppression in America*. New York: Harper & Row, 1972.

Blocker, Jack S. "Black Migration to Muncie, 1860–1930." *Indiana Magazine of History* 92 (1996): 297–320.

Blommaert, Jan. "Workshopping: Notes on Professional Vision in Discourse." 1997. africana_rug.ac.be/texts/research-publications/publications_on-line/workshopping.htm.

Bloom, Alan D. *The Closing of the American Mind*. New York: Simon and Schuster, 1987.

Bobo, Lawrence, James R. Kluegel, and Ryan A. Smith. "Laissez-Faire Racism: The Crystallization of a Kinder, Gentler, Anti-Black Ideology." In *Racial Attitudes in the 1990s: Continuity and Change*, edited by Steven A. Tuch and Jack K. Martin, pp. 15–42. Westport, Conn.: Praeger, 1997.

Bogardus, Emory S. "A Race-Relations Cycle." *American Journal of Sociology* 35, no. 4 (January 1930): 612–617.

Boggs, Ralph Steele. *Bibliografía del folklore mexicano*. Mexico, D.F.: Instituto Panamericano de Geografía e Historia, 1939.

Bonilla, Frank, and Robert Girling, eds. *Structures of Dependency*. East Palo Alto, Calif.: Nairobi Bookstore, 1973

Bonilla-Silva, Eduardo. *Racism without Racists: Color-Blind Racism and the Persistence of Racial Inequality in the United States*. Lanham, Md.: Rowman & Littlefield, 2003.

Boyer, Ernest L. *Scholarship Reconsidered*. Carnegie Foundation for the Advancement of Teaching. San Francisco: Jossey-Bass, 1990.

Brennan, James F. "Racist Culture." In *The History and Systems of Psychology*. 3rd ed. Englewood Cliffs, N.J.: Prentice Hall, 1991.

Brittan, Arthur, and Mary Maynard. *Sexism, Racism and Oppression*. New York: Blackwell, 1994.

Brock, Rochelle. "Using Critical Thinking to Understand a Black Woman's Identity." In *Critical Thinking: An Encyclopedia*, edited by Danny Weil and Joe Kincheloe. New York: Greenwood, 2003.

Brodkin, Karen. "How Jews Became White Folks." In *White Privilege: Essential Readings on the Other Side of Racism*, edited by Paula S. Rothenberg, pp. 35–48. New York: Worth Publishers, 2002.

———. *How Jews Became White Folks and What That Says about Race in America*. New Brunswick, N.J.: Rutgers University Press, 1998.

Broyles-Gonzales, Yolanda. *El Teatro Campesino: Theater in the Chicano Movement*. Austin: University of Texas Press, 1994.

Bruner, J. *The Culture of Education*. Cambridge, Mass.: Harvard University Press, 1996.

Bui, James D., Shirley Suet-Ling Tang, and Peter N. Kiang. "The Local/Global Politics of Boston's Viet-Vote." *AAPI Nexus: Policy, Practice & Community* 2, no. 2 (2004): 10–18.

Bulmer, Martin, and John Solomos. *Researching Race and Racism*. London: Routledge, 2004.

Bulosan, Carlos. *America Is in the Heart*. New York: Harcourt, Brace, 1943.

Burbules, Nicholas, and Rupert Berk. "Critical Thinking and Critical Pedagogy: Relations, Differences, and Limits." In *Critical Theories in Education*, edited by Thomas Popkewitz and Lynn Fendler. New York: Routledge, 1999.

Burgess, Ernest W. "Social Planning and Race Relations." In *Race Relations: Problems and Theory*, edited by Jitsuichi Masuoka and Preston Valien, pp. 13–25. Chapel Hill: University of North Carolina Press, 1961.

Buroway, Michael. *Global Ethnography*. Berkeley: University of California Press, 2000.

Burawoy, Michael, et al. *Ethnography Unbound: Power and Resistance in the Modern Metropolis*. Berkeley: University of California Press, 1991.

Busby, Margaret. *Daughters of Africa: An International Anthology of Words and Writings by Women of African Descent; From the Ancient Egyptian to the Present*. New York: Pantheon, 1992.

Buss, Fran Leeper. *Forged under the Sun/Forjado Bajo del Sol: The Life of Maria Elena Lucas*. Ann Arbor: University of Michigan Press, 1993.

Butler, Johnnella E. "African American Literature and Realist Theory: Seeking the 'True-True.'" In *Identity Politics Reconsidered*, edited by Linda Martín Alcoff, Michael Hames-García, Satya Mohanty, and Paula Moya. Palgrave Press, forthcoming.

———, ed. *Color-Line to Borderlands: The Matrix of American Ethnic Studies*. Seattle: University of Washington Press, 2001.

———. "Ethnic Studies as a Matrix for the Humanities, the Social Sciences, and the Common Good." In *Color-Line to Borderlands: The Matrix of American Ethnic Studies*, edited by Johnnella E. Butler. Seattle: University of Washington Press, 2001.

———. "*Mumbo Jumbo*, Theory, and the Aesthetics of Wholeness." In *Aesthetics in a Multicultural Age*, edited by Emory Elliott, Louis Freitas Caton, and Jeffrey Rhyne, pp. 175–193. New York: Oxford University Press, 2002.

Butler, Johnnella E., and John C. Walter. *Transforming the Curriculum: Ethnic Studies and Women's Studies*. New York: SUNY Press, 1991.

Butler, Judith. *Gender Trouble: Feminism and the Subversion of Identity*. New York: Routledge, 1990.

Caccamo, Rita. *Back to Middletown: Three Generations of Sociological Reflections*. Stanford, Calif.: Stanford University Press, 2000.

Calderón, José. "Multi-Ethnic Coalition-Building in a Diverse School District." *Critical Sociology* 21 (Spring 1995): 101–111.

———. "Partnership in Teaching and Learning: Combining the Practice of Critical Pedagogy with Civic Engagement and Diversity." *Peer Review* 5, no. 3 (Spring 2003): 6–9.

Calderón, José, Suzanne Foster, and Silvia Rodriguez. "Organizing Immigrant Workers: Action Research and Strategies in the Pomona Day Labor Center." In *Latino Los Angeles: Transformations, Communities, and Activism*, edited by Enrique C. Ochoa and Gilda Laura Ochoa, pp. 279–299. Tucson: University of Arizona Press, 2005.

Camacho, Patricia. "An Interpersonal Process: Redefining Traditional and Nontraditional Roles of Women Supporters and Leaders in the UFW." Senior thesis, Pitzer College, Claremont, Calif., 1995.

Candelaria, Cordelia. "Go 'Way from My Window, La Llorona." In *Infinite Divisions: An Anthology of Chicana Literature*, edited by Tey Diana Rebolledo and Eliana Rivero. Tucson: University of Arizona Press, 1993.

Cannon, K. *Black Womanist Ethics*. Atlanta, Ga.: Scholars Press, 1988.

Cantor, Jeffrey A. *Experiential Learning in Higher Education: Linking Classroom and Community*. Report no. 7. Washington, D.C.: George Washington University, 1995.

Capra, Fritjof. *The Web of Life: A New Scientific Understanding of Living Systems*. New York: Anchor, 1996.

Carmichael, Stokely, and Charles V. Hamilton. *Black Power: The Politics of Liberation in America*. New York: Vintage, 1967.

Carr, Leslie G. *'Color-Blind' Racism*. Thousand Oaks, Calif.: Sage Publications, 1997.

Carson, Clayborne. *In Struggle: SNCC and the Black Awakening of the 1960s*. Cambridge, Mass.: Harvard University Press, 1981.

Carson, Josephine. *Silent Voices: The Southern Negro Woman Today*. New York: Delacorte Press, 1969.

Carter, Roymieco. "Visual Literacy: Critical Thinking with the Visual Image." In *Critical Thinking: An Encyclopedia*, edited by Danny Weil and Joe Kincheloe. New York: Greenwood, 2003.

Carter, Robert T. "The Relationship between Racism and Racial Identity among White Americans: An Exploratory Investigation." *Journal of Counseling and Development* 69 (1990): 46–50.

Cary, Richard. "Art and Aesthetics." In *Critical Thinking: An Encyclopedia*, edited by Danny Weil and Joe Kincheloe. New York: Greenwood, 2003.

Castillo, Ana, ed. *Goddess of the Americas: La Diosa de las Américas; Writings on the Virgin of Guadalupe*. New York: Riverhead Books, 1996.

———. *So Far from God*. New York: W.W. Norton, 1993.

Center for Improvement of Teaching. *Diversity Research at an Urban Commuter University*. Monograph. Boston: University of Massachusetts, Boston, 1999.

Champagne, Duane. "Toward a Multidimensional Historical Comparative Methodology: Context, Process, and Causality." In *Race and Ethnicity in Research Methods*, edited by John H. Stanfield and Rutledge M. Dennis, pp. 223–253. Newbury Park, Calif.: Sage Publications, 1993.

Champagne, Duane, and Jay Stauss, eds., *Native American Studies in Higher Education: Models for Collaboration between Universities and Indigenous Nations*. Walnut Creek, Calif.: AltaMira Press, 2002.

Chan, Jeffery Paul, Frank Chin, Lawson Fusao Inada, and Shawn Wong, eds. *The Big Aiiieeeee! An Anthology of Chinese American and Japanese American Literature*. New York: Meridian, 1991.

Chan, Sucheng. *Asian Americans: An Interpretive History*. Boston: Twayne, 1991.

———, ed. *Hmong Means Free: Life in Laos and America*. Philadelphia: Temple University Press, 1994.

Cheah, Pheng, and Bruce Robbins, eds. *Cosmopolitics: Thinking and Feeling beyond the Nation*. Minneapolis: University of Minnesota Press, 1998.

Cheatham, Harold, and James Stewart, eds. *Black Families: Interdisciplinary Perspectives*. New Brunswick, N.J.: Transaction Books, 1990.

Cheng, Anne. *The Melancholy of Race*. New York: Oxford University Press, 2000.

Cheung, King-Kok, ed. *The Interethnic Companion to Asian American Literature*. Cambridge: Cambridge University Press, 1997.

———. "The Woman Warrior versus the Chinaman Pacific: Must a Chinese American Critic Choose between Feminism and Heroism?" In *Maxine Hong Kingston's The Woman Warrior: A Casebook*, edited by Sau-Ling Cynthia Wong. New York: Oxford University Press, 1999.

Chicago Commission on Race Relations. *The Negro in Chicago: A Study of Race Relations and a Race Riot*. Chicago: University of Chicago Press, 1922.

Chin, Frank, Jeffery Paul Chan, Lawson Fusao Inada, and Shawn Hsu Wong, eds. *Aiiieeeee! An Anthology of Asian-American Writers*. Garden City, N.Y.: Anchor, 1975.

Chodorow, Nancy. *The Reproduction of Mothering.* Berkeley: University of California Press, 1978.
Chomsky, Noam. *9-11.* New York: Seven Stories Press, 2001.
Christian, Barbara. *Black Feminist Criticism: Perspectives on Black Women Writers.* New York: Pergamon, 1985.
———. *Black Women Novelists: The Development of a Tradition, 1892–1976.* Westport, Conn.: Greenwood Press, 1980.
Chun-Hoon, Lowell, Lucie Hirata, and Alan Moriyama. "Curriculum Development in Asian American Studies." In *Proceedings of National Asian American Studies Conference II*, edited by George Kagiwada, Joyce Sakai, and Gus Lee, pp. 83–90. Davis, Calif.: University of California, Davis, 1973.
Churchill, Ward. *Struggle for the Land.* Monroe, Maine: Common Courage Press, 1998.
———. "The Tragedy and the Travesty: The Subversion of Indigenous Sovereignty in North America." In *Contemporary Native American Political Issues*, edited by Troy R. Johnson. Walnut Creek, Calif.: AltaMira Press, 1999.
Cisneros, Sandra. *The House on Mango Street.* New York: Vintage, 1991.
———. *Woman Hollering Creek and Other Stories.* New York: Random House, 1991.
Clark Hine, Darlene, ed. *Black Women's History: Theory and Practice.* Brooklyn, N.Y.: Carlson Publishers, 1990.
Clark Hine, Darlene., Elsa Barkley Brown, and Rosalyn Terborg-Penn, eds. *Black Women in America: An Historical Encyclopedia.* Brooklyn, N.Y.: Carlson Publishers, 1993.
Clark Hine, Darlene, and Kathleen Thompson. *A Shining Thread of Hope: The History of Black Women in America.* New York: Broadway Books, 1998.
Clarke, Edwin L. *The Art of Straight Thinking: A Primer of Scientific Method for Social Inquiry.* New York: D. Appleton, 1929.
Collier-Thomas, Bettye. *Daughters of Thunder: Black Women Preachers and Their Sermons, 1850–1979.* San Francisco: Jossey-Bass, 1998.
Collier-Thomas, Bettye, and Vincint Franklin, eds. *Sisters in the Struggle: African-American Women in the Civil Rights–Black Power Movement.* New York: New York University Press, 2001.
The Combahee River Collective. "A Black Feminist Statement." In *Capitalist Patriarchy and the Case of Socialist Feminism*, edited by Zillah R. Eisenstein. New York: Monthly Review Press, 1979.
———. "The Combahee River Collective Statement." In *Theorizing Feminism: Parallel Trends in the Humanities and Social Sciences*, edited by Anne C. Hermann and Abigail J. Stewart. Boulder, Colo.: Westview Press, 1994.
Cone, James H. *For My People: Black Theology and the Black Church.* Maryknoll, N.Y.: Orbis Books, 1984.
Conyers, James, ed. *Afrocentricity and the Academy: Essays on Theory and Practice.* Jefferson, N.C.: McFarland, 2003.

Cooper, Anna Julia. *A Voice from the South, by a Black Woman of the South.* New York: Negro Universities Press, 1969.
Corpi, Lucha. *Black Widow's Wardrobe.* Houston, Tex.: Arte Público Press, 1999
———. "Marina." In *Infinite Divisions: An Anthology of Chicana Literature*, edited by Tey Diana Rebolledo and Eliana Rivero. Tucson: University of Arizona Press, 1993.
Cose, Ellis. *Color Blind.* New York: HarperCollins, 1997.
Coulburn, Rushton, and W. E. B. Du Bois. "Mr. Sorokin's Systems." *Journal of Modern History* 14 (1942): 500–521.
Crenshaw, Kimberlé W., Neil Gotanda, Gary Peller, and Kendall Thomas, eds. *Critical Race Theory: The Key Writings That Formed the Movement.* New York: New York University Press, 1995.
Cross, William. *Shades of Black, Diversity in African American Identity.* Philadelphia: Temple University Press, 1991.
Cruse, Harold. *Plural But Equal.* New York: William Morrow, 1987.
Cypess, Sandra Messinger. *La Malinche in Mexican Literature: From History to Myth.* Austin: University of Texas Press, 1991.
Dahlbom, Bo. "Going to the Future." 1998. www.viktoria.infomatik.gu.se/~max/bo/papers.html
Darder, Antonia. *Reinventing Paulo Freire: A Pedagogy of Love.* Boulder, Colo.: Westview Press, 2002.
Dasgupta, N., D. E. McGhee, A. G. Greenwald, and M. R. Banaji. "Automatic Preference for White Americans: Eliminating the Familiarity Explanation." *Journal of Experimental Social Psychology* 36 (2000): 316–328.
Dasgupta, Shamita Das, ed. *A Patchwork Shawl: Chronicles of South Asian Women in America.* New Brunswick, N.J.: Rutgers University Press, 1998.
Davis, Angela. *Women, Race and Class.* New York: Random House, 1981.
Death Runs Riot. Insignia and WETA, producers. Television series episode. In *The West*, edited by West Film Project and WETA. Washington, D.C.: Insignia and WETA, 1996.
DeBonis, Steven. *Children of the Enemy: Oral Histories of Vietnamese Amerasians and Their Mothers.* Jefferson, N.C.: McFarland, 1995
Degenaar, J. "Myth and the Collision of Cultures." *Myth and Symbol* 2 (1995).
Dei, George. "Indigenous Knowledge as an Empowerment Tool." In *Empowerment: Toward Sustainable Development*, edited by Naresh Singh and Vangile Titi. Toronto: Fernwood Press, 1995.
De Jong, David H. *Promises of the Past: A History of Indian Education.* Golden, Colo.: North American Press, 1993.
Del Castillo, Adelaida. "Malintzin Tenepal: A Preliminary Look into a New Perspective." In *Essays on La Mujer*, edited by Rosaura Sánchez and Rosa Martínez Cruz, pp. 124–149. Chicano Studies Center Publications, University of California, Los Angeles, 1977.
Del Castillo, Richard Griswold, and Richard A. Garcia. *Cesar Chavez: A Triumph of Spirit.* Norman: University of Oklahoma Press, 1995.

Delgado, Richard, ed. *Critical Race Theory: The Cutting Edge*. Philadelphia: Temple University Press, 1995.

———. *The Coming Race War? And Other Apocalyptic Tales of America After Affirmative Action and Welfare*. New York: New York University Press, 1996.

Delgado, Richard, and Jean Stefancic. *Critical Race Theory: An Introduction*. New York: New York University Press, 2001.

———, eds. *Critical White Studies: Looking behind the Mirror*. Philadelphia: Temple University Press, 1997.

Delgado Bernal, Dolores. "Learning and Living Pedagogies of the Home: The Mestiza Consciousness of Chicana Students." *Qualitative Studies in Education* 14, no. 5 (2001): 623–639.

———. "Using a Chicana Feminist Epistemology in Educational Research." *Harvard Educational Review* 68, no. 4 (1998): 555–582.

Delgado-Gaitán, Concha. "Researching Change and Changing the Researcher." *Harvard Educational Review* 63, no. 4 (1993): 389–411.

Delgado-Gaitán, Concha, and Henry Trueba. *Crossing Cultural Borders: Education for Immigrant Families in America*. London: Falmer Press, 1991.

Del Valle Arizpe, Artemio. *Leyendas y sucedidos del México colonial*. Mexico City: El Libro Español, 1963.

Denzin, Norman K., and Yvonna S. Lincoln, eds. *Handbook of Qualitative Research*. 2nd ed. Thousand Oaks, Calif.: Sage Publications, 2000.

Devault, Marjorie. "Talking Back to Sociology: Distinctive Contributions of Feminist Methodologies." *Annual Review of Sociology* 22 (1996).

Devine, Patricia G., and Andrew J. Elliot. "Are Racial Stereotypes Really Fading? The Princeton Trilogy Revisited." *Personality and Social Psychology Bulletin* 21 (1995): 1139–1150.

Dewey, John. *Democracy and Education: An Introduction to the Philosophy of Education*. New York: Macmillan, 1916.

Díaz del Castillo, Bernal. *Verdadera historia de la conquista de la Nueva España*. Mexico City: Editorial Porrúa, 1967.

Dicks, Bella, and Bruce Mason. "Hypermedia and Ethnography: Reflections on the Construction of a Research Approach." *Sociological Research Online* 3 (1998): 3.

Dill, Bonnie Thornton. "'The Means to Put My Children Through': Child-Rearing Goals and Strategies among Black Female Domestic Servants." In *The Black Woman*, edited by LaFrances Rodgers-Rose, pp. 107–123. Beverly Hills, Calif.: Sage Publications, 1980.

———. "Race, Class, and Gender: Prospects for an All-Inclusive Sisterhood." *Feminist Studies* 9 (1993):131–150.

Diop, Cheikh Anta. *The African Origin of Civilization: Myth or Reality*. Edited and translated by Mercer Cook. Westport, Conn.: Lawrence Hill, 1974.

———. *The Cultural Unity of Black Africa*. Chicago: Third World Press, 1990.

Draine, S. C., and A. G. Greenwald. "Replicable Unconscious Semantic Priming." *Journal of Experimental Psychology* 127 (1998): 286–303.

D'Souza, Dinesh. *Illiberal Education: The Politics of Race and Sex on Campus*. New York: Vintage, 1991.

Du Bois, W. E. B. "The Atlanta Conferences." *Voice of the Negro* 1 (March 1904): 85–90.

———. "The Beginnings of Slavery." *Voice of the Negro* 2 (February 1905): 104–106.

———. *The Black Flame: A Trilogy*. Vol. 1, *The Ordeal of Mansart*. Vol. 2, *Mansart Builds a School*. Vol. 3, *Worlds of Color*. New York: Mainstream Publishers, 1957, 1959, 1961.

———. "The Conservation of Races." American Negro Academy Occasional Papers, no. 2, 1897. Reprinted in *W. E. B. Du Bois Speaks: Speeches and Addresses 1890–1919*, edited by Philip Foner, pp. 73–85. New York: Pathfinder Press, 1970.

———. "Economic Disfranchisement." *Crisis* 37 (August 1930): 281–282.

———. *The Education of Black People: Ten Critiques, 1906–1960*. New York: Monthly Review Press, 1973.

———. "The Evolution of the Race Problem." *Proceedings of the National Negro Conference*. New York, 1909. Reprinted in *W. E. B. Du Bois Speaks: Speeches and Addresses 1890–1919*, edited by Philip Foner, pp. 196–210. New York: Pathfinder Press, 1970.

———. "The Field and Function of the Negro College." Alumni reunion address, Fisk University, 1933. Reprinted in *W. E. B. Du Bois: The Education of Black People, Ten Critiques 1900–1960*, edited by Herbert Aptheker, pp. 83–102. Amherst: University of Massachusetts Press, 1973.

———. "My Evolving Program for Negro Freedom." In *What the Negro Wants*, edited by Rayford Logan, pp. 31–70. Chapel Hill: University of North Carolina Press, 1944.

———. *The Philadelphia Negro: A Social Study*. Philadelphia: University of Pennsylvania Press, 1899.

———. Postscript to *The Ordeal of Mansart*. Originally published in 1957. Millwood, N.Y.: Kraus Thomson, 1976.

———. "The Social Origins of Negro Art." *Modern Quarterly* 3, no. 1 (1925): 53–56.

———. *The Souls of Black Folk*. Chicago: A. C. McClurg, 1903.

———. *The Souls of Black Folk*. New York: Library of America, 1986.

———. "The Study of the Negro Problems." *Annals of the American Academy of Political and Social Science* 11 (January 1898): 1–23.

———. *The World and Africa: An Inquiry into the Part Which Africa Has Played in World History*. Originally published in 1946. New York: International Publishers, 1968.

Dueñas Contreras, Tomasa, et al. "Transnational Latina Youth and Low-Intensity Conflict: Tempering the Forces of Assimilation." Paper presented as part of a panel, "Internal Wars in Education: *Llegaste a Jugar Entre Las Strawberry Fields y Nada*—You Walked into a Minefield." National Association for Chicana and Chicano Studies Annual Conference, Los Angeles, California, April 2003.

Dueñas Tovar, Tomasa, et al. "*Recordando Mis Raíces y Viviendo Mis Tradiciones* [Remembering My Roots and Living My Traditions]: The Making of a Transnational Bilingual Children's Book." Panel at the Reading the World Conference, University of San Francisco, March 2003.

Dumas, Michael. "Critical Thinking as Black Experience." In *Critical Thinking: An Encyclopedia*, edited by Danny Weil and Joe Kincheloe. New York: Greenwood, 2003.

Durán, Fray Diego. *Historia de las Indias de Nueva España y Tierra Firme*. First published in 1579. Mexico City: Imprenta de J. M. Andrade y F. Escalante, 1867–1880.

During, Simon, ed. *The Cultural Studies Reader*. New York: Routledge, 1993.

Eagleton, Terry. *Literary Theory*. Oxford: Blackwell, 1996.

Eckel, P., B. Hill, and M. Green. *On Change: En Route to Transformation*. Washington, D.C.: American Council on Education, 1998.

Edid, Marilyn. *Farm Labor Organizing: Trends & Prospects*. Ithaca, N.Y.: ILR Press, 1994.

Elbaz, Gilbert. "The Sociology of AIDS Activism: The Case of Act up/New York, 1987–1992." Ph.D. dissertation. City University of New York, 1992.

Eldin, Max, and Morton Levin. "Cogenerative Learning: Bringing Participation into Action Research." In *Participatory Action Research*, edited by William Foote Whyte, pp. 127–142. Newbury Park, Calif.: Sage Publications, 1991.

Elenes, C. Alejandra, Francisca E. González, Dolores Delgado Bernal, and Sofia Villenas. "Introduction: Chicana/Mexicana Feminist Pedagogies; *Consejos, Respeto y Educación* in Everyday Life." *Qualitative Studies in Education* 14, no. 5 (2001): 595–602.

Elliott, Michael, and Claudia Stokes. "What Is Method and Why Does It Matter?" 2003, www.nyupress.org/webchapter/0814722156intro.pdf.

Ellis, Trey. "The New Black Aesthetic." *Callaloo* 38 (Winter 1989): 233–243.

Embree, Edwin. *Brown America, the Story of a New Race*. New York: Friendship Press, 1936.

Emerson, Robert M., Rachel I. Fretz, and Linda L. Shaw. *Writing Ethnographic Fieldnotes*. Chicago: University of Chicago Press, 1995.

Eng, David L. *Racial Castration: Managing Masculinity in Asian America*. Durham, N.C.: Duke University Press, 2001.

English, Fenwick W. "A Critical Appraisal of Sara Lawrence-Lightfoot's Portraiture as a Method of Educational Research." *Educational Researcher* 29, no. 7 (October 2000): 21–26.

Entman, Robert M., and Andrew Rojecki. *The Black Image in the White Mind: Media and Race in America*. Chicago: University of Chicago Press, 2000.

Erdrich, Louise. *Love Medicine*. New York: Bantam, 1989.

Erler, Mary, and Maryanne Kowaleski, eds. *Women and Power in the Middle Ages*. Athens: University of Georgia Press, 1988.

Espinosa, Alex. "The Development of Critical Consciousness through a Praxis of Reflection and Involvement." Senior thesis, Pitzer College, Claremont, Calif., 1999.

Espiritu, Yen Le. *Asian American Panethnicity: Bridging Institutions and Identities.* Philadelphia: Temple University Press, 1992.

———. *Filipino American Lives.* Philadelphia: Temple University Press, 1995.

Essed, Philomena, and David Goldberg, eds. *Race Critical Theories.* Malden, Mass.: Blackwell, 2002.

Eyler, Janet, and Dwight E. Giles. *Where's the Learning in Service Learning?* San Francisco: Jossey-Bass, 1999.

Faggins, Barbara. *Africans and Indians: An Afrocentric Analysis of Contacts between Africans and Indians in Colonial Virginia.* New York: Routledge, 2001.

Fals-Borda, Orlando, and Muhammad Anisur Rahman. *Action and Knowledge: Breaking the Monopoly with Participatory Action Research.* New York: Apex Press, 1991.

Fanon, Frantz. *The Wretched of the Earth.* London: Penguin, 1967.

———. *The Wretched of the Earth.* New York: Grove Press, 1968.

Feagin, Joe R., and Clairece Booth. *Racial and Ethnic Relations and Searching for the Uncommon Group.* 6th ed. Upper Saddle River, N.J.: Prentice Hall, 2003.

Feagin, Joe R., Hernan Vera, and Pinar Batur. *White Racism: The Basics.* 1st ed. New York: Routledge, 1995.

———. *White Racism: The Basics.* 2nd ed. New York: Routledge, 2001.

Fenwick, T. "Experiential Learning in Adult Education: A Comparative Framework." www.ualberta.ca/~tfenwick/ext/aeq.htm.

Figueroa, Julie L. "Out of the Neighborhood and Into the Ivory Tower: Understanding the Schooling Experiences of Latino Male Undergraduates as a Process of Negotiation and Navigation." Unpublished dissertation. University of California, Berkeley, 2002.

Fine, Michelle, Louise Weis, Susan Weseen, and Loonmun Wong, "For Whom? Qualitative Research, Representations, and Social Responsibilities." In *Handbook of Qualitative Research*, 2nd ed., edited by Norman K. Denzin and Yvonna S. Lincoln, pp. 107–131. Thousand Oaks, Calif.: Sage Publications, 2000.

Fischer, Frank. "Beyond Empiricism: Policy Inquiry in Postpositivist Perspective." *Policy Studies Journal* 26, no. 1 (1998): 129–146.

Flores, William V. "Citizens vs. Citizenry: Undocumented Immigrants and Latino Cultural Citizenship." In *Latino Cultural Citizenship: Claiming Identity, Space, and Rights*, edited by William V. Flores and Rina Benmayor, pp. 252–277 and 289–290. Boston: Beacon Press, 1997.

Flores, William V., and Rina Benmayor, eds. *Latino Cultural Citizenship: Claiming Identity, Space, and Rights.* Boston: Beacon Press, 1997.

Fogel, Robert. *Without Consent or Contract: The Rise and Fall of American Slavery.* New York: W. W. Norton, 1989.

Fogel, Robert, and Stanley Engerman. *Time on the Cross: The Economics of American Negro Slavery.* 2 vols. Boston: Little, Brown, 1974.

Foley, Neil. "Becoming Hispanic: Mexican Americans and Whiteness." In *White Privilege: Essential Readings on the Other Side of Racism*, edited by Paula S. Rothenberg, pp. 49–60. New York: Worth Publishers, 2002.

———. *White Scourge: Mexicans, Blacks, and Poor Whites in Texas Cotton Culture.* Berkeley: University of California Press, 1997.

Foner, Nancy. *From Ellis Island to JFK: New York's Two Great Waves of Immigration.* New Haven, Conn.: Yale University Press, 2000.

Fong, Timothy P. "Reflections on Teaching about Asian American Communities." In *Teaching Asian America: Diversity & the Problem of Community,* edited by Lane Hirabayashi, pp. 143–150. Lanham, Md.: Rowman & Littlefield, 1998.

Fong, Timothy P., and Larry H. Shinagawa, eds. *Asian Americans: Experiences and Perspectives.* Upper Saddle River, N.J.: Prentice Hall, 2000.

Fontana, Andrea, and James H. Frey. "Interviewing: The Art of Science." In *Collecting and Interpreting Qualitative Materials,* edited by Norman K. Denzin and Yvonna S. Lincoln, pp. 47–78. London: Sage Publications, 1998.

Forbes, Jack D. *Afro-Americans in the Far West.* Berkeley: Far West Laboratory, 1967.

———. *Apache, Navaho and Spaniard.* Norman: University of Oklahoma Press, 1960, 1994.

———. *Aztecas del Norte: The Chicanos of Aztlan.* New York: Fawcett, 1973.

———. *Black Africans and Native Americans: Race, Caste and Color in the Evolution of Red-Black Peoples.* Oxford: Blackwell, 1988. Reprinted in May 1993 by University of Illinois Press in a paperback edition as *Africans and Native Americans: The Language of Race and the Evolution of Red-Black People,* with an improved index and a few other changes.

———. *Columbus and Other Cannibals: The Wetiko Disease of Exploitation, Imperialism and Terrorism.* New York: Autonomedia/Semiotexte, 1992.

——— *The Indian in America's Past.* Englewood Cliffs, N.J.: Prentice-Hall, 1964.

———. *Native Americans of California and Nevada.* Healdsburg, Calif: Naturegraph, 1969. Revised edition 1982.

———. *Warriors of the Colorado: The Quechans and Their Neighbors.* Norman: University of Oklahoma Press, 1965.

Ford, Nick. "Black Studies Programs." *Current History* 67, no. 399 (1974): 224–227.

Foster, Frances. *Written by Herself: Literary Production by African American Women, 1746–1892.* Bloomington: Indiana University Press, 1993.

Foster, Roxie. "Addressing Epistemologic and Practical Issues in Multimethod Research: A Procedure for Conceptual Triangulation." *Advances in Nursing Education* 202, no. 2 (1997).

Foucault, Michel. *The Archaeology of Knowledge.* Translated by A. Sheridan Smith. New York: Pantheon, 1972.

———. *Discipline and Punish: The Birth of the Prison.* New York: Vintage, 1977.

———. *The History of Sexuality: An Introduction.* Vol. 1. New York: Vintage, 1978.

Franklin, John Hope. *The Color Line.* Columbia: University of Missouri Press, 1993.

Frazier, E. Franklin. "Is the Negro Family a Unique Sociological Unit?" *Opportunity* 5 (1927): 165–168.

———. *Race and Culture Contacts in the Modern World*. New York: Knopf, 1957.

———. "Theoretical Structure of Sociology and Sociological Research." *British Journal of Sociology* 4, no. 4 (December 1953): 293–311.

Freeman, James M. *Hearts of Sorrow: Vietnamese-American Lives*. Stanford, Calif.: Stanford University Press, 1989.

Freire, Paulo. *Pedagogy of the Oppressed*. New York: Herder and Herder, 1970.

Freire, Paulo. *Pedagogy of the Oppressed*. Revised 20th-century edition. New York: Continuum, 1993.

Friedman, Susan. "(Inter) Disciplinarity and the Question of the Women's Studies Ph.D." *Feminist Studies* 24, no. 2 (1998).

Fuchs, Lawrence. *The American Kaleidoscope*. Hanover, N.H.: Wesleyan University Press, 1990.

Fuentes, Emma, Daniel Liou, Patricia Sánchez, and Andrea Dyrness. "Interim Report from the English Language Learner Committee," Diversity Project, University of California, Berkeley, Spring 2000.

Fujitani, T., et al., eds. *Perilous Memories: The Asia-Pacific War(s)*. Durham, N.C.: Duke University Press, 2001.

Funk & Wagnalls Standard Dictionary of Folklore, Mythology, and Legend. New York: Funk and Wagnalls, 1950.

Fusco, Coco. *English Is Broken Here: Notes on Cultural Fusion in the Americas*. New York: New Press, 1995.

Gaertner, Samuel L., and John F. Dovidio. "The Aversive Form of Racism." In *Prejudice, Discrimination, and Racism*, edited by John F. Dovidio and Samuel L. Gaertner, pp. 61–89. San Diego, Calif.: Academic Press, 1986.

Gaines, Ernest. *A Lesson before Dying*. New York: Vintage, 1993.

Gaines, Kevin K. *Uplifting the Race: Black Leadership, Politics, and Culture in the Twentieth Century*. Chapel Hill: University of North Carolina Press, 1996.

Galloway, A. M., T. B. Gutkin, A. Saunders, J. E. Gonzalez, G. Yetter, and R. R. Sobansky. "White Racial Attitudes: A Synthesis of Extant Literature and Scale Development." Poster presented at the American Psychological Convention, Boston, Mass., August 1999.

Gamson, Zelda F. "Higher Education & Rebuilding Civic Life." *Change*, January–February 1997, 10–13.

Garcia, Eugene E. *Hispanic Education in the United States: Raíces y Alas*. Lanham, MD: Rowman & Littlefield, 2001.

Garcia, Eugene E., Francisco A. Lomelí, and Isidro D. Ortiz, eds. *Chicano Studies: A Multidisciplinary Approach*. New York: Teachers College Press, 1984.

Gates, Henry Louis, Jr., and Anthony Appiah. *Identities*. Chicago: University of Chicago Press, 1995.

Geeland, D., and P. Taylor. "Writing Our Lived Experience: Beyond the (Pale) Hermeneutic." *Electronic Journal of Science Education* 5 (2000). unr.edu/homepage/crowther/ejse/geelanetal.html.

Geertz, Clifford. *The Interpretation of Cultures: Selected Essays*. New York: Basic Books, 1973.

Giddings, Paula. *When and Where I Enter: The Impact of Black Women on Race and Sex in America*. New York: William Morrow, 1984.

Gidley, Mick, ed. *Representing Others: White Views of Indigenous Peoples*. Exeter: University of Exeter Press, 1994.

Gilens, Martin. *Why Americans Hate Welfare: Race, Media, and the Politics of Antipoverty Policy*. Chicago: University of Chicago Press, 1999.

Gilkes, Cheryl Townsend. "From Slavery to Social Welfare: Racism and the Control of Black Women." In *Class, Race, and Sex: The Dynamics of Control*, edited by Amy Smerdlow and Helen Lessinger, pp. 288–300. Boston: G. K. Hall, 1981.

———. "'Holding Back the Ocean with a Broom': Black Women and Community Work." In *The Black Woman*, edited by LaFrances Rodgers-Rose, pp. 217–231. Beverly Hills, Calif.: Sage Publications, 1980.

———. "'Together and in Harness': Women's Traditions in the Sanctified Church." *Signs* 10 (1985): 678–699.

Gilroy, Paul. *Against Race: Imagining Political Culture beyond the Color Line*. Cambridge, Mass.: Belknap Press of Harvard University Press, 2000.

———. *The Black Atlantic: Modernity and Double Consciousness*. Cambridge, Mass.: Harvard University Press, 1993.

Giroux, Henry. *Pedagogy and the Politics of Hope: Theory, Culture, and Schooling*. Boulder, Colo.: Westview Press, 1997.

Glaser, Barney. *Theoretical Sensitivity*. Mill Valley, Calif.: Sociology Press, 1978.

Glaser, Barney, and Anselm. Strauss. *The Discovery of Grounded Theory*. Chicago: Aldine, 1967.

Glassick, C. E., M. Taylor Huber, and G. I. Maeroff. *Scholarship Assessed*. Ernest L. Boyer Project of the Carnegie Foundation for the Advancement of Teaching. San Francisco: Jossey-Bass, 1997.

Glenn, Evelyn Nakano. *Unequal Freedom: How Race and Gender Shaped American Citizenship and Labor*. Cambridge, Mass.: Harvard University Press, 2002.

Goldberg, David Theo. *The Racial State*. Malden, Mass.: Blackwell, 2002.

———. *Racist Culture: Philosophy and the Politics of Meaning*. Oxford: Blackwell, 1993.

Gonzales-Berry, Erlinda. *Paletitas de guayaba*. Albuquerque, N.Mex.: El Norte Publications, 1991.

González, Francisca. "Haciendo que hacer—Cultivating a Mestiza Worldview and Academic Achievement: Braiding Cultural Knowledge into Educational Research, Policy, Practice." *Qualitative Studies in Education* 14, no. 5 (2001): 641–656.

González, Norma. *"I Am My Language": Discourses of Women and Children in the Borderlands*. Tucson: University of Arizona Press, 2001.

Goodall, Hurley. "Writing Muncie's African American Community: How We Wrote the Other Side of Middletown." Address presented at the Union Baptist Church, Muncie Ind., April 17, 2003.

Gordon, Avery F., and Christopher Newfield, eds. *Mapping Multiculturalism.* Minneapolis: University of Minnesota Press, 1996.
Gordon, Lewis R. *Bad Faith and Anti-Black Racism.* Atlantic Highlands, N.J.: Humanities Press, 1995.
Gordon, Vivian. *Black Women, Feminism, Black Liberation: Which Way?* Revised ed. Chicago: Third World Press, 1987.
Gould, Mark. "Race and Theory: Culture, Poverty, and Adaptation to Discrimination in Wilson and Ogbu." *Sociological Theory* 17, no. 2 (1999): 171–200.
Grant, J. *White Women's Christ and Black Women's Jesus: Feminist Christology and Womanist Response.* Atlanta, Ga.: Scholars Press, 1989.
Grant, Madison. *The Passing of the Great Race; or, the Racial Basis of European History.* New York: Charles Scribner's Sons, 1916.
Gray, Cecil Conteen. *Afrocentric Thought and Praxis: An Intellectual History.* Trenton, N.J.: Africa World Press, 2001.
Greenwald, A. G., D. E. McGhee, and J. L. K. Schwartz. "Measuring Individual Differences in Implicit Cognition: The Implicit Association Test." *Journal of Personality and Social Psychology* 74 (1998): 1464–1480.
Greenwood, Davydd J., and Morten Levin. *Introduction to Action Research: Social Research for Social Change.* Thousand Oaks, Calif.: Sage Publications, 1998.
Gresson, Aaron. *America's Atonement.* New York: Peter Lang, 2004.
———. *The Recovery of Race in America.* Minneapolis: University of Minnesota Press, 1991.
Grewal, Inderpal, and Caren Kaplan, eds. *Scattered Hegemonies: Postmodernity and Transnational Feminist Practices.* Minneapolis: University of Minnesota Press, 1994.
Groden, Michael, and Martin Kreiswirth, eds. *The Johns Hopkins Guide to Literary Theory and Criticism.* Baltimore: Johns Hopkins University Press, 1994.
Grossberg, Lawrence, et al., eds. *Cultural Studies.* New York: Routledge, 1992.
Guajardo, Miguel A. "Education for Leadership Development: Preparing a New Generation of Leaders." Unpublished doctoral dissertation, University of Texas, Austin, 2002.
Guajardo, Miguel A., Patricia Sánchez, Elisa Fineman, and James Joseph Scheurich. "Labores de la Vida/The Labors of Life: A Description of a Video Documentary of Mexican-American Adults Who Were Migrant Agricultural Workers as Children." In *Anti-Racist Scholarship: An Advocacy,* edited by J. J. Scheurich. Albany, N.Y.: SUNY Press, 2002.
Guinier, Lani, and Susan Sturm. *Who's Qualified?* Boston: Beacon Press, 2001.
Guiner, Lani, and Gerald Torres. *The Miner's Canary: Enlisting Race, Resisting Power, Transforming Democracy.* Cambridge, Mass.: Harvard University Press, 2002.
Gunaratnam, Yasmin. *Researching "Race" and Ethnicity: Methods, Knowledge and Power.* Thousand Oaks, Calif.: Sage Publications, 2003.
Gutierrez, Ramon. "Ethnic Studies: Its Evolution in American Colleges and Universities." In *Multiculturalism: A Critical Reader,* edited by David Theo Goldberg. Cambridge, Mass.: Blackwell, 1994.

Guy-Sheftall, Beverly. Introduction to *Words of Fire, an Anthology of African-American Feminist Thought*, edited by Beverly Guy-Sheftall, pp. 1–22. New York: New Press, 1995.

Gwaltney, John Langston. *Drylongso: A Self-portrait of Black America*. New York: Vintage, 1980.

———. "The Black Woman and Child Rearing." In *The Black Woman*, edited by LaFrances Rodgers-Rose, pp. 79–88. Beverly Hills, Calif.: Sage Publications, 1980.

———. *Drylongso: A Self-portrait of Black America*. New York: Vintage, 1980.

Hagey, Rebecca S. "The Use and Abuse of Participatory Action Research." *Chronic Disease of Canada* 18, no. 1 (1997).

Haig, Brian. "Grounded Theory as Scientific Method." *Philosophy of Education* 1995, 1. www.ed.uiuc.edu/EPS/PES-Yearbook/95_docs/haig.html.

Hale, Charles R., ed. *Engaging Contradictions: Theory, Politics and Methods of Activist Scholarship*. Berkeley: University of California Press, forthcoming, 2008.

Hale, Janice. "The Black Woman and Child Rearing." *The Black Woman*, edited by Francis, Rodgers-Rose Beverly Hills Calif.: Sage, 1980.

Haley, Alex. *The Autobiography of Malcolm X*. New York: Ballantine Books, 1965.

Hall, Budd L. "From Margins to Center? Development and Purpose of Participatory Research." *American Sociologist* 23, no. 4 (1992).

Hall, Donald E. *Literary and Cultural Theory: From Basic Principles to Advanced Applications*. Boston: Houghton Mifflin, 2001.

Hall, Perry. *In the Vineyard, Working in African American Studies*. Knoxville: University of Tennessee Press, 1999.

Hall, Stuart. "The West and the Rest: Discourse and Power." In *Formations of Modernity*, edited by Stuart Hall and Bram Gielben, pp. 276–320. Cambridge: Polity Press and Open University, 1992.

Hames-García, Michael, and Paula Moya, eds. *Reclaiming Identity: Realist Theory and the Predicament of Postmodernism*. Berkeley: University of California Press, 2000.

Harden, Jacalyn D. *Double Cross: Japanese Americans in Black and White Chicago*. Minneapolis: University of Minnesota Press, 2003.

Hardiman, Rita, and William Cross. *White Identity Theory: Origins and Prospect*. Videorecording. North Amherst, Mass.: Microtraining, 1991.

Harding, Sandra. "Comment on Hekman's 'Truth and Method: Feminist Standpoint Theory Revisited': Whose Standpoint Needs the Regimes of Truth and Reality?" *Signs* 22, no. 2 (1997): 382–391.

Harding, Sandra, and Merrill Hintikka, eds. *Discovering Reality: Feminist Perspectives on Epistemology, Metaphysics, Methodology, and the Philosophy of Science*. Dordrecht: Kluver, 1983.

Harding, Vincent. "Power from Our People: The Sources of the Modern Revival of Black History." *Black Scholar* 18, no. 1 (January–February 1987).

Hare, Nathan. "The Battle of Black Studies." *Black Scholar*, May 1972, 32–37.

Harley, Sharon, and Rosalyn Terborg-Penn, eds. *The Afro-American Woman, Struggles and Images*. Port West, N.Y.: National University, 1978.

Harper-Bolton, Charlyn. "A Reconceptualization of the Black Woman." *Black Male/Female Relationships*, Winter 1982, 32–42.

Harris, Jerome, and William McCullough. "Quantitative Methods and Black Community Studies." In *The Death of White Sociology*, edited by Joyce Ladner, pp. 331–343. New York: Random House, 1973.

Harris, Robert. "Coming of Age: The Transformation of Afro-American Historiography." In *Paradigms in Black Studies. Intellectual History, Cultural Meaning, and Political Ideology*, edited by Abdul Alkalimat, pp. 53–72. Chicago: Twenty-First Century Books, 1990.

Hartsock, Nancy M. "The Feminist Standpoint: Developing the Ground for a Specifically Feminist Historical Materialism." In *Discovering Reality: Feminist Perspectives on Epistemology, Metaphysics, Methodology, and the Philosophy of Science*, edited by Sandra Harding and Merrill Hintikka, pp. 283–310. Dordrecht: Kluver, 1983.

Hayes, Floyd W., III., ed. *A Turbulent Voyage: Readings in African American Studies*. San Diego, Calif.: Collegiate Press, 2002.

Hekman, Susan. "Truth and Method : Feminist Standpoint Theory Revisited." *Discovering Reality: Feminist Perspectives on Epistemology, Metaphysics, and Philiosphy of Science*, edited by Sandra Harding and Merrill Hinyikka. Dordrecht: Reidel, 1983.

Helms, Janet E. *Black and White Racial Identity: Theory, Research and Practice*. Westport, Conn.: Greenwood Press, 1990.

———. "Toward a Theoretical Explanation of the Effect of Race on Counseling: A Black and White Model." *Counseling Psychology* 12 (1984): 153–165.

Helms, Janet E., and Robert T. Carter. "White Racial Identity Attitude Inventory." In *Black and White Racial Identity: Theory, Research and Practice*, edited by Janet E. Helms, pp. 62–80. Westport, Conn.: Greenwood Press, 1990.

Herman, E., and N. Chomsky. *Manufacturing Consent: The Political Economy of Mass Media*. New York: Pantheon, 1988.

Herrera-Sobek, María, ed. *Chicana Literary and Artistic Expressions: Culture and Society in Dialogue*. Santa Barbara, Calif.: Center for Chicano Studies Publication Series, 2000.

———. "In Search of La Malinche: Pictorial Representations of a Mytho-Historical Figure." In *Feminism, Nation and Myth: La Malinche*, edited by Rolando Romero and Amanda Nolacea Harris, pp. 112–133. Houston, Tex.: Arte Público Press, 2005.

———, ed. *Santa Barraza: Artist of the Borderlands*. College Station: Texas A&M University Press, 2001.

Hesford, Wendy S., and Wendy Kozol, eds. *Haunting Violations: Feminist Criticism and the Crisis of the "Real."* Urbana: University of Illinois Press, 2001.

Higginbotham, Elizabeth. "Laid Bare by the System: Work and Survival for Black and Hispanic Women." In *Class, Race, and Sex: The Dynamics of Control*, edited by Amy Smerdlow and Helen Lessinger, pp. 200–215. Boston: G. K. Hall, 1993.

———. "Race and Class Barriers to Black Women's College Attendance." *Journal of Ethnic Studies* 13 (1985): 89–107.

———. "Two Representative Issues in Contemporary Sociological Work on Black Women." In *But Some of Us Are Brave*, edited by Gloria T. Hull, Patricia Bell Scott, and Barbara Smith, pp. 93–98. Old Westbury, N.Y.: Feminist Press, 1982.

Hiley, D., S. Kennedy, and S. Robbins. "Faculty Roles and Collective Responsibilities." *Metropolitan University* 8, (1997): 242–252.

Hill Collins, Patricia. *Black Feminist Thought: Knowledge, Consciousness, and the Politics of Empowerment*, 2nd ed. New York: Routledge, 1991.

Hing, Bill Ong, and Ronald Lee, eds. *Reframing the Immigration Debate*. Los Angeles: University of California, Los Angeles, Asian American Studies Center and LEAP, 1996.

Hinson, Glenn. *Fire in My Bones: Transcendence and the Holy Spirit in African American Gospel*. Philadelphia: University of Pennsylvania Press, 2000.

Hintzen, Percy C. *The Costs of Regime Survival: Racial Mobilization, Elite Domination, and Control of the State in Guyana and Trinidad*. New York: Cambridge University Press, 1989.

Hirabayashi, Lane. "Back to the Future: Re-framing Community-Based Research." *Amerasia Journal* 21, nos. 1 and 2 (1995): 103–118.

———. *The Politics of Fieldwork: Fieldwork in an American Concentration Camp*. Tucson: University of Arizona Press, 1999.

———, ed. *Teaching Asian America: Diversity & the Problem of Community*. Lanham, Md.: Rowman & Littlefield, 1998.

Hirabayashi, Lane, and Marilyn Alquizola. "Asian American Studies: Reevaluating for the 1990s." *The State of Asian America: Activism and Resistance in the 1990s*, edited by Karin Aguilar-San Juan. Boston: South End Press, 1994.

Hoban, G., and G. Erickson. "Frameworks for Sustaining Professional Learning." Paper presented at the Australasian Science Education Research Association, Darwin, Australia, 1998.

hooks, bell. *Ain't I a Woman: Black Women and Feminism*. Boston: South End Press, 1981.

———. *From Margin to Center*. Boston: South End Press, 1984.

———. *Killing Rage: Ending Racism*. New York: Henry Holt, 1995.

———. *Teaching to Transgress: Education as the Practice of Freedom*. New York: Routledge, 1994.

Horn, Raymond. *Teacher Talk: A Postformal Inquiry into Educational Change*. New York: Peter Lang, 2000.

Horton, John. *Politics of Diversity*. With the assistance of José Calderón et al. Philadelphia: Temple University Press, 1995.

Houston, Velina Hasu, ed., *The Politics of Life: Four Plays by Asian American Women.* Philadelphia: Temple University Press, 1993.

Houts, Leslie A., and Joe R. Feagin. "Review of *Racing Research, Researching Race.*" *Contemporary Sociology* 30, no. 5 (2001): 570–571.

"How Race is Lived in America." *New York Times.* June –July 2000. www.nytimenews.com/race

Howley, A., E. Pendarvis, and C. Howley. "Anti-intellectualism in U.S. Schools." *Education Policy Analysis Archives* 1, no. 6 (1993).

Huang, Xiaozhao. *A Study of African-American Vernacular English in America's "Middletown": Evidence of Linguistic Convergence.* Lewiston, N.Y.: E. Mellen Press, 2000.

Hu-DeHart, Evelyn. "Ethnic Studies in U.S. Higher Education." In *Handbook of Research on Multicultural Education*, 2nd ed., edited by James A. Banks and Cherry A. McGee Banks, pp. 869–881. San Francisco: Jossey-Bass, 2004.

———. "The History, Development, and Future of Ethnic Studies." *Phi Delta Kappan* 75, no. 1 (1993): 50–54.

———. "The Undermining of Ethnic Studies." *Chronicle of Higher Education*, October 20, 1995, sec. 2.

Hudson, Berkley. "Monterey Park's Mix Lures Researchers." *Los Angeles Times*, October 23, 1988, IX, 1.

Hudson-Weems, Clenora. *Africana Womanism: Reclaiming Ourselves.* Troy, Mich.: Bedford Publishers, 1993.

———. "Africana Womanism and the Critical Need for Africana Theory and Thought." *Western Journal of Black Studies*, Summer 1997, 70–84.

———. "Cultural and Agenda Conflicts in Academia: Critical Issues for Africana Women's Studies." *Western Journal of Black Studies* 13, no. 4 (1989): 181–189.

Huggins, Nathan. *Afro-American Studies: A Report to the Ford Foundation.* New York: Ford Foundation, 1985.

Hull, Gloria T., Patricia Bell Scott, and Barbara Smith. *All the Women Are White, All the Blacks Are Men, But Some of Us Are Brave: Black Women's Studies.* Old Westbury, N.Y.: Feminist Press, 1982.

Hulse, Carol. "Lott's Praise for Thurmond Echoed His Words of 1980." *New York Times*, December 10, 2002. Retrieved December 16, 2002, from www.nytimes.com.

Hune, Shirley. "Rethinking Race: Paradigms and Policy Formation." In *Contemporary Asian America: A Multidisciplinary Reader*, edited by Min Zhou and James V. Gatewood, pp. 667–676. New York: New York University Press, 2000.

Hurtado, Aída. "Plenary Session on Chicana Positioning." National Association for Chicana and Chicano Studies Annual Conference. Los Angeles, Calif., April 5, 2003.

Husseini, S. "A Media Crusade." *Globalspin.* 2001. http://www.globalspin.org/media_crusade.html.

Hytten, K. "John Dewey and Critical Thinking." In *Critical Thinking: An Encyclopedia*, edited by Danny Weil and Joe Kincheloe. New York: Greenwood, 2003.
Ignatiev, Noel. "Abolitionism and the White Studies Racket." *Race Traitor: Treason to Whiteness Is Loyalty to Humanity* 10 (1999): 3–7.
———. *How the Irish Became White*. Cambridge, Mass.: Harvard University Press, 1995.
Inayatullah, S. "Deconstructing and Reconstructing the Future: Predictive, Cultural, and Critical Epistemologies." 1995. www.scu.edu.au/schools/sawd/futures/secure/module1/1.5-sohail-inayatullah.html.
Ivancevich, J. M., and J. A. Gilbert. "Diversity Management: Time for a New Approach." *Public Personnel Management* 29 (2000): 75–92.
Jackson, Irene. *More Than Dancing: Essays on Afro-American Music and Musicians*. Westport, Conn.: Greenwood Press, 1985.
Jackson, Jacquelyn. "Black Female Sociologists." In *Black Sociologists*, edited by James B. Blackwell and Morris Janowitz, pp. 267–298. Chicago: University of Chicago Press, 1974.
Jackson, M. "Toward a Sociology of Black Studies." *Journal of Black Studies* 1, no. 2 (1970): 131–140.
Jacoby, Barbara. *Service Learning in Higher Education*. San Francisco: Jossey-Bass Publishers, 1996.
Jaimes, M. Annette. "American Indian Studies: Toward an Indigenous Model." *American Indian Culture and Research Journal* 11, no. 3 (1987): 1–16.
Jenkins, Adelbert. *Psychology and African Americans, a Humanistic Approach*. 2nd ed. Needham Heights, Mass.: Allyn & Bacon, 1995.
Johnson, Yvonna. *The Voices of African American Women: The Use of Narrative and Authorial Voice in the Works of Harriet Jacobs, Zora Neale Hurston, and Alice Walker*. American University Studies 14: American Literature. Washington, D.C.: American University, 1999.
Jones, Jacqueline. *Labor of Love, Labor of Sorrow: Black Women, Work, and the Family from Slavery to the Present*. New York: Vintage, 1986.
Joseph, May. *Nomadic Identities: The Performance of Citizenship*. Minneapolis: University of Minnesota Press, 1999.
Kang, Laura Hyun Yi. *Compositional Subjects: Enfiguring Asian/American Women*. Durham, N.C.: Duke University Press, 2002.
Kaplan, Amy, and Donald E. Pease, eds. *Cultures of United States Imperialism*. Durham, N.C.: Duke University Press, 1993.
Karenga, Maulana. *Introduction to Black Studies*. 1st ed. Los Angeles: University of Sankore Press, 1982.
———. *Introduction to Black Studies*. 2nd ed. Los Angeles: University of Sankore Press, 1993.
Kasinitz, Philip. *Caribbean New York: Black Immigrants and the Politics of Race*. Ithaca, N.Y.: Cornell University Press, 1992.

Katrak, Ketu. *Politics of the Female Body: Postcolonial Women Writers of the Third World.* New Brunswick NJ: Rutgers University Press, 2006.

Katz, D., and K. W. Braly. "Racial Prejudice and Racial Stereotypes." *Journal of Abnormal and Social Psychology* 30 (1935): 175–193.

Kearney, Michael. "La Llorona as a Social Symbol." *Western Folklore* 28 (1969): 200.

Keller, Evelyn Fox. "Gender and Science." In *Discovering Reality*, edited by Sandra Harding and Merrill Hintikka, pp. 187–206. Boston: D. Reidel, 1983.

Keller, Gary, ed. *Contemporary Chicana and Chicano Art.* Vols. 1 and 2. Tempe, Ariz.: Bilingual Review/Editorial Bilingüe, 2002.

Kelley, Robin D. G. *Yo' Mama's Disfunktional! Fighting the Culture Wars in Urban America.* Boston: Beacon Press, 1997.

Kellner, Douglas. *Media Culture: Cultural Studies, Identity and Politics between the Modern and Postmodern.* New York: Routledge, 1995.

Kellogg Commission on the Future of State and Land-Grant Universities. *Returning to our Roots: The Engaged Institution.* 3rd report. February 1999.

Keto, C. Tsehloane. *Vision and Time: Historical Perspective on an Africa-Centered Paradigm.* Lanham, Md.: University Press of America, 2001.

Kiang, Peter N. "After the Initiative: Envisioning Diversity Research Sustainability." In *Diversity Research at an Urban Commuter University*, Center for the Improvement of Teaching, pp. 85–104. Boston: University of Massachusetts, Boston, 1999.

———. "Linking Strategies and Interventions in Asian American Studies to K–12 Classrooms and Teacher Preparation." *International Journal of Qualitative Studies in Education* 17, no. 2 (2004): 199–225.

———. "Long-Term Effects of Diversity in the Curriculum: Analyzing the Impact of Asian American Studies in the Lives of Alumni from an Urban Commuter University." In *Diversity on Campus: Reports from the Field*, pp. 23–25. NASPA: Student Affairs Administrators in Higher Education, 2000.

———. "Pedagogies of Life and Death: Transforming Immigrant/Refugee Students and Asian American Studies." Duke University Press. *Positions* 5, no. 2 (1997): 529–555.

———. "Persistence Stories and Survival Strategies of Cambodian Americans in College." *Journal of Narrative and Life History* 6, no. 1 (1996): 39–64.

———. "Stories and Structures of Persistence: Ethnographic Learning through Research and Practice in Asian American Studies." In *Ethnography and Schools: Qualitative Approaches to the Study of Education*, edited by Yali Zou and Henry T. Trueba, pp. 223–255. Lanham, Md.: Rowman & Littlefield, 2002.

———. "Voicing Names and Naming Voices: Pedagogy and Persistence in an Asian American Studies Classroom." In *Crossing the Curriculum: Multilingual Learners in College Classrooms*, edited by Vivian Zamel and Ruth Speck, pp. 207–220. Mahwah, N.J.: Lawrence Erlbaum, 2003.

———. "Writing from the Past, Writing for the Future: Healing Effects of Asian American Studies in the Curriculum." *Transformations: A Resource for Curriculum Transformation and Scholarship* 9, no. 2 (Fall 1998): 132–149.

Kiang, Peter N., and Kenneth Wong. "The Status of Asian Americans in Public Higher Education in Massachusetts: Asian American Studies in the Curriculum." Unpublished report. Institute for Asian American Studies, University of Massachusetts, Boston, 1996.

Kifner, John. "Lott, and the Shadow of a Pro-White Group." *New York Times*, Nation, July 14, 1999.

Kikumura, Akemi. *Through Harsh Winters: The Life of a Japanese Immigrant Woman*. Novato, Calif.: Chandler and Sharp, 1981.

Kincheloe, Joe. "Describing the Bricolage: Conceptualizing a New Rigor in Qualitative Research." *Qualitative Inquiry* 7, no. 6 (2001): 679–692.

———. *Getting beyond the Facts: Teaching Social Studies/Social Sciences in the Twenty-first Century*. New York: Peter Lang, 2001.

———. "Into the Great Wide Open: Introducing Critical Thinking." In *Critical Thinking and Learning: An Encyclopedia*, edited by Joe Kincheloe and Danny Weil. Santa Barbara, Calif.: ABC-Clio.

Kincheloe, Joe, and Kathleen Berry. *Rigour and Complexity in Qualitative Research: Conceptualizing the Bricolage*. London: Open University Press, 2004.

Kincheloe, Joe, and Peter McLaren. "Rethinking Critical Theory and Qualitative Research." In *The Handbook of Qualitative Research*, edited by Norman K. Denzin and Yvonna S. Lincoln. 3rd ed. Thousand Oaks, Calif.: Sage Publications, 2004.

Kincheloe, Joe, and Shirley Steinberg. *Changing Multiculturalism*. London: Open University Press, 1997.

Kincheloe, Joe, and Shirley Steinberg. *The Miseducation of the West: Constructing Islam*. New York: Greenwood, 2004.

Kincheloe, Joe, and Danny Weil, eds. *Critical Thinking and Learning: An Encyclopedia*. New York: Greenwood, 2003.

Kincheloe, Joe, Shirley Steinberg, and Patricia Hinchey, eds. *The Post-formal Reader: Cognition and Education*. New York: Falmer Press, 1999.

Kincheloe, Joe, Shirley Steinberg, Nelson Rodriguez, and Ronald Chennault. *White Reign: Deploying Whiteness in America*. New York: St. Martin's, 1998.

King, Mae. "The Politics of Sexual Stereotypes." *Black Scholar* 4 (1973): 12–23.

King, Martin Luther, Jr. *Why We Can't Wait*. New York: Mentor Books, 1964.

Kingston, Maxine Hong. *Woman Warrior: Memoirs of a Girlhood among Ghosts*. New York: Random House, 1976.

Kirtley, Bacil F. "La Llorona and Related Themes." *Western Folklore* 19 (1960): 155–168.

Kivel, Paul. *Uprooting Racism: How White People Can Work for Racial Justice*. Philadelphia: New Society Publishers, 1996.

Klein, Julie Thomson. *Crossing Boundaries: Knowledge, Disciplinarities, and Interdisciplinarities*. Charlottesville: University Press of Virginia, 1996.

———. *Interdisciplinarity: History, Theory, and Practice*. Detroit, Mich.: Wayne State University Press, 1990.

Klinkner, Philip A., and Roger M. Smith. *The Unsteady March: The Rise and Decline of Racial Equality in America.* Chicago: University of Chicago Press, 1999.

Knowles, Caroline. *Race and Social Analysis.* Thousand Oaks, Calif.: Sage Publications, 2003.

Kogawa, Joy. *Obasan.* New York: Anchor, 1994.

Kovel, Joel. *White Racism: A Psychohistory.* New York: Columbia University Press, 1984.

Krieger, Susan. *Social Science and the Self: Personal Essays on an Art Form.* New Brunswick: Rutgers University Press, 1991.

Kuhn, Thomas S. *The Structure of Scientific Revolutions.* 2nd ed. Chicago: University of Chicago Press, 1970.

Kulis, Stephen, Karen A. Miller, Morris Axelrod, and Leonard Gordon. "Minority Representation of U.S. Departments." *ASA Footnotes* 14 (1986): 3.

Ladner, Joyce. *Tomorrow's Tomorrow: The Black Woman.* Garden City, N.Y.: Anchor, 1971.

Ladson-Billings, Gloria. "Racialized Discourses and Ethnic Epistemologies." In *Handbook of Qualitative Research,* 2nd ed, edited by Norman K. Denzin and Yvonna S. Lincoln, pp. 257–277. Thousand Oaks, Calif.: Sage Publications, 2000.

Lafaye, Jacques. *Quetzalcoatl and Guadalupe: The Formation of Mexican National Consciousness, 1531–1813.* Chicago: University of Chicago Press, 1976.

Lahiri, Jhumpa. *The Interpreter of Maladies: Stories.* Boston: Houghton Mifflin, 1999.

Lai, David C. "Introduction" and "Retrospect and Prospect." In *Chinatowns: Towns within Cities in Canada,* pp. 1–11 and 273–285. Vancouver: University of British Columbia Press, 1988.

LaLone, Mary, ed. *Appalachian Coal Mining Memories: Life in the Coal Fields of Virginia's New River Valley.* Blacksburg, Va.: Pocahontas Press, 1997.

Lapani, B. "Information Literacy: The Challenge of the Digital Age." 1998. www.acal.edu.au/lepani.htm.

Larana, Enrique, Hank Johnston, and Joseph R. Gusfield. *New Social Movements: From Ideology to Identity.* Philadelphia: Temple University Press, 1994.

Lassiter, Luke Eric. "From 'Reading over the Shoulders of Natives' to 'Reading alongside Natives,' Literally: Toward a Collaborative and Reciprocal Ethnography." *Journal of Anthropological Research* 57 (2001): 137–149.

Lassiter, Luke Eric. *Invitation to Anthropology.* Walnut Creek, Calif.: AltaMira Press, 2002.

Latina Feminist Group. *Telling to Live: Latina Feminist Testimonios.* Durham, N.C.: Duke University Press, 2001.

Latucca, Lisa R. *Creating Interdisciplinarity.* Nashville, Tenn.: Vanderbilt University Press, 2001.

Laundry, Bart. *The New Black Middle Class.* Berkeley: University of California Press, 1987.

Lawrence, Charles. "The Id, the Ego, and Equal Protection: Reckoning with Unconscious Racism." *Stanford Law Review* 39 (1987): 317–322.

Lawrence, Charles R., III, and Mari Matsuda. *We Won't Go Back: Making the Case for Affirmative Action*. Boston: Houghton Mifflin, 1997.
Lawrence-Lightfoot, Sara. *I've Known Rivers: Lives of Loss and Liberation*. Reading, Mass.: Addison-Wesley, 1994.
Lawrence-Lightfoot, Sara, and Jessica Hoffman Davis. *The Art and Science of Portraiture*. 1st ed. San Francisco: Jossey-Bass, 1997.
Leal, Luis. "The Malinche-Llorona Dichotomy: The Evolution of a Myth." In *La Malinche*, edited by Rolando Romero. Houston, Tex.: Arte Público Press, 2004.
Leddy, Betty. "La Llorona in Southern Arizona." *Western Folklore* 7 (1948): 272.
Lee, Alfred McClung. *Toward Humanist Sociology*. Englewood Cliffs, N.J.: Prentice-Hall, 1973.
Lee, Mary Paik. *Quiet Odyssey: A Pioneer Korean Woman in America*. Seattle: University of Washington Press, 1990.
Lee, R. A. "The Evolution of Affirmative Action." *Public Personnel Management* 28 (1999): 393–408.
Lefebvre, Henri. *The Production of Space*. Cambridge, Mass.: Blackwell, 1991.
Lentricchia, Frank, and Thomas McLaughlin, eds. *Critical Theory for Literary Study*. Chicago: University of Chicago Press, 1995.
Lewis, Diane. "A Response to Inequality: Black Women, Racism and Sexism." *Signs* 3 (1977): 339–361.
Lim, Genny. *Paper Angels*, in *The Unbroken Thread: An Anthology of Plays by Asian American Women*, edited by Roberta Uno, pp. 11–52. Amherst: University of Massachusetts Press, 1993.
Lim, Imogene L., and John Eng-Wong. "Chow Mein Sandwiches: Chinese American Entrepreneurship in Rhode Island." In *Origins and Destinations*, pp. 417–436. Los Angeles: Chinese Historical Society of Southern California, 1994.
Limón, José. "La Llorona, the Third Legend of Greater Mexico: Cultural Symbols, Women, and the Political Unconscious." *Renato Rosaldo Lecture Series Monograph*. Tucson: University of Arizona, Mexican American Studies and Research Center, 1986.
Lincoln, Yvonna. "An Emerging New *Bricoleur*: Promises and Possibilities—a Reaction to Joe Kincheloe's 'Describing the Bricoleur.'" *Qualitative Inquiry* 7, no. 6 (2001): 693–696.
Lipsitz, George. *The Possessive Investment in Whiteness: How White People Profit from Identity Politics*. Philadelphia: Temple University Press, 1998.
———. "Who'll Stop the Rain? Youth Culture, Rock 'n' Roll, and Social Crises." In *The Sixties: From Memory to History*, edited by David Farber. Chapel Hill: University of North Carolina Press, 1994.
Liu, John. "Towards an Understanding of the Internal Colonial Model." In *Counterpoint: Perspectives on Asian America*, edited by Emma Gee. Los Angeles: UCLA Asian American Studies Center, 1976.
Loewenberg, Bert, James Bogin, and Ruth Bogin, eds. *Black Women in Nineteenth-century Life*. University Park: Pennsylvania State University Press, 1976.

Lofland, John, and Lyn Lofland. *Analyzing Social Settings: A Guide to Qualitative Observation and Analysis.* Belmont, Calif.: Wadsworth Publishing, 1995.

Loo, Chalsa, and Don Mar. "Research and Asian Americans: Social Change or Empty Prize?" *Amerasia Journal* 12, no. 2 (1985–1986): 85–93.

Lopez, Gerardo R., and Laurence Parker, eds. *Interrogating Racism in Qualitative Research Methodology.* New York: Peter Lang, 2003.

Lopez, Ian F. *White by Law: The Legal Construction of Race.* New York: New York University Press, 1996.

López, Montserrat, et al. "No me quiero ir pero no me quiero quedar: Transnational Latina Youth and Participatory Research." Panel at the Center for Popular Education and Participatory Research Annual Conference, Berkeley, Calif., February 2002.

Lorde, Audre. "The Master's Tools Will Never Dismantle the Master's House." In *This Bridge Called My Back: Writings by Radical Women of Color*, 3rd ed., edited by Cherríe L. Moraga and Gloria E. Anzaldúa, pp. 106–109. Berkeley, Calif.: Third Woman Press, 2002.

———. *Sister Outsider: Essays and Speeches.* Trumansburg, N.Y.: Crossing Press, 1984.

Lowe, Lisa. *Immigrant Acts: On Asian American Cultural Politics.* Durham, N.C.: Duke University Press, 1996.

———. "The International within the National: American Studies and Asian American Critique." *Cultural Heritage* 40 (1998) 29–47.

Lowe, Lisa, and David Lloyd, eds. *The Politics of Culture in the Shadow of Capital.* Durham, N.C.: Duke University Press, 1997.

Luibhéid, Eithne. *Entry Denied: Controlling Sexuality at the Border.* Minneapolis: University of Minnesota Press, 2002.

Lutz, Kristin, Kim Jones, and Judy Kendall. "Expanding the Praxis Debate: Contributions to Clinical Inquiry." *Advances in Nursing Science* 20, no. 2 (1997).

Lynd, Robert S., and Helen Merrell Lynd. *Middletown: A Study of Contemporary American Culture.* New York: Harcourt, Brace, 1929.

———. *Middletown in Transition: A Study in Cultural Conflicts.* New York: Harcourt, Brace, 1937.

Lynton, Ernest A. *Making the Case for Professional Service.* Washington, D.C.: American Association for Higher Education, 1995.

Macedo, Donaldo. *Literacies of Power: What Americans Are Not Allowed to Know.* Boulder, Colo.: Westview Press, 1994.

Maguire, Patricia. "Challenges, Contradictions, and Celebrations: Attempting Participatory Research as a Doctoral Student." In *Voices of Change: Participatory Research in the United States and Canada*, edited by P. Park, M. Brydon-Miller, B. Hall, and T. Jackson. Westport, Conn.: Bergin & Garvey, 1984.

Malewski, Erik. "Queer Sexuality—The Trouble with Knowing: Standards of Complexity and Sexual Orientations." In *Standards and Schooling in the United States: An Encyclopedia*, edited by Joe Kincheloe and Danny Weil. 3 vols. Santa Barbara, Calif.: ABC-CLIO, 2001.

Manalansan, Martin F., IV. "Introduction." In *Cultural Compass: Ethnographic Explorations of Asian America*, edited by Martin F. Manalansan, IV, pp. 1–13. Asian American History and Culture series. Philadelphia: Temple University Press, 2000.

Manley, Theodoric, Jr. "Teaching Race and Ethnic Relations: Do the Right Thing." *Ethnic and Racial Studies* 17, no. 1 (1994): 135–163.

Mannheim Karl. *Ideology and Utopia: An Introduction to the Sociology of Knowledge.* New York: Harcourt Brace, 1936.

Marable, Manning. *Beyond Black and White: Transforming African-American Politics.* New York: Verso, 1995.

———. *The Crisis of Color and Democracy: Essays on Race, Class and Power.* Monroe, Maine: Common Courage Press, 1992.

———. *Dispatches from the Ebony Tower.* New York: Columbia University Press, 2000.

———. *From the Grassroots: Essays toward Afro-American Liberation.* Boston: South End Press, 1980.

———. *How Capitalism Underdeveloped Black America: Problems in Race, Political Economy, and Society.* Boston: South End Press, 1983.

———. "The Modern Miseducation of the Negro: Critiques of Black History Curricula." In *Black Studies Curriculum Development Course Evaluations*, Institute of the Black World, Conference I, C1–C28. Atlanta, Ga.: Institute of the Black World, 1981.

———. *Race, Reform and Rebellion: The Second Reconstruction in Black America, 1945–1982.* Jackson: University Press of Mississippi, 1984.

Marijuan, Perdo. "Information Revisited." Paper presented to the First Conference on the Foundations of Information Science, Madrid, Spain, 1994.

Marx, Marcia. Review of *Color-Line to Borderlands*, by Johnnella E. Butler. *Journal of American Ethnic History*, Summer 2003, 113–114.

Masequesmay, Gina. "Everyday Identity Work at an Asian Pacific AIDS Organization." *Cultural Compass: Ethnographic Explorations of Asian America*, edited by Martin F. Manalansan, IV. Philadelphia: Temple University. Press, 2000.

———. "Negotiating Multiple Identities in a Queer Vietnamese Support Group." *Journal of Homosexuality* 45, no. 2–4 (2003) 193–215.

Massey, Doreen. "Politics and Space/Time." In *Place and the Politics of Identity*, edited by Michael Keith and Steve Pile, pp. 141–161. London: Routledge, 1993.

Massey, Douglas S., and Nancy N. Denton. *American Apartheid: Segregation and the Making of the Underclass.* Cambridge, Mass.: Harvard University Press, 1993.

Matthews, Fred H. *Quest for an American Sociology: Robert E. Park and the Chicago School.* Montreal: McGill-Queen's University Press, 1977.

Maturana, Humberto, and Francisco Varela. *The Tree of Knowledge.* Boston: Shambhala, 1987.

Maurial, Mahia. "Indigenous Knowledge and Schooling: A Continuum between Conflict and Dialogue." In *What Is Indigenous Knowledge? Voices from the Academy*, edited by Ladislaus Semali and Joe Kincheloe. New York: Falmer Press, 1999.

Maurrasse, David J. *Beyond the Campus: How Colleges and Universities Form Partnerships with Their Communities.* New York: Routledge, 2001.

May, T. *Between Genealogy and Epistemology: Psychology, Politics, and Knowledge in the Thought of Michel Foucault.* University Park: Pennsylvania State University Press, 1993.

Mayer, Milton. "The Issue is Miscegenation." *The Progressive,* 23 (September 1959), pp. 8–18.

Mazama, Ama. *The Afrocentric Paradigm.* Trenton, N.J.: Africa World Press, 2003.

McCauley, Clark, M. Wright, and M. Harris. "Diversity Workshops on Campus: A Survey of Current Practice at U.S. Colleges and Universities." *College Student Journal* 34 (2000): 100–114.

McClendon, William. "Black Studies: Education for Liberation." *Black Scholar* 6, no 1 (1974): 15–20.

McClintock, Anne. *Imperial Leather: Race, Gender and Sexuality in the Colonial Conquest.* New York: Routledge, 1995.

McConahay, John B. "Modern Racism, Ambivalence, and the Modern Racism Scale." In *Prejudice, Discrimination and Racism,* edited by John F. Dovidio and Samuel L. Gaertner, pp. 91–125. Orlando, Fla: Academic Press, 1986.

McGougan, Jill. "The Internal and External Factors Impacting a Day Labor Center as Part of a Social Movement." Senior thesis, Pitzer College, Claremont, Calif., 2000.

McLaren, Peter. "Bricklayers and Bricoleurs: A Marxist Addendum." *Qualitative Inquiry* 7, no. 6 (2001): 700–705.

McLaren, Peter, Rhonda Hammer, Susan Reilly, and David Scholle. *Rethinking Media Literacy: A Critical Pedagogy of Representation.* New York: Peter Lang, 1995.

McLeod, John. "Qualitative Research as Bricolage." Paper presented at the Society for Psychotherapy Research annual conference, Chicago, 2000.

McRorie, Sally. "Pentimento: Philosophical Inquiry as Research in Art Education." Unpublished manuscript. 1999.

Meador, Kyle, project coordinator. "Hiram Johnson High School & Will C. Wood Tutorial Program." *Ethnic Studies Department Project.* Sacramento: California State University Press, 2003.

Memmi, Albert. *The Colonizer and the Colonized.* Boston: Beacon Press, 1967.

Mercado, C., and Luis C. Moll. "The Study of Funds of Knowledge." *Centro* 9, no. 9 (1997): 26–42.

Merton, Robert K. "Insiders and Outsiders: A Chapter in the Sociology of Knowledge." *American Journal of Sociology* 78 (1972): 9–47.

Messer-Davidow, Ellen. *Disciplining Feminism: From Social Activism to Academic Discourse.* Durham, N.C.: Duke University Press, 2002.

Messer-Davidow, Ellen, et al., eds. *Knowledges: Historical and Critical Studies in Disciplinarity.* Charlottesville: University Press of Virginia, 1993.

Miller, Elaine K.. *Mexican Folk Narratives from Los Angeles.* Austin, Tex.: American Folklore Society, 1973.

Minnich, Elizabeth. *Transforming Knowledge*. Philadelphia: Temple University Press, 1991.

Miramontes, H. "Requiring Ethnic Studies." 2003. gladstone.uoregon.edu/~hmiramon/writing%20121/esreqtograduate.rtf.

Mitchell, Alison. "Survivors of Tuskegee Study Get Apology from Clinton." *New York Times*, May 17, 1997, p. 9.

Mohanty, Chandra. *Feminism without Borders: Decolonizing Theory, Practicing Solidarity*. Durham, N.C.: Duke University Press, 2003.

———. "Under Western Eyes: Feminist Scholarship and Colonial Discourses." *Feminist Review* 30 (Autumn 1988): 61–88.

Mohanty, Chandra, et al., eds. *Third World Women and the Politics of Feminism*. Bloomington: Indiana University Press, 1991.

Mohanty, Satya. "The Epistemic Status of Cultural Identity: On *Beloved* and the Postcolonial Condition." In *Reclaiming Identity: Realist Theory and the Predicament of Postmodernism*, edited by Paula Moya and Michael Hames-García, pp. 29–66. Berkeley: University of California Press, 2000.

———. *Literary Theory and the Claims of History*. Ithaca, N.Y.: Cornell University Press, 1997.

Moll, Luis C., C. Amanti, D. Neff, and Norma González. "Funds of Knowledge for Teaching: Using a Qualitative Approach to Connect Homes and Classrooms." *Theory into Practice* 31, no. 2 (1992): 132–141.

Monteith, Margo J., Julia R. Zuwerink, and Patricia G. Devine. "Prejudice and Prejudice Reduction: Classic Challenges, Contemporary Approaches." In *Social Cognition: Impact on Social Psychology*, edited by P. G. Devine, D. L. Hamilton, and T. M. Ostrom, pp. 323–346. New York: Academic Press, 1994.

Montoya, Margaret E. "Academic Mestizaje: Re/Producing Clinical Teaching and Re/Framing Wills as Latina Praxis." *Harvard Latino Law Review* 2 (1997): 349.

Mora, Juana, and David R. Diaz. *Latino Social Policy: A Participatory Research Model*. Binghampton, N.Y.: Haworth Press, 2004.

Mora, Pat. *Chants*. Houston, Tex.: Arte Público Press, 1984.

Moraga, Cherríe. *The Hungry Woman: A Mexican Medea*. Los Angeles: West End Press, 2001.

Moraga, Cherrie L., and Gloria E. Anzaldúa, eds. *This Bridge Called My Back: Writings by Radical Women of Color*. 3rd ed. Berkeley, Calif.: Third Woman Press, 2002.

Morales, Alejandro. *Caras viejas y vino nuevo*. Mexico City: Joaquín Mortiz, 1975.

Morawski, Jill. "The Science behind Feminist Research Methods." *Journal of Social Issues* 53, no. 4 (1997): 667–682.

Morrison, Toni. *The Bluest Eye*. New York: Washington Square Press, 1972.

———. *Playing in the Dark: Whiteness and the Literary Imagination*. Cambridge, Mass.: Harvard University Press, 1992.

Morton, Keith. "The Irony of Service: Charity, Project, and Social Change in Service Learning." *Michigan Journal of Community Service Learning* 2 (1995): 19–32.

Moses, Wilson Jeremiah. *The Golden Age of Black Nationalism, 1850–1925*. New York: Oxford University Press, 1978.

Moses, Yolanda T. Forward to *The Other Side of Middletown: Exploring Muncie's African American Community*, edited by Luke Eric Lassiter, Hurley Goodall, Elizabeth Campbell, and Michelle Natasya Johnson. Walnut Creek, Calif.: AltaMira Press, 2004.

Mosha, R. Sambuli. *The Heartbeat of Indigenous Africa: A Study of the Chagga Educational System*. New York: Garland, 2000.

Moya, Paula M. *Learning from Experience: Minority Identities, Multicultural Struggles*. Berkeley: University of California Press, 2002.

Mulkay, Michael. *Science and the Sociology of Knowledge*. Boston: Allen & Unwin, 1979.

Mullings, Leith. "Anthropological Perspectives on the Afro-American Family." *American Journal of Social Psychiatry* 6 (1986): 11–16.

———. *On Our Own Terms: Race, Class and Gender in the Lives of African American Women*. New York: Routledge, 1997.

———. "Uneven Development: Class, Race and Gender in the United States before 1900." In *Women's Work, Development and the Division of Labor by Gender*, edited by Eleanor Leacock and Helen Safa, pp. 41–57. South Hadley, Mass.: Bergin & Garvey, 1986.

Muñoz, Carlos, Jr. *Youth, Identity, Power: The Chicano Movement*. London: Verso, 1989.

Murillo, Enríque, Jr. "How Does It Feel to Be a Problem? 'Disciplining' the Transnational Subject in the American South." In *Education in the New Latino Diaspora: Policy and the Politics of Identity*, edited by Stanton Wortham, Enrique Murillo, Jr., and Edmund T. Hamman, pp. 215–239. Westport, Conn.: Ablex Publishing, 2002.

Murphie, A. "Cyberfictions and Hypertext: What Is Happening to Text?" 1998. www.mcs.elm.mq.edu.au/staff/Andrew/307/hypeprt.html.

Murray, Pauli. "The Liberation of Black Women." In *Voices of the New Feminism*, edited by Mary Lou Thompson, pp. 87–102. Boston: Beacon Press, 1970.

Myers, Lena Wright. *Black Women: Do They Cope Better?* Englewood Cliffs, N.J.: Prentice-Hall, 1980.

Nagel, Joane. "Ethnicity and Sexuality." *Annual Review of Sociology* 26 (2000): 107–133.

———. *Race, Ethnicity, and Sexuality: Intimate Intersections, Forbidden Frontiers*. New York: Oxford University Press, 2003.

Naisbitt, John, and Patricia Aburdene. *Megatrends 2000, Ten New Directions for the 1990's*. New York: William Morrow, 1990.

Nandy, Ashis. *The Intimate Enemy: Loss and Recovery of Self under Colonialism*. Delhi: Oxford University Press, 1989.

Naples, Nancy A. *Feminism and Method: Ethnography, Discourse Analysis and Activist Research*. New York: Routledge, 2003.

Nardi, Peter M., and Beth E. Schneider, eds. *Social Perspectives on Lesbian & Gay Studies*. London: Routledge, 1998.
Nee, Victor G., and Brett de Bary Nee. *Longtime Californ': A Documentary Study of an American Chinatown*. New York: Pantheon, 1972.
Neihardt, John G., ed. *Black Elk Speaks*. Lincoln: University of Nebraska Press, 1961.
Nelson, Cary, and Dilip Gaonkar, eds. *Disciplinarity and Dissent in Cultural Studies*. New York: Routledge, 1996.
Nelson, Dana D. *National Manhood: Capitalist Citizenship and the Imagined Fraternity of White Men*. Durham, N.C.: Duke University Press, 1998.
Ness, Carol. " S. F.'s Diversity Comeuppance." *San Francisco Chronicle*. April 1, 2000.
———. "33, 871, 648 Hispanics Now Make Up Third of Californians." *San Francisco Chronicle*. March 30, 2000.
Neville, H. A., and M. Furlong. "The Impact of Participation in a Cultural Awareness Program on the Racial Attitudes and Social Behaviors of First-Year College Students." *Journal of College Student Development* 35 (1994): 371–377.
Neville, H. A., M. J. Heppner, C. E. Louie, C. E. Thompson, L. Brooks, and C. E. Baker. "The Impact of Multicultural Training on White Racial Identity Attitudes and Therapy Competencies." *Professional Psychology: Research and Practice* 27 (1996): 83–89.
Newland, Paul. "Logical Types of Learning." 1997. www.envf.port.ac.uk/newmedia/lecturenotes/EMMA/at2n.htm.
Noone, Lynne, and Patricia Cartwright. "Doing a Critical Literacy Pedagogy: Trans/forming Teachers in a Teacher Education Course." 1996. www.atea.schools.net.au/ATEA/96conf/noone.html.
Norment, Nathaniel, Jr., ed. *African-American Studies Reader*. Durham, N.C.: Carolina Academic Press, 2001.
Nyden, Philip, Anne Figert, Mark Shibley, and Darryl Burrows. *Building Community: Social Science in Action*. Thousand Oaks, Calif.: Pine Forge Press, 1997.
Nygreen, Kysa, Soo Ah Kwon and Patricia Sánchez. "Urban Youth Building Community: Social Change and Participatory Research in Schools, Homes, and Community-Based Organizations. "*Journal of Community Practice* 14, 1–2 (2006) 105–21.
Okada, John. *No No Boy*. Rutland, Vt.: C. E. Tuttle, 1976.
Okihiro, Gary Y. *The Columbia Guide to Asian American History*. New York: Columbia University Press, 2001.
Okihiro, Gary Y., ed. *Ethnic Studies*. New York: M. Wiener Publications, 1989.
———. *Margins and Mainstreams: Asians in American History and Culture*. Seattle: University of Washington Press, 1994.
———. "Oral History and the Writing of Ethnic History: A Reconnaissance into Method and Theory." *Oral History Review* 9 (1981).
Olson, Lynne. *Freedom's Daughters: The Unsung Heroines of the Civil Rights Movement from 1830 to 1970*. New York: Scribner, 2001.

Omi, Michael, and Dana Takagi, eds. "Thinking Theory in Asian American Studies." Special issue, *Amerasia Journal* 21, nos. 1–2 (1995): viii.

Omi, Michael, and Howard Winant. *Racial Formation in the United States: From the 1960s to the 1980s.* New York: Routledge & Kegan Paul, 1986.

———. *Racial Formation in the United States: From the 1960s to the 1990s.* 2nd ed. New York: Routledge, 1994.

Omolade, Barbara. *The Rising Song of African American Women.* New York: Routledge, 1994.

Ong, Aihwa. *Flexible Citizenship: The Cultural Logics of Transnationality.* Durham, N.C.: Duke University Press, 1999.

Orozco, Cynthia. "Sexism in Chicano Studies and the Community." In *Chicana Voices: Intersections of Class, Race, and Gender,* edited by Teresa Córdova et al. Austin: University of Texas, Center for Mexican American Studies, 1986.

Ostrow, James, Gary Hesser, and Sandra Enos. *Cultivating the Sociological Imagination: Concepts and Models for Service-Learning in Sociology.* Washington, D.C.: American Association of Higher Education, 1999.

O'Sullivan, Edmund. *Transformative Learning: Educational Vision for the 21st Century.* London: Zed, 1999.

Ottavi, T. M., D. B. Pope-Davis, and J. G. Dings. "Relationship between White Racial Identity Attitudes and Self-Reported Multicultural Counseling Competencies." *Journal of Counseling Psychology* 41 (1994): 149–154.

Padilla, Felix M. *The Struggle of Latino/Latina University Students: In Search of a Liberating Education.* New York: Routledge, 1999.

Palmer, Carole. "Information Work at the Boundaries of Science: Linking Library Services to Research Practices." *Library Trends* 44, no. 2 (1996): 165–192.

Papa, Lee, and Luke Eric Lassiter. "The Muncie Race Riots of 1967, Representing Community Memory through Public Performance, and Collaborative Ethnography between Faculty, Students, and the Local Community." *Journal of Contemporary Ethnography* 32 (2003): 147–166.

Paris, Peter J. *The Social Teaching of the Black Churches.* Philadelphia: Fortress Press, 1985.

Park, Robert E. "Behind Our Masks." *Survey* 56, no. 3 (May 1, 1926).

———. "Human Migration and the Marginal Man." *American Journal of Sociology* 23, no. 6 (May 1928): 881–893.

———. *Race and Culture.* Glencoe, Ill.: Free Press, 1950.

Park, Robert E., and Ernest W. Burgess. *Introduction to the Science of Sociology.* Chicago: University of Chicago Press, 1921.

Parmar, P. "Critical Thinking and Rap Music: The Critical Pedagogy of KRS-One." In *Critical Thinking: An Encyclopedia,* edited by Joe Kincheloe and Danny Weil. New York: Greenwood, 2003.

Parrillo, Vincent N. *Strangers to These Shores.* Boston: Allyn and Bacon, 2003.

Paulson, R. "Mapping Knowledge Perspectives in Studies of Educational Change." In *Transforming Schools,* edited by Peter Cookson, Jr., and Barbara Schneider. New York: Garland, 1995.

Pearson, Charles H. *National Life and Character*. London: Macmillan, 1893.
Persons, Stow. *Ethnic Studies at Chicago, 1905–1945*. Urbana: University of Illinois Press, 1987.
Pettigrew, Thomas F. "Race and Class in the 1980s: An Interactive View." *Daedalus* 110, no. 2 (1981): 233–255.
Pfohl, Stephen. *Images of Deviance and Social Control: A Sociological History*. 2nd ed. New York: McGraw-Hill, 1994.
Phan, Aimee. *We May Never Meet: Stories*. New York: St. Martin's, 2004.
Pickering, John. "The Self Is a Semiotic Process." *Journal of Consciousness Studies* 6, no. 4 (1999): 31–47.
Pierson, Ruth Roach, and Nupur Chaudhuri, eds. *Nation, Empire, Colony: Historicizing Gender and Race*. Bloomington: Indiana University Press, 1998.
Pinar, William. "The Researcher as Bricoleur: The Teacher as Public Intellectual." *Qualitative Inquiry* 7, no. 6 (2001): 696–700.
Pizarro, Marc. "'Chicana/o Power!' Epistemology and Methodology for Social Justice and Empowerment in Chicana/o Communities." *Qualitative Studies in Education* 11, no. 1 (1998): 57–80.
Pope-Davis, D. B., and T. M. Ottavi. "The Relationship between Racism and Racial Identity among White Americans." *Journal of Counseling and Development* 72 (1994): 293–297.
Prashad, Vijay. *Everybody Was Kung Fu Fighting: Afro-Asian Connections and the Myth of Cultural Purity*. Boston: Beacon Press, 2001.
Progler, Yusef. "Social Studies—Social Studies Standards: Diversity, Conformity, Complexity." In *Standards and Schooling in the United States: An Encyclopedia*, edited by Joe Kincheloe and Danny Weil. 3 vols. Santa Barbara, Calif.: ABC-Clio, 2001.
Quiñónez, Naomi. "La Llorona." In *Infinite Divisions: An Anthology of Chicana Literature*, edited by Tey Diana Rebolledo and Eliana Rivero. Tucson: University of Arizona Press, 1993.
Ramaley, Judith A. "Supporting Public Scholarship." *Peer Review* 2, no. 1 (Fall 1999): 13–14.
Raushenbush, Winifred. *Robert E. Park: Biography of a Sociologist*. Durham, N.C.: Duke University Press, 1979.
Reardon, Kenneth M. "Participatory Action Research as Service Learning." *New Directions for Teaching and Learning* 73 (Spring 1998): 57–64.
Report of the National Advisory Commission on Civil Disorders. New York: Bantam, 1968.
Rich, Adrienne. "Living the Revolution." *Women's Review of Books* 3, no. 12 (September 1986).
———. *Of Woman Born: Motherhood as Experience and Institution*. New York: W. W. Norton. 1976.
Richards, Dona. "European Mythology; The Ideology of 'Progress.'" In *Contemporary Black Thought*, edited by Molefi Kete Asante and Abdulai S. Vandi, pp. 59–79. Beverly Hills, Calif.: Sage Publications, 1980.

Richardson, Frank, and Robert Woolfolk. "Social Theory and Values: A Hermeneutic Perspective." *Theory and Psychology* 4, no. 2 (1994): 199–226.

Richardson, Laurel. "Narrative and Sociology." *Journal of Contemporary Ethnography* 19, no. 1 (April 1990): 116–135.

Riva Palacio, Vicente, and Juan de Dios Peza. "La Llorona." In *Tradiciones y leyendas mexicanas*. Mexico City: Manuel Porrúa S.A., Librería, 1977.

Rivers, W. H. R. *Social Organization*. New York: Knopf, 1924.

Rivkin, Julie, and Michael Ryan, eds. *Literary Theory: An Anthology*. Oxford: Blackwell, 1998.

Robeson, Paul. "I Want Negro Culture." In *Paul Robeson Speaks: Writings, Speeches, Interviews, 1918–1974*, edited by Philip Foner, pp. 96–98. New York: Brunner/Mazel Publishers, 1978. Originally published in the *London News Chronicle*, May 30, 1935.

Robinson, Armstead L., Craig C. Foster, and Donald H. Ogilvie, eds. *Black Studies in the University: A Symposium*. New Haven, Conn.: Yale University Press, 1969.

Robinson, Dean E. *Black Nationalism in American Politics and Thought*. New York: Cambridge University Press, 2001.

Rochfort, Desmond. *Mexican Muralists: Orozco, Rivera, Sequeiros*. San Francisco: Chronicle Books, 1993.

Rodríguez, Clara E. *Changing Race: Latinos, the Census, and the History of Ethnicity in the United States*. New York: New York University Press, 2000.

Rodriguez, Luis. *Always Running: La Vida Loca; Gang Days in L. A.* Willimantic, Conn.: Curbstone Press, 1993.

Rodriguez, Nelson, and Leila Villaverde. *Dismantling White Privilege*. New York: Peter Lang, 2000.

Roediger, David R. *Colored White: Transcending the Racial Past*. Berkeley: University of California Press, 2002.

———. *Towards the Abolition of Whiteness*. London: Verso, 1994.

———. *The Wages of Whiteness: Race and the Making of the American Working Class*. The Haymarket Series, edited by Michael Davis and Michael Sprinker. New York: Verso, 1991.

Rogers, Jane. "The Function of the La Llorona Motif in Rudolfo Anaya's *Bless Me, Ultima*." *Latin American Literary Review* 5, no. 10 (Spring–Summer 1977): 64.

Rollins, Judith. *Between Women, Domestics and Their Employers*. Philadelphia: Temple University Press, 1985.

Romero, Rolando, and Amanda Nolacea Harris, eds. *Feminism, Nation and Myth: La Malinche*. Houston, Tex.: Arte Público Press, 2005.

Root, Maria P. P., ed. *The Multiracial Experience: Racial Borders as the New Frontier*. Thousand Oaks, Calif.: Sage Publications, 1996.

———, ed. *Racially Mixed People in America*. Newbury Park, Calif.: Sage Publications, 1993.

Rosaldo, Michelle Z. "Moral/Analytic Dilemmas Posed by the Intersection of Feminism and Social Science." In *Social Science as Moral Inquiry*, edited by Norma

Hann, Robert N. Bellah, Paul Rabinow, and William Sullivan, pp. 76–96. New York: Columbia University Press, 1983.

Rose, Karel, and Joe Kincheloe. *Art, Culture, and Education: Artful Teaching in a Fractured Landscape.* New York: Peter Lang, 2003.

Rose, Margaret. "Traditional and Nontraditional Patterns of Female Activism in the United Farm Workers of America, 1962 to 1980." *Frontiers* 11, no. 1 (1990): 25–32.

Ross, Fred. *Conquering Goliath: Cesar Chavez at the Beginning.* Keene, Calif.: Taller Grafico, 1989.

Ross, Robert H. and Emory S. Bogardus. "The Second-Generation Race Relations Cycle: A Study in *Issei-Nisei* Relationships." *Sociology and Social Research* 24, no. 4 (March–April 1940): 357–363.

Rothenberg, Paula S., ed. *White Privilege: Essential Readings on the Other Side of Racism.* New York: Worth Publishers, 2002.

Rottenberg, Dan, ed. *Middletown Jews: The Tenuous Survival of an American Jewish Community.* Bloomington: Indiana University Press, 1997.

Rubin, Herbert J. and Irene S. Rubin. *Qualitative Interviewing: The Art of Hearing Data.* Thousand Oak Calif.: Sage, 1995.

Rudman, L. A., A. G. Greenwald, D. S. Mellott, and J. L. K. Schwartz. "Measuring the Automatic Components of Prejudice: Flexibility and Generality of the Implicit Association Test." *Social Cognition* 17 (1999): 437–465.

Russell, Joseph. "Afro-American Studies: From Chaos to Consolidation." *Negro Education Review* 26, no. 4 (1975): 181–189.

Sahagún, Bernardo de. *Florentine Codex: General History of the Things of New Spain.* Translated by Arthur J. O. Anderson and Charles E. Dibble. Santa Fe, N.Mex.: School of American Research, 1950.

———. *Historia general de la Nueva España.* Mexico City: Editorial Porrúa, 1956.

Said, Edward W. *Covering Islam: How the Media and the Experts Determine How We See the Rest of the World.* New York: Pantheon, 1981.

———. *Culture and Imperialism.* New York: Vintage, 1993.

———. *Orientalism.* New York: Random House, 1979.

———. *The World, the Text and the Critic.* Cambridge, Mass.: Harvard University Press, 1983.

Saldívar, Ramón. "Multicultural Politics, Aesthetics, and the Realist Theory of Identity: A Response to Satya Mohanty." *New Literary History* 32 (2001): 853.

Salinas, Raul. "A Trip through the Mind Jail." In *We Are Chicanos, Anthology of Mexican American Literature*, edited by Phillip D. Ortego, pp. 195–200. New York: Washington Square Press, 1973.

Sánchez, Patricia. "At Home in Two Places: Second-Generation *Mexicanas* and Their Lives as Engaged Transnationals." Unpublished dissertation, University of California, Berkeley, 2004.

———. "Quinceañera." In *Mexico and the United States*, edited by Lee Stacy Leney and Gordon Leney. Tarrytown, N.Y.: Marshall Cavendish, 2002.

Sánchez, Patricia, et al. "Achieving Equity in 'Other' Educational Sites: Redistributing the Power of Knowledge through Youth Activism, Social Change, and Participatory Research." Panel at the American Educational Studies Association Annual Convention, Kansas City, Mo., November 2004.

———. "Cultural Authenticity and Transnational Latina Youth: Constructing a Metanarrative across Borders." *Linguistics and Education* 18, 3–4 (2007) 258–82.

———. "Promoting the Life Experiences and Funds of Knowledge of Transnational Families: Writing Ourselves in(to) the Research and Children's Literature." Panel at the California Association for Bilingual Education (CABE) Annual Conference, Los Angeles, Calif., February 2003.

———. "Urban Immigrant Students: How Transnationalism Shapes Their World Learning." *Urban Review* 39, 5 (2007) 489–517.

Sandoval, Chela. "Mestizaje as Method: Feminists of Color Challenge the Canon." In *Living Chicana Theory*, edited by Carla Trujillo, pp. 352–370. Berkeley, Calif.: Third Woman Press, 1998.

Sandoval, Chela. *Methodology of the Oppressed*. Minneapolis: University of Minnesota Press, 2000.

San Juan, E., Jr. *Racial and Cultural Studies*. Durham, N.C.: Duke University Press, 2002.

———. *Racial Formations, Critical Transformations*. Atlanta Highlands, N.J.: Humanities Press, 1992.

Sawicki, Jana. *Disciplining Foucault: Feminism, Power, and the Body*. New York: Routledge, 1991.

Scering, G. "Themes of a Critical/Feminist Pedagogy: Teacher Education for Democracy." *Journal of Teacher Education* 48, no. 1 (1997): 62–69.

Scharlin, Craig, and Lilia V. Villanueva. *Philip Vera Cruz: A Personal History of Filipino Immigrants and the Farmworkers Movement*. Los Angeles: UCLA Labor Center and Asian American Studies Center, 1994.

Scheper-Hughes, Nancy. *Death without Weeping: The Violence of Everyday Life in Brazil*. Berkeley: University of California Press, 1992.

Scheurich, James J. "The Destructive Desire for a Depoliticized Ethnographic Methodology: Response to Harry Wolcott." In *Anti-Racist Scholarship: An Advocacy*, edited by James J. Scheurich, pp. 153–157. Albany, N.Y.: SUNY Press, 2002.

Scheurich, James J., and Michelle D. Young. "Coloring Epistemology: Are Our Research Epistemologies Racially Biased?" In *Anti-Racist Scholarship: An Advocacy*, edited by James J. Scheurich, pp. 51–73. Albany, N.Y.: SUNY Press, 2002.

Schevitz, Tanya. "California Minorities Become Majority: Census Reflects Surge Among Latinos, Asians." *San Francisco Chronicle*. August 30, 2000.

Schlesinger, M. *The Disuniting of America*. New York: Norton, 1992.

Schneider, Carol Geary. "Changing Practices in Liberal Education; What Future Faculty Need to Know." *Peer Review* 6, no. 3 (Spring 2004): 4–7.

Schuman, Howard, Charlotte Steeh, Lawrence Bobo, and Maria Krysan. *Racial Attitudes in America: Trends and Interpretations*. Revised ed. Cambridge, Mass: Harvard University Press, 1997.

Schutz, Alfred. "The Stranger: An Essay in Social Psychology." *American Journal of Sociology* 49 (1944): 499–507.

Scott, Joseph. "Polygamy: A Futuristic Family Arrangement among African Americans." *Black Books Bulletin* 4 (1976): 13–19.

Scott, Joan W. "Experience." In *Feminists Theorize the Political*, edited by Judith Butler and Joan W. Scott. New York: Routledge, 1992.

Scott, Otis L. *Lines, Borders and Connections*. Dubuque, Iowa: Kendall/Hunt, 1997.

———. *The Veil: Perspectives on Race and Ethnicity in the United States*. Minneapolis/St. Paul, Minn.: West Publishing, 1994.

Scott, Patricia Bell. "Debunking Sapphire: Toward a Non-racist and Non-sexist Social Science." In *All the Women are White, All the Blacks are Men, But Some of Us Are Brave*, edited by Gloria T. Hull, Patricia Bell Scott, and Barbara Smith, pp. 85–92. Old Westbury, N.Y.: Feminist Press, 1982.

Sears, David O. "Symbolic Racism." In *Eliminating Racism: Profiles in Controversy*, edited by P. A. Katz and D. A. Taylor, pp. 53–84. New York: Plenum, 1988.

Seidman, Steven. *Difference Troubles: Queering Social Theory and Sexual Politics*. Cambridge: Cambridge University Press, 1997.

———. "Introduction (Queer Theory/Sociology)." In *Queer Theory/Sociology*, edited by Steven Seidman, pp. 1–29. Twentieth-Century Social Theory. Cambridge: Blackwell, 1996.

Selfe, Cynthia, and Richard Selfe. "The Politics of the Interface: Power and Its Exercise in Electronic Contact Zones." 1994. www.hu.mtu.edu/~cyselfe/texts/politics.html.

Semali, Ladislaus. *Literacy in Multimedia America: Integrating Media across the Curriculum*. New York: Garland, 1997.

Semali, Ladislaus, and Joe Kincheloe. *What Is Indigenous Knowledge? Voices from the Academy*. New York: Falmer Press, 1999.

Shor, Ira. *Critical Teaching and Everyday Life*. Boston: South End Press, 1980.

———. *Empowering Education: Critical Teaching for Social Change*. Chicago: University of Chicago Press, 1992.

Silko, Leslie Marmon. *Ceremony*. New York: Penguin Books, 1986.

Simmel, Georg. "The Sociological Significance of the 'Stranger.'" In *Introduction to the Science of Sociology*, edited by Robert E. Park and Ernest W. Burgess, pp. 322–327. Chicago: University of Chicago Press, 1921.

Simms, M., and J. Julianne Malveaux, eds. *Slipping through the Cracks: The Status of Black Women*. New Brunswick, N.J.: Transaction Books, 1986.

Simon, Julian L. *Basic Research Methods in Social Sciences: The Art of Empirical Investigation*. 2nd ed. New York: Random House, 1978.

Simpson, Douglas, and Michael Jackson. "John Dewey and Educational Evaluation." In *Standards and Schooling in the U.S.: An Encyclopedia*, edited by Joe Kincheloe and D. Weil. Santa Barbara, Calif.: ABC-Clio, 2001.

Singleton, Sharon E., Cathy A. Burack, and Deborah J. Hirsch. *Faculty Service Enclaves: A Summary Report*. New England Resource Center for Higher Education, February 1997.

Sleeter, Christine. "How White Teachers Construct Race." In *Race, Identity, and Reproduction in Education*, edited by Cameron McCarthy and Warren Crichlow. New York: Routledge, 1993.

Smith, Barbara, ed. *Home Girls: A Black Feminist Anthology*. New York: Kitchen Table, Women of Color Press, 1983.

———. *The Truth That Never Hurts: Writings on Race, Gender and Freedom*. New Brunswick, N.J.: Rutgers University Press, 1998.

Smith, David. "On Enfraudening the Public Sphere: The Futility of Empire and the Future of Knowledge after America." *Policy Futures in Education* 1, no. 3 (2004): 488–503.

Smith, Dorothy. "Comment on Hekman's 'Truth and Method: Feminist Standpoint Theory Revisited.'" *Signs* 22, no. 2 (1997): 392–398.

———. *The Everyday World as Problematic: A Feminist Sociology*. Toronto: University of Toronto Press, 1987.

———. "Women's Perspective as a Radical Critique of Sociology." *Sociological Inquiry* 44 (1974): 7–14.

Smith, John K., and Deborah K. Deemer. "The Art and Practices of Interpretation, Evaluation, and Representation." In *Handbook of Qualitative Research*, 2nd ed., edited by Norman K. Denzin and Yvonna S. Lincoln, pp. 870–896. Thousand Oaks, Calif.: Sage Publications, 2000.

Smith, Linda Tuhiwai. *Decolonizing Methodologies: Research and Indigenous Peoples*. New York: St. Martin's, 1999.

Smith, V. *Not Just Race, Not Just Gender: Black Feminist Readings*. New York: Routledge, 1998.

Sollars, Werner, ed. *The Invention of Ethnicity*. New York: Oxford University Press, 1989.

Solorzano, Daniel, and Dolores Delgado Bernal. "Academic Language and Chicana/o Activist Scholars: Balancing the Academy and Community One Hopes to Serve." *International Journal of Educational Reform*, no. 6 (1997): 226–231.

Soto, Lourdes, ed. *The Politics of Early Childhood Education*. New York: Peter Lang, 2000.

Sowell, Thomas. *Ethnic America*. New York: Basic Books, 1981.

Soyinka, Wole. *The Burden of Memory, the Muse of Forgiveness*. New York: Oxford University Press, 1999.

Spencer, Jon Michael. *The New Colored People: The Race Movement in America*. New York: New York University Press, 1997.

Spillers, Hortense J. "Mama's Baby, Papa's Maybe: An American Grammar Book." *diacritics*, Summer 1987, 65.

Spindler, George, and Louise Spindler. "Roger Harker and Schönhausen: From Familiar to Strange and Back Again." In *Doing the Ethnography of Schooling: Educational Anthropology in Action*, edited by George Spindler, pp. 21–43. Prospect Heights, Ill.: Waveland Press, 1988.

Spivak, Gayatri Chakravorty. "Can the Subaltern Speak?" in *Colonial Discourse and Post-colonial Theory: A Reader*. New York: Columbia University Press, 1994.

Spradley, James P., and David McCurdy. *The Cultural Experience: Ethnography in Complex Society*. Prospect Heights, Ill.: Waveland Press, 1972.

Stake, Robert E. *The Art of Case Study Research*. Thousand Oaks, Calif.: Sage Publications, 1995.

Stanfield, John H. "Epistemological Considerations." In *Race and Ethnicity in Research Methods*, edited by John H. Stanfield and Rutledge M. Dennis, pp. 16–36. Newbury Park, Calif.: Sage Publications, 1993.

———. "The Ethnocentric Bias of Social Science Knowledge Production." *Review of Research in Education* 12: 387–415.

———. "Methodological Reflections, an Introduction." In *Race and Ethnicity in Research Methods*, edited by John H. Stanfield and Rutledge M. Dennis, pp. 3–36. Newbury Park, Calif.: Sage Publications, 1993.

Stanfield, John H., and Rutledge M. Dennis, eds. *Race and Ethnicity in Research Methods*. Thousand Oaks, Calif.: Sage Publications, 1993.

Staples, Robert. "What Is Black Sociology? Toward a Sociology of Black Liberation." In *The Death of White Sociology*, edited by Joyce Ladner, pp. 161–172. New York: Vintage, 1973.

Staples, Robert, and Alfredo Mirande. "Racial and Cultural Variations among American Families: A Decennial Review of the Literature on Minority Families." *Journal of Marriage and the Family* 42, no. 4 (1980): 887–903.

Steady, Filomena Chioma. "African Feminism: A Worldwide Perspective." *Women in Africa and the African Diaspora.*, edited by R. Terborg-Penn et al. Washington DC: Howard University Press, 1989.

———. "The Black Woman Cross-culturally: An Overview." In *The Black Woman Cross-culturally*, edited by Filomina Chioma Steady, pp. 7–42. Cambridge, Mass.: Schenkman, 1981.

Steele, Shelby. *The Content of Our Character*. New York: Harper Perennial, 1991.

Steinberg, Shirley, ed. *Multi/intercultural Conversations*. New York: Peter Lang, 2001.

Steinberg, Stephen. *Turning Back*. Boston: Beacon Press, 1995.

Steiner, Jesse Frederick. *The Japanese Invasion: A Study in the Psychology of Inter-Racial Contacts*. Chicago: A. C. McClurg, 1917.

Stewart, James. "Alternative Models of Black Studies." *UMOJA* 5 (1981): 17–39.

———. "Foundations of a "Jazz" Theory of Africana Studies." In *Flight in Search of Vision*, by James Stewart, pp. 191–202. Trenton, N.J.: Africa World Press, 2004.

———. "Perspectives on Black Families from Contemporary Soul Music: The Case of Millie Jackson." *Phylon*, March 1980, 57–71.

———. "Perspectives on Reformist, Radical, and Recovery Models of Black Identity Dynamics from the Novels of W. E. B. Du Bois." In *Flight in Search of Vision*, by James Stewart, pp. 107–127. Trenton, N.J.: Africa World Press, 2004.

———. "Reaching for Higher Ground: Toward an Understanding of Black/Africana Studies." *Afrocentric Scholar* 1, no. 1 (1992): 1–63.

Stoddard, Lothrop. *The Rising Tide of Color against White World-Supremacy*. New York: Charles Scribner's Sons, 1920.

Stoecker, Randy. *Research Methods for Community Change: A Project-Based Approach*. Thousand Oaks, Calif.: Sage Publications, 2005.

Strand, Kerry, et al. *Community-Based Research and Higher Education*. San Francisco: Jossey-Bass, 2003.

Strauss, Anselm, and Juliet Cobin. *Basics of Qualitative Research: Grounded Theory Procedures and Techniques*. Newbury Park, Calif.: Sage Publications, 1990.

Strong, Josiah, *Our Country: Its Possible Future and Its Present Crisis*. New York: Baker & Taylor, 1885.

Sumida, Stephen H. "Postcolonialism, Nationalism, and the Emergence of Asian/Pacific American Literatures." In *The Interethnic Companion to Asian American Literature*, edited by King-Kok Cheung, pp. 274–288. Cambridge: Cambridge University Press, 1997.

Sunstein, Bonnie Stone, and Elizabeth Chiseri-Strater. *Fieldworking: Reading and Writing Research*. 2nd ed. Boston: Bedford/St. Martin's, 2002.

Suyemoto, Karen L., and Peter N. Kiang. "Diversity Research as Service Learning." *Academic Exchange Quarterly* 7, no. 2 (Summer 2003): 71–75.

Takaki, Ronald A. *A Different Mirror: A History of Multicultural America*. Boston: Little, Brown, 1993.

Tan, Amy. *The Joy Luck Club*. New York: Ballantine Books, 1989.

Tang, Shirley. *An Assessment of Khmer American Community Needs in Lynn, Massachusetts*. Research report. Lynn, Mass.: Khmer Association of the North Shore, 2005.

———. "Challenges of Policy and Practice in Under-Resourced Asian American Communities: Analyzing Public Education, Health, Development Issues with Cambodian American Women." *Asian American Law Journal* 13 (Spring 2008).

Tate, Claudia. *Black Women Writers at Work*. New York: Continuum, 1983.

Tedlock, Barbara. "From Participant Observation to the Observation of Participation: The Emergence of Narrative Ethnography." *Journal of Anthropological Research* 47 (1991): 69–94.

Tedlock, Dennis. *The Spoken Word and the Work of Interpretation*. Philadelphia: University of Pennsylvania Press, 1983.

Terborg-Penn, Rosalyn. "Black Male Perspectives on the Nineteenth-Century Woman." In *The Afro-American Woman: Struggles and Images*, edited by Sharon Harley and Rosalyn Terborg-Penn. Port Washington, N.Y.: Kennikat Press, 1978.

Te Runanga o Ngati Awa. *Nga Karoretanga o Mataatua Whare* [The Wanderings of the Carved House, Mataatua]. Whakatane, New Zealand: Ngati Awa Research Report 2, 1990.

Thandeka. *Learning to Be White.* New York: Continuum, 1999.
Thayer-Bacon, B. *Transforming Critical Thinking: Thinking Constructively.* New York: Teachers College Press, 2000.
Thomas, Gary. "The Myth of Rational Research." *British Educational Research Journal* 24, no. 2 (1998).
Thomas, Jim. *Doing Critical Ethnography.* Newbury Park, Calif.: Sage Publications, 1993.
Thomas, William I., and Florian Znaniecki. *The Polish Peasant in Europe and America: Monograph of an Immigrant Group.* 5 vols. Chicago: University of Chicago Press, 1918–1920.
Thompson, Vincent Bakpetu. *The Making of the African Diaspora in the Americas, 1441–1900.* New York: Longman, 1987.
Ting, Jennifer. "Bachelor Society: Deviant Heterosexuality and Asian American Historiography." In *Privileging Positions: The Sites of Asian American Studies,* edited by Gary Y. Okihiro et al., pp. 271–279. Pullman: Washington State University Press, 1995.
Tocqueville, Alexis de. *Democracy in America.* Translated by Arthur Goldhammer. New York: Library of American, 2004.
Tong, Rosemarie. *Feminist Thought: A Comprehensive Introduction.* Boulder, Colo.: Westview Press, 1989.
Toomer, Jean. *Cane.* (1923). New York: Liveright, 1993.
Toulmin, Stephen. *Human Understanding.* Vol. 1. Princeton, N.J.: Princeton University Press, 1972.
Tresaugue, Matthew. "Pomona OKs Labor Center." *Daily Bulletin,* July 31, 1997.
Trexler, Richard C. *Sex and Conquest: Gendered Violence, Political Order, and the European Conquest of the Americas.* Ithaca, N.Y.: Cornell University Press, 1995.
Turner, Frederick Jackson. *The Frontier in American History.* New York: Henry Holt, 1920.
U.S. Bureau of the Census. Statistical abstract. Washington, D.C.: U.S. Government Printing Office, 1960–2000.
Uno, Roberta, ed. *The Unbroken Thread: An Anthology of Plays by Asian American Women.* Amherst: University of Massachusetts Press, 1993.
Urrieta, Luis, Jr. "Las Identidades También Lloran, Identities Also Cry: Exploring the Human Side of Indigenous Latina/o Identities." *Educational Studies* 34, no. 2 (2003): 148–168.
Valdes, Francisco, Jerome McCristal Culp, and Angela P. Harris, eds. *Crossroads, Directions, and a New Critical Race Theory.* Philadelphia: Temple University Press, 2002.
Valencia, Richard, ed. *The Evolution of Deficit Thinking: Educational Thought and Practice.* Washington, D.C.: Falmer Press, 1997.
Valenzuela, Angela. *Subtractive Schooling: U.S.-Mexican Youth and the Politics of Caring.* Albany, N.Y.: SUNY Press, 1999.
Van Ausdale, Debra, and Joe R. Feagin. *The First R: How Children Learn Race and Racism.* New York: Rowman & Littlefield, 2001.

Van Boven, Leaf. "Pluralistic Ignorance and Political Correctness: The Case of Affirmative Action." *Political Psychology* 21 (2000): 267–276.

Van Dijk, Teun. "Analyzing Racism through Discourse Analysis." In *Race and Ethnicity in Research Methods*, edited by John H. Stanfield and Rutledge M. Dennis, pp. 92–134. Newbury Park, Calif.: Sage Publications, 1993.

Varela, Francisco. *Ethical Know-How: Action, Wisdom, and Cognition.* Stanford, Calif.: Stanford University Press, 1999.

Vaz, Kim. "Making Room for Emancipatory Research in Psychology: A Multicultural Feminist Perspective." In *Spirit, Space & Survival, African American Women in (White) Academe*, edited by Joy James and Ruth Farmer, pp. 83–98. New York: Routledge, 1993.

Villenas, Sofia. "The Colonizer/Colonized Chicana Ethnographer: Identity, Marginalization, and Co-optation in the Field." *Harvard Educational Review* 66, no. 4 (1996): 711–731.

———. "Reinventing Educación in New Latino Communities: Pedagogies of Change and Continuity in North Carolina." In *Education in the New Latino Diaspora: Policy and the Politics of Identity*, edited by Stanton Wortham, Enrique Murillo, Jr., and Edmund T. Hamman, pp. 17–35. Westport, Conn.: Ablex Publishing, 2002.

Vo, Linda Trinh. "Performing Ethnography in Asian American Communities: Beyond the Insider-versus-Outsider Perspective." In *Cultural Compass: Ethnographic Explorations of Asian America*, edited by Martin F. Manalansan, IV, pp. 17–37. Asian American History and Culture series. Philadelphia: Temple University Press, 2000.

Vo, Linda Trinh, and Rick Bonus. *Contemporary Asian American Communities: Intersections and Divergences.* Philadelphia: Temple University Press, 2002.

Wakukawa, Ernest K. *A History of the Japanese People in Hawaii.* Honolulu: Toyo Shoin, 1938.

Wal, Jessika ter, and Maykel Verkuyten. *Comparative Perspectives on Racism.* Aldershot, UK: Ashgate, 2000.

Walker, Alice, ed. *I Love Myself When I Am Laughing . . . A Zora Neal Hurston Reader.* Westbury, N.Y.: Feminist Press, 1979.

Walker, Alice. "In Search of Our Mothers' Gardens." In *In Search of Our Mothers' Gardens*, pp. 231–243. New York: Harcourt Brace Jovanovich, 1974.

Walker, Sheila, ed., *African Roots/American Cultures: Africa in the Creation of the Americas.* Lanham, Md.: Rowman & Littlefield, 2001.

Wall, Cheryl. *Changing Our Own Words: Essays on Criticism, Theory, and Writing by Black Women.* New Brunswick: Rutgers University Press, 1989.

Walters, Ronald. "Toward a Definition of Black Social Science." In *The Death of White Sociology*, edited by Joyce Ladner, pp. 190–212. New York: Vintage, 1973.

Wang, Ling-chi. "Curriculum Transformation at UC Berkeley: Our Past, Present, and Future." 1991. amercult/berkeley.edu/geninfo/wang.html.

Weber, Devra. *Dark Sweat, White Gold: California Farm Workers, Cotton, and the New Deal.* Berkeley: University of California Press, 1994.

Wei, William. *The Asian American Movement*. Philadelphia: Temple University Press, 1993.

Weinstein, Mark. "Critical Thinking? Expanding the Paradigm." 1995. www.chss.montclair.edu/inquiry/fall95/weinste.html.

Weiss, Robert S. *Learning from Strangers: The Art and Method of Qualitative Interview Studies*. New York: Free Press, 1994.

Weissinger, Thomas. "Black Studies Scholarly Communication: A Citation Analysis of Periodical Literature." *Collection Management* 27, nos. 3–4 (2002): 45–56.

Welarantna, Usha. *Beyond the Killing Fields: Voices of Nine Cambodian Survivors in America*. Stanford, Calif.: Stanford University Press, 1993.

Wells, Miriam J. *Strawberry Fields: Politics, Class, and Work in California Agriculture*. Ithaca, N.Y.: Cornell University Press, 1996.

Welsh-Asante, Kariamce, ed. *The African Aesthetic: Keeper of the Tradition*. New York: Greenwood, 1993.

———. *African Dance: An Artistic, Historical, and Philosophical Inquiry*. Trenton, N.J.: Africa World Press, 1996.

Westkott, Marcia. "Feminist Criticism of the Social Sciences." *Harvard Educational Review* 49 (1979): 422–430.

White, Deborah Gray. *Ar'n't I a Woman? Female Slaves in the Plantation South*. New York: W.W. Norton, 1985.

White, E. Frances. "Listening to the Voices of Black Feminism." *Radical America* 18 (1984): 7–25.

White, Richard. *The Roots of Dependency: Subsistence, Environment, and Social Change among Choctaws, Pawnees, and Navajos*. Lincoln: University of Nebraska Press, 1983.

Whyte, William Foote. *Participatory Action Research*. Newbury Park: Calif.: Sage Publications, 1989.

Wilcox, Preston. "Black Studies as an Academic Discipline." *Negro Digest*, March 1970.

Wilentz, Sean. "Integrating Ethnicity into American Studies." *The Chronicle of Higher Education*, November 29, 1996, A56.

Williams, Brackette F. "Skinfolk, Not Kinfolk: Comparative Reflections on the Identity of Participant-Observation in Two Field Situations." In *Feminist Dilemmas in Fieldwork*, edited by Diane L. Wolf, pp. 72–95. Boulder, Colo.: Westview Press, 1996.

Williams, George W. *History of the Negro Race in America from 1619 to 1880*. 2 vols. New York: G. P. Putnam's Sons, 1883.

Williams, Patricia. *The Alchemy of Race and Rights*. Cambridge, Mass.: Harvard University Press, 1991.

Williams, Raymond. *The Country and the City*. London: Paladin, 1973

Williams, S. "Truth, Speech, and Ethics: A Feminist Revision of Free Speech Theory." *Genders* 30 (1999). www.genders.org.

Williamson, Joel. *New People: Miscegenation and Mulattoes in the United States*. Baton Rouge: Louisiana State University Press, 1995.

Willis, Paul, and Mats Trondman. "Manifesto for Ethnography." *Ethnography* 1, no. 1 (2000): 1–16.
Wilson, Rob, and Wimal Dissanayake, eds. *Global/Local: Cultural Production and the Transnational Imaginary*. Durham, N.C.: Duke University Press, 1996.
Wilson, William J. *The Declining Significance of Race: Blacks and Changing American Institutions*. Chicago: University of Chicago Press, 1978.
Winant, Howard. "Race and Race Theory." *Annual Review of Sociology* 26 (2000): 169–185.
———. *Racial Conditions*. Minneapolis: University of Minnesota Press, 1994.
Winddance Twine, France, and Jonathan W. Warren, eds. *Racing Research, Researching Race: Methodological Dilemmas in Critical Race Studies*. New York: New York University Press, 2000.
Wissler, Clark. *Man and Culture*. New York: Crowell, 1923.
Wittig, M. A., and L. Molina. "Moderators and Mediators of Prejudice Reduction in Multicultural Education." In *Reducing Prejudice and Discrimination*, edited by S. Oskamp, pp. 295–318. Mahwah, N.J.: Lawrence Erlbaum, 1999.
Wolcott, Harry F. *The Art of Fieldwork*. Walnut Creek, Calif.: AltaMira Press, 1995.
Wolf, Diane L., ed. *Feminist Dilemmas in Fieldwork*. Boulder, Colo.: Westview Press, 1996.
Wong, K. Scott, "'The Eagle Seeks a Helpless Quarry': Chinatown, the Police, and the Press—The 1903 Boston Chinatown Raid Revisited." *Amerasia Journal* 22, no. 3 (1996): 81–103.
Wong, Sau-Ling Cynthia. "Denationalization Reconsidered: Asian American Cultural Criticism at a Theoretical Crossroads." *Amerasia Journal* 21, nos. 1 and 2 (1995): 1–27.
Wong, Sau-Ling Cynthia, and Stephen H. Sumida. *A Resource Guide to Asian American Literature*. New York: MLA, 2001.
Woodhouse, Mark. *Paradigm Wars: Worldviews for a New Age*. Berkeley, Calif.: Frog, 1996.
Woodson, Carter G. *The Miseducation of the Negro*. Nashville: Winston-Derek, 1990.
Yamamoto, Eric, et al. *Race, Rights and Reparation: Law and the Japanese American Internment*. New York: Aspen, 2001.
Yang, Phillip Q., ed. *Introduction to Ethnic Studies*. Dubuque, Iowa: Kendall-Hunt, 1999.
Yep, Gust A. "From Homophobia and Heterosexism to Heteronormativity: Toward the Development of a Model of Queer Interventions in the University Classroom." *Journal of Lesbian Studies* 6, no. 3–4 (2002): 163–176.
Young, T. R., and James Yarbrough. "Reinventing Sociology: Mission and Methods for Postmodern Sociologists." Red Feather Institute. Transforming Sociology Series, 1993.
Yu, Amanda. "Asian American Studies Course Offerings in Massachusetts Colleges and Universities." Unpublished document, University of Massachusetts, Boston, 2002.

Yu, Henry. *Thinking Orientals: Migration, Contact, and Exoticism in Modern America.* New York: Oxford University Press, 2001.

Yudice, George. "Neither Impugning nor Disavowing Whiteness Does a Viable Politics Make: The Limits of Identity Politics." In *After Political Correctness*, edited by Christopher Newfield and Ronald Strickland. Boulder, Colo.: Westview Press, 1995.

Yu-Wen Shen Wu, Jean, and Min Song, eds. *Asian American Studies: A Reader.* New Brunswick, N.J.: Rutgers University Press, 2000.

Zack, Naomi. *Race and Mixed Race.* Philadelphia: Temple University Press, 1993.

Zavella, Patricia. "Feminist Insider Dilemmas: Constructing Ethnic Identity with Chicana Informants." In *Feminist Dilemmas in Fieldwork*, edited by Diane L. Wolf, pp. 138–159. Boulder, Colo.: Westview Press, 1996.

Zinsser, William. *On Writing Well: The Classic Guide to Writing Nonfiction.* 25th ed. New York: Quill, 2001.

Zlotkowski, Edward, ed. *Successful Service-Learning Programs.* Bolton, Mass.: Anker Publishing Company, 1998.

Zou, Yali, and Henry T. Trueba, eds. *Ethnography and Schools: Qualitative Approaches to the Study of Education.* Lanham, Md.: Rowman & Littlefield, 2002.

Index

Abram, Renzie, Jr., 474
absence, bricolage and, 325–27
academia: art metaphors in, as exclusionary, 143–77; black women and, 110–14; bricolage and, 314; and community, 80–81; cultural practice and, 162–69; inequality in, 368–69; marginality in, 95, 166–68, 170; pedagogy of, 411–12; placement of ethnic studies programs in, 23, 86–87, 244, 251, 267–68; and politics, 29; scholars of color in, effects of, 110–14, 222–23
activism: Africana studies and, 179, 183–84, 210; black feminist thought and, 106–7; Chicana epistemology and, 161–62; ethnic studies and, 4–5, 27–29, 263; Forbes and, 80–81; and methodology, 319–21; and research, 353–66; term, 106. *See also* service learning
activist ethnography, 219–39; advantages and limitations of, 231–34; definition of, 229
Acuña, Rodolfo, 283
advanced undergraduates, and research, case study on, 376–84

Africalogy, definition of, 208
African Americans: in Muncie, 469–89; and reparations, 276n7. *See also under* black
African American studies, 34, 248; and development of ethnic studies, 38–39, 79–80
Africana studies: dimensions of, 179; methodology in, 179–217; and politics, 185–89; research directions for, 201–9; subject areas in, 193–94
African diaspora studies, 205–7; and literature studies, 270–73
African worldviews, 330–31
Afrocentricity, 207–9
Afrogenic perspective, definition of, 206
agency: and development of ethnic studies, 44–45; and methodology, 319–21
Aguilar, Gerónimo de, 296
Alarcón, Norma, 298, 300
Alcoff, Linda Martín, 243, 409
Alexie, Sherman, 410, 423
Alkalimat, A., 186
Allen, Robert L., 50
Alquizola, Marilyn, 466
Alurista, 284, 289–90

539

American, term, 88, 282
American Association for Higher Education, 368
analytical methods, in black/Africana studies, 182
Anaya, Rudolfo, 291
Andean worldviews, 331–33
Anderson, Julius, 474
Anderson, Michelle, 474
Angelou, Maya, 358
Anzaldúa, Gloria, 249
Apess, William, 79
Apffel-Marglin, Frederique, 332
Appadurai, Arjun, 271
Appiah, Anthony, 245, 254n4
applied research teams (ARTs), 384–93; term, 385
Aquinas, Thomas, 131
Arreguín, Afredo, 300
art: black/Africana studies and, 189–92; bricolage and, 345–46; Chicana, images in, 281–312; metaphor of research as, 143–77; in tutoring program, 463. *See also* creative expression; literatures; music
ARTs. *See* applied research teams
Asante, Molefi, 26, 206–8
Asian American(s): demographics of, 268, 453; term, 274
Asian American literature, 36, 257–79; critical reading practices for, 268–75; diversity within, 269
Asian American studies: community research methods in, 367–98; effects of, survey on, 389–92
assimilation, and development of ethnic studies, 42, 60
Association of American Colleges & Universities, 368
Atlanta University, 185
authorship, multiple, approaches to, 195–96

autonomy, ethnic studies programs and, 23
ayllu, term, 333
Aztec culture, 283–85
Aztlán, 284; term, 80–81
Azuela, Mariano, 282

Baker, H., 196
Ball, Virginia B., 472
Ball State University, collaborative ethnic research project, 469–89
BAM. *See* Black Arts Movement
Banda, Dan, 299
banking concept of pedagogy, 353–54
Banks, Joseph, 137–38
Baraka, Amiri, 190
Barnett, Ida Wells, 100
Barnett, Teresa, 463
Barraza, Santa, 292, 299
Bartholomae, David, 411
Bartleson, Phyllis, 474
Bateson, Gregory, 333
Bell, Derrick, 258
Bennett, L., 184–85
Berry, Kathleen, 340
Beveridge, William I. B., 172n5
Bhabha, Homi K., 423–24
bias: Forbes on, 67–69, 71; PC movement on, 428
biracial movement, 205
black/Africana studies: and art, 189–92; history of, 180–96; methodology in, 179–217
Black Arts Movement (BAM), 189–90
Black Atlantic movement, 205
Black Elk, 80
black English, 190
black feminist thought, 93–121, 203; definition of, 95; sociological significance of, 107–14; themes in, 95–107. *See also* feminist theory
Blyden, Edward, 38
Bogardus, Emory, 41–42

Bolton, Herbert Eugene, 78
Booth, Jessica, 474
Borah, Woodrow, 78
borderlands constructs, 244–45; Chicana epistemology and, 168–69; in ethnic studies, 19; Forbes on, 64–67, 73–74; and race and sexuality, 226
Bounds, Brandy, 474, 488n13
Boyer, Ernest, 368
Bricker, Sarah, 474, 479–80
bricolage: concept of, 318–19; and ethnic studies research, 313–50; and meaning making, 324–25; steps in, 340–46; subversive nature of, 321–23
bricoleurs: term, 318; types of, 320
Brittan, Arthur, 119n32
Brushchipus, Kaspar, 284
Bulmer, Martin, 7
Bulosan, Carlos, 410
Burawoy, Michael, 228–29
Burke, Carla, 474
Burns, Geraldine, 474, 480
Bush, George W., 35
Butler, Johnnella E., 31n6, 243–56, 401
Butler, Judith, 247

Caccamo, Rita, 471
Calderon, Jose Z., 353–66
Caldwell, Russell, 64
California: demographics of, 453; politics in, 24, 29, 31n12, 32n23; service learning in, 453–67
California Indian Education Association, 82
California State University at Sacramento, Department of Ethnic Studies, 453–67
Campbell, Elizabeth (Beth), 472–73, 475, 480, 483
Campus Comjpact, 369
Candelaria, Cordelia, 291–92

Carby, Hazel, 260
Carmichael, Stokely, 49
Carnegie, Andrew, 253
Carnegie Foundation, 369
Carreón, Héctor, 309
Carter, Melanie, 6
Castillo, Ana, 291, 410
Centeotl, 302
center: in colonial vocabulary, 136, 137t; community as, 369–72
Center for California Cultural and Social Issues, 362
Césaire, Aimé, 38
chacras, term, 332–33
Chagga peoples, 330
Chan, Sucheng, 3
Chanecas, 288
Chapman, Tracy, 436
charity models, versus service learning, 361–63
Chavez, Cesar, 359
Cheung, King-Kok, 270–71
Chicanos/as: in California, 453; epistemology, and qualitative research, 151–57; literary and visual arts, images in, 281–312; term, 80. *See also* Latino studies
Chicomecoatl, 302
Chiseri-Strater, Elizabeth, 481
Choy, Curtis, 377–78
Chun-Hoon, Lowell, 367–68
Cihuacóatl, 284–87, 302
Cihuateto, 293
Cisneros, Sandra, 291, 295, 309, 358
Citlalicue, 302
Ciuateteo, 287
Ciupipltin, 287
civil rights movement: and Chicanos/as, 282; and ethnic studies movement, 18, 82–83; Muncie and, 471; and race studies, 261–62; and racism, 427–28; Virgin of Guadalupe and, 303

class, and intersectionality, 271
Clifford, James, 261
Clinton, Bill, 3
cliometrics, definition of, 182
Coatlicue, 285, 287
collaboration: and research, 469–89; and service learning, 453–67
colonialism: and Asian American literature, 269; critique of, Smith on, 125–41; internal, 7–8, 37; and La Malinche, 296–300; problem approach and, 43; and racial theories, 223; spatial vocabulary of, 136, 137*t*
colonization, phases of, 128
color blindness, ethnic studies and, 24
Combahee River Collective, 48
Comíte de Padres Latinos (COPLA), 152
community: academia and, 80–81; Asian American studies coursework and, 367–98; centering commitments to, 369–72; Chicana epistemology and, 161–62; definition of, 362–63; ethnic studies and, 2, 26–27, 45, 263; intersectionality and, 219–39; Latino research and, 143–77; of practitioners, and sociological paradigms, 109; Western research and, 130–33. *See also* service learning
Companeros, Oscar, 272
conceptual interdisciplinarity, 252
conceptual maps, 109; in bricolage, 340–41
confidentiality, 233–34
consciousness: black feminist thought and, 106–7; bricolage and, 320; in Cartesian thought, 330; double, 415–16; indigenous concepts of, 331
constructions: definition of, 70; validation of, 70–72

conversations: in collaborative research, 476–85; postformal, 338
Cooper, Anna Julia, 26, 102–3
COPLA, 152
Corbin, Juliet, 154
Corpi, Lucha, 291, 298–99
corrective agenda, ethnic studies and, 19
Cortés, Hernan, 76, 296, 299–300
creative expression: Africana studies and, 189–92; black feminist thought and, 105; Chicana, images in, 281–312; and intersectionality, 265; and pedagogy, 402; in tutoring program, 463. *See also* art; literatures; music
Crenshaw, Kimberly, 258, 267
critical ethnography, 228
critical pedagogy, 353–66
critical race studies, and ethnic studies research, 258
critical reading practices, for Asian American literature, 268–75
Cruse, Harold, 49
cuentos, 158, 164–65, 177n57
cultural analysis, 187
cultural hegemony, 272
cultural identity, formation of, 421–22
cultural intuition, 154
cultural practice, 170–71; in action, 162–69; definition of, 157–59; as ethnic epistemology and methodology, 161–62; metaphor of, 159–61
culture: Africana studies and, 189–92; black feminist thought and, 103–7; elements of, 103; and Western research, 127–28
curriculum: Butler on, 253–54; in ethnic studies, 400–404; whiteness and, 86
Cutter, Donald C., 64
Cypess, Sandra Messinger, 300

Darwinism, social, 133
Davis, Jessica Hoffman, 148
de Dios Peza, Juan, 288
del Castillo, Adelaida, 298, 300
Delgado Bernal, Dolores, 151–52, 154–55, 157
Delgado-Gaitán, Concha, 151–53, 155–56
Delpha, Abigail, 474
del Valle Arizpe, Artemio, 288
Dennis, Rutledge M., 5
Denzin, Norm, 320, 322, 329
dependency, concept of, 52n15
depth, in research project, 380–81
Descartes, René, 131, 330, 333
de Tocqueville, Alexis, 7
diaspora studies, 205–7; and literature studies, 270–73
Díaz del Castillo, Bernal, 76, 296
dichos, 158, 171, 177n65
Diego, Juan, 301–2
difference: bricolage and, 325, 333–36; and PC movement, 428; politics of, 337–39
Dill, Bonnie Thornton, 102, 105, 107, 116n3
Diop, Cheikh Anta, 207
disciplinarity, bricolage and, 327–33
discipline, versus subject area, 194
discourse theory, and Africana studies, 199–200
distance: art metaphor and, 146–47; bricolage and, 320; concept of, 139
diversity research teams, 385
documentary arts, in tutoring program, 463
domination: bricolage and, 344–45; definition of, 239n40; and dehmanization, 99; knowledge work and, 317; matrix of, 220. *See also* power
Dortch, Jarrod, 474
double consciousness, 415–16

Douyon, Andre, 455
D'Souza, Dinesh, 34–35
dualism, 50; academia and, 111; black feminist thought on, 101–2; Cartesian, 131, 330; and racism, 119n32
Du Bois, W. E. B., 79, 192, 211, 224; on double consciousness, 415–16; and interdisciplinarity, 199–200; and methodology, 182–85
Durán, Diego, 286

Eagle Rock, 61–62
Efaw, Eric, 474
Einstein, Albert, 334
Elbaz, Gilbert, 228
Eliot, T. S., 274
empiricism, critique of: Forbes on, 65; Smith on, 125–41
empowerment: ethnography and, 153, 155; Masequesmay on, 221
enactivism, Santiago theory of, 322, 336
Eng, David, 271
Englatino, 88, 91n16
Enlightenment, 138–39
epistemology: crisis in, 265; cultural practice as, 161–62; definition of, 219; ethnic, in Latino qualitative studies, 143–77; feminist thought and, 126; and identity, 422; and imperialism, 316; and racism, 149–50
Erdrich, Louise, 358
Espiritu, Yen Le, 268, 274–75
essentialism: marginalized persons and, 234; Moya on, 247; student controversy on, 420
ethical codes, for ethnography, 484–85
ethnic, term, 87
ethnicity, definition of, 261
ethnic literatures: Asian American, 36, 257–79; Chicana, images in,

281–312; methodology and, 257–79; pedagogy and, 399–426; testimonial, 400
ethnic studies: characteristics of, 19; current status of, 22–25; epistemological stance in, 220–21; future of, 25–30, 85–87; historiography and, 59–91; history of, 18–21; and interdisciplinarity, 243–56; origins of, 59–61; pedagogy for, 399–426; placement in academia, 23, 86–87, 244, 251, 267–68; recommendations for, 47–51; term, 87–89
ethnic studies movement, 18–19
ethnic studies research, 1–14; bricolage and, 313–50; concepts in, 2–5; history of, 1–2; literature review on, 5–8; sites of, 394–95; versus traditional disciplines, 262
ethnographic methodology: Forbes on, 74; and intersectionality, 219–39
ethnography: collaborative, 469–89; critical, 228; potentials and limitations of, 486–87; writing, 482–85
ethnology, term, 88
ethnomusicology, 191
ethnopoetics, 482
European thought: centering of, academia and, 267; critique of, 77–80, 125–41; and curriculum, 86; and development of ethnic studies, 37–38, 59–60; Forbes on, 66, 74–77, 87; images in, 281; Kristol on, 246–47; literature review on, 7; and reading ethnic literatures, 260–61
evidence: Africana studies and, 193; Forbes on, 67–70, 72–77
experience: and Africana methodology, 186; of Chicanas, 163–65; and Chicano epistemology, 156; and cultural identity, 421; and cultural practice, 157; and development of ethnic studies, 44–45; postpositive realist theory on, 406–7
extended case method, 228–29
external colonialism, 7

Fabionar, James, 463
families: black feminist thought on, 113–14; gender and, 129; interdisciplinary study of, 194–95; time and, 138
Fanon, Frantz, 141n18, 283
Far West Laboratory, 82
Faulkner, Edgar, 474
feedback, in bricolage, 341
feminist theory, 278n24; bricolage and, 337; and development of ethnic studies, 36–37; intersectionality and, 273; and methodology, 50; Western, 126. *See also* black feminist thought
Ferguso, Rosa Linda, 267
fictive, term, 326
Fields, Mia, 474
fieldwork, cultural practice and, 162–69
Figueroa, Julie L., 143–77
Flores, Bill, 379
Fong, Timothy P., ix–xii, 1–14
Forbes, Jack D., 59–91
Foucault, Michel, 127, 134, 260
Franco, Victoria F., 306f
Frazier, E. Franklin, 79, 187
Freire, Paulo, 325, 357–58
Freud, Sigmund, 225, 431
Fuller, Hoyte, 246–47
Future of Minority Studies Project, 245–46, 255n6

Gaines, Ernest, 410, 413–16
garbage, Forbes on, 67–69

Garfinkel, Harold, 239n41
Gates, Henry Louis, Jr., 245, 254n4
Gawlowski, Danny, 474
Gayle, Addison, 190
Geertz, Clifford, 259, 265
gender: Africana studies and, 188; definition of, 129; and discourse, 199; intersectionality and, 128–30
geographic information systems (GIS), 188, 195
George, Rosemary, 261, 272
Gibbon, Edward, 62
Giddings, Paula, 118n25
Gilkes, Cheryl, 96, 104
Gilroy, Paul, 48, 206, 260–61
GIS. *See* geographic information systems
globalization, Africana studies and, 184
Goldberg, David Theo, 128, 258, 272
Gonzales-Berry, Erlinda, 299
Goodall, Hurley, 469, 471, 473–75, 480–81, 488n18
Gopinath, Gayatri, 261
Gordon, Lewis, 412–13
Gorman, Carl and Mary, 80
Greek culture: images in, 281; philosophy, 131
grounded theory, 155, 187–88
Gunaratnam, Yasmin, 7
Gwaltney, John, 97

Habermas, Jürgen, 239n40
Hagedorn, Jessica, 271, 410
Hale, Janice, 105
Haley, Alex, 358
Hall, Donald, 258–59
Hall, Stuart, 126–27, 130, 192, 196, 260–61
Hardiman, Rita, 434
Harding, Sandra, 219–20, 236n7
Harding, Vincent, 33
Harper, Frances Ellen, 100
Harrington, M. R., 63

Harris, R., 181–82
Harstock, Nancy, 220
Hatch, Barry, 355
Hawaii, colonialism and, 274
Healthy Start, 453, 457, 459–60
Hedstrom, Julia, 463
Hegel, G. W. F., 131–32
hegemony, cultural, 272
Hemispheric Initiative of the Americas, 88
Henderson, Stephen, 190
Herodotus, 59, 70
Herrera-Sobek, María, 281–312
Hick, John, 63
Hidalgo y Costilla, Miguel, 303
higher education reform, 368–69
Hill Collins, Patricia, 93–121, 204, 220, 249
Hinson, Glenn, 482
Hirabayashi, Lane, 466
Hiram Johnson High School, 453–56; neighborhood issues and, 457–59, 458t–459t; tutoring program for, 460–64
Hirata, Lucie Cheng, 367–68
historiography: and black/Africana studies, 181–85; and ethnic studies, 59–91; Forbes and, 61–63
Hogan, Linda, 410
Holiwski, Frank, 427–49
homosexuality, 219–39
Hong, Grace, 267
hooks, bell, 36, 94, 101, 402, 404, 409
Horn, Ray, 338
Hu-DeHart, Evelyn, 4
Huerta, Dolores, 360
human ecology model, 187
humanism: black feminist thought and, 102–3, 119n35; Greek philosophy and, 131; and interdisciplinarity, 244, 254n2
humility, and ethnic studies research, 66–67

Hune, Shirley, 222
hunter, and evidence, 72–77
Hurston, Zora Neal, 94
Hwang, David Henry, 36, 271
hybridity: and diaspora studies, 205; and literature studies, 272

identity: Butler on, 243–56; concept of, 243–44; cultural, formation of, 421–22
identity politics, versus ethnic studies, 46
identity work, 230–31
IGERT Program, 256n21
immigration: and diaspora studies, 205; and intersectionality, 227; and literature studies, 269; and race relations study, 39–40, 262, 264–65
imperialism, 316–17; Forbes on, 71; and literature studies, 269, 271–72
Implicit Association Test, 445
indigenous, term, 87
indigenous knowledges, 330–33
indigenous perspective: Forbes on, 64–67; Maori, 129–33, 135–36
individual: race relations study on, 45; Western research and, 130–33
Indochinese Women's Conference, 35
informed disciplinarity, 252
insider perspectives, 5; challenges to, 228; remaining, 109; service learning and, 384
Integrative Graduate Education and Research Training (IGERT) Program, 256n21
integrity, in research project, 381–82
interdisciplinarity: Africana studies and, 192–202; approaches to, 196–202; bricolage and, 313–50; and collaborative research, 474; current state of, 251–52; ethnic studies and, 243–56; jazz and, 190–91; and literature studies, 257, 262–68; typology of, 252
interdisciplinary, concept, 263–66
internal colonialism, 7–8, 37
internationalism, and development of ethnic studies, 35, 37–39, 48–49
intersectionality: elements of, 264; and literature studies, 271; and methodology, 219–39; and reading ethnic literatures, 263–68; Smith on, 128–30
interviews, in collaborative research, 476–85
Ixtabay, 287

Jackson, I., 191
Jackson, Millie, 200
James, C. L. R., 79
Janvier, Thomas A., 286
Japanese Americans, and reparations, 276n7
jazz, 190–91; and interdisciplinarity, 190–91, 197–99
Johnson, Charles S., 41
Johnson, Eric, 474, 480
Johnson, Hiram, 454
Johnson, Lyndon B., 43
Johnson, Michelle Natasya, 473, 475, 480, 483
journals, on applied research, 387

Kang, Laura Hyun Yi, 257, 263, 269, 271
Karenga, Maulana, 180–81, 185–86, 189–90, 193–94, 207–8, 251
Katrak, Ketu H., 257–79
Kearney, Michael, 287
Kellner, Douglas, 329
Kennedy, Robert, 82
Kiang, Peter Nien-Chu, 367–98
Kincheloe, Joe L., 313–50
King, Mae, 96
Kingston, Maxine Hong, 260

Kinsey, Alfred, 225, 238n30
Kirtley, Basil F., 284–85
Kissel, Carrie, 474
Klein, Julie Thompson, 263, 265–66
knowledge: indigenous, 330–33; restructuring of, 265; subjugated, 334, 336–37
knowledge production, difference and, 333–36
knowledge work: and dominant ideologies, 317; postapocalyptic, 329–30
Knowles, Caroline, 7
Kogawa, Joy, 259
Kondi, Jason, 465
Kraemer, Anne, 474
Krieger, Susan, 149
Kristol, Irving, 246–47
Kuhn, Thomas S., 108–9

labor: black feminist thought on, 113; black women and, 93–94, 115n2; time and, Western thought on, 138
Ladson-Billings, Gloria, 150
Lafaye, Jacques, 301
LaFlesche, Francis, 79
Lahiri, Jhumpa, 260, 410
La Llorona, 284–95; and Chicana writers, 289–92; and Chicano/a visual arts, 292–95, 293f; and Chicano writers, 289–91; historical antecedents of, 284–89
La Malinche, 296–300; and Chicana painters, 299; and Chicana writers, 291, 298–99; historical antecedents of, 285–86, 289, 296–98; term, 296
Lamia, 287
Lassiter, Luke Eric, 469–89
Latino studies: ethnic epistemology in, 143–77. *See also* Chicanos/as
Latucca, Lisa R., 252
la vitrina, 159–61
Lawrence-Lightfoot, Sara, 148–49

Leal, Luis, 285
Leddy, Betty, 288
Lefebvre, Henri, 134
legal studies: and ethnic studies research, 258; and literature studies, 269
Leong, Russell, 271
lesbian/gay/bisexual/transgender (LGBT). *See* queer studies
A Lesson before Dying (Gaines), 410, 413–16
Levine, Ellis, 63
liberatory pedagogy, 402, 421
librarians, 62
lifeworlds, 228
Lilith, 286–87
Lim, Genny, 260
Limón, José, 294
Lincoln, Yvonna, 320, 322, 326, 329
line, in colonial vocabulary, 136, 137t
Lipsitz, George, 50, 261, 421
literatures: Asian American, 36, 257–79; Chicana, images in, 281–312; methodology and, 257–79; pedagogy and, 399–426; testimonial, 400
Livingston, Richard, 63
Logan, Rayford W., 79
López, Alma, 309
Lopez, Gerardo R., 5
Lopez, Ian F., 434
López, Yolanda M., 304–5, 306f–308f
Lorde, Audre, 8, 39, 120n46
Lott, Trent, 429
Lottinville, Savoie, 89n4
Lowe, Lisa, 257, 261, 264–67, 269, 272, 417
Luibheid, Eithne, 227
Lynd, Robert S. and Helen M., 469–71, 475, 481, 487
Lynton, Ernest, 368

M., Rosa, 293
Mankekar, Purnima, 261

Manley, Theodoric, Jr., 427–49
Maori worldview, 129–33, 135–36
Marable, M., 181, 184–85
marginality: in academia, 95, 166–68, 170; and black feminist thought, 93–121; intersections of race and sexuality and, 219–39
Marina. *See* Malinche
Mark, Gregory Yee, 453–67
Mark Keppel High School, 355–57
Martinez, Silva, 465
Marx, Marcia, 244–45
Masequesmay, Gina, 219–39
Mataatua, 135–36
Matlacihuatl, 288
Matlaziwa, 288
Matsumoto, Lorene, 465
Maturana, Humberto, 322, 334
Mayan culture, 283, 285
Maynard, Mary, 119n32
McLaren, Peter, 320
McNeary, Edward, 474
McNickle, D'arcy, 79
McWilliams, Carey, 83
Meador, Kara, 465
meaning making, bricolage and, 324–25
measurement: and space, 134; and understanding, 125
Memmi, Albert, 38–39
Mendieta, Eduardo, 243
Merton, Robert K., 110
metaphors, for research: art as, 143–77; la vitrina as, 159–61
method, definition of, 219
methodology, 6; agency and, 319–21; art and, 190; in black/Africana studies, 179–217; Butler on, 243, 253–54; of collaborative research, 473–76; cultural practice as, 161–62; decolonizing, 125–41; definition of, 219; historical, 60, 64–65, 71–77; in reading ethnic literatures, 257–79; thesis with

illustrations, Forbes on, 65–66
Mexico, literary and visual arts of, 281–312
Meyer, Milton, 80
Middletown, 469–71, 475, 481, 487; African Americans in, 469–89
Miller, Elaine, 288
Mills, C. Wright, 229
minority, term, 87
Mohanty, Chandra, 267, 271
Mohanty, Satya, 399, 406, 408
Monacans, 76
monocultural scholarship, 320, 322; questioning, 330–33
Monterey Park, CA, 355–57, 364n3
Moore, Ashley, 474
Mora, Pat, 295
Moraga, Cherríe, 249, 292
Morales, Alejandro, 290
Moriyama, Alan, 367–68
Morrison, Toni, 358, 410
Mosha, R. Sambuli, 330
motherhood, black feminist thought and, 104–5
movement, and pedagogy, 404
Moya, Paula, 246–47, 399, 404–8, 413, 421–22
Mulkay, Michael, 109
Mullings, Leith, 103
multiculturalism: critical theory in, 315–17; versus ethnic studies, 46; term, 315
multidimensionality, Africana studies and, 179
multidisciplinarity, versus interdisciplinarity, 192–96
multiple authorship, approaches to, 195–96
multiple perspectives, in research project, 381
Muncie, IN, 469–89
music, Africana studies and, 190–91, 197–99

mutualism, 333–36
Myers, Lena Wright, 98

Nagel, Joane, 224, 226
names, lesson plan on, 372–74
Nandy, Ashis, 128
Naples, Nancy, 219
narrative methods, in black/Africana studies, 182
nationalism: and development of ethnic studies, 35–39, 48, 59; and literature studies, 270
National Review Board for the Scholarship of Engagement, 368
Native American studies: Eurocentric assumptions and, 74–77; Forbes and, 59–91; future of, 85–87; and publication, 78; recommendations for, 80
needs assessment research project, 457
negritude, 38–39
neoconservatism, 246–47
neutrality, critique of, ethnic studies research and, 4
New Zealand, 129–33, 135–36; colonial vocabulary in, 137*t*
Ngati Awa, 136
Nietzsche, Friedrich, 329
No No Boy (Okada), 358, 410, 416–17
Nowatzki, Robert, 483
Nunez, Fabian, 361

Oakes, Richard, 82
objectivity, critique of: Butler on, 245–49; ethnic studies research and, 4; Saldívar on, 408–9; Simmel on, 94
Okada, John, 358, 410, 416–17
O'Keeffe, Georgia, 149
Okihiro, Gary Y., 33–57
Omi, Michael, 45–46, 224, 268
Ô-Môi, 219–39; findings on, 229–31

oppression: black feminist thought on, 99–103, 118n25; evidence of, 69; interlocking nature of, 100–103, 118n25, 220, 237n23
oral history, 44; Chicana epistemology and, 164–65; Forbes on, 69–70
Orozco, 299
Otago Museum, 136
outside, in colonial vocabulary, 136, 137*t*
outsider perspectives, 5; benefits of, 94; challenges to, 228; and Chicana epistemology, 166–68; disadvantages of, 116n11; ethnic studies and, 20; Hill Collins on, 93–121

pan-Africanism, 38
pan-Americanism, Forbes on, 64–67
pan-Asian ethnicity, 274–75
Papa, Lee, 472
paradigms: definition of, 108; shifts, in jazz, 197; sociological, elements of, 108–9
Park, Robert E., 40–42, 116n11
Parker, Laurence, 5
Parmenter, Adrian, 82
participatory research, 353–66; in collaboration, 478–80
past, existence of, Forbes on, 65
pausing, 72
Paz, Ignacio, 297
Paz, Octavio, 297
PC. *See* politically correct movement
Pearson, Charles H., 37
pedagogy: banking concept of, 353–54; Carnegie Foundation and, 369; critical, 353–66; for ethnic studies, 399–426; liberatory, 402, 421
peer helper program, 463–64
Pennsylvania, 179
Pérez, Domino Renee, 294
perspectivism, 329

Peterson, Cari, 474
Pfohl, Stephen, 227–28
Phan, Aimee, 278n26
philosophy: bricolage and, 343–44; Greek, 131
Pillow, Wanda, 6
Pinar, William, 327
Pitzer College, 359–60, 362
Pizarro, Marc, 151, 155–57
poetry: and ethnography, 482; Forbes and, 84
point of entry text (POET), in bricolage, 340–46
politically correct (PC) movement, 428–33
politics: Africana studies and, 185–92; Chicano/a arts and, 284; of difference, 337–39; ethnic studies and, 23–24, 29; and jazz, 198; Masequesmay and, 221–22; Virgin of Guadalupe and, 303
polyrhythms, in jazz, 197
Pomona Economic Opportunity Center, 360–61, 365n15
portraiture, research as, 148–49
positivist social research, critique of: art metaphor and, 147; Calderon on, 353; ethnic studies research and, 4; Smith on, 125–41
postcolonialism: and Chicano/a arts, 283; and literature studies, 271–72, 274
postformal conversations, 338
postmodernism: and diaspora studies, 205; and literature studies, 258, 270; Moya on, 246–47
postpositivist realist theory: and literature studies, 399, 405–9; Moya on, 249, 424n6
poststructuralism: and literature studies, 258, 270; Moya on, 406
power: bricolage and, 313, 327–29, 344–45; Eurocentric assumptions and, 75; Smith on, 126. *See also* domination
Powhatan, 75–76
problems approach: to race relations study, 39–43, 50; researcher and, 154
protective agenda, ethnic studies research and, 3
Pryor, Delores, 474
Pskegdemus, 287
publication: in Africana studies, 210; Forbes and, 77–80, 83–85

qualitative research: in Africana studies, 187–88, 199; Latino, ethnic epistemology in, 143–77; and reading ethnic literatures, 259
quantitative research, in Africana studies, 188
queer studies, 219–39
Queer theory, 223, 226, 234, 236n10, 239n46
Quilaztli, 285
Quiñónez, Naomi, 291–92
quoting, in jazz, 197

race: conceptualizing, 222–27, 261; intersectionality and, 128–30, 219–39, 273; movement beyond, 47–51; and sexuality, 226–27; theoretical development on, 223–25
race relations study: and development of ethnic studies, 45; problems approach to, 39–43, 50
racial identity, Butler on, 243
racial state, 258, 272
racism: critique of, effects of, 79–80; dualistic thinking and, 119n32; Du Bois on, 224; epistemological, 149–50; ethnic studies and, 24; instruction on, effects of, 427–49; new, 429–30; problem approach and, 43; reduction of, strategies for,

432–33; term, 412–13; unconscious, 430–32
Radhakrishnan, R., 272
Ralston, Pamela, 399–426
rationality, 188–89; bricolage and, 334–35
reading: in collaborative research, 480–82; critical practices in, 268–75; ethnic literatures, methodology for, 257–79
realist theory. *See* postpositivist realist theory
Recahekrians, 76
recipes, 109
reciprocity, and Chicana epistemology, 169
reconstruction, term, 70
redemptive agenda, ethnic studies and, 19
reductionism, bricolage and, 321–23
reflexivity, 228; in research project, 381–82
reinterpretation, ethnic studies research and, 3
relevance: ethnic studies and, 27–28; Masequesmay on, 221; in research project, 381
religion, black feminist thought and, 104, 120n39
research: as art versus cultural practice, 143–77; participatory, 353–66; project guidelines, 380–82; and social theory, 318–19
Revilla, Linda, 453–67
Rhinehart, Carl, 474, 480
Rhinehart, Dolores, 474, 480
Rich, Adrienne, 50, 116n3
rigor, bricolage and, 314, 321–24, 326–30, 335
Riva Palacio, Vicente, 288
Rivera, Diego, 299
Robertson, Rosalie, 483
Robinson, Ella, 63

Rodgers, Carolyn, 190
Rodriguez, Luis, 358
Roediger, David, 409
Rogers, Jane, 291
Rollins, Judith, 99
Roman culture, images in, 281
Rousseau, Jean-Jacques, 132–33
rules: Foucault on, 127; term, 126
Rustin, Bayard, 49

Sacramento: neighborhood characteristics in, 457, 458*t*–459*t*; service learning in, 453–67
Sahagún, Bernardino de, 285
Said, Edward, 283
Saldívar, Ramón, 408–9
saludos, 163
Sánchez, Patricia, 143–77
Sandoval, Chela, 6
San Francisco State College (University), 1, 82
Santiago theory, 322, 336
savage: concept of, 128; Rousseau on, 133
scanning, 72
scars, as evidence, 69
Scheper-Hughes, Nancy, 148
Scheurich, James J., 149
Schlesinger, Arthur, 66
Schomburg Center for Research in Black Culture, 401, 424n1
Schutz, Alfred, 109
science, term, 188
Scott, Joan W., 44–46, 247
Scott, Otis L., 17–32
Scott, Patricia Bell, 112
Seidman, Stephen, 225
self-definition, in black feminist thought, 96–100
self-determination, Masequesmay on, 221
self-valuation, in black feminist thought, 96–100

September 11, 2001: and nationalism, 35; and xenophobia, 24–25, 29–30, 60
service learning: Calderon on, 353–66; versus charity models, 361–63; in elementary school, 383–84; ethnic studies and, 26–27; Mark on, 453–67; students on, 465
Sevill, Eduardo, 465
sexuality: conceptualizing, 222–27; intersectionality and, 219–39, 273; and race, 226–27; theoretical development on, 225–26; Virgin of Guadalupe and, 309
Shange, Ntozake, 98
Shor, Ira, 357
Shukla, Sandhya, 268
silencing: art metaphor as, 145; voice approaches and, 44–46, 269
Silko, Leslie Marmon, 358
Simon, Julian L., 145
sisterhood, 104
small learning communities (SLC), 462
Smith, Barbara, 100
Smith, David G., 316
Smith, Dorothy, 220, 230
Smith, John, 75–76
Smith, Linda Tuhiwai, 7, 125–41, 159
Smith, Willie Mae Ford, 105
Sobredo, James, 453–67
social change: focus on, ethnic studies research and, 4–5; service learning and, 353–66. *See also* transformation
social Darwinism, 133
social theory, research and, 318–19
society, Western research and, 130–33
sociology: art metaphors in, as exclusionary, 143–77; black feminist thought and, 107–14; black women and, 110–14; paradigms in, elements of, 108–9; and politics of Africana studies, 185–89
solidarity, ethnic studies and, 35–39
Solomos, John, 7
Southwest Museum, 63
space, Western thought on, 133–36
Stake, Robert E., 147
Standing Bear, Luther, 79
standpoint theory, 220–21, 236n7
Stanfield, John, 5, 187
state, race and, 258, 272
Steinberg, Shirley, 315
stereotypes: black feminist thought on, 96–98; PC movement on, 428; Tan on, 419–20
Stewart, James B., 179–217
Stewart, Margaret F., 307f
Strachey, John, 75
stranger status: Simmel on, 94–95; in sociology, 110
Strauss, Anselm, 154
Strong, Josiah, 37–38
struggle. *See* activism
Struths, Mary, 457, 459–60
students: and controversial works, 418–20; and ethnographic research, 469–89; and research, case study on, 372–76; on service learning, 465; and tutoring program, 460–64
subaltern, term, 87
subcultural, term, 87
subjects of research: collaboration with, 469–89; confidentiality and, 233–34; and development of ethnic studies, 43–45; treatment of, black feminist thought on, 112–13
subjugated knowledges, 334, 336–37
Suman, Alvaro, 293f, 294
Sumida, Stephen, 272, 274
Sunstein, Bonnie Stone, 481
superficiality, 327–28
Suyemoto, Karen L., 367–98

Synhorst, Kara, 465
synthetic interdisciplinarity, 252

Tafoya, Lynne, 461
Takagi, Dana, 268
Takaki, Ronald, 251
Tan, Amy, 358, 418–20
Tang, Shirley Suet-Ling, 367–98
Taylor, Alistair, 63
Taylor, Charles H., Jr., 34
Taylor, John, 297
teaching: case studies on, 372–93; with community research methods, 367–98; in ethnic studies, 399–426; on white racism, effects of, 427–49
ter Wal, Jessika, 7
testimonial literature, 400
text selection, for ethnic studies, 400, 410, 426n21
textual analysis, recommendations for, 77
theory: Africana studies and, 193; in community-based research, 465–66; critical multiculturalist, 315–17; Forbes on, 67–69; and literature studies, 259–61; and pedagogy, 409–24
Third World Liberation Front, 1–2, 83, 455
Thomas, Jim, 363
Thomas, William I., 40
Thurmond, Strom, 429
time, Western thought on, 136–40
tinkering, 319, 328
Toci, 302
Tonantzin, 302
Toomer, Jean, 403
Torquemada, Juan de, 286
Totopotomoy, 76
Toulmin, S., 188–89
Touraine, Alain, 228
Toure, Kwame, 49

transformation: bricolage and, 324–25; difference and, 337–39; ethnic studies and, 19–21, 34; pedagogy and, 400–404
transinterdisciplinarity, 252
Trueba, Henry T., 155
trust, and Chicana epistemology, 169
Truth, Sojourner, 100
Tubman, Harriet, 48
Turner, James, 204
Tuskegee Syphilis Study, 3
tutoring program, 460–64
Twine, France Winddance, 5

understanding: bricolage and, 321; measurement and, 125; struggle and, 422
United Farm Workers' Union, 359–63
United Native Americans, 82
United States: and imperialism, 269, 271–72, 316–17; internal colonialism in, 37; white racism in, instruction on, effects of, 427–49
University of California at Berkeley, 82
University of California at Davis, 83, 85–86
University of Chicago, 40–42, 49–50, 187
Uong, Chanrithy, 383

Valdez, Luis, 284
Van Dijk, T., 197, 199
Varela, Francisco, 322, 331, 334
Velasco, Pete, 359–60, 365n13
Verkuyten, Maykel, 7
victim approach, critique of: Africana studies and, 179; D'Souza on, 34
Victorio, Andres, 464
Villenas, Sofia, 151–54, 156–57
Virginia B. Ball Center for Creative Inquiry, 469, 472–73, 477, 483, 487n12

554   INDEX

Virgin of Guadalupe, 300–309; historical antecedents of, 301–4; and visual arts, 304–9
visibility approaches, 44–46; black feminist thought on, 99, 112
vitrina, 159–61
voice approaches, 44–46; Kang on, 269

Wahunsonacock, 75–76
Waitangi Tribunal, 129–30, 136, 140n13
Wakukawa, Ernest K., 44
Walker, Alice, 98, 105
Wallbank, T. Walter, 63
Warren, Jonathan W., 5
Washburn, Jason J., 427–49
wa Thiongo, Ngugi, 206
Weigman, Robyn, 409
Western research: critique of, Smith on, 125–41; cultural formations of, 127–28
White, Deborah Gray, 104
White, E. Frances, 94
White, Nancy, 97, 100
White, Phyllis, Joanne, 474
White Racial Attitudes Scale (WRAS), 438–40; evaluation of, 440–43; pretest and posttest means and standard deviations, 443*t*
White Racial Identity Attitude Inventory (WRIAI), 437–38; evaluation of, 440–43; pretest and posttest means and standard deviations, 441*t*–442*t*; subtest means profile, 439*f*
white racism, instruction on, effects of, 427–49

Wilhelm II, kaiser of Germany, 37
Will C. Wood Middle School, 453, 456; neighborhood issues and, 457–59, 458*t*–459*t*; tutoring program for, 460–64
Williams, Patricia, 258
Williams, Terry Tempest, 265
Winant, Howard, 45–46, 224, 261–62
Winnemucca, Sarah, 81
Wissler, Clark, 470, 487n3
women of color: and development of ethnic studies, 48–49. *See also* black feminist thought
women's studies: Africana, 202–4. *See also* feminist theory
Wong, James, 461
Woodson, Carter G., 79
world studies: versus ethnic studies, 59–91; term, 88
WRAS. *See* White Racial Attitudes Scale
WRIAI. *See* White Racial Identity Attitude Inventory
writing: in ethnic studies course, 411; ethnography, 482–85
written texts, bias toward, Forbes on, 68–69

xenophobia, 60, 88–89; ethnic studies and, 24–25
Xtabay, 285

Yep, Gust A., 237n23
Young, Michelle D., 149
Young-El, John, 474

Zilonen, 302
Zinsser, William, 482

Contributors

Johnnella E. Butler is professor of comparative women's studies and provost and vice president for academic affairs at Spelman College. For the balance of her career, she has served as chair of African American studies at Smith College and chair of American ethnic studies at the University of Washington, Seattle, with appointments in English and women's studies. Before moving to Spelman College, she served as associate dean and associate vice-provost in the Graduate School, University of Washington. She specializes in curriculum transformation, particularly in ethnic studies and women's studies, and publishes in these fields as well as in literary studies. Her most recent book is the edited volume *Color-Line to Borderlands: The Matrix of American Ethnic Studies* (2001).

Jose Z. Calderon is professor of sociology and Chicano studies at Pitzer College in Claremont, California. He has a long history of connecting his academic work with community organizing, student-based service learning, participatory action research, critical pedagogy, and multiethnic coalition building. As a participant ethnographer, he has published numerous articles and studies based on his community experiences and observations. He is the editor of *Race, Poverty and Social Justice: Multidisciplinary Perspectives through Service Learning* (2007).

Patricia Hill Collins is the Wilson Elkins Professor of Sociology at the University of Maryland. She is a social theorist whose research and scholarship have dealt primarily with issues of race, gender, social class, sexuality and/or nation. Her first book, *Black Feminist Thought: Knowledge,*

Consciousness, and the Politics of Empowerment, published in 1990, with a revised tenth-year anniversary edition published in 2000, won the Jessie Bernard Award of the American Sociological Association for significant scholarship in gender, and the C. Wright Mills Award of the Society for the Study of Social Problems. Her second book, *Race, Class, and Gender: An Anthology* (1992, 1995, 1998, 2001, 2004) edited with Margaret Andersen, and with a sixth edition currently in preparation, is used in undergraduate classrooms in over 200 colleges and universities. She also published *Fighting Words: Black Women and the Search for Justice* (1998); *Black Sexual Politics: African Americans, Gender, and the New Racism* (2004); and *From Black Power to Hip Hop: Racism, Nationalism, and Feminism* (2006).

Julie Figueroa is assistant professor in the Department of Ethnic Studies at California State University, Sacramento. Applying a sociocultural lens, Dr. Figueroa examines higher education through the issues of access, academic success, and retention in terms of the experience of first generation college students. Her recently published work includes a coauthored chapter, "Tracing Institutional Racism in Higher Education: Academic Practices of Latino Male Undergraduates" (2006). Dr. Figueroa works in the areas of qualitative research, teaching and learning, and educational policy.

Timothy P. Fong is professor of ethnic studies at California State University, Sacramento. His research specialties include comparative race and ethnic relations, immigration history, politics and public policy, community studies, and qualitative methodology (ethnography and oral history). He has authored and edited several books including *The First Suburban Chinatown: The Remaking of Monterey Park, California* (1994), *Asian Americans: Experiences and Perspectives* with Larry H. Shinagawa (2000), and *The Contemporary Asian American Experience: Beyond the Model Minority* (1998, 2002, and 2007). Dr. Fong is also the editor of the Critical Perspectives on Asian Pacific Americans Series, published by AltaMira Press.

Jack D. Forbes is professor emeritus and former chair of Native American studies at the University of California at Davis, where he has served since 1969. He is of Powhatan-Renápe, Delaware-Lenápe, and other background. In 1960–1961 he developed proposals for Native American studies programs and for an indigenous university. In l971 the D-Q University came into being as a result of that proposal. He is also a poet, a writer of fiction, and a guest lecturer in Russia, Japan, Britain, Netherlands, Germany, Italy, France, Canada, Belgium, Switzerland, Norway, Mexico, and elsewhere. Forbes has also been active in grassroots organizing, founding the Native American Movement in the early 1960s and co-founding United Native Americans in 1968. He has served as editor of *Warpath*, the UNA newspaper, in 1968–1969, and as editor of *Attan-Akamik*, the Powhatan periodical. He is the author of some 450 published works, including books, monographs, articles, poems, and short stories

Maria Herrera-Sobek is Associate Vice Chancellor for Diversity, Equity, and Academic Policy, Luis Leal Endowed Chair (1997 to the present), and professor of Chicana and Chicano studies, University of California, Santa Barbara. She has published over 175 articles, book chapters, reviews, poetry, and books, including *Power, Race and Gender in Academe: Strangers in the Tower?* with Shirley Geok-lin Lim (1999); *Santa Barraza: Artist of the Borderlands*; and *Chicano Renaissance: Contemporary Cultural Trends* with David Maciel and Isidro D. Ortiz (2006), and Chicano Folklore: A Handbook (2006). Presently she is working on a book, *Constructing Nationhood and Ethnicity: La Malinche, the Virgin of Guadalupe, and La Llorona*.

Frank Holiwski received his M.A. and Ph.D. in clinical-community psychology from DePaul University. He has taught various diverse topics in psychology, and has had research published in the areas of health psychology and social psychology. He is currently assistant professor of psychology at South Georgia College. His primary interests are in white racial identity formation and eradicating white racism; other interests include gender identity, sexual identity, and the influences various components of the identity matrix have on each other.

Ketu H. Katrak, originally from Bombay, India, is professor of humanities at the University of California, Irvine. She is the author of *Politics of the Female Body: Postcolonial Women Writers of the Third World* (2006); co-editor of *Anti-Feminist Harassment* (1996); and "South Asian American Literature" in King-Kok Cheung (ed.), *Interethnic Companion to Asian American Literature* (1997), as well as other essays published in *Amerasia Journal* and *Modern Fiction Studies*, among others.

Peter Nien-chu Kiang is professor of education and director of the Asian American Studies Program at the University of Massachusetts, Boston, where he has taught since 1987. He is currently co-president of the Chinese Historical Society of New England and chair of the Massachusetts Advisory Committee for the United States Commission on Civil Rights.

He holds a B.A., Ed.M., and Ed.D. from Harvard University, and is a former Community Fellow in the Department of Urban Studies and Planning at MIT.

Joe L. Kincheloe is the Canada Research Chair of Critical Pedagogy at McGill University. He is the founder of The Paulo and Nita Freire International Project for Critical Pedagogy. He is the author of numerous books and articles about pedagogy, cultural studies, ethnic studies, education and social justice, racism, class bias, and sexism, issues of cognition, cultural context, and educational reform. His books include *Teachers as Researchers: Qualitative Inquiry and the Path to Empowerment* (2003), *The Sign of the Burger: McDonald's and the Culture of Power*, *The Critical Pedagogy Primer* (2002), *Rigour and Complexity in Educational Research: Conceptualizing the Bricolage with Kathleeen Berry* (2004). His co-edited works include *The Praeger Handbook of Education and Psychology* (Four Volumes) with Raymond A. Horn (2006), *The Miseducation of the West: How the Schools and Media Distort Our Understanding of Islam* with Shirley Steinberg (2004), and the Gustavus Myers Human Rights award winner, *Measured Lies: The Bell Curve Examined* with Shirley Steinberg. Kincheloe is very concerned with the politics of knowledge as it relates to the socio-cultural , ethnic, political, psychological, and educational dimensions of contemporary life. In this context he utilizes multi-perspective research methods (bricolage) and multiple theoretical frameworks to study these issues.

Luke Eric Lassiter is director of the Graduate Humanities Program at the Marshall University Graduate College in South Charleston, West Virginia. He has authored and coauthored several books, including *Invitation to Anthropology* (2006) and *Signifying Serpents and Mardi Gras Runners* with Celeste Ray (2003). Dr. Lassiter was also the recipient of the 2005 Margaret Mead Award from the Society of Applied Anthropologists for his book, *The Other Side of Middletown: Exploring Muncie's African American Community* with Hurley Goodall, Elizabeth Campbell, and Michelle Natasya Johnson (2004).

Theodoric (Ted) Manley, Jr. is currently associate professor of sociology at DePaul University and executive director of the Hoop Institute, a not-for-profit community-based organization serving people of color and poor white communities. He has a B.A. in sociology, philosophy, and religion from Tarkio College in Tarkio, Missouri; an M.A. in sociology with an emphasis in community development and applied sociology from Colorado State University in Fort Collins, Colorado, and a Ph.D. from the

University of Chicago in the areas of urban sociology and race and ethnic relations.

Gregory Mark is professor and former chair of the Ethnic Studies Department at California State University, Sacramento. He is also the director and principle investigator at the Asian/Pacific Islander Youth Violence Prevention Center in the John A. Burns School of Medicine at the University of Hawaii, Manoa.

Gina Masequesmay is a 1.5 generation Vietnamese American, lesbian sociologist. She is currently associate professor in Asian American studies at California State University, Northridge. Her research interests include Vietnamese Americans, sexualities, negotiating multiple identities, race and ethnicity, and immigrant adaptation.

Gary Y. Okihiro is professor of international and public affairs at Columbia University, where he was the founding director of the Center for the Study of Ethnicity and Race. His research interests are Asian American studies and southern Africa. He is the author of nine books in U.S. and African history, six of which have won prizes. His most recent books include *The Columbia Guide to Asian American History* (2001) and *Common Ground: Reimagining American History* (2001). Others include *A Social History of the Bakwena and Peoples of the Kalahari of Southern Africa, 19th Century* (2000); *Storied Lives: Japanese American Students and World War II* (1999); *Whispered Silences: Japanese Americans and World War II* (1996); and *Margins and Mainstreams: Asians in American History and Culture* (1994). His latest book is *Impounded: Dorothea Lange and the Censored Images of Japanese American Internment* with Linda Gordon (2006).

Pamela Ralston received her Ph.D. from the University of Washington in 2000. She is the program chair for written communications and developmental studies at Tacoma Community College in Washington. She teaches developmental and college-level composition, literature, and American ethnic and gender studies, and her research interests are in American ethnic studies, pedagogy, and curriculum design.

Linda Revilla is a 2.5 generation Filipino American. She has a Ph.D. in developmental psychology from the University of California, Los Angeles, and teaches ethnic studies and child development at California State University, Sacramento. Her research interests include ethnic identity, Asian American family and mental health issues, and community service-learning. A national trustee of the Filipino American National Historical Society, she served as associate producer, associate writer, and principal scholar for the award-winning documentary, "An Untold Triumph" (2002) on the First and Second Filipino American Regiments in Word War II.

Otis L. Scott is dean of the College of Social Sciences and Interdisciplinary Studies at California State University, Sacramento. His research interest is in developing descriptive and prescriptive ethnic-based social science/humanities models for better understanding and addressing the complexities of life among people of color. Dean Scott's publications include *The Veil: Perspectives on Race and Ethnicity in the United States* (1994); *Teaching from a Multicultural Perspective* (1994); and *Lines, Borders and Connections* (1997).

Patricia Sánchez is assistant professor in the Division of Bicultural-Bilingual Studies at the University of Texas at San Antonio. In her research, Dr. Sánchez uses a sociocultural lens to examine issues related to globalization, transnationalism, and immigrant students and families. Her recently published work includes a co-authored book on social policy, *Beyond "Bilingual" Education: New Immigrants and Public School Policies in California* (2004). Dr. Sánchez has also published in such journals as *Discourse: Studies in the Cultural Politics of Education* and the *Journal of Community Practice*.

Linda Tuhiwai Smith is professor of education and joint director of Nga Pae o te Maramatanga, the National Institute for Research Excellence in Maori Development and Advancement at the University of Auckland. Her research interests include young people and their participation in society and the economy, Maori social justice issues, Maori education policy and practice, and oral histories. She has a deep interest in indigenous methodologies and ways of knowing. Dr. Smith has served on a number of national advisory bodies and committees, including the New Zealand Planning Council, the National Advisory Council for the Employment of Women, the Tertiary Education Advisory Commission, and the Maori Tertiary Reference Group. Her publications include *Decolonising Methodologies: Research and Indigenous Peoples* (1999) and "On Tricky Ground: Researching the Native in the Age of Uncertainty," which is a chapter in *The Handbook of Qualitative Research, 3rd edition*, edited by Norman K. Denzin and Yvoanna S. Lincoln (2005).

James Sobredo is associate professor in the Asian American Studies Program, Ethnic Studies Department at California State University, Sacramento. Dr. Sobredo specializes in immigration, Supreme Court history, sixteenth-century economics, and the Manila galleon trade, and he teaches ethnic studies from a world history perspective. He is the co-author of *Studies in Pacific History: Economics, Politics and Migration* with Dennis O. Flynn and Arturo Giraldez (2002) and *European Entry into the Pacific: Spain and the Acapulco-Manila Galleons* with Dennis Flynn and Arturo Giraldez (2001).

Karen L. Suyemoto is associate professor in psychology and Asian American studies at the University of Massachusetts, Boston. She has published and presented on topics related to racial and cultural identity, particularly in multiracial and Asian American peoples, and feminist applications and connections with multicultural understandings in psychology. Dr. Suyemoto is the current vice president of the Asian American Psychological Association (AAPA), served as the program cochair of the 2004 national conference of the Association for Asian American Studies and the codirector of the New England Center for Inclusive Teaching, and has consulted with local and national community and counseling organizations and agencies regarding service to Asian Americans and other people of color.

James B. Stewart is professor of labor studies and industrial relations, African and African American studies, and management and organization at Penn State. He previously served as vice provost for educational equity and director of the Black Studies Program. Stewart served two terms as president of the National Council for Black Studies (1997–2001) and directed the NCBS Summer Faculty Institute from 1989 to 1991. His book *Flight in Search of Vision* (2004) chronicles the evolution and liberatory potential of Black/Africana studies. Stewart has also produced nine other monographs, and has published over seventy articles in economics and Black studies professional journals.

Shirley Suet Ling Tang is assistant professor in the Asian American studies and American studies programs at the University of Massachusetts, Boston. Her work examines race, (im)migration, development, and the social consequences of war. Her research/teaching interests include: comparative urban cultural history; Southeast Asian American community studies; and creative expressions at local and transnational levels. She is currently writing a book on the development and displacement of the Khmer (Cambodian) American community in Revere, Massachusetts.

Jason J. Washburn holds a B.A. in psychology and sociology from the State University of New York at Fredonia and an M.A. and Ph.D. in clinical psychology from DePaul University. He completed his clinical internship training at the University of Washington School of Medicine, his postdoctoral clinical training at the University of Michigan Medical School, and his postdoctoral research training as the Robert Wood Johnson Scholar for the Northwestern Juvenile Project. He is currently a research assistant professor of psychiatry and behavioral sciences at Northwestern University Feinberg School of Medicine, director of clinical outcomes at Alexian Brothers Behavioral Health Hospital, and in private practice. His clinical and research activities focus on child and adolescent psychology, evidence-based practice, juvenile delinquency, and white racism.